MW00861531

"The pandemic of 2020 has made th
transformation ever more urgent. As th
what should take its place? The Next ~ ~~~~ ~~~~ ~~~~ ~~~ ~~ the
most fruitful efforts to articulate possible paths forward. This collection—a
veritable who's who of visionaries—is a must-read for anyone interested in
creating an egalitarian, sustainable, and humane successor to capitalism."

—Juliet Schor, author, *After The Gig: How the*
Sharing Economy Got Hijacked and How to Win It Back

"Aged to perfection, Gus Speth is a global treasure. He and Kathleen Courrier have assembled 38 of the top systems thinkers to offer a multitude of provocative paths toward a radically better future for people and the planet."

—John Cavanagh, Director, Institute for Policy
Studies and co-editor of *Alternatives to Economic*
Globalization: A Better World is Possible

"This impressive collection of essays was completed a little before the Coronavirus pandemic shook up all our ways of living in the present and viewing the future. The book offers numerous suggestions on how to build truly new and resilient systemic changes in the economic, social and environmental spheres. Each of the 28 essays addresses issues that are urgently needed to reach the sustainable future we have been dreaming about for the past decades. It is now crystal clear that small adjustments to the existing system will no longer suffice. The systemic transformation needed must be global, courageous, inclusive and provide for previously disconnected issues to be considered together. *The New Systems Reader* is well positioned to play an important role in helping us move rapidly to create a new way forward for our planet and all of its inhabitants."

—Julia Marton-Lefèvre, Former Director General,
International Union for Conservation of Nature (IUCN)

"*The New Systems Reader* puts to rest, once and for all and not a moment too soon, the most nefarious of lies: There is no alternative. Its pages present compelling alternatives that promise a more fair, more healthy, more thriving economy, along with road maps to get there. The only thing missing is a people-powered movement strong enough to bring these visions to fruition. That's up to us, so read this book and let's go!"

—Annie Leonard, Executive Director, Greenpeace US

"This book could not be emerging at a better moment: many more of us now realize that we need new models for our collective life, and it will come as a relief to many readers to know those models are out there, with people hard at work figuring out how we can build them to scale in time. A landmark book!"

—Bill McKibben, author of *Deep Economy*

The New Systems Reader

The recognition is growing: truly addressing the problems of the 21st century requires going beyond small tweaks and modest reforms to business as usual—it requires "changing the system." But what does this mean? And what would it entail? *The New Systems Reader* highlights some of the most thoughtful, substantive, and promising answers to these questions, drawing on the work and ideas of some of the world's key thinkers and activists on systemic change. Amid the failure of traditional politics and policies to address our fundamental challenges, an increasing number of thoughtful proposals and real-world models suggest new possibilities, this book convenes an essential conversation about the future we want.

James Gustave Speth is senior fellow and co-chair of The Next System Project at The Democracy Collaborative. Formerly dean of the Yale School of Forestry and Environmental Studies, administrator of the United Nations Development Programme, and chair of the UN Development Group, he served as a senior adviser on environmental issues to Presidents Carter and Clinton. He is the author, co-author, or editor of seven books including *America the Possible: Manifesto for a New Economy* (2012); and most recently, the 2014 memoir *Angels by the River*, which traces his path from mainstream environmental insider to a champion of fundamental systemic change in our political and economic institutions.

Kathleen Courrier retired in 2016 from her position as vice president of communications at the American Institutes for Research. Before that, she was vice president of communications at the Urban Institute in Washington for 14 years, publications director at World Resources Institute from its inception, communications head and then acting director of the Center for Renewable Resources, a writer/editor for the Academy for Educational Development, and a freelance writer/editor. She is past president of Washington Book Publishers and a former book columnist for *SIERRA* magazine. Her articles and reviews have appeared in *The Washington Post*, *Columbia Journalism Review*, *Issues in Science and Technology*, *Los Angeles Times*, and *MIT's Technology Review*.

The New Systems Reader

Alternatives to a Failed Economy

Edited by
James Gustave Speth
and Kathleen Courrier

 Routledge
Taylor & Francis Group

NEW YORK AND LONDON

First published 2021
by Routledge
52 Vanderbilt Avenue, New York, NY 10017

and by Routledge
2 Park Square, Milton Park, Abingdon, Oxon, OX14 4RN

Routledge is an imprint of the Taylor & Francis Group, an informa business

Library of Congress Cataloging-in-Publication Data
A catalog record for this title has been requested

ISBN: 978-0-367-31338-8 (hbk)
ISBN: 978-0-367-31339-5 (pbk)
ISBN: 978-0-367-31340-1 (ebk)

Typeset in Bembo
by codeMantra

Contents

Contributors

Kali Akuno is a co-founder and co-director of Cooperation Jackson, which was established to advance the development of economic democracy in Jackson, Mississippi by building a solidarity economy anchored by a network of cooperatives and other types of worker-owned and democratically self-managed enterprises. He is also co-editor of *Jackson Rising: The Struggle for Economic Democracy and Black Self-Determination in Jackson, Mississippi*. He was previously the director of special projects under Jackson Mayor Chokwe Lumumba, where his work included cooperative development and environmental sustainability.

Michael Albert is founder of South End Press, Z Magazine, and ZNet/ZCommunications, among various other projects (such as the online school World Institute for Social Change, or WISC, and an activist organization, International Organization for a Participatory Society, or IOPS). Albert, an activist since the 1960s, is the author of more than 20 books and hundreds of articles and has spoken in countries around the world. He is co-author, and advocate, with Robin Hahnel, of the economic vision *Participatory Economics*, and the social vision, *Participatory Society*. Besides books on economic and social vision and strategy, he has written a memoir, *Remembering Tomorrow*.

Gar Alperovitz is co-founder of the Democracy Collaborative and co-chair of its Next System Project. He is a former Fellow of King's College, Cambridge, and Lionel R. Bauman Professor of Political Economy at the University of Maryland. His long career as a historian, political economist, activist, writer, and government official includes authorship of several critically acclaimed books; testimony before numerous congressional committees; and helping to lead in Youngstown, Ohio the first modern attempt to covert a steel mill into worker ownership. Among his recent books are *America Beyond Capitalism*, *What Then Must We Do?*, and *Principles of a Pluralist Commonwealth*.

Hans A. Baer is associate professor and a principal honorary research fellow in the School of Social and Political Sciences and the Centre of

Health and Society at the University of Melbourne. He is an anthropologist and development studies specialist who has published 20 books, including four related to climate change. His latest book is *Democratic Eco-Socialism as A Real Utopia: Transitioning to an Alternative World System.*

David Bollier is director of the Reinventing the Commons Program at the Schumacher Center for a New Economics in Great Barrington, Massachusetts and co-founder of the Commons Strategies Group, an advocacy/consulting project that assists the international commons movement. Bollier has written or edited several books on the commons, including *Think Like a Commoner: A Short Introduction to the Life of the Commons* (2014). His latest book, *Free, Fair, and Alive: The Insurgent Power of the Commons,* was scheduled for release in the fall of 2019.

Marvin T. Brown is an author and educator focused on developing the conditions for good conversations in the workplace, in civic settings, and in an unjust world. He is the author of *Working Ethics* (1990), *The Ethical Process* (1993), *Corporate Integrity* (2005), *Civilizing the Economy* (2010), and *Learning through Disagreement* (2014). He holds a PhD from Graduate Theological Union in Berkeley, Calif., an MD from Union Theological Seminary in New York City, and a BA from Nebraska Wesleyan University. He has been honored with Teacher of the Year and Faculty Service awards from the University of San Francisco, where he served as adjunct professor, and an Alumni Achievement Award from Nebraska Wesleyan University.

Jenny Cameron is an associate professor in geography and environmental studies at the University of Newcastle, Australia. Her work focuses on the development of economic alternatives, such as cooperatives and community enterprises. She teaches courses on global poverty and development, globalization, and geographies of development. She is a founding member of the Community Economies Collective.

Libbie Cohn is the manager of development and communications at the Center for Economic Democracy, where she works with grassroots, nonprofit, and funding partners to strengthen community-led economies. She has previously worked as an independent documentary filmmaker and legal services paralegal supporting low-income Asian immigrants. Raised in Hong Kong, Beijing, and the United States, Libbie holds a certificate in regenerative ecological design from Ecosa Institute and a master's degree in city planning from MIT.

Andrew Cumbers is professor of regional political economy at the University of Glasgow. He has written extensively on the problems and the prospects for a more democratic and egalitarian economy and society. He is currently working on a project funded by The Economic and Social Research Council to create an Economic Democracy Index. His book *Reclaiming Public Ownership* (Zed) won the 2015 Gunnar Myrdal Prize for Evolutionary Political Economy.

Kelly Dombroski is a lecturer in human geography at the University of Canterbury, Christchurch, New Zealand. Her research is focused on rethinking the ways that humans live with the earth in light of resource depletion, climate change, and unequal access to life's necessities and pleasures. Recent work includes "Hybrid Activist Collectives: Reframing Mothers' Environmental and Caring Labour" in the *International Journal of Sociology and Social Policy*, and "Seeing Diversity, Multiplying Possibility: My journey from Post-feminism to Post-development with J.K. Gibson-Graham," in W. Harcourt (Ed.), *The Palgrave Handbook of Gender and Development*. With J.K. Gibson-Graham, she is co-editing the forthcoming Edward Elgar *Handbook of Diverse Economies.*

Riane Eisler, JD, PhD is a systems scientist and cultural historian best known as author of *The Chalice and the Blade: Our History, Our Future* (now in its 57th US printing and 26 foreign editions) and *The Real Wealth of Nations: Creating a Caring Economics.* She is co-founder and president of the Center for Partnership Studies (CPS) and editor-in-chief of the Interdisciplinary Journal of Partnership Studies. Her most recent book is *Nurturing Our Humanity: How Domination and Partnership Shape Our Brains, Lives, and Future* (Oxford University Press).

Nia K. Evans is the director of the Boston Ujima Project. Her educational background is in labor relations, education leadership, and public policy. Her advocacy includes a focus on eliminating the barriers that come between analysts and the lived experiences of everyday people as well as gaining more acknowledgement of the value of diverse types of expertise in policy. She has a BS in industrial and labor relations from Cornell University and a Master of Arts in education leadership, with a course of study in leadership, policy, and politics from Teachers College at Columbia University. She also studied abroad at the University of New South Wales in Sydney, Australia, where she focused on international labor relations.

Christian Felber is an international speaker, contemporary dancer, and founder of the Economy for the Common Good movement. He has written or coauthored fifteen books; the most recent include *Change Everything, Money—The New Rules of the Game* and *Trade for Good.* He teaches at several universities and is affiliate scholar of the Berlin-based think tank IASS.

Lorenzo Fioramonti is full professor of political economy at the University of Pretoria (South Africa), where he directs the Centre for the Study of Governance Innovation. He is also senior fellow at the Centre for Social Investment of the University of Heidelberg and at the Hertie School of Governance (Germany) and associate fellow at the United Nations University. He is the founder of the Action Research Network for a Wellbeing Economy in Africa and the author of more than 60 scientific articles and 10 books, the most recent of which are *Wellbeing Economy: Success in a World Without Growth* (MacMillan 2017) and *The World After GDP: Economics, Politics and International Relations in the Post-Growth Era* (Polity 2017).

J.K. Gibson-Graham is a pen name shared by feminist economic geographers Katherine Gibson and the late Julie Graham (Professor of Geography, University of Massachusetts Amherst), who together founded The Community Economies Research Network and the Community Economies Collective. Katherine Gibson is currently a research professor at the Institute for Culture and Society, Western Sydney University, Australia. Books by J.K. Gibson-Graham include *The End of Capitalism (As We Knew It): A Feminist Critique of Political Economy* (1996) and *Take Back the Economy: An Ethical Guide for Transforming our Communities*, with J. Cameron & S. Healy (2013).

Jessica Gordon Nembhard is a political economist and professor of community justice and social economic development in the Africana Studies Department at John Jay College, City University of NY. Her research includes a particular focus on cooperative economics. She has served as an affiliate scholar with the Centre for the Study of Co-operatives, University of Saskatchewan, Canada and has been active with numerous organizations, including the Grassroots Economic Organizing (GEO) collective, the US Federation of Worker Cooperatives, the Association of Cooperative Educators, and the US Solidarity Economy Network. She has published numerous articles on cooperative economics, community economic development, credit unions, wealth inequality, community wealth, and Black political economy. She is also author of the book *Collective Courage: A History of African American Cooperative Economic Thought and Practice.*

Gus Hagelberg is presently a board member of the Economy for the Common Good management team.

Robin Hahnel is an economist and political activist best known as co-creator, along with Michael Albert, of a radical alternative to capitalism known as participatory economics, or parecon. He is professor emeritus of economics at American University in Washington, where he taught from 1976 to 2008, and a visiting professor in economics at Portland State University in Portland, Oregon, where he resides with his family. In addition to a dozen book chapters and more than three dozen articles in academic journals, he has published ten books, including *Quiet*

Revolution in Welfare Economics and *The Political Economy of Participatory Economics* with Princeton University Press, *Economic Justice and Democracy* with Routledge, and most recently *Green Economics: Confronting the Ecological Crisis* with ME Sharpe (Routledge, 2014).

Sacajawea Hall is also a founding member of Cooperation Jackson and currently co-leads the Land and Housing Initiative, including the development of a Community Land Trust. She is a Black feminist activist with more than ten years of experience leading political mobilizations, direct actions, conferences, fundraising initiatives, and communications for numerous organizations, coalitions, and networks throughout the United States.

Stephen Healy is a senior research fellow at the Institute for Culture and Society, Western Sydney University, Australia. His work includes health care reform policy, the role of cooperatives in regional development, and the solidarity economy movement. His most current research project (with Katherine Gibson, Jenny Cameron, and Jo McNeill) focuses on the role that cooperatives, social enterprises, and ecologically oriented enterprise might play in reconfiguring manufacturing.

Tim Jackson is professor of sustainable development at the University of Surrey and director of the Centre for the Understanding of Sustainable Prosperity (CUSP), which aims to explore the moral, cultural, social, political, and economic dimensions of prosperity on a finite planet. Over the past two decades, he has undertaken numerous advisory roles for business, government, civil society, and inter-governmental agencies. Between 2004 and 2011, he was economics commissioner on the UK Sustainable Development Commission, where his work culminated in the publication of *Prosperity without Growth—economics for a finite planet* (Routledge 2009, 2017). He was awarded the Hillary Laureate for exceptional international leadership in 2016.

Zitto Kabwe is a Tanzanian opposition member of Parliament representing the constituency of Kigoma-Ujiji. He has served in the Tanzanian Parliament since 2005. From 2008 to 2015, he chaired the Public Accounts Committee. In 2014, he founded the opposition party Alliance for Change and Transparency, ACT-Wazalendo, which champions a socialist vision in Tanzanian politics as outlined in its founding policy document, the Tabora Declaration.

Emily Kawano is co-director of the Wellspring Cooperative Corporation, which aims to use anchor institution purchases to create a network of worker-owned, inner-city cooperative businesses in Springfield, Massachusetts that will provide job training and entry-level jobs to unemployed and underemployed residents. Kawano also serves as coordinator of the US Solidarity Economy Network. An economist by training, Kawano served as the director of the Center for Popular Economics from 2004 to 2013. Before that, she taught at Smith College, worked as the National Economic Justice Representative for the American Friends Service Committee and, in Northern Ireland, founded a popular economics program with the Irish Congress of Trade Unions.

Lane Kenworthy is professor of sociology and Yankelovich Chair in Social Thought at the University of California, San Diego. He studies the causes and consequences of living standards, poverty, inequality, mobility, employment, economic growth, social policy, taxes, public opinion, and politics in the United States and other affluent countries. He is the author of *Social Democratic Capitalism* (2019), *How Big Should Our Government Be?* (2016, with Jon Bakija, Peter Lindert, and Jeff Madrick), *Social Democratic America* (2014), *Progress for the Poor* (2011), *Jobs with Equality* (2008), *Egalitarian Capitalism* (2004), and *In Search of National Economic Success* (1995).

David C. Korten is the founder and president of the Living Economies Forum; co-founder, board member, and board chair emeritus of *YES! Magazine;* an associate fellow of the Institute for Policy Studies; and a full member of the Club of Rome. He is best known for his books that frame a new economy for what he calls the "ecological civilization" to which humanity must now transition, including the bestseller *When Corporations Rule the World* (1995, 2001, 2015) and his latest, *Change the Story, Change the Future: A Living Economy for a Living Earth* (2015). He is a co-founder and until 2016 was co-chair, of the New Economy Working Group. He serves on the advisory boards of the Institute for Postmodern Development of China, Toward Ecological Civilization, the Center for Child Honoring, and the American Independent Business Alliance.

Michael T. Lewis is executive director of the Canadian Centre for Community Renewal and the editor of its journal, *i-4* ("inspire, innovate, incite, invent"). He is well known in Canada and internationally as a practitioner, author, educator, and leader in the field of community economic development and the social economy. He has built and advised a broad range of businesses, organizations, and governments in Canada and internationally, linking practice with policy. He is also leader of the BALTA Social Economy Research Alliance, a consortium in British Columbia and Alberta that conducts research relevant to strengthening the social economy in the region.

Henning Meyer is managing director and editor-in-chief of Social Europe Publishing & Consulting GmbH, a digital media and consulting company that publishes "cutting-edge thinking" on economics and politics. He is also research associate of the Public Policy Group at the

London School of Economics and Political Science (LSE) and a visiting fellow at Cambridge University's Centre for Business Research. He has appeared as a commentator on various news channels around the globe and his writing has appeared in such news publications as *The Guardian, DIE ZEIT, The New York Times, and El País.*

Ethan Miller is a lecturer in politics, anthropology, and environmental studies at Bates College in Lewiston, Maine. His recent book, *Reimagining Livelihoods,* focuses on challenging problematic distinctions between "economy," "society," and "environment" in regional development and on developing cross-cutting and integrative conceptual tools to strengthen transformative, post-capitalist organizing efforts. Ethan has also worked in an array of cooperative and ecological livelihood projects.

Paul Raskin is the founding president of the Tellus Institute, where he has focused on the development of visions and strategies for a transformation to more resilient and equitable forms of social development. He has served as a lead author for the US National Academy of Science's Board on Sustainability, the Intergovernmental Panel on Climate Change, the Millennium Ecosystem Assessment, the Earth Charter, and UNEP's Global Environment Outlook. In 1995, he convened the Global Scenario Group to explore the requirements for a transition to a sustainable and just global civilization. He holds a PhD in theoretical physics from Columbia University. His most recent publication is *Journey to Earthland: The Great Transition to Planetary Civilization.*

John Restakis is an independent researcher and consultant on international co-op and community economic development. He also lectures widely on globalization, regional development, and systems change. He was previously executive director of the Community Evolution Foundation and the BC Co-op Association, both based in Vancouver. His professional background includes community organizing, adult and popular education, and co-op development. John is co-founder of Synergia Co-operative Institute, adjunct professor at the Centre for Sustainable Development at Simon Fraser University, and research associate for Co-operatives UK. He is the author of *Humanizing the Economy: Co-operatives in the Age of Capital.*

David Schweickart is professor of philosophy at Loyola University Chicago. He holds PhDs in mathematics and philosophy. His primary focus has been on developing and defending a socialist alternative to capitalism that he calls "economic democracy." He is the author of three books, including *After Capitalism* (2002, 2011). He has also authored numerous articles in social-political philosophy. His work has been translated into Chinese, Spanish, French, Norwegian, Slovak, Farsi, and Catalan.

Michael H. Shuman is an economist, attorney, author, and entrepreneur, and director of local economy projects for Neighborhood Associates Corporation. He's also an adjunct instructor at Bard Business School in New York City, a fellow at Cutting Edge Capital and the Post-Carbon Institute, and a founding board member of the Business Alliance for Local Living Economies. He has authored, coauthored, or edited ten books, including *The Small Mart Revolution: How Local Businesses Are Beating the Global Competition* (Berrett-Koehler, 2006), winner of the bronze prize from the Independent Publishers Association for best business book. His most recent book is *The Local Economy Solution: How Innovative, Self-Financing Pollinator Enterprises Can Grow Jobs and Prosperity* (Chelsea Green, 2015).

Richard Smith is a founding member of System Change Not Climate Change. He is the author of *Green Capitalism: the God that Failed* (World Economic Association Press 2015) and *China's Engine of Ecological Collapse* (Verso, 2017). He has published numerous articles about the Chinese economy as well as about capitalist economic theory and the environment. He has held postdoctoral appointments at the East-West Center in Honolulu and at Rutgers University New Brunswick.

James Gustave ("Gus") Speth is distinguished fellow and co-chair of The Next System Project at The Democracy Collaborative and associate fellow at the Tellus Institute. His work to combat environmental degradation and promote sustainable development has included being a co-founder of the Natural Resources Defense Council and founder of the World Resources Institute. He has also served in leadership roles on environmental issues in the administration of President Jimmy Carter and at the United Nations. He is the author, co-author, or editor of seven books, including the award-winning *The Bridge at the Edge of the World: Capitalism, the Environment, and Crossing from Crisis to Sustainability*, and *Red Sky at Morning: America and the Crisis of the Global Environment*. His most recent book is *America the Possible: Manifesto for a New Economy* (Yale Press, 2012).

Aaron Tanaka, the co-founder and director of the Center for Economic Democracy, is a Boston-based community organizer, philanthropic advisor, and impact investor. He helps steer resources to social movement collaboratives that advance alternatives to capitalist economics in the United States. Previously, he served as the startup manager for the Boston Impact Initiative, the co-founding executive director of the Boston Workers Alliance and was a former fellow with Business Alliance for Local Living Economies (BALLE), Echoing Green and Tufts Department of Urban Planning. He serves on multiple boards, including the Asian American Resource Workshop, Neighborhood Funders Group, and the New Economy Coalition.

Peter A. Victor, author of *Managing without Growth: Slower by Design, not Disaster,* is a professor in environmental studies at York University, where he was dean of environmental studies from 1996 to 2001. He has worked for nearly 50 years in Canada and abroad as an academic, consultant, and public servant on economic and environmental issues. He received the Molson Prize in the Social Sciences by the Canada Council for the Arts in 2011 and the Boulding Memorial Prize from the International Society for Ecological Economics in 2014, and was elected to the Royal Society of Canada in 2015. He was the founding president of the Canadian Society of Ecological Economics and is a past president of the Royal Canadian Institute for the Advancement of Science.

Ed Whitfield is co-managing director of the Fund for Democratic Communities (F4DC), which works to strengthen democracy within communities by helping grassroots organizations develop deep roots in the communities where they work and rely mainly on those communities for support. F4DC nurtures alternatives in response to the escalating hardships arising from the convergence of economic collapse with political collapse, social and cultural collapse, and ecological collapse. A longtime advocate and activist working for social and economic justice, Whitfield is a native of Little Rock, Arkansas and has lived in Greensboro, South Carolina since 1970. He regularly speaks and writes on such issues as cooperatives, economic development, education, and social responses to racism. He also serves on the boards of the *New Economy Coalition, The Working World*, and the *Southern Reparations Loan Fund*.

Richard D. Wolff is the founder of Democracy at Work, a nonprofit producer of media and live events that analyzes capitalism critically as a systemic problem and advocates for democratizing workplaces as part of a systemic solution. He is professor of economics emeritus at the University of Massachusetts, Amherst and a visiting professor at the New School in New York City. He has also taught economics at Yale University, the City University of New York, and the Sorbonne. His latest books include *Occupy the Economy: Challenging Capitalism* (2012), *Democracy at Work: A Cure for Capitalism* (2012), *Capitalism's Crisis Deepens* (2016), and *Understanding Marxism* (2019). He produces and hosts the weekly program *Economic Update,* which airs nationwide on Free Speech TV and on more than 95 radio stations.

Preface

Systems have a way of making us forget they exist.

I grew up in a pleasant town in the American South in the 1940s and 1950s—pleasant enough if you happened to be white. It took me until my undergraduate years to appreciate fully the depths of injustice inherent in the system of life there and to understand that, as a system, it was rotten and untenable.

The moment when the scaffolding of your cultural life and your upbringing collapse around you is certainly disorienting—what you were brought up to believe in and take as natural and inevitable disappears. But it is also a liberating experience.

To understand that a system exists is to imagine the possibility of it being otherwise. To further understand that the system is fundamentally flawed is to imagine the possibility of something much better—a next system.

My subsequent trajectory through and beyond the mainstream environmental movement led me, later in life, to a similar moment. As the founder of the World Resources Institute, as a co-founder of Natural Resources Defense Council, as a presidential advisor, environmental school dean, and United Nations administrator, I proceeded for decades under the assumption that we could correct dangerous disregard for the environmental health of our planet by working for reforms within the system. It was an unexamined presupposition that our political economy was mostly a given, and that the task before the environmental movement was to press hard on the levers of policy and politics to impede unsustainable practices within that system while promoting more sustainable ones.

Thank goodness we have won significant battles, but we are steadily losing the war. Decades of this work—all good, all worthwhile, but all ultimately unsuccessful in moving us away from a path toward climate and ecological catastrophe—led to another, slower epiphany, a realization that the outcomes we as an environmental movement were powerless to hold back were due not only to bad actors or bad policies but to deeper flaws in our economic and political system itself. These flaws are baked into the very fabric of our political economy, so that fighting for a bright future for people and planet within that system will be a losing proposition in the end. This, like my earlier moment coming to terms with the horrors of systemic racism, was not an easy lesson to take. But it was a necessary and ultimately liberating one.

In particular, it led me to begin the work that resulted in the book you now have before you, which asks the question; What does it really mean to "change the system"?

Why Systems Matter

The starting point for this book is the inability of traditional politics and policies to address fundamental challenges. Our goal is not to offer visions of alternative systems because it is an intellectually interesting thought experiment, but as visions whose urgency is demanded by our historical moment. As Abraham Lincoln put it: "If we could first know where we are... we could better judge what to do and how to do it."

Truly addressing the economic, ecological, and political problems of the 21st century requires going beyond business as usual. In the United States, where most of our contributors ground their work, stagnating outcomes around individual and community well-being are showing the limits of the current system. A very rich nation by conventional measures, the United States has, measured against the 19 other "advanced democracies" in the Organization for Economic Cooperation and Development (OECD), the greatest inequality of both incomes and wealth; the highest rates of incarceration, poverty, and infant mortality; and the shortest life expectancies. In the United States and elsewhere around the globe, the inability of the current system to deliver a future worth believing in fuels the resurgence of dangerous authoritarian and nationalist tendencies.

Beyond national borders, we are hitting, with the onrushing disaster of the climate crisis, the first of what systems theorist Donella "Dana" Meadows and her collaborators termed "limits to growth." (It won't be the last.)

Recognizing the system is broken, however, is only a first step. If one remains bound by the wrongheaded idea that "there is no alternative," a broken system is only an occasion for cynicism, despair, and reaction. It is also be the occasion for the cynical "I'm going to get all I can while I can." Our goal in this reader is to dispel the deadly notion that nothing can be done—that today's corporate capitalism as we know it is the best and, in any case, the only possible option.

Thankfully, many alternative visions exist, buttressed by the work of individual thinkers and increasingly sophisticated networks of research and reflection. These thoughtful proposals suggesting new political-economic possibilities—sometimes in considerable detail—map out potential futures for us to consider. We have endeavored here to select and present a representative sample of the most important proposals. We have focused especially on those that stem from a sustained line of inquiry, research, and advocacy—for all of our contributors, the system question in one form or another, is core to their work.

The contours of the different systems also converge around an at least partially shared vision of key outcomes. Here are a few of those outcomes as I see them:

- The lifeblood of the dominant enterprise type is not profit and growth, but public benefit, social purpose, and a decent living for those involved, while the ownership and control of productive enterprise has shifted decisively to workers, the public, and economic democracy generally.
- The imperative to protect the planet and its climate, and the need to restore the environment back to health, governs economic enterprise and government action. An ethos of nature as a commons for the shared benefit of all life replaces the practice of privatized resource extraction, with benefits hoarded by the few and the costs borne by the many, usually the poorest and most marginalized.
- Investments are made in accordance with democratically determined priorities, with shareholders replaced by stakeholders and with social and environmental returns taking priority over financial ones.
- The aim of economic policy is no longer tied to growth of GDP, but to promote national and international well-being and the common good.
- Equal justice truly exists for all people in all spheres of life, and reparative justice to address the historic and continuing damage caused by systemic racism is core to the work of ensuring that the benefits of economic activity are widely and equitably shared.
- Popular sovereignty—democratic government of, by and for the people—is restored, concomitant with the expansion of democracy into the economy, reversing the takeover of government by the corporate sector.

We hope that the convictions and deep engagement of our contributors with the design of "what comes next" can help shake loose any lingering but profoundly unhelpful belief that we have somehow arrived at the end of history. Our current corporate capitalist system can be superseded by a next system that is equitable, green, democratic, and just.

Comparative analysis of the systems presented here can help us on the difficult path to synthesis—and one of our goals in assembling this collection was to ask our contributors to evaluate their own work with respect to a shared set of analytical categories. (We've reproduced that schema as an appendix in this volume.) The prevalence of planning, the role of the state, the scale of relevant geographies, the organization of work, the relation to nature and environment, all of these provide useful handholds to put these systemic visions in relation. We can demand of each of these systems what they can tell us about growth, justice, leisure, gender, race, consumerism, democracy, or any other of a litany of key challenges. Are their answers incidental, or core to the dynamic drivers of the system proposed?

Importantly, these are not visions of systems that promise inevitable, utterly predictable outcomes. Dana Meadows taught us that human systems are inherently unpredictable. She believed that hoping to design a perfect system in which we are omniscient conquerors is a fool's errand. "The future can't be predicted," she wrote in her essay "Dancing with Systems," "but it can be envisioned and brought lovingly into being. Systems can't be controlled, but they can be designed and redesigned. We can't surge forward with certainty into a world of no surprises, but we can expect surprises and learn from them and even profit from them. We can't impose our will upon a system. We can listen to what the system tells us and discover how its properties and our values can work together to bring forth something much better than could ever be produced by our will alone."[1]

Many Alternatives

The rich diversity of systemic visions we have assembled here presents a new challenge, leading us to our second goal in assembling this volume. All of the thinkers and activists we have enlisted start from a similar recognition of the problems in the current system—but they all end up somewhere different. The paths they identify also vary considerably— from local self-regulation to top-down reconstruction, from the rewiring of values to the rewiring of ownership, and everywhere in between. There are many alternatives—so which one do we want to build toward? And what questions are at stake in this choice?

Do we need to change everything? Essays by Lane Kenworthy, Henning Meyer, and Michael H. Shuman propose visions grounded in significant reforms that stop short of a truly revolutionary transformation—drawing on the social democratic and liberal traditions, and the promise of markets grounded in local communities. Even here, they present significant choices. Can a country as culturally and ideologically diverse as the United States be led to embrace unity under a European-style "good society," as Kenworthy and Meyer suggest, or do we concede that a system of radical localism will mean that different communities will make different decisions about how they order their lives, as Shuman does, and that's OK? Still, the virtue of these proposals lies in their closeness to reality.

The distance to travel to their new systems is far from trivial, but it doesn't require us to imagine a total rewiring of our political economic system.

Other proposals insist on more fundamental changes, down to the foundational level of the values that drive how and to what end systems work. For instance, Christian Felber and Gus Hagelberg propose a system built around alternative measures of social and economic value based on an assessment of the common good and stewardship of the planet. Marvin T. Brown echoes that perspective, but raises the challenge to think beyond traditional market frameworks driven by individual desires to imagine markets driven by community well-being. Riane Eisler contributes another layer by calling for a break with the dominant value system of patriarchal dominance, replacing it with a system centered on partnership and on properly valuing such social roles as caregiving. The way David C. Korten frames the debate is a choice between a "money is sacred" story and a "life is sacred" story. Paul Raskin offers a glimpse into the future to show how the world might transition from where it is today to one that is more equitable and environmentally sustainable. His cosmopolitan vision differs sharply from Shuman's localism.

As the climate crisis intensifies, a particular dimension of interest is how systemic visions engage with the constraints of ecology—contributions from Tim Jackson and Peter A. Victor, Lorenzo Fioramonti, Hans A. Baer, and Richard Smith all address this environmental dimension head-on, arriving at some starkly different answers. There is little debate about the need for an environmental accounting of our economic activity, and such an accounting in and of itself has implications for how markets and societies will function. But can either capitalist or socialist societies as currently constituted adapt to the structural changes that such an accounting would demand?

Who owns a new system? Answering "we do" is a start, but it begs new questions. David Schweickart, Richard D. Wolff, and Andrew Cumbers interrogate the dynamics of democratizing ownership as a key facet of a systemic transition, focusing on worker and public ownership. Here we are called by Schweikart to imagine a world in which workers control their jobs and workplaces, and investment decisions are made collectively by society. Richard D. Wolff shows how cooperatives can model the way forward. Cumbers looks at how various forms of public ownership can be strategically deployed to support the successful collective management of a new system.

How do the pieces of a new system fit together? Tracing how community-based alternatives can be knitted together into larger scale systemic visions, my own contribution, that of my Next System Project co-chair Gar Alperovitz, as well as Jessica Gordon Nembhard, Emily Kawano, Ed Whitfield, and Michael T. Lewis, explore the architectures of composition and assemblage that can hold a systemic alternative together. What you will see in these essays is Alperovitz delving into the importance of building community while I explore what it means to have an economy centered on bringing "joy"—not just the superficial pleasure of having things but an inner contentment that comes though mutually beneficial relationships. Nambhard adds the critically important dimension of the need to repair the damage done by centuries of systemic racism and sexism in order to build a truly cooperative solidarity economy. Kawano, Whitfield, and Lewis discuss the existing and emergent models we might use to build a new system with racial and gender justice at its core.

What are the ways in which people connect to and feel a part of a new system? One path would involve rethinking the scope of "the commons"—the domain of resources shared and collectively managed by the people, as David Bollier suggests, rather than privately extracted and traded on the market. John Restakis supplements an expansive definition of the commons with the idea that the deployment of capital is also socially controlled, primarily directed to support cooperatives and collectives. Writings by Michael Albert and Robin Hahnel explore how to deepen democratic processes in both the political and economic realms, so that the idea of decision-making by the people closest to and most affected by the decision is not a slogan but is a routine practice.

Finally, we present a set of visions of systemic transformation grounded in concrete organizing. One essay by J.K. Gibson-Graham, Jenny Cameron, Kelly Dombroski, Stephen Healy, and Ethan Miller looks at the hidden registers of system change beneath the surface of today's economy. Then Kali Akuno and Sacajewa Hall, Tanaka-Evans-Cohn, and Zitto Kabwe each offer a perspective grounded in contemporary social movement building, from the Deep South of the United States to Tanzania. These essays show how real people are grappling with the challenges of bringing an audacious vision of systemic change into reality.

Choices on the Road to Synthesis

"There is no alternative" threatens us with expulsion to a barren desert if we dare to demand some set of arrangements that transcend the possibilities of our current capitalist configuration. But as the plenitude of alternative, visions we have collected in the pages that follow show, far from a desert, what we have is a thriving, diverse ecosystem, an intellectual ecology of mutual relation and overlapping concern. Indeed, this forest of ideas is so thick that the problem is trying to forge a meaningful path through it, to see the trees in their particularity and relation, to understand what is shared—common emergent themes that can unify our work—and what remains irreconcilable, difficult choices to be faced with intellectual honesty and in good faith.

We know a lot—too much!—about how the gross-domestic-product-maximizing, corporate-profit/shareholder-value-focused economic system courts disaster for people and planet. We know—again, too well!—all that is externalized and made invisible by this system, from the rights of nature to the value of the caring labor that reproduces our social life. And we know quite a bit about how the major 20th-century attempt to find a different path resulted in the historical tragedy of statist socialism. So, we know what to ask of a systemic design, the criteria it must fulfill, the traps it must avoid.

But what are we to make of this volume's diversity in tactics and strategy? Karl Marx famously once wrote that he shouldn't, as a critic of the existing economic order, be responsible for writing "recipes for the cookshops of the future." It's *possible* to agree with this judgment and view the diversity of systemic visions presented here as a kind of fascinating kaleidoscope of possibility—each turn offering a new aspect in which design principles of one reflect upon, resonate with, or contradict another—without continuing with the intellectual and empirical work necessary to understand which synthesis presents a truly operative way forward. The ideas here *could* remain utopias, fantastic visions of possibility that help us think through the limits of the present without asking us to take them seriously.

Ultimately, though, we believe that such a sanguine dismissal of the design criteria of a new system is not appropriate. First, historical experience—especially the long and painful collapse of the Soviet experiment—has shown just how deadly it can be to embark on a revolutionary journey without a solid understanding of your destination. Second, the enemies of freedom and equity have never hesitated to create their own recipes for futures we don't want. Corporate neoliberalism's coordinated advance was made possible, in no small part, because it knew where it was going and how it might get there. Finally, we don't have the luxury of time; an accelerating climate and other crises documented here are demanding, *now*, that we begin to shift the underlying dynamics of our economic system in fundamental ways. With the human suffering of the COVID-19 pandemic mounting as I write, the manifold failings of our current system cry even louder for fundamental change. Indeed, the many movements for a new, democratic economy directly inspiring the authors contributing here are already beginning to work toward making such shifts in practice.

Our hope is that this volume provides a set of places to begin this important and urgent conversation about what comes next.

James Gustave Speth

Note

1 Donella Meadows, "Dancing with Systems," *Academy for Systems Change*, http://donellameadows.org/archives/dancing-with-systems/.

Acknowledgments

It is common to refer to team efforts, but producing this book required an unusually big one.

Shortly after The Next System Project (NSP) was launched as a project of The Democracy Collaborative in early 2015, its executive director, Joe Guinan, and I saw that we had an opportunity to pull together a group of the best thinkers to address an essential question: if today's system of political economy is failing across a broad front, what next systems are possible that would truly serve people, place, and planet?

Joe and I had creative inputs and strong encouragement from my NSP co-chair and co-founder of The Democracy Collaborative, Gar Alperovitz, and from Ted Howard, The Democracy Collaborative's president. NSP's research director, Thomas Hanna, was also quite helpful in this regard. Dana Brown, who directs the Next System Project and the many, many strands of incredibly important work happening there, was indispensable at keeping all the balls in the air as we juggled this book and many other projects.

I wish to thank abundantly the 38 authors who responded to our call. I had the great pleasure and privilege of working as editor with almost all of them, and their work was of the highest order. Along the way, two of the finest writer-editors in the United States, Joni Praded and Kathleen Courrier, assisted admirably in developing the essays forward into what you see in this book. The good folks at Solidarity Research Center also provided some essential assistance helping proofread these essays.

It is a complex process getting all the moving pieces working together, and that task fell to the talented Isaiah J. Poole, NSP's editorial manager, and before him to Carla Santos Skandier, now co-director of NSP's Climate and Energy Project. John Duda, The Democracy Collaborative's communications director during this project, skillfully managed the outreach and communication for each of the essays and also had responsibility for shepherding the book through the publication process with Routledge. We also want to thank Dean Birkenkamp at Routledge, whose thoughtful feedback helped us understand how best to assemble and present this potential cacophony of systemic perspectives as a coherent whole.

Finally, we want to thank the organizations and individuals whose financial support made this volume possible: Cary Brown, Christina Lee Brown, The Kendeda Fund, Sydney Lea, Robin Barone, NoVo Foundation, Open Society Foundations, Steven Rockefeller, Heather Ross, Shift Foundation, Lisa Steele, Edward Strohbehn, and The Summit Foundation.

On behalf of The Next System Project, a very big thank you to all.

James Gustave Speth
Co-chair, The Next System Project

About The Democracy Collaborative and The Next System Project

The Democracy Collaborative (democracycollaborative.org) is a research and development lab for the democratic economy, a national and international hub for the conception and implementation of transformative economic solutions. Launched in 2000, it now has a global network of staff and fellows developing the theory, policy, and practice for economies centered on community wealth building. The Democracy Collaborative's approach to local economic development, using such strategies as worker cooperatives, community land trusts, and other forms of democratic and community ownership and harnessing the economic power of anchor institutions such as hospitals and universities, is increasingly being incorporated into the toolbox of municipal governments and community advocates.

The Next System Project (thenextsystem.org) was launched by The Democracy Collaborative with the support of more than 300 leading scholars and activists to promote systemic solutions for an age of systemic crisis. Working with a broad group of researchers, theorists, and activists, the Next System Project combines the best research, understanding and strategic thinking with on-the-ground organizing and development experience to promote visions, models, and pathways for a "next system" capable of delivering social, economic, and ecological outcomes superior to those of the failed systems of the past and present.

Part I

Social Democracy and Radical Localism

Any discussion about why billions of people globally struggle (and often fail) to meet their basic needs, and why even many who nominally succeed see themselves as cogs in an economy that drains their humanity, must eventually come to the question of how the economic system is designed. What is the economy designed to do? Who is it designed to benefit? Who or what powers it?

Capitalism and socialism offer sharply different answers to these questions. But societies built around the precepts of both ideologies have come up short in distributing wealth, rewarding work, encouraging innovation and creativity, and making the opportunity for a life of well-being universal. Is the answer a better form of capitalism? A better form of socialism? A mix of the two?

This part features three approaches to building a different economy. None calls for a full break from capitalism, and all involve a market economy. But they offer different structures based on different governing principles from what we see today.

Lane Kenworthy, a sociology professor at the University of California, San Diego, drawing inspiration from the Scandinavian countries, models "social democratic capitalism"—market capitalism aimed at the full realization of economic security, equality of opportunity, and shared prosperity. In his view, government should play a key role in improving economic and living conditions, and minimizing inequality. The details of that role include using a progressive income tax structure to cover the cost of an income floor for the less well-off. "Getting closer to the good society doesn't require a radical break from our historical path," he writes. "It simply requires continuing along that path."

Henning Meyer, editor in chief of *Social Europe* and a research associate of the Public Policy Group at the London School of Economics and Political Science, also posits a social democratic system, but his version has a mixed economy. The production and sale of some goods, like consumer electronics, would happen in a profit-seeking market while such vital public goods as healthcare services would not. His "Good Society" is values-driven, emphasizing inclusivity and democratic decision-making and "seek[ing] to combine an activist cosmopolitan outlook on global issues with a re-foundation of social democracy's communitarian roots." Henning calls for prioritizing enlightened politics over economic interests, and for embracing diverse ownership models, including models that better suit the production of public goods.

Economist and entrepreneur Michael H. Shuman, director of local economy projects at Neighborhood Associates Corporation, proposes radical localism to create "a million utopias." Pointing to the economic, social, and environmental achievements of highly decentralized Switzerland, Shuman argues that a compelling possible direction for systemic transformation of the United States is through the principle of subsidiarity, in which decisions are made closest to the people—at the state and local level. He also envisions open markets coupled with robust antitrust enforcement to keep enterprises "diverse, small, and competitive," even though the public sector's scope and power would generally be minimal. Given the toxicity of 21st-century US politics, he writes, the strongest argument for decentralization as a path to systemic change "is that it is happening already."

Chapter 1

Social Democratic Capitalism

The Nordic Experience and Beyond

Lane Kenworthy

To this point in history, the most successful societies have been those that feature capitalism, a democratic political system, good elementary and secondary (K-12) schooling, a big welfare state, employment-conducive public services, and moderate regulation of product and labor markets. I call this set of policies and institutions "social democratic capitalism." All rich longstanding-democratic nations have the first three of these— capitalist economies, democratic political systems, and good-quality K-12 education. The distinguishing feature of social democratic capitalism is its addition of expansive and generous public insurance programs along with aggressive promotion of high employment via public services and modest rather than stringent regulation of product and labor markets.[1]

The aims of a good society include community, democracy, economic equality, economic opportunity, economic prosperity, economic security, economic stability, education, employment, environmental quality and sustainability, family, finance, freedom, good government, happiness, health, housing, knowledge, law and order, openness and support for other peoples, privacy, and safety. Social democratic capitalist countries have done better than others at achieving economic security (decent living standards for the least well-off and stability of income and expenses) and equality of opportunity. And they have done so without sacrificing the many other things we want in a good society, from liberty to economic growth to health and happiness and much more. Social democratic capitalism has proved more effective than existing alternatives at helping the least well-off and just as effective as those alternatives at achieving other aims.

The chief practitioners of social democratic capitalism have been the Nordic countries—Denmark, Finland, Norway, and Sweden. Contrary to what some presume, there is no good reason to think social democratic capitalism will work well only in these countries. Its success almost certainly is transferable to other affluent democratic nations. Indeed, all of those nations already are partial adopters of social democratic capitalism.

The American Way Forward

What changes are needed in the current system to achieve social democracy? In the contemporary United States, the chief changes needed lie in the realm of social policy. The United States has many public insurance programs and government services already. For the most part, they work very well. We should adjust and expand some of them and add others because the experience of other rich democratic nations shows us that there are other policies and programs that would be good for Americans and because we face new economic and social challenges that didn't exist or were less consequential in earlier eras.

What exactly should we do? We should add or improve the following:

- Health insurance
- Paid parental leave
- Child allowance
- Unemployment insurance and wage insurance
- Sickness insurance
- Disability insurance
- Social assistance
- Criminal justice
- Pensions
- Elder care
- Housing assistance
- Early education
- Apprenticeships
- College
- Affirmative action
- Full employment
- Minimum wage
- Earned income tax credit
- Profit sharing
- Infrastructure and public spaces
- Paid vacation days and holidays

Why rely on government programs rather than such intermediary institutions as families, civic organizations, and labor unions? One reason is that these institutions don't cover everyone. There has never been a society in which all children grow up in stable two-parent families, all workers enjoy union-negotiated wages and benefits, and civic associations serve the needs of all the disadvantaged. Moreover, these institutions have been steadily weakening for half a century. Americans marry later and divorce more frequently. Fewer children grow up in a home with both of their original parents. Participation in voluntary organizations has been declining.

And barely one in ten employed Americans is a union member. Even more problematic, these changes have a class tilt: families, community organizations, and union membership have weakened most among those with less education and income. Advocates for revitalizing these institutions offer lots of hope, but little evidence here or from other rich nations that revival is possible.

On a spectrum from imminently practicable to purely speculative, social democracy lies at the imminently practicable end. It exists to varying degrees in the four Nordic countries. Many other rich nations have some of the policies in force already, and some of those countries have been changing or adding policies to move closer to social democratic ones. Since the United States has perhaps the longest road to travel among the world's rich longstanding democracies, it might take half a century to put in place the full array of policies used in today's Nordic nations.

The notion of a social democratic United States will strike some observers of US politics as a pipe dream. But in the realm of public social policy, the distance between the United States today and Denmark or Sweden today is smaller than the distance between the United States a century ago and the United States today. In the past 100 years, we've put in place a host of public programs that contribute to economic security, opportunity, and shared prosperity. Getting closer to the good society doesn't require a radical break from our historical path; it simply requires continuing along that path.

Progress will be incremental, coming in fits and starts. But steps forward will have staying power. New programs and expansions of existing ones will mostly persist, as they have in the past, because programs that work well become popular and because the array of veto points in the US political system makes policy changes difficult. Small steps and the occasional big leap, even coupled with some backsliding, will cumulatively increase the breadth and generosity of government social programs.

This isn't a prediction about the timing or conditions under which specific policy advances will occur. It's a hypothesis about a probabilistic process. Over the long run, new programs occasionally will be created and existing ones intermittently expanded, and these additions and expansions are unlikely to be reversed. This pattern, in fact, aptly describes the history of US social policy over the past century.

Good Society Economics

Much remains unknown about how best to run an economy. We have virtually no evidence, for instance, about whether a large-scale democratically planned economy could function effectively. The same is true of a basic income grant at a level high enough to make employment genuinely optional. One of the strongest arguments for social democratic capitalism is that we have real-life experience with this model and that experience offers reason for optimism that the model can achieve a host of goals.

Here are some specifics, as they exist in the contemporary Nordic countries:

A significant share of all productive assets and businesses are privately owned, though in some sectors, such as health care, most or all may be state-owned. Most investment decisions are made by firms. Private firms keep profits, but are taxed at a fairly high rate, as are the income and consumption of individuals.

Markets play the leading role in allocating not only investment but also labor, goods, and services. Government regulates these markets, extensively in some sectors. And government may be a large employer; in some Nordic countries, nearly a third of employment is public. Planning of the national economy is limited mainly to steering resources toward certain sectors ("industrial policy").[2]

Social democracy is compatible with a range of firm sizes and corporate governance arrangements. Firm ownership might be dominated by larger shareholders who provide patient capital or by small shareholders favoring shorter time horizons. Firm boards could be elected entirely by shareholders or by a mix of shareholders and employees ("codetermination").

Labor unions play an important role in determining wage levels and wage differences in social democratic countries. Unionization rates in the Nordic nations remain among the world's highest. If unions were to continue to weaken significantly, as they have in many other rich democratic nations, government would need to take a more active role in wage determination, via a statutory minimum wage (which none of the Nordic countries currently has) or Australia-style wage tribunals. Most medium-sized and large firms are required to have an employee-elected workers council, which negotiates with management about working conditions, hours, and other non-pay matters.

Consistent with their embrace of competition and their concern for the least well-off, social democratic countries typically favor economic globalization—particularly trade of goods and services. They have been more ambivalent about immigration, though in recent decades Sweden has been a world leader in accepting refugees and its foreign-born population share is now higher than in the United States.

Social democracy constricts economic freedom in one respect: government takes money from us and spends it to ensure economic security, expand opportunity, and enhance living standards. This isn't especially objectionable. Only diehard libertarians believe individual liberty should trump all other considerations, and virtually everyone supports government paternalism in the form of property protection, traffic lights, and food safety regulations, to mention just a few examples. Beyond that, many people support public social programs. When basic needs are met, we tend to prefer more security, broader opportunity, greater fairness, and confidence that living standards will improve over time. We are willing to allocate some of our present and future income to guarantee these desirable outcomes and to allow government to take on that task. That's why public social programs tend to expand in size and scope as nations grow richer.

At the same time, a social democratic government can have a relatively light regulatory touch. In the Nordic nations, government sets basic standards for employee and consumer protections, but it seldom tells economic actors how to comply. The aim is to maximize individual opportunity and provide security for those who fail while impinging as little as possible on competition and flexibility.

An expansion of public insurance and public services in the United States will come with a price tag. Roughly, adding or extending the various programs listed earlier would require a rise in government spending of 10 percent of GDP. If that sounds beyond the pale, note that if our government expenditures rise from today's 38 percent of GDP to around 48 percent we will be only a little above the current norm among the world's rich nations. And an increase of 10 percent of GDP would be much smaller than the increase that occurred in the United States between 1920 and today.

Raising the Floor

The Nordic countries have so far kept inequality at a modest level, ensuring a high and rising income floor for the least well-off and boosting opportunity for persons from less advantaged families and neighborhoods. How?

First, in keeping poverty and income inequality in check, government transfers rather than taxes do most of the work. All rich nations, including the Nordic countries, have tax systems that are roughly proportional: households up and down the income ladder pay approximately the same share of their pretax income in taxes. Consequently, taxes don't much alter the distribution of income. But government transfers do. Countries that provide larger income transfers to low- and middle-income households typically reduce poverty and income inequality more. In fact, pre-transfer income for households on the bottom fifth of the income ladder is about the same in Sweden and Denmark as in the United States. But transfers make the income of these households higher in Denmark and Sweden than in the United States. If we were to count the value of free or low-cost public services, the difference between the Nordic countries and the United States would be even greater.

Taxes play a role in redistributing income mainly by providing the funds for transfers. The key difference between America's tax system and those of highly redistributive countries, such as Denmark and Sweden, isn't that US taxes are less progressive. It's that US tax rates are lower, so that tax system raises less revenue. While making America's tax system more progressive is a good idea, we can't get the revenues we need—another 10 percent of GDP—solely from households at the top. Doing that would require increasing the effective tax rate paid by the top 1 or 5 percent of households to a level far exceeding that at any point in the past half century. An American social democracy will require larger tax payments from both the rich and the middle class.

Second, government transfers do more than secure a high income floor for the least well-off. They also raise that floor over time so economic growth is broadly shared. We often think of the trickle-down process as economic growth raising earnings via more work hours and higher wages. But in almost every affluent nation, the earnings of low-end households have increased little, if at all, since the late 1970s. Instead, increases in net government transfers—transfers received minus taxes paid—have driven most increases in incomes. Sometimes increasing transfers requires no policy change because benefit levels rise automatically as the economy grows. This happens when, for instance, pensions, unemployment compensation, and related benefits are indexed to average wages. Increases in other transfers, such as social assistance, require periodic policy updates.

What's the right level for the federal minimum wage? Fifteen dollars per hour, the goal of the "Fight for $15" movement, might be too high. A $15 minimum wage isn't likely to reduce employment much or at all in such cities as New York or San Francisco, but in Mississippi and Arkansas there's a good chance it would. A federal minimum of $12 per hour, indexed to prices to accommodate inflation over time, seems more likely to work. States and cities could still set their own minimum higher than the federal level, as many currently do. And people in low-end service jobs need not have a low income even if they are paid a low wage. A subsidy such as the Earned Income Tax Credit can boost household incomes while encouraging employment.

Should we try to minimize low-end service jobs? One way to do that is to make the wage floor very high, perhaps supplemented by heavy payroll taxes, to reduce employer demand for low-end positions. But why not welcome low-end service jobs? High-end services can't employ everyone. Imagine a high-skill, high-employment economy of the future with 85 percent of the working-age population in paid work. Suppose 65 percent finish college and end up in high- or middle-paying service jobs. That optimistic scenario still leaves 20 percent in other jobs. A few will work in manufacturing or farming, but for the rest we'll need low-end service jobs.

As we get richer, most of us happily outsource more tasks that we don't have the time, expertise, or desire to do ourselves—changing the oil in the car, mowing the lawn, cleaning, cooking, caring for children and other family members, advising, educating, organizing, managing, coaching, transporting. And improved productivity and lower costs abroad will reduce the price we pay for food, manufactured goods, and some services, leaving us with more disposable income. So we'll want more people teaching preschool children, coaching and mentoring teenagers, helping adults navigate the labor market or a midlife career transition, caring for the elderly, preparing and serving food, cleaning public spaces, delivering packages, and so on.

Should we instead pay out a basic income grant—an annual transfer of, say, $15,000 to every adult, not conditional on employment? This would significantly enhance people's economic freedom. And if it replaced social assistance programs like Temporary Assistance to Needy Families and Supplemental Nutritional Assistance Program ("food stamps"), it would reduce both government administrative costs and the stigma attached to receiving benefits. The hitch is that a grant large enough to allow adults to live without earnings almost certainly would reduce employment, and we need high employment to keep the tax base large enough to pay for generous social programs and government's other functions. Moreover, a program that reduces employment might further widen the political divide, endangering other public social protections.

For some, a low-end service job might be a career. Others will want a service position to be merely a stepping stone. Such jobs can be especially valuable for the young and immigrants. Besides organizing formal job ladders, government can help ensure that people move themselves up by providing health care, early education, elementary and secondary schooling, lifelong learning opportunities, retraining, job placement assistance, special services for the mentally or physically disabled, language assistance for immigrants, targeted programs for the young and the elderly, and assistance with transportation.

Mobility between jobs need not be confined to upward moves. It's difficult to predict at age 18 or even 22 what kinds of interests and capabilities you will have at age 35 or 50. Policy should help people change their job, occupation, or entire line of work at various points in life, even if the switch is simply to something different, rather than something better. This calls for counseling, mentoring, and perhaps several year-long paid sabbaticals. It also means eligibility for pensions, unemployment insurance, sickness insurance, parental leave, and holidays, and other nonwage benefits should be contingent on employment, but not on a particular job or employer.

If most people are expected to be employed, policy also ought to improve the quality of work-life. Low-end service jobs may offer limited mental stimulation or opportunity to participate in decision-making, and some are stressful. Some of these jobs will never provide more than limited stimulation, but we should push firms to do what's possible. More generally, we should aim to improve working conditions in all jobs and not assume that only higher-skilled, better-paying positions automatically come with decent work quality. Consider here an auditing procedure whereby government sets outcome standards for work conditions, leaves it up to firms to decide how to meet the standards, and monitors efforts to do so.

Policy also ought to limit the degree to which job inequality spills over into social inequality and segregation. In a good society, inequalities are modest, not severe. Jobs inevitably come with inequalities of status. If pay differences are large too, social segregation and inequality of respect might result. Policy should push against this. Neighborhoods should be designed or redesigned to encourage class mixing. Parks, beaches, libraries, and public transport ought to be attractive to all. And we might consider a mandatory year of national service to ensure that everyone gets an experience of genuine social mixing as they embark on adulthood.

So far I've focused on the distribution of wages, jobs, and incomes. What is the best way to reduce inequality of opportunity? Many institutions and policies can help, but evidence increasingly points to a key role for universal high-quality affordable early education. Schools help to offset the massive differences among families.[3] Having children enter school earlier in life could reduce disparities among kindergarteners. Indeed, some analysts conclude that the impact of schooling is larger before kindergarten than after.

Social Democracy's Political Road Ahead

Social democracy in the United States is compatible with varying degrees of political centralization, with some use of direct democracy (referendums), and with varying foreign policies. Although the shift wouldn't require any constitutional changes, two would be helpful. One is switching from our winner-take-all presidential-parliamentary system of elections and government to a single parliament with proportional representation elections. The other is taxing wealth directly while wealth holders are alive (wealth tax) rather than only when they die (estate tax).

An important question is whether a strong union movement and a well-organized social movement are needed. True, differences in union strength help account for why the United States lags behind the Nordic countries in public insurance programs and public services. But over the past century, the United States has nevertheless added a host of valuable programs, and unions and social movements weren't always critical to their creation. Even so, organized labor resurgence would help, as would better organized and more persistent social movements. The "Fight for $15" movement may signal a shift in this direction.

The Nordic countries haven't gotten everything right. Each has at one time or another gone too far with social policy generosity and made mistakes in macroeconomic management, and each has struggled to embrace and successfully manage large-scale immigration. Even so, their experience shows that adding public insurance and public services to a capitalist economy can enhance economic security and equality of opportunity without sacrificing liberty, economic dynamism, health, happiness, or the many other things we want in a good society.

Notes

1 For details, evidence, and references, see Lane Kenworthy, *Social Democratic Capitalism* (New York: Oxford University Press, 2019); Lane Kenworthy, *Social Democratic America* (New York: Oxford University Press, 2014).

2 Bernie Sanders proposed essentially this in his 2016 presidential bid. Sanders calls himself a "democratic socialist," but he doesn't want to nationalize firms or industries or shift from private to public ownership. His chief proposals are to create some new public insurance programs (paid parental leave, sickness insurance) and expand some others (Social Security, Medicare), to create some new publicly funded services (early education) and expand some others (health care, training, job placement), to reduce user fees for some services (public colleges), and to increase the minimum wage. This is social democracy, not socialism.

3 We know this from two pieces of evidence. First, at kindergarten entry, children from poor homes tend to have much lower measurable skills than children from affluent homes. Given the huge variation in home and neighborhood circumstances, we would expect that gap to continue to widen throughout childhood. But it doesn't; it's about the same size at the end of high school as at the start of kindergarten. This tells us that schools have an equalizing effect. Second, during summer vacations, when children are out of school, those from lower-income families tend to fall farther behind compared to those from higher-income families.

Chapter 2

The Good Society 2.0

Henning Meyer

When the global financial crisis hit in 2007–2008, many social democrats in Europe (and beyond) believed that their time had finally come. Deregulated financial markets had developed into a self-referential system that was becoming ever more detached from the wider economy. And when the finance industry collapsed, the consequences reverberated widely, given global economic interdependency. The Wall Street crash not just brought down other financial centers, including the City of London, but also plunged the global economy into a deep crisis that has still not been resolved.

It also became clear, quite quickly, that this global meltdown would have significant political repercussions. Surely this should have been a "social democratic moment," as the Oxford historian David Marquand mused. Wasn't it social democracy that had always stood for appropriate regulation to steady inherently unstable markets? Wasn't this unregulated spasm what had happened? Real-world evidence emerged to confirm that one main plank of social democratic theory *is* right: markets need to be regulated to function properly.

More than a decade on, it is fair to conclude that the "social democratic moment" never happened. In Europe, the crisis' political repercussions have materialized as substantial political volatility and permanent emergency politics. The problems of the financial sector also corresponded with major shortcomings in the construction of the Euro. What started as a financial crisis quickly morphed into a crisis of the entire Eurozone and the European Union. Meanwhile, the refugee crisis added another dimension to the plethora of unresolved questions. The resulting political discontent has not benefitted social democrats. Why and what does this mean for the future of social democratic politics?

Answering these questions requires understanding the development of European social democracy in the decades before the economic crisis. In the 1990s and 2000s, social democratic parties assessing their situation tried to determine why they had been losing electoral appeal since the late 1970s. Along with many country-specific explanations was one common concern: against the backdrop of the emerging free-market doctrines, traditional social democratic politics looked outdated. The old ways were blamed for declining electoral fortunes.

Reacting to this self-appraisal, and inspired by the experiences of the New Democrats and President Bill Clinton in the United States, many social democratic parties started a renewal process to adjust their political programs. This "Third Way" adjustment period basically led to different forms and degrees of social democratic accommodation to the neoliberal mainstream. Britain's New Labor and Germany's *Neue Mitte* are just two examples of the various "Third Ways" that emerged all over Europe.

The term "Third Way" had, of course, been used for a long time and had several different meanings. In the 1990s context, it was basically understood as a middle way between old-style social democracy and neoliberalism. This middle way approach often came up in the presumed distinction between means and ends. Social democratic values were viewed as permanent ends, but the means to achieve them were adaptable to new circumstances. "Good policy is what works" was an often-heard phrase. Yet, means and ends necessarily interact, and it is far from obvious "what works." And who decides the criteria of what works and doesn't? Since politics usually involves trade-offs, for whom does a policy work and for whom not? Such issues have always dogged overly simplistic definitions of effective policy.

This programmatic renewal of social democracy had several consequences. Since it meant moving toward, rather than challenging, neoliberal political orthodoxy, the development of real political alternatives and visions was neglected. This was especially true of the acceptance of the "economization" of almost all political arenas, including social policies, which made political discourse monolithic. Political renewal is always necessary and, naturally, social democracy should learn lessons from conservative, green, and liberal ideas. But the extent of this political adjustment process in many cases led to the accusation—still heard today—that social democratic parties have sacrificed their core beliefs and have become almost indistinguishable from their political competitors.

In electoral terms, the Third Way worked well for a time. By the late 1990s, all but a few EU member states had governments led by social democrats. Many of them had implemented bold policy agendas based on their new politics. The Third Way seemed to have won the day.

Eventually, however, cracks started to appear. Fundamental problems emerged when the financial crisis revealed that all the old-fashioned social democratic talk about the inherent instability of markets was not that outdated after all, and that we were entering a period of global economic turmoil.

At this point, what seemed like strengths before the economic collapse became fundamental weaknesses. Since social democrats hadn't developed an alternative political program in the previous decades, they were intellectually unprepared when the crisis hit. There simply was no real political alternative on offer. Even worse, many social democrats in government had pushed through deregulation agendas, so they were not seen just as politically clueless, but as collaborators in a failing system. A bare cupboard and bad faith led to the breakdown of trust and further alienated significant parts of the traditional social democratic support—groups already disaffected by unpopular policy measures. Against this backdrop, social democrats simply were not to be the political beneficiaries of the financial crisis, and new questions, such as how to deal with the Eurozone and refugee crises, have since reinforced this lack of political orientation.

The reasons why the "social democratic moment" never happened trace to the contemporary challenges of social democracy. European social democrats struggle with the rapid change taking place around them. The Eurozone crisis requires bold decisions and further steps toward European integration that seemed unthinkable only a few years ago. The refugee crisis requires coordinated European action too. The alternative to deeper integration is renationalization, which has been equally unthinkable until recently but has, some commentators say, already started.

This political storm requires bold leadership and has caught social democrats ill prepared. The Third Way period is over, but a genuinely new social democratic politics has not been established yet. The list of urgent tasks is daunting: social democrats have to redefine their political offering, rebuild credibility and trust, and, as if this was not enough, must achieve this tall order in the most turbulent political times in decades.

But not all is gloomy. Clarity about the task ahead will help to address it. A group of thinkers and practitioners from all over Europe has been working on a new social democratic politics for several years now. What has been developed under the concept of the Good Society is a new social democratic narrative that takes a thorough, value-driven analysis of our current economic and political problems as a starting point to craft a new politics.

A New Politics

The goal of this new community of action-oriented thinkers is to define the Good Society to make a "better society" possible and sketch the political way toward it. Such a value-driven political compass is an important tool for navigating today's stormy political seas, just as it's a useful starting point for addressing wider challenges.

The idea of a Good Society is based on democracy, community, and pluralism. It is democratic because only the free participation of every citizen can guarantee true freedom and progress. It is based on a community approach because it recognizes our mutual interdependencies and joint interests. And it is pluralistic because it draws vitality from the diversity of political institutions, economic activities, and cultural identities.

The Good Society approach also breaks with some of the political techniques that have run their course. During the Third Way's heyday, policy-making was rather transactional. Based on political research and focus groups, a political offer was tailored to the electoral customer's identified needs. The resulting politics was reactive rather than transformational. But now that the limits and constraints of our current economic and political systems have become all too obvious, a more ambitious politics is needed.

In practical terms, creating this society means reestablishing the primacy of enlightened politics over economic interests. It means defending and expanding citizen rights, where possible, and transforming the relationship between individuals and the state into a new democratic partnership, one that strengthens transparency and accountability on all levels. The primacy of society means the supremacy of general social goods—such as inclusion, education, and health—over market interests. It also means redistributing wealth and power. The economic philosophy of the Good Society is rooted in the idea of ecologically sustainable and just economic development that benefits the whole of society, not just a few at its top.

Besides serving justice and environmental sustainability, a new values-driven approach such as the Good Society is needed to revive European social democracy. Since societies are becoming more diverse, it's just logical that trying to generate electoral success by targeting specific social segments with transactional politics amounts to chasing ever smaller and more differentiated groups. Politics is thus becoming narrower and more exclusive. A values-based political agenda should, in contrast, be able to foster broad buy-in and unite otherwise diverse social groups drawn in by a positive social and economic vision.

Political change is, however, a slow process that takes place in small steps alongside the necessities, and within the constraints, of day-to-day politics. Creating a new distinctive social democratic agenda is also difficult because the political competition is not static and because in an interdependent world it is simply not good enough to build a Good Society in a European shell, let alone within national borders. For this reason, the Good Society's global dimension deserves special attention.

Of course, many of today's most important issues—such as rising inequality, workplace problems, and environmental degradation—simply cannot be addressed on a national or European scale. The Good Society project thus aims to revitalize the internationalist tradition of social democracy and to build global alliances. So many political issues are global in reach now that citizens are politically experienced, albeit in different ways, in countries everywhere.

Clearly, reaching out and building bridges to other progressive traditions around the world is a vital part of the Good Society project. But how are the same or similar political issues perceived in different parts of the world? What other progressive solutions to these problems exist? And where are there connection points for discursive and political alliances that can help all conceptualize and address today's pressing issues in mutually reinforcing ways? Embracing these crucial questions gives the Good Society a truly global dimension, one that social democracy has neglected in recent decades.

I have discussed the Good Society with thinkers and practitioners in Asia (South Korea, China, and Japan) and from Latin America. There is openness and curiosity in Asia, where solid public welfare systems are largely missing and missed. The experience with Latin America has been more sobering. Even though "*buen vivir*" and "21st century socialism" are discussed, the political content associated with these terms seems very traditional and dogmatic. The obvious candidates for joint discussion in the future are the United States and Canada, especially against the backdrop of current political developments in these countries.

A new regional political dimension is also a constitutive part of the Good Society. Be it in Europe, Asia, Latin America, or Africa, a new quality of regional integration of political ideas and discourses is needed to effectively address today's pressing issues. The Good Society project is a hub for creating better regional connections, nurturing and inspiring the development and exchange of ideas.

Finally, national Good Society activities should also be adapted to fit national circumstances. A great strength of the Good Society is that it is not a one-size-fits-all approach for implementing the same policies everywhere, regardless of specific circumstances and national traditions. Instead, the Good Society is a political toolbox of best practices and general policy guidance. These policies share common roots in the analysis of today's pressing problems and the social democratic values underpinning this analysis. That makes continuous adaptation of the Good Society to different national circumstances an important line of work.

Social democracy is in transition and it needs to adapt to the current political and economic circumstances. Small or simply rhetorical adjustments will not suffice, and the digital revolution, the most transformative economic and social development in decades but one replete with distributional issues, is adding a completely new dimension. That explains why we are now talking about the "Good Society 2.0."

The Good Economy 2.0

The Good Economy would be a mixed economy. Different forms of ownership and organization would exist alongside each other. A key would be defining public goods. Once everybody understood and internalized that, it would be perfectly fine to create, say, a profit-seeking consumer electronics firm that seeks to maximize profit and get ahead in a competitive landscape, but probably not a profit-seeking healthcare system since smartphones aren't public goods and healthcare is. In other words, profit-seeking gets in the way of healthcare. If health security is the aim, a nonprofit collective solution aimed at dispersing risk and providing needed services is a much better and more efficient system. An object lesson here might be the US healthcare cost structure. In any case, we need to define the guiding logic of different parts of the economy and create structures to match.

The idea of a mixed economy also distinguishes social democracy from what is often referred to as socialism or democratic socialism. All these terms are linguistic minefields and get used in different ways in different countries and at different times. But, as a rule of thumb, democratic socialists emphasize general public ownership of the means of production while social democrats advocate a mixed economy approach.

Investment decisions in the Good Economy would be made the conventional way, though governments urgently need to rediscover their role in proactive fiscal policies. In many countries, especially in Europe, the misguided dogma of austerity has led governments to significantly underuse fiscal policy and to underinvest in critical (digital) infrastructure and other public assets.

Monetary policy would remain as it is. But the functioning of financial markets and institutions needs to be reformed to avoid the kind of speculation and capital misallocation we have witnessed. There is nothing inherently good or bad about finance. It is a tool that should also be used for social purposes, not just private gain. Progressives too often dismiss finance rather than trying to use it for progressive objectives. Fortunately, some people are waking up to those possibilities. Various activities in Europe under the banner of "progressive finance" have aimed to recapture this tool.

As for capital, its structural inequality is one of two drivers likely to widen the gap between haves and have-nots. The other is the potential polarization of labor markets due to the digital revolution. Both make shaping the digital revolution and rethinking taxation and capital ownership crucial.

We could moderate inequality in the primary and secondary distribution of income via taxes and institutions. But if Thomas Piketty's analysis in *Capital in the Twenty-First Century* is right and we have a structural distributional imbalance in the relationship between growth and capital returns, then capital ownership needs to be rethought. Maybe workers could be part-owners of companies and maybe we need a financial vehicle such as a sovereign wealth fund to resocialize capital returns across the wider economy.

For wage setting, a conducive regulatory environment is crucial. The Good Economy would have national and international minimum wages and strong worker representation in the company and in the wider economy to make sure productivity gains are shared fairly. Market functions need not be dismantled. But it is crucially important to design a political economy that produces the desired outcomes in both the primary and the secondary distribution of income.

The digital revolution is likely to challenge our historic ideas about jobs and employment. And three trends that will play out in varying ways in different countries need to be widely understood: job substitution, job augmentation, and job creation.

In the digital age, we will see many more forms of cooperation and economic activity. Depending on how we decide to distribute the likely productivity gains born of the digital revolution, we can also expect somewhat more leisure time in the future.

If productivity gains are used to reduce working hours, work arrangements will become much more flexible. The end result might be fewer hours worked per week and across the work life. There could be adjustments in hours, for instance, from early to middle to late career to take health, child-rearing, leisure, and other interests into account. As for job displacement, the very big fly in the ointment, trade unions are key to making sure that worker concerns are heard in the time of disruption ahead. Their organizational problems aside, unions will be indispensable if the digital society is shaped fairly.

More generally, we are moving into a much more colorful economic life in which the traditional economic categories of wage labor (reduced hours) and leisure sit alongside elements of the sharing economy (financial interest) and a new form of digital commons (not-for-profit). If the digital revolution is shaped well, our social and economic lives could be much more adaptable and much richer.

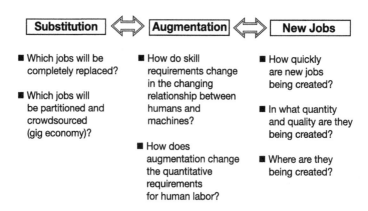

Figure 2.1 Key questions about job substitution, augmentation, and job creation in the digital economy.

the United States who was elected in 2016 and his Senate were committed to radically paring back national government, perhaps the only space left open for creative change is at the state and local levels.

Subsidiarity

Even though Americans wax enthusiastic about "states' rights," few truly want to "let Oregon be Oregon, and let Alabama be Alabama." Almost all, left and right, dream about imposing their visions of utopia on everyone else. That's why American politics has become so toxic and why, in a country of 330 million diverse views, the only utopia possible may be a local one built by like-minded neighbors pursuing their own dreams.

The principle at decentralization's core is *subsidiarity*, a fancy word for DIY ("do it yourself"). If you can accomplish your own goals without harming anyone else, subsidiarity encourages you to act. The concept is infused with an expansive notion of personal freedom and natural rights, tapping the power of the local "commons" that David Bollier defines as "a self-organized system by which communities manage resources…with minimal or no reliance on the market or State."[5] Start collective initiatives in your community and if none works, then—and only then—bump it up to the state level. If that fails, then and only then move it to the national level. A world embracing subsidiarity has powerful local governments, less powerful state or regional governments, weak national governments, and highly circumscribed international institutions.

Subsidiarity has several virtues. It is biased toward action and catalyzes participatory democracy in the locales people care about most. It's efficient, mobilizing collective action without involving unnecessary decision-makers or bureaucrats. But it's also flexible and pragmatic, recognizing that a few decisions, like nuclear weapons deployment, must be made higher up.

Yet, Americans are surprisingly skeptical of this pure form of decentralization. Our brief early history under the Articles of Confederation, when states had their own currency, trade practices, and foreign policies, was and remains regarded as a chaotic time when we were vulnerable to recapture by the British monarchy. Progressives more recently point out how "states' rights" historically have provided a cover for slavery, secession, and segregation, and for today's exclusionary voting practices. Conservatives, even some self-styled constitutionalists, are equally eager to wield central power to wipe out such progressive local initiatives as abortion clinics, pro-LGBT ordinances, municipal minimum wages, or the sanctuary cities that protect illegal immigrants from detention and deportation.

The Bill of Rights must remain a cornerstone of a decentralized United States. Federalism must be synchronized with decentralism. In the US democracy's formative years, such Federalists as James Madison and Alexander Hamilton advocated greater centralization while such anti-federalists as Patrick Henry called for greater decentralization. Yet, both groups found common ground, constructing a *relatively* decentralized system that protected minorities from majority abuse. In that vein, subsidiarity works best in a system of rights protecting citizens against encroachment by hostile national, state, or local laws.

Subsidiarity also requires an open marketplace, where entrepreneurs and small businesses flourish. It would be preposterous to grant communities political freedom if they weren't economically free to materially sustain it. But because the United States must also manage corporations that operate in many states or globally, higher levels of power are necessary to break up monopolies and ensure robust local competition. Here, Switzerland, with its gigantic and often secretive banks, is not a particularly reassuring model. Better to imagine the era of President Theodore Roosevelt, who used antitrust tools to break up giants like Standard Oil. Decentralizing power means doing everything possible to keep businesses in every sector diverse, small, and competitive.

An open market implies minimizing the public sector's scope and power. For example, all corporate subsidies would be eliminated. In *Systems of Survival*, the late economist Jane Jacobs argued that when the guardian sector (her term for the appropriate role of government) took on the functions of the mercantile sector (business), "monstrous hybrids" resulted.[6] Indeed, corporate subsidies exemplify wasteful government overreach that too often greases the wheels of corrupt transactions between politicians and businesspeople.[7]

The United States has a relatively free market, but not only Milton Friedman fundamentalists see enormous room for improvement. Corporate welfare is now running at several hundred billion dollars per year at the national level, and at least at $80 billion at the state and local levels.[8] Anti-trust laws need to be bolstered and dominant corporate players like Walmart, Bank of America, and Tyson Foods broken apart. American conservatives understandably complain about high business taxes that drive many of the largest US corporations offshore, and in a more decentralized system federal business taxes could and should be greatly reduced.

Another core goal of subsidiarity is self-reliance, which is important for economic, political, and environmental reasons. Contrary to simplistic critiques from free-traders, local self-reliance does not mean withdrawing from the national or global economy. It means engaging the world from a position of strength. Local self-reliance enables a community to grow income, wealth, and jobs through diversification, which in turn multiplies the number of sectors that can both meet local demand and penetrate global markets.[9]

Self-reliance runs deep in the American character. It found expression in early American writers like Ralph Waldo Emerson and Henry David Thoreau and survives in "buy-local" and community resilience

Finally, the Good Society needs a broader set of indicators. The far too narrow focus on GDP, which undervalues whatever is hard to measure or intangible, has led to an incomplete view of what is important. In recent years, various new indicators to measure different elements of happiness and well-being have been developed. And another exciting development in public policy is "nudging," or guiding people toward rational decisions in their own interest by intervening in the choice architectures that are necessarily parts of our everyday lives whether we realize it or not. Utilizing a wider set of indicators and tools such as nudges in addition to traditional policies is part of the Good Society' broader approach to politics.

Will Only Crises Open Doors?

The Good Society approach is about changing direction rather than achieving any final state of affairs. That could happen reasonably quickly. And it's feasible, especially if introduced internationally and everywhere at the same time.

The most likely scenario for change would be a reaction to a new crisis, such as the aftermath of the financial crisis in 2008. We saw then that internationally coordinated policy responses are indeed possible under extreme pressure—however short-lived the cooperation.

Yet, social movements can play a crucial role in agenda setting and getting a topic debated in political circles. However short-lived, movements such as Occupy Wall Street and others have managed to get inequality, for instance, firmly on the political agenda. Even when policy reactions are grindingly slow or incomplete, working within the framework of broad progressive alliances to get issues on the political agenda is an important initial step.

Finally, while waiting for crisis to strike and doing what we can to avert it, we must change the way policies are created. What we have seen too often in Western countries in recent decades is a transactional policy-making approach driven primarily by electoral concerns—a reversal of means and ends. The result has been intellectual emptiness and a loss of trust in progressive parties that polarizes people or invites apolitical ennui. Gaining office should be a means to implementing a policy agenda that has won support in a democratic election, not an end in itself.

In the Good Society 2.0, policy is transformative. It starts with an analysis of what is wrong and what kind of values-based policies could help improve the situation and in this way moves us closer to a values-based society. To be clear, we will never reach the "Good Society." The means to establish whether we live in a good society or not don't even exist and societies are by definition dynamic and constantly changing. The Good Society as a political narrative provides a political compass rather than a description of a fixed destination. The goal is the journey and beginning it is the imminent political task.

Chapter 3

The Promise of a Million Utopias

Michael H. Shuman

Here's a fun question guaranteed to stump friends, family, and party guests: can you name Switzerland's leader? Trust me—no one ever knows the answer. That's because it hardly matters.

Switzerland is arguably the world's most decentralized nation. Each of its 26 states, called "cantons," governs its own affairs autonomously. Cantons have their own official languages, constitutions, and parliaments, and each has radically differing policies for education, labor, welfare, and the economy. Within the cantons are 3,000 relatively autonomous local governments, called "communes," and they are the most important political units in the lives of the eight million Swiss.

Swiss direct democracy is practiced through frequent federal- and canton-level referenda. A national referendum, ballot-worthy with just 50,000 signatures, can overturn any act of parliament, and 100,000 signatures can bring a grassroots-authored proposition to a national vote. The president comes from a collegial seven-member Federal Council, chosen for a four-year term by an elected two-body legislature. Council members typically serve for only one term, and the president has no more power than the other six members. Federal powers are largely restricted to matters that absolutely require national coordination, such as currency and railways. The presidency holds highly limited power, even in foreign policy.

By many metrics, the country's performance is exceptional. Swiss per capita Gross Domestic Product or GDP (in real dollars) is the world's second highest.[1] The country ranked third in the United Nations' 2015 *Human Development Report*, which measures income, education, and life expectancy.[2] The 2016 Environmental Performance Index places Switzerland 16th for safeguarding the environment.[3] According to the *CIA World Factbook*, Switzerland currently ranks 18th in income equality.[4]

Switzerland is no utopia. But its decentralized structure suggests a compelling possible direction for systemic transformation of the United States. Indeed, given our embrace of states' rights—reflected in the Constitution's Tenth Amendment—the Swiss model could be considered deeply in tune with American history and values. Moreover, given that the president of movements. Yet, outside major cities, most Americans live in highly specialized, highly dependent economies. Even after years of local food promotion, almost no area grows locally more than a few percentage points of the raw foodstuffs it consumes.[10] Economic development "experts" who pushed communities into finding and filling a handful of globally competitive niches—and ignoring the rest of the economy—have succeeded all too well.[11] The next system envisioned here counsels the opposite: diversify your economy to increase your self-reliance and, ultimately, multiply your competitive niches for export.

The final core goal of a decentralized United States should be solidarity with the rest of humanity. This is another departure from the Swiss, whose steadfast neutrality has by some reckonings made them accomplices to war crimes. Subsidiary demands that challenges that cannot be addressed at lower levels must be addressed at higher ones, and fighting some global problems—drugs, child pornography, arms trade, pandemics like Ebola, and climate disruption—requires global collaboration. Under the system envisioned here, every community has a solemn duty to engage with other communities worldwide to solve these problems. Total isolationism is morally impermissible.

Devolution American Style

Meaningful devolution in the United States will require invoking federalism to carefully shrink the national government and carefully expand state and local governments. For instance, subsidiarity will require a fundamentally narrower approach to "preemption," a court's determination that a federal law is superior to a state law. Today, federal courts sometimes knock out state laws that might conflict with federal law or intrude on a field that the federal government has "occupied." A narrower approach to preemption would permit any state and local law unless a federal law *expressly* forbids it or compliance with the federal and state laws is *impossible* (as when federal law mandates stores to stay open on Sunday and a state law orders them to close). The Supreme Court could narrow grounds for preemption, but recent court decisions (knocking out local campaign-financing laws) seem to go in the opposite direction.[12] The faster recourse might be for Congress to pass a law stating very narrow criteria for preemption, which a non-activist Court might treat as binding.

Ultimately, however, shrinking the federal government will require overhauling entitlements and the military. Of the $4.7 trillion in the 2020 federal budget, entitlement programs (primarily Social Security and Medicare) add up to $2.8 trillion (or 60 percent) and the military and intelligence programs total $989 billion dollars (or 21 percent).[13] Another 10 percent goes to pay interest on the debt. In short, all the heated arguments between Democrats and Republicans on nonmilitary spending are over a measly 9 percent of the budget.

Decentralizing the United States could mean eliminating core entitlement programs, but these instead should gradually be handed over to state and local governments to administer more wisely. For example, if the Social Security trust fund were divided up on a per capita basis and given to 50-plus state administrators, they might invest the funds in local businesses or state economic development projects. Progressive states might expand residents' retirement benefits while assessing greater annual contributions; conservative states might give residents more discretion over how much they save and where they invest their savings.

Similar two-step shifts could be made in other entitlement programs, such as SNAP food benefits. How? First, return to states' programmatic funds proportional to their populations and allow them greater leeway in spending their share to achieve the same goals. Second, gradually roll back the federal contribution and allow states to expand, contract, or revamp their programs as they see fit, so long as they do not harm constitutionally protected minorities.

As for cutting military expenditures, it's hard to imagine this happening if Americans don't redefine "security." Many widely held beliefs fuel today's bloated military establishment: that security requires unilateral deployment of the world's largest military force, that military solutions to global problems trump economic or ecological ones, and that serving as the world's police force is the United States' unique right and responsibility. Reducing spending on this goliath to what the neutrality-loving Swiss spend (0.7 percent of their GDP) would be a stretch. But even scaling military ambitions to, say, the British or the French levels (about 2 percent of GDP, compared to 4.7 percent in the United States today) would save more than half a trillion dollars per year.[14]

What would ultimately remain under federal jurisdiction would be those functions that enjoy the American public's broad support and require some national coordination. Besides a smaller military force, think here of the federal courts, highways, air traffic control, oversight of interstate commerce, the preparation of national statistics, border enforcement, air quality standards, and public health programs. Even in these realms, however, regulations could be simplified and more details left to the states. With a stronger presumption against federal preemption, states would have fewer fears that devolution might upend their local quality of life.

Scaling Down

US decentralization as envisioned here could take place within the 50 states, and their more than 3,000 counties and 36,000 localities. Appealing as regional or bioregional governance may seem, these are just fanciful ideas. There are sound historical, legal, and cultural reasons for today's divisions. Why impose restructuring on an already ambitious decentralization agenda?

That said, nothing prevents two or more localities, counties, or states from voluntarily combining into a regional body to realize greater economies of scale. The constitution's Compact Clause already facilitates thousands of interstate agreements on ports, border enforcement, and utility management. In a decentralized United States, such agreements among cities or counties would become more common.

Decentralization should not stop at the state's border. An embrace of subsidiarity might lead some states to move some programs to their counties or municipalities. Perhaps retirement funds or anti-poverty programs could be devolved to the local level, where residents could shape these programs to better fit local needs. Devolution within a state, however, ultimately requires expanding local tax power to fund increased responsibilities.

A decentralized United States would sign only those treaties that protect local rights. Many of the trade agreements signed over the past generation shifted from the worthy objective of tariff reduction to the indefensible objective of regulatory harmonization. Specifically, provisions in the World Trade Organization (WTO) and the North American Free Trade Agreement (NAFTA) overrode state and local environmental laws deemed "unscientific" by corporate-influenced judges, restricted government agencies' ability to buy or invest locally, and prevented communities from labeling products possibly containing GMOs or made by child labor.[15] These agreements would need to be repudiated or revamped so localities could set any nondiscriminatory standards they wish, buy and invest in local businesses just like corporations can, and label anything they want as an exercise of free speech. This framework is consistent with the US Constitution and Supreme Court jurisprudence on the Commerce Clause.

A Robust Small-Business Sector

Even though Switzerland is known for its big banks, its small business sector is vast, competitive, and powerful. Indeed, the world's largest complementary currency system, run by the WIR Bank, is Swiss. Its assets exceed $5 billion. Four-fifths of the system's 80,000 members are small- and medium-scale businesses. Since 1934, the network has facilitated loans and sales among members by using an internal currency (alongside Swiss francs) guaranteed by member assets.

A Swiss-inspired economic model for a decentralized United States would be rooted in a highly competitive market economy dominated by small- and medium-scale businesses—a recipe, growing evidence suggests, for regional prosperity. For example, authors of a 2010 study in the *Harvard Business Review*[16] wrote that "regional economic growth is highly correlated with the presence of many small, entrepreneurial employers—not a few big ones." A 2013 paper by the Federal Reserve in Atlanta found statistically significant "evidence that local entrepreneurship matters for local economic performance... [T]he percent of employment provided by resident, or locally-owned, business establishments has a significant positive effect on county income and employment growth and a significant and negative effect on poverty..."[17]

But can smaller businesses compete in a globalized world economy? Broadly speaking, local businesses have done remarkably well at competing, despite economic developers' neglect and subsidies for global competitors. Two basic facts underscore this conclusion. First, when the spectacular growth of home-based businesses in the United States is properly accounted for, there has been no shift whatsoever from the local half of all jobs to the non-local half for almost a generation.[18] Second, local businesses' profit rates haven't dropped below those of big businesses. In fact, Internal Revenue Service data show that net revenue from sole proprietors, which most small businesses either are or start out as, generated three times more net income per receipt dollar than C corporations.[19] Canada's most profitable businesses have 10–20 employees and are 63 percent more profitable than big businesses.[20]

Within this framework, competitive state economies could still structure their rules in creative new ways. For example, states might:

- Enact tougher antitrust laws;
- Have large public sectors leading industries like healthcare and banking, or keep their public sectors tiny;
- Provide tax incentives to companies that formed as Benefit corporations (embracing high labor and environmental standards), as low-profit companies, or as cooperatives;
- Adopt aggressive economic planning mechanisms, or remain highly laissez-faire; or
- Issue their own currency (as many locales did during the Great Depression).

The biggest impediment to the spread of local business is, arguably, capital. Even though locally owned businesses constitute slightly more than half of the US economy, they receive far less than half of all banking capital and almost none of the securities capital (which is five times greater) tied up in pension funds, mutual funds, and insurance funds. This constitutes a huge capital market failure.

Various state reforms could make more capital available to local business. Among the most interesting:

- Create a state-owned bank, like the Bank of North Dakota, that places unspent public funds and federal transfer payments on deposit in local banks and credit unions, which are three times more likely than global banks to lend to locally owned business.
- Expand the crowdfunding reforms already afoot in more than 35 states that make it cheaper and easier for local businesses to issue intrastate securities.
- Create a state stock exchange, as Michigan committed itself to exploring, to facilitate the resale of intrastate securities.
- Make it easier for grassroots groups to create neighborhood-scale investment funds, as the Canadian province of Nova Scotia did in 1998, and allow residents to put tax-deferred retirement savings in them.[21]
- Enact a tax credit for investments in locally owned business. The Canadian province of New Brunswick gives residents a 50 percent credit on provincial taxes when they invest at least 1,000 Canadian dollars in a local business.

Only some states would embrace these ideas. Others will approach reforms in radically different ways, including taking a pass. The only absolute requirement is the reform of federal securities laws to *permit* states to implement new ideas. Some of these reforms—for public banking, crowdfunding, and tax credits—are clearly legal now. Others, such as reforms of the Exchanges Act of 1934 or the Investment Company Act of 1940, might require "no-action" regulatory initiatives from the Security Exchange Commission or congressional action.

What will happen when trillions of dollars of investment capital, which have so far gone automatically to Wall Street, get shifted to Main Street? Lower investor demand could depress Fortune 500 stock prices, which might prompt even more Americans to move their money into the local economy. Given the underlying competitiveness and profitability of local small businesses, economic decentralization might then proceed surprisingly swiftly.

A Diversity of Social Policies

The Swiss social safety net provides various kinds of national insurances (including retirement, unemployment, health, accident, and disability), but social programs beyond those vary enormously by canton. Generally, Swiss social policy emanates from nonprofits funded by local governments, and when programs are prove effective, they may be taken up by the canton or federal government.[22] For example, publicly supported nursery school begins when children are anywhere from the ages of four to six, and publicly supported child-care programs are robust in some communities and skeletal in others.

In a decentralized United States, the social policies of the 50 states would also be as diverse as their economies. Some states might embrace Swedish-style social programs (financed by significantly higher taxes) while others might embrace private sector models. Whatever choices are made, the prerequisite for successful social programs is a strong economy because a strong private sector minimizes burdens on the public sector and, in principle, allows for generous funding of social programs.

While many different kinds of antipoverty programs are defensible, here are some particularly interesting ideas for states to consider:

- Grow the retirement programs they inherit from the national government and expand the mandatory contribution that all workers make to their savings. Make savings fully portable from job to job (or to self-employment).

- Adopt and expand the earned-income tax credits to maximize the incentive of the poor to work.

- Provide employers with tax credits to maximize their incentive to hire the chronically poor, including residents with disabilities and prison records.

- Keep making benefits available to the chronically poor, whether through cash supplements or in-kind benefits, but on condition that recipients accept low-wage jobs, provided if necessary by the government as the employer of last resort. Organize some of these jobs around meeting basic needs—say, in community gardens and greenhouses integrated with public housing.

Although a decentralized America would still have a strong Bill of Rights protecting Americans from discriminatory laws based on race, religion, ethnicity, and gender, even this arena needs state innovation. A decentralized union would permit a state to enact stronger protections of rights than those afforded under the US Constitution. The Supreme Court in principle recognizes this. For example, California was permitted to grant greater free speech rights to protestors in a private shopping mall than the US Constitution would provide.[23] And states were permitted to allow same-sex marriage before it became a national standard. Similarly, "blue states" might strengthen the rights of women, non-heterosexuals, and immigrants while "red states" might strengthen the rights of the unborn and religious practice in public places.

A decentralized union might also with luck see states showing more tolerance of communities that deviate from state norms. For example, red Texas might still permit bluish Austin to set a higher minimum wage and make abortion services more accessible. Or blue Maryland might still permit a reddish Salisbury to try ways of remedying discrimination other than affirmative action.

Those unhappy with the utopian inclination of their community or state could always move, a time-honored American tradition. This may seem cold-hearted toward those too poor to uproot, but US history is filled with migrations by people with strong grievances and limited means. And this pursuit of alternatives is happening anyway, as Americans sort themselves into more ideologically homogeneous communities. The overarching point is that a real democracy, and a decentralized democracy especially, always lets its members choose whether to change, accept, or flee local policies they don't like.

BIMBY, Not NIMBY

Local self-reliance offers a powerful new way to think about sustainability. A local economy that that becomes highly self-reliant by using its own labor and natural resources by definition imposes fewer demands on other localities' resources. Energy self-reliant states, for example, won't want to go to war in the Mideast to protect "our oil."

We should extend this thinking further to protect other global commons. In 1987, the Brundtland Commission, arguing for urgent global action to deal with dramatic global environmental deterioration, defined *sustainability* as meeting the current generation's needs without impairing future generations' ability to meet theirs.[24] Through a more decentralist lens, sustainability might be redefined as every community meeting its own needs, present and future, without impairing the ability of other communities to do the same.[25] Adding place to sustainability drives home the value of global solidarity.

Skeptics, of course, can point to communities that will do as little as possible to manage their resources, world be damned. The phrase NIMBY, which refers to "not in my backyard," is about communities that refuse to do their part to solve collective problems—like providing land for their own garbage disposal. In a highly decentralized United States, NIMBY would be frowned upon but accepted, provided that the NIMBY community was not imposing new environmental problems on its neighbors. For those that were, higher-level legislation would be needed.

Far more important than the challenge of NIMBY is the opportunity of BIMBY—those communities that proclaim "*begin* in my backyard." For example, in the late 1980s, I helped organize a group of two dozen American and Canadian communities that entered into a quasi-treaty with one another called the Stratospheric Protection Accord (SPA).[26] Frustrated with the lack of national action to reduce emissions of the chlorofluorocarbons (CFCs) and halons puncturing Earth's protective ozone layer, these communities used their local regulatory authority to slash local emissions. This local action ultimately prompted both national governments to convene the Montreal Protocols. Today's largely aspirational treaty on climate, signed in Paris 2015, will become meaningful only if comparable local initiatives emerge to reduce specific greenhouse gases. Fortunately, governors and mayors responded quickly to President Trump's repudiation of the Paris agreement by doubling down on their own commitments.

In a decentralized United States, BIMBY would expand dramatically as communities shared with one another technologies, policies, and business models for increasing local sustainability. They would rely on such vanguard organizations as ICLEI—the International Council for Local Environmental Initiatives.[27]

Local Foreign Policy

"All politics is local," House Speaker Tip O'Neill said. So is political engagement's most genuine form. Moving the locus of political power downward means more empowerment opportunities for the grassroots. Today's *Hunger Games* politics, characterized by phony, anonymous, top-down manipulation by corporations, billionaires, sclerotic political parties, pollsters, television ads, and staged events, can finally give way to genuine deliberation and action by people who actually know one another. The ideas promulgated by such scholars as the late Benjamin Barber in *Strong Democracy* would stand a chance of really materializing.[28]

A decentralized union could also change politics at the top. Switzerland's microscopic presidency is probably not the ticket in the United States anytime soon. But, within the American constitutional order, the size and ambitions of the federal government could be shrunk as states and localities took up more of its functions. To facilitate a smooth transition to this model, a smart federal government might narrow grounds for preemption by the federal courts, broaden state and local discretion for assessing taxes to cover increased responsibilities, and ensure that responsibilities and commensurate power devolve together and that for at least a few transition years states are spared unfunded mandates.

Also needed: broad "compact" authority for noncontiguous states or towns to strike collaborative agreements with one another whenever they need larger economies of scale. Indeed, any matter appropriate for state action should be made permissible through interstate compacts. Even where oversight must be national—such as immigration, water pollution, or currency—decentralization through compacts would make getting results easier.

Even in foreign policy. Despite legalistic pronouncements that states and localities have no role in it, they have been active players since the early days of the US Constitution, which enumerates and protects these activities:

- The First Amendment guarantees the right of local elected officials to speak out on foreign policy, using such tools as public education, lobbying, and resolutions.

- The Fifth Amendment accords local elected officials a privilege to travel internationally, as they frequently have to enter trade agreements, push human rights causes, and oppose wars.
- The "market participant" exemption of the commerce clause allows (though recent trade agreements chip away) state and local governments broad authority to invest in or contract with foreign entities they like and to divest from and avoid doing business with those entities they detest.[29]
- While state and local authorities are forbidden from entering international treaties, they can enter federally permitted international "compacts" and almost any international contracts.
- The Constitution's militia clause gives states a modest role in US military policy.
- And the Tenth Amendment reminds us that all ambiguities should be resolved in favor of state power.

We've already seen profound instances in which state and local governments have changed US foreign policy. Nuclear freeze resolutions by city councils brought the Reagan Administration to the negotiating table with the then Soviet Union around nuclear arms control. Divestment campaigns upended Reagan's policy of "constructive engagement" with apartheid South Africa and brought Nelson Mandela to power. Sister cities with Nicaragua held back US efforts to overthrow the Sandinistas. The list goes on and on.

True, state and local authorities lack viable military options for their foreign policy, but this is a plus. After all, if an objective of a decentralized United States is to reduce military spending, it will want all levels of government— including state and local officials—to mobilize more nonmilitary means like persuasion, education, trade, aid, and exchanges. Benjamin Barber makes this powerful argument in *If Mayors Ruled the World*.[30]

Political engagement, of course, is never automatic, even at the local level. States and localities will need to implement new institutions to engage citizens more effectively, including citizen advisory commissions, online discourse between civil servants and citizens, apps that increase the flow of practical grassroots information, and participatory budgeting. Whatever the next system of the United States, decentralization makes the adoption of such valuable innovations more likely.

Steps toward a Grand Bargain

The transition envisioned here will likely take a generation given how dysfunctional Washington politics have become. But, shy of that, perhaps national politicians can agree to give states *permission* to experiment. As that experimentation bears fruit, the virtues of a grand bargain around decentralization might hit home: *Red states can become redder if blue states can become bluer.*

Permission to innovate might, for instance, be useful in tax reform. A powerful argument is now being made across the political spectrum to shift taxes away from "goods" we want more of (like income, sales, property development, and value-adding business) to "bads" we want less of (like tobacco, pollution, carbon emissions, nonrenewable resource use, and high-frequency stock trading). For fairness' sake, some states and localities might also opt for a greatly simplified but progressive individual income tax to compensate "losers" from such a tax shift, though many other approaches are imaginable. Invoking the Commerce Clause of the Constitution, producers of oil, gas, and coal will almost surely challenge any state's carbon tax. But Congress' simple declaration that a state carbon tax is permissible would—at no federal cost—be binding on the courts and ease experimentation.

The framework suggested here doesn't *require* states and localities to change their tax systems. It simply opens the *possibility* of exploring alternatives. If legislators allowed states more latitude to do things they might find abhorrent in their own states, local conversations about what really works might deepen.

If Washington's current stalemate persists much longer or if the federal government dismantles programs many deem essential, states and localities will see that they will have to act on their own. If federal entitlement programs go bankrupt, states will have to create their own programs (as many have already, in the form of portable, state-managed 401-Ks). If the federal government continues to underfund infrastructure programs, states will have no choice but to repair their own bridges with their own money. Dysfunction at the top may naturally accelerate innovation and action below.

Two seasoned political observers, Thomas Mann and Norman Ornstein, recently argued that not since right after the Civil War has the United States had a less functional federal government.[31] But even if the federal government functioned better, it's probably too big now to do much, and the more populous the country gets, the harder involving citizens in a meaningful democratic process becomes.

Engagement, participation, and creativity increasingly require local groups to work on local problems. It's no mere coincidence that most governors are less ideological and more pragmatic than their peers in Washington. Instead of bloviating ideologically, state leaders are expected to get things done. Subsidiarity's rationale—that political action is quicker, smarter, and less polarized at the state and local levels—is for this reason interesting to both conservatives and progressives.

Most decentralists detest any attempt to nationalize healthcare, even a milquetoast, insurance-based program like Obamacare. Reform proceeded because a national consensus coalesced that preventing patients with preexisting conditions from obtaining any insurance at all—the previous reality—was morally unacceptable. But the Obama administration then overreached with its national solution and paid a huge political price. It would have been smarter to have learned from its decentralist neighbor to the north.

Canada's first socialized medical system was in Saskatchewan, geographically and politically proximate to Montana. In 1946, that cowboy province guaranteed free hospital care for most of its residents.[32] Eleven years later, the national government passed the Hospital Insurance and Diagnostic Services Act, thereafter paying for half of any provincial healthcare reform that met certain basic characteristics, including comprehensiveness, universality, and portability. By 1961, ten provinces were participating, each experimenting with reforms consistent with the national objectives. This experience brought about a Canadian consensus that the government should gradually expand its coverage into a national system that still allows provinces substantial flexibility. Today, all of Canada's political parties back this program, though their reform proposals differ.

A decentralist-minded Obama administration might have reformed healthcare by setting broad goals for coverage and inclusion of the uninsured, offering states matching funds, and leaving implementation to governors and state legislatures. Some states would have chosen, like Massachusetts, to expand the private insurance system through subsidies. More progressive states might have created a statewide public insurance pool or even a state-run medical system. Conservative states might have created an expansive system of medical savings accounts. States choosing similar systems might then have been encouraged to form interstate pools to achieve better economies of scale. This way, every state would have had a positive, creative incentive to construct a medical system based on its own values. Interestingly, this is what former Senate leader Tom Daschle and former Republican House Speaker Newt Gingrich recently proposed.[33]

The Obamacare debate proves that whenever a national mega-plan is shoved down the throats of recalcitrant states, the losers will do everything in their power to block it. Devolution offers a chance to channel the vast hot air that goes into blocking national legislation into constructive experimentation in 50 "laboratories of democracy." Many conservative solutions—public education vouchers, flat taxes, cash-based welfare programs—arouse my skepticism, but we should all be curious to see how these ideas might work when given a chance.

Decentralization also better inoculates the country against crises. The growing discourse around resilience worldwide is really about how to help communities handle the unexpected, whether earthquakes, manmade climate disruptions, capital flights, or pandemics. A country of increasingly self-reliant communities is, by definition, better equipped to cope with unexpected catastrophes. When one community is overwhelmed, more self-reliant neighboring communities will have the capacity to help.

Conclusion

Perhaps the strongest argument for US decentralization is that it is happening already. With the federal government hopelessly gridlocked, state and local governments have increasingly had to step into the void to meet their citizens' needs. Looming cuts of the federal government will only hasten this trend. Shouldn't we move power and resources to those levels of government mindfully rather than haphazardly?

Readers who still imagine their own ideology prevailing no doubt bristle at this vision. Progressives dream of a national political realignment that will enable the United States to look more like northern Europe. Conservatives are excited to remake the United States into a highly deregulated, business-friendly nation. To all of you, let me offer one final bucket of ice water: the chance of any of you succeeding politically in a country of more than 330 million people rooted in some state and local autonomy is slim to none.

The best any of us will achieve in a large, diverse country is the opportunity to remake our own community into exactly the place where we would like to live. Whatever your community looks like, rest assured that most of your fellow Americans won't want to live there. But if each of us can move just a little closer to our own utopias, we will all be more satisfied and embrace that famous French expression, "Viva la difference!"

Notes

1 Statistica, "The 20 Countries with the Largest Gross Domestic Product per Capita in 2016," http://www.statista.com/statistics/270180/countries-with-the-largest-gross-domestic-product-gdp-per-capita/.
2 United Nations Development Programme, *Human Development Report 2015* (New York: UNDP, 2015), 208.
3 Yale Center for Environmental Law and Policy, *Global Metrics for the Environment* (New Haven, CT: YCELP, 2016), 18.
4 Central Intelligence Agency, "The World Factbook," https://www.cia.gov/library/publications/the-world-factbook/rankorder/2172rank.html.
5 David Bollier, "The Commons, Short and Sweet," July 15, 2011, www.bollier.org/commons-short-and-sweet.
6 Jane Jacobs, *Systems of Survival* (New York: Vintage, 1994).
7 Matt Zapotosky, Rosalind S. Helderman, and Rachel Weiner, "Robert F. McDonnell Sentenced to Two Years in Prison," *The Washington Post*, January 6, 2015, https://www.washingtonpost.com/local/virginia-politics/robert-f-mcdonnell-sentenced-to-two-years-in-prison-in-corruption-case/2015/01/06/e51520ca-9049-11e4-ba53-a477d66580ed_story.html. The Supreme Court subsequently overturned McDonnell's conviction.

8 Louise Story, "As Companies Seek Tax Deals, Governments Pay High Price," *The New York Times*, December 1, 2012, http://www.nytimes.com/2012/12/02/us/how-local-taxpayers-bankroll-corporations.html?pagewanted=all&_r=0.

9 Jane Jacobs, *The Economy of Cities* (New York: Vintage, 1969).

10 This observation comes from my nearly three dozen studies of local economies and local food economies in US cities. See, e.g., Michael H. Shuman, *The 25% Shift: The Benefits of Food Localization for Boulder County and How to Realize Them* (Boulder, CO: Transition Colorado, February 2012).

11 Michael E. Porter, *Competitive Advantage of Nations* (New York: Free Press, 1990).

12 See, e.g., *McComish (Arizona Free Enterprise) v. Bennett*, 131 S.Ct. 1672 (2011), which invalidated Arizona's Clean Elections Act provision matching a candidate's funds if his or her opponent exceeded a statutorily set threshold.

13 See https://www.thebalance.com/current-u-s-federal-government-spending-3305763.

14 The World Bank, "Data: Military Expenditure as a Percentage of GDP," http://data.worldbank.org/indicator/MS.MIL.XPND.GD.ZS.

15 Michael H. Shuman, *The Small-Mart Revolution: How Local Businesses Are Beating the Global Competition* (San Francisco, CA: Berrett-Koehler, 2006), 178–183.

16 Edward L. Glaeser and William R. Kerr, "The Secret to Job Growth: Think Small," *Harvard Business Review*, July-August 2010, https://hbr.org/2010/07/the-secret-to-job-growth-think-small.

17 Anil Rupesingha, "Locally Owned: Do Local Business Ownership and Size Matter for Local Economic Well-Being?" Federal Reserve Bank of Atlanta, *Community and Economic Development Discussion Paper* 01-13 (August 2013), http://www.microbiz.org/wp-content/uploads/2013/10/Local-Ownership-and-Ec-Well-Being.pdf.

18 See historic data produced by the Bureau of Labor Statistics.

19 See IRS "Tax Stats – Integrated Business Data," Table 1 on "Selected Financial Data on Businesses," at https://www.irs.gov/uac/soi-tax-stats-integrated-business-data.

20 Statistics Canada, "Firm Dynamics: Variation in Profitability across Canadian Firms of Different Sizes, 2000–2009," Publication 11-622-M, 26 (December 2013).

21 See, Novia Scotia Community Economic Development Funds, http://novascotia.ca/business/CEDIF/.

22 Nathalie Kakpo and Sandro Cattacin, "Local Welfare in Switzerland: Housing, Employment, and Child Care," University of Geneva, WILCO Publication 7 (2011).

23 Pruneyard Shopping Center v. Robins, 447 U.S. 74 Supreme Court of the United States, 1980, *Supreme Court Collection*. Legal Information Inst., Cornell U. Law School, n.d.

24 World Commission on Environment and Development, *Our Common Future* (Oxford: Oxford University Press, 1987).

25 Of course, some believe that protection of nature should not be up to any community to decide and should simply be a foundational principle of governance. In a decentralized United States, some communities would be free to implement more demanding conceptions of sustainability.

26 George Moffett, "Cities Dabble in Foreign Affairs," *Christian Science Monitor*, February 8, 1995.

27 For more on the ICLEI and their work, see: http://www.iclei.org/.

28 Benjamin R. Barber, *Strong Democracy: Participatory Politics for a New Age* (Berkeley: University of California Press, 2004).

29 See discussion in Shuman, *The Small-Mart Revolution*, 178–183.

30 Benjamin R. Barber, *If Mayors Ruled the World: Dysfunctional Nations, Rising Cities* (New Haven, CT: Yale University Press, 2014).

31 Thomas E. Mann and Norman J. Mann, *It's Even Worse than It Looks: How the American Constitutional System Collided with the New Politics of Extremism* (New York: Basic Books, 2013).

32 For more information on healthcare in Canada, see: Wikipedia, "Health Care in Canada," https://en.wikipedia.org/wiki/Health_care_in_Canada#History.

33 Newt Gingrich and Tom Daschle, "How to Make Both Parties Happy through the Affordable Health Care Act," *Washington Post*, February 3, 2016, https://www.washingtonpost.com/opinions/how-to-make-both-parties-happy-through-the-affordable-care-act/2016/02/03/7641c3ca-c9e0-11e5-a7b2-5a2f824b02c9_story.html.

Part 2

New System Values

What value system should drive an economic system? Some would argue that "values"—specifically, ethics and moral principles—have no fundamental place in the discussion of an economic system and that the only relevant question is how best to optimize the production and exchange of goods and services to meet human desires and needs. Others argue that the key question is who makes the decisions about how the economy functions and that making sure that the right cross-section of people have their hands on the economy's levers will invariably lead to right outcomes. Yet, questions about how we structure an economy for more socially desirable outcomes invariably center on age-old questions of how we are to live together as a human species and what our obligations are to each other. From that viewpoint, economics cannot be amoral, and democratic decision-making structures are insufficient.

Chapters in this part explore how values can and should shape system design and outcomes.

Christian Felber and Gus Hagelberg of the organization Economy for the Common Good offer a plan for an "ethical market economy." Focusing on increasing the quality of life for everyone, promoting human dignity and rights, and ensuring ecological responsibility and social justice, they argue that the economy will serve the public good when these values are exercised through a system of inclusive "sovereign democracy." They propose a "new bottom line": instead of accumulation of wealth as measured by gross domestic product, a "common good product" would measure quality of life, the meeting of basic needs, and environmental stewardship. Already, 400 companies have created "Common Good Balance Sheets," and the authors propose policy changes, mandates, and new legislation that would allow for their vision to be fully realized.

Marvin T. Brown, an educator who has written several books on ethics and human relations, presents a model in which economic activity is based not solely on property ownership or the free market but on civic membership in a "global civil society." He advocates reframing our social structures around civic relations, such as those within families and communities. The wealth of families and communities would be at the center of the economy's purpose rather than wealth accumulation by individuals or nation-states. A "civic economy of provisions" would ensure that all people have access to food, housing, health care, and education, and would address difficult social and economic issues by asking participants to "draw on their shared humanity to listen and learn from one another."

Cultural historian and author Riane Eisler, co-founder of the Institute for Partnership Studies, looks to the study of "relational dynamics" to define the fundamental choice driving total system change, a choice not between such typically referenced dualities as capitalism and socialism but between a "domination" model and a "partnership" model. Changing our economic systems, she writes, involves understanding and changing the dominant social context from which they derive. The partnership model she envisions is characterized by democratic decision-making rather than authoritarianism, gender equality rather than the subordination of women and of caregiving, an end to the institutionalized and idealized forms of violence used to maintain hierarchies of domination, and support for empathetic and mutually respectful relationships.

David C. Korten, founder and president of the Living Economies Forum and co-founder of *Yes!* magazine, contrasts a "suicide economy" with a "living Earth economy." The suicide economy values life only for its market value and prioritizes profit over community well-being. Its "money is sacred" story pervades economics, law, and democracy. The living Earth economy's story—that "life is sacred"—is centered in reconnecting with nature and with one another. Emphasizing these values, Korten calls for a system transformation that shifts power from global corporations to largely self-reliant and deeply democratic, self-governing, bioregional living communities.

Paul Raskin, the founding president of the Tellus Institute, offers a "dispatch from the future" in "Earthland." Set in 2084, the world has emerged from a period of crises and has moved toward a radically different system where "resilient economies channel and constrain markets to function within more compassionate social norms and well-established environmental limits." Politically, Earthland is organized through "constrained pluralism," based on the principle of subsidiarity—a recognition of globalism ("One World") with a parallel focus on local diversity ("Many Places"). Regions adopt different models in accordance with their cultural and political leanings. As futuristic tales often do, this one offers readers words from the future to give hope to the present: "Another world was possible."

Chapter 4

The Economy for the Common Good

A Workable, Transformative, Ethics-Based Alternative

Christian Felber and Gus Hagelberg

The Economy for the Common Good (ECG) is a comprehensive and co-herent economic model up and working in hundreds of businesses, universities, municipalities, and local chapters across Europe and South America. An alternative to both capitalism and communism, it emerges from a holistic worldview and the concept of "sovereign democracy"—a stronger democracy than exists today. The model has five underlying goals:

1   Encouraging business decisions that promote human rights, justice, and sustainability
2   Transitioning to an economic system that primarily serves the "common good" and that honors such universal constitutionally established values as dignity, social justice, sustainability, and democracy
3   Measuring business' success according to the values outlined above
4   Setting the cornerstones of the economy's legal framework through democratic processes that yield concrete recommendations for re-forming and reevaluating national constitutions and international treaties
5   Closing the gaps between feeling and thinking, economy and ethics, mankind and nature, science and spirituality

Rewarding "good" behavior and making "poor" behavior more visible to the public and less profitable will transform the economy. Results will include greater cooperation among business partners and less runaway de-structive growth. Companies will find their optimal size, and business profits will increasingly be used to improve products, infrastructure, and working conditions and less for increasing investor dividends. The incessant drive for ever more profits and market share will slowly fade.

ECG encourages private enterprise but only within the confines of a common good framework. We will continue to have a free market economy, but not capitalism.

The ECG's tools and methods—including a new public-good approach to money, banking, and financial services—can be applied at all economic and political levels. Various city and state governments have endorsed the principles of the ECG and are implementing its tools. The European Union and some European countries are considering applying ECG tools in new laws on nonfinancial reporting, public procurement, investment guidelines, and other activities. ECG's performance tool has been successfully implemented by over 500 businesses and by some banks, universities, and NGOs.

The ECG is based on a proposal for sovereign democracy that provides citizens with "sovereign rights." People have the exclusive rights to change the constitution, replace the government, and overturn laws they oppose. These rights return power to the people, reduce political apathy, and involve voters more deeply in their communities and their workplaces.

The ECG cooperates with other social and new economy movements to create synergies, connect to the current economic policy, and transform our political system. Ten principles embody the ideas and concepts underlying the ECG movement:

1   The ECG strives toward an ethical market economy designed to increase the quality of life for all, not increase the wealth of a few.
2   The ECG helps promote human dignity, human rights, and ecological responsibility in day-to-day business practice.
3   The Common Good Matrix—continually improved in an open, democratic process—indicates to what extent a company practices these values.
4   The Matrix provides companies the basis for creating a Common Good Balance Sheet. The Common Good Report describes and makes public the company's record implementing these universal values. Both tools are externally audited.
5   Common Good companies benefit in the marketplace through consumer choice, cooperation partners, and common-good–oriented lending institutions.
6   To offset higher costs resulting from ethical, social, and ecological activities, Common Good companies should receive advantages in taxation, bank loans, and public grants and contracts.
7   Business profits strengthen and stabilize a company and ensure the long-term income of owners and employees, but profits should not serve the interests of external investors. Freed of pressure to maximize the return on investment, entrepreneurs have more flexibility to work for the common good.
8   No longer forced to grow, companies can design business to improve the quality of life and help safeguard the natural world. Mutual appreciation, fairness, creativity, and cooperation can better thrive in such a working environment.

9 Reducing income inequality is mandatory to assure everyone equal economic and political opportunities.

10 The ECG movement invites you to take part in creating an economy based on these values.

What Is the Economy?

A central concern of the ECG is to end the confusion of means and ends in our economic system. Money and capital should no longer be the goal or end of economic activity, but rather the means of improving the common good. This is by no means a new concept. The Greek philosopher Aristotle differentiated between *oikonomia*, the art of sustainably managing the "house" (economy for the common good), and *chrematistike*, the art of making money (capitalism). In his concept of *oikonomia*, money serves only as a means.

Many Western constitutions echo Aristotle in defining the goal of the economy. The constitution of Bavaria, Germany, for example, declares: "Economic activity in its entirety serves the common good." The Spanish Constitution says: "The entire wealth of the country in its different forms, irrespective of ownership, shall be subordinated to the general interest." The Colombian constitution says that "Private economic enterprise ... may not be carried out against the common good." The preamble to the US Constitution states that one goal is to "promote the general Welfare."

Measuring the New Bottom Line

ECG is redefining success in terms of a company's contribution to the common good. Today's faulty system measures economic success strictly according to such monetary indicators as the Gross Domestic Product (GDP) for countries or financial profit for businesses. The satisfaction of basic needs, quality of life, or environmental protection count for nothing. In a new economy, the Common Good Product will indicate a country's success in meeting universal values while the Common Good Balance Sheet will show how much a company contributes to the common good.

Banking and finance will also reorient their priorities. Value-oriented indicators will determine whether a person or company is creditworthy. Financial institutions, individuals, and corporations will still need monetary evaluations, and GDP, financial balance sheets, and credit risk analyses will remain. But all will be less important than common good indicators.

At the national level, the Common Good Product should be defined by the sovereign citizens. Perhaps in local assemblies, citizens would identify 20 most relevant aspects of quality of life and well-being and convert them to a measurable and comparable indicator that tells us much more than the GDP. The Organization for Economic Co-operation and Development's

(OECD) "Better Life Index," Bhutan's "Gross National Happiness," and the Happy Planet Index all exemplify alternatives to GDP.

At the business level, the Common Good Balance Sheet measures a company's adherence to such key constitutional values as human dignity, solidarity, justice, sustainability, and democracy. Balance Sheet questions include, for instance:

- Do products and services satisfy human needs?
- How humane are working conditions?
- How environmentally friendly are production processes?
- How ethical is the sales and purchasing policy?
- How are profits distributed?
- Do women receive equal pay for equal work?
- How involved are employees in core, strategic decision-making?

Business owners, managers, and interested workers who have taken on a Common Good Balance Sheet work through a catalogue of indicators and describe their related activities. If asked, certified ECG business consultants help the company address the issues, gather the information, and determine compliance. Either way, independent auditors examine the results and a Common Good Report is published. The current average score, around 300, indicates considerable room for improvement. The admittedly utopian maximum, 1,000 points, would signal peace, no poverty or unemployment, a clean environment, gender justice, and engaged and motivated workers.

Companies with high balance sheet scores could be rewarded with tax benefits, lower tariffs, better terms on loans, and priority in public procurement. These measures would make ethical and environmentally friendly products and services cheaper than ethically questionable ones. Instead of suffering a competitive disadvantage due to higher costs and prices, as is the case today, responsible businesses would have a market advantage. In Spain, Italy, Germany, and Austria, some cities and state legislatures already accord preferential treatment and grants to common good-oriented companies.

Use of Profits

Profits, like money or capital, are economic tools. How a company uses its profits should be completely transparent and limited in scope. Society regulates business and individual activity in a multitude of ways, from speed limits on highways to safety regulations in manufacturing industries. The use of profits should be no exception.

A company should be free to use its profits for:

- Investments in the business
- Reserves for future losses

- Investments in capital reserves
- Dividend payouts to employees
- Loans to other businesses

For other activities, a company's use of financial surpluses should be restricted to:

- Investments in financial services
- Dividend payouts to proprietors and shareholders who do not work in the company

Some practices could be outlawed, including:

- Hostile takeovers and mergers
- Donations to political parties or PACs

These proposals would help halt the relentless drive toward profit maximization and continual growth. Reorienting profits would encourage businesses to contribute more to society and the environment. Businesses would no longer fear failure if they did not increase shareholder value. The compulsion to grow and continuously gain more market share would also disappear, freeing businesses to determine their optimal size and focus on producing great products and services. Private companies and entrepreneurship would have their place, but they need to be reoriented to serve the public good and further human rights, human dignity, cooperation, sustainability, and democracy. The result is a free market economy in which capital accumulation is not the driving force.

From "Counter-petition" to Cooperation

One cornerstone of the capitalist market economy is the concept that competition drives business. Nobel Prize laureate Friedrich August von Hayek wrote that competition is "in most circumstances the most efficient method known." This widely held belief has yet to be scientifically proven, but research *has* shown that cooperation outperforms competition in motivating workers—the key to innovation and efficiency.

Competition does, of course, motivate people, as proven by capitalism. But where one person succeeds only if another person fails, the main motivation is the fear that permeates market capitalism. Millions fear losing their jobs, their incomes, their social status, and their places in the community. Why encourage this state of mind and affairs? More philosophically, competition elicits delight in outshining others. But the purpose of our actions and work should not be besting others but, rather, performing our tasks well, enjoying our work, and seeing that it is helpful and valuable. Isn't feeling better because others are worse off just plain sick?

The word "competition" derives from the Latin word for "searching together." ECG fosters true competition according to its original meaning of working together.

Structural Cooperation

In the Economy for the Common Good, competition would not disappear. But its darker side would show up in a company's Common Good Balance Sheet. Aggressive behavior against competitors, such as hostile takeovers, price dumping, advertising via mass media, or enclosure of intellectual property, would earn companies' low marks on their ethical scorecard and inhibit market success. Conversely, treating customers well or sharing know-how, resources, and the means of production openly with competitors would raise business's common good score. The current win-lose paradigm would give way to a win-win paradigm if enterprises were rewarded for cooperation.

Pursuing an optimal company size instead of simply growth would encourage enterprises to cooperate. A right-sized firm is more apt to share know-how and even pass on contracts it cannot fulfill. As the theory of evolution informs us, not all species endlessly grow until they die. In Harvard mathematician and biologist Martin Nowak's words, "cooperation is the chief architect of evolution."[1]

Like other ideas proposed here, these reforms would change the economy's legal framework. In practice, governments and parliaments should first be encouraged to implement the reform proposals directly through legislation. If the political mandate is still too weak, the reforms will have to be brought about by the "sovereign assemblies" described below, through referendums—that is, by the people.

Property and Inequality

Private Property

The starting point here is a historical dualism. Socialist economic theories value public property very highly while capitalism makes private property the supreme form of property. The Economy for the Common Good doesn't rank property types but aims (through limits and conditions) to prevent the excessive concentration of private property. Government furthers the common good by providing such basic infrastructure as water, energy, and transportation or health services and education, but the production of, say, furniture, clothes, or food might be best left to private companies provided that their size is regulated, their common good balance sheets are compulsory, and inheritance is limited.

The commons, another form of property, should also be protected by law. Collectively owned companies should be controlled by their stakeholders—workers, customers, suppliers—not outside investors.

One important exception to property rights involves nature. To respect our origins and our fertile earth, ECG proposes the limited and conditional use of nature and an end to commercial ownership rights. This approach would prevent land grabbing, real estate speculation, intellectual property rights on living organisms, and such resource degradation as massive deforestation.

Property Type	Public Property	Personal Property	Collective Property	Community Property	Usage Rights (Not Property)
Function	Schools, local governments, central bank, money	Bicycle, home, company	Meadows, fisheries, seeds, software	Large production facilities	Water, energy, land
Limits	Infrastructure	Consumer goods	Commons	Consumer goods	Nature
Conditions	Privatization only with public consent	Limits and conditions	Clear rules and sanctions	Vital for society's needs	Ecological human rights

These reflections and proposals and the property typology in the table are rooted in the idea that all property and property rights must serve such higher values as social justice.

Income and Wealth Inequality

A linchpin of the ECG is limiting inequality. Limits could be placed on income, property, inheritance, or company size. A *Financial Times* survey and Harris Poll found that 78 percent of US respondents felt that inequality had increased too much. In the UK, it was 79 percent, in China 80 percent, and in Germany 87 percent.[2]

As for how to set limits, the international ECG movement uses systemic consensus. This effective variant of consensus decision-making measures resistance to a proposal within a committee or larger group. Such "rehearsals" of democratic rights can help usher in the "sovereign democracy" discussed below. In systemic consensus, the first step is presenting all proposals to a committee or group and then measuring opposition or aversion by a vote. Arms down means no aversion or resistance. One arm up signals some opposition. Both arms up is an unambiguous "no" vote. The proposal with the least opposition wins.

ECG speakers have tried this voting method with about 50,000 citizens from Sweden to Chile. On the issue of limiting inequality and capping income levels within a company, participants proposed various maximum incomes—three, five, seven, ten, twelve, fifteen, twenty, fifty, or hundred times higher than the lowest paid worker. Usually, a factor of ten was the most popular. The extremes of unlimited inequality as well as full equality frequently meet with strong resistance. In the ECG, minimum wage and maximum income are legal limits while everything in between can be negotiated in a free market.

Money and Finance

Money as a Public Good

Just as business needs to view profits as the means and the common good as the end, priorities need to change in the realm of money and finances. Money too should be only a means to reach a higher goal.

Making money a public good means first and foremost that sovereign citizens set the rules of the monetary system. In democratically organized assemblies, the people define the new monetary and financial system. Its guiding principles would include:

- The central bank is a public institution whose organs are composed by all relevant stakeholders of society.
- Monetary policy's mandate and the objectives are determined by voters.
- Only the central bank can issue money; private banks are simply intermediaries of "sovereign" money.
- The people decide where new money goes, whether to government to alleviate public expenditures or directly to citizens, but most goes to the public.
- Certified banks' goal must be to serve the public's interests (not distribute profits to owners).
- Loans can be granted only for investments in the real economy that do not harm the public or the environment (not for buying on the financial market).
- Loan requests will be assessed not only according to financial risks but, more important, according to their common-good creditworthiness.

"Return on Investment" Reexamined

Economists and finance experts deem an investment successful if it generates a financial return, the higher the better. This one-dimensional concept of success is flawed. We cannot know how the investment affects the environment and natural resources, working conditions, human rights, cultural diversity, or democratic principles.

Financial institutions in an Economy for the Common Good will behave differently. The loan plan's impacts on a community, the environment, and working conditions will come to light, and banks won't lend unless the business or individual is ethically (not just financially) creditworthy and can prove that the loan will not harm the common good. Borrowing costs go down when the ethical value of an investment program goes up, and borrowers reap rewards for proving that their project will benefit the public good and the environment.

If an investment is found to benefit the common good but the financial assessment is negative and the credit risk too high, the bank will probably refuse to grant the loan. But it could hand the loan plan over to cooperative banks or a crowd-investment platform. Loan seekers with socially good but financially risky projects could go forward even though lenders may never see a dime.

All in all, this new financial system will discourage investment decisions that endanger our fundamental values and encourage the investments that further the common good. The rewards include peace of mind, regional employment, meaningful jobs, strong and resilient local economies, reduced inequality and exclusion, and a large range of commons and companies that increase the common good.

Rewarding Ethical Investments

These concepts need not remain theoretical. The policy recommendations made here can be implemented locally or regionally now and nationally and internationally in the future.

To keep operating in the market, banks can be given a choice. They can either become community-oriented, ethical, or cooperative banks, or they can enter the free market. That means they will not be refinanced by (public) central bank, they will be excluded from business with public authorities, they would not be covered by any public deposit insurance, and their bailout with taxpayer's money would be illegal. Few would survive under such circumstances, and those "too big to fail" would most likely downsize or disappear.

More Diverse Business Entities and an Ethics-Based Economy

In three ways, the ECG represents a new type of market economy. First, it is fully ethical. Economic success will no longer be judged in strictly financial terms so a social, sustainable, cooperative, democratic, human market economy will emerge. Second, it will be a truly liberal insofar as all market players will have equal rights, liberties, and opportunities.

Third, markets will provide space for alternative cultural practices and alternative economic models that satisfy human needs. The care economy, gift economy, barter systems, local collaboration networks, urban gardening, peer-to-peer production, and the commons will become more socially recognized and important.

As the principles and tools of the Economy for the Common Good are implemented, business entities should become more diverse. We expect to see more smaller companies, new forms of legal businesses, stronger commons, and more cooperatives, social businesses, benefit corporations, and common-good companies.

Meanwhile, the average working time spent in waged jobs within formal markets could gradually shrink dramatically without endangering livelihoods. With, say, a 20-hour workweek, people will find more time for leisure, family caregiving, and community work. They will also have more time for democratic decision-making—key because ECG's "sovereign democracy" model is much more participatory and co-creative than today's democracy, requiring commensurately more time and energy.

Sovereign Democracy and Trade

Many argue that democracy in Western countries is failing. The English political scientist Colin Crouch describes today's democracy as "post democracy." But don't we actually live in "pre-democracy" since a true form of democracy has never existed?

In a true democracy, the sovereign people would be the highest authority and hold the ultimate power, standing above the legislature, the government, every international treaty, and every law. Sovereign citizens could directly modify the constitution, laws, economy, and institutions if they had "sovereign rights" to

1 Draft a constitution (elect a constitutional convention and vote on the results)
2 Change the constitution
3 Elect a government
4 Vote out a government
5 Correct legislative decisions
6 Directly put bills to vote
7 Directly control and regulate essential utilities
8 Issue money
9 Define the framework for negotiating international treaties and vote on the results of negotiations

For three reasons, the right to draft a constitution matters most. First, the ultimate democratic document should be written only by the highest authority—the people. Second, we must avoid the danger of indirect representatives awarding themselves additional powers and stripping people of their sovereign rights. Third, the people could build fundamental cornerstones and guidelines for the economy and democratic institutions directly into the constitution. Given the constitution's preeminence, people would create the constitution and legislative bodies, the laws embodying it.

Today, we see a great divide between public opinion and public policy. Public opinion surveys show that in virtually no country does the majority approve of banks becoming too big to fail and getting bailed out by taxpayers. Nor do people support the transfer of capital to tax havens, patents on living organisms, or unlabeled genetically modified food. Sovereign rights would eliminate such policy divergences from public opinion.

Decision-Making in a Sovereign Democracy

To practice the right to draft and amend the constitution, constitutional or "sovereign assemblies" can be created first locally, then regionally, and finally nationally. Sovereign assemblies would discuss and settle only fundamental questions since legislatures would handle legal implementation and details. Such questions include:

- Do we want *okonomia* or *chrematistike*—an economy for profits or economy for the common good?
- Should the central benchmark of economic policy be GDP or a Common Good Product?
- Should money become a public good?
- Should companies seeking operating licenses be required to publish non-financial reports like the Common Good Balance Sheet?

Most people seem to prefer a Common Good Product to the GDP. In a representative survey ordered by Germany's Federal Ministry of Environment, only 18 percent of Germans wanted the GDP to remain the main benchmark for economic and social policy; just over two-thirds preferred a more comprehensive life-quality indicator.

Exercising their sovereign rights, the people could vote on a compulsory Common Good Balance Sheet for all companies. Other authors, including Joel Bakan (*The Corporation*), fellow Next System Project contributor David C. Korten (*When Corporations Rule the World*), and George Monbiot (*The Age of Consent*), contend that major corporations should receive an operating license *only* if their social, ecological, and ethical performance passes muster.

Sovereign citizens could also conduct a referendum to limit income inequality. Public opinion be damned, excessive pay is the global reality. In Austria, top executives are paid 1,150 times as much as the lowest paid workers. In Germany, it's 6,000 times more, and in the United States one chief executive, Amazon CEO Jeff Bezos, in 2018 reportedly earned well over 1.2 million times a worker earning the federal minimum wage.[3] Clearly, sovereign citizens would pick a less disturbing differential.

International Trade

Related to democratic sovereign rights, international trade and its strong effects on local and national economies are also critical issues in the transition to a common-good economy. "Free" trade agreements embody the premise that the more trade the better and—just like money, profits, and growth—trade is embraced as an end in itself. The World Trade Organization (WTO), the Bilateral Investment Treaty, the Trans-Pacific Partnership (TTP), the Comprehensive Economic and Trade Agreement (CETA), and the Trans-Atlantic Trade and Investment Partnership (TTIP) all blindly encourage more trade without judging its impact on democratic values.

Yet, trade is simply a tool for furthering human rights, justice, sustainability, and democracy. Thus, these and similar questions should be asked in all trade negotiations:

- Will the agreement comprehensively protect human and labor rights, and do the trade partners respect these rights?
- Does it enhance sustainable development and reduce the ecological footprint?
- Does the agreement make wealth distribution more just social cohesion stronger?
- Will it help close the gender gap and broaden inclusion of disadvantaged people?

If such questions can be answered affirmatively, more trade should be welcomed. If not, less trade would be better.

To determine whether the signatories satisfy a particular trade agreement's requirements, such instruments as UN resolutions, human rights conventions, the Kyoto Protocol, and the International Labor Organization (ILO) could be used. Countries that ratify and respect these agreements could trade more freely while countries that violate them could expect progressively assessed tariffs.

Countries with higher standards could also protect their Ethical Common Market by asking companies seeking access to provide a Common Good Balance Sheet. Their "ethical score" could mean free access to the market, more costly access, or blocked access. The European Union is now formulating a "European Ethical Market"[4] along similar lines.

Ecology and Education

Environment and Ecological Human Rights

The Common Good Balance Sheet is not meant to replace other sustainable development policies. The challenge of deep sustainability, especially given climate change, is so big that a highly diverse policy mix is needed. Unfortunately, most policy measures to date, from carbon taxes to subsidies for renewable energy and organic agriculture, have been relatively ineffectual. More ambitious proposals, like global resource management, haven't yet caught on.

A radical but liberal measure would be creating and allocating ecological human rights. Mother Earth's annual gift of natural resources and ecosystem services could be divided by the total number of human beings, priced sustainably, and allocated as a global per capita resource budget. Each consumer's personal "ecological credit card" would be reloaded annually. Once its balance reaches zero, further consumption would be forbidden (though, of course, nobody would be allowed to starve or freeze). With this equal ecological right for all, consumers would enjoy freedom of choice so long as they don't endanger the common good.

One such method, the "doughnut model" developed by Oxfam's Kate Raworth, which expands upon the "planetary boundaries" concept of the Stockholm Resilience Center (Johan Rockström et al.), combines two limiting factors at the boundary of an imaginary biosphere. The first limitation, the outer circle, is Mother Earth's yearly gift to mankind—the "biological limit." The inner circle encompasses the resources human beings need to meet their basic needs—the "social limit." The art of an ecologically efficient economy is keeping humankind's consumption of natural resources and our "ecological footprint" within these two limits. For example, the per capita consumption represented by the inner circle could become an unconditional, non-negotiable, and inalienable human right and the amount between the two circles could be negotiable, allowing the poor to sell unused consumption chits to the rich and the frugal to sell to hedonists. This general approach extends German philosopher Immanuel Kant's categorical imperative to nature. As Kant might say today, we humans should choose a lifestyle that all human beings could choose without threatening the opportunities of others and those of future generations.

Substantial scientific research has shown that consuming fewer resources and material goods need not diminish quality of life.[5] On the contrary, using less energy, oil, electricity, pesticides, and harmful additives can have palpable benefits:

- Rivers, lakes, forests, and meadows could offer more recreational value.
- Homes wouldn't need oil or gas because they would be well insulated, made of natural materials, and intelligently designed.

- Building materials would smell of natural wood, pleasant to the eye and touch.
- Food would be healthier, providing more nutrients and energy.
- Essential daily errands could be run on foot or using convenient and comfortable public transportation.
- Our work environment would be more stress-free.
- Poverty could disappear once everyone had equal opportunities and rights.

If everyone could rest assured that their lifestyle did not rob people living in other places and future generations of their sustenance, life would simply be better.

Education

A flourishing Economy for the Common Good requires conveying new values, sensitizing people on all levels, rehearsing social and communicative competence, and setting an example for respecting nature. For this reason, all levels of education should cover:

Understanding feelings. Children would gain more experience perceiving feelings, taking them seriously, not being ashamed of them, talking about them, and regulating them consciously. Society has failed to help children and young adults learn these skills; as research has shown, myriads of conflicts in relationships remain unresolved because people can't understand their feelings and needs.

Understanding values. Attitudes toward values would be imparted and discussed. Children would become aware of subconsciously held biases and prejudices. Students would learn that they can compete against and cooperate with each other and to expect different effects with each approach. They would study the fundamental ethical principles of important philosophical ideas and religions.

Understanding communication. Children would start by learning how to listen, pay regard to others, take them seriously, and discuss matters objectively without resorting to personal insult or judgments. This might seem obvious, but we are light years away from an appreciative, democratic, and nonviolent culture of public discourse characterized by respectful communication among adversaries and by intelligent and cohesive arguments.

Children would also learn how to become more aware of gender roles and avoid mistakes and injuries in interactions and discourse. Similarly, children would come to see that intercultural misunderstandings are normal and that creating understanding takes effort.

Understanding democracy. Democracy is highly valued in Western societies, but schools don't teach ways to live and sustain it or show its vulnerabilities. Understanding democracy could include exploring:

- Ways to incorporate varied interests into one law or regulation
- Decision-making that doesn't leave a large minority unheard
- Open, respectful encounters with others holding different views as a prerequisite for decisions supported by a large majority
- Commitment by all to keep special interests in check
- Democratic responsibility (which cannot be delegated) versus the power to implement decisions (which can)

Experiencing nature and understanding wildlife. An economy hooked on constant increases in money, income, assets, and material goods has lost all sense of proportion. Fortunately, the trouble many people have relating to themselves, other human beings, their natural environment, and the larger scheme of things can be healed by embracing, nurturing, and balancing relationships.

Nature's healing power will also give children peace of mind. Wind and rain, clouds and water, stars, flowers, the mountains—whoever is deeply connected to these will likely find little appeal in shopping centers, the stock market, and, perhaps, automobile ownership. In any case, experiencing a year of reduced material consumption can enhance life's intensity and quality.

Crafts. The "couch potato" generation spends increasing amounts of time in a virtual world that separates human beings from nature—from encounters with material, tools, shapes, colors, and smells in the natural world. All of us should all have the experience of producing something manually and giving it to someone who can use it. Rudolf Steiner, the founder of anthroposophy, advocated developing a comprehensive program for exposing pupils to the "practice" of life, and Steiner-inspired Waldorf schools offer internships in forestry, trades, and social institutions. Gradually, such activities connect the inner self with the task at hand and unleash young people's creative potential.

Sensitizing the body. The Argentinian revolutionary leader Che Guevara reportedly said "solidarity is the tenderness of the people." How can we expect governments and politicians to encounter each other with tenderness if we aren't tender to ourselves? Many of us eat poorly, exercise little, show scant physical affection, or rarely give or receive a relaxing massage. Yet, we all have it in us to sense things so acutely that each step and each contact with an object can spark a deep sensual experience and make the salves of consumption and drugs unnecessary.

For this reason, children should be encouraged to develop an attentive and appreciative relationship to their own body, their creativity, and authenticity. Beginning with games, dance, and group acrobatics, this program can be expanded after puberty to include bodywork, massage, energy work, and yoga.

True Universities and Economics

The word "university" literally means "turned into one." Accordingly, a true university would offer universal science as a "single" (uni-) science at the core of every field of study. First, students acquire an overview of all disciplines and their interconnections, analogies, and common patterns. Later, they specialize in, for example, "holistic economics" to finally become an ethical entrepreneur, commons manager, or banker.

Such a holistic university would offer three advantages over today's higher education institutions. First, all who have attended university would have a common ground and basis for conversation with everyone else. Second, the danger that technical studies would be separated from nature, or economics from ethics, would shrink. Third, such university studies might be much more engaging than today's curriculum.

Real-World Examples, Experiments, and Comparable Models

The international movement "Economy for the Common Good" began in 2010 on the initiative of a dozen companies in Austria. Since then, some 2,700 businesses from 50 nations have joined the movement, and 500 of them have implemented the Common Good Balance Sheet. Three banks and such public institutions as the University of Applied Sciences of Burgenland, Austria, which recently elected a "Common Good Officer," or the health insurer Pro Vita that was awarded the Global Challenge Award at the UN Climate Change Conference (COP24) in Katovice, Poland for encouraging its clients to eat less meat, number among the pioneers. The Universities of Flensburg and Kiel in Germany have concluded a three-year research project on implementing the Common Good Balance Sheet in large corporations; three companies listed on the German stock exchange (DAX) participated. The University of Valencia, Spain established a chair dedicated to the Economy for the Common Good in 2017 and concluded a first empirical study on 206 companies with a Common Good Balance Sheet (CGBS). The result is that the CGBS has a positive impact on the ethical performance of the pioneer companies. The University of Barcelona was the first university that implemented a CGBS, and the University of Salamanca initiated a country-wide collaboration among universities on the research and teaching of the ECG model. In addition, the pioneering universities have integrated the model into their curriculum or completed the CGBS themselves.

European municipalities are also joining the movement. Some are becoming common-good cities, while others are encouraging companies to complete the Balance Sheet. The region of Valencia, Spain passed a law to promote the model; it created a public register for audited companies that is open to other audits and certifications as well. Also, the German state of Baden-Württemberg endorsed the ECG model. More and more cities and regions are considering giving companies with an audited balance sheet (and a good score) priority in public procurement, start-up financing, and other forms of assistance.

The ECG movement enjoyed a major success with the European Union in 2015. The European Economic and Social Committee, a 350-member advisory body to the Commission and the Parliament, declared by an 86 percent majority that "the Economy for the Common Good (ECG) model is conceived to be included both in the European and the domestic legal framework."[6]

The ECG movement now boasts some 150 local chapters in 20 countries. Dozens of permanent working groups ("hubs") are dedicated to such tasks as improving the content of the Common Good Balance Sheet, supporting common good businesses, training consultants, and bringing the common good into public education. Delegates from local chapters and hubs assemble yearly to vote consensually on strategic decisions. Thirty-one legal associations have been founded, and the International Federation for the ECG established in 2018 coordinates global activities.

Real-World Examples

The 500 companies using the balance sheet started the process of creating more transparent, worker-friendly, sustainable, and social businesses.

The steps can be small. The Italian hotel "La Perla," for example, introduced one meat-free day per week.[7] Some ECG-certified companies have started using renewable energy and recycling paper. Or they finance public transport of their employees, promote car-sharing, and switch to electric cars.

Changes can also be big. When the Balance Sheet was implemented by one single-owner Salzburg-based company, the employees' opinions and critiques spawned positive changes and results throughout the company. Now, most employees are co-owners. The municipality of Kirchanschöring, Germany is phasing out new zoning for single-family homes. Building permits are granted only for innovative types of co-housing.

Changes resulting from the Common Good Balance Sheet can also be small steps. A medium-sized furniture manufacturer reoriented his sell-sell-sell marketing strategy after considering the ECG's ethical sales indicator, deciding from then on to sell his customers only what they really needed. This policy change exemplifies a shift from the growth and maximization paradigm to a "de-growth" or steady-state paradigm. The Sparda Bank from Munich, Germany eliminated its whole bonus system.[8]

Common-good–oriented companies have also begun cooperating more with competitors, sharing know-how, staff, and even financial liquidity. Likewise, they are starting to collaborate with such ethical banks as the Banca Etica (Italy), GLS Bank (Germany), or Triodos (the Netherlands). The Austrian "cooperative for the common good" followed the examples of ethical banks in other European countries but went farther, banning the distribution of financial profit to the owners while instituting common good examinations for all loan plans on its crowdfunding platform. Since May 2019, it offers—in collaboration with an ethical bank—the first common good current account in Austria. Apart from financial services, it also runs an academy on alternative monetary and financial systems and a think tank for the common good.

Another real-world example of progress toward a better way of living and doing business is Bhutan's Gross National Happiness (GNH) index. Every two years, several thousand Bhutanese households are quizzed about all aspects of quality of life—from subjective well-being, health, and education to social relations, trust, and safety. Not just an indicator, GNH is a tool for strategic political decisions (such as whether to enter the World Trade Organization).

Costa Rica decided to live without an army and to enjoy "pura vida." Sikkim in India is the first region in the world to declare itself 100 percent organic in agriculture—other Indian regions are following! In Iceland, the Parliament is debating a "positive money reform" that would vest the central bank with the exclusive right to create money.

Today, ethical initiatives like these are only a drop in the global capitalist bucket. But, by implementing the methods described here—such as an ethical creditworthiness check and the Common Good Balance Sheet—they can become mainstream.

Comparable Models, Collaboration

Margaret Thatcher was wrong when she declared that "There is no alternative" (TINA) [to capitalism]. We counter with "TAPAS" or "There are plenty of alternatives!" The ECG movement's many collaborators include the commons movement, the social and solidarity economy, the Degrowth Network, the Post Growth Alliance, Transition Town, Circular Economy, ethical banking, Fair Trade, B Corps, Convivialism, *Buenvivir*, GNH movement, and many others.

Besides networking, reinforcing, and spreading the word for the others, ECG provides a framework integrating, implementing, and creatively combining parts of alternative models. For instance, the framework could include ECG proposals to reduce the average workweek, a Common Good Balance Sheet for cooperatives, or the idea of "ecological human rights," but also integrate concrete proposals from ECG partners' initiatives.

Creating an Economy for the Common Good

Despite its appeal and spread, ECG's economic model is far from realized, and voluntary measures won't turn the tide. Policy changes, mandates, and new legislation will be required. Four steps will be essential to trigger deep-rooted systemic change:

1   More businesses must voluntarily create common good balance sheets.
2   The public must increasingly pressure local, state, national, and international legislators to mandate ethics-based balance sheets as legally binding as financial balance sheets.
3   Municipalities and regional governments must endorse the ECG, become Common Good cities and regions, do the balance sheet for themselves, and then require Common Good Balance Sheets from companies receiving government contracts and initiate or support democratic citizen assemblies.
4   Local democratic assemblies must be established at the national and supranational level so the people can amend the constitution to create a new legal economic framework aligned with their values.

Notes

1 Martin Nowak, *Supercooperators: Beyond the Survival of the Fittest: Why Cooperation, Not Competition, Is the Key to Life* (Edinburgh: Canongate Books Ltd., 2012).
2 John Thornhill, "Income Inequality Seen as the Great Divide," *Financial Times*, May 19, 2008.
3 Hillary Hoffower, "We Did the Math to Calculate How Much Money Jeff Bezos Makes in a Year, Month, Week, Day, Hour, Minute, and Second," *Business Insider*, https://www.businessinsider.com/what-amazon-ceo-jeff-bezos-makes-every-day-hour-minute-2018-10.
4 "Economy for the Common Good," *European Economic and Social Committee*, September 2015, http://www.eesc.europa.eu/?i=portal.en.eco-opinions.34923.
5 Richard Layard, *Happiness: Lessons from a New Science* (London: Penguin, 2005); Richard Wilkinson and Kate Pickett, *The Spirit Level. Why More Equal Societies Almost Always Do Better* (London: Penguin, 2010).
6 "Economy for the Common Good," 2015.
7 Hote Laperla, http://www.hotel-laperla.it/en/pills/common-welfare-economy/14-699.html.
8 Sparda-Bank, https://www.sparda-m.de/gemeinwohl-oekonomie.php.

Chapter 5

A Civic Economy of Provisions

Marvin T. Brown

Many of us agree that the economy we have is not the economy we want. There are many worthy alternatives: a solidarity economy, a sharing economy, a local economy, an ownership economy, and so on. As an additional alternative, consider a *civic economy* based on civic relations rather than property relations and designed to make provisions for all rather than money for the few.[1] A civic economy would not ignore our social differences but would use our common humanity as a basis for engaging in civic conversations about how to redesign our social and economic worlds so they are just and sustainable.

Capitalism, as it has come down to us over the past three centuries, violates the principle of a common humanity by splitting off from its story the burden borne by the real providers of wealth, both human and otherwise. There is no better illustration of this duplicity than Adam Smith's silence on the role of enslaved people in creating the wealth his nation enjoyed.[2] Capitalism originated in the Atlantic triangle trade connecting Europe, Africa, and the Americas. Soon, new theories of property and property relations were developed to explain and justify the Atlantic economy, which involved the enslavement of more than 11 million Africans to supply the labor for the growing economies of Europe and white America. Enslaved people, at the time, were treated as property. They received no more sympathy and consideration than cattle or horses. This is a hard truth about capitalism that is usually overlooked or denied.

The refusal to integrate this history into our views of modern economics prevents us from telling the truth about the current destruction of the environment, or to acknowledge—really acknowledge—the misery of workers today who provide us our goods. Facing this history, and thus reconnecting with the real providers of wealth, is the only way out of the property-based economics of capitalism and into a civic economy of different systems of provision that could save the future for our children and grandchildren. A *civic* economy of provisions could give us a chance to repair the violations of our common humanity and to restore the basic practices of all human communities.

Basic Practices of Human Communities

The framework of a civic economy of provision integrates the three basic practices of any human community: providing for one another, protecting one another, and creating meaning together. This idea of a civic economy of provision has both classical and modern adherents. In Aristotle, we see the origins of the idea that the economy belongs to the civic sphere. More recently, Julie A. Nelson has written in *Economics for Humans* that the economy "is about the provisioning of goods and services to meet our material needs."[3] Daniel W. Bromley, in his philosophical work on subjective pragmatism, also writes that economics should be about "how societies organize themselves for their provisioning."[4] Although neither author dwells on the notion of provisioning, they open the door to such an approach. Taking this idea farther, then the civic economy should be one in which all people, organized together in many ways, are able to provide for their families and communities.

If we are to provide one another with the basics for a good life, we will need to also protect providers—the planet and people, common resources, and cooperative activities. Instead of focusing on property rights, we need to focus on human rights. Instead of seeing the natural world as a commodity, we need to recognize it as a living being that gives us life. If we do create this type of economy, we will also create a way of living together that gives us meaningful relationships and self-worth. In short, the civic economy of provision seeks, as a priority, to return our thinking about the economy to first principles and to focus our conversations about and with each other on what truly matters most to us.

In the economics-of-property tradition, the focus has been on the individual or economic man, who acts in his self-interest and tries to maximize his good fortune. The economics of provision offers an alternative. It follows Virginia Held's suggestion that the image of the mother and child more correctly represents our human nature.[5] This image highlights a relationship of attachment instead of isolation and allows us to acknowledge the parent's labor in providing for the child. This mental picture also helps us imagine a relationship of mutual identity, rather than one based on each individual's self-interest. As Nancy Folbre argues in *The Invisible Heart*, the family has been largely eliminated from economic thinking, and yet it is in the family mainly where we provide and care for one another.[6] True, individuals do want to provide for themselves, but we do this in community with others. Just as it is a mistake to isolate individuals from their communities, it is also a mistake to isolate the economy from the systems to which it belongs.

The Systemic Context of the Economy

A civic economy of provision belongs to three distinct systems: the ecological system of the biosphere, the social system of human societies, and the civic system of discourse. The ecological system sustains us and other living things. We belong to it—are nested in it. As the context of our common humanity, this ecological system provides resources for the making of provisions for families and communities.

Social systems comprise sets of relationships that unite and divide us, including the traditionally defined economy. All organizations and institutions belong to society, including businesses, governments, and so-called "civil society" organizations. Instead of ignoring the social identity of civil society organizations, a civic approach sees them within the matrix of social differences and conflicts. Like other social organizations and institutions, their purpose is to play their role in creating communities where members can provide for and protect one another.

The civic is grounded in our common humanity and emerges through conversations that arise primarily from potentially illuminating disagreements about how to handle our social differences. Civic conversations take up controversial social and economic issues in ways that let participants draw on their shared humanity to listen and learn from one another. These civic conversations can take place in a variety of forums, from neighborhood meetings and workplace sessions to city council workshops, with processes for scaling up to larger groupings and geographies.

If we are to base the economy on civic relations instead of property relations, then we need to use reciprocity as the moral foundation for making exchanges. In specific exchanges, people should receive in proportion to what they have given. More generally, a just humane system based on reciprocity will continually aim for what Lawrence Becker has called "balanced social relationships."[7] Balanced social relations require coherence, inclusion, and integrity instead of chaos, exclusion, and fragmentation, which means that current social relationships need re-balancing. The civic system of discourse depends on and yet can also change our relations to the natural system of the biosphere and our various social worlds, as it draws on different resources for designing systems of provision.

Designing Systems of Provision

In our modern economy, providing for families and communities is accomplished through various systems of provision, such as the food- or the health-care system. These systems of provision could be organized to make provisions for all. How, of course, is a major question. Many people see only two organizing options: capitalism or socialism. A civic economy of provision is another option. As citizens guided by such civic norms as reciprocity and moral equality, we can engage in civic conversations to turn economic systems toward sustainability and justice. If we are smart citizens, we will not discard things that can work, such as markets and property rights, but we will also not allow them to control our fate.

Whether we use markets for making provisions or property rights for managing resources depends on how we decide to live together. Markets should never violate the civic principle of reciprocity, and property rights should never override our common rights to natural resources. Still, sometimes markets can be useful in meeting people's preferences and paying for resource use. Private ownership can encourage personal stewardship. The point is to ensure that the economy fulfills its purpose of making provisions justly and sustainably.

In a civic economy, citizens would decide how to distribute provisions, and the production and distribution of some provisions would rely more on markets than others. Market competition can be effective when it is contained by rules and assumptions based on civic cooperation, as well as the principles of moral equality and reciprocity. If some basic provisions, such as food or housing, are distributed through competitive markets, then citizens should have access to a basic income so they can participate in such markets.

That said, we must remember that most property-based wealth is not created by competitive markets, but by non-competitive salaries such as CEO stock options, by fees such as those for financial services, or by various forms of unearned income, such as increase in land value.

As for private property, in the civil economy the Lockean tradition of ownership trumping civic membership is reversed and civic membership is a condition for ownership. Instead of assuming that possession implies ownership that the state then acknowledges and protects, in the framework of civic economics of provision, the state is the origin of ownership and owning property is like having a concession to use a common resource.

As with a managed commons, which can be maintained indefinitely without abuse, community members together develop governance rules but the resource can still provide commercial benefits. Farmers could own their farm but citizens could develop policies (on, say, regulating pesticide use) that would protect all farmland for future generations, and increased land values would be taxed so that the value added would go to the community instead of becoming unearned income for farmers.[8]

Instead of dividing the economy into different sectors, the economy would be divided into different systems of provision. Banks, for example, would not belong to a financial sector, but to various systems of provision, and bank owners wouldn't determine bank functions. Instead,

Figure 5.1 Civic systems of provision.

civic policies would define money's role. In many cases, citizens would probably opt for public or cooperative banks rather than privately owned banks.

Civic systems of provision can be seen as three concentric circles, as illustrated in Figure 5.1.

In the inner circle, citizens engage in conversations about how to make provisions for all. Guided by civic norms of moral equality and reciprocity, these conversations would aim to design systems of provision that would create and maintain balanced social relationships.

The middle circle represents the basic process of an economics of provision, which would be the same for all provider systems: human providers transform natural provisions to provisions for our families and communities. Each entry in the outer circle represents a system of provision, and each system includes all the social organizations and institutions that help us provide what we as families and communities need and deserve.

Applying this civic economics framework to the just and sustainable provision of food looks like Figure 5.2.

Here too, the inner circle, civic conversations, is where citizens deliberate and decide how human providers will transform natural resources into provisions for families and communities, and the interactions in the middle circle are the same as in the general model. The outer circle shows the groups and agencies likely to be involved in the provision of food.

Let's look more closely how such civic systems of provision draw on and change the natural, social, and civic worlds in which we live, beginning with the idea of civic conversations.

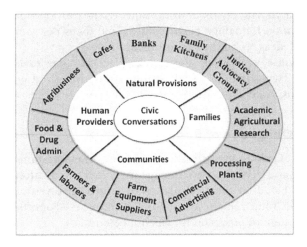

Figure 5.2 Civic system of providing food.

Civic Conversations

The realization of civic systems of provision depends on our ability to develop a civic consciousness that is grounded in our common humanity and our capacity to engage in conversations with others who bring different stories and alternative points of view. Such a consciousness can emerge from actual encounters with others who have diverse pasts and a common future, and success often depends on getting the right people in the room (or other space) together.

In civic conversations, all differences are recognized as sources of knowledge, including racial, ethnic, and religious differences. Participants in these conversations are invited to explore how to repair violations of our common humanity by the economics of slavery and its legacy, opening the way to creating the humility necessary to address social inequality and climatic destruction. Real progress in creating a viable system of provision and protection will not happen until we address issues of white superiority and impunity. By the same token, the civic would not be dominated by any religion, but would invite all believers to become members. The civic is grounded in our common humanity, and diverse religions inform us about what it means to be human and to live in a human community. If we can engage in such civic conversations, we can then work together to change our economic system to one based on civic membership rather than property ownership.

Civic conversations are based on Benjamin Barber's notion of a "strong" or participative democracy.[9] The principle of subsidiarity is at work here too. In local settings, direct democracy is possible. In larger settings, representative democracy would work. Since civic conversations are based on our common humanity, participants would focus not so much on the exchange of ideas, as on the improvement of ideas.

These civic conversations always take place in some social setting or institution. Two common social settings are business and governmental organizations. A civic perspective would focus on civic obligations.

The Civic Obligation of Business

Any system of provision, such as food, housing, or entertainment, involves both public and private actors and agencies. Private investors may make investments based on their calculation of return on investment. But the business itself must remain focused on its purpose—contributing to the particular system of provision to which it belongs.

General Motors, for example, belongs to the transportation system. General Foods belongs to the food system. Blue Cross belongs to the health-care system. A business' civic purpose depends on its particular system of provision, not on its investors, although investors may hope or expect to get a good return. For the most part, corporate obligations would grow out of whatever functions their respective systems of provision perform.

Since corporations are legal or civic creations, citizens can change them by changing their charters. For this reason, a civic economics of provision would vest civic conversations with determining the design of corporations. Corporations would be confined to their own system of provision—those where they have some socially valuable expertise—and restrained in other systems where other agents should control the agenda, such as electoral politics. Instead of businesses deciding what they will "give back to the community" through their Corporate Social Responsibility programs, elected agencies would determine their "Corporate Civic Obligations"[10] within the mix of enterprises in the various systems of provision.

In the future, corporate boards should represent all stakeholders so their corporate decisions will match their civic obligations. All innovative corporate forms are possible from a civic perspective *if* they are based on civic norms, address the violations of our common humanity, enhance the making of provisions, and advance justice and sustainability. If the aim is to provide food in an urban area, for example, the participants in the system would include local food markets and restaurants, food suppliers and processors, food producers and growers, government agencies on the local, state, and national levels, food advocacy groups, banks and transportation agencies (see Figure 5.2). Answering the question of how to provide good food for all justly and sustainably could require invitations to any of these groups, and others, to get a bead on how best to make the desired changes.

Generally, increased value created by any system of provision belongs to the whole system, even though it may appear in just one part, such as business corporations. In a civic system of provision model, this increased value should be distributed throughout the whole system through taxes because the owner is the system, not the corporation or its stockholders.

In the international business sphere, our current ideology of comparative advantage puts developing nations at a disadvantage in terms of creating self-governing public institutions. In the civil economy, international trade would aim to make all communities more self-sustaining. Given the long history of colonialism and exploitation, which continues to infect global trade policies, we need to repair the violations of our common humanity through new policies that will benefit peoples in former colonies, focusing on economic systems of provision that are for the people rather than for international corporations.

The Civic Workplace

So, what about the workplace? Can workers and managers engage in civic deliberation? They certainly have conflicts, but are these conflicts based on different interests? In the old economics of property-oriented business model, they are, since the conflict is about the value or price of different properties (labor, land, and money). But, if we switch to a new economics of provision based on civic relations, the picture looks much different. The role or purpose of the business organization changes from getting a return on investment to making provisions. In this model, all members of the organization are "employed" to fulfill the mission of providing quality goods and services. They may disagree about how best to do that, but not about the company's purpose. In fact, this common purpose gives them a shared vision that enables them to deliberate on how best to realize it.

Civil conversations on work issues would, as now, also cover workplace conditions and pay. If wages were based on the civic principle of reciprocity, requiring that a good day's work gets a good day's pay, that would be enough income to "make a living" for one's family. Wages or salaries that go beyond this moral minimum would be largely determined by the market.

Systemic change almost always requires citizens to organize to hold those in administrative positions accountable.[11] The struggle of labor unions for recognition and fair wages is an important legacy of our current social systems. Their effectiveness in moving current systems toward justice and sustainability also depends on their contribution to the creation of meaningful civic conversations.

In time, we will need to move toward something like a basic income for all, simply because a sustainable economy must produce less rather than more. For that—the subject of another civic conversation—we can design life-work models where people use local currencies to trade with neighbors for perhaps 20 percent of their needs, receive a basic income for 30 percent, and work two or three days a week for the other 50 percent. The work of designing such an economy will be possible only when government functions as both a facilitator and a protector of inclusive civic conversations.

Government Involvement

Government is also a social institution, in some respects no more grounded today in the civic than other social organizations. But, that means the chances of reforming government are no slimmer than those of reforming other social institutions either.

Government's role is central to the civic economics of provision. Every system of provision needs a multitude of organizations to make provisions for all, and the role of government would vary by system. The provision of health care will probably be largely a government program and food would be a mixture. Entertainment would be mostly nongovernmental, though cities may want to develop community-supported museums and music halls after a broad-based conversation with citizens about preferences.

Decisions by local and beyond-local participants in civic conversations should also determine how much of the economy government should control. If we allow government to create money as needed to pay for real work, then government expenditure depends on social conditions. Some communities might decide to use voluntary food banks to provide sustenance to those without the money to purchase from markets, or communities might decide to provide government food stamps instead. The question is how to involve in these conversations the people who know how to develop the best approach. The variety of approaches, however, does not change the moral imperative of protecting the basic sources of our provisions: the biosphere.

The Environmental Moral Imperative

In this model of the civil economy, a distinction is drawn between social and natural systems. Social systems (including the economy) are verbal and non-verbal communication patterns that create trends subject to positive and negative feedback loops. Natural systems are cyclical and self-organizing, which is aptly illustrated by the role of photosynthesis in the carbon cycle. Social systems need corrective human interference. Natural systems need to be protected from abusive human interference.

As the picture of the food system illustrates, the environment is a natural provider that human providers transform into provisions for families and communities. The civic approach places our common humanity in both the natural environment and society. The civic space emerges between our human nature and our social differences. This vantage helps us recognize that we belong to the natural environment, instead of the natural environment belonging to us. Thus, a civic approach to environmental issues is not merely utilitarian, but also ontological.

Nature is a provider for human and nonhuman communities. Both natural and human providers must be protected from abuse and treated with gratitude for their gifts. The global striving for continual "economic growth" almost ridicules such a stance toward nature. So, we need to engage in civic conversations on how to move toward an appropriate relationship between the environment and the people.

One promising approach for consideration is the United Nations' Natural Step partnership.[12] This program for moving strategically toward sustainability bids us to begin with an image of what a sustainable global community would look like and then together figure out together how to move in that direction. Natural Step can work at many levels, and, at the highest, would entail nations with greater capacity for making changes helping those with less capacity.

Because of colonialism and its legacy, the contemporary property-based social system now dominates the world, so most responses to environmental challenges are based on utilitarian calculations. A civic approach would argue that these calculations should never override the moral principle of protecting the natural provisions from destruction.

The civil economy model proposes that instead of treating land (the environment) and labor (humans) as commodities, we treat them as providers. The perpetuators of the commodification of living beings endanger both the environment and our humanity.

Upending Trends, Changing Direction

The changes needed now will be disruptive and disturbing, especially for those benefitting from current social systems. And though disruption has to come before transformation, not every disruption or every social movement is positive. For that, we must go deeper to the level of our shared humanity, which emerges through civic conversations and breaks through the wall of silence—the silence of privilege.

More theoretically, if we understand social systems as sets of social trends influenced by positive and negative feedback loops, then changing systems requires us to examine what is supporting current trends and then to change it to support trends that move in a different direction.

Do we have the power to make such changes? We do if we remember that power today resides mostly in the design of organizations and institutions.[13] If you redesign the organization, you change the location of power and power relations. If we want to eliminate the influence of billionaires in electoral politics, we must change the political structure. Kenneth Boulding has argued that three different types of power maintain social systems: integration, exchange, and threat.[14] If we can change the beliefs (integration), incentives (exchanges), or laws and rules (threats) of current trends, we will change the trends. All three changes are necessary. That said, changing our picture of what a just and sustainable economy would look like is only part of the work ahead.

A civic economics of provision requires, above all else, a strong notion of citizenship—of membership in a global civil society. With this common identity, we can allow civic rather than property relationships to define our bonds with each other—at work, in our neighborhoods, in our cities, and in global communities. A civic economy would ensure that making provisions, not accumulating property, is at the core of our economic thinking.

What We Need to Transition to a Civic Economy

- Switch the basis of the economy from property relations and ownership to civic relations and civic membership.
- Place the wealth of families and communities at the center of the economy's purpose, rather than the wealth of isolated individuals or nation-states.
- Change the goal of the economy from economic growth to making provisions for all.
- Associate, rather than dissociate, Europe and white America's wealth with the misery of slavery, colonialism, and its legacy.
- Treat labor and land as providers rather than properties.
- Use civic norms, such as reciprocity, to determine economic exchanges.
- Treat people at work as citizens with the rights of voice, representation, and respect.
- Locate the primary function of money in different systems of provision rather than in financial markets.
- Treat money as a civic means for making provisions rather than as a commodity/property.
- Engage in conversations that aim to repair the past violations of our common humanity, instead of assuming that one can create a new future without accounting for the past.
- Recognize ourselves as a part of nature, rather than seeing ourselves apart from nature.

Notes

1 Marvin T. Brown, *Civilizing the Economy: A New Economics of Provision* (New York: Cambridge University Press, 2010).
2 Brown, *Civilizing the Economy*, 19–33.

3 Julie A. Nelson, *Economics for Humans* (Chicago: The University of Chicago Press, 2006), 1.
4 Daniel W. Bromley, *Sufficient Reason: Volitional Pragmatism and the Meaning of Economic Institutions* (Princeton, NJ: Princeton University Press, 2009), 180.
5 Virginia Held, *Feminist Morality: Transforming Culture, Society, and Politics* (Chicago, IL: The University of Chicago Press, 1993), 72.
6 Nancy Folbre, *The Invisible Heart: Economics and Family Values* (New York: The New Press, 2001), xii.
7 Lawrence C. Becker, *Reciprocity* (Chicago, IL: The University of Chicago Press, 1986), 107.
8 As proposed by Henry George in *Progress and Poverty* (New York: Robert Schalkenback Foundation, 1997).
9 Benjamin Barber, *Strong Democracy: Participatory Politics in a New Age* (Berkeley: University of California Press, 2004).
10 Brown, *Civilizing the Economy*, 210–221.
11 See Jeffrey Stout, *Blessed Are the Organized: Grassroots Democracy in America* (Princeton, NJ: Princeton University Press, 2012).
12 "The Natural Step," http://www.thenaturalstep.org/.
13 Marvin T. Brown, *Corporate Integrity: Rethinking Organizational Ethics and Leadership* (New York: Cambridge University Press, 2005), 91.
14 Kenneth Boulding, *Three Faces of Power* (New York: Sage Publications, 1990).

Chapter 6

Whole Systems Change

A Framework and First Steps for Social/Economic Transformation

Riane Eisler

Today's nuclear and biological weapons give us destructive powers once attributed only to a vengeful God. Fossil fuels combined with our species' exponential population growth are decimating our natural life-support systems. A technological shift, as seismic as that from foraging to farming and from agriculture to manufacturing, is hurling us into the postindustrial, knowledge-service age. Jobs are disappearing, and many more soon will be lost to robotics and artificial intelligence. The chasm between haves and have-nots is again widening within and between nations. Religious fanaticism is resurging, promising heavenly rewards for terrorizing, maiming, and killing. Yet, the vast majority of people, including most national leaders, academics, and mass media, remain in a kind of trance, insulated by old ways of thinking.

Fortunately, people in growing numbers are reexamining not only what was and is, but also what can, and must, be done. They understand that solving our unprecedented problems calls for more than just tinkering at the edges of failing systems—that we need whole systems change, and that this, in turn, requires a fundamental cultural transformation.

This chapter outlines such a cultural transformation—a new conceptual framework, the actions needed for whole systems change, and references to successful pilot programs.

From Old to New Thinking

After the fall of the Soviet Union, some people contended that capitalism would bring peace and a more equitable world. But it has instead widened the gap between those on the top and those at the bottom and accelerated environmental degradation. In reaction, some propose socialism even though the mass applications of Marx's socialist theories in the former Soviet Union and China led to enormous repression, violence, and environmental problems. Still others say that the solution to our ills is democratic elections, but elections don't prevent oligarchies from ruling or, as happened after the "Arab Spring," authoritarianism from ascending.

Finally, some would have us return to prescientific Western times or replace Western secularism with Eastern religions, forgetting that the religious European Middle Ages were cruel and repressive, that some Eastern religions have helped perpetuate inequality and oppression, and that today's fundamentalist religious regimes are brutally violent and oppressive.

All these approaches have one thing in common: they derive from old thinking. They look at societies from the perspective of such old categories as capitalist versus socialist, religious versus secular, Eastern versus Western, rightist versus leftist, and industrial versus pre- or postindustrial. All ignore the lessons of history and none answers the most critical question for our future: *what kind of social configuration supports the expression of our human capacities for consciousness, caring, and creativity—or, alternatively, our capacities for insensitivity, cruelty, and destructiveness?*

A New Method of Analysis

The *study of relational dynamics* is a new method for analyzing social systems.[1] It focuses on two primary relational dynamics: the kinds of relations— from intimate to international—that a culture encourages or discourages and the interactive relationships that maintain a culture's basic character. This trans-disciplinary analysis draws from systems, complexity, and self-organizing theories—the study of how different components of living systems interact to maintain one another and the larger whole of which they are a part, and how they can change.[2] Cross-cultural anthropological and sociological surveys and studies of individual societies; writings by historians; analyses of laws, moral codes, art, and literature; scholarship from psychology, economics, education, political science, philosophy, religious studies, archeology, myths, and legends; and data from such newer fields as primatology, neuroscience, gender studies, women's studies, and men's studies all feed into this new form of inquiry.[3]

Unlike most social analysis, relational dynamics doesn't focus only on political, economic, and other "public" institutions. Its integrative approach, drawing from biological and social science, shows the critical importance of the "private" sphere of family and other intimate relations in shaping beliefs, behaviors, and even brain development.[4]

Two Underlying Social Configurations

The social configurations identified by the study of relational dynamics transcend familiar categories, such as religious or secular, leftist or rightist, socialist or capitalist, Eastern or Western, Northern or Southern, and industrial or pre- or post-industrial. While descriptions of a society's ideology, technology, economics, or location are important, they tell us nothing about how a society constructs the gender and parent-child relations where children first experience, observe, and learn what is considered normal and moral in human relations. Nor do such descriptions tell us anything about what kinds of relations in all spheres—from the family, education, and religion to politics and economics—a society's beliefs, guiding values, and institutions support or inhibit.

Examining societies from the perspective of relational dynamics reveals social configurations that conventional siloed, uni-disciplinary approaches can't discern. New social categories—called the *domination model* and the *partnership model*—reveal otherwise invisible connections. Think, for example, about the connection between whether violence is considered normal in childrearing and whether a society is warlike or peaceful (see Figure 6.1). On the most basic level, these categories help us see what kinds of social systems support our human capacities for consciousness, empathy, caring, and creativity instead of our capacities for insensitivity, cruelty, exploitation, and destructiveness.[5]

The Domination Social Configuration

Hitler's Germany (a technologically advanced, Western rightist society), Stalin's USSR (a secular, leftist society), Khomeini's Iran, the Taliban of Afghanistan, ISIS in Iraq and Syria (Eastern religious societies), and Idi Amin's Uganda (a tribalist society) have been some of the past century's most brutally violent and repressive societies. As different as they may appear by conventional perspectives, all share the core configuration of the four interactive, mutually supporting components of the domination model:

1   A structure of rigid top-down rankings in both the family and the state or tribe, and all institutions in between
2   The rigid ranking of the male half of humanity over the female half, and a system of gendered values that devalues such traditionally "feminine" traits and activities as caring, caregiving, and nonviolence
3   Culturally accepted abuse and violence—from child- and wife-beating to pogroms to lynchings and chronic warfare—that maintain hierarchies of domination, be they man over woman, man over man, race over race, religion over religion, tribe over tribe, or nation over nation
4   The belief that all of the above are inevitable, normal, and even moral

The Partnership Configuration

The partnership model configuration also has four interactive components:

1   A democratic structure in *both* the family and the state or tribe, and all institutions in between

2 Equal partnership between women and men, and a high valuing in all people and policy of such qualities and behaviors as non-violence, nurturance, and caregiving denigrated in domination systems

3 Abuse and violence are not institutionalized or idealized since they are not needed to maintain rigid rankings of domination

4 Beliefs about human nature that support empathic and mutually respectful relations—with insensitivity, cruelty, and violence not considered inevitable, much less moral

The Partnership System

Democratic and economically equitable structure

Equal valuing of males and females and high regard for stereotypical feminine values

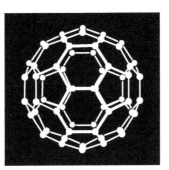

Mutual respect and trust with low degree of violence

Beliefs and stories that give high value to empathic and caring relations

The Domination System

Authoritarian and inequitable social and economic structure

Subordination of women and "femininity" to men and "masculinity"

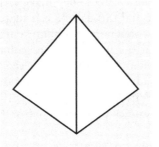

High degree of abuse and violence

Beliefs and stories that justify and idealize domination and violence

Figure 6.1 "Partnership" vs. "domination". From Riane Eisler, *The Real Wealth of Nations: Creating a Caring Economics*.

As with societies toward the domination end of the partnership/domination continuum, societies orienting to the partnership end transcend conventional categories, such as religious or secular, Eastern or Western, industrial or postindustrial, and so on. To illustrate, in contrast to domination-oriented tribal societies, where family violence is customary and may include such brutal rituals as female genital cutting/mutilation, the forest Teduray of the Philippines rear their children non-violently, women play major social roles, and such stereotypically feminine values as caring and nurturing are valued in both women and men.[6]

The agrarian Minagkabau in Sumatra are another example.[7] As Sanday writes:

> The Minagkabau subordinate male dominion and competition, which we consider basic to human social ordering and evolution, to the work of maternal nurture, which they hold to be necessary for the common good and the healthy society ... Social well-being is found in natural growth and fertility according to the dictum that the unfurling, blooming, and growth in nature is our teacher.[8]

On the other side of the planet, such Nordic nations as Sweden, Finland, and Norway also orient more toward partnership. These technologically advanced societies are not ideal, but they have more democracy in *both* the family and the state, with no huge gaps between haves and have-nots. Women hold high political offices (40–50 percent of national legislatures)[9] raising the status of the "feminine." Nurturance is supported by fiscal policy through such measures as universal health care and childcare, respectful elder care, stipends to help families care for children, and generous paid parental leave.[10]

These more partnership-oriented societies support activities that model and promote empathy and caring. They make large investments in caring for their own people and through NGOs support people in far-away places. They have many cooperative economic enterprises, and have been leaders in environmental sustainability. Not coincidentally, these more partnership-oriented nations have also been at the forefront of the movement to leave behind traditions of violence and domination. They have decoupled "masculinity" from its association with domination and violence, pioneered peace studies programs, and outlawed physically disciplining children at home.[11]

Are these advances toward greater democracy, equity, and reduced violence possible simply because the Nordic countries are small and homogenous, as some argue? Other small, homogeneous nations, such as Saudi Arabia, are undemocratic and rigidly male-dominated. In some, wealth and power are concentrated in a small elite, and violence (including "honor" murders and public beheadings) is used to maintain top-down control in both family and state. So the difference is not a matter of size or homogeneity, but of culture. Indeed, the Nordic countries (market economies and not "democratic socialist" as they are frequently mislabeled) often call themselves "caring societies"—another way of describing partnership-oriented cultures.

Caveats

"Partnership" was chosen to describe the social configuration that supports relations of mutual respect, accountability, and benefit because mutuality is, at least in theory, the basis for relations among business partners. The distinction between the partnership and the domination model is *not* that there is cooperation in the first and not the second. People cooperate all the time in domination-oriented systems. Members of monopolies, invading armies, criminal gangs, and terrorist groups all work together.

A second caveat is that partnership structures are not flat. Every society requires parents, teachers, managers, and leaders—so there are hierarchies. But instead of *hierarchies of domination*, they are *hierarchies of actualization*— more flexible structures in which the ideal norm is not *power over* but *power to* and *power with*.

A third caveat is that the difference between domination and partnership systems is not that there is no competition in the latter. There is competition in both, but rather than dog-eat-dog competition aimed at destroying or putting competitors out of business, in partnership systems achievement by others spurs excellence.

Another caveat is that while a major difference between domination and partnership systems is whether both genders are equally valued, this difference is not about anything inherent in women or men. As men embrace "feminine" roles, feeding and diapering babies, and women become leaders in once exclusively male preserves, gender roles become more fluid.

Nor are partnership systems conflict-free. But in domination systems, conflict is suppressed until it explodes in violence, and violent struggle is idealized. In partnership systems, conflict is nearly always nonviolent, and handling conflict is an opportunity to find creative solutions. That said, the shift to the partnership side of the continuum must be global so that partnership-oriented nations won't be overrun if they can't protect themselves from societies (like Nazi Germany) on the domination end of the continuum.

In short, these models aren't based on such simplistic notions as "all would be well if people only cooperate" or "we must avoid conflict." Rather, they describe social configurations that support two different kinds of relations, beliefs, and institutions—providing information vital for cultural transformation.

Cultural Transformation

The domination model has always entailed terrible damage to people and nature. But at today's level of technological development, the mix of high technology and an ethos of domination and conquest threatens our survival. But with the disequilibrium kindled by the Industrial Revolution and stoked by the rapid move into the knowledge-service era, old beliefs and institutions were destabilized and the possibility of fundamental change opened up.

This takes us to another outcome from the study of relational dynamics: *cultural transformation theory*.[12] Like chaos theory,[13] it holds that living systems can undergo transformative change during times of great disequilibrium. As explored in *The Chalice and the Blade, Nurturing Our Humanity*, and other works, tension between the partnership model and the domination model courses through our cultural evolution.[14] Gathering-hunting cultures were oriented more to the partnership side of the continuum, studies of contemporary gathering-hunting societies and archeological finds show.[15] The same was true of many cultures in the early Neolithic or farming age and up to, in some places, the Bronze Age.[16] Then, domination systems formed during a period of disequilibrium brought about by climate changes, mass migrations, and other dislocations.[17] Thereafter, the domination model became the norm for much of recorded history, despite periodic countercurrents. But during another period of great disequilibrium brought by the gradual shift from the agrarian to the industrial and now postindustrial age, the partnership movement has been gaining momentum, at least in some regions.

The 17th- and 18th-century Enlightenment "rights of man" movement challenged the so-called divinely ordained right of kings to rule. The 18th- and 19th-century feminist movement challenged the supposedly divinely ordained right of men to rule women and children in the "castles" of their homes. The 19th- and 20th-century abolitionist, civil rights, and anticolonial movements challenged another "divinely ordained" right—that of "superior" races to rule over "inferior" ones. The movement for economic justice challenges top-down economic rule. The peace movement and the movement to end violence against women and children challenge the use of violence to impose one's will on others. The environmental movement challenges the once-hallowed conquest and domination of nature.[18]

However, progress toward partnership has not been linear. It can best be imaged as an upward spiral countered by dips or periodic regressions.[19] One important factor behind these regressions is that most progressive movements have paid almost exclusive attention to the so-called public sphere of economic and political relations: the "men's world" from which women and children are excluded in domination systems. Changing parent-child and woman-man relations in the so-called private sphere received far less attention. Consequently, domination systems had the foundations needed to keep rebuilding themselves.

Consider that for the most repressive modern regimes—from Hitler's Germany and Stalin's USSR to ISIS in Iraq and Syria—a top priority has been maintaining or reinstating family relations based on domination and submission. Today's religious fundamentalists—be they Muslim, Hindu, Jewish, or Christian—emphasize returning to a "traditional family" in which men dominate women and children learn never to question even unjust orders. This domination-based family structure provides the foundation for the repressive theocratic system these regimes want to impose.

In addition, even though our global population explosion drives resource depletion and other environmental crises, fundamentalist leaders fiercely oppose reproductive freedom for women. Indeed, male control over women typifies rigid domination systems, whether secular or religious. Stalin halted small steps taken toward gender equity in families, re-criminalized abortion, and made top leadership exclusively male again.[20]

Regressive leaders also refuse to acknowledge the full spectrum of sexual orientation, asserting that a household headed by a male who controls women and children is the God-given order. These same leaders promulgate parenting that inculcates absolute obedience to authority, in the United States recommending spanking to prevent "spoiling" and urging parents to force eight-month-old babies to sit still with their hands on their high-chair trays—effectively terrorizing them so they automatically submit to domination as adults.[21]

It is also no coincidence that those who fiercely oppose government regulations limiting the power of mega-corporations and the super-rich also try to deny women's reproductive freedom, equal employment protection, and an equal say in families. Subjugating one half of humanity reinforces the top-down economic system rearguard leaders support.

Foundations for Whole Systems Change

The new conceptual framework sketched here helps us see that there are today many important efforts to accelerate the shift toward the partnership side of the continuum worldwide. However, regressions will continue, with disastrous effects, unless we build the missing foundations for a partnership future.

The First Cornerstone: Childhood

Although people can change throughout life, early experiences and relations are critical. Our brains' neural pathways are not set at birth: they are largely formed in interaction with our early experiences and observations.[22]

When family relations based on chronic violations of human rights are considered normal and moral, they provide mental and emotional models for condoning such violations in other relations. If these relations are violent, children learn that violence from the more powerful toward the less powerful is an acceptable way of dealing with conflicts and problems. Although many people reject these teachings, many others replicate them in intimate relations—and national and international ones.[23] Coercive, inequitable, and violent childrearing thus undergirds a coercive, inequitable, and chronically violent social organization.

This calls for a global campaign against abuse and violence in childhood relations.[24] Key elements include:

- *Education*: providing both women and men the knowledge and skills for empathic, sensitive, nonviolent, authoritative rather than authoritarian childrearing (see the Center for Partnership Studies' *Caring and Connected Parenting Guide*[25])
- *Laws*: enacting and enforcing laws criminalizing child abuse, including invoking such international laws as the Rome Statute to protect children and women from family violence[26]
- *Media*: eliminating the idealization of violence in action entertainment and "sitcoms" where family members abuse and humiliate each other
- *Morality*: engaging religious leaders to stand against the intimate violence that every year blights, and often takes, the lives of millions of children and women, and models violence for all relations[27]

The Second Cornerstone: Gender

When people learn to equate difference—beginning with the fundamental male/female form difference—with superiority or inferiority, dominating or being dominated, being served or serving, they internalize a template automatically applicable to a different race, religion, ethnicity, sexual orientation, and so forth. The social construction of gender roles and relations also shapes a society's guiding values. With the subordination of the female half of humanity comes the subordination of caring, caregiving, nonviolence, and other traits and activities stereotypically associated with femininity. This gendered system of values adversely affects quality of life, as documented in an 89-nation study—*Women, Men, and the Global Quality of Life*—by the Center for Partnership Studies.[28] The World Economic Forums' *Gender Gap* reports also confirm the correlation between the status of women and economic success.[29] Clearly, depriving half the population of equal opportunities deprives societies of enormous contributions. And as long as women are devalued so also are policies considered "soft" or "feminine" in domination systems.

A four-dimensional (education, laws, media, and morality) global campaign for equitable and nonviolent gender relations will accelerate forward movement. Along with progressive leaders, foundations too should prioritize empowering girls and women and promoting women's leadership worldwide.

The Third Cornerstone: Economics

As documented in *The Real Wealth of Nations: Creating a Caring Economics*, we urgently need new post-capitalist, post-socialist economic thinking.[30] If we reexamine the critique of capitalism as unjust and exploitive from the perspective of the partnership-domination continuum, we see that it is actually a critique of the beliefs, institutions, and relationships inherent in domination systems.

To understand, and change, current economic systems, we must understand and change the domination social context from which they derive. Today's winner-take-all economics harks back to earlier domination traditions—from pharaonic Egypt to ancient Chinese empires, India's caste system, Middle Eastern warlord raiding, and European feudalism. Remember too that Adam Smith developed capitalism's economic model in the 18th century, when rigid top-down rankings were even more entrenched. Karl Marx's socialist theory also reflected dominator assumptions—including using force to impose the "dictatorship of the proletariat."

For both Marx and Smith, nature was there to be exploited. Smith's statement that wealth derives from a nation's land and labor has been interpreted to mean that he valued our natural environment.[31] However, rather than recognizing nature's limitations, Smith contended that wealth would grow endlessly as self-interest guided the "invisible hand of the market." Similarly, attempts to ally Marx with nature[32] don't convince given his emphasis on the "commodification of labor" and his blindness to industrialization's devastating impact on nature.[33] In short, caring for nature is not part of either capitalist or socialist theory.

Smith and Marx considered caregiving "women's work"—"reproductive" not "productive" labor. This false distinction has been roundly criticized for perpetuating a gendered economy that severely disadvantages women and children.[34] Yet, despite mounting evidence that environmental neglect is potentially suicidal and that caring for people from early childhood on is key to producing the "high-quality human capital" essential for the postindustrial knowledge/service economy, this distinction between "productive" and "reproductive" labor still colors current economic thinking and policies.[35]

Without leaving everything from capitalism and socialism behind, we must discard their domination elements and preserve their partnership elements. Beyond that, we must create a new economic model that recognizes that the most important human work is caring for people and nature. As we move into the postindustrial knowledge-service economy, we urgently need a far more accurate and realistic economic map than we have had to guide us (see Figures 6.2 and 6.3).

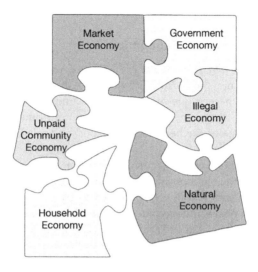

Figure 6.2 Old economic map. Includes market, government, and illegal economies only. From Riane Eisler, *The Real Wealth of Nations: Creating a Caring Economics.*

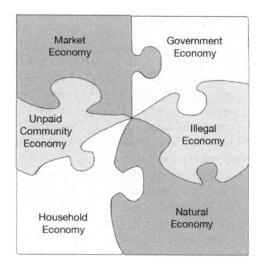

Figure 6.3 New economic map. Also includes unpaid community, household, and natural economies. From Riane Eisler, *The Real Wealth of Nations: Creating a Caring Economics.*

The Real Wealth of Nations: Creating a Caring Economics proposes an economic map that includes all six of the sectors that actually compose economic systems:

- The household economy
- The unpaid community economy
- The market economy
- The illegal economy
- The government economy
- The natural economy[36]

This *full-spectrum* economic map provides the basis for a new economic paradigm that accords visibility and value in its metrics, policies, and practices to the essential work of caring for people and Earth.[37] The new theoretical framework for economics that this map will help us develop won't come together all at once, but as the demand for more caring structures and rules grows worldwide, we can gradually revise economics to support positive changes in policies and practices.

An important early step is demonstrating that caregiving work in both the market and household is essential to producing the "high-quality human capital" needed for economic success in the knowledge-service age. This case-making is also essential for cutting through the disproportionate poverty of women whose work is poorly paid in the market and unpaid at home worldwide. Even in the rich United States, women over the age of 65 are, according to US Census statistics, almost twice as likely to be poor as men over 65,[38] largely because most of these women are or were caregivers.

To change these dismal realities, pilot testing of effective steps toward solutions is vital. The Center for Partnership Studies' Caring Economy Campaign (CEC) substantiates the return from investing in care-taking through such policies as paid parental leave, support for high-quality childcare, caregiver tax credits, and Social Security for caregivers.[39] This program's *Social Wealth Economic Indicators* (SWEIs) document the economic benefits of investing in care, and the consequences of devaluing it, especially for marginalized populations in the United States.[40] The center's CEC addresses systemic issues, such as the need for rethinking what productive work is as automation and other technological breakthroughs rapidly take over jobs. The CEC's online training for change-agents worldwide prepares participants to advocate effectively for government and business policies that help people move out of poverty and away from the stress of trying to balance family and employment.

The Fourth Cornerstone: Narratives/Language

Since we humans live by stories, cultural transformation requires more accurate stories than we have now about our personal, social, and economic possibilities. Religious stories about "original sin" and secular stories about "evolutionary imperatives" claim that humans are innately selfish and violent—and must be rigidly controlled. Yet, neuroscience is demonstrating that humans are "wired" more for empathy and caring than for cruelty and violence.[41] We are also learning about human nature's great flexibility and our environment's (and, by extension, culture's) impacts on which genetic capacities we express or inhibit.[42]

Spreading new narratives, including new theories about our past, present, and the possibilities for our future, requires educators, artists, writers, and scholars to work together. One such effort is the *Interdisciplinary Journal of Partnership Studies*, an online, peer-reviewed open-access journal for sharing scholarship and creating connections "for cultural transformation to build a world in which all relationships, institutions, policies and organizations are based on principles of partnership."[43] In addition, we must recognize findings from linguistic psychologists that the categories provided by our language channel our thinking, and adopt the new language of partnership systems, domination systems, hierarchies of domination, hierarchies of actualization, and other terms that show that we can move to a more just and caring society.

Partnership-oriented stories about spirituality and morality are also essential. We must show that spirituality can be a path to creating a better world right here on Earth, instead of just an escape from "this vale of tears" to otherworldly realms.

Conclusion

We cannot move forward unless we identify our alternatives. The struggle for our future is not between East and West, North and South, religious and secular, rightist and leftist, capitalist or socialist, or more and less technologically developed societies. It is a struggle *within* all these kinds of societies between those embracing a partnership-oriented system and those pushing us back to rigid rankings of domination.

We have been taught that our only options are dominating or being dominated. Influential religious leaders such as St. Augustine preached that God assigned us a fixed place in society and that wishing to change this is like a finger wanting to be an eye.[44] And the idea of a fixed social order of inferiors and superiors dies hard.

If we can leave the domination model behind and stop marginalizing women and children to bring about whole systems change, our world still won't be perfect. But it will be much more equitable, peaceful, and sustainable—and might look something like this:

> Neuroscience's findings on the importance of good care for human development have made sound education for childcare, primary school teaching, and other caring professions a top social priority. These jobs are highly respected and well paid, parenting education is prioritized, and schools teach boys and girls how to care for self, others, and nature.
>
> As automation, robotics, and artificial intelligence replace more and more jobs, new economic inventions gradually replace our unsustainable overconsumption-driven economic systems. As we move toward a caring economy, childcare in families is supported by the whole society through caregiver tax credits and stipends, paid parental leave, and Social Security credit for the first seven years of childcare—whether the caregiver is female or male. These supports are funded by savings from investing in care and from taxes on harmful activities and products.
>
> Instead of being used for destruction and domination, new technological breakthroughs and older technologies are employed to better sustain and enhance life. As material, emotional, and spiritual needs are increasingly met, crime, terrorism, and warfare decrease. As women gain reproductive freedom, education, and equal rights, population growth slows. Without "masculine" social priorities such as domination and conquest, nations are more peaceful and the danger of nuclear or biological annihilation gradually diminishes.
>
> Caring for nature is a basic economic and social principle. Policy makers also recognize that investing in people, starting early on, is key to a just and prosperous economic system.
>
> As the value of caregiving is recognized and supported by policy, the roles of women and men are fundamentally rebalanced. Men and women share paid positions, household tasks, childcare, and other roles.
>
> Companies understand that caring for children, the elderly, and the sick is productive work and caring practices are rewarded with tax breaks and other benefits. Workplaces provide flexible-time, job-sharing, and other partnership inventions.
>
> Poverty and hunger ebb because women are rewarded for caregiving. Care for the elderly is facilitated by adequate monetary pensions, including those for caregivers.
>
> Respect for human rights is modeled and taught as fundamental in all relations—from intimate to international. Since difference is not equated with dominating or being dominated, racism, anti-Semitism, and other ugly old isms gradually fade away.

Creativity flourishes in music, literature, and the arts, providing a more hopeful and realistic picture of what being human can mean. New social and economic inventions greatly humanize business, policy, and day-to-day life.

Gaps between haves and have-nots shrink as people are no longer driven to amass enormous wealth as substitutes for caring connection, creativity, and meaning. And spirituality is no longer so focused on an afterlife, but instead on building a world where the wonder and beauty latent in every child can be realized right here on Earth.

As caring is valued more, women receive greater respect. Women comprise half of the national legislatures, and many head governments. There is real representative democracy.

The good news is that, despite fierce resistance, the partnership movement has been gaining momentum. Yet, even this forward movement is still largely guided by old beliefs and theories lingering on from times that oriented more closely to the domination side of the continuum. That is why the need for a new conceptual framework that makes visible the interactive, mutually supporting, elements of partnership systems is so urgent. Also urgent is concerted action to build foundations for whole systems change.

Clearly, we must continue, and intensify, our work toward positive environmental, economic, and social change. But we will greatly advance this work by together building the missing four cornerstones focused on childhood, gender, economics, and narratives/language.

My colleagues and I invite you to join us in our efforts to this end. The Center for Partnership Studies' webinars and online courses are good "on-ramps" for getting started and becoming part of the movement.[45] We also invite you to join with us in further developing our Social Wealth Economic Indicators into an international index, as well as adapting them for state and local use.[46]

Moving to a world that orients primarily to the partnership rather than domination model is a long-term enterprise. Time, perseverance, and the courage to challenge established beliefs and structures will be needed. But if we are to build a future where all children can realize their capacities for consciousness, caring, and creativity—the capacities that make us fully human—we have to start constructing its foundations now.

Notes

1 Riane Eisler, *The Chalice and the Blade: Our History, Our Future* (San Francisco, CA: Harper & Row, 1987); Riane Eisler and Douglas Fry, *Nurturing Our Humanity: How Domination and Partnership Shape Our Brains, Lives, and Future* (New York: Oxford University Press, 2019).
2 Frederick Emery and Eric Trist, *Toward a Social Ecology: Contextual Appreciation of the Future and the Present* (New York: Plenum Press, 1973); Humbert

Maturana and Francisco Varela, *Autopoeisis and Cognition: The Realization of the Living* (Boston, MA: Reidel, 1980); Ilya Prigogine and Isabelle Stengers, *Order Out of Chaos* (New York: Bantam, 1984).

3 Eisler and Fry, *Nurturing Our Humanity*; Eisler, *The Chalice and the Blade*; Riane Eisler, *Sacred Pleasure: Sex, Myth, and the Politics of the Body* (San Francisco, CA: Harper Collins, 1995); Riane Eisler, *Tomorrow's Children: A Blueprint for Partnership Education in the 21st Century* (Boulder, CO: Westview Press, 2000); Riane Eisler, *The Power of Partnership: Seven Relationships That Will Change Your Life* (Novato, CA: New World Library, 2002); Riane Eisler, *The Real Wealth of Nations: Creating a Caring Economics* (San Francisco, CA: Berrett-Koehler, 2007); Riane Eisler, "Economics as if Caring Matters," *Challenge* 55, 2 (2012): 58–86; Riane Eisler, "Protecting the Majority of Humanity: Toward an Integrated Approach to Crimes Against Present and Future Generations," in *Sustainable Development, International Criminal Justice, and Treaty Implementation*, edited by Sebastien Jodoin (Cambridge: Cambridge University Press, 2013); Riane Eisler and Daniel Levine, "Nurture, Nature, and Caring: We Are Not Prisoners of Our Genes," *Brain and Mind* 3, 1 (April 2002): 9–52.

4 Eisler and Fry, *Nurturing Our Humanity*; Deborah Niehoff, *The Biology of Violence: How Understanding the Brain, Behavior, and the Environment Can Break the Vicious Cycle of Aggression* (New York: Free Press, 1999); Bruce Perry, "Childhood Experience and the Expression of Genetic Potential," *Brain and Mind* 3, 1 (April 2002): 79–100; Rena L. Repetti, Shelley E. Taylor, and Teresa E. Seeman, "Risky Families: Family Social Environments and the Mental and Physical Health of Offspring," *Psychological Bulletin* 128, 2 (2002): 330–366.

5 Eisler and Fry, *Nurturing Our Humanity*; Eisler, *The Chalice and the Blade*; Eisler, *Sacred Pleasure*; Eisler, *The Power of Partnership*; Eisler, *The Real Wealth of Nations*; Riane Eisler and Teddie Potter, *Transforming Interprofessional Partnerships: A New Framework for Nursing and Partnership-Based Health Care* (Indianapolis, IN: Theta Tau International, 2014).

6 Stuart Schlegel, *Wisdom from a Rainforest* (Athens: University of Georgia Press, 1998).

7 Peggy Sanday, *Women at the Center* (Ithaca, NY: Cornell University Press, 2002).

8 Sanday, *Women at the Center*, 22–24.

9 Drude Dahlerup, "Women in Nordic Politics—A Continuing Success Story?" The Danish Center for Research and Information on Gender, Equality and Diversity. Retrieved from: http://kvinfo.org/history/women-nordic-politics-continuing-success-story.

10 Eisler, *The Real Wealth of Nations*.

11 Eisler, *The Real Wealth of Nations*.

12 Eisler, *The Chalice and the Blade*; Eisler and Fry, *Nurturing Our Humanity*.

13 Prigogine and Stengers, *Order out of Chaos*.

14 Eisler, *The Chalice and the Blade*; Jiayin Min, *The Chalice and the Blade in Chinese Culture* (Beijing: China Social Sciences Publishing House, 1995).

15 Douglas Fry, editor, *War, Peace, and Human Nature: The Convergence of Evolutionary and Cultural Views* (New York: Oxford University Press, 2013).

16 Nicolas Platon, *Crete* (Geneva: Nagel Publishers, 1966); James Mellaart, *Çatal Hüyük* (New York: McGraw Hill, 1967); Marija Gimbutas, *The Goddesses and Gods of Old Europe* (Berkeley: University of California Press, 1992); Nanno Marinatos, *Minoan Religion: Ritual, Image, and Symbol* (Columbia: University of South Carolina Press, 1993); Ian Hodder, "Women and Men at Catalhoyuk," *Scientific American*, 290 (January 2004): 77–83.

17 Mellaart, *Çatal Hüyük*; Gimbutas, *The Goddesses and Gods of Old Europe*; J.P. Mallory, *In Search of the Indo-Europeans: Language, Archaeology and Myth* (London: Thames and Hudson, 1989); Gerda Lerner, *The Creation of Patriarchy* (New York: Oxford University Press, 1989); Samuel Kramer and John Maier, *Myths of Enki, The Crafty God* (New York: Oxford University Press, 1989); James DeMeo, "The Origins and Diffusion of Patrism in Saharasia, c.4000 B.C.E.: Evidence for a Worldwide, Climate-Linked Geographical Pattern in Human Behavior," *World Futures* 30, 4 (1991): 247–271.

18 Eisler, *The Real Wealth of Nations*.

19 Eisler, *The Real Wealth of Nations*; Eisler and Fry, *Nurturing Our Humanity*; Riane Eisler, David Loye, and Kari Norgaard, *Women, Men, and the Global Quality of Life* (Pacific Grove: Center for Partnership Studies, 1995).

20 Eisler and Fry, *Nurturing Our Humanity*; Eisler, *The Real Wealth of Nations*; Eisler, *Sacred Pleasure*; Eisler, *Protecting the Majority of Humanity*.

21 Elizabeth Thompson Gershoff, "Corporal Punishment by Parents and Associated Child Behaviors and Experiences: A Meta-analytic and Theoretical Review," *Psychological Bulletin* 128, 4 (2002): 539.

22 Eisler and Fry, *Nurturing Our Humanity*; Niehoff, *The Biology of Violence*; Perry, "Childhood Experience and the Expression of Genetic Potential."

23 Eisler and Fry, *Nurturing Our Humanity*; Michael Milburn and Sheree Conrad, *The Politics of Denial* (Cambridge, MA: MIT Press, 1996).

24 Eisler, *Protecting the Majority of Humanity*.

25 Licia Rando, *Caring and Connected Parenting: A Guide to Raising Connected Children* (Pacific Grove: Center for Partnership Studies, 2010), www.centerforpartnership.org.

26 Eisler, *Protecting the Majority of Humanity*.

27 See Spiritual Alliance to Stop Intimate Violence, www.centerforpartnership.org.

28 Eisler, Loye, and Norgaard, *Women, Men, and the Global Quality of Life*.

29 See "Global Gender Gap Report," http://reports.weforum.org/global-gender-gap-report-2015/report-highlights/.

30 Eisler, *The Real Wealth of Nations*.

31 Patrick Frierson, "Adam Smith and the Possibility of Sympathy with Nature," *Pacific Philosophical Quarterly* 87, 4 (2006): 442–480.

32 Paul Burkett, *Marxism and Ecological Economics* (Chicago: Haymarket Books, 2009).

33 Ted Benton, "Marxism and Natural Limits," *New Left Review* 178 (November/December 1989): 51–86; Karl Polanyi, *The Great Transformation* (New York: Farrar & Rinehart, 1944).

34 Diane Elson, *Male Bias in the Development Process* (Manchester: Manchester, 1991); Naila Kabeer, *Gender Mainstreaming in Poverty Eradication and the Millennium Development Goals* (Pall Mall, London: The Commonwealth Secretariat, 2003); Eisler, *The Real Wealth of Nations*; Eisler, "Economics as if Caring Matters."

35 Eisler, "Economics as if Caring Matters."

36 Eisler, *The Real Wealth of Nations*.

37 Eisler, *The Real Wealth of Nations*.

38 12.1 percent of women and 7.4 percent of men over age 65 lived in poverty in 2014 (https://www.census.gov/hhes/www/poverty/data/incpovhlth/2014/figure6.pdf).

39 See the Center for Partnership Studies, "Caring Economy Campaign," http://caringeconomy.org/.

40 See the Center for Partnership Studies, "Social Wealth Economic Indicators," http://caringeconomy.org/newindicators/.

41 Eisler and Fry, *Nurturing Our Humanity*; Frans De Waal, *The Age of Empathy: Nature's Lessons for a Kinder Society* (New York: Random House, 2009); Fry, *War, Peace, and Human Nature*.

42 Eisler and Fry, *Nurturing Our Humanity*; Perry, "Childhood Experience and the Expression of Genetic Potential"; James Leckman, Catherine Panter-Brick, and Rima Salah, editors, *Pathways to Peace: The Transformative Power of Children and Families* (Cambridge, MA: MIT Press, 2014).

43 See the *Interdisciplinary Journal of Partnership Studies*, http://pubs.lib.umn.edu/ijps/.

44 Roy Baumeister, "How the Self Became a Problem: A Psychological Review of Historical Research," *Journal of Personality and Social Psychology* 52, I (1987): 169.

45 See www.centerforpartnership.org.

46 See Social Wealth Economic Indicators at www.centerforpartnership.org.

Chapter 7

A Living Economy for a Living Earth

David C. Korten

As an MBA student decades ago, I was taught to look at the big picture. Treat the visible downstream problem—a defective product or an under-performing employee—as the symptom of an upstream system failure. If the cause of the system failure is not resolved, the problem will recur.

We humans must now apply that lesson, on a much larger scale, to the greatest challenge we have faced since our earliest ancestors walked the plains of Africa. As a now-global species, we have embraced money as our defining goal and created a system of culture, institutions, technology, and infrastructure that is driving us to self-extinction. We must transform that system or bear the ultimate consequence of failed collective choices thousands of years in the making.

There is no magic-bullet solution and marginal adjustments will not suffice. A viable human future depends on a complete system remake, rethinking and reinventing from the bottom up the culture, institutions, technology, and infrastructure of our failed system.

It all turns on our reawakening to a simple truth that our ancestors understood and we seem to have forgotten: we are living beings born of and nurtured by a living Earth. We must navigate a rapid transition to a living economy for a living Earth.

Core Goals

The goal is a "living" economy designed and managed to serve three core goals:

- **Ecosystem Health and Balance**: Valuing life above all else, it must restore and enhance the generative capacity of Earth's biosphere as we learn to live within Earth's limits.
- **Shared Prosperity**: It must support resource sharing to secure material sufficiency and spiritual abundance for all people.
- **Living Democracy**: It must give each and every person an active voice in the decisions that affect their life, and support the just and nonviolent resolution of conflict through inclusive and transparent processes.

The system failure of the sharply contrasting "suicide" economy now in place rests on three fatal errors:

- **It counts ecosystem destruction for financial gain as wealth creation.** Devoted to what Pope Francis calls the "idolatry of money," it values life only for its market price and creates "wealth" by depleting Earth's capacity to support life to grow the financial assets of the already wealthy.
- **It drives a growing global class division between the profligate and the desperate.** It encourages and celebrates excessive and wasteful consumption by the few while reducing the many to increasing desperation and excluding them from life's essentials—including clean air, drinking water, fertile soils, and a place to live.
- **It limits meaningful participation in rule-making to the winners in a rigged game.** A corporate dominated, money-driven political system concentrates rule-making power in the hands of those who profit from environmental destruction and economic exclusion, thus reinforcing political choices that assure ultimate system collapse.

The terminally destructive outcomes of the suicide economy—also known as capitalism—are not acts of nature. They result from human cultural, institutional, technological, and infrastructure choices. We can make different choices. The essential choices, however, are collective—not individual—and require collective corrective action based on authentic understanding of our human needs and nature.

Two System Design Errors

The suicide economy's system design has two fatal flaws. First, it values life only for its market price. Second, it prioritizes corporate profits over community well-being.

It Values Life Only for Its Market Price

The reality of humanity's existential bias for money—and its devastating consequences for life—came to me in November 1992 at a mountain retreat in the Philippines with leaders of six major Asian nongovernmental organizations. We found common agreement that the "Asian development miracle" much touted by the World Bank and free market economists was more illusion than reality.

Surface appearances of prosperity masked a deeper reality of impoverishment and spreading disruption of the region's social and ecological foundations. Economic development was monetizing relationships once based on a sense of mutual caring and obligation between people and between people and the land. One evening after dinner an image came to my mind of development as a pool of money, spreading out across the Asian countryside like an alien being, consuming whatever life it touched to grow itself.

Yet, money is just a number created by humans. It has no substance, intrinsic value, or will. Indeed, it is not even recognizable by anything outside the human mind. Yet, the consequences are evident and real. Ultimately, I realized that the only possible source of the motive drive in this evil scenario is our misdirected human will. As Pogo says, "We have met the enemy and he is us."

This misdirection is the consequence of an illusion that money is wealth and the measure of our individual and societal worth. What we call economic development is largely a process of monetizing relationships, thus alienating us from the bonds of caring for one another and the living lands and waters that are the ultimate means of our living.

The more dependent we become on money to obtain food, water, shelter, energy, and other basics we once provided for ourselves in mostly cooperative nonmonetary engagement with one another and nature, the more we embrace money as our defining value. And the more subservient we become to the corporations on which we depend for the money they provide us as wages and loans and then demand in payment for access to these essentials—while taking their cut on every transaction.

In rich countries, we submit to the same process when we hire out the care of our children and elderly to corporations, while working at corporate jobs to earn the money to pay the fees. GDP grows in tandem with our corporate servitude.

Our salvation from this travesty lies in recognition that life is sacred. Money is just a number, sometimes useful as an accounting chit to facilitate exchange. Once we recognize this distinction, we can more readily see the opportunities for redirecting our life energy from serving the suicide economy to serving life through the systems of a living Earth economy.

It Prioritizes Corporate Profits over Community Well-Being

Many years ago, I asked Sixto Roxas, a distinguished Filipino economist and former international bank executive, why economists so often promote policies that have such disastrous consequences for people and nature. He answered without hesitation:

> That's easy. They choose the firm rather than the household as their basic unit of analysis. The word economics comes from the ancient Greek word *okionomia*, meaning "household management." The classical economists viewed the economy through that lens. When the founders of contemporary economics sought to raise economics to the stature of a science by basing it on a mathematical model, they chose

the firm because its transactions are monetized and therefore already quantified. Economists have since viewed the economy through the lens of the [profit-seeking] firm rather than that of the [life-seeking] household.

He noted there was a time when the household and the firm were one and the same and connected to place. A household commonly accommodated an extended family and was an economic entity that produced and consumed most essentials and engaged in regular exchange with neighbors grounded in recognition that the well-being of each depended on the well-being of all.

He further noted that contiguous households had a common interest in their neighboring forest as a source of beauty, food, firewood, building materials, shade, fresh water, soil stability, air purification, filtration of dust, and employment from tourism and sustained-yield forest management.

The "advance" of economic development has changed all that in so many ways in countries both rich and poor.

Now the household and the firm are competing itinerate entities that lack long-term ties and commitment to the natural health and beauty of any place. The household wants well compensated jobs for all its members who seek employment. The firm wants to hire as few workers as possible at the lowest possible cost. The international timber corporation views the forest simply as a commodity to harvest and sell for profit on its way to the next forest. The fewer the workers hired, the less their pay, and the shorter their employment tenure, the greater the firm's profit.

Now growing numbers of households in "advanced" countries have only a single occupant or a single parent with child and have become simply a place to eat an occasional meal, have a bed for the night, and store personal belongings. Contact with neighbors is rare and often contentious. Money mediates most exchanges on terms set by transnational corporations. Masses of people struggle alone for daily survival devoid of joy or meaning.

We acquiesce because the system offers us ever fewer options and corporations consolidate their political power to block humanizing reforms. Many corporations have become so big and complex that they now operate largely beyond human accountability, even to their CEOs.

Fortunately, we have the means to liberate ourselves from servitude to this deadly system of our own making.

Learning to Live as a Global Earth Community

The earliest humans recognized a foundational truth that science now affirms and documents in increasing detail. Life exists only in communities of living organisms that self-organize to create and maintain the conditions of their own existence. We have only begun to understand how it works and the implications.

Reconnecting with Nature

The roots of our current human disconnect from nature trace back 10,000 years to the initial human transition from organizing as small roaming bands of hunter-gatherers to organizing as settled agricultural societies. Hunter-gatherers migrated with the herds and seasons. They understood and respected nature's seasonal flows and cycles. They depended on human and animal muscle, sunlight, and firewood (stored sunlight) for energy. And they traveled light.

With settled agriculture came the nascent belief that humans stand above and apart from other species. With the coming of the modern coal-fueled steam engine in 1765 came the Industrial Revolution. Earlier civilizations destroyed their living Earth foundations only in the places they dominated. Initially, the damage was sufficiently limited and isolated that Earth generally recovered.

The Industrial Revolution, however, cut the capitalist genie loose. To feed its appetite for energy, materials, and chemicals, human societies ever more aggressively mined the carbons and toxins that nature had sequestered deep underground over billions of years to create conditions on Earth's surface suited to more complex and intelligent organisms. Enthralled by our seeming power over nature and unmindful of the consequences for our health and well-being, we released these carbons and toxins back into Earth's atmosphere and soils in our mindless pursuit of power and money.

Soon, we were engaged in the unrestrained disruption and depletion of Earth's species, soils, waters, coral reefs, herds, fisheries, and forests in the global suicide economy's quest for unprecedented growth—material excess, military domination, and human population growth.

Economists, who ignore capitalism's social and environmental costs, assure us that we are getting richer because GDP is growing. Where does that leave us now? The Global Footprint Network estimates that it would take 1.7 Earth planets to sustain current levels of human consumption. And this takes no account of the daily struggles and unmet needs of the billions of people who after decades of "economic development" continue to struggle for a bare subsistence living. The more intense the competition for what remains of Earth's bounty, the faster we deplete Earth's capacity to support life in any form and the more people we thrust into lives of desperation.

Reconnecting with One Another

Early human societies assigned people distinctive roles by age and gender, but social stratification was inherently limited since everyone shared both the work and the harvest. Significant class divisions became possible only once settled agricultural societies began to produce a consequential surplus, thus sowing the seeds of monarchy that began to take root around 3000 BC in the Tigris-Euphrates and Nile River valleys, as aspiring tyrants learned to expropriate and exploit the surplus for their personal ends. Domination by race, religion, gender, and class became the human norm.

Thousands of years later, populist demands for democracy eventually drove the kings and emperors from their thrones. With time, we came to believe that democracy had triumphed over monarchy and assumed that was the end of the story. It wasn't. Deeper forces were at work.[1]

In 1600, the British crown issued the first modern corporate charter to the British East India Company to exploit colonial territories for private gain, free from parliamentary oversight. That was an early attempt by the oligarchs to circumvent through the institutions of *corporatocracy* the populist effort to limit the powers of the nobility.

The corporatocracy's methods are more sophisticated and less visible than those of monarchy, but at least as oppressive and even more pervasive. By the late 20th century, transnational corporations possessed rights and powers that placed them beyond accountability to any democratic nation-state while further consolidating power that now allows them to largely dictate the policies of even the world's strongest nation-states.

We did see one hopeful pause in this relentless march. According to a study by the Organisation for Economic Co-operation and Development (OECD), within-country global inequality fell sharply between 1950 and 1980 before returning to historic levels.[2] Those 30 years were a time of strong unions, a progressive political culture, and progressive public policies. The United States led the way in this historical departure. The elitist political forces again rallied, however, and took control of US power and credibility to advance the cause of corporatocracy throughout the world and restore the longer-term norm of inequality.

The 30-year anomaly demonstrated that democracy and technological advance can create a more just and prosperous world for all. But a dangerous delusional fantasy came with it—a belief that GDP growth could go on forever and would one day raise consumption levels everywhere until they equaled or surpassed those of the now increasingly profligate and shrinking US middle class.

Still largely in thrall to that illusion, the world has returned to its historical norm. The ruling class and the top ranks of the retainer class appropriate all of Earth's regenerative surplus—and more—to live in opulent luxury while forcing the rest of humanity into a struggle for survival *and* depleting the regenerative systems on which all Earth life depends. The promise that sustained GDP growth will eventually lift all the world's people to material affluence is pure deception, as ever more people now realize.

The essential transformation of our unjust, destructive, and grotesquely wasteful institutional system depends on bridging the divisions that have long kept the many, who seek peace and justice for all, divided against one another. The communications revolution that has stripped away the barriers of geography creates the potential for humanity to unite in a common awareness that human possibilities are bounded by a finite Earth. With that awareness, we can together create institutions that organize around radically democratic, life-seeking, place-based communities to provide material sufficiency and spiritual abundance for all.

Ours is a historic challenge of epic proportion. Deep transformation is already under way as people everywhere experience the consequence of social and environmental breakdown and mobilize to bring forth the culture and institutions of the next system.

Principal Means

Moving beyond the failed system of the suicide economy requires replacing the four foundational pillars on which it rests:

1   A *"Money Is Sacred" Story*: The corporatocracy's self-serving belief that money is wealth and making money is wealth creation
2   A *"Money Is Sacred" Economics*: A phantom wealth economics that presents an immoral and dysfunctional ideology as settled science
3   A *"Money Is Sacred" Law*: A legal system that gives incorporated pools of financial assets more rights and powers than living people and communities
4   A *"Money Is Sacred" Democracy*: A one-dollar, one-vote democracy that favors monopolistic concentrations of absentee ownership to serve money at the expense of life

The task before us now is replacing the four pillars of the suicide economy with the four pillars of a living Earth economy:

1   A *Life Is Sacred Story*: A sacred life and living Earth story that affirms our true nature as living beings who survive and prosper only as responsible members of a living Earth community.
2   A *Life Is Sacred Economics*: A pragmatic, values-based, real-wealth economics discipline that recognizes that life is the foundation of all real wealth, serving life is an economy's only legitimate purpose, and money is a tool, not a purpose.
3   A *Life Is Sacred Law*: A system of natural rights law based on recognition that without nature, there are no people; without people, there are no corporations; and the only legitimate reason for a corporation to exist is to serve the living community that chartered it.
4   A *Life Is Sacred Democracy*: A one-person, one-vote political democracy secured by an economic democracy grounded in the Jeffersonian ideal that each person should hold an ownership stake in the means of producing his or her living.

Each of these pillars represents a high-leverage point of intervention to advance the essential system transition from a suicide to a living economy.

A Life Is Sacred Story

We humans live by shared stories that embody the common values and understandings needed to organize as coherent groups, communities, and societies. Our most important stories express our deepest beliefs about our human nature, origin, purpose, and the truly sacred. If we get our story right, we can get our future right. As theologian Thomas Berry observed in *Dream of the Earth*, "The deepest crises experienced by any society are those moments of change when the story becomes inadequate for meeting the survival demands of a present situation."[3]

We live at a time between stories. We are in deep trouble because we organize as a global society around a sacred money-and-markets story fabricated and propagated by corporate-funded advertising, education, and public relations designed to create and maintain an individualistic money-worshiping consumer culture. So long as we continue to organize around this story, we will get the same self-destructive result.

System change necessarily begins with a new story. Fortunately, the failed sacred money-and-markets story is fast losing credibility, and a sacred life and living Earth story is emerging. The new story, with its ancient roots, affirms our true nature as living beings who survive and thrive only as contributing, cooperative members of a living Earth community. It reminds us that time is life, real wealth is living wealth, and the economy's only legitimate purpose is to serve living communities.

This is an authentic story that the institutions of empire have historically sought to suppress. It lives in the human heart, and for most people needs only to be affirmed. (For more on the living Earth story, including its implications for science, education, media, and religion, see *Change the Story, Change the Future: A Living Economy for a Living Earth*.[4])

A Life Is Sacred Economics

Economics is the branch of knowledge concerned with managing the household to best fulfill the needs of its members. The often-cited founders of modern economics, such as Adam Smith, David Ricardo, Henry George, Thomas Malthus, and Karl Marx, sought to understand how societies organize and manage their labor and natural endowments to best meet the needs of their people.

As documented by science historian Robert Nadeau in *Rebirth of the Sacred*, a group of economists in the mid-1800s turned away from this grand intellectual tradition.[5] Consumed by a bad case of physics envy, these economists appropriated a mathematical model from physics, substituted economic variables for the physical variables, declared economics a values-free science, and dismissed other streams of economic thought as unscientific heresy.

Inappropriately applying a mathematical model with no evident relationship to economic reality and no way to incorporate such intangibles as political power and the health of social and environmental systems, contemporary mainstream (neoliberal/phantom wealth) economists promote policies that increase economic inequality, destroy nature, and undermine democracy. Failing to distinguish between the phantom-wealth money and the real wealth that money can buy, most economists call financial assets "capital" and treat it as the foundational asset essential to human well-being and progress and the ultimate economic constraint. All other assets, by their reckoning, are substitutable and therefore expendable.

Escaping their notice is what economists themselves call a fallacy of composition—inappropriately assuming that what is true for the individual is also true for society. For the individual, a lack of money is generally the primary constraint on consumption and investment. Yet, any nation with its own currency and a central bank can create money in any quantity it chooses with a few computer keystrokes.

For a nation, money never need be in short supply and therefore should never be a nation's defining constraint. The actual constraints are human capital (workers' health and skill), social capital (the bonds of trust and caring essential to healthy communities), and biosystem capital (the living systems comprising Earth's capacity to support life). The suicide economy systematically depletes all three to create money. Thus, it transforms real capital into phantom financial capital. The rich get richer, and we all slip toward self-extinction.

The real drivers of suicidal economic policies, however, are not the phantom wealth economists who promote an elitist ideology as science. Credentialed economists merely provide intellectual cover for corporatist oligarchs to advance their economic self-interest, assuring the public that maximizing corporate profits will maximize GDP growth and that maximizing GDP growth will maximize benefits to all.

In their promotion of this misdirection, most economists deny or ignore ten essential, observable real-world truths:

- The economy's only valid purpose is to serve life.
- Money is a useful means as a token of exchange, not the economy's purpose.
- All real wealth begins with the generative systems of a living Earth.
- Equality is an essential foundation for healthy human communities and for healthy co-productive relationships with the rest of nature.
- The first test of an economy's performance is how well it maintains and enhances the health of biosystem capital.

- The household that seeks to secure its members' well-being is a more ethical and practical basic unit of economic organization than the corporation.
- Community-based living economies are most secure, stable, productive, and innovative when they organize to meet their own needs with their own resources while freely sharing ideas and technology and trading their natural surplus in balanced exchange with their neighbors.
- Living communities are strongest and healthiest when monetary exchange takes place within a strong framework of relationships based on mutual trust, caring, and sharing.
- Real investment is long term and produces real value for society; speculation is short term and contributes nothing of value to society. Support the former and bar the latter.
- A human-scale business owned by local stakeholders, who know and care about the community they serve, is more likely to serve that community's interests than a transnational corporation that claims its only obligation is to grow the financial assets of absentee owners trading shares at light speed in global financial markets.

Embracing these ground truths, real-wealth economists favor:

- The evaluation of economic performance based on indicators of the health and sustained generative capacity of individuals, communities, and living Earth
- Strict limits on the concentration of economic power
- Restoration of the household as a social unit and of relationships based on mutual caring, trust, and responsibility
- Local decision-making
- Self-reliant use of local resources to meet local needs
- Stable, long-term local ownership
- Secure employment for all job seekers doing beneficial work
- An equitable distribution of income consistent with individual contributions to the community's health and well-being
- Worker ownership of enterprises so workers and owners are not separate classes with opposing interests competing for the returns to enterprise
- Tax policies that support an equitable distribution of wealth consistent with fair rewards for labor and investment contributions and that penalize speculation and other forms of predatory investment

There is little evidence that the economics discipline can or will transform itself from within. The pay and status of its practitioners are at risk if its deceptions are exposed. There are, however, hopeful signs that change may be forthcoming. George Soros has funded the solutions-seeking Institute for New Economic Thinking.[6] The International Student Initiative for Pluralism in Economics, an alliance of 82 associations of economics students from 31 countries, is demanding that university economics courses offer more diverse perspectives.[7] Economics for the Anthropocene (E4A), an intellectual partnership organized by McGill University, the University of Vermont, and York University,[8] aims to improve how the social sciences and humanities connect to scientific realities about human–Earth relationships.

In parallel, an applied real-wealth economics is being created through practice by the many millions of people who are taking practical steps to bring a real-wealth economy into being. While creating a new living Earth economy from the bottom up, they are also building an applied real-wealth living Earth economics and growing an emerging crop of self-educated living-Earth economists (who may or may not call themselves economists).

A Life Is Sacred Law

An essential function of a legal system is to provide for the rule-based resolution of disputes over conflicting rights and interests. In our time, few would dare to defend a system of law based on the divine right of kings—the theory that the monarch's authority derives directly from God's will so cannot be subject to earthly dispute or the will of the people. Yet, contemporary legal practice features a roughly equivalent principle, what author and community-wealth expert Marjorie Kelly calls "the divine right of capital"—the presumed right of capital's owners to pursue profit without regard to the consequences for society and living Earth.[9]

This legal doctrine is the product of decisions by a corporatist US Supreme Court, extended and codified by global agreements (misleadingly labeled trade pacts) and promoted by corporate lobbyists hellbent to place corporations ever farther beyond democracy's reach. This perversion of life, law, and justice obstructs the transition to democracy, peace, justice, sustainability, and a living economy.

Yet, there are no people without the rest of nature and there are no corporations without people. Well-organized citizen campaigns are gaining traction to strip away the legal fiction that corporations are entitled to the same rights as natural-born persons. So too, global campaigns to secure legal rights for nature are gathering force. Some current local initiatives in the United States combine the two.

Indigenous peoples and environmental organizations brought the rights of nature frame to the debates of the 2012 United Nation's Rio+20 environmental conference. Wall Street interests argued that the best way to save nature is to price natural resources and sell them to corporations to manage for private financial return.

Leaders from indigenous and environmental communities countered that living Earth is the sacred source of our birth and nurture and her care is a scared obligation of humanity beyond financial calculation. A Rights of Nature provision is now included in Ecuador's constitution.[10] More than 200 US communities have passed ordinances granting rights to nature.[11] Similar initiatives are springing up all around the world.

At its foundation, Western jurisprudence views society atomistically as an aggregation of discrete individuals, each with individual property rights and each entitled to do with his or her individually owned land anything not specifically prohibited by law. In "life is sacred" law, rights will always be coupled with corresponding responsibilities for community well-being.

In all things, balance between individual and community interests must be maintained. Capitalism and communism both fail to achieve an appropriate balance. Capitalism because it recognizes only individual interests. Communism because it recognizes only community interests. Both ignore the reality that the interests of the individual and the community are inseparably linked.

The fallacies of individualism devoid of community responsibility are especially evident in the Western concept of property rights. They ignore the reality that the boundaries of natural ecosystems do not correspond to the artificial legal boundaries of individually owned parcels of land—or of towns, cities, states, and nations. We've barely begun to address the implications.

As the tension grows in Western law between protecting the presumed right of owners to use their parcels as they wish and the realization that we depend on and must care for Earth's living systems, we must rethink and restructure our laws and their administration accordingly.

A Life Is Sacred Democracy

Who will choose the rules and the methods of their enforcement? The consensus favors democracy, which to most of us means each person has an equal voice in the decisions affecting his or her life. That would be a democracy of persons. What we have now is a democracy of money in which few politicians can win elections without the support of corporate money.

The institutions the dominate our daily lives are not the governments ruled by elected politicians. They are transnational corporations in which employees have no rights and are subject to instant and arbitrary dismissal. In theory, these corporations are accountable to their owners. Most titular owners of corporate shares, however, have no idea what corporations they own and they have no part in nor bear any personal liability for corporate actions or their consequences.

When powerful institutions acquire a political voice independent of the voices of real people, democracy becomes a sham. That's why initiatives to get corporations and big money out of politics merit high priority. Promising initiatives would strip away the fiction of corporate personhood, bar corporations from political engagement, eliminate independent political action committees, limit individual political donations, advance public financing of elections, and reinstate equal time rules for media using public airways. All are needed since our current "democracy" is little more than a primitive electoral system appended onto the classic hierarchical institutional structures of imperial rule.

Amid democracy's historic challenge to monarchy, Adam Smith and Thomas Jefferson both advocated a liberal vision of a society of independent small farmers and artisans who secure their voice and their freedom through the ownership of their own land and the tools of their trade. To Smith, small, local, independently owned businesses were the foundation of a healthy market economy; to Jefferson, small, local, independent farmers were the foundation of a healthy democracy. Both abhorred the monopolization of power by either public or private institutions.

As the liberal democratic vision of Smith and Jefferson gained public support, the champions of oligarchy sought to co-opt it through their influence within the institutions of government, education, religion, and media. They embraced the vision of private ownership and markets, but removed the small and the local.

As formerly colonialized nations gained their independence following World War II, and began the embrace of democracy, the corporate oligarchs again mobilized—this time to integrate local and national economies into a seamless global economy, consolidating global corporate monopoly power beyond the reach of democratically elected governments.

Monopolization of access to the means of producing our livelihoods mocks Smith's markets and Jefferson's democracy. It is also contrary to the foundational organizing principles of healthy living systems. There is no equivalent in nature to the concentrated hierarchical power of either the state or the corporation. Living systems have no central decision-maker, no command-and-control structure. Living systems, including superorganisms like the human body with its tens of trillions of cooperatively interconnected cells, self-organize within a frame of community in which decision-making is everywhere local and shaped by countless feedback loops.

In a truly democratic world, the stronger the sense of community and the more democratic the distribution of power, the more varied the mechanisms of spontaneous cooperation and the less the need for coercive regulation and intervention by a central authority to constrain antisocial behavior.

Designing the next system frame for an authentic living Earth democracy requires us to revisit the most basic questions about democracy, property rights, economic justice, and the corporation as an institutional form. It is a challenge as daunting as that faced by those who rebelled against the divine right of kings many generations ago. It is, in fact, the same struggle with the outcome still in question.

★ ★ ★

We are a species of enormous potential gone badly astray. Hope lies in our rapid awakening to our nature and potential as living beings with a profound responsibility as creative, loving, contributing members of the living Earth community that birthed and nurtures us. The misadventures of our species' adolescence now present us with a challenge of epic proportions: to create a new system of culture, institutions, technology, and infrastructure that aligns us with the responsibilities of that membership.

The Living Economy in a Populous World

The denser the population relative to the resource base, the greater the imperative to share essential resources. Population relative to the resource base is now denser than at any time in human history. Yet, as a recent study concluded, globally, the current distribution of wealth is the most unequal. We are also arguably more isolated from one another in single-person homes and cars, with less sharing of space, tools, and care.

Facing the need for redistribution and reconnection, we must understand that this extreme maldistribution is largely the product of monopolistic concentrations of power, financial speculation, fraud, public subsidies and bailouts, exploitation of labor, usury, abuses of eminent domain for private benefit, and privatization of the commons—much of it illegal.

The redistributive path away from these ills requires, among other actions:

- Closed access to offshore tax havens
- Taxes on financial transactions to eliminate high-speed trading
- A 100 percent capital gains tax on profits from investments held less than a month
- A sharply progressive tax on large estates with the proceeds directed to providing every 21-year-old person with a trust fund to invest in home ownership and the productive assets on which his or her living depends
- Full-cost usage fees for access to common property resources

(Continued)

Money and Banking in the Living Economy

The system of well-regulated, locally rooted, and accountable financial institutions in the United States before the 1970s provides a reasonable first approximation of the money creation and management system needed now. In this system, local financial institutions provide the communities they serve with a capacity to mobilize funding in response to local needs and opportunities by aggregating local savings and directing them into productive investments. (See the New Economy Working Group report, *How to Liberate America from Wall Street Rule.*[12])

To create a healthy system of money creation and allocation, the current banking system must be restructured to limit its function to basic banking. This will require rebuilding the money and banking system from the bottom up as a well-regulated community-accountable public utility. Necessary measures include restoring tax and regulatory rules that restrict bank size, limit public guarantees and subsidies to financial institutions engaged exclusively in performing basic banking functions, and render extractive finance illegal or unprofitable.

The normal process by which the banking system leverages reserves to create more credit can enable communities to create financing beyond their own savings, in response to local needs and opportunities. With proper transparency, public oversight, restrictions on bank size, and a preference for cooperative ownership of banking institutions, the same capacity that Wall Street has abused to fuel speculation and consolidate monopolies can become a powerful and beneficial community tool for building vibrant local economies.

A central bank, responsible for money supply management, is essential to any modern economy. The Federal Reserve in the United States, for instance, has the power to create money by the trillions of dollars and to direct those dollars to the beneficiaries of its choosing. Under current rules, it does so with no public accounting or oversight. It considers its primary mandate to be ensuring the solvency and profitability of Wall Street's megabanks—a badly misplaced priority since these banks are managed to maximize their top managers' compensation packages, not to serve the public interest. That said, a transparent and publicly accountable national central bank with substantial political independence is essential to manage the money supply and oversee banking functions.

The following recommendations are adapted from a proposal that William Greider spells out in "Dismantling the Temple."[13]

- Reorganize the Federal Reserve to function as a true independent federal agency, subject to strict standards of transparency, public scrutiny, audit by the General Accounting Office, and Congressional oversight. The board of governors should continue to be appointed by the president and confirmed by Congress, and the Fed should remain responsible for managing the national money supply to maintain full employment and the value of the currency.
- Relieve the Fed of its regulatory function and, instead, create a new regulatory body responsible for regulating commercial banks and the "shadow banking system" of hedge funds, private equity firms, and others.
- Create a Federal Recovery and Reconstruction Bank to which a restructured Federal Reserve would direct newly created money to in turn allocate to Congressionally approved green infrastructure projects under provisions that favor local contractors and suppliers who procure locally and hire local workers.

The money that this proposal directs to building essential infrastructure would flow directly to local communities as local wages and profits. Recipients would use the money to make mortgage payments, put food on the table, pay off credit card debt, meet payroll, and pay taxes. New tax revenues would flow into governments to fund public programs, and new deposits would flow into the banking system at the bottom to fund home ownership and local business.

Creating money to generate employment through infrastructure investment in a bottom-up economy with large-scale un- and under-employment and unutilized productive capacity is not inflationary. If only three to four trillion dollars of the twelve trillion dollars in keystroke US currency created by the Federal Reserve following the 2008 crisis as an economic stimulus had been spent on building an energy-efficient green physical infrastructure, the United States would now have a booming national economy and a start on securing the future of our children.[14]

Notes

1 David C. Korten, *The Great Turning: From Empire to Earth Community* (Oakland, CA: Berrett-Koehler, 2006).
2 "Breaking the Camel's Back," *The Economist*, October 4, 2014, http://www.economist.com/news/finance-and-economics/21621908-what-impressive-work-economic-history-tells-you-about-inequality-breaking.
3 Thomas Berry, *The Dream of the Earth* (San Francisco, CA: Sierra Club Books, 1988), xi.
4 David C. Korten, *Change the Story, Change the Future: A Living Economy for a Living Earth* (Oakland, CA: Berrett Koehler, 2015).
5 Robert L. Nadeau, *Rebirth of the Sacred: Science, Religion, and the New Environmental Ethos* (New York: Oxford University Press, 2013), chapter 7.
6 See *Center for New Economic Thinking*, http://ineteconomics.org/.
7 See *International Student Initiative for Pluralism in Economics*, http://www.isipe.net.
8 See *Economics for the Anthropocene*, http://e4a-net.org/.
9 Marjorie Kelly, *The Divine Right of Capital* (San Francisco, CA: Berret-Koehler Publishers, 2001).
10 See "Rights of Nature Articles in Ecuador's Constitution," *The Rights of Nature*, https://therightsofnature.org/wp-content/uploads/pdfs/Rights-for-Nature-Articles-in-Ecuadors-Constitution.pdf.
11 See Community Environmental Legal Defense Fund, "U.S. Communities," http://celdf.org/join-the-movement/where-we-work/u-s-communities/.
12 David C. Korten, "How to Liberate America from Wall Street Rule," *New Economy Working Group*, July 2011, http://www.yesmagazine.org/pdf/liberateamericadownload.pdf.
13 William Greider, "Dismantling the Temple: How to Fix the Federal Reserve," *The Nation*, July 15, 2009, http://www.thenation.com/article/dismantling-temple/.
14 Korten, "How to Liberate America from Wall Street Rule," 31.

Chapter 8

Earthland
Scenes from a Civilized Future

Paul Raskin

In this dispatch from the future, we visit the flourishing planetary
civilization of 2084 that has emerged out of the great crises and struggles that today still lie before us. The essay is excerpted from Journey
to Earthland: The Great Transition to Planetary Civilization.[1] The
book's initial sections set the essential context for the visionary "destination" presented here as a stand-alone piece. History has entered
the Planetary Phase of Civilization with strands of interdependence
weaving humanity and Earth into the overarching proto-country of
Earthland. In this century, social evolution will play out on a world
stage where perils are many and the outcome deeply uncertain. Can
we reach the kind of civilization envisioned here? Our fictive essayist
reports that it's possible—if we citizens of Earthland make it so. The
author could be your child or grandchild, or you, young Earthlander.

Mandela City, 2084

This brief treatise considers the state of planetary civilization in 2084, sketch-
ing its complex structure, social dynamism, and unfinished promise—and,
yes, celebrating how far we have come. The portrayal may strike some
readers as overly burnished, but this author, a proud veteran of the battle
for the 21st century, makes no apology. Yet he has no illusions: we live in
Earthland—not Shangri-La—where real people confront real problems.
Still, who would deny that the world today stands as living refutation of the
apocalyptic premonitions that once haunted dreams of the future?

One Hundred Years That Shook the World

Our snapshot of 2084 can glimpse only a single frame in the moving
picture of 21st-century history. That history is the subject of an ocean
of literature plumbing the roots and meaning of the Great Transition.
A potted history will suffice here for locating the contemporary world in
the context of the unfolding transition. The "five-stage theory" introduced in the seminal chronicle *One Hundred Years That Shook the World*
offers a useful framework (Figure 8.1).

		General		Commonwealth of
Takeoff	Rolling Crisis	Emergency	Reform Era	Earthland

| 1980 | 2001 | 2023 | 2028 | 2048 | 2084 |

Figure 8.1 Major stages of the Great Transition.

Takeoff of the Planetary Phase (1980–2001)

A unitary social-ecological global system began to crystallize, signaling the onset of a major new epoch. This holistic phenomenon found multiple expressions, among them economic globalization, biospheric disruption, digital connectivity, transnational civil society, and global terrorism. The process accelerated after the collapse of the bipolar Cold War order in 1989, as global capitalism gained hegemony, lubricated by "Washington Consensus" policies of deregulation, free trade, privatization, and retrenchment of government services. In response, massive protests erupted, but they could only slow, not reverse, the juggernaut of corporate-led globalization. In parallel, burgeoning cross-border marketing and entertainment industries spurred consumerism among the affluent, yearning among the have-nots, and thwarted expectations among the young and angry. A dissonant cacophony—dot-com bubbles bursting, towers crashing, dogs of war barking, glaciers collapsing—rang in the new millennium, shattering dreams of market utopia.

Rolling Crisis (2001–2023)

Freewheeling turbo-capitalism segued into an unrelenting drumbeat of war, violence, displacement, pandemic, recession, and environmental disruption. The rat-a-tat of bad news came to be understood as discrete manifestations of an overarching structural crisis. Correspondingly, critiques grew more systemic and radical, and collective resistance gathered momentum. As the crisis surged, the "global citizens movement" (GCM) convened its inaugural Intercontinental Congress in 2021, where it adopted the landmark Declaration of Interdependence that captured the growing consensus on the "character of the historic challenge," "principles of unity," and "visions of Earthland." The GCM's message spread virally through a vast lattice of affiliated nodes, spawning circles of engagement across the planet. The movement became a living socio-political experiment in creating an Earthlandic community. By 2023, movement "circles" were ubiquitous, advancing local strategies linked to the wider shift. The popular rising came too late to reverse the global tailspin, but without it, the future surely would have been far bleaker.

General Emergency (2023–2028)

The multipronged crisis rolled on, gathering into a mighty chain reaction of cascading feedbacks and amplifications. Every cause was an effect, every effect a cause. The poor suffered most acutely, though no one could fully insulate themselves from the cauldron of disruption. This was a tragic period by any measure, yet could have been even worse had the world not mobilized in response. The GCM, its strength surging, played a critical role by prodding befogged and irresolute governments into acting on the comprehensive UN sustainability and climate goals that had languished since 2015. This mobilization quelled the chaos and thwarted the New Earth Order (NEO), an elite alliance preparing to proclaim an emergency World Authority. The world pulled back from the brink, leaving the "NEOs" ample time to ponder their miscalculations during their long years of incarceration.

The Reform Era (2028–2048)

As the upheaval abated, the old order began to reassert itself. But a new generation of leaders, well-schooled in the mistakes of the past, understood the necessity for strong government stewardship, lest history repeat itself. The UN established the New Global Deal, the apotheosis of enlightened international governance, which included a hard-hitting ensemble of policies, institutions, and financing to deliver on the aspirational goals of the old sustainability agenda. At the heart of the NGD was the push for "resilience economies" that would channel and constrain markets to function within more compassionate social norms and well-established environmental limits. Over the vehement objection of its impatient radical wing, the GCM put its considerable political weight behind this defanging of free-market capitalism, deeming "planetary social democracy" a necessary way station on the path of Great Transition. However, by the 2040s, Policy Reform's "alliance of necessity" became untenable: retrogressive forces, stoked by well-funded revanchist campaigns, grew stronger, and the old pathologies of aggressive capitalism, consumerist culture, and xenophobic nationalism recrudesced. Progressives everywhere anxiously asked, is reform enough? The answer resounded across the continents: "Earthland Now!" The GCM was prepared, harnessing discontent into effective strategy, and gaining decisive political influence in a growing roster of countries and international bodies. The movement's internal deliberative body, the Earthland Parliamentary Assembly (EPA), was repurposed as the core body for democratic global governance.

Commonwealth of Earthland (2048–present)

The current stage of the Great Transition began when the EPA adopted by consensus the world constitution of 2048, formally establishing the

Commonwealth of Earthland. Resistance flared among sectoral interests and nativist bases, but masses of ordinary people mobilized to defend the Commonwealth. After a tumultuous decade, the new institutional structures began to stabilize, and the revolutionary turn toward planetary civilization was in full swing.

What Matters

The tangible political and cultural expressions of the Great Transition were rooted in a parallel transition under way in the intangible realm of the human heart. People returned to the most fundamental questions: how shall we live? Who should we be? What matters? The collective grappling for fresh answers provided the moral compass for the journey through the maelstrom of planetary change.

The entire edifice of contemporary civilization rises on a foundation of compelling human values. The prevailing pretransition ethos— consumerism, individualism, and anthropocentrism—has yielded to a different triad: quality of life, human solidarity, and ecocentrism. These values spring from a yearning for wholeness as individuals, as a species, and as a community of life. To be sure, our diverse regions and cultures invest these values with unique shades of meaning and varying weights. But they remain the *sine qua non* nearly everywhere.

The enhancement of the "quality of life," rather than the old obsession with GDP and the mere quantitative expansion of goods and services, has come to be widely understood as the only valid basis for development. This conviction now seems so self-evident that it must be remembered that over the eons the problem of scarcity and survival—what Keynes called the "economic problem"—had dominated existence. Then, the industrial cornucopia opened the way to a post-scarcity civilization, but the dream was long deferred as deeply inscribed class divisions instead brought overconsumption for the privileged and deprivation for the excluded. Now, the synergy of two ethical factors—material sufficiency ("enough is enough") and equitable distribution of wealth ("enough for all")—has enabled ways of living more satisfying than the work-and-buy treadmill for the affluent and desperation for the economically marginal. Today, people are as ambitious as ever, but fulfillment, not wealth, is the primary measure of success and source of well-being.

The second pillar of the contemporary zeitgeist—human solidarity— bolsters the strong connection we feel toward strangers who live in distant places and descendants who will inhabit the distant future. This capacious camaraderie draws on wellsprings of empathy that lie deep in the human psyche, expressed in the Golden Rule that threads through the great religious traditions, and in the secular ideals of democracy, tolerance, respect, equality, and rights. This augmented solidarity is the correlative in consciousness of the interdependence in the external world. The Planetary Phase, in mingling the destinies of all, has stretched esprit de corps across space and time to embrace the whole human family, living and unborn.

Ecocentrism, our third defining value, affirms humanity's place in the web of life, and extends solidarity to our fellow creatures who share the planet's fragile skin. We are mystified and horrified by the feckless indifference of earlier generations to the integrity of nature and its treasury of biodiversity. The lesson was hard won, and much has been lost, but the predatory motive of the past—the domination of nature—has been consigned to the dustbin of history. Now our relationship to the earth is tempered by humility, which comes with understanding our dependence on her resilience and bounty. People today hold deep reverence for the natural world, finding in it endless wonder, sustenance, and enjoyment.

One World

The enlarged sense of place has buoyed an ethos of globalism as strongly felt as nationalism once was, perhaps more so. After all, gazing down from orbital flights and space excursions, we behold an integral planet, not imaginary state boundaries. Social prophets had long envisioned one human family, but the dream of One World had to await its unsentimental partner: mutual self-interest. The Planetary Phase ignited cosmopolitan aspirations, meshing them with the exigency for cooperation in a world of shared risks. The subjective ideal was now anchored in objective conditions.

Thus, it has become axiomatic that the globe is the natural political unit for managing common affairs: sustaining the biosphere and keeping the peace, of course, but also cultivating an organic planetary civilization in its many dimensions. Indeed, Earthland's thriving world culture and demos stand as the apotheoses of the transformation.

The quartet of principles underpinning our global political community has roots in the great struggles of our forebears for rights, peace, development, and environment. The 2048 World Constitution builds on this indispensable heritage, codified in milestone agreements such as the 1948 Universal Declaration of Human Rights, the 1992 Earth Summit's Agenda 21, and the 2000 Earth Charter. Its preamble draws heavily from the GCM's 2021 Declaration of Interdependence, with its call for an Earthland of rights, freedom, and dignity for all within a vibrant and sustainable commonwealth. Ultimately, the keenly felt sense of solidarity with people and the larger living world binds and sustains our planetary society.

Many Places

This resolute commitment to One World is matched by an equal commitment to Many Places. The celebration of both unity and diversity animates our "politics of trust" with its two prongs: the toleration of proximate differences and the cultivation of ultimate solidarity. The Great Transition has demonstrated that the tension between globalism and localism, although very real, need not be antagonistic. Indeed, the two are mutual preconditions for a stable and flourishing political culture. On the one hand, the integrity of One World depends on vibrant regions for cultural innovation, community cohesion, and democratic renewal. On the other, the vitality of Many Places depends on the global political community to secure and enrich our shared civilization and planet.

A century ago, it was common to speak of a unitary project of "modernity" in which all nations would eventually replicate the institutions, norms, and values of advanced industrial societies. The theory (and ideology) that all countries would converge toward the dominant model contained a kernel of truth. Capitalism's expansionary logic sought to incorporate peripheries and transform them in its own image. At least, that is, to the degree it was given free rein. But the crisis of the world system put the final nails in the coffin of such historical determinism. The Commonwealth is confirming on the ground the counterproposition that multiple paths to modernity are available. Today, the paramount ideals of modernity—equality, tolerance, reason, rule of law, and active citizenship—are ubiquitous, but find sundry expression across a variegated social landscape.

Earthland is a tapestry woven of hundreds of distinct places. Many regions took shape around existing national boundaries or metropolitan centers; some traced the perimeters of river basins or other "bioregions"; and a few had been semiautonomous areas within old nation-states. They come in all sizes and varieties from small, homogenous communities, to large, complex territories, themselves laced with semiautonomous subregions.

The consolidation of Earthland's regional map over the past several decades was not without conflict. Social tensions and land disputes were inevitable, some flaring around stubborn boundary controversies inherited from the past, and some engendered by more porous borders, as global citizenship liberalized the right to resettle. Aided by the simple alchemy of time that turns yesterday's strangers into today's neighbors, and assuaged by the Commonwealth's persuasive mediation and financial inducements, our constellation of regions has largely stabilized. Sadly, though, lingering discord in a handful of hotspots remains a painful sore on the body politic, and a protracted challenge for World Court adjudications.

What is the character of Earthland's regions? It is useful to organize the kaleidoscope of places into a manageable taxonomy. A world traveler today is likely to encounter three types of regions: *Agoria, Ecodemia,* and *Arcadia.* These coinages rely on Greek roots to evoke the classical ideal of a political community—active citizens, shared purpose, and just social relations—that inspires all our regions.

In ancient Athens, the agora served as both marketplace and center of political life; thus, commerce and consumption figure prominently in Agoria. The neologism Ecodemia combines the word roots of economy and democracy; thus, economic democracy is a priority in these regions. Arcadia was the bucolic place of Greek myth; thus, the local community and simpler lifestyles are particularly valued here. Of course, specific places deviate from these idealizations in enumerable ways. Still, the three archetypes capture distinctions critical for understanding Earthland's plural geographic structure.

Agoria, with its more conventional lifestyle and institutions, would be most recognizable to a visitor from the past (indeed, some radical critics refer to these regions disparagingly as "Sweden Supreme"). Ecodemia, with its collectivist ethos and socialized political economy, departs most fundamentally from classical capitalism. Arcadia accentuates self-reliant economies, small enterprises, face-to-face democracy, frugality, and reverence for tradition and nature. In fact, all are late 21st-century social inventions unique to our singular time.

Some reactionary social critics argue that our regions are mere perversions of the three great political "isms" of the past: capitalism, socialism, and anarchism. Not surprisingly, this facile provocation has been roundly lambasted in the popular media and excoriated by a small army of scholars. But give the devil his due: the thesis has a degree of validity. After all, Agoria's market emphasis does give it a capitalist tonality, Ecodemia's insistence on the primacy of social ownership echoes classical socialism, and Arcadia's small-is-beautiful enthusiasm channels the essence of the humanistic anarchist tradition.

However, these associations with past ideologies mask as much as they reveal. Agoria's dedication to sustainability, justice, and global solidarity is of a different order than the most outstanding social democracies of the past ("SwedenX10" to Agorian enthusiasts). Ecodemia's commitment to democracy, rights, and the environment bears little resemblance to the autocratic socialist experiments of the 20th century. Arcadia's highly sophisticated societies are enthusiastic participants in world affairs, not the simple, pastoral utopias of the old anarchist dreamers.

The stress on regional difference should be balanced by a reminder of shared features. Compared to nations of a century ago, nearly all regions are socially cohesive and well-governed. All offer citizens a healthy environment, universal education and healthcare, and material security as a basis for the pursuit of fulfilling lives. Almost all are at peace. Most importantly, One World binds the Many Places as a planetary civilization. We are regional denizens with allegiance to place, and also global citizens building a world community.

Governance: The Principle of Constrained Pluralism

Of course, the harmonious ideal of One World, Many Places must inevitably alight in the discordant reality of contentious politics. The Commonwealth's greatest quandary has been to fashion workable arrangements for balancing the contending imperatives of global responsibility and regional autonomy. The early political debate on this question split along old dualities: cosmopolitanism versus communalism, statism versus anarchism, and top down versus bottom up. The solution for overcoming these polarities was remarkably simple, but difficult to see through the old nationalist mystifications.

Earthland's political philosophy rests on the *principle of constrained pluralism*, comprised of three complementary subprinciples: *irreducibility, subsidiarity,* and *heterogeneity*. Irreducibility affirms One World: the adjudication of certain issues necessarily and properly is retained at the global level of governance. Subsidiarity asserts the centrality of Many Places: the scope of irreducible global authority is sharply limited and decision-making is guided to the most local level feasible. Heterogeneity grants regions the right to pursue forms of social evolution consonant with democratically determined values and traditions, constrained only by their obligation to conform to globally mandated responsibilities.

The principles of constrained pluralism are enshrined in the World Constitution, and few find them objectionable. However, philosophical consent can mask ideological devils that lurk in the details. The application of the framework in the political sphere has been a battleground of public contestation (almost always peaceful). The most controversial question—what should be considered irreducibly global?—has provoked a tug-of-war between contending camps advocating for either a more tight-knit world state or a more decentralized federation.

The debate on the proper balance between One World and Many Places has not abated; indeed, it may never find resolution. Nevertheless, a wide consensus has been established on a minimal set of legitimate, universal concerns that cannot be effectively delegated to regions. The irreducible "Spheres of Global Responsibility" are summarized in the chart (Figure 8.2).

Constrained pluralism is the concrete political expression of the old slogan "unity in diversity." The commitment to unity implies that the planetary governance sets "boundary conditions" on regional activity to ensure the congruence of aggregate outcomes and global goals. The commitment to diversity bars central authorities from dictating how these conditions are met, leaving wide scope for regions to adopt diverse approaches compatible with cultural traditions, value preferences, and local resources. In turn, each region contains a hierarchy of subregional entities,

Rights	Civil liberties; political participation; education, health, and material well-being
Biosphere	Shared resources; climate, ecosystems, and biodiversity; refuges and parks
Security	Disarmament; dispute resolution; emergency planning; disaster relief; humanitarian intervention
Economy	Trade and finance; communications and transport; development aid; consumer protection
Culture	Space exploration; heritage preservation; world university system; intellectual property

Figure 8.2 Spheres of global responsibility.

nested like Russian matryoshka dolls from provinces down to hamlets; the principle of constrained pluralism applies at each level. Up and down the line, our political system delegates decision-making to the most local level possible, retaining authority at larger levels where necessary.

In the environmental realm, the Commonwealth's regulation of greenhouse gas emissions illustrates the way the principle of constrained pluralism works in action. Total emissions are capped globally and allocated to regions in proportion to population; regional policies for meeting these obligations may accentuate market mechanisms, regulation, technological innovation, or lifestyle changes. Examples abound in the social realm, as well. For instance, the "right to a decent standard of living for all" provision of the World Constitution is universally applicable, operationalized globally as a set of minimum targets, then implemented regionally through such diverse strategies as ensured employment, welfare programs, and guaranteed minimum income.

All decision-making processes reflect the Commonwealth's core governance principles of democracy, participation, and transparency; any politician tempted to bend the rules can expect to be held accountable by a vigilant public. Outside officialdom, civil society networks assiduously work to educate citizens, influence decision-makers, and monitor business practices and governmental behavior—and, when necessary, organize protests. And of course, the GCM did not vanish after the glory days of 2048. The movement remains a potent force for challenging the status quo and prodding change, to the chagrin of its many detractors, who deem its radical idealism an atavistic nuisance.

The World Assembly sits at the pinnacle of the formal political structure. Its membership includes both regional representatives and at-large members selected by popular vote in world-wide elections. At-large representation gives voice to "One World" politics by stimulating the formation of world parties as a counterweight to regional parochialism. Strong regional representation ensures that the "Many Places" are not forgotten. Together, they constitute an effective safeguard against tyranny from above or below.

Within regions, the forms of democracy vary, including the representational systems typical of Agoria, the workplace nodes prominent in Ecodemia, and direct engagement in Arcadia. Ultimately, Earthland's vitality and legitimacy come from the informed involvement of ordinary people, a goal mightily enabled by advanced communication technology that shrinks psychic space between polities and dissolves language barriers. The physical principle at the foundation of modern cyberspace—quantum entanglement—echoes the political entanglement of the global demos.

Economy

The size of the world economy has quadrupled since the early years of this century, in itself nothing to crow about because, all else equal, greater output correlates with greater environmental damage. What is worth celebrating is that the economic pie became more equally shared as income distributions tightened both between and within regions. Everyone has the right to a basic standard of living, and absolute destitution has been nearly eradicated, with the very few exceptions found in vanishing pockets of dysfunction.

The material well-being of the typical world citizen today is far higher than it was at the turn of the century, when Earthland was a failed proto-state inhabited by an obscenely wealthy few and impoverished billions. True, in certain places, like the North American region, average income is somewhat lower than it once was. However, the comparison is misleading in two important ways. First, in those days, average income was elevated by the bygone class of super-rich. Second, old GDPs were bloated by market transactions ("exchange value") that did not contribute to human well-being ("use value"), such as expenditures on the military, environmental cleanup, and personal security. Correcting for these factors, the real income of a typical family has actually increased slightly.

The size of the market (GDP) was always a poor proxy for a society's well-being, although that disconnect hardly deterred pre-Commonwealth politicians from making growth the be-all and end-all of public policy. Now, although the economic standard of living still matters, so do environmental quality, community cohesion, democratic participation, and human rights, health, and happiness. Holistic measures confirm quantitatively what everyday life tells us intuitively: the state of world development has never been higher and continues to climb.

Zooming down to the regional scale provides a more textured view of the variety of economic arrangements. In Agoria, private corporations continue to play a major role, and investment capital for the most part is still privately held. But corporations have been rechartered to put social purpose at the core of their missions and to require the meaningful participation of all stakeholders in their decision-making. Moreover, they operate in a comprehensive regulatory framework designed to align business behavior with social goals, stimulate ecological technology, and nudge households to moderate consumerism. Governments channel Agoria's market economies toward building equitable, responsible, and environmental societies. Radical social democracy works and works well.

Ecodemia's system of "economic democracy" takes protean forms as it mutates and evolves in distinct cultural and political settings. The common feature is the expulsion of the capitalist from two key arenas of economic life: firm ownership and capital investment. Large-scale corporations based on private owners and hired employees have been replaced by worker- and community-owned enterprises, complemented by nonprofits and highly regulated small businesses. In parallel, socialized investment processes have displaced private capital markets. Publicly controlled regional and community investment banks determine how to recycle social savings and tax-generated capital funds, and rely on decision-making processes that include ample opportunity for civil society participation. These banks are mandated to review proposals from capital-seeking entrepreneurs, and to make approval subject to a demonstration that the projects are financially viable and advance society's larger social and environmental goals.

Small privately held enterprises comprise the backbone of Arcadia's relatively independent economies. But even in the land of small-is-beautiful, natural monopolies like utilities, ports, and mass transport are big-is-necessary exceptions. Place-based in spirit, Arcadia actively participates in world affairs and cosmopolitan culture. Some regions boast world-class centers of innovation in human-scale technologies: small-farm ecological agriculture, modular solar devices, human-scale transport systems, and much more. Churning with artistic intensity, Arcadia adds more than its share to Earthland's cultural richness. Exports of niche products and services, along with eco-tourism, support the modest trade requirements of these relatively time-rich, slow-moving societies.

And let us not forget the labor-intensive "people's economy" that flourishes alongside the high-technology base, producing a breath-taking array of aesthetic goods and skilled services. This informal marketplace supplements the incomes of many households, while offering artisans of a thousand stripes an outlet for creative expression. The people's economy continues to be enabled and encouraged by social policies that promote "time affluence," especially decreased work weeks and assured minimum income. Its role will surely grow in significance in the steady-state economy of the future as technological advance further reduces the labor requirements of the formal economy.

Whatever the regional economic architecture, a common principle guides policy: economies are a means for attaining social and environmental ends, not an end in themselves. Correspondingly, responsible business practices, codified in law and enforced by strong regulatory processes, are the norm for all enterprises. Approval of capital investments depends on a showing of compatibility with the common good, a determination made directly by public banks in Ecodemia or indirectly through the participatory regulatory and legal mechanisms in Agoria and Arcadia. Dense networks of civil society organizations, prepared to bring miscreants to task, diligently monitor detailed social-ecological performance reports and respond accordingly.

World Trade

Lest our regional focus leave the misapprehension that the world economy is no more than the sum of its parts, it is worth reiterating the essential role of global-scale institutions. World bodies marshal and organize the flow of "solidarity funds" to needy areas, implement transregional infrastructure projects, conduct space and oceanic exploration, and promote education and research for the common good. Moreover, world trade remains an important, if controversial, feature of our interdependent economy.

How much trade is desirable? How should the system be designed? A few small anti-trade parties advocate extreme autarky, but most people believe rule-governed trade can make important contributions to Earthland's core values. First, interregional exchange can augment global solidarity by countering anachronistic nationalisms—when goods stop crossing borders, it has been said, bullets start to. Second, it can contribute to individual fulfillment by giving access to resources and products that are unavailable locally, thereby enriching the human experience. Third, it can foster win-win transactions that reduce environmental stress: food imports to water-parched areas, solar energy exports from deserts, and livestock exports from lands where sustainable grass-fed grazing is feasible.

For these reasons, the consensus is strong that, in principle, Earthlandic trade has a legitimate role. But in practice, the debate can be fierce on how to set the rules. The fundamental conundrum of world trade persists: how best to balance the pull toward open economic intercourse with the rights of localities to shield themselves from the disruptive power of unbridled markets. Trade negotiations bring all the tension between globalism and regionalism to the surface, leaving no easy resolution.

The tilt today is toward a circumscribed trade regime that seeks an equilibrium between cosmopolitan and communitarian sensibilities. Strictly enforced rules proscribe unfair regional barriers, but do permit interdicting imports that would undercut legitimate local plans and aspirations. The Commonwealth's dispute resolution system is busy, indeed, mediating the fuzzy boundary between perverse and virtuous protectionism.

As with much else, policy on trade varies across regions. Cosmopolitan Agorians tend to support it, welcoming the economic vitality and product diversity it brings. At the other extreme some Arcadian places have erected towering barriers to imports. Most regions fall in between free trade and protectionist poles, and all, of course, must adhere to globally adjudicated strictures and rules.

In aggregate, world trade, while still important, plays a lesser role than in globalization's heyday at the turn of the century. The attention to the rights of regions to protect the integrity of their social models has bounded the scope for market exchange. Likewise, the rise in transport costs, as fuel prices came to fully incorporate environmental externalities, has added an economic advantage to the push for greater localization. Finally, the Commonwealth's tax on traded goods and services, and cross-border monetary and financial transactions, restrains trade while generating revenue for global programs.

The Way We Are

Let us turn to the social dimensions of Earthland, and the people who live here.

People

Earthland's population has now stabilized at just under eight billion people. Admittedly, this is a large number for a resource-hungry species on a small planet, but we are far fewer than the pre-transition projection of perhaps 11 billion people by the end of this century. By any measure, this has been a remarkable demographic shift made all the more impressive by the sharp increases in average life expectancy. The youth of today, who will benefit from further advance in biomedical science, can expect to be fighting fit at 100 years of age. And we present-day centenarians, born at the inception of the Great Transition, have every intention of participating in its next phase.

Of course, the story of population stabilization had a dark side—the decades of crisis and fear that cost lives and discouraged procreation—that must not be forgotten. Still, the primary and lasting impetus has been widespread social progress. Women elected to have fewer offspring in response to three intertwined factors: female education and empowerment, access to birth control, and the elimination of poverty, which correlated with the demographic shift, as it always has.

Earthlanders reside in roughly equal numbers in Agoria, Ecodemia, and Arcadia. Current regional population distributions reflect the considerable interregional resettlement as people were drawn to congenial places in the years after the Commonwealth was established. The flow has now largely abated, but immigrants continue in a trickle to exercise their right, as citizens of Earthland, to relocate. Thankfully, the old drivers of dislocation—desperate poverty, environmental disruption, and armed conflict—have largely vanished.

Agoria tends to be highly urbanized, Arcadians mostly cluster around small towns, and Ecodemia exhibits a mixed pattern. The "new metropolitan vision" that guides urban design has a central aim of creating a constellation of neighborhoods that integrate home, work, commerce, and leisure. This proximity of activities strengthens the cohesiveness of these towns-within-the city, while diminishing infrastructure and energy requirements. For many, these urban nodes ideally balance the propinquity of a human-scale community with the cultural intensity of a metropolis. But others are drawn to the lure of rural life, an especially powerful sentiment in Arcadia.

Family structures have evolved over the years to accommodate changing demographic realities, notably longer lives and fewer children. Naturally, Earthland's socially liberal ethos welcomes a full spectrum of ways of living together, with the caveat that participation not be coerced. The traditional nuclear family endures, especially in Agoria, adjusting to highly fluid gender and caretaking roles as women gain equal status in all realms—or at least are moving in that direction in traditionally chauvinist cultures. Alternative arrangements proliferate as well, notably Ecodemia's intentional communities and Arcadia's mélange of communal experiments. Diversity in living choices, sexual orientation, and gender identity is part and parcel of the age of tolerance and pluralism. The approaches may vary, but a social priority—care for children, the elderly, and the needy—is a constant.

Time

A core objective of the "new paradigm" has been to fashion societies that enable people to lead rich and fulfilling lives. This endeavor has had economic and cultural prongs. In its early decades, the Commonwealth focused on the economic preconditions of assuring secure, adequate living standards for all. This steadfast effort has radically reduced inequality and poverty, guaranteed a basic income, and increasingly provided people with more leisure time.

The cultural prong of nourishing human potentiality remains a work in progress, and may forever so be. Still, never have so many pursued so passionately the intellectual, artistic, social, recreational, and spiritual dimensions of a well-lived life. Most Earthlanders, and nearly all youth, opt for lifestyles that combine basic material sufficiency with ample time for pursuit of qualitative dimensions of well-being. The few who are still enthralled by conspicuous consumption are generally considered rather unevolved aesthetically and spiritually.

The contemporary way of life depends on the abundance of a once scarce commodity: free time. Today's citizens are highly "time affluent" relative to their forebears with workweeks in the formal economy typically range from 12 to 18 hours. Correspondingly, the social labor budget—and, therefore, the necessary work-time per person—has steadily decreased. The arithmetic is straightforward. On the output side of the economic equation, technological progress has increased productivity (the quantity of goods and services produced in an hour of work). On the demand side, lifestyles of material moderation require fewer consumer products, and those products are built for longevity. Moreover, such once-prominent unproductive sectors as advertising and the military-industrial complex have shriveled, further reducing socially necessary labor time.

What do people do with their free time? Many craftspeople and service providers devote considerable effort in the labor-intensive "people's economy." But nearly everyone reserves ample space in their day for non-market endeavors. The pursuit of money is giving way to the cultivation of skills, relationships, and the life of the mind and spirit. The cynics of yesteryear, who feared the indolent masses would squander their free time, stand refuted. The humanists, who spoke of our untapped potential to cultivate the art of living, were the prescient ones. The limits to human aspiration and achievement, if they exist, are nowhere in sight.

Education

If it is true that education turns mirrors into windows, Earthland is becoming a house of glass. We have grasped well history's lessons: an informed citizenry grounds real democracy; critical thinking opens closed minds; and knowledge and experience are the passports to a life lived fully. These convictions fuel peoples' passion for learning, and society's commitment to deliver a rich educational experience to all our young, and bountiful opportunity for lifelong learning.

The educational mission at all levels has expanded and shifted in the course of the transition. Here, we profile higher education, since, prodded and inspired by the eruption of the GCM, universities played a vital role educating students, spreading public awareness, and generating knowledge for a world in transformation. Core curricula began to emphasize big systems, big ideas, and big history, thereby connecting cosmology and social history to the understanding of the contemporary condition and underscoring the problem of the future. Preparing students for a life of the mind and appreciation of the arts became the foundation for disciplinary focus and vocational preparation. Cutting-edge programs trained new generations of sustainability professionals equipped to manage complex systems, and scientists, humanists, and artists keen to enrich Earthlandic culture.

In parallel with this pedagogic shift came the equally significant epistemological shift that brought an emphasis on transdisciplinary study of the character and dynamics of social-ecological systems. Needless to say, all the old specialized fields continue to thrive, albeit with some, like economics and law, undergoing root-and-branch reconstruction. But the race goes not to inhabitants of disciplinary islands but to explorers of integrative knowledge frameworks. This new scientific revolution transcends the reductive and mechanistic models of the old one to place holism and emergence at the frontiers of contemporary theory.

Beyond serving as a font of ideas and center of learning, the new university became an important player in the transition unfolding outside its walls. Academic specialists brought a systemic perspective to advising governments and citizens groups on the transformation. Diverse public programs raised consciousness on the great challenges of global change. Most significantly, educational institutions were engines of change and loci of action. They still are, not least through educating tomorrow's leaders, social entrepreneurs, and citizen-activists. The fully humanistic university has arrived, synergistically pursuing a triple mission—mass education, rigorous scholarship, and the common good—once thought to be contradictory.

Spirituality

The transition has left no aspect of culture untouched, and the forms of religion and spiritual practice are no exception. This is the way of the world: social transformations cause—and in turn are caused by—transformations in belief systems. When the Planetary Phase began roiling cultures in the decades around the turn of the century, decidedly illiberal streams pervaded most religions. Fundamentalism surged in reaction to the penetration of disruptive capitalism, which dissolved the consolations of tradition with the dubious promise of a purse of gold. In the vacuum of meaning that ensued, religious absolutism bubbled up, offering comfort for the lost and solace for the disappointed—and a banner of opposition for the zealous.

To this day, atavistic fundamentalist sects still practice their rigid customs and proffer literal interpretation of holy texts. These small groups may reject Earthland's core principles of tolerance and pluralism, but nevertheless benefit from them. Their rights are strictly protected, subject only to the prohibition against the coercive imposition of beliefs on others. Late 21st-century fundamentalism, a curious throwback to a less enlightened era, reminds us of the timeless longing for unattainable certainty.

In the mainstream of the Great Transition, people were adjusting values and questioning assumptions. The search for new forms of the material and spiritual, and equipoise between them, led many beyond both hedonistic materialism and religious orthodoxy. The awakening spawned three central tendencies: *secularization, experimentation,* and *reinvention.*

Organized spiritual practice finds fewer adherents as interest wanes with each new generation. Suspicious of received authority and supernatural assumptions, more of us seek sources of meaning and transcendence in the wondrous marvels of art, life, and nature. Scholars debate the reasons for the diminishing draw of institutionalized religion (they have since the trend surfaced in Western Europe and elsewhere in the 20th century). What is indisputable is that secularization has correlated with improved education and enhanced security—and, of course, with the expanding explanatory power of natural science.

As traditional forms contracted, new religious systems have proliferated, some created out of whole cloth and others as syncretic blends of ancient, modern, and New Age traditions. The breathtaking variety of this experimentation reflects the wide scope of spiritual ferment and cultural exploration stimulated by the transition. Each theology offers its disciples a unique metaphysics and, perhaps most importantly, a community of shared beliefs, rituals, and identity. The new religions come and go, metamorphosing as they evolve and spread.

All the while, the old religions were transmogrifying and reinventing themselves as the strong bearers of planetary values that they have become. The Great Transition was in no small measure a struggle for the soul of the church, mosque, temple, and synagogue. By the early 21st century, prophetic voices in every religion were delving into traditional doctrine for roots of the modern agenda—tolerance, equity, ecology, fraternity—and finding anticipations. As the transition unfolded, the voices became choruses of interfaith ensembles spreading the word and marching in the streets.

Social Justice

By any measure, Earthland has become more equitable and tolerant than any country of the past, the fruit of the long campaign to mend deep fissures of class privilege, male domination, and bigotry of all shades. The triumph is real, but with the work of amelioration unfinished, it is too soon to declare the conquest of prejudice complete. Civil libertarians are right to warn of the dangers of apathy and retrogression.

Still, Earthland's stunning erasure of grotesque disparities between rich and poor should not be minimized. Notably, income distributions have become far tighter than in the past and the wealth gap between haves and have-nots has been closed by paring both the top and the bottom. Caps on total personal assets and limits on inheritance have made the super-rich an extinct species, while redistributive tax structures and a guaranteed minimum standard of living have nearly eradicated destitution.

Of course, economic justice is but one prong of social equity. The struggle for equal rights, regardless of gender, race, religion, ethnicity, and sexual orientation, has a long and arduous history. Earthland's egalitarianism and muted class distinctions opened a new front in this fight by dissolving entrenched structures of power. Perhaps most significantly, universal material security and access to education have reduced fear and ignorance, the primary ingredients that feed xenophobia and intolerance.

At the deepest level, the prevailing ethos of solidarity forms the bedrock for a culture of respect and care for every member of the human family. At last, the dream of full equality is close to fulfillment, and our vibrant rights movements deserve much of the credit. This towering landmark on the path of social evolution would not be on the horizon without their persistence and vigilance, and even now would remain vulnerable to stagnation or reversal. Prejudice and domination, the old nemeses of justice, are finally on the run.

Environment

From its inception, Earthland has confronted the terrible legacy of a degraded biosphere and destabilized climate. The ecological emergency of the first decades of this century threatened to remold the planet into a bubbling cauldron of disruption, pain, and loss. Fortunately, this near calamity for civilization awakened the world's people to the dire peril of drifting complacently in conventional development mode, and spawned the vibrant environmentalism central to the Great Transition movement.

Not content just to mourn the lost treasury of creatures and landscapes, activists mobilized to protect and restore what remained, and to set our damaged planet on the long path to recovery. The formation and consolidation of the Global Assembly for Integrated Action ("GAIA") in the 2020s was a milestone in creating a powerful unified front for this effort. Its multipronged campaign—"the moral equivalent of war"—became the flagship collective initiative of the early Commonwealth, an endeavor that continues to this day.

A measure of GAIA's success has been the significant contraction of the human ecological footprint, even as the world economy has grown. This sharp decoupling of economic scale and environmental impact was of critical importance to meeting and reconciling the goals of ecological sustainability and global equity. The key enabling factor was the change in culture and values that moderated the craving for tangible products. The shift in consumption patterns brought a corresponding shift in economic structure wherein sectors light on the environment—services, arts, health, knowledge—have become more prominent at the expense of industries highly dependent on natural resources.

In parallel, a host of technological innovations, such as nanotechnology and biofabrication, brought leaner, longer-lasting products, while soaring carbon costs and rapid improvements in renewable energy and bioapplications turned out the lights on the fossil fuel age. The "waste stream" has been converted from a river of effluents to a primary input flow to industry. Ecological farming and mindful diets are the twin pillars of our sustainable agriculture system. Advanced techniques for removing atmospheric carbon from the atmosphere through enriched soils, bioenergy and sequestration, and carbon-fixing devices have been ramping up as well.

These hard-hitting climate actions have set us on a trajectory to reach atmospheric carbon concentrations of 350 ppm in the foreseeable future, a target once scoffed at by turn-of-the-century "realists." Indeed, climate visionaries recently launched 280.org, a 100-year campaign to return concentrations to pre-industrial levels. Other milestones are on the horizon, as well. Freshwater use is gradually coming into balance with renewable water resources nearly everywhere. As terrestrial ecosystems and habitats recover, species are being removed one by one from the endangered list. The oceans, the lifeblood of the biosphere, are healthier than they have been in decades—less acidic, less polluted, and home to more, and more varied, sea life.

The project of restoring the richness, resilience, and stability of the biosphere remains a vast collective cultural and political enterprise. At last, humanity understands the moral and biophysical imperative to care for the ecosphere, a hard-learned lesson that shall not be forgotten. In our time, the wounded earth is healing; someday, the bitter scars from the past will fade away like yesterday's nightmare.

In Praise of Generations Past

The state of the Commonwealth is strong and our grandchildren's prospects are bright. But complacency would be folly. The immediate task is to heal the lingering injuries of the past—eradicating the last pockets of poverty, quelling old antagonisms that still flare across contested borders, and mending nature's still-festering wounds. Strengthening educational programs and political processes is vital to solidifying Earthland's ideals in minds and institutions. Social capital is the best inoculation against resurgence of the merchants of greed, demagogues of hate, and all who would summon the dark hobgoblins from the recesses of the human psyche.

The turning wheel of time no doubt will reveal 22nd-century challenges now gestating in the contemporary social fabric. Human history has not ended; in the fullest sense, it has just begun. We are entrusted with the priceless legacy of a hundred millennia of cultural evolution and emancipatory struggle that loosened the shackles of ignorance and privation. Now, we stand at the auspicious—and perhaps improbable—denouement of a century with an unpromising beginning. The timeless drama of the human condition continues in triumph and tragedy, but who among us would trade the theater of historical possibility that now opens before us?

How different is the ringing sense of expectation that surrounds us from the ominous soundtrack that rattled our grandparents' youth when the world careened toward calamity? But even then, those who listened could hear the chords of hope and feel the quickening rhythm of change. The Planetary Phase was relentlessly forging a single community of fate, but who would call the tune? Would the people of the world dance together toward a decent future?

Victor Hugo once noted that nothing is so powerful as an idea whose time has come. In the Planetary Phase, the idea of One World had finally arrived, but the reality did not fall from the sky. It took a tenacious few to sow the seeds as social conditions enriched the soil; the rest, as they say, is history. With profound gratitude, we honor the pivotal generations of the transition that rose to the promise of Earthland when the century was still young. Living in yesterday's tomorrow, we proudly confirm what they could only imagine: another world was possible!

Note

1 Paul Raskin, *Journey to Earthland: The Great Transition to Planetary Civilization* (Boston, MA: Tellus Institute, 2016), http://www.greattransition.org/publication/journey-to-earthland.

Part 3

A Planetary Economy

The climate crisis has prompted a major rethinking of the imperatives of economic growth. Traditional economic discourse typically measures growth in terms of goods produced and resources consumed, the more the better. But the scientific facts behind the planetary warming and the broader ecological crisis created by our production and consumption practices give rise to questions rarely confronted before: will our efforts to mitigate the worst effects of fossil fuels and chemical toxins without changing the basic structures of capitalism be enough to avert ecological collapse? What does "economic growth" mean in a world up against its ecological limits? Do we change how we define and measure it? Can we really improve the living standards for billions of people around the world without totally destroying the only planetary home we have?

The chapters in this part offer a range of possibilities for enabling people to, in the words of authors Tim Jackson and Peter A. Victor, "flourish on a finite planet." A fundamental question is whether capitalism is up to the task of combining broad prosperity with environmental sustainability. Not in its current state, they all agree, but how radically different the economies of the future must be is a matter of debate.

Jackson, director at the Centre for Understanding of Sustainable Prosperity and a professor of sustainable development at the University of Surrey, and Victor, professor and former dean of environmental studies at York University, outline the need for a new ecological macroeconomic model that accurately reflects the real economy's structure, takes full account of the ecological and resource constraints at the national scale, and incorporates a "consistent description of the financial economy." Adopting the model would mean changing the nature of enterprise, the purpose and structure of work, the structure of investments, and the operation of our debt-based money and finance systems. Elements of the new system, they write, already exist in places like farmers' markets, cooperatives, and even library systems.

One issue that Lorenzo Fioramonti, who directs the Centre for the Study of Governance Innovation at the University of Pretoria, tackles is the "framework of measurement by which the economy is controlled." Instead of using "gross domestic product" to measure economic growth and progress, he calls for a "dashboard" of indicators to measure the well-being of people, taking into account "the negative contributions of pollution and waste and the benefits coming from households' and families' work, small businesses, and nonprofit organizations." Doing so, he argues, would encourage the development of public, collective, and shared ownership models, create new identities in the marketplace ("prosumers"), address gender-based discrimination, and eliminate the economic need for international trade agreements and austerity programs.

Hans A. Baer, associate professor and honorary research fellow at the University of Melbourne, describes a system of "democratic eco-socialism" that he says would take into account the fragility of the planet and its limited resources through equitable distribution mechanisms. It would emerge, he writes, through "system-challenging reforms" that address historical failings of both capitalist and socialist societies. Key features of Baer's democratic eco-socialism include public ownership of the means of production and a representative and participatory democracy. He distinguishes between "growth"—an ever-increasing demand for more production and consumption—and "development," a way to provide all people with adequate food, shelter, clothing, health, education, and recreation. Eco-socialism would aim to meet people's basic needs, protect the environment, and create a high degree of social equality—a sharp contrast to today's growth-oriented capitalist economies.

In "Six Theses for Saving the Planet," Richard Smith, a founding member of System Change Not Climate Change, challenges the notion that green economy proposals or "degrowth" strategies alone will save us from global ecological collapse. Instead, he argues, the only way to save the planet is to replace capitalism with "global eco-socialist democracy." Six theses make up the heart of Smith's proposed system: substantial cuts in fossil fuel consumption; a "dignified" and sustainable living standard for all; production of goods that are more rebuildable, recyclable, and shareable; investments in public needs, including renewable energy, infrastructure, and public education; systemic approaches to managing waste and toxics; and assurances of quality jobs for displaced workers. Acknowledging that the path to a mostly publicly owned economy is steep, Smith asks "what other choice do we have but to try?"

Chapter 9

Toward a New, Green Economy—Sustainable and Just—at Community Scale

Tim Jackson and Peter A. Victor

Green economy is still a contested concept.[1] At its worst, it simply provides cover for business as usual—the escalation of unsustainable corporate practices that threaten the integrity of the natural world and undermine the resource base for future prosperity. At its best, green economy offers a positive blueprint for a new economics firmly anchored in principles of ecological constraint, social justice, and lasting prosperity. A premise of this piece is that such a blueprint is worth articulating.

Explorations of the green economy have until now mostly taken place at a national or international level. Our own work—both individually and together—has mainly been directed toward this task.[2] Our aim here is to address the implications of the green economy at the local level. We draw substantially in what follows on the understandings we have gleaned from working at the national scale. But we also explore the lessons to be learned for the green economy from numerous small-scale, community-based initiatives for social and ecological change.[3] In particular, we offer a set of conceptual foundations for more sustainable, people-friendly community-based economic activities in order to explore the implications of the green economy at community scale.

It seems clear that the strength and character of communities lie less in the technologies they employ and more in the social relations they engender. The green economy is not just about resource-efficient technology—"treading lightly on the earth." It also encompasses matters of democratization and voice, of social inclusion and justice, and of policy, power, and governance. These more foundational questions are logically prior to questions about specific industrial sectors like food, energy, transport, or waste. They also speak more closely to the first principles of system change at the economic level. The kinds of questions that orient our inquiry include:

- How is enterprise to be organized?
- How is labor to be employed?
- What is the structure of investment?
- What kind of financial systems are appropriate?
- What sort of governance structures are relevant?

These questions also lie at the heart of community. Perhaps the most fundamental point of all concerns the ends or purpose our economies are supposed to serve. What is the nature of prosperity itself and how should the economy attempt to deliver this at community scale?

Foundations for the Green Economy

The green economy is not an end in itself; rather, it is a means toward a shared and lasting prosperity. The economy must deliver the capabilities for people to thrive and for communities to flourish. Beyond simply delivering goods and services, this task involves maintaining and enhancing social and environmental well-being. In the following sections of this chapter, we will explore in more detail how it might be possible to shape the economic institutions that support these conditions. First, however, we must address a more basic question: what is the nature of prosperity? What does it mean for people and communities to prosper? What exactly are the end goals of the green economy?

It is not unusual to find the answer to these questions hashed out in purely economic terms. Increased prosperity is about having more money in our pockets. Rising incomes mean better choices, richer lives—an improved quality of life for those who benefit from them. Or so the story goes. This response clearly has an appealing logic when it comes to the world's poorest people. A meaningful approach to prosperity must certainly address the plight of two billion people across the world still living on less than $2 a day. But to cash out prosperity entirely in terms of money has some obvious drawbacks. Not the least of these is that it fails to answer the underlying question: what is that we aspire to achieve with ever-increasing incomes?

It is interesting to note that when local communities come together to address their own well-being, they tend to adopt a far wider view of prosperity than the one adopted by economists in describing the progress of society. Typically, their focus includes health, education, and the strength of the community itself. It rapidly becomes clear that the dimensions of prosperity are much more complex than—and cannot really be measured by—money alone. More is not always better. Quality is not the same as quantity. Prosperity is not entirely or even primarily material in nature. It has vital social and psychological dimensions.

To do well is in part about our ability to give and receive love, to enjoy the respect of our peers, to contribute useful work, to feel secure in the face of uncertainty, and to have a sense of belonging and trust in our community. There is a critical social dimension to prosperity: individual prosperity is curtailed in the presence of social calamity. That things are going well for me personally is of little consolation if my family, my friends, and my community are all in dire straits.

Our sense of things going well also requires some notion of continuity. We aren't inclined to think that life is going swimmingly if we confidently expect things to fall apart tomorrow. Prosperity is not a momentary sensation. It demands conditions and circumstances that are expected to endure. Though, as consumers, we are often tempted to focus on instant gratification, satisfaction today means nothing if it undermines the conditions on which tomorrow's well-being depends.

These two dimensions of prosperity—its shared nature and its longevity over time—come together in relation to environmental concerns. A fair and lasting prosperity cannot be isolated from the ecological conditions and resource availabilities on which our collective well-being depends. The levels of prosperity to which as a species we can aspire are physically bounded by the capacity of the planet to support us. To ignore these natural bounds to material flourishing is to condemn our descendants— and our fellow creatures—to an impoverished planet. But in defining prosperity as a social and psychological condition, as much as a material one, we have opened up an intriguing possibility: that material bounds do not in themselves constrain prosperity itself. Perhaps by having less stuff, we can lead better and richer lives. Perhaps we could live better by consuming less.

The idea that humans can flourish and at the same time consume less is clearly tantalizing. It would be foolish to think that it is easy to achieve. But, equally, it should not be given up lightly. It may well offer the best underlying vision we have for the green economy: prosperity as the art of living well on a finite planet.

We can now identify three foundations for the green economy. The first is prosperity itself. The pursuit of human well-being lies at the heart of the green economy; it motivates economic activity and justifies economic output. The second is the set of biophysical boundaries within which economic activity must take place, not just for human well-being but also for the well-being of other species with whom humans share the planet. Economic activity that undermines ecological and mineral assets and other natural systems on which prosperity tomorrow depends is unsustainable. The final concept is social justice. Prosperity that provides only for the few and fails to alleviate the plight of the poor and disadvantaged, where there is a clear mismatch between effort and reward, or where the opportunities for advancement are restricted unfairly, diminishes the quality of society and leads eventually to social instability. To put things even more simply, the objective of the green economy is to achieve a shared (socially just) and a lasting (environmentally sustainable) prosperity.

So far so good. But what does all this mean for the structure of the economy itself. What does enterprise look like in the green economy? How is work organized? What role does investment have and how does it differ from the conventional economy? Last but not least, how does the money system function, enabling local communities to finance the kinds of projects that will lead to a lasting and sustainable prosperity? In the following sections, we address each of these factors in turn.

Enterprise for the Community

In the broadest sense, we can define the role of enterprise as providing the capabilities for people to prosper and for communities to thrive. Within this framing, it is possible to identify a number of clear operational principles that enterprises should fulfill in the green economy. They should:

• Provide an equitable distribution of the goods and services needed for prosperity
• Use as little as possible in the way of materials and energy
• Cause as little damage as possible to ecosystems
• Offer people meaningful employment and the opportunity to participate in society
• Contribute to the vitality of the community

Guided by these criteria, it is instructive to ask two important questions about enterprise in the green economy:

• Are there specific sectors of economic activity that should be encouraged in the green economy?
• What organizational form should enterprise take in the green economy?

Numerous responses to the first question have identified such technological sectors as energy efficiency, renewable energy, and resource productivity as central to the green economy. This response accords with the technological view of the green economy: an economy more or less like the existing one, but in which investment transforms the energy infrastructure to low-carbon alternatives. Clearly, this makes some sense. In a green economy, we need new energy companies to produce and supply green electricity, energy-efficient lights and appliances, and so on.

There are numerous examples of such companies in Canada and abroad, particularly in the energy sector. Bullfrog Power is a Canadian company offering green electricity and natural gas to households and businesses across the country.[4] Good Energy is a similar provider in the UK.[5] For several reasons, most of these new energy companies are smaller—and often more embedded in the community—than conventional providers. In the first place, many of the green energy companies are recent startups, developing new approaches to energy supply and energy efficiency more or less from scratch, unencumbered by sunk capital or entrenched mind-sets. Also, renewable, sustainable energy sources tend to be local as do the solutions that will make people's homes and businesses more energy efficient.

Many of these new community-based energy companies are established as "energy service companies" or ESCOs. Here, the focus is not simply on supplying megawatts, but on delivering the energy services that households and businesses need: heat, light, and motive power. Though at first sight the distinction between energy and energy services might seem opaque, it turns out to be a vital element in the reinvention of enterprise for the green economy.

The critical point is this: it is the services that energy can provide—thermal comfort, visual comfort, access—that contribute to our prosperity rather than oil, gas, or electricity for their own sake. It is entirely possible, for instance, to achieve the same level of thermal comfort in all sorts of ways. Wearing thin clothes in a draughty house and burning lots of gas is one way. Wearing warm clothes in a well-insulated house and installing an air source heat pump powered by renewable energy is another. In terms of prosperity, these options may well be equivalent. In terms of resource intensity and environmental impact, they are completely different.

This re-framing of the role of energy companies as energy service companies offers us a kind of blueprint for enterprise more generally. The distinction between the throughput of material commodities and the delivery of services mirrors precisely the distinction we introduced earlier between material affluence and our ability to flourish—not just in material ways. Beyond our material needs, prosperity is as much about social and psychological functioning—identity, affiliation, participation, creativity, and experience—as it is about material stuff.

Often, of course, we try to employ material artifacts to satisfy these needs, with greater and lesser degrees of success.[6] But the needs themselves are not inherently material, and it is a mistake to cast enterprise solely in terms of the throughput of material products. Rather, we should construe enterprise in the green economy in terms of delivering the "human services" that improve the quality of our lives: health, social care, education, leisure, recreation, and the maintenance and protection of physical and natural assets.

The seeds for this new economy already exist in local, community-based social enterprise: community energy projects, local farmer's markets, cooperatives of many types, sports clubs, libraries, community health and fitness centers, local repair and maintenance services, craft workshops, writing centers, outdoor pursuits, music and drama, yoga, martial arts, meditation, hairdressing, gardening, and the restoration of parks and open spaces.

Perhaps the most telling point of all is that people often achieve a greater sense of well-being and fulfillment both as producers and as consumers of these activities than they do in the time-poor, materialistic, supermarket economy in which much of our lives is spent.[7] Nor is it simply the outputs from these activities that make a positive contribution to flourishing. As we've seen above, the form and organization of our systems of provision also matter. Economic organization needs to work with the grain of community and the long-term social good, rather than against it.

Jobs Worth Having

Insights into the role and nature of work are not new. Drawing on insights from Buddhist philosophy, the Indian philosopher Kumarappa argued that when the nature of work is properly appreciated, "it will stand in the same relation to the higher faculties as food is to the physical body. It nourishes and enlivens the higher [self]."[8] Picking up on the same theme, the economist E.F. Schumacher argued that "properly conducted in conditions of human dignity and freedom, work blesses those who do it and equally their products."[9]

By contrast, the conventional economic view sees work as a sacrifice of our time, leisure, and comfort, and wages are "compensation" for that sacrifice. This leads to perverse outcomes for both workers and entrepreneurs. As Schumacher points out, "the ideal from the point of view of the employer is to have output without employees, and the ideal from the point of view of the employee is to have income without employment."[10]

This perverse dynamic is internalized in the modern economy through the pursuit of increasing labor productivity: the desire continually to increase the output delivered by each hour of working time. Rising labor productivity is often viewed as the engine of progress in modern capitalist economies. But the relentless pursuit of increased labor productivity also presents society with a profound dilemma. As each hour of working time becomes more "productive," fewer and fewer people are needed to deliver any given level of economic output. When economic growth is hard to come by, for whatever reason, the dynamic of rising labor productivity is a harsh mistress.[11]

There are, broadly speaking, two avenues of intervention through which to escape from this "productivity trap."[12] One is to accept productivity growth in the economy and reap the rewards in terms of reduced hours worked per employee—or, in other words, to share the available work among the workforce. The second strategy is to ease up on the gas pedal of ever-increasing productivity—to shift economic activity to more labor-intensive sectors. Interestingly, both these avenues have some precedence in the history of economic ideas.

As it turns out, societies have often taken some of the economy's labor productivity gains in the form of increased leisure time (Figure 9.1). Paid working hours in the United States have declined by 8 percent since 1961.

In France, it's over 30 percent; Sweden, 15 percent, and in Canada the average paid working hours have fallen by around 17 percent since 1961.[13] In the absence of these declines, the rate of unemployment in these countries would have been much higher.[14] It may not be the workaholic's choice, but sharing the available working time by reducing working hours is an important strategy for ensuring that everyone has access to a livelihood, particularly when growth is hard to come by.[15]

Work share makes good sense for both employees and employers. However, simple arithmetic suggests a second avenue for keeping people in work when demand is rising less quickly. Reining back the relentless increase in labor productivity offers a compelling option. By shifting to a lower productivity economy, we have within our grasp the arithmetical means to maintain or increase employment, even as the economy ceases to grow.

If this second option sounds perverse at first, it is largely because we have become so conditioned by the language of efficiency. After all, it's our ability to generate more output with fewer people that's lifted our lives out of drudgery and delivered us the cornucopia of material wealth—iPhones, hybrid cars, cheap holiday flights, plasma screen TVs—which even the poorest now aspire to. Leaving aside here momentarily the environmental

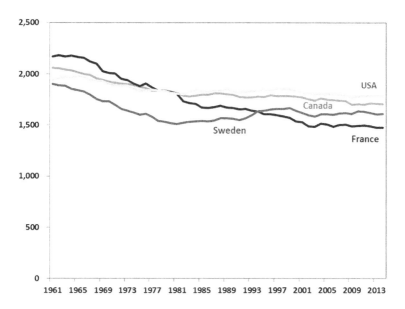

Figure 9.1 Trends in working hours in Canada, France, Sweden, and the United States during 1961–2014. Organization for Economic Co-operation and Development, OECDStat database.

impacts of this massive explosion of material goods, it is clear that rising labor productivity has in some cases made our lives definitively better. At least in the short term. Who now would rather keep their accounts in longhand, wash hotel sheets by hand, or mix concrete with a spade?

But there are places too where chasing labor productivity growth makes much less sense. Certain kinds of tasks rely inherently on the allocation of people's time and attention. The care and concern of one human being for another, for instance, is a peculiar "commodity." It cannot be stockpiled. It cannot be degraded through trade. You cannot substitute away from it. It is not deliverable by machines. Its quality rests primarily on the attention paid by one person to another.[16] In seeking to make care work more "efficient," we undermine not only the value of the care but also the experience of the carer. Compassion fatigue is a rising scourge in a health sector hounded by meaningless productivity targets.

Care is not the only profession to suffer at the hands of productivity goals. Craft is another. It is the accuracy and detail inherent in crafted goods that endows them with lasting value. It is the attention paid by the carpenter, the tailor, and the designer that makes this detail possible. Likewise, it is the time spent practicing, rehearsing, and performing that gives art its enduring appeal. Not much is to be gained from asking the New York Philharmonic to cut down on rehearsal time and play Beethoven's ninth Symphony faster and faster each year.[17] The performance of music itself and the appreciation of that performance through various media rely inherently on the musicians' time and dedication to their art.

Care, craft, and culture are basically the same "human services" that sit at the heart of the vision of enterprise set out above. Services inherently resist the logic of productivity growth precisely because the value of the services provided is tied intimately to the contribution of people's time, skill, and labor. It is a naturally employment-rich sector that contributes immensely both to individual well-being and to the vibrancy of our communities.

Since these activities are built around the value of human services rather than the relentless throughput of material stuff, they also offer a half decent chance of making the economy more sustainable. In short, achieving full employment in the green economy may have less to do with chasing after endless productivity growth and more to do with building local economies based around care, craft, and culture, and in doing so, restoring the value of decent work to its rightful place at the heart of society.

Investing in the Future

Investment may be the single most important element in the green economy: it embodies the relationship between the present and the future. The fact that people set aside a proportion of their income for investment at all reflects a fundamentally prudential aspect of human nature. We care not just about our present happiness but also about our future well-being.[18] Investment is the vehicle through which we build, protect, and maintain the assets on which tomorrow's prosperity depends.

Of course, it is always possible for this relationship between present and future to become distorted. We can become too short sighted—both as individuals and as a society. We sometimes privilege risky speculation— practices that are fundamentally gambling—over the investments that create and maintain solid, long-lasting physical, social, and environmental assets. We may create rules that privilege asset holders at the expense of the poorest in society. Our investment architectures are sometimes so complex that individuals and communities find it impossible to manage their own long-term financial security. We set aside too little to protect the most important long-term assets of all: those provided by natural ecosystems.

It is important to understand both how these mistakes can become institutionalized and how to correct them. Corrective measures at a federal or provincial level need to be complemented by workable alternatives that can return a measure of resilience to local communities. The green economy needs not just a coherent vision of sustainable investment, but a way of translating this vision into practice at community scale.

In simple terms, we can characterize "real investment" in the conventional economy as pursuing three main objectives.[19] First, it aims to maintain (and, where necessary, replace or expand) the existing stock of fixed assets. Second, it attempts to improve the productivity of those assets—most often, as we have noted, through the pursuit of increased labor productivity. Finally, investment is directed toward the process of "creative destruction"—the creation and re-creation of new markets for new products, the continual throwing over of the old in favor of the new. In short, conventional investment strategy is a crucial part of the architecture of the *unsustainable* economy and offers little in the way of a reliable basis for the green economy.[20]

So, what should investment look like? The green economy cannot simply be characterized as more of the same with a smattering of clean-tech investments thrown in. Certainly investments in low-carbon, resource-light technologies rightly belong in a green investment portfolio. But a more thorough rethink of the portfolio as a whole is also needed. The starting point for this rethink is to recall these three simple principles:

- Prosperity consists in our ability to flourish as human beings—now and in the future.
- Enterprise concerns the organization of economic services that deliver the capabilities we need to flourish.
- Investment is the process of setting aside income in the present in order to maintain, protect, and enhance the assets from which future prosperity will flow.

This vision allows us to identify the outlines of a green investment "portfolio." It makes clear that we need to invest, for example, in health, education, social care, leisure, and recreation; in green spaces, lakes and rivers, parks and gardens; in community halls, concert halls, theatres, museums, and libraries. Investment in the green economy needs to be focused on the protection and maintenance of the assets on which future prosperity depends. The portfolio of green investment must, of course, include the low-carbon technology and infrastructure typically associated with the green economy. But it must also include wider investments in resource productivity, in building human and social capital, in the protection of ecological systems, in the building of community infrastructures, and in the maintenance of public spaces.

Clearly, the conventional relationship between investment expenditure and productivity no longer holds in the same way for green investment. The ecology of investment will itself have to change in the green economy. Investment in long-term, public goods will have to be judged against criteria other than financial market success. This may also mean rethinking the ownership of assets and the distribution of surpluses from them. But perhaps the biggest challenge for this new portfolio of investment is the question of financing. It is to this subject that we now turn.

Making Money Work

So far, our concern here has mainly been with what is sometimes called the "real economy": the patterns of employment, production, consumption, government spending, and investment in the economy. But it is useful to distinguish the real economy from the financial or "money economy": the wider set of financial flows on which the real economy depends. This wider set of financial accounts includes the flow of money into and out of different economic sectors, the processes of borrowing, lending, and creating money (the money supply), and the changes in the financial assets and liabilities of different economic actors. These money flows are essential to the financing of investments in the real economy.

Ignoring what was happening in the money economy was one of the decisive errors contributing to the financial crisis and subsequent global recession. The real economy appeared to be doing well and GDP growth looked strong in the run up to the crisis. But the weakening of company balance sheets and the over-indebtedness of households in many OECD countries were a contributing cause of the fragility and eventual instability in the financial system.[21]

Few economists foresaw, for instance, how the massive expansion of commercial debt-based money (Figure 9.2) could destabilize the money system as a whole. To many non-economists, the existence of a debt-based money system itself comes as a complete surprise. We tend to think of

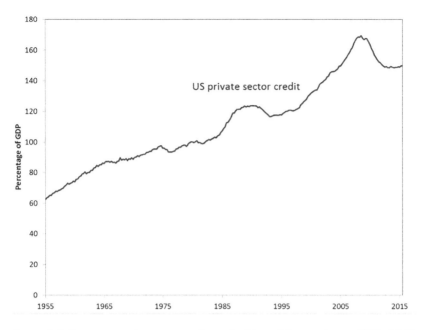

Figure 9.2 Expansion of private credit in the United States during 1955–2015.
Source: Adapted from Jackson, *Prosperity without Growth* 2017, Figure 2.[27]

money as something printed by the central bank more or less under the control of the government. The reality is that in most advanced economies, less than 5 percent of the money supply is created in this way. Most money circulating in the economy today is created as "credit"—loans advanced to companies and households by commercial banks, almost literally "out of nothing."

This process is said to "expand the balance sheet," but it doesn't in itself change the financial net worth (the difference between assets and liabilities) of the bank. Any change in the financial worth of the bank from making a loan depends on what happens after the loan is created: how much interest is charged on it, whether and when the loan is repaid, how much of the deposit is spent, where it is spent, where that money ends up in the economy. If the loan is repaid in good time at an interest rate favorable to the bank, it increases bank profits and boosts its financial worth. If the borrower defaults on the loan, the transaction will leave the bank with "toxic" assets—loans that are non-recoverable—which will reduce its financial worth.

One important implication of this debt-based money system is that the investments needed by the green economy must generally prove their creditworthiness on entirely commercial grounds and must compete for capital with all sorts of commercial investments. So, for example, green investments must compete with financial speculation in commodities, property, or financial assets. They must compete with unsustainable consumer lending—in which repayment (and punishment for non-payment) is reinforced by legal institutions. They must compete with investments in dirty, extractive industries that degrade the environment, and operate through supply chains profitable only because they involve child labor.

The social benefits of green investment are rarely factored into the commercial market. Neither are the social costs of unsustainable investment (including the huge cost of unrestrained speculative trading). Worse still, these social costs are often ultimately borne by the taxpayer rather than by the investors.

So how much can communities do to improve their ability to finance green investments? There are, of course, a small number of "ethical banks" aiming to offer savers a way of investing their money for good causes. Triodos Bank in Europe is one such bank. Investing in renewable energy, energy efficiency, and community-based social projects, it has shown that it is possible to be a successful bank and still to hold to the principles of sustainable prosperity.

Communities might also look to attract public funding from community development financial institutions and credit unions, as well as federal, provincial, or municipal governments. The benefits to the nation as a whole from having strong, resilient, and sustainable communities are self-evident, and some federal and provincial government schemes do offer finance. A prime example is Sustainable Development Technology Canada (SDTC), a federally funded not-for-profit organization that supports innovative green technologies for climate change, clean air, water quality, and soils.

Inevitably, the ability of government to engage in community financing is dependent on its own fiscal position; and this, in turn, depends partly on the performance of the national economy. When economic growth is harder to come by, government tax receipts are lower and social security and employment insurance costs tend to be higher. Deficit spending is likely to rise; the national debt increases and, under the existing system in which government itself must also compete for funding on commercial money markets, the interest payments on the debt further constrain government spending.

This is particularly true in a monetary system in which sovereign (national) debt must be financed from open money markets at commercial interest rates. There is a clear risk that the costs to the taxpayer of maintaining the public debt are paid to precisely the people who benefit most from its existence. The combination of a debt-based money supply and an accumulation of private financial assets is deeply regressive. It also makes financing green investment very difficult.

However, there are some clear signals about the appropriate direction to turn to improve the situation. Here, we highlight three particularly important social innovations that are supported strongly by this analysis. The first is impact investing—the reinvestment of private net savings into the green economy. The second is community banking and credit unions—the implementation of local savings and investment vehicles that plough benefits directly back into the community. The third is the reconfiguring of the money supply itself, reclaiming control of the money supply from commercial interests and returning it to either the public sector (government) or the community, giving them access to debt-free money.

The good news is that there are positive examples in support of each of these innovations. Impact investing—the channeling of investment funds toward ethical, social, and sustainable companies, technologies, and processes—is an increasingly important element in the architecture of the green economy. This kind of investment was once seen as philanthropy. But as the Capital Institute has remarked, it should be seen as a vital complement both to philanthropy and to government funding: "a way to leverage secure philanthropic and public sector dollars, while harnessing the power of social entrepreneurs and market-based solutions to solve some of the world's most intractable problems."[22]

Perhaps the most popular model for community investment is the credit union—financial institutions in which individual members pool their savings to provide loans to other members. Although subject to many of the same regulations as banks, credit unions are typically smaller, more local, and designed specifically to be nonprofit institutions. They therefore offer a particularly appropriate vehicle for green investment at community scale and are beginning to be adopted for this purpose.

Our final suggestion for leveraging finance toward green investment at community scale concerns the money supply itself. There are some rather strong arguments in favor of changing the existing debt-based money system and returning more control of the money supply to the government. Some of these arguments have a surprising pedigree.

The so-called Chicago plan—which calls for 100 percent backing of deposits with government-issued money—was first put forward in the 1930s and was supported most notably by the Nobel laureate Irving Fisher. The idea has been revived in a working paper from the International Monetary Fund that points to several advantages of the plan, including its ability to better control credit cycles, eliminate bank runs, dramatically reduce both government debt and private debt, and allow the government to invest directly in communities without punitive interest payments.[23]

Obviously, this strategy lies outside the capacity of individual communities to achieve. It would require brave political leadership at the federal level to regain public control of the money supply. Nonetheless, it is clearly a strategy that requires public support, which could quite reasonably be gathered first at the community level. Versions of the same idea have been put forward recently in a variety of places at the federal level. In Switzerland, a proposal to do just this was put to a public vote 2018 and gathered surprising public support—although, sadly, not enough to pass the proposal into law.[24]

Another strategy for financing innovations in the green economy with a rather long pedigree is the creation of local currencies. Local exchange and trading systems (LETS) have emerged over the last few decades as an alternative to mainstream currencies. There are now over 1,500 LETS schemes worldwide. One example is the Berkshares scheme providing local currency to the Berkshire region in Canada.[25] Another is the Peterborough LETS, established in 1994 to provide a currency basis—green dollars—for the exchange of local goods and services in the Peterborough area.[26]

It is unclear to what extent such examples can be scaled up (either in scope or in number) to form the basis of a genuine transformation of the larger financial system. They are clearly consistent with our findings about financial architecture from the macroeconomic level and they also point the way toward more far-reaching changes. But they also depend to some extent on broader system-level change for their success. Thus, there is also a legitimate role for the local community in campaigning for change, as we have begun to see happening for example in the Extinction Rebellion movement in Europe.

Clearly, the green economy demands a different financial landscape from the one that led to the financial crisis of 2008/2009. Reforming this system is vital. Long-term security has to be prioritized over short-term gain. Social and ecological returns must be factored into investment decisions alongside conventional financial returns. Improving the ability of people to invest their savings locally, to the benefit of their own community, is paramount. In short, reforming capital markets is not just the most obvious response to the financial crisis but also an essential foundation for a new green economy at community scale.

Building Sustainable Communities

Our broad aim here has been to explore the implications of emerging ideas about the "green economy" as they apply to local communities. The starting point for this exploration was a vision of prosperity as a shared endeavor: the ability to live well on a finite planet. We have highlighted both the shared, social dimensions of prosperity and the importance of longevity over time. We have also explored the demands that this vision of prosperity places on the economic structure and institutions of the green economy. Four specific features emerged from this exploration:

- The nature of enterprise
- The organization of work

- The structure of investment
- The role of money economy

It will not have gone unnoticed that many of the interventions envisioned here cannot be implemented at will without more far-reaching changes in the broader political and economic framework. The question of governance, broadly defined, becomes critical to the delivery of the green economy.

Much of the motivation for exploring the green economy comes from recognizing the growing impacts of humans on the biosphere, globally and regionally. Some of these impacts, such as climate change, arise from the increasing use of fossil fuels and the efforts to obtain them from remote and risky locations in oil sands, deep rock formations, and under the sea. Other impacts, though often ubiquitous—in the sense that they are happening all over the world—are nonetheless local in impact. Scarcity of fresh water is one example. Urban air pollution is another. The speed and scale of losses in biodiversity have both local and global impacts.

All of these problems are ultimately experienced by people living in communities, even though they cannot be solved entirely (and in many cases, not mainly) by action at the community level. Wider levels of government play a key role in framing the issues, setting the agenda, and providing initiatives. To a large extent, governments at the provincial, state, and the national levels determine which policy issues are up for discussion and action and which are not. But the range of possible policy avenues is extensive. It includes the influence of the state on:

- Incentive structures (taxes, subsidies, penalties)
- Facilitating conditions and situational factors (access to infrastructures for recycling, public transport, etc.)
- Institutional context (rules, regulations, market structures)
- Social and cultural context (strength of community, family stability, etc.)
- Business practices and their impact on both consumers and employees
- Communities' ability and autonomy to help themselves
- Government's own environmental and social performance

Critically, government's role as lawmaker is not confined to punitive regulation. Changes to labor law that incentivize employers and give employees rights to shorter hours can be critical to providing decent work and maintaining high employment levels. Of particular importance to the green economy is government's role in financing investments in infrastructure with long time horizons and significant non-financial returns.

In short, a concerted strategy is needed to make change possible to: ensure that incentive structures and institutional rules favor the green economy; enable access to appropriate infrastructures, technologies, and opportunities; engage people in initiatives to help themselves; and exemplify the desired changes within government's own policies and practices.

Admittedly, the challenges of implementing the green economy at community scale are significant. The apparent intractability of human behavior is in part a function of the policy model that has dominated conventional thinking on pro-environmental and pro-social change. But the evidence suggests that this model is inaccurate. Despite the rhetoric of modern "hands-off" governance, policy intervenes continually in the behavior of individuals both directly (through taxes, regulations, and incentives) and (more importantly) through its extensive influence over the social and institutional context. Governments are not just innocent bystanders in the negotiation of economic progress. They influence and co-create the culture of change. A genuine understanding of the social and institutional context of the green economy opens up a much more creative vista for policy innovation than has hitherto been recognized. Expanding on these opportunities is an urgent responsibility of government.

In summary, there is a meaningful concept of the green economy that has clear relevance at community scale and this concept has specific implications for how enterprise is conceived, how work is organized, how investment is structured, and how the money system can be made to operate in the service of society. These concrete proposals for change are not only implementable, but are already in many places actually being implemented, improving the quality of people's lives and increasing the resilience of their communities.

Clearly, there is no silver bullet, no universal fix that will easily transform communities for the better. But identifying and implementing action for change is never simple in reality. Rather, the points of intervention will be diverse and depend on both the needs of the community and the skills and opportunities of those involved.

For some, the route to a green economy may involve setting up a local food cooperative or improving the quality and quantity of urban gardens. For others, it might mean establishing a community-based renewable energy project. For entrepreneurs, the process may start with a simple inquiry into the sustainability of the supply chain or the social value of the product. For teachers, it might involve changes in the curriculum. For health professionals, it might mean getting involved in community health. For investors, it might start by drawing a line in the sand: shifting money from speculative or environmentally destructive portfolios toward positive investments in change. Individual choices about what to buy, or how to travel, or where to save have cumulative impacts on the boundaries of possibility. For the activist, change might mean protest; for the policy-maker, it may involve painstaking reform.

For academic economists, the process of change might well start by asking the simple question: how does an economy work when it isn't being driven by relentless growth in material consumption? This is the question that we first asked ourselves over a decade ago. It led us to work together in defining the conditions for a green economy both at the national level and at community scale. We believe that task is as urgent now as it has ever been.

Notes

1 For more skeptical views, see Clive L. Spash, "Green Economy, Red Herring," *Environmental Values* 21, 2 (2012): 95–99; Barbara Unmüssig, Lili Fuhr, and Thomas Fatheuer, "Critique of the Green Economy: Toward Social and Environmental Equity," *Publication Series on Ecology* 22 (2012), Berlin: Heinrich Böll Stiftung, https://www.boell.de/sites/default/files/Critique_of_the_Green_Economy.pdf.

2 Tim Jackson, *Prosperity without Growth: Economics for a Finite Planet* (London: Earthscan/Routledge, 2009, 2017); Peter Victor, *Managing without Growth: Slower by Design, Not Disaster* (Cheltenham: Edward Elgar, 2008, 2018); Tim Jackson and Peter Victor, "Managing without Growth: Exploring Possibilities", in *Managing without Growth: Slower by Design, Not Disaster*, edited by P. A. Victor (Cheltenham: Edward Elgar, 2008, 2018), pp. 271–301. Tim Jackson, "The Post-Growth Challenge: Secular Stagnation, Inequality and the Limits to Growth" *Ecological Economics* 156 (2019): 236–246. Tim Jackson and Peter Victor, "Does Slow Growth Lead to Rising Inequality? Some Theoretical Reflections and Numerical Simulations." *Ecological Economics* 121 (2016): 206–219. Tim Jackson and Peter Victor, "Productivity and Work in the Green Economy: Some Theoretical Reflections and Empirical Tests," *Environmental Innovation and Societal Transitions* 1, 1 (2011): 101–108.

3 For the purposes of this report, we understand community to mean a group of people located in proximity to one another with shared values and interests.

4 Bullfrog Power, http://www.bullfrogpower.com/about/mission.cfm.

5 Good Energy, http://www.goodenergy.co.uk/.

6 See Jackson, *Prosperity without Growth* (2009/2016), Chapter 6 for a more extensive discussion of this point.

7 See Davy Castel, Claude Lemoine, and Annick Durand-Delvigne, "Working in Cooperatives and Social Economy: Effects on Job Satisfaction and the Meaning of Work," *Perspectives interdisciplinaires sur le travail et la santé* 13-2 (2011), http://pistes.revues.org/2635.

8 Quoted in Ernst Friedrich Schumacher, *Small Is Beautiful* (London: Vintage Books, 1973), 40.

9 Schumacher, *Small Is Beautiful*.

10 Schumacher, *Small Is Beautiful*.

11 For a fuller discussion of this, see Jackson, *Prosperity without Growth* (2009/2016); Victor, *Managing without Growth*.

12 See Tim Jackson and Peter Victor, "Productivity and Work in the Green Economy: Some Theoretical Reflections and Empirical Tests," *Environmental Innovation and Societal Transitions* 1, 1 (2011): 101–108.

13 Data from the Organisation for Economic Co-operation and Development (OECD), OECDStat database, online at: http://stats.oecd.org/Index.aspx?DatasetCode=ANHRS.

14 See Victor, *Managing without Growth*, 157–158.

15 Anna Coote, Jane Franklin, and the New Economics Foundation, "Time on Our Side: Why we All Need a Shorter Working Week" (London: New

Economics Foundation, 2013), http://neweconomics.org/sites/neweconomics.org/files/About_Time_conference_note.pdf.

16 This is not to suggest, of course, that material and technical advances in the caring professions are insignificant. On the contrary, some of these represent a direct contribution to improved quality of care. Our point is only to note that these advances should not tempt us to sacrifice the quality of care that comes from the time spent by caregivers.

17 Tim Jackson, "Let's Be Less Productive," *The New York Times*, May 26, 2012, http://www.nytimes.com/2012/05/27/opinion/sunday/lets-be-less-productive.html?_r=0.

18 It is interesting to note that prudential behavior is not restricted to the human species. Many species exhibit behaviors which might broadly be regarded as investment behaviors. Beavers build dams; squirrels horde nuts; camels store water. Each of these activities carries a current cost, but reaps future dividends. Nor is this behavior restricted to mammals; nest-building is a basic activity for birds, bees, termites, ants, and wasps. Even plants invest: the energy that is required to produce brightly colored flowers carries a vital return for plants in terms of pollination.

19 As in section three, we distinguish "real investment"—as the flow of capital into fixed (physical) assets—from speculative financial investment—the trading of commodities, property, and financial assets. We explore this distinction further in section seven.

20 When, in addition, we consider speculative investment, conventional investment portfolios appear even more destructive, contributing not only to resource depletion and environmental degradation but even—as we say in the global financial crisis—to financial instability.

21 The reader interested in more detail on the workings of the money economy might usefully refer to several recent publications in this field, including: Josh Ryan-Collins, Tony Greenham, and the New Economics Foundation, *Where Does Money Come From?* (London: New Economics Foundation, 2012); Andrew Jackson and Ben Dyson, *Modernising Money—Why Our Monetary System Is Broken and How It Can Be Fixed* (London: Positive Money, 2012); Randall Wray, *Modern Money Theory* (Oxford: Palgrave Macmillan, 2012).

22 Capital Institute, "The Patient Capital Collaborative—Field Study No 3. Field Guide to Investing in a Regenerative Economy," http://fieldguide.capitalinstitute.org/uploads/1/3/9/6/13963161/ppcepub.pdf.

23 Jaromir Benes and Michael Kumhof, "The Chicago Plan Revisited," International Monetary Fund Working Paper, August 2012, https://www.imf.org/external/pubs/ft/wp/2012/wp12202.pdf.

24 See Jackson and Dyson, *Modernising Money—Why Our Monetary System Is Broken and How It Can Be Fixed*; See also: Positive Money, http://positivemoney.org/; on the Swiss initiative, see Vollgeld-Initiative, http://www.vollgeld-initiative.ch/english; see also http://www.initiative-monnaie-pleine.ch/.

25 See for example http://www.lets-linkup.com/. For more information on Berkshares, see http://www.berkshares.org/heroes/mohicans.htm.

26 The Peterborough Local Economic Trading System, http://ptbolets.50webs.com/greendollars.html.

27 Data are from the Bank for International Settlements, http://www.bis.org/statistics/totcredit/credpriv_doc.pdf.

Chapter 10

Well-Being Economy

A Scenario for a Post-Growth Horizontal Governance System

Lorenzo Fioramonti[1]

For the past half century, Western societies have defined the route to development narrowly as economic growth. Growth has become an end in itself. As a result, the true meaning of development has been lost. Rather than an end goal, development should be viewed as a process toward an improved state of existence for humanity and our ecosystems.

The concept of well-being, with its multidimensional character, far better describes this improved state. Good, enjoyable, and fulfilling lives cannot be achieved through industrial output alone. Indeed, such output can easily endanger human progress, leading to the deterioration of the social relationships and environmental balance on which well-being depends.

The question is: how do we build economies designed to achieve holistic well-being? Can we find better channels for pursuing well-being than the destructive model of growth-driven development on which we are hooked? To do so, we must redesign our social organization, starting by restructuring the economy, which will trigger profound changes in both political institutions and society.

From a governance perspective, the economy is a decision-making system. The economic "rules of the game" shape behaviors, define incentives, and guide collective action. They ensure predictability, acceptability, and compliance. As such, the economic and political systems are closely enmeshed, at times competing for relevance and at times depending on each other. However, the economic rules frequently dictate political decision-making, so the economy can be seen as the ultimate rules-making system for creating and maintaining social order. For instance, by dividing responsibilities between producers and consumers, organizing the distribution of goods and services, and designing a monetary system for exchange, the economy becomes the arbiter of social organization. Its rules and roles are so ingrained that order is easily maintained, even without an overarching political authority. If we can successfully alter those economic governance rules, it follows we stand a real chance of reorganizing society, both politically and socially.

From the Old to the New: Which Changes and What Scope?

Our current model of economic organization can be described as a vertical structure in which wealth created by growth at the pyramid's top is "expected" to trickle down to the lower layers. The separation of production and consumption roles puts consumers at the receiving end of the growth process. The model is reinforced by the predominant economic growth measurement, gross domestic product (GDP). By statistical design, GDP's definition of production and assets unduly restricts the range of activities considered economically valuable. For instance, the vertical economy recognizes only the contribution of formal economic processes to the national income while ignoring the important contribution of the so-called non-money economies.

Because GDP measures "price-able" output without any consideration for both negative and positive "externalities"—that is, impacts on society and nature—the vertical economy overemphasizes the performance of large corporations at the expense of small businesses, in which production levels are relatively lower in terms of market prices but with enormous positive social and environmental impacts. In rewarding economies of scale by portraying them as cost effective, it disregards such negative externalities as overproduction and environmental destruction, which are not deducted from the GDP measurement of economic activity.

In the vertical economy, natural systems (and the wealth therein) have no value unless owned and exploited. To contribute to development, nature requires top-down control (ideally, via a large company that can maximize output) and must be commercialized through market channels. Neither preserving natural beauty to enhance the welfare of ecosystems nor managing natural resources for the common good allows the vertical economy to grow. The reverse is equally true. As the World Resources Institute observes: "A country could exhaust its mineral resources, cut down its forests, erode its soil, pollute its aquifers, and hunt its wildlife and fisheries to extinction, but measured income would not be affected as these assets disappeared."[2]

Policies designed to support the vertical economy replace informal systems (such as street vendors, small-scale farming, local markets, family businesses, and the unpaid productive work that people carry out for themselves, their families, and their communities) with formal structures (say, shopping malls, industrial-scale farming, and large infrastructure projects). Natural resources are commercialized and sold off: the higher the volume, the better for the economy, regardless of the social and environmental costs. Growing trees does not add to economic growth, but cutting and selling them off does. While some profit from this "creation" of monetary wealth, many are left behind and even harmed.

Two main reasons account for this state of affairs. First, top-down management is by definition limited to a few gatekeepers. Second, as open resources are brought under proprietary control, the communities that used to access them freely no longer can. The Organisation for Economic Co-operation and Development (OECD) has confirmed the close link between rising inequality and the worldwide growth of the vertical economy, an effect amplified across much of Africa and Asia, where the informal economy provides a fundamental safety net to many poor households.[3] The economist Thomas Piketty has provided time-series data over two centuries to show how income inequality rises in the absence of corrective policies, progressive taxation, and redistribution mechanisms.[4] In reality, the so-called "trickle-down effect," a key characteristic of the vertical economy that was often used to make the social case for 20th-century economic policies, fails the litmus test of hard data in the 21st century. The old adage that "a rising tide lifts all boats" no longer applies (if it ever did!).

An economy designed to promote well-being needs to be adaptable, integrative, and empowering. *Adaptable* because the new economy will operate like a network, abandoning the conventional vertical structure to expand horizontally and build resilience against external shocks through a system of nodes. *Integrative* because it locates systems of production and consumption within the broader biosphere. And *empowering* because its users will take control, rather than assuming the passive role of "consumers."

The convergence of crises, including environmental degradation, rising inequality, mass migration, and resource depletion, is making the unsustainability and gross inefficiency of the current model self-evident. And it is also triggering innovation. Pockets of experimentation are mushrooming around the globe, where a technological revolution in peer-to-peer software and hardware, 3D printing, decentralized renewable energy systems (blockchain-operated microgrids), and agroecology is advancing a new economic model based on collaboration rather than reductive competition. These possibilities for increasing innovation's scale and impact at the global level are unprecedented.

We may expect changes in geopolitical trends, too, especially insofar as globalization is concerned. One reason for this change is the need to avoid catastrophic climate change. Following the Paris climate deal at the United Nations Conference of the Parties (COP21) in 2015, the world will need to introduce regulations to curb carbon emissions, which will certainly affect global markets and long-distance transportation systems. Energy projections also point in this direction. The International Energy Agency (IEA) believes that conventional crude output will fall "by more than 40 million barrels per day by 2035."[5] As a consequence, out of 790 billion barrels of total production required to meet projected demand over this period, "more than half is needed just to offset declining production."[6] As for natural gas, a nonrenewable resource often touted as the magic bullet to deal with shrinking oil reserves, the IEA forecasts some growth in the next decade (mostly in North America), with uncertainty about "whether gas can be made available at prices that are attractive to consumers while still offering incentives for the necessary large capital-intensive investments in gas supply."[7] Even if we dispute such projections, the climate change imperative will still make it unlikely that these polluting resources will continue powering globalization, especially considering that natural gas production generates a greenhouse gas (methane) that is far more polluting than CO_2. At the same time, such renewable energy systems as solar, wind, hydro, and geothermal (which are expected to grow exponentially in the coming years) can hardly come to the rescue of globalization since they are hard to transport long distances.

Against this backdrop, the IEA believes the global economy requires an immediate reduction in energy-related emissions if the world is to stand even the smallest chance of remaining within the two degrees Celsius margin, given that the climate-compatible carbon budget will be exhausted by 2040.[8]

While the current form of globalization will not be able to continue in this scenario, a networked economy that scales horizontally will thrive in a climate-compatible economic system. The localization and blending of production and consumption will result in a better circular system, reducing waste and negative externalities. Moreover, adaptability to local conditions will improve the connection between supply and demand, minimizing environmental and social impacts. Instead of striving for ever-growing scale, businesses will seek "the right size," just like cells in an organism do. Environmental and social considerations will become an integral part of successful businesses since customers, no longer only on the receiving end, will play an active role in the production process.

This "next" economy is also likely to continue operating transnationally, challenging the potential inward-looking nationalistic trends that global economic contraction might trigger. For, while production and consumption will be increasingly localized, exchange will happen across the nodes of the network with scant regard for political borders. This effect will be particularly strong in South America, Europe, Africa, the Middle East, and East Asia, where common languages and culture, as well as similar ecological conditions, favor cross-border interaction.[9]

How to Get There? A Theory of Change

The key to change lies in shifting institutional frameworks. By modifying rewards, incentives, and sanctions in line with a different approach to prosperity, we will empower innovative businesses and social actors to champion the new economy.

Gross domestic product (GDP) is not simply an economic metric, but a performance assessment tool for society that goes well beyond its superficial objective of summarizing attainments. (The political and policy implications of GDP are discussed at length in two of my previous books.[10]) From the perspective of institutional economics, GDP is an institution in its own right, controlling behaviors and decisions to ensure compliance by establishing the overarching framework for policymaking. It follows that to go "beyond GDP," redirecting its institutional leverage by introducing new performance assessment tools, is likely to trigger a cascade effect throughout society.

For instance, an institutionalized system of accounting that emphasized the full social and environmental costs of highly centralized, polluting, and wasteful production would reveal that many large corporations are commandeering wealth from society rather than adding value, thus reducing their acceptability and political influence. Such a system would also highlight the economic contributions and external benefits of production forms that GDP either downplays or ignores. If unpaid household activity and the social benefits of small, distributed businesses are fully accounted for, unconventional economic actors will gain a much stronger voice in society. Civil society will also benefit: its activities will no longer be perceived as marginal (implicit in such definitions as "nonprofit" and "third sector"), but rather as key drivers of well-being.

In the same way, looking beyond GDP in economic performance can disrupt the balance of opposing forces in a number of key sociopolitical disputes. Opponents of fossil fuel industries and others fighting climate change will find their moral and ethical arguments underpinned by solid economic indicators, as will groups mobilized against austerity policies or such international trade agreements as the Transatlantic Trade and Investment Partnership (TTIP) and the Trans-Pacific Partnership (TPP). Current arguments for unfettered free trade rest almost entirely on GDP measurements that promote volume over quality in economic activity and ignore international trade's negative environmental and social externalities. Further, austerity policies currently dividing Europe and other world regions enforce punitive debt-to-GDP ratios that prevent social investment. A new approach to measuring economic performance will inevitably turn the tables of influence on all these fronts.

Beneficiaries of a shift beyond GDP include families, communities, cooperatives, informal and small businesses, organic farmers, fair trade networks, and many similar groups. Even high-tech companies, and especially online service providers from Google to Facebook, have much to gain. From a GDP perspective, these companies' only value derives from selling advertising space, while their overall societal impact in terms of connectivity, social networking, and information sharing has no economic value in GDP terms because it is provided free of charge or at a marginal cost close to zero. This means that the contribution to economic dynamism and well-being of information-sharing technologies, some of which provide public goods from free phone calls to global maps to library services, is grossly underestimated by the vertical GDP model.

The "beyond GDP" debate is now high on the agenda. Many international agencies, including the United Nations (UN), the OECD, the World Bank, and the European Union, are actively engaged, as are many national governments. Moreover, the UN 2015 Sustainable Development Goals, albeit with somewhat contradictory objectives, provide at least an entry point for global institutional change. As more social actors become aware of how a move beyond GDP can further their causes, chances are that grassroots social pressure will also grow, connecting bottom-up movements for change with top-down political reform. The pace is quickening, and radical change within the next decade can be anticipated if pressure is maintained.

Ideally, GDP should be replaced by a "dashboard" of indicators that integrate the key dimensions of human and ecological well-being. This integration would need to be done carefully, combining monetary measurements with non-monetary ones. For starters, the economy should be measured in terms of genuine progress, which will require introducing monetary units for dimensions that do not involve formal transactions, such as natural and social capital. This change would make it clear that both ecosystems and household contributions are valuable for economic success. At the same time, the economy's operating boundaries should be determined by non-monetary measurements of social and environmental well-being, indicating the ecological ceiling and the social floor that cannot be breached without endangering well-being. Not allowing econometric calculations to simply offset losses in one field with gains in another (what economists call the "perfect substitutability" of different types of capital) fully respects the strong version of sustainability. In this accounting system, continuous improvements in well-being come without jeopardizing social and ecological conditions.

Economics, Politics, and Society in the Well-Being Economy

In a well-being economy, production and asset boundaries differ greatly from those imposed by the GDP framework. While the latter recognizes only assets and productive capacity that are under the institutional control of a proprietor, the well-being economy takes a holistic approach, taking account of economic activity's positive and negative external impacts. It also values "goods" (such as those related to the biosphere) that, while not owned by anyone in particular, significantly contribute to human and environmental well-being.

While proprietorship will continue to have its place, the roles of public, collective, and shared ownership will grow significantly with the recognition of the centrality of the nurturing of common resources to human well-being. By introducing genuine progress indicators, as well as their corporate applications, both in terms of natural capital accounting and environmental profit and loss metrics (which report corporate activities' ecological impacts in monetary terms), certain economic activities that enjoy respect and support in the GDP economy will be revealed as unprofitable. Think here of fossil fuel companies whose negative impact on society and the environment largely exceeds the profits shown in their balance sheets, as recently revealed by studies conducted in partnership with the United Nations Environment Programme.[11] Against this backdrop, it is not surprising that polluting industries have traditionally opposed any reform in economic accounting methods, challenging the deduction of environmental losses from GDP back in the 1990s, when the US government proposed a reform.[12]

As using new measurements reconfigures rewards and sanctions, some business models will have to change to stay profitable and socially acceptable, while those with the most negative effects will need to be phased out. Limited liability—a foundation of the GDP economy and a powerful instrument in the creation of giant unaccountable corporations that seek economies of scale without reference to social or environmental consequences—will have to be reconsidered in light of the new parameters of well-being. In the future, limited liability status may be granted only to companies supporting improvements in well-being while complying fully with social and environmental responsibilities. Patterns of ownership will change accordingly, with social enterprises and hybrid organizations that connect for-profit with nonprofit activities becoming more common as well-being is incorporated into economic accounting and social capital becomes a clear driver of economic prosperity. This momentum will build on current regulatory innovations, such as the introduction of L3Cs (low-profit limited-liability companies), which have become increasingly common in the USA. These organizations draw on foundation and nonprofit funding to operate as socially oriented businesses—well-being organizations blurring the boundaries between nonprofit and for-profit.

With the distinction between entrepreneurial profit and well-being blurred, the parallel difference between producer and consumer (and the transactional, profit-driven activities that separate them) will begin to fade. The emergence of the new "prosumer" will change the very meaning of work, demonstrating how human beings can be productive in ways that transcend the traditional framework of paid employment. According to the Inclusive Wealth Index—a "beyond GDP" tool developed by the UN—the real wealth driving development across the world is not produced capital, but human and natural capital.[13] Investing in people and nature is what promises the best returns in a well-being economy.

To reflect this reality, the new economy will embrace and value the whole range of an individual's activities—as teacher, caregiver, parent, maker, community leader, and many other roles carrying both monetary and social rewards (well beyond the reductive category of "jobs"). The importance of socially useful leisure activities, particularly in relation to maintaining physical and mental health, will be fully acknowledged, while women, on whose unpaid and undervalued contribution to personal and social well-being the GDP economy has been free riding for so long, will emerge as the true champions of well-being–based development.

With households equally integrated as firms in economic performance accounting, families will play a central role in the new economy. Family time will be perceived as adding to both society's public good and economic dynamism. Moreover, the blurring of professional and leisure activities could liberate both women and men from their traditional social roles. The household will become a locus of collaboration rather than segregation. It will also become a focus for activity within local economic communities for whom the arbitrary divisions between state, market, and civil society will be increasingly irrelevant. State institutions will continue to have a role in planning and legislation, but families, communities, and small businesses will become the real drivers of development. Their political power will grow accordingly.

With the emergence of a new economy based on the prosperity generated by collaborative "horizontal" entrepreneurial initiatives, a new well-being politics will develop to promote sharing and cooperation in political processes. Breaking with the production and consumption cycle, individuals will have more time to devote to well-being enhancing (and therefore economically valuable) activities. Representative forms of participation, such as traditional party politics, may change profoundly, giving way to local governance structures based on direct participation, which integrate seamlessly with the new socially responsible economic frameworks. Over time, the nation-state's primacy will erode. As powers are increasingly devolved to the local level, cities may pioneer the transition to well-being economics. More broadly, the established economic and political distinctions between "capitalists" and "working class," "proprietary" and "public," as well as "market" and "public sphere" will dissolve as the activities of the new economy increasingly straddle these traditional fault lines.

This new approach may ultimately lead to a profound reorganization of our money system. Although monetary theory generally describes money as a unit of account, a currency, and a store of value, money is primarily a tool of social organization. Money coordinates economic activity, making transactional outcomes predictable, especially in societies with limited interpersonal trust and reciprocity. Money systems, however, are not neutral, and invariably favor some forms of production and consumption over others. Today's dominant system, like the economy it serves, is highly centralized and narrowly controlled. It gives enormous power to private commercial and investment banks, devolving to them control over the money supply through the issuance of debt, leaving ordinary citizens on the receiving end of monetary governance.

In a well-being economy, the money system will need to follow the same distributed model of governance as the economy itself to provide appropriate levels of local, national, and international economic stimulus and control. Local currencies would underpin regional prosperity and economic resilience, straddling arbitrary national borders to reflect economic and social networks. A national network of currencies could replace the national currency so communities could trade with each other. In Germany, for instance, a network of local currencies called Regiogeld (regional money) connects over 70 nonprofit local currency projects, emitting the equivalent of 800,000 euros in value. Alternatively, a national currency could continue alongside local currencies. Globally, a complementary system of crypto-currencies would facilitate the worldwide interchange of ideas and knowledge (the so-called "light economy").

In theory, the GDP economy can operate only within the boundaries of social acceptance and planetary resource capacity. As an extractive system, according no value to unexploited resources and making no judgment about the qualitative value of production and consumption, its growth must ultimately conflict with natural and social equilibria. In practice, these boundaries have not been respected, creating the rampant inequality, social dislocation, and environmental destruction that presently beset our world.

In contrast to this destructive path, the well-being economy model is designed to strengthen social and natural capital while generating human development. A "virtuous circle" is created whereby value, measured in terms of well-being, feeds the improvements in the human and natural capital upon which the value creation depends. The negative environmental impacts will be greatly reduced as the "circular economy" model of resource recycling and systems for upcycling are integrated into mainstream business models. The services that the GDP model considers to be provided free of charge by nature (so-called "ecosystem services," including a myriad of fundamental "economic" functions ranging from rainfall to pollination, carbon sequestration, and irradiation that are essential to any form of production) will become fully valued components of society's infrastructure, supported by new horizontal structures of governance that connect people more closely to the natural ecosystems in which they live and work. Economic "growth" in this model comes not from exploiting natural and human resources, but from improving the quality and effectiveness of human-to-human and human-to-ecosystem interactions, supported by appropriate enabling technologies.

Conclusion: Can This Really Happen?

The convergence of transformative technological innovation with a systemic crisis—as evidenced by global warming, mass migrations, and rising inequality—demands and creates the conditions for a profound restructuring of the economic system at the global, national, and local levels. The key to unlocking this process lies in the framework of measurement by which the economy is controlled. Today's GDP-based framework is increasingly questioned by experts and citizens, by international institutions, and by national political leaders. The currents of change are beginning to flow and, as social, political, and economic pressures build, the opportunity is emerging for convergence on a new economic paradigm: the well-being economy.

Pockets of this future system are already well embedded. Local currencies have been growing across the globe since the 2008 financial crisis, connecting through networks and involving hundreds of thousands of users. Technologies are breaking down industrial monopolies at an accelerating rate, especially across the Internet, where such nonprofit initiatives as Wikipedia and Mozilla have outcompeted traditional centralized forms of production. For-profit and nonprofit "sharing economy" ventures are entering the mainstream, as are business models inspired by the concepts of the circular economy and upcycling. As noted by such technology commentators as Jeremy Rifkin and Chris Anderson, this technological revolution is moving from software to hardware, with production value chains being "reshored," shortened, and localized while maintaining high efficiency levels and low costs.[14]

Natural capital accounting, environmental profit and loss, and ecosystem services valuations are being promoted by the UN (through projects like the Economics of Ecosystems and Biodiversity), the World Bank (through such initiatives as Wealth Accounting and Valuation of Ecosystem Services), the OECD (through its Better Life Index), and many third-sector institutions. Well-being indicators are being integrated in the statistical systems of both regional institutions and national governments, particularly in view of the proceedings of a 2009 commission chaired by Nobel laureates Joseph Stiglitz and Amartya Sen and by French economist Jean-Paul Fitoussi.

Centralized forms of business are increasingly under attack—not only because of their high social and environmental costs but also because their business model pits productivity against employment, leading inevitably to joblessness in an era of low economic growth. Decentralized systems for producing and consuming renewable energy through solar, wind, and geothermal technology are available to millions of users, often also through such grassroots action plans as the so-called "transition initiatives" in Europe and North America and the "smart villages" in the developing world. The very notion of a corporation may soon be altered as regulatory systems, accounting methods, and new technologies converge and open up the possibility for massively diffusing a model that University of Michigan's Gerald Davis calls "locavorism."[15] In Davis' words:

> Locavorism has taken hold in many places, as an indigenous-but-networked movement...Technologies for "locavore power production" from solar, wind, and other sources are also likely to prompt the creation of community-based power grids...Legal forms that serve as alternatives to the corporation have experienced a swell of innovations and global competition. Several states have adopted Benefit Corporation enabling legislation that allows corporations to be chartered with explicit social benefit goals, giving safe harbor to skirt the perceived requirement to serve primarily shareholder interests, while increasing the standards for providing other social goods.[16]

The well-being economy is a vision that unites all these and many other streams of governance innovation into a coherent narrative, placing fundamental change within our reach.

Notes

1 I would like to thank my colleague Martin Whitlock for his comments and precious editorial assistance.
2 Robert Repetto et al., *Wasting Assets: Natural Resources in the National Income Accounts* (Washington, DC: World Resources Institute, 1989), V.
3 Organisation for Economic Co-operation and Development (OECD), *Divided We Stand: Why Inequality Keeps Rising* (Paris: Organisation for Economic Co-operation and Development, 2011); Organisation for Economic Co-operation and Development, *Growing Unequal? Income Distribution and Poverty in OECD Countries* (Paris: Organisation for Economic Co-operation and Development, 2008).
4 Thomas Piketty, *Capital in the 21st Century* (Cambridge, MA: Harvard University Press, 2014).
5 International Energy Agency (IEA), *World Energy Outlook 2013: Executive Summary* (Vienna: International Energy Agency, 2013), 4.
6 International Energy Agency (IEA), *World Energy Outlook 2014: Executive Summary* (Vienna: International Energy Agency, 2014), 3.
7 International Energy Agency, *World Energy Outlook 2014*, 3.
8 International Energy Agency, *World Energy Outlook 2014*, 2.
9 Lorenzo Fioramonti, "A Post-GDP World? Rethinking International Politics in the 21st Century," *Global Policy* (2015), doi: 10.1111/1758-5899.12269.
10 Lorenzo Fioramonti, *How Numbers Rule the World: The Use and Abuse of Statistics in Global Politics* (London: Zed Books, 2014); Lorenzo Fioramonti, *Gross*

Domestic Problem: The Politics behind the World's Most Powerful Number (London: Zed Books, 2013).

11 Trucost, *Natural Capital at Risk: The Top 100 Externalities of Business* (London: Trucost and TEEB, 2013).

12 Fioramonti, *Gross Domestic Problem*.

13 United Nations University International Human Dimensions-Programme (UNU–IHDP) and United Nations Environment Programme (UNEP), *Inclusive Wealth Report 2014: Measuring Progress toward Sustainability* (Cambridge: Cambridge University Press, 2014).

14 Jeremy Rifkin, *The Zero Marginal Cost Society: The Internet of Things, the Collaborative Commons, and the Eclipse of Capitalism* (New York: St. Martin's Press, 2014); Chris Anderson, *Makers: The New Industrial Revolution* (New York: Crown Publishing Group, 2012).

15 Gerald Davis, "After the Corporation," *Politics & Society* 1, 2 (2013): 283–308.

16 Davis, "After the Corporation," 300.

Chapter 11

Toward Democratic Eco-socialism as the Next World System

A Vision for the Future

Hans A. Baer

This essay is guided by two questions: How do we live in harmony with each other on a fragile planet of limited and unevenly distributed resources? And how do we live in harmony with nature, particularly as humanity lurches into an era of potentially catastrophic climate change that is largely a by-product of the capitalist world system? Social systems—whether local, regional, or global—do not last forever.

Capitalism, as a globalizing political economic system committed to profit-making and continual economic growth, has created a treadmill of production and consumption that depends heavily on fossil fuels use, which drives climate change. While capitalism has produced numerous impressive but very unevenly distributed technological innovations, some beneficial and others destructive, it is a system fraught with contradictions, including: growing social disparities within most nation-states, authoritarian and militarist practices, depletion of natural resources, environmental degradation, climatic changes, species extinction, and population growth. Even more than in capitalism's earlier stages, transnational corporations and such associated bodies as the World Bank, the International Monetary Fund, and the World Trade Organization to varying extents make or break governments and politicians around the world. Although capitalism has been around for about 500 years, it has become increasingly clear that it must be replaced by a "next system" or an alternative world system oriented to social parity and justice, democratic processes, and environmental sustainability.

Reconceptualizing Socialism

Numerous observers see the collapse of Communist regimes in the former Soviet Union and Eastern Europe as evidence that capitalism constitutes the end of history and that socialism was a bankrupt experiment that led to totalitarianism, forced collectivization, gulags, ruthless political purges, and inefficient centralized planned economies. But the efforts of Lenin, Trotsky, and other Bolsheviks to germinate a process that they hoped would result in socialism occurred under extremely adverse conditions, including poverty and constant external threat. Although the Bolsheviks, particularly under Stalin's dictatorship, did transform the Soviet Union into an industrial powerhouse by the 1930s, such external forces as World War II and the Cold War combined with such internal forces as a centralized command economy and a one-party political system to prevent socialist democracy from developing.

With some modifications, the model of bureaucratic centralism was adopted by various other post-revolutionary societies after World War II, starting with China in 1949. The contradictory nature of Leninist regimes imploded first in Eastern Europe in 1989, highlighted by the fall of the Berlin Wall, and in the Soviet Union in 1991. In China, Communist leaders embraced capitalist structures as a means of rapid development to the point that, some scholars argue, that it now constitutes a state capitalist society, entailing tremendous social inequalities and environmental devastation.

The collapse of Communist regimes created a crisis for many leftists throughout the world. Many progressives had hoped that somehow these various societies would undergo changes that would transform them into democratic and ecologically sensitive socialist societies.

Democratic Socialism

Due to the shortcomings of efforts to create socialism in the 20th century, the notion of socialism has been discredited in many quarters. This seeming dead end has prompted various progressive scholars and social activists who wish to preserve such socialist ideals as collective ownership, social equality, and representative and participatory democracy to refer to their visions of a better world in such terms as *radical democracy*, *global democracy*, and *Earth democracy*. Regardless, unless progressive people come to terms with the historical discrepancies between the ideals of socialism and the realities of what passed for it, they can't reconstruct a viable global socialist system that is both regional and local, highly democratic, environmentally sustainable and equipped to ensure that all people have access to basic resources. In my view, *post-revolutionary societies* or what some term *actually-existing socialist societies* did or still display both positive and negative (even sometimes tragic and horrific) features.

Framed in whatever guise, authentic socialism remains very much a vision. Some Marxian scholars assert that democracy is an inherent component of socialism. According to Ralph Miliband in *Socialism for a Skeptical Age*, three core propositions define socialism: democracy, egalitarianism, and socialization or public ownership of a predominant part of the economy.[1] Although a socialist society would require some centralized planning and coordination, democratic socialism recognizes the need for decentralized economic, political, and social structures that would permit maximal popular participation in decision-making. Besides workplace democracy, socialist democracy would involve citizens in operating educational institutions, health facilities, housing associations, and other organizations that impact people's lives. Miliband envisions three distinct economic sectors:

- a predominantly and varied public sector
- a sizable cooperative sector
- a sizeable private sector consisting primarily of small and medium companies providing goods, services, and amenities[2]

Complementing Miliband's scheme, Tariq Ali agues in *The Idea of Communism* that twenty-first century socialism should include political pluralism, freedom of speech, access to the media, the right to form trade unions, and cultural liberty.[3]

Eco-socialism

With such notable exceptions as Herbert Marcuse, Erich Fromm, E.P. Thompson, and Andre Gorz, Marxists have paid scant attention to environmental factors. But over the past three decades or so, some leftists have awakened to environmental travesties in developed and developing capitalist societies and in post-revolutionary societies. Indeed, John Bellamy Foster argues in *Marx's Ecology* that Karl Marx himself recognized that capitalism's *metabolic rift* with nature.[4]

Eco-socialism seeks to come to grips with capitalism's inherent growth paradigm, including in post-revolutionary societies.[5] In China, eco-socialism has made some headway among Marxist scholars. Ariel Salleh, an Australian sociologist, has been a long-time proponent of socialist eco-feminism and Indian eco-feminist. Vandana Shiva in *Earth Democracy* asserts that all beings, human and nonhuman, have a natural right to sustenance and that a just society is based on a living commons and economic democracy.[6]

Democratic Eco-socialism

In the concept of *democratic eco-socialism*, earlier concepts of democratic socialism and eco-socialism merge. The imperative for progressives is to reinvent socialism by recognizing that we live on a planet with limited resources that must be equitably distributed to provide everyone now and in the future with enough, but not too much. As delineated in *Medical Anthropology and the World*, a textbook that I co-authored with Merrill Singer and Ida Susser, democratic eco-socialism entails:

- An economy oriented to meeting basic social needs—namely, adequate food, clothing, shelter, education, health, and dignified work
- A high degree of social equality
- Public ownership of the means of production
- Representative and participatory democracy
- Environmental sustainability[7]

Democratic eco-socialism rejects a statist, growth-oriented, productivist ethic. The vision closely resembles what world systems theorists Terry Boswell and Christopher Chase-Dunn in *The Spiral of Capitalism and Socialism* term *global democracy*, which entails these components:

- An increasing movement toward public ownership of productive forces at local, regional, national, and international levels
- An economy oriented toward meeting social needs, such as basic food, clothing, shelter, and health care, and environmental sustainability rather than profit-making
- The eradication of health and social disparities and the redistribution of human resources between developed and developing societies and within societies
- The curtailment of population growth that would largely follow once the previously mentioned conditions were achieved
- The conservation of finite resources and the development of renewable energy resources
- The re-design of settlement and transport systems to reduce energy demands and greenhouse gas emissions
- The reduction of wastes through recycling and transcending the reigning culture of consumption[8]

Democratic eco-socialism constitutes what sociologist Erik Olin Wright calls a real utopia, one that is achievable but only through much theorizing and social experimentation.[9] As today's capitalist world system continues to self-destruct, democratic eco-socialism seeks to provide a vision to mobilize people around the world to prevent ongoing human socioeconomic and environmental destruction.

While Stalin's highly authoritarian and draconian social system made a mockery of Marxian socialism, other experiments are closer to the mark. In keeping with Trotsky's notion of the "permanent revolution," the creation of socialism requires a global process, the beginnings of which we may be seeing rekindled in the Bolivarian Revolution in Latin America (albeit an experiment with numerous contradictions) and the emergence of new left parties in Europe, particularly Syriza in Greece in 2015 and Die Linkeu in the German Bundestag. As global capitalism finds itself in deepening economic and ecological crises, democratic eco-socialism provides a radical vision for mobilizing people around the world to struggle for the next system.

Anti-systemic movements are sure to be a permanent feature of the world's political landscape so long as capitalism remains a hegemonic political-economic system. Various anti-systemic movements, particularly the labor, ethnic and indigenous rights, women's, anti-corporate globalization, peace, environmental, and climate movements are a crucial component of moving humanity to an alternative world system. But there are no guarantees, especially given the disparate nature of these movements.

Transitional System-Challenging Reforms

Reforms, even well-intentioned ones, may prolong capitalism's life. Given this reality, Andre Gorz in *Socialism and Revolution* differentiates between "reformist reforms" and "non-reformist reforms."[10] The first designates the conscious implementation of minor material improvements that don't alter the existing social system's basic structure. Between the poles of reformist reform and complete structural transformation, Gorz identifies a category of applied work, or non-reformist reform—efforts to permanently realign power. In practice, the distinction between these two types of reforms can be elusive. But one important difference might be whether they are initiated by the powers that be or by the working class, other subaltern groups, or anti-systemic social movements.

The transition to a democratic eco-socialist world system is not guaranteed and will require taking a tedious, even convoluted, path. Marx viewed blueprints as a distraction from political tasks that needed to be undertaken in the present moment, and pressing issues are indeed paramount. But history counsels that there always will be immediate struggles that must be addressed. Often, people asking what a transition to a democratic eco-socialist world system would take are seeking basic guidelines on how to do more than merely bumble along. Here are some suggestions:

- Creating new progressive, anti-capitalist parties designed to capture the state
- Implementing at production sites greenhouse gas emissions taxes that include measures to protect low-income people
- Increasing public ownership, socialization, or nationalization in various means of production
- Expanding social equality within and among nation-states and achieving a sustainable global population
- Building workers' democracy

- Creating meaningful work and shortening the work week
- Achieving a net-zero-growth economy
- Adopting energy efficiency, renewable energy sources, and green jobs
- Expanding public transportation and greatly curbing reliance on private motor vehicles and air travel
- Developing sustainable food production and forestry
- Resisting the culture of consumption, opting instead for sustainable and meaningful consumption
- Introducing sustainable trade
- Building sustainable settlement patterns and local communities

These transitional steps constitute loose guidelines for shifting human societies or countries toward democratic eco-socialism and a safe climate. But meeting both goals will entail a global effort, including the creation of a progressive global climate-governance regime. To work, the transitional reforms suggested here will have to be adapted by many countries, both developed and developing, around the world.

New Left Parties Designed to Capture the State

The shift to a democratic eco-socialist world will require a revolution that will have to be played out in different ways by different nations. Obviously, the capitalist class and its political allies will resist such a revolution. The larger question is whether a democratic eco-socialist-oriented revolution can be achieved largely through peaceful measures or whether it will entail violence or perhaps both, depending on the country. There is no easy answer to this question. Nevertheless, while Karl Marx and Friedrich Engels envisaged an armed overthrow of capitalism in some situations, they also saw reforms within the bowels of capitalist societies as vehicles for peacefully transiting from capitalism to socialism.

Ultimately, achieving most of the 13 transitional reforms delineated above may require that new left parties or socialist-oriented parties come to power and in a sense "capture the state" so we have the political resolve needed guarantee their implementation. For example, nationalizing the means of production would be difficult without a leftist political party in power. Until the election of Syriza in Greece in 2015, the possibility of new left parties coming to power appeared remote. Even with victory, as events have already revealed, the Syriza government must struggle to meet various demands as a member of the European Union. But given the gravity of both the global economic and ecological crisis, including climate change, political tipping points—like the tipping points climate scientists say have set off irreversible climatic events—shouldn't be ruled out.

Other prominent examples of new left parties are Left Front in France, Left Unity in the UK, and Podemos in Spain. In Australia, a new left party could comprise disaffected Australian Labor Party-types, many Greens, members of various socialist groups, and independent socialists and anarchists. At some critical point, new left parties could theoretically merge into a global left party, a notion found mostly in such science fiction as W. Warren Wagar's *A Short History of the Future*.[11]

Emissions Taxes

An emissions tax can serve as a progressive climate change mitigation strategy. Humanity must figure out ways to reduce greenhouse gas emissions quickly to keep the planet in a relatively safe state. Much ink has been spilled on how to reduce greenhouse gas emissions, including weighing the pros and cons of emissions taxes and trading schemes. Unfortunately, current trading schemes, including those in the U.S., the Kyoto Protocol, and the E.U., essentially grant corporations and developed countries property rights to emit greenhouse gas emissions. The carbon permit prices under the E.U. Emissions Trading System have fluctuated wildly, from a high of 30 euros in April 2006 to three cents at the end of 2007, to 30 euros during 2008, then down to 6.04 euros in April 2012, and up to 9.80 euros in August 2012, and, fortunately, up to 21.55 euros in March 2019.

A carefully crafted emissions tax could serve as a transitional reform. Retired NASA climate scientist James Hansen has called for a steep carbon tax at the production site to quickly reduce greenhouse gas emissions. Ultimately, the record on the few emissions tax schemes so far has been modest or mixed in terms of curtailing emissions or promoting renewable energy use. Emissions taxes are, at best, only a short-term solution, and they might not be necessary if energy production and mining were universally publicly owned. But governments would have to agree not to prop up corporate endeavors but instead to seek social parity and environmental sustainability.

Public Ownership of the Means of Production

In an era of increasing privatization of social and health services, and even military activities and prisons, raising the specter of public ownership, nationalization, or socialization of the means of production is taboo in conventional economic and political circles. Privatization is often justified as efficient economically. Yet, many publicly owned enterprises do operate relatively efficiently. Public ownership options include state ownership, worker-owned enterprises, and cooperatives.

Common misunderstandings aside, public ownership or nationalization of the means of production does not itself constitute socialism. After World War II, Britain nationalized heavy industry that had been in decline for over 50 years, but kept previous owners on in managerial positions. Historically, public ownership of various productive forces in Australia was extensive, including utilities, banks, manufacturing operations, communication networks, airlines such as Qantas Airlines, and transportation systems.

In *The Rise of the Green Left*, Derek Wall maintains that eco-socialism is founded on the principle of common property rights.[12] With that principle in mind, we need to guard against the increasing privatization of water resources. Supposedly through public-private partnerships, a small number of multinational corporations assert that they are not buying or selling water per se, simply managing its delivery. The drive in many countries to privatize electricity production, communications, health care, and an array of other services also needs to be resisted.

Workers' Democracy

Workers' economic or participatory democracy would constitute an integral component in a shift toward democratic eco-socialism. Democratic planning needs to be built into the production process, determining which goods are needed and whether they are environmentally sustainable, for instance. Michael Albert and Robin Hahnel in *The Political Economy of Participatory Economics* delineate a model of participatory economics, *Parecon*, that would entail a network of workplace and consumer-based councils.[13] Parecon, compatible with the notion of democratic socialism, seeks solidarity, diversity, equity, and self-management. A revised iteration of Parecon also entails environmental protection and restoration.

As for worker compensation, Frank Stilwell in *Changing Track* argues that a 3:1 ratio of the highest to lowest incomes would be a tolerable standard for a socialist society.[14] Taxation will be needed as long as we still have wealthy corporations and individuals collecting more than their fair share, but meanwhile emphasizing compensations for work other than material rewards (whether intellectual and even physical stimulation, or the sense that one has contributed to the greater good) is a good idea.

Socialism is committed to the notion of unalienated, fulfilling, or meaningful work. Satisfying work contributes to positive self-esteem and a sense that one is contributing to society while unemployment for some can be psychologically devastating. Even for people over the traditional retirement age, work or employment can be fulfilling and meaningful. A shorter work week would permit everyone to be employed and thus eliminate the "industrial reserve army" that is an inherent feature of capitalist economies. What Juliet Schor describes in *The Overworked American* applies to Australian culture, its stereotype as laid back aside.[15]

It's hard to say what the optimal work week would be. To some degree, it would vary by individual. Marx characterized humans as *Homo Faber* or "Man the worker," but he was thinking of unalienated labor, where work and play are intricately interwoven, as they often are in foraging societies. In *The German Ideology*, Marx and Engels envisioned a society in which one would "hunt in the morning, fish in the afternoon, rear cattle in the evening, criticize after dinner."[16] Working life would never totally end as long as a person had the mental and physical capacity and the desire to engage in it. Thus, people should be given the option of phasing into "retirement" rather than simply going from full-time employment to full-time retirement.

A Steady-State or Net-Zero-Growth Economy

A growing number of neo-Marxian scholars as well as non-Marxian scholars have been questioning the economic growth paradigm. For too long, many socialists have, like mainstream economists and business people, bought into the growth paradigm, remaining oblivious to its ecological impacts. A serious redistribution of the world's resources would ensure an adequate living standard for everyone on the planet, but this shift would require serious discussion of how much is enough and, with the elimination of poverty, the recognition that the global population would begin to dwindle, easing strain on the ecosystem.

Obviously, some large sectors of developed societies and smaller sectors of developing societies need to shrink while the abjectly poor of developing societies and developed countries—such as homeless people or indigenous peoples living on reservations in North America and Australia—need greater access to nutritious food, decent housing and sanitation, health care, and education, which requires some sort of development. Ultimately, issues of growth, de-growth, development, and underdevelopment are intricately interwoven with the redistribution of resources. Partly following Herman Daly and John B. Cobb, Jr. in *For the Common Good*, I distinguish between growth and development.[17] Growth entails using ever more resources on the capitalist treadmill of production and consumption. Development entails providing all people with adequate food, clothing, shelter, health care, education, and recreation.

Beyond a certain point, more food, clothing, and shelter are superfluous and environmentally unsustainable. How much health care is necessary would depend upon each individual's physical and mental states, which are interwoven and highly variable. Health can be defined as access to and control over the basic material and nonmaterial resources that sustain and promote life at a high level of individual and group satisfaction. In a socialist society or a society seeking to construct socialism, preventive health care would be emphasized more than curative health care.

Energy Efficiency, Renewable Energy Sources, and Green Jobs

Given the demands of global capitalism to continually expand, under a business-as-usual scenario humanity will need ever more energy to fuel the treadmill of production, consumption, and population growth. In a steady-state economy, energy requirements could theoretically level out or even eventually decline. Although energy efficiency is often hailed as a mechanism for transitioning to a green-energy economy, due to the Jevons Paradox or the "rebound effect," increased efficiency in capitalist countries is associated with *increased* economic growth and consumption. In short, efficiency gains cancel out the benefits of energy savings. Energy efficiency is still a desirable goal, this means, but environmental sustainability requires coupling it with a steady-state or zero-growth economy.

A planned centralized economy could facilitate the transition to renewable energy sources—particularly solar, wind, geothermal energy, and possibly ocean-wave energy—and mitigate climate change. Solar photovoltaic cells and panels could provide local power in such sunny remote areas as sub-Saharan Africa or Australia, while large offshore wind farms could provide energy to the Baltic Sea nations, for instance. Geothermal energy as a renewable energy source is already being harnessed in such volcanic regions as Iceland, El Salvador, Kenya, the Philippines, and Costa Rica.

While acknowledging renewables' potential usefulness, various scholars have observed that these energy sources are no panacea for mitigating climate change. Renewable energy enthusiasts seldom ask "how much energy do we really need in the first place?" particularly in developed countries. A large-scale transition to renewable energy sources must be coupled with a decline in per capita consumption among the world's affluent while allowing the poor to draw on these new energy sources to access basic resources. Besides addressing this equity concern, a shift to renewable energy sources will require an integrated approach to grapple with technical issues, too—say, the intermittence of solar and wind energy.

More generally, eco-socialism needs to develop "socialist technology." Many of its component parts to some extent already exist in capitalist societies but haven't attracted capital because they are less profitable than conventional energy development. We have the technology to make products last instead of break down fairly quickly on the built-in path to obsolescence. Bicycles, smaller cars, trains, trams, and buses—but not large cars—could all be part of a socialist or an appropriate technology.

A shift to democratic eco-socialism will also entail creating *green jobs* that are environmentally sustainable and cater to people's social, educational, recreational, and health care needs. Such job creation must be accompanied by a "just transition," which means retraining displaced workers from obsolescent and environmentally destructive industries and enterprises to assume jobs in environmentally sustainable ones.

Sustainable Public Transportation and Travel

In *Ecotopia*, Ernest Callenbach describes a fictional place in northern California, Oregon, and Washington State that has transcended cars.[18]

Here and now, too, the negative environmental effects of private motor vehicles underscore the dire need for sustainable public transportation. A new urbanism that seeks to make cities more livable and environmentally sustainable has emerged around the world and begun to permeate urban planning. Singapore, Hong Kong, Zurich, Copenhagen, Freiburg, Vancouver, Toronto, Boston, and others are encouraging residents to rely more on public transportation, including trains, trams, and buses. A global movement to make inner cities car-free is also afoot. Besides limited car use, sustainable transportation would mean smaller and more energy-efficient cars, a ban on four-wheel-drive or sport utility vehicles except in rugged areas or under special circumstances, and drastically limited air travel.

Switching to, say, intercity trains, suburban trains, trams, or light-rail systems would diminish greenhouse gas emissions, as would reinstating more comprehensive passenger rail in North America and Australia. But none of these modes of transportation is a panacea, and which is the best in urban areas depends on the situation, as does the related issue of how to connect small towns and rural areas with cities.

In capitalist societies, "time is money," and this dictates rapid movement between places. Conversely, in a more leisurely paced eco-socialist world, people might find slower train travel—although faster than it is today in most of North America and Australia—a good excuse to read, chat with fellow passengers, enjoy the passing countryside, reflect, and even sleep. Airships, which travel at speeds of 150 to 200 kilometers per hour, afford another slower travel option.

Other transportation alternatives need a hearing too. Vacations or holidays would entail trips much closer to home, by train or bus, rather than to far-off places by plane or car. Cheap package holidays by airplane could become a thing of the past. Transoceanic ships fitted with kites or solid sails could harness wind power. Teleconferencing could make much air travel undertaken for business or conferences unnecessary.

Sustainable Food Production and Forestry

Shifting food production away from heavy reliance on meat, particularly livestock, to organic farming, vegetarianism, and even veganism would be more environmentally sustainable and would mitigate climate change and health problems. So would shifting toward agro-ecology, which relies on farmers' extensive knowledge of local ecosystems and seeks to transcend dependence on chemical, oil-based agriculture. Crops such as maize, wheat, sorghum, millet, and vegetables can be grown in forested areas that provide shade, improve water availability, prevent soil erosion, and add nitrogen to soils. More generally, most small-scale organic farming is more fuel-efficient than industrial agriculture, which relies heavily on petroleum, chemical fertilizers, and pesticides, and is also more water-efficient.

Agro-forestry blends trees and shrubs with perennial crops and the production of cattle, poultry, and other animals. The Coalition for Rainforest Nations campaigns for cash incentives for developing countries to conserve their forests. Permaculture integrates concepts from organic farming, sustainable forestry, no-till management, and the village design techniques of Indigenous peoples.

Urban farming needs to be expanded too, especially in the developing world. Laws prohibiting farming in cities must go. Much food can be raised on rooftops, perhaps coupled with strategic placement of solar panels.

Despite horror stories about the enforced collectivization of agriculture in the Soviet Union during the Stalinist era, Saral Sarkar in *Eco-Socialism or Eco-Capitalism?* asserts that collective agriculture needs to be revisited. Based this time around on decentralized planning and respect for regional variation within a country,[19] it would realize numerous economies of scale.

Replacing the Culture of Consumption

Obviously, all humans need food, clothing, and shelter to survive. But capitalism converts "needs" into "wants" through nonstop advertising and these wants become sops for people alienated in the workplace and everyday social life. Fred Magdoff and John Bellamy Foster in *What Every Environmentalist Needs to Know about Capitalism* argue that a democratic and egalitarian economic system must limit consumption levels to significantly less than they generally are now for most middle-class people in developed societies.[20] Unfortunately, at least in developed societies, only niche groups have gotten the message. Even many middle-class environmentalists who see population growth as the principal ecological problem appear to want to maintain something like their present material standard of living, albeit on a planet with far fewer people. (Bringing down population growth will require eradicating poverty first.).

Jonathan Neale in *Stop Global Warming: Change the World* warns climate activists not to talk about sacrifice by ordinary people.[21] In reality, though, most people in developed societies and the more affluent sectors in developing societies will need to scale back their consumption of material goods and destination travel.

Sustainable Trade

Over the past two centuries, global production has resulted in the tremendous cross-border trade of goods and services. While free trade agreements and lower transport costs facilitate international trade, it relies heavily upon oil and shipping contributes heavily to greenhouse gas emissions. Then too, while China and other developing countries get criticized for increasing greenhouse gas emissions, an appreciable amount of total emissions comes from imports to developed countries of cheap resources and manufactured goods from developing countries. Also, international aviation and marine fuels are exempt from international taxation.

The global food system has seen a tremendous rise in "food miles"—a measurement of the distance that sustenance travels from where it is produced to where it is consumed. Vandana Shiva in *Soil Not Oil* maintains that humanity can reduce food miles by eating diverse, local, and fresh foods, rather than increasing greenhouse gas emissions through the spread of corporate industrial farming, nonlocal supplies, and processed and packaged food.[22] Relying on green shipping and on railroads and waterways would use less energy.

Sustainable Settlement Patterns and Local Communities

Modern cities have evolved largely to serve capitalism's need for manufacturing, financial, commercial, distribution, and communication centers, as well as the government bureaucracy's administrative demands. As they have grown, cities have gobbled up precious farmland and natural areas along with huge amounts of energy to operate office buildings, industries, residences, shopping centers, recreational facilities, restaurants, educational institutions, hospitals, residences, highways, parking lots, airports, and so on.

While green-cities advocates often argue that urban density can foster environmental sustainability, they downplay the complex relationship between density and economic growth. Cities' ecological and carbon footprints vary considerably by nation (developed versus developing country), neighborhood (McMansions versus slum dwellings), and transportation mode (excellent public transportation system versus a highly car-dependent one). These footprints extend far beyond city limits since such voluminous resources are produced and brought in from outside for residents.

Theoretically, cities could become much greener than they are now. During the early 20th century, various socialists and anarchists pioneered efforts, such as the Karl Marx-Hof in Red Vienna and the Bauhaus housing experiments in Germany, to make metropolises more socially and environmentally livable. Going forward, new urbanists need to work harder to be socially inclusive and counteract gentrification, which marginalizes low-income people.

The development of green cities constitutes a highly imaginative endeavor, one that will require drawing insights from architecture, building construction, urban planning, transportation development, the social sciences, and other fields. For architects, current focal points include green roofs and walls, fritted glazing, solar panels, and more efficient lighting. City and energy planners are exploring medium-density housing, easy access to public transport, walkability and minimal reliance on automobiles, and good connections to other cities. A new field, *eco-psychology*, stresses the need for people, including urban dwellers, to have contact with the natural environment. Eco-villages springing up in urban and rural parts of developed and developing societies constitute pre-figurative social experiments in developing more sustainable settlement patterns.

Another question is the optimal maximum population of a metropolis. The huge size of some municipalities almost defies the imagination. The world already has 33 megacities, metropolises with more than 10 million people: Tokyo has 37.4 million people, Delhi 28.5 million, Shanghai 25.6 million, Sao Paulo 21.7 million, Mexico City 21.6 million, and Cairo, 20 million.[23] What size is best has no easy answer since that depends on the national context and notions of acceptable population density.

Conclusion

The transitional steps delineated here constitute loose guidelines for shifting human societies or countries toward democratic eco-socialism. Not intended to be comprehensive, these ideas can be starting points as humanity enters an era of increasingly dangerous climate change accompanied by tumultuous environmental and social consequences. Together, we should all be imaging and creating a more socially just, democratic, and generally environmentally sustainable world society while protecting our shared climate.

To reiterate one last time, democratic eco-socialism rejects the capitalist treadmill of production and consumption, and its associated growth model. Instead, it recognizes that humans live on an ecologically fragile planet with limited resources that must be sustained and renewed as much as possible for future generations. For the immediate or even the foreseeable future, the notion that democratic eco-socialism may eventually be implemented in any society, developed or developing, or in numerous societies, may appear absurd. However, history tells us that social changes can occur very quickly once social, structural, and environmental conditions have reached a tipping point.

As the 21st century unfolds, our survival as a species appears to be ever more precarious. Some climate activists say that we do not have enough time to transcend global capitalism so we can create a safe climate for humanity and that climate activists have no choice but to collaborate with more supposedly progressive corporate leaders and politicians within the parameters of the current global political economy. But combatting climate change and global capitalism go hand in hand. The more enlightened corporate elites and their political allies may permit some climate change mitigation, but they will certainly not let go of global capitalism and embrace an emerging democratic eco-socialist world system. As I argue in *Global Capitalism and Climate Change*, green capitalism and today's climate regimes alone won't seriously mitigate climate change.[24] The system that created the problem isn't likely to solve it.

Most likely, things will get worse before they get better, and there is no guarantee that they will get better. Nevertheless, numerous cracks are emerging in the entrenched capitalist world system. In his Commentary No. 205 of March 15, 2007, Immanuel Wallerstein argues that in terms of the foreseeable future:

> I do not believe that our historical system is going to last much longer, for I consider it to be in a terminal structural crisis, a chaotic transition to some other system (or systems), a transition that will last twenty-five to fifty years. I therefore believe it could be possible to overcome the self-destructive patterns of global environmental change into which the world has fallen and establish alternative patterns. I emphasize however my firm assessment that the outcome of this transition is inherently uncertain and unpredictable.[25]

Presenting a precise timeline of transition from the capitalist world system to a democratic eco-socialist world system is extremely difficult, probably impossible. But stabilization of the Earth's climate system needs to occur within the next two or three decades lest large swathes of land become uninhabitable for human beings and other species.

Despite the daunting difficulties that much of humanity currently faces, progressive people must keep challenging the system in their conversations, teachings, and writings while also struggling against the current system to create new left parties, point out alternative ways of organizing the world along democratic eco-socialist principles, and listening to critical input from other progressive perspectives, including eco-anarchism, eco-feminism, and Indigenous voices. As humanity finds itself in ever more dire straits, counter-hegemonic voices will, we can only hope, be better received than they are now and will inspire ordinary people to become more politically involved in creating a much-needed new world.

Humanity is obviously at a crossroads. We perhaps have three choices. One is business as usual. Another is a shift to some variant of the green capitalism that has gained much support among people left of center. A third is an eco-socialist vision that while muted right now will become stronger as the need for more sweeping change becomes more apparent to more people.

Notes

1 Ralph Miliband, *Socialism for a Sceptical Age* (Cambridge: Polity Press, 1994), 3.
2 Miliband, *Socialism for a Sceptical Age*, 93–94.
3 Tariq Ali, *The Idea of Communism* (London: Seagull Books, 2009).

4 John B. Foster, *Marx's Ecology: Materialism and Nature* (New York: Monthly Review Press, 2000).
5 John B. Foster, *The Ecological Revolution: Making Peace with the Planet* (New York: Monthly Review Press, 2009).
6 Vandana Shiva, *Earth Democracy: Justice, Sustainability, and Peace* (Cambridge, MA: South End Press, 2005), 84.
7 Hans A. Baer, Merrill Singer, and Ida Susser, *Medical Anthropology and the World System: Critical Perspectives* (Santa Barbara, CA: Praeger, 2013), 358.
8 Terry Boswell and Christopher K. Chase-Dunn, *The Spiral of Capitalism and Socialism: Toward Global Democracy* (Boulder, CO: Lynne Rienner Publishers, 2000).
9 Erik O. Wright, *Envisioning Real Utopias* (London: Verso, 2010).
10 André Gorz, *Socialism and Revolution* (London: Allen Lane, 1975).
11 Warren Wagar, *A Short History of the Future* (Chicago: University of Chicago Press, 1989).
12 Derek Wall, *The Rise of the Green Left: Inside the Worldwide Ecosocialist Movement* (London: Pluto Press, 2010).
13 Michael Albert and Robin Hahnel, *The Political Economy of Participatory Economics* (Princeton, N.J: Princeton University Press, 1991).
14 Frank Stillwell, *Changing Track: A New Political Economic Direction for Australia* (Annandale: Pluto Press, 2000).
15 Juliet Schor, *The Overworked American: The Unexpected Decline of Leisure* (New York: Basic Books, 1991).
16 Karl Marx, Friedrich Engels, C. J. Arthur, *The German Ideology* (London: Lawrence & Wishart, 1974 (1845)).
17 Herman Daly, John B. Cobb, and Clifford W. Cobb, *For the Common Good: Redirecting the Economy toward Community, the Environment, and a Sustainable Future* (Boston, MA: Beacon Press, 1989).
18 Ernest Callenbach, *Ecotopia: The Notebooks and Reports of William Weston* (Berkeley, CA: Banyan Tree Books, 1975).
19 Saral Sarkar, *Eco-Socialism or Eco-Capitalism? A Critical Analysis of Humanity's Fundamental Choices* (London: Zed Books, 1999).
20 Fred Magdoff and John B. Foster, *What Every Environmentalist Needs to Know about Capitalism: A Citizen's Guide to Capitalism and the Environment* (New York: Monthly Review Press, 2011).
21 Jonathan Neale, *Stop Global Warming: Change the World* (London: Bookmarks, 2008).
22 Vandana Shiva, *Soil Not Oil: Environmental Justice in a Time of Climate Crisis* (Cambridge, MA: South End Press, 2008).
23 United Nations, Department of Economic and Social Affairs, Population Division, *The World's Cities in 2018—Data Booklet* (2018), 4.
24 Hans A. Baer, *Global Capitalism and Climate Change: The Need for an Alternative World System* (Lanham, MD: AltaMira Press, 2012).
25 Immanuel Wallerstein, "The Ecology and the Economy: What Is Rational?" *Review (Fernand Braudel Center)* 27, 4 (2204): 273–283.

Chapter 12

Six Theses on Saving the Planet

Richard Smith

Since the Industrial Revolution's beginning, workers, trade unionists, radicals, and socialists have fought the worst depredations of capitalist development: intensifying exploitation, increasing social polarization, persistent racism and sexism, deteriorating workplace health and safety conditions, environmental ravages, and relentless efforts to suppress democratic political gains. Now, global capitalist development has thrown up an unprecedented threat to our very survival as a species, and this threat has no possible solution within the framework of capitalism. Only overthrowing the social order and instituting a global eco-socialist democracy stands a chance of preventing global ecological collapse and perhaps even our own extinction. Our only hope is a world economy composed of communities and nations of self-governing associated producer-consumers, cooperatively managing their mostly planned, mostly publicly owned, and globally coordinated economies to serve the common good and humanity's future needs.

Racing to Extinction

In Stanley Kramer's great post-apocalyptic drama *On the Beach* (1959), young men hurtle their race cars around a course at faster and faster speeds seemingly oblivious to danger. Indeed, as one by one they crash and burn, the others just race on by determined, apparently, to commit suicide. Why? Because thermonuclear war has just obliterated the northern hemisphere, and clouds of radioactive fallout are headed south, dooming these Australians too. The government is handing out suicide pills, so if you're a race-car driver why not die doing something you enjoy instead of slowly succumbing to radiation poisoning?

To a stranger from another world, looking down on Earth today, our own situation might look similar. Despite ever more alarming reports by our top climate scientists, the Intergovernmental Panel on Climate Change (IPCC), credible international authorities, major insurers, and others, all warning that temperatures could soar by four to six degrees

Celsius by century's end if we don't immediately start cutting greenhouse gas emissions and that global ecological collapse and our civilization's end could result, we seem hell-bent on racing to collective suicide, cooking the planet, and wiping out the ecological bases of human life.

It's not that we don't know what we have to do to save ourselves. A recent 40-country poll found that large majorities support limiting greenhouse gases—69 percent in the USA, 71 percent in China.[1] And it's not that we lack the technical means to brake the race to collapse. *Mostly what we have to do is just stop doing what we're doing.* And yet:

- Instead of suppressing fossil fuel production, producers are frantically pumping oil and gas from one end of the earth to the other. Amid an oil glut, they are opening new fields and inventing new technologies to revive old fields. Coal production is still climbing, not only in China and India but even in self-styled "green" Germany.[2]

- Instead of minimizing fossil fuel consumption, consumers seem bent on maximizing it. The world auto fleet surpassed one billion in 2014, and in the USA cheap fuel has encouraged more people to drive luxury trucks and SUVs that get worse mileage than trucks in the 1950s.[3] Air travel is now the fastest growing source of global CO_2 emissions—small wonder when an ad in the New York subway reads, "Cheap Flights Make It Easy to Say, Phuket … Let's Travel." We're burning more fuels generating electricity to power the iPhones, iPads, electric cars, and the Internet of Things. As temperatures rise, we're burning still more fuel to cool off, globally consuming more fossil fuel to run air conditioners than to heat our homes.[4]

- Instead of responsibly limiting emissions, governments carry on in denial. Since the Rio Summit in 1992, every annual Conference of the Parties (COP) has ended in abject failure to adopt binding limits on CO_2 emissions. Today, we face the prospects of emissions soaring to ever higher levels and global temperatures breaking new records year after year, with 2016 registering the warmest average global temperatures ever. And yet, Paris COP21 copped out again, with soaring rhetoric and promises that are meaningless without legally binding commitments to reduce greenhouse gas emissions.

- Instead of minding nature's wealth, companies and nations everywhere are plundering the planet's last readily accessible resources to turn them all into "product."[5] We're mining the Arctic for minerals and oil, strip-mining ocean floors for fish and minerals, and leveling tropical forests to make cheap flooring and grow biofuels to power gas hogs. From New York to Shanghai to Abu Dhabi, construction companies are building airports, highways, vanity skyscrapers, ever more luxurious condos and McMansions, gilded palaces and resorts nonstop. Between 2011 and 2014, Chinese construction companies

poured 6.6 gigatons of cement, building superfluous dams, highways, and "ghost cities"—about half again as much as went into all of
America's infrastructure and cities in the 20th century.[6]

• Instead of inventing ways to minimize resource consumption,
our smartest companies work day and night to invent superfluous
"needs"—everything from drones and hover boards to virtual reality
devices, toilet seats that wash your butt, and pointless "apps" to waste
your time.[7] All in the end just unnecessarily convert more of nature
into products.

• Instead of making necessary products durable, long lasting, and recyclable, top companies like Apple set their brightest engineers, de-
signers, and marketers to devising ways to make products wear out
and become obsolete faster. We consume more, faster, more often,
and without purpose, and most of our economy is geared to produce
waste. As an American retail analyst famously wrote in 1955:

> Our enormously productive economy demands that we make
> consumption our way of life, that we convert the buying and use
> of goods into rituals, that we seek our spiritual satisfactions, our
> ego satisfactions, in consumption... We need things consumed,
> burned up, worn out, replaced, and discarded at an ever increas-
> ing pace."[8] As Giles Slade asks with Egypt's great monuments in
> mind, after we collapse, "Will America's pyramids be pyramids
> of waste?[9]

What's Going on Here?

Why are we cooking the climate, consuming the future? Why don't we
stop? The problem is rooted in our economic system's very nature. Large
corporations are destroying life on earth, but they can't change enough
to save the planet and we live under a system largely of their making, so
we all keep pouring on the gas instead of slamming on the brakes. The
only alternative—impossible as this may seem—is to replace this global
economic system and the governments of the 1 percent that prop it with
a global bottom-up economic democracy, an *eco-socialist civilization*. Six
theses explain why:

I. Capitalism Is Overwhelmingly the Main Driver of Planetary Ecological Collapse and It Can't Be Reformed Enough to Save Humans.

For the ten millennia preceding capitalism's birth, most people lived in
completely or largely self-sufficient village farm communities. Peasant
families grew their own food, built their own houses, fabricated most of

their own crude tools, made their own clothes, and made do with animal power for farm work and transportation. Productivity was low with little real change over centuries, and production was geared to direct use, not the market.

In some places, agrarian ruling classes on mostly self-sufficient estates extracted rents, but spent the excess on military arms and fortifications and on conspicuous consumption. Cities were small, markets and trade limited. Wealth consisted of manors, farms, and rents—not money in the bank.

Before capitalism's rise, consumption and global population remained low and grew slowly. Gradually, population growth and the division of land parcels among children made subsistence precarious. Over centuries, repeated cycles of slow growth increased population density and led to collapse and famine, followed by revived growth as reduced populations found abandoned lands to farm again. Surplus extraction combined with stagnant productivity and unscientific farm management sometimes brought down entire civilizations—Mesopotamia, the Mayans, and others.[10]

The transition to capitalism changed all that. From the mid-15th century, English peasants were gradually cleared off the land in enclosure movements and proletarianized. Landlords and new capitalist farmers with hired labor began specializing in single crops—wheat, wool, or flax— for sale in markets where competition governed prices. (Hell is other pig farmers!) To compete, farmers needed to seek cheaper inputs and labor, bring in new technology, crop patterns, and economies of scale, and *develop the forces of production*. This specialized production for markets has shaped economic development up until today. Indeed, the rise of capitalism was virtually synonymous with economic development.

The Tragedy of the Commodity

Greater production called forth greater demand. In England, the capitalist agricultural revolution of the 15th through 17th centuries entrained the Industrial Revolution of the next two centuries. Commercial farmers sought better tools, wool carders better machines, merchants better means of transport, and so on. In turn, capitalist competition gave rise to an economy of permanent change, ceaseless technological revolution, and systematic application of science to production.

Rising productivity and medical advances also propelled the "demographic revolution," as the human population surged from one billion in 1800 to two billion by 1927, to three billion by 1960, and so on. Capitalism replaced cycles of underproduction with periodic crises of "overproduction." Cyclically, booms culminated in crises and collapse and the destruction of capital and labor, followed by renewed growth based on cheaper labor and capital. For better and worse, capitalist development has profoundly transformed our lives. It has also savaged the planet.

2. Solutions to our ecological crisis are blindingly obvious and at hand, but so long as we live under capitalism, we can't prevent ecological collapse tomorrow without precipitating economic collapse today.

What to do? Since the 1970s, mainstream ecological economists have tried to deal with the problem of capitalist growth in one of two ways.[11] The first approach, inspired by Herman Daly's idea of a "steady state economy" and Serge Latouche's call for "degrowth," imagined that capitalism could be reconstructed so it would stop growing, or degrow, while continuing to *develop* internally.[12] The second approach, exemplified by Paul Hawken, Lester Brown, and other "sustainable development" proponents, held that capitalism could keep growing indefinitely and be rendered environmentally benign through an eco-entrepreneur-led "green industrial revolution," green subsidies, carbon taxes, penalties for polluters, etc.

Pro- or antigrowth, both approaches assume that capitalism is so malleable that corporations can be induced to subordinate profit-making to "saving the earth." But what really unites both schools of thought is the *a priori* rejection of alternatives to capitalism—whether economic planning or socialism. That is where the mainstream is wrong because there is no possible solution to our crisis within any conceivable capitalist framework.

Why "Steady State" and "Degrowth" Are Incompatible with a Viable Capitalist Economy

While we do need degrowth, the tendency toward growth would remain in any conceivable capitalist economy, "green" or otherwise.[13] Private, family-owned, or closely held companies not beholden to shareholders are exceptions, as are public utilities with guaranteed profits. But most US companies are investor-owned corporations, owned by mutual funds, investment banks, pension funds, and so on. For them, growth is an inescapable requirement.

Why? First, producers depend on the market for selling their commodities and buying raw material inputs and the means of production. Second, competition drives economic development by forcing producers to systematically cut costs, find cheaper inputs, innovate, adopt new technology, and reinvest much of their surpluses in production. Third, "grow or die" is a survival law in the marketplace. Companies face irresistible and relentless pressure from shareholders to maximize profits. CEOs have no choice but to constantly seek to grow sales and grow the market. Bigger is also safer because wealthier companies can better take advantage of economies of scale, dominate markets, and set market prices. In short, the growth imperative is virtually an iron law of successful capitalist competition. It is not "subjective," optional, or dispensable.

Why "Green Capitalism" Can't Save the World

Companies can't prioritize people and planet over profits because CEOs and corporate boards are responsible to private shareholders, not society. Corporations may embrace environmentalism so long as doing so increases profits (by, for example, recycling, reducing waste, or introducing "green" products). But saving the world requires more than recycling and installing LED light bulbs. It requires that the pursuit of profits be systematically subordinated to ecological concerns, and this corporations cannot do.[14] No corporate board can sacrifice earnings, let alone put itself out of business to save humans. As Milton Friedman wrote, "there is one and only one social responsibility of business—to use its resources and engage in activities to increase its profits."[15] Indeed, that's their one and only legal obligation.[16]

Climate scientists advise us that if we hope to contain global warming within two degrees Celsius above preindustrial levels, we must phase out fossil fuel burning by 7–10 percent per year every year from 2015 through 2050.[17] But how could we ever do this in an economy based on huge investor-owned corporations? Imagine the ExxonMobil's CEO telling his investors:

> Sorry, but to save the planet, we cannot grow profits next year and we have to cut production (and thus profits) by 7–10 percent next year and every year thereafter, for the next three and a half decades, by which time we will be basically out of business.

How long would it take retirement funds to dump that stock? Cutting fossil fuel use by 7–10 percent annually for decades would also rapidly bankrupt the auto industry, the aircraft and airlines industries, tourism, petrochemicals, agricultural chemicals and agribusiness, synthetic fibers, textiles, plastics of every sort, construction, and more. What company is going to commit economic suicide to save the planet? And, what unions would support de-growth involving massive layoffs?

And what government? When California's former governor Jerry Brown and the California Senate Democrats proposed legislation halving the state's petroleum use by 2030, the oil industry hollered bloody murder. The Western States Petroleum Association said that a 50 percent mandate would mean job losses, and increased fuel and electricity costs. Advertisements paid for by the oil industry asserted "that it could lead to fuel rationing and bans on sport utility vehicles," reported *The New York Times*.[18] Facing revolt in the State Assembly, erstwhile green Governor Brown caved.[19]

In fact, the oil companies were right. Fossil fuel consumption cuts like those Brown proposed would mean massive layoffs in affected industries, gasoline rationing, and bans on gas-hogs. Yet, if we're going to save humans, we must do just that. Capitalism affords no way around this conundrum. That's why we need to radically restructure the economy.

We all know what we have to do, and what needs doing doesn't require any big technological breakthroughs. But we can't stop or even slow down. While global warming will kill us in the long run, ending overconsumption will kill us in the short run by precipitating economic collapse, mass unemployment, and starvation. This is the ultimate fatal choice of capitalism: we have to destroy our children's tomorrow to hang on to our jobs today.

Corporations aren't necessarily evil. They're doing what they're supposed to do for the benefit of their owners. But this means that so long as the global economy is based on capitalist private and corporate property and on competitive production for the market, we're doomed to collective social suicide. No amount of tinkering with the market can apply the brake to the drive to global ecological collapse. We can't green-shop our way to sustainability because individual choice in the marketplace won't turn the tide. Only collective democratic control over the economy to make it put social and environmental needs first will, and that requires national and international economic planning to reorganize the economy and redeploy labor and resources to these ends.

3. If capitalism can't help but destroy the world, then what choice is there but to socialize most of the world's industrial economies and plan them directly for the common good?

Since capitalism's rise 300 years ago, more and more of the world has come to be run on the basis of market anarchy, on Adam Smith's maxim that every individual should just seek his/her own economic self-interest and that the "common good" would take care of itself.[20] Well, that hasn't worked out so well.

The problems of "planet management" can't be solved by individual choice in the marketplace. They require conscious rational planning, international cooperation, and collective democratic control over the economy—not market anarchy. Climate scientists tell us we need a global plan to suppress fossil fuel emissions, and we need it NOW.[21] Ocean scientists call for a global Five-Year Plan to save the oceans.[22] We need rational, comprehensive, legally binding plans to save the world's remaining forests, to protect and restore rivers, lakes, and fisheries, to save millions of imperiled species, and to conserve natural resources of all kinds.

And we need a plan to save humans. We need to make the needs of humanity, the environment, other species, and future generations our highest priorities. Private, self-interested corporations can't do that. The only way forward is with public control over planning at all levels, investment, and technological change. Planning a world economy can't be left to a few people either. This is going to require the creativity and input of a world of peoples together tackling a "to do" list that would include at least the following:

1. We would have to radically suppress fossil fuel consumption in industrialized nations across the economy from energy generation to transportation, manufacturing, agriculture, and services. Globally, on average, electricity generation and heating account for around 25 percent of greenhouse gas emissions; industry, 21 percent; transportation, 14 percent; and agriculture, forestry, and other land use (mainly deforestation), 24 percent.[23] This means we not only need to rapidly phase out fossil fuel-powered utilities and shift to renewables, but we also need to suppress manufacturing (starting with useless, disposable, and destructive products). We would have to limit construction to socially necessary essentials. We would have to replace fossil fuel-dependent industrial agriculture with organic farming, halt deforestation worldwide, and implement reforestation programs. We would have to sharply curb motor vehicle use, air travel, and other GHG-emitting services.

If technical miracles don't enable us to grow our economies without consuming more fossil fuels and other resources, then our only option is to halt economic growth in the industrialized economies. This would mean industrial closures and retrenchments across the economy.[24] Companies like ExxonMobil, General Motors, Boeing, Apple, Monsanto, United Airlines, and other producers of unsustainable and destructive products and services can hardly be expected to put themselves out of business and throw their workers on the streets. They would have to be nationalized or socialized, bought out, or expropriated so they could be decommissioned, retrenched, or repurposed. Their excessed employees could be reemployed in socially beneficial, ecologically sustainable, and perhaps more personally fulfilling work. This doubtless sounds extreme, but global heating of four to six degrees Celsius by 2100 is more extreme—and irreversible.[25] So do we save GM and ExxonMobil for a few decades or save humans? This is the sort of question we as a society need to be discussing.

2. We would have to "contract and converge" production around a globally sustainable and workable average that can provide a dignified living standard for all the world's peoples. We would have to slam the brakes on out-of-control growth in the global North. We would need to retrench or shut down unnecessary, resource-hogging, wasteful, and polluting industries. We would have to discontinue industrial agriculture, fishing, logging, and their like. We would have to close down many unnecessary services—the banking industry, Wall Street, credit card, retail, public relations, and advertising "industries" built to underwrite and promote overconsumption. We would have to abolish the military-surveillance-police state industrial complex, and all its manufacturers. We just can't keep squandering our social surplus on such waste.

At the same time, we would be obliged to redirect considerable resources to ramping up sustainable development in the global South. We in the North have a responsibility to help the South build basic infrastructure, electrification, sanitation systems, public schools, health care, and so on. We would help their citizens achieve a comfortable material standard of living without repeating all the disastrous wastes born of capitalist consumerism in the North. If the industrialized North stopped looting and thereby impoverishing it, the South could use its natural resource wealth for its own sustainable development.

For example, China's stupendously wasteful overproduction and overconstruction since the 1990s has been heavily dependent on importing vast quantities of iron ore, coal, oil, lumber, and other raw materials from Africa, Latin America, Asia, and Australia. The result is extensive ecological destruction. Africans, Asians, and Latin Americans could use those resources for themselves if they didn't have to ship them to China in exchange for disposable plastic junk and payoffs to dictators.[26]

Similarly, oil revenues provide virtually all government revenue in the Oil Belt, from Libya to Saudi Arabia. If we have to suppress global oil production to save humans, then entire economies are going to have to be reconstructed. But, again, what's the alternative?

3. We would have to revolutionize the production of the goods and services to minimize resource consumption and produce things that are durable, rebuildable, recyclable, and shareable. We're seven going on nine or ten billion people on one small planet with depleted resources. We won't survive much longer with a global economy geared to consuming more resources per capita. We need an economy geared to minimizing resource consumption per capita, while producing enough material goods and services for all of humanity to live comfortably and leave enough for future generations, other fauna, and flora.

Instead of products designed to be used up, worn out, and tossed as quickly as possible, we need to produce shoes that can be re-soled, wellmade and long-lasting clothes, durable and repairable appliances, and up-gradable smartphones. We need to phase out the private car in favor of shared vehicles, bicycles, and public transportation.[27] And we need to make basic cars that last decades. We need to erect buildings engineered to last centuries, like those in old European cities. Here again, such deindustrialization and restructuring would cashier not just factories here and there, but in some cases entire industries. This would eliminate pointless luxuries and wasteful disposables (think "fast fashion" or iPhones 6, 7, 8).

4. We need to steer investments into things society does need— renewable energy, organic farming, public transportation, public water systems, environmental remediation, public health, and

quality schools. All these priorities would be commonsensical if the profit motive hadn't distorted the economy. Why would anyone waste money on bottled water if the municipal water supplies were better quality?[28] Or waste hours slogging to work in cars if they had the option of convenient, comfortable, clean, and efficient public transport? And so on. We have more than enough social wealth to restructure our economies along these lines. It's just that it's wasted on wars, subsidies to undeserving oil companies, tax giveaways to the rich, and more. Just the trillions of dollars that the US government has thrown away on its criminal wars in the Middle East since 1991 could easily have paid for converting the entire country to renewable energy.[29]

5. We need to devise a rational and systematic approach to handling and eliminating waste and toxics as far as possible. We need to abolish production of disposable products (save for critical uses, like medical) and most packaging; bring back refillable containers; generalize mandatory composting, recycling, and so on.[30] We need to stop making so many chemicals, most of which have trivial uses anyway. Pesticides should be banned altogether. In general, society should enshrine and live by the precautionary principle already embraced by scientists, doctors, and grassroots anti-toxics organizations.[31] Again, such rational reorganization of the economy in the interests of public health requires the visible hand of planning, not the invisible hand of market anarchy.

6. We must provide equivalent jobs for all workers displaced by necessary shutdowns because it is just and also because, without guaranteed employment, these people can't support the huge structural changes needed to save humans. Given capitalism, any retrenchment, let alone mass industrial closures, would mean large-scale unemployment. That's why the environmental movement has such difficulty talking to workers who intuitively grasp the connection. And yet, we're doomed if we don't close down polluting industries. The only way to deal with this contradiction is to take it head on, to concede that radical restructuring will mean massive displacement. Only an eco-socialist economy can immediately and rationally provide alternative employment for excessed workers in unsustainable polluting industries.[32]

Happily, grabbing the bull by the horns this way is not "austerity." This is a huge *opportunity* to replace alienated commodification with worthwhile, interesting, and self-fulfilling work. The vast majority of US workers are employed in alienating, often dangerous, and harmful work. The transition to eco-socialism presents the opportunity to abolish idiotic jobs in banking and advertising, assembly line manufacturing, arms production, and more. Moreover, ceasing production of useless or harmful products opens the way to a shortened workday and reduced workweek. In other words, managed de-industrialization emancipates labor.

Planning Can't Work?

It has been a standard shibboleth of capitalist economists, from Milton Friedman to Paul Krugman, that economic planning "can't work." Business editors never tire of recalling Soviet central planning's failures as proof. But those failures prove nothing about the potentials of planning *per se* because in the Stalinist states planning was *of, by, and for* the party bureaucracy.[33] These were totalitarian states, not democracies. Central planners shut workers and everyone else out of the planning process, dictating production targets and quotas from the top down. Workers had no way or incentive to contribute knowledge and creativity to the planning process. Planning will be rational and efficient only when it's in everyone's interests, and when there are material or other rewards and costs.

Governments "Can't Pick Winners"?

For years after the 2011 bankruptcy of solar startup Solyndra Corporation, bankrolled by the Obama administration, the *Wall Street Journal* editors kept reminding their readers of this demonstrated proof that government can't pick winners.[34] But Solyndra didn't fail because solar is a losing technology. It failed because it couldn't compete against lower-cost, state-owned, state-directed, and state-subsidized competitors in *China*.[35]

Besides, since when do capitalists have a crystal ball? CEOs and corporate boards bet on "loser" technologies and products all the time. The ever-lengthening list of misplaced private bets includes everything from the Israeli electric car start-up Fisker Automotive to Sony's Betamax, Ford's Edsel, and the White Star Lines Titanic. Besides picking losing technology and products, CEOs and boards lose money for their shareholders and drive successful companies into bankruptcy every day. Consider the misadventures of JP Morgan Chase, Lehman Brothers, Washington Mutual, Enron, WorldCom, Pan American Airways, and Swissair.[36] Government-backed Solyndra lost $535 million. But when Jamie Dimon lost two *billion dollars* for JP Morgan Chase, the *Wall Street Journal* didn't howl that capitalists "can't pick winners." When Enron collapsed, we heard no blanket condemnation of the private sector's "inevitable incompetence." When Royal Dutch Shell Arctic ceased drilling in September 2015, conceding it had wasted seven billion dollars of shareholders' money, the *Wall Street Journal* didn't blame Shell's CEO but did say that "backing away from the arctic is a step in the right direction."[37]

So much for the free market's unerring wisdom in picking winners. Hypocrisy is stock and trade of capitalists, lazy media, and fact-averse capitalist economists eager to make the facts fit their simpleminded model, no matter the truth. Indeed, the *Wall Street Journal* rarely, if ever, applauds government for picking *indisputable winners*—when, for instance, government-funded and government-directed applied research produced nuclear weapons, nuclear energy, radar, rockets, the jet engine, the transistor, the microchip, the internet, GPS, and breakthrough biotechnology; when government scientists and industries first landed a man on the moon and then a government-built state-of-the-art science lab the size of a Mini Cooper within a mile and a half of its target on *Mars*; and so on. Clearly, government has picked some winners.

Capitalist Planning Sure Works

Within their own enterprises, capitalists rarely dispute the potentials of rational planning. Just the opposite. Today, the revenues of the world's largest corporations are bigger than many national economies. According to the Institute for Policy Studies, 51 of the world's 100 largest economic entities are corporations, the rest countries.[38] Aside from banks, which don't produce anything, most of the top companies are oil and auto companies. Walmart has 2.2 million employees.[39]

If companies with revenues greater than the GDPs of most countries can rationally and efficiently plan their economies—think here of airplane manufacture or oil exploration, refinement, and distribution—why can't nations? Why can't we rationally plan the world's industrial economy to meet the needs of the world's peoples? Of course, planning a national economy and coordinating global economies is harder than planning production, sale, and maintenance of airplanes. But no technological barrier stands in the way, and we don't have a choice. It's plan or die.

Saving Small Producers

Even though large-scale industrial planning is the only feasible alternative to unplanned market anarchy, there is no need to nationalize family farms, farmers' markets, artisans, groceries, local restaurants, repair shops, worker cooperatives, and similar small businesses. Large-scale corporations are destroying the world, not small producers. If we want to save humans, the corporations would have to be nationalized, socialized, and completely reorganized. Many must be closed down, others scaled back or repurposed. But within the framework of a larger planned economy, small-scale, local, independent producers could carry on more less unchanged if they work within the limits of what's sustainable, respect pollution limits and resource conservation mandates, and don't grow beyond reasonable, agreed-upon maximum sizes. We don't need to plan the entire economy, and we have bigger problems to worry about.

4. Rational planning requires democracy.

The only way to plan the economy for the common good is doing it ourselves, democratically. Solar or coal? Frack the planet or work our way off fossil fuels? Drench the world's farms in toxic pesticides or return to organic agriculture? Mainly public transportation or private cars? Let's vote, giving everyone a say in decisions that affect us all.

The problem with capitalism is that the economy isn't up for a vote. Huge decisions that affect all of us, and millions of other species—even the fate of life on earth—are *private* decisions, made by corporate boards on behalf of self-interested investors. Polls show that 93 percent of Americans want GMO labeling on foods and 57 percent consider such foods unsafe to eat.[40] So why they don't get to vote on whether we get GMOs in our food or whether GMOs are labeled? The House of Representatives, which claims to represent the electorate, passed a bill to prevent mandatory labeling.[41] This is capitalist "democracy," with politicians more often than not representing the companies and the rich who fund political campaigns. Polls show that 69 percent of Americans, 71 percent of Chinese, 77 percent of Nigerians, and 88 percent of Brazilians want binding limits imposed on CO_2 emissions.[42] But corporations don't, so they bribe or browbeat politicians to keep limits off limits.

What kind of democracy is this? Why don't we get to vote or hold national referenda on these questions? We don't have to be experts to make such decisions. Corporate board members aren't experts; they are major investors and prominent, often politically connected VIPs. Corporate boards decide and vote on what they want to do, then hire experts to figure out how to get it done. Why can't society do the same, but in the interest of the common good instead of Wall Street investors?

How do we know people would vote for the common good? We don't. After all, people routinely vote against their own interests. Yet, on closer inspection it's not so surprising, given the limited choices they're offered in capitalist democracy. What we see is that *in the abstract*, people would vote their conscience on environmental issues. If 69 percent of Americans favor binding limits on CO_2 emissions and 93 percent want GMO labeling, it shows that people have pretty good instincts about the environment. But when the issue is framed as a choice between environment versus jobs and other pocketbook issues, people very often vote for the economy and against the environment.

For example, in 2012 Californians voted on Proposition 37, which would have required labeling of GMO content in foods. Huge majorities favored labeling, polls showed, but the measure didn't pass, probably because its opponents, including Monsanto, E.I. Dupont, BASF Plant Science, and other industries, outspent the pro-labeling forces by more than five to one and paid for disingenuous propaganda ads claiming the bill would increase family grocery costs by as much as $400 per year. This is a common pattern with a long history.[43] Yet, even so, the measure was only barely defeated.[44]

The initiative process is direct democracy in action. But when corporate interests are free to spend unlimited money to influence voting, and especially when jobs or living standards are threatened, democracy is sabotaged. If we want democracy to work, we would have to publicly fund elections and referenda balloting 100 percent, arrange for open debate on issues, show zero tolerance for propagandistic media, and guarantee workers in dismantled capitalist industries new comparable jobs.

Planet Democracy: Creating Institutions of Economic Democracy

We would have to establish democratic institutions to plan and manage our social economy: local, regional, national, continental, and international planning boards. Not just workers, the direct producers, but entire communities, consumers, farmers, peasants—everyone—would be involved. As a rule, the more direct the democracy, the closer it hews to the public's will. And direct democracy need not be limited to local economies or issues. Many referenda must be national, even global, because they deal with universal, planet-wide issues. Should we build more coal-fired power plants or close them and shift to renewable power? Should we ban large gas-hogs and, as needed, revive the equivalent of 1960s VW Beetles, Citroen 2CVs, and Fiat 500s? Should we fish the oceans to extinction or manage them sustainably? Such questions need to be addressed both globally and locally. We have the Internet now and models aplenty: the Paris Commune, the Russian workers councils of 1917–1919, Poland's Solidarity trade union in 1980–1981, Brazil's participatory planning, La Via Campesina, and others.[45] Direct democracy at the base and delegated authority with right of recall for higher level planning boards—what's so difficult about that?

The Example of Public Regulation of Utilities

Surprisingly, the USA has a working example of something like a proto-socialist planning model. As the authors of *Democracy and Regulation: How the Public Can Govern Essential Services* note, the USA may be the world's leading champion of the free market, but a large and indispensable sector of the US economy is not governed by the free market, but is instead democratically run by public oversight—and that sector is utilities, the provision of electricity, heating fuel, water and sewerage, and local telephone service. Not only that, the authors write, but these are the world's most efficient and cheapest utility systems:

...every aspect of US regulation is wide open to the public. There are no secret meetings, no secret documents. Any and all citizens and groups are invited to take part: individuals, industrial customers, government agencies, consumer groups, trade unions, the utility itself, even its competitors. *Everyone affected by the outcome has a right to make their case openly, to ask questions of government and utilities, to read all financial and operating records in detail.* In public forums, with all information open to all citizens, the principles of social dialogue and transparency come to life. It is an extraordinary exercise in democracy–and it works... [and] the US holds to the strictest, most elaborate and detailed system of regulation anywhere...[46]

"No regulatory Garden of Eden," as the authors put it, this set-up has many failings. Regulation is constantly under attack by promoters of market pricing, and the public interest and the profit motive of investor-owned utilities often conflict, with negative consequences for the public. But even so, this successful democratic public regulation of large-scale industries offers us a real-world practical example of "proto-socialism." Why couldn't something like this model of democracy and transparency be scaled up to encompass the entire industrial economy?

Of course, we would have to do much more than just regulate industries. We would have to completely reorganize and reprioritize the whole economy, indeed the whole global industrial economy. Retrenching and closing down resource-consuming and polluting industries, shifting resources out of them, and starting new industries are huge tasks, beyond the scope of even the biggest corporations. So who else could do this but self-organized masses of citizens, the whole society acting in concert, democratically?

5. Democracy requires rough socioeconomic equality.

When during the Great Depression that great "People's Lawyer," Supreme Court Justice Louis Brandeis, said *"We can either have democracy in this country or we can have great wealth concentrated in the hands of a few, but we can't have both,"* he was more right than he knew. Today's concentration of wealth is the greatest ever. Worldwide, Oxfam found, just 80 individuals own as much wealth as the bottom half, 3.6 billion of the world's population.[47] So it's hardly surprising that today we have the weakest and most corrupt democracies since the Gilded Age.

To achieve real democracy, we would have to abolish "the great wealth concentrated in the hands of the few." More would have to go than just capitalist private property in the means of production; so would extremes of income, exorbitant salaries, accumulated wealth, great property, and inheritance. The only way to prevent the corruption of democracy is to create a society with neither rich nor poor. If it's illegal to be rich, then there's little or no incentive to be corrupt. Brandeis was right.

Does that mean we would all have to dress in blue Mao suits and dine in communal mess halls? Hardly. Lots of studies, notably Wilkinson and Pickett's *Spirit Level*, have shown that people are happier, life is better, and there's less crime and violence and fewer mental health problems in societies where income differences are small and concentrated wealth is limited.[48] Gandhi was right that "the world has enough for everyone's needs, but not everyone's greed." The wasteful consumerist lifestyle of the American middle and upper classes couldn't be universalized, but there is more than enough wealth to provide every human being on Earth with safe water and sanitation, quality food, housing, public transportation, great schools, and health care—all the *authentic* necessities. These should all be guaranteed *as a matter of right*. Indeed, most were already declared so in articles 22–25 of the United Nations' Universal Declaration of Human Rights of 1948.

The Promise of Eco-socialism

Freeing ourselves from the toil of producing unnecessary and harmful commodities would free us to shorten the workday, enjoy the leisure promised but never delivered by capitalism, and *redefine "standard of living" to connote a way of life that is actually richer, while consuming less.* In a society in which all have easy access to basic necessities and live comfortably and can count on guaranteed employment and a basic income, we can realize our fullest potential instead of wasting our lives in mindless drudgery and shopping. Artists can do art instead of advertising. Carpenters like myself can build sturdy aesthetically pleasing housing for people who need it, instead of trophy homes. Scientists and inventors can build a better world instead of the next iThing or killer drone. Wall Street bankers can find socially worthwhile work. We can all build a beautiful world to pass on while leaving space and resources for the wonderful life forms that share this amazing blue planet with us now. This is the potential of eco-socialism.

6. Impossible? Perhaps, but what's the alternative?

The "planetary emergency" we face is no joke. As Jared Diamond reminds us in *Collapse*, in the past civilizations went belly up individually whereas today we face the prospect of planet-wide ecological collapse, the collapse of civilization, and perhaps even our own extinction.[49] What gives us an edge here is that capitalism has no solution whatsoever to this crisis; its answer to every problem is more of same planet-wrecking growth and overconsumption. A market solution to our crisis eludes capitalism because every "solution" has to be subordinated to maximizing growth. But what difference does it make if Germany gets almost 30 percent of its electricity from solar and wind, when German industry uses this power to manufacture millions of globe-warming cars? What does it matter if Apple powers its Chinese plants with "100 percent renewable energy" when what it manufactures in China is ecologically disastrous and costly disposable products—billions of iPhones, iPads, and the rest? But, of course, manufacturing durable, repairable, updatable phones would put Apple out of business fast.

This is why green capitalism can go only so far. As one by one the pro-market stratagems—the cap and trades, carbon taxes, the REDDs, and the "green growth" delusions of perpetual growth without perpetually growing resource consumption—all prove counterproductive or too feeble to radically suppress resource consumption and pollution, people will become more open to radical alternatives.

Capitalism has had a good 300-year run. But economic systems come and go, as do governments. There is no gainsaying the magnitude of the changes we must make to save ourselves. Closing the book on capitalism and moving on to a higher stage of civilization—eco-socialism—by replacing the culture of acquisitive individualism with a culture of sharing, community, and love, is humanity's greatest challenge yet. We may fail. But what other choice do we have but to try? Unlike the Australians in Stanley Kramer's dystopian film, we still have a chance.

Notes

1 Sewell Chan, "Poll finds Global Consensus on the Need to Curb Emissions," *New York Times*, November 6, 2015.
2 Germany shut down its nuclear power plants, but replaced electricity generation mainly with coal-fired power plants to power its industries. Auto manufacturing is the country's leading export. And, with car companies, it's "big car big profit, small car small profit." So the Germans burn coal to produce gas guzzlers. Germany's government is even demolishing renewable-powered medieval villages to mine coal. See Tony Paterson, "Green Village to be Bulldozed and Mined for Lignite in Germany's Quest for Non-nuclear Fuel," *The Independent*, September 29, 2014, http://www.independent.co.uk/environment/green-living/green-village-to-be-bulldozed-and-mined-for-lignite-in-germanys-quest-for-non-nuclear-fuel-9760091.html.
3 Trucks in 1950 got 8.4mpg whereas in 2010 they got 6.4mpg. See http://www.eia.gov/totalenergy/data/annual/showtext.cfm?t=ptb0208. Demand for fuel-efficient cars is falling and such hybrid/electric powered cars as the Prius and Leaf account for an infinitesimal and falling percentage of new car sales, while demand for gas-hogs is rising. See Mike Ramsey and Christina Rogers, "Surging Demand for Pickups Tests new EPA Rules," *Wall Street Journal*, August 4, 2015. It hardly matters since electric cars are mostly coal-oil-gas powered since fossil fuels dominate in electricity production. See "What Is US Electricity Generation by Energy Source," last modified March 31, 2015, https://www.eia.gov/tools/faqs/faq.cfm?id=427&t=3. In China, the world's largest car market, virtually all cars are fossil fuel-powered. Same in India.

4 John Schwartz, "Deadly Heat Is Forecast in Persian Gulf by 2100," *New York Times*, October 26, 2015, based on a report by Jeremy S. Pal and Elfatih A. B. Eltahir, "Future Temperature in Southwest Asia Projected to Exceed a Threshold for Human Adaptability," *Nature Climate Change* 6 (October 26, 2015): 1–4.

5 Michael T. Klare, *The Race for What's Left: The Global Scramble for the World's Last Resources* (New York: Picador, 2012); Ugo Bardi, *Extracted: How the Quest for Mineral Wealth Is Plundering the Planet* (White River Junction: Chelsea Green, 2014); Craig Simons, *Devouring Dragon: How China's Rise Threatens Our Natural World* (New York: St. Martins, 2013); Elizabeth C. Economy and Michael Levi, *By All Means Necessary: How China's Resource Quest Is Changing the World* (New York: Oxford, 2015); Simon Romero, "Countries Rush for Upper Hand in Antarctica," *New York Times*, December 29, 2015.

6 China's astounding resource overconsumption is in a class by itself. To understand why, see my "China's Communist-Capitalist Ecological Apocalypse," *Real-World Economics Review* 71 (June 2015): 19–63, http://www.paecon.net/PAEReview/issue71/Smith71.pdf.

7 Helen Lewis, "Never Mind the Pointless Apps–Our Best Minds Should Be Solving Real Problems," *Guardian*, November 11, 2015, http://www.theguardian.com/commentisfree/2015/nov/11/laundry-ninjas-free-market-science; Hu Yongqi, "As Phone Sales Cool, HTC Bets on VR Devices," *China Daily*, January 5, 2016, http://www.chinadaily.com.cn/business/tech/2016-01/05/content_22932829.htm; Gao Yuan, "Virtual Reality, the Next Big Thing for Future-Minded Tech Firms," *China Daily*, January 5, 2016, http://usa.chinadaily.com.cn/epaper/2016-01/05/content_22941357.htm.

8 Retailing consultant Victor Lebow quoted by Vance Packard in his brilliant and sardonic classic *The Waste Makers* (Philadelphia: David McKay, 1960), 24.

9 Giles Slade, *Made to Break: Technology and Obsolescence in America* (Boston, MA: Harvard, 2006), 7.

10 Warren O. Ault, *Open-Field Farming in Medieval England* (London: George Allen & Unwin, 1972); Alan Mayhew, *Rural Settlement and Farming in Germany* (New York: Barnes & Noble, 1973); B.H. Slicher Van Bath, *The Agrarian History of Western Europe A.D. 500–1850* (London: Edward Arnold, 1963); Jack Goody et al., *Family and Inheritance: Rural Society in Western Europe 1200–1800* (Cambridge: Cambridge University Press, 1976). Robert Brenner, *The Brenner Debate*, T.H. Aston and C.H.E. Philpin, eds. (Cambridge: Cambridge University Press, 1985).

11 For more information, see Richard Smith, *Green Capitalism: The God That Failed* (World Economic Association Press, 2015), http://www.world economicsassociation.org/downloads/green-capitalism-the-god-that-failed/.

12 Herman Daly, *Beyond Growth: The Economics of Sustainable Development* (Boston, MA: Beacon, 1996); Serge Latouche, *Farewell to Growth* (Cambridge: Polity, 2009).

13 Smith, *Green Capitalism*, chapter 2.

14 Smith, *Green Capitalism*, chapter 3.

15 Milton Friedman, "The Social Responsibility of Business Is to Increase its Profits," *The New York Times Magazine*, September 13, 1970.

16 On the responsibilities of corporations, see Joel Bakan, *The Corporation: The Pathological Pursuit of Profit and Power* (New York: Free Press, 2004).

17 Intergovernmental Panel on Climate Change (IPCC), Climate Change 2014: Synthesis Report. Contribution of Working Groups I, II, and III to the Fifth Assessment Report of the Intergovernmental Panel on Climate Change (Geneva: IPCC, 2014), http://www.ipcc.ch.

18 Adam Nagourney, "California Democrats Drop Plan for 50 Percent Oil Cut," *New York Times*, September 10, 2015.

19 Brent Kendall and Amy Harder, "Industry, States Set to Fight EPA Greenhouse Gas Rules," *Wall Street Journal*, August 9, 2015.

20 Smith, *Green Capitalism*, chapter 1.

21 IPCC, *Climate Change 2014: Synthesis Report*.

22 Jenna Iacurci, "Report Calls for Five-year Plan to Save World's Over-Fished Oceans," *Nature World News*, June 24, 2014, http://www.natureworldnews.com/articles/7735/20140624/report-calls-for-five-year-plan-to-save-worlds-over-fished-oceans.htm; Also: J.-P. Gattuso et al., "Contrasting Futures for Ocean and Society from Different Anthropogenic CO2 Emissions Scenarios," *Science* 349, 6243 (July 3, 2015).

23 World Resources Institute, Climate Analysis Indicators Tool (CAIT) 2.0, accessed May 2014, http://cait.wri.org.

24 Smith, *Green Capitalism*, chapter 2.

25 World Bank, *Turn Down the Heat: Why a 4° Warmer World Must Be Avoided* (Washington, DC: World Bank, 2012), http://documents.worldbank.org/curated/en/2012/11/17097815/turn-down-heat-4°c-warmer-world-must-avoided; Mark Lynas, *Six Degrees: Our Future on a Hotter Planet* (Washington, DC: National Geographic, 2008).

26 See Smith, "China's Communist-Capitalist Ecological Apocalypse."

27 "Germany Opens Bicycle-Only Autobahn," *Bicyling*, December 29, 2015, http://www.bicycling.com/culture/advocacy/germany-opens-bicycle-only-autobahn.

28 Consumer Reports News, "Bottled Water: $346 per Year. Tap Water: 48 Cents. Any questions?" *Consumer Reports*, July 12, 2011, http://www.consumerreports.org/cro/news/2011/07/bottled-water-346-per-year-tap-water-48-cents-any-questions/index.htm.

29 Mark Z. Jacobson et al. "100% Clean and Renewable Wind, Water, and Sunlight (WWS) All-Sector Energy Roadmaps to the 50 United States," *Energy & Environment Science* 8 (2015): 2093–2117, http://web.stanford.edu/group/efmh/jacobson/Articles/I/USStatesWWS.pdf; Eliot Chang, "Infographic: How Much Would it Cost for the Entire Planet to Switch to Renewable Energy?" *Inhabitat* (and the sources cited therein), September 24, 2013, accessed January 8, 2016, http://inhabitat.com/infographic-how-much-would-it-cost-for-the-entire-planet-to-switch-to-renewable-energy/.

30 See Heather Rogers, *Gone Tomorrow: The Hidden Life of Garbage* (New York: New Press, 2005); Giles Slade, *Made to Break: Technology and Obsolescence in America* (Cambridge, MA: Harvard, 2007); Charles Moore and Cassandra Phillips, *Plastic Ocean: How a Sea Captain's Chance Discovery Launched a Determined Quest to Save the Oceans* (New York: Penguin, 2011).

31 See the Louisville Charter for Safer Chemicals, http://smartpolicyreform.org/the-charter/the-louisville-charter; Safer Chemicals Healthy Families, http://www.saferchemicals.org; Smith, *Green Capitalism*, chapter 2.

32 For more detail, see Smith, *Green Capitalism*, chapter 4.

33 Smith, *Green Capitalism*, chapter 5.

34 For example, "The Solyndra Economy," *Wall Street Journal*, October 11, 2011, http://www.wsj.com/articles/SB1000142405297020452460457661097288233
49418.

35 Smith, *Green Capitalism*, chapter 5.

36 Matt Egan, "16 Firms Worth Billions Despite Losing Money," *CNN Money*, January 23, 2015, http://money.cnn.com/2015/01/23/investing/shazam-tech-startups-lose-money/.

37 Helen Thomas, "Why Shell Has Gone Cold in the Arctic," *Wall Street Journal*, September 28, 2015.

38 John Cavanaugh and Sarah Anderson, "Top 200: The Rise of Corporate Global Power," Institute for Policy Studies, 2010, http://www.ips-dc.org/top_200_the_rise_of_corporate_global_power/.

39 Walmart, Company Facts, corporate.walmart.com/newsroom/company-facts.

40 Monica Anderson, "Amid Debate over Labeling GM Foods, Most Americans Believe They're Unsafe to Eat," *Pew Research Center*, Facttank, August 11, 2015, http://www.pewresearch.org/fact-tank/2015/08/11/amid-debate-over-labeling-gm-foods-most-americans-believe-theyre-unsafe/.

41 Mary Clare Jalonick, "House Passes Bill to Prevent Mandatory GMO Food Labeling," *Associated Press*, July 23, 2015, http://www.pbs.org/newshour/rundown/house-passes-bill-prevent-mandatory-gmo-food-labeling/.

42 Sewell Chan, "Poll Finds Global Consensus on a Need to Tackle Climate Change."

43 See Carl Lutrin and Allen Settle, "The Public and Ecology: The Role of Initiatives in California's Environmental Politics," *Western Political Science Quarterly* 28, 2 (June 1975): 352–371.

44 For the industry-backed opponents, see Jeffrey M. Smith's speech on GMOs, Chemtrails Conference, August 17, 2012, https://www.youtube.com/watch?-feature=player_embedded&v=P5B62cbwP_E; for the pro-labeling forces, see Stacy Malkan, "Statement about Bogus Economic Analysis of GMO Labeling Costs – Yes on Prop 37," August 31, 2012, http://www.carighttoknow.org/cost_statement; Also: Common Dreams Staff, "Pesticide Giants Pour Millions into Campaign to Defeat California Prop. 37," October 4, 2012, CommonDreams.org, http://www.commondreams.org/news/2012/10/04/pesticide-giants-pour-millions-campaign-defeat-californias-prop-37.

45 For example, Poland's Solidarity trade union opposed the Polish Communist Party's monopoly of the economy by proposing a comprehensive economic program based around "social," state, cooperative, private, and mixed enterprises operating in a mixed economy in which "socialized planning should be operated on the principle that the final decision belongs to the representative, not executive bodies." From: Network of Solidarity Organizations in Leading Factories, *Position on Social and Economic Reform of the Country* (1981), p. 4, quoted in Horst Brand, "Solidarity's Proposals for Reforming Poland's Economy," *Monthly Labor Review* (May 1982): 43–46. Unfortunately, Solidarity never got to try out these reforms because it was crushed and its leaders jailed for years, after which capitalism was restored in Poland.

46 Greg Palast, Jerrold Oppenheim, and Theo MacGregor, *Democracy and Regulation: How the Public Can Govern Essential Services* (London: Pluto, 2003), 1–4 (italics are mine).

47 Mona Chalabi, "Meet The 80 People Who Are As Rich As Half the World," *FiveThirtyEight*, January 18, 2015, http://fivethirtyeight.com/datalab/meet-the-80-people-who-are-as-rich-as-half-the-world/.

48 Kate Pickett and Richard Wilkinson, *The Spirit Level: Why Greater Equality Makes Societies Stronger* (London: Bloomsbury, 2011).

49 Jared Diamond, *Collapse: How Societies Choose to Fail or Succeed* (London: Penguin, 2011).

Part 4

Ownership and Economic Democracy

The challenge for advocates of socialism as a model for a new economy is that "socialism" today evokes images of countries where a government bureaucracy manages most or all aspects of the economy—often disregarding the will of the people. Viewed strictly through this lens, if the central flaw of capitalism is that it is controlled by and operates for a tiny elite, a socialism that begins and ends with government control of the means of production can just as easily be one controlled by and operated for a tiny elite.

What alternative, then, allows for true "power to the people"—in which economic decisions are made collectively by everyone for the common good? If the answer to the question "who should own the economy" is "all of us," what structure would make that possible and practical?

The three chapters in this part explore options for bringing the economy, the government, the financial sector, and the workplace under democratic control. The solutions proposed seek to escape the binary confines of the capitalist-socialist debate, instead inviting people to work together to shape an economy that meets their needs and reflects their values.

David Schweickart, philosophy professor at Loyola University Chicago, proposes an "economic democracy" that extends democracy into the workplace and the linked spheres of finance and investment. In place of private ownership of the means of production under capitalism, or state ownership and planning under socialism, the basic structure of economic democracy is socially owned, worker-controlled firms in a competitive market. The model has neither capital markets nor labor markets in the usual sense. Workers would control their own jobs and workplaces, while productive resources would become the collective property of society and investment decisions would be under social control. Schweickart's framework includes a right to employment, reconstruction of the financial sector, an "entrepreneurial-capitalist" sector to drive marketplace innovation, and a "social tariff" to encourage healthy, fair trade between nations while discouraging race-to-the-bottom trade deals.

Richard D. Wolff, economics professor emeritus at the University of Massachusetts and the host of a weekly television show, "Economic Update," describes a next economic system centered on worker-directed cooperatives. Wolff argues that transitioning to a non-capitalist system requires changing the "who and the why of key economic decision-making." By creating Worker Self-Directed Enterprises (WSDEs), workers become their own bosses, responsible for democratically deciding what, how, and where goods are produced; how to distribute or reinvest profits; and, with democratic organizations of residential communities, how to take into account health, community wealth, and solidarity. According to Wolff, WSDEs represent both the goal of a new system and the mechanism for reaching it.

While Schweickart and Wolff focus on worker ownership, Andrew Cumbers, professor of regional political economy at the University of Glasgow, examines public ownership as a way for workers, consumers, and citizens to participate in economic decision-making and exercise community control over resources. He calls for a "de-centered" political economy that disperses decision-making authority and knowledge broadly among different actors. Cumbers explores seven broad types of public ownership—full state ownership, partial state ownership, regional/subnational state ownership, local/municipal state ownership, employee-owned firms, producer and consumer cooperatives—and how they could be strategically incorporated across the economy. Public ownership of oil production in Norway and renewable energy in Denmark exemplify his model. While the public sector has come under political attack in recent decades, public ownership remains popular—a hopeful sign of what is possible.

Chapter 13

Economic Democracy

Ethical, Economically Viable Socialism

David Schweickart

> The big challenges that capitalism now faces … include issues of inequality (especially that of grinding poverty in a world of unprecedented prosperity) and of "public goods" (that is, goods people share together, like the environment). The solution to these *problems will almost certainly call for institutions that take us beyond the capitalist market economy* (italics added).[1]

So wrote Nobel Laureate economist Amartya Sen, nearly two decades ago. The intervening years since then have only strengthened his thesis—inequality and environmental degradation have gotten much worse and grinding poverty persists. But does a viable alternative exist? Is there a way to go beyond the capitalist market economy—a new system that would preserve the strengths of competitive capitalism while eliminating, or at least mitigating, its worst features?

The clear and unequivocal answer is "Yes." And the way forward is simple enough to state: we need to extend democracy to the economy itself. To sloganize, we need to "Democratize Labor!" "Democratize Capital!" and "Democratize Democracy!"

Economic Democracy: The Basic Model

Today's economic system, free market capitalism, consists essentially of three kinds of markets:

- Markets for goods and services: Enterprises compete with one another to provide consumers what they need or want.
- Labor markets: Working requires access to the "means of production." One's "capacity to work" (one's "labor-power" as Marx called it) is a commodity like any other, to be bought and sold. People must compete for jobs, and, once hired, do what they are told.

- Capital markets: Private financial institutions raise money from those who have excess and allocate it to businesses promising the highest profitability.

This model has proven strengths, but also grievous weaknesses. What might an economically viable, ethically desirable alternative look like?

Let us imagine an economic system, *Economic Democracy*, that keeps the first set of markets, competitive markets for goods and services, but replaces most wage labor with cooperative labor and replaces our out-of-control financial markets with a more democratic mechanism for handling investment. It will be a form of socialism, although structurally different from past and present examples of existing socialism, and from those versions of welfare-state capitalism that are sometimes designated socialist.

Let's begin with the basic model, a simplified version of an alternative non-capitalist economy. Real-world economies will always be more complicated than the models that describe them, but only through modeling can we comprehend an economic system's essential dynamic. Just as the model of capitalism that Marx gave us remains indispensable for grasping our current system, our new model helps us see how a different system, perhaps the "next system," would work.

What would the basic institutions of Economic Democracy look like?

Historical experience makes clear that *competitive markets* are a necessary component of any economically viable alternative to capitalism. Central planning does not work for a sophisticated economy. Quite simply, the knowledge and incentive problems are too great. But markets in Economic Democracy will be largely confined to goods and services. There will be regulations to protect health, safety, and the environment, but enterprises will compete with one another in selling goods and services to consumers. (Not all goods and services. Health care, education, and others may be designated tax-payer–funded "public goods," provided without charge to all who need them, as is the case, to varying degrees, in most forms of contemporary capitalism.)

Most enterprises in Economic Democracy, however, are quite different from what they are in capitalism. They are not entities that can be bought or sold, but are instead communities. When you join a firm, you have the right to vote for members of a worker council, just as you have the right now to vote for the city or town council governing your place of residence. This council appoints upper management and oversees major enterprise decisions. Although managers are granted some autonomy, ultimately they answer to the workforce.

As for income, all workers share in the enterprise's profits. These shares need not be equal, but everyone's income is tied directly to the firm's performance, so everyone is incentivized to work diligently and efficiently— and to see to it that co-workers do the same.

Besides democratizing labor, Economic Democracy also democratizes capital. Some sort of democratic control of investment is essential if an economy is to develop rationally. Given the ecological terrors we now face, rational development has never been more urgently needed. Investment decisions made today shape fundamentally our collective future, making democratic control essential.

But democratic control of investment is impossible if we must rely on private investors to generate and allocate the funds. Instead of counting on private investors to do either, let's generate our investment funds publicly via a *capital-assets tax*—a flat-rate property tax on all businesses. This tax replaces the interest and dividend payments to shareholders and creditors in a capitalist economy, as well as the corporate income tax. The revenue this tax generates constitutes the *national investment fund*. All such revenue is reinvested in the economy. (An income and/or consumption tax will fund other government services and ongoing expenses.)

These publicly generated funds are allocated according to a combination of national, regional, and local planning as well as market criteria. A certain portion of the national investment fund is set aside for national public projects while the rest is allocated to all regions of the country. Regions do not compete for capital. Instead, each region receives, as a matter of right, each and every year, its *fair share*—generally its *per-capita* share—of the investment fund. The national legislature can make exceptions, but these would likely be rare; since investment allocation is a zero-sum game, a higher per-capita share to one region means lower per-capita shares to others.

Some of these regional funds are set aside for public investments that are regional in scope. The remainder goes to communities, also on a *per-capita* basis, where it is channeled to *public investment banks* that lend it to enterprises to upgrade their technologies, restructure their business, and/or expand production, and to individuals to start new businesses. These loans reflect both economic and social criteria—including, importantly, employment creation and environmental impact (negative or positive). They are repaid with interest, with the interest rate generally the same as the capital-assets tax rate.

This public investment system makes coherent long-term investment planning at the national, regional, and community levels possible. The allocative mechanism is straightforward and transparent (unlike today's utterly opaque, Wall Street-dominated institutions) and, hence, readily subject to democratic oversight and control.

Economic Democracy: The Extended Model

Markets for goods and services, workplace democracy, and democratic control of investment constitute the defining features of Economic Democracy, but other structures should also be part of our "next system." Briefly, four are particularly important.

The Government as Employer of Last Resort

A long-held tenet of socialism is that everyone who wants to work should have access to a job. In Economic Democracy, everyone should have a genuine *right to work* that government ensures. If a person cannot find work elsewhere, the government will provide one—low-wage but decent, doing something useful.

Socialist Savings and Loan Associations

Economic Democracy separates two functions that capitalist financial institutions conflate: investment funding and saving/borrowing for personal consumption. The first is central to long-term societal development, and thus is subject to democratic control. The second need not be so controlled since private savings are not needed for investment capital.

Independent savings and loan associations, structured as credit unions or worker cooperatives, can benefit people without causing significant harm. S&Ls will offer individuals consumer credit so they can take out loans and pay them off over time with interest. (Housing would doubtless comprise a major portion of these loans, allowing individuals to buy homes before saving up the full purchase price.) Money for these loans would come from private savers. Their savings would be protected and pay interest.

An Entrepreneurial-Capitalist Sector

His unsurpassed critique of capitalism notwithstanding, Marx did neglect the function of the *entrepreneur* in society. Marx's analysis of capitalism focuses on the capitalist *qua* capitalist—the provider of capital. This provision of capital is a *passive* function, which the state can readily take over, as it does in our basic model.

Another part now played by *some* capitalists is a creative, *entrepreneurial* role. It is played by a large number of "petty capitalists" who set up their own small businesses, but also by a smaller number of "grand capitalists," who turn innovative ideas into major industries. Even though workplace democracy will be the norm throughout society in the new model, not *all* businesses need conform. Anything but parasitic, the petty capitalist works hard, bringing energy, initiative, and intelligence to the task of running a small business. Together, small businesses provide jobs for large numbers of people, and goods and services to even more. They would continue to play a vital role in the new system.

What petty capitalists *don't* typically provide is much technological or organizational innovation. There is, for that reason, an honorable role in our new system for *entrepreneurial capitalists* who operate on a grander scale. This class need not pose a serious threat to the democratic structures of our economy. Nor should democratic firms, when they have equal access to investment capital, fear competition from capitalist firms. On the contrary, since capitalist firms must compete with democratic firms for workers, they will be under pressure to at least partially democratize their own operations through, for example, profit sharing and more participatory work relations.

A rather simple legal mechanism could also help keep this capitalist class in check. The basic problem with capitalists under capitalism is not their active entrepreneurial role (which relatively few actually play), but their passive role as richly rewarded suppliers of investment capital (and their active role as forces in political life, having little else to do with their vast fortunes). Since Economic Democracy transparently and rationally substitutes a capital-assets tax for the savings-of-the-wealthy-as-the source-of-investment-capital, the trick is to develop a mechanism that would prevent the active entrepreneurial capitalist from becoming a passive parasitic one.

The mechanism: a simple law with two parts. The law would stipulate that an enterprise developed by an entrepreneurial capitalist could be sold at any time, but, *if it exceeds a certain size*, sold only to the state, at a price determined by the value of its capital-assets. (Smaller firms can be sold to other private individuals.) It would further stipulate that an enterprise beyond a certain size *must* be sold to the state when the owner retires, dies, or moves on to another venture. When the state purchases an enterprise, it turns it over to the enterprise's workers to be run democratically. (Of course, an entrepreneur who must sell their firm will most likely introduce forms of participatory governance prior to departure to ensure that their creation will not fall apart without them.)

In Economic Democracy, entrepreneurial capitalists incubate innovation *and* new democratic enterprises. Clearly, entrepreneurial capitalists have an honorable role to play in our new socialist system.

Socialist Protectionism

The institutions of Economic Democracy discussed so far apply to a national economy. But what about economic relations with other countries? Since democratic firms won't relocate abroad, and since funds for investment are publicly generated and by law must be reinvested in domestic firms, neither jobs nor capital will be "exported." And because there are no stocks nor private enterprises (apart from small businesses) to buy, not much foreign capital (if any) will flow into the country either.

Foreign trade in and of itself is not objectionable—so long as the trade is "fair." An economically democratic country can trade freely with countries whose worker incomes and environmental regulations resemble their own. But for countries with lower worker incomes or laxer social or environmental regulations, an Economic Democracy will pursue fair trade, not free trade. The aims are to allow for healthy competition but not race-to-the-bottom, destructive competition and acknowledge our human obligation to strive to eliminate poverty, environmental degradation, and other social injustices everywhere.

Our main economic mechanism for meeting these obligations is *socialist protectionism*. This approach requires imposing a *social tariff* on imported goods to compensate for low wages and/or lack of commitment in exporting countries to socially beneficial practices (protecting the environment, worker health and safety, etc.), then rebating all these tariff proceeds back, either to exporting-country governments or, perhaps more likely, to organizations working to improve conditions within the countries.

Rich countries operating as Economic Democracies might address global poverty in other ways as well. They will be encouraged to make their "intellectual property" freely available to poor countries, devote a portion of their publicly funded research to addressing problems faced by poor countries, and help create "intermediate technologies" that make work easier and more satisfying without destroying jobs.

Over time, these social protectionist policies would allow poor countries to devote fewer of their resources to producing for wealthy-country consumption and more to satisfying their own people's needs. The point of socialist protectionism is not to protect one's own workforce at the expense of workers elsewhere, but to protect one's own workers to enhance the life prospects of people everywhere—and of the planet itself.

Conclusion

The system outlined here would be economically viable, and it could steer clear of the massive evils of contemporary capitalism—staggering inequality, intractable unemployment, overwork among the employed, "irrational" economic instability divorced from natural causes, and massive environmental degradation. (See my *After Capitalism* for the evidence and arguments.)[2]

That said, overcoming these defects requires more than the institutional changes advocated here. It is important to emphasize that we do not live in a democratic society now. The massive economic inequality that capitalism has generated has severely compromised our political system, making a mockery of the concept of "rule by the people"—hence, the need to "Democratize Democracy!"

Consider too that democratizing institutions will produce a just and sustainable society only if the majority wants to live in such a society. Democratic institutions must always face the "garbage in, garbage out" problem. If the majority of a population is racist or sexist or homophobic or addicted to mindless consumption, then democratic institutions will give us racist, sexist, homophobic, ecologically destructive outcomes. Proposals for Economic Democracy are only part of the global movement now developing to create a just and sustainable world.

An impetus to action is the realization that the massive evils and many dysfunctions we see all around us today cannot be resolved within a capitalist framework. We need different institutions. We need a "system change" if we are going to survive and flourish as a species. We need a new economic system if we, our children, and our grandchildren are going to live in a just, humane, peaceful, and sustainable world. To quote from a Carolyn Forché poem written decades ago, but now more telling than ever:

> It is either the beginning or the end of the world.
> The choice is ourselves or nothing.[3]

Notes

1 Amartya Sen, *Development as Freedom* (New York: Knopf, 1999).
2 David Schweickart, *After Capitalism* (Lanham, NJ: Rowman and Littlefield, 2011).
3 Carolyn Forché, *The Country between Us* (New York: Harper Perennial, 1982), 55.

Chapter 14

The Next System

Workers Direct Themselves

Richard D. Wolff

Capitalism as an economic system has been prone to instability (recurring cycles) and inequality. This has provoked challenges, criticism, and opposition. In defensive responses, capitalism found and made use of a variety of economic forms and reforms. These worked well and repeatedly to pacify critics and opponents. However, eventually capitalism's instability and inequality always resurfaced to produce another round of conflict over the system.

The multiple forms and reforms over time clarified the difference between them all and the core economic substance of capitalism. They also exposed the need to change that substance if we are to get beyond the endless reforms that have never finally solved its problems. Among key forms, history shows us capitalisms where one person or a family plays the role of employer but also capitalisms where a non-kinship collective of individuals plays that role (as in a corporate board of directors). Private individuals may own a capitalist enterprise, a state apparatus may do so, or combinations of both kinds of owners may coexist. Owners of capitalist enterprises may include its employees (ESOPs), much as corporate boards of directors may include representatives elected by its employees (Germany's *Mitbestimmung*).

Similarly, distributions of productive resources and products may occur via exchange in market transactions or via planned distributions. Exchange ratios—or prices—may be negotiated within markets or else assigned by planning authorities. Capitalist organizations of production have coexisted with all of these and still other distribution mechanisms.

What all these forms and reforms do is draw our attention to the basic substance of capitalism. A kind of core remains whose forms can and do vary. That core is the relationship among the people engaged in producing the goods and services upon which life depends. In capitalism, that relationship is captured in terms of employer and employee: two different groups of people within capitalist enterprises that collaborate and conflict.

In this core relationship, capitalism both resembles and differs from slavery and feudalism as alternative systems for producing goods and services.

In slavery, the core relationship was master and slave. In feudalism, it was lord and serf. Like capitalism, slavery and feudalism exhibited varieties of forms and reforms across their histories. Slaves, for example, could be owned by an individual or a group, by private individuals, or state officials. Slaves could own other slaves, and so on. The same applied to lords and serfs; state feudalism could coexist with private feudalism. The varieties of its forms help us focus on the core relationship that defines each system: master/slave, lord/serf, employer/employee. Capitalism shares the duality of the other two systems; yet, its duality differs from theirs.

For us, a new system should not be another reformation of the basic dualities noted above. It should not leave in place the employer–employee relationship at capitalism's core. For the last two centuries, new-system-type debates have centered on capitalism versus socialism understood chiefly in terms of private versus state forms of the same employer-employee relationship we identify as the core of capitalism. History has moved beyond the debate between private and state forms of capitalism, whether or not verbalized as capitalism versus socialism.

Instead, the next system should, we at Democracy at Work argue, collapse the difference between two groups of people within enterprises and unite them as one. The employees of capitalism should become their own employers. We call the result "workers self-directed enterprises" (WSDEs). We underscore *self-directed* as a metaphorical reference to the role of the board of directors within capitalist corporations. That board is the employer, structurally and legally, who hires the employees, pays them, directs their labor, and organizes the enterprise's activities as a whole. The new system we envisage—prefigured in some of the worker co-ops that have existed in the past and present—makes employees and employers the same group of people running as well as working within each enterprise.

Within WSDEs, each employee/employer has one vote in deciding what the enterprise produces, what technology it uses, where production is located, and what is to be done with the enterprise's revenues. In a next system based on WSDEs, democracy would finally have been brought into the enterprise. There, capitalism had always excluded it. Democracy inside the enterprise could and would reinforce democracy outside in residential communities where it might then become substantive, not merely formal. Indeed, a codetermination of economic and political democracies would be enabled by means of a change to a WSDE-based economy. We might then actually construct interdependent, socially democratic decision-making in and by economic and political spheres of social life.

This focus on the micro-level of society differs from the earlier prioritization of macro-levels (as in private versus social ownership of means of production, market versus planned economy, and so on). The mode of promoting this new system entails the slogan "democratize the enterprise." For this slogan, the traditional enemies of a new system beyond capitalism are very unprepared. A key insight conveyed through that slogan is that previous reforms of capitalism—including state capitalisms—did not change enterprises' basic employer-employee relationships and therein lay their central flaw and inadequacy. The macro-level changes state capitalisms did often achieve could not endure in large part because their unchanged micro-level structure of employer versus employee undid them.

A new system based on WSDEs in factories, offices, and stores could be good partners for buyers' co-ops, sellers' co-ops, owners' co-ops, and the other types of cooperative activities. They might well be necessary partners for their survival and growth. Likewise, WSDEs would enable and support political democracy within residential communities that interact with the WSDEs.

In our organization, Democracy at Work, we advocate for WSDEs and a basic economic change from undemocratic capitalist relations to democracy within all enterprises. We share the many diverse aspirations for a better "next system" that animate our colleagues in this volume. Our reason for focusing on and targeting changing the internal employer-employee relationship of the capitalist enterprise is not that this relationship is more important for, or determinant of, that better system than its other economic and noneconomic dimensions. We focus on it because it has not been adequately appreciated and analyzed.

Chapter 15

Diversifying Public Ownership

Constructing Institutions for Participation, Social Empowerment, and Democratic Control

Andrew Cumbers

This chapter advocates a form of economic democracy based on diverse forms of public ownership. No single scale is given priority. Instead, importance is accorded to decentralized forms of public ownership—to encourage greater public participation and engagement—mixed with higher-level state ownership for strategic sectors and planning for such key public policy goals as tackling climate change. Public ownership, defined pluralistically here, includes state ownership and the role that cooperatives and employee ownership could play in a more democratic economy.

The proposal outlined here would enhance democratic participation and collective knowledge formation in relation to the economy. The guiding principle is that increased privatization of the economy is leading to growing inequalities, inappropriate policy formation, and decision-making in the interest of wealthy elites at the expense of a broader common good. In contrast, considerable evidence shows that greater collective ownership of the economy leads to more progressive, egalitarian, and socially just outcomes that also offer more effective solutions to such critical public policy problems as dealing with the effects of climate change.[1]

Against Trend

The modern contemporary economy is increasingly owned and controlled by a wealthy elite. Since the mid-1980s, a global privatization agenda has entrenched power by further concentrating ownership. Although this global phenomenon includes the United States, the trends' best exemplar is the United Kingdom, where the privatization programs pursued by Conservative governments have diminished individual shareholding and increased corporate and foreign ownership of the economy (see Figure 15.1). Ironically, much of this concentration of wealth is accounted for by foreign state-owned, or partially stated-owned, corporations (e.g., French energy corporation EDF or the German firm RWE) behaving much like private multinationals. More recently, financial interests' growing influence in economic ownership, notably hedge funds, private equity, and

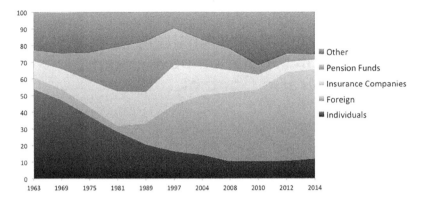

Figure 15.1 Ownership of share capital in UK's quoted companies, 1963–2014.
Source: UK Office of National Statistics.[19]

other investment vehicles, has further entrenched short-term rent-seeking on behalf of vested interests.

In opposition to these trends, the model proposed here involves developing alternative and more democratic economic structures and constructing new and diverse forms of public ownership. A mixed economy of varied forms of public ownership, in both planned and regulated market sectors, would co-exist with small privately owned firms. Different forms of public ownership are advocated for different parts of the economy, but all would implement democratic and decentered institutional frameworks.

Critical here, the idea of a "decentered" political economy should not be confused with decentralization per se. Decentering can be defined as developing a political economy in which decision-making powers and knowledge formation are functionally and geographically dispersed among different actors, rather than concentrated within particular groups. Both older forms of socialist central planning and the modern capitalist economy agglomerate power within elite groups, under both public and private ownership.

An economy organized around public ownership should, unlike these older forms, also disperse administrative units, knowledge production, and competence. The new economy should also comprise a plurality and diversity of organizations—mutual bodies, trade union research networks, small business associations, government, and autonomously funded think tanks—offering alternative and competing interpretations of economic problems. Of course, there are no guarantees in any economic system that elite or special interests cannot capture policy agendas to the detriment of the common good, but dispersing functions, knowledge, and institutional capacity countervails those tendencies.

Pursuing Public Ownership

Public ownership is defined broadly here, and "commons" is used instead of "common ownership." The use of the term "public" is advocated as an alternative to "private" in relation to economic ownership and the social relations that underpin the economy. The point is that the pursuit of public ownership, in its strongest sense, implies an economy that is primarily owned collectively and, more importantly, subject to collective decision-making—in opposition to corporate or financialized forms of ownership. Key to what follows here is that "public" includes both state forms of collective ownership and such non-state forms as cooperatives and worker-owned enterprises. While small private firms drive innovation and entrepreneurship, helping to ensure indispensable dynamism, an agreed-upon size threshold could be used to introduce forms of collective public ownership beyond a certain point. This cap could, in turn, help prevent labor appropriation, or the emergence of a class of corporate vested interests.

Principles Underpinning a Public Ownership Model

Four underpinning principles should undergird a publicly owned democratic economy.[2] The first is that economic decision-making should be dispersed and decentralized as democratically as possible across society, rather than concentrated and centralized in a corporate and financial oligarchy or a board of directors running state enterprises at arm's length from democratic control (the so-called Morrisonian model of postwar British nationalization). Second is a requirement for tolerance, respect, and engagement with different traditions of collective and public ownership. Third is the need for institutional economic forms that promote knowledge, innovation, and deliberation in economic practice. And last is the integration of the second and third principles into a requirement for diversity and pluralism in organizational forms.

To deliver on these principles in the current global economy, public ownership should have the following aspirations:

- To promote greater participation by workers, consumers, and citizens in general economic decision-making
- To take into public ownership industries too strategically important to be in private hands, such as banking, energy, and other utilities
- To facilitate greater local community control over resources, in contradistinction to such increasingly destructive forms of ownership as private equity firms and other asset-stripping forms of private ownership

- To redistribute income and wealth through cross-subsidization among sectors and social groups
- To secure such key environmental and social goals as combating climate change and addressing growing inequalities

Forms of Ownership

Table 15.1 details seven broad types of public ownership already present in the contemporary economy. In practice, a range of hybrids can also be adopted, as could more loosely networked organizational forms that link localities and communities to broaden support and resources. Interesting examples from Latin America include partnerships between trade unions, municipal governments, and consumer groups in some re-municipalized public utility sectors such as water. Table 15.1 also provides an assessment of varying public ownership forms in promoting democratic engagement and fulfilling key public policy goals, based on country case studies developed at greater length in my book, *Reclaiming Public Ownership.*

Historical experience tells us much about the effects of different forms of public ownership. Full public ownership of entire sectors at higher scales—such as full state ownership (FSO) or regional state ownership (RSO)—like that in many capitalist and communist countries between 1945 and 1979, can deliver effective public control to achieve long-term strategic investment and key policy outcomes, as evidenced in countries from France to South Korea.[3] More decentralized forms of public ownership, such as local/municipal state ownership (LMO) and cooperatives, are evident in Germany and Denmark, in the successful community-based shift toward renewable energy.

Importantly, a wide range of different models of public ownership can meet key public policy objectives and still be democratically accountable. Also, a trade-off exists between delivering very democratic and participatory economic institutions to the local community—(e.g., LMOs, producer cooperatives (PCs), employee ownership (EO))—and having higher national or even international level institutions—FSO, partial state ownership (PSO)—that can deal strategically with the broader issue of tackling equality and injustice. RSOs at the subnational regional level (e.g., Hydro-Quebec, Scottish Water) might combine the best of both worlds—with capacity for higher geographical strategic coordination and closer social proximity to citizens than national level organizations. Overall, we should aspire to democratically controlled public ownership at higher levels while leaving control of most other activities to communities. Whatever form of ownership is chosen, the aspiration should be toward democratic decision-making and giving employees, consumers, user groups, and local communities a voice.

Table 15.1 How Effective Are Various Forms of Public
Ownership in Achieving Desired Objectives?

Objective	Form of Ownership	Rating
Securing public control of the economy's strategic sectors ("commanding heights")	FSO	++
	RSO	+
	PSO	+
	LMO	+
	PC	=
	CC	−
	EO	−
Achieving greater local community control over decision-making	FSO	−
	RSO	+
	PSO	−
	LMO	++
	PC	+
	CC	+
	EO	+
Achieving distributional justice (equal and fair provision across a national/regional territory)	FSO	++
	RSO	+
	PSO	+
	LMO	+
	PC	−
	CC	+
	EO	−
Achieving environmental sustainability and tackling climate change	FSO	++
	RSO	++
	PSO	+
	LMO	++
	PC	=
	CC	=
	EO	=
Developing greater participation in decision-making	FSO	=
	RSO	+
	PSO	=
	LMO	+
	PC	++
	CC	++
	EO	++

Source: Cumbers, *Reclaiming Public Ownership*, 2012, 165.
Key:
  + positive effect.
  − negative effect.
  = neutral.
  FSO = full state ownership.
  RSO = regional state ownership.
  PSO = partial state ownership.
  LMO = Local/municipal state ownership.
  PC = producer cooperative.
  CC = consumer cooperative.
  EO = employee ownership.

In theory, taking an industry into FSO will meet the objectives of influencing key sectors and undertaking longer-term strategic planning to secure such important goals as dealing with climate change and building and maintaining modern electricity or transport systems. Largely resulting from partial privatization, PSO like we see in many European countries is perhaps today's most common form of state ownership. FSOs and PSOs are less likely to secure greater participation by the ordinary citizen, so over time the elite could capture them and trigger the principal agent problems that have beset earlier nationalizations. In the United Kingdom in the 1950s, for example, the state-owned electricity generation sector embarked with minimal public engagement on a very costly program of nuclear power station construction, subordinating energy generation to military objectives.[4] However, some argue, greater managerial autonomy makes state-owned entities more efficient.

In practice, such issues can never be fully eradicated, but the problems can be minimized where management and the workforce have operational freedom but remain more broadly democratically accountable to clearly specified public goals. The Norwegian state oil company Statoil was a good example in the 1970s of an FSO with day-to-day managerial autonomy but a broader remit to pursue progressive social and environmental policies.[5]

While local municipal ownership models are spatially closer to local communities and citizens, they also run the risk of capture by elite groups. In particular, city governance could develop boosterish projects (e.g., gentrification, event-led regeneration, such as Olympic Games hosting) that may benefit particular groups, not the more general interest. Cooperative and employee-owned firms (EO, PO, CO) clearly score highest in terms of democratic participation and involvement but arguably will do less well at securing broader policy objectives. While an economy completely composed of decentralized cooperative firms will most likely shift overall economic values toward more socially progressive ends, without countervailing forms of ownership that model could also create new hierarchies if employees, producer interests, or other groups monopolize decision-making at the expense of others—say, pensioners or the unemployed.

Hybrid Public Ownership

Recent years have seen considerable experimentation with new forms of public ownership. A pronounced trend is toward more hybrid forms that combine state and non-state forms of collective ownership. Examples of this abound in Latin America, where resistance to privatization and re-municipalization following successful campaigns have led to the establishment of new public organizations that seem to broaden participation and democracy. *Aguas Argentinas SA* was founded in greater Buenos Aires in response to failed privatization by a US-led consortium of multinational corporations; this cooperative's shares were held jointly by the local authority and the water and sanitation workers trade union. Another example is the *Mittlegrunden* wind farm, constructed off Copenhagen's coast in 2001 and providing 3 percent of the Danish capital's electricity needs. Ownership of the wind farm was originally divided equally between the city's own municipal energy company and a specially created cooperative that has since bought the city council's stake. Some 8,700 residents now own shares, administered through the cooperative.

Geographic and Historical Scope

Globalization since 1980 has in many ways undermined the sovereignty of national states to effectively manage the economy. The growth of multinational corporations, the increased complexity of commodity chains, and the deregulation (mostly by central state governments) of financial markets have all made it harder to construct effective national-scaled organizational models and systems. However, as the recent financial crisis and subsequent wave of bank nationalizations demonstrated, nations remain the only political actors capable of using their legislative and regulatory powers to enact broader systemic change when economic crises strike. Only within the European Union have national governments effectively ceded power completely to higher-level supra-state disciplining mechanisms. But even then, dominant national states, notably Germany, control macroeconomic decision-making.

With such caveats in mind, the model proposed here places alternative forms of public ownership in the national state economic space, but takes account of today's multi-scalar economic realities. Since there is no one-size-fits-all institutional design, a diverse set of spatial configurations reflects both social needs and the economy's technical requirements across different sectors.

Strategies for democratic public ownership will also need to be sensitive to geographical and historical contingency and work with the grain of current public ownership practice. More decentralized forms of public ownership organized around cooperatives and local state ownership might work better in federal systems with strong traditions of local mutualism, in countries such as Germany and the United States, than in more centralized economic systems, such as the United Kingdom, where older forms of public ownership have been highly centralized. But again, ownership forms will vary by sector.

While democracy is best served by attempting to disperse rather than centralize economic decision-making, globalization and the complexities of advanced economies mean that there is often, in practice, a trade-off between higher-level coordination and local autonomy and participation. The way around this trade-off is through confederal structures—for example, national publicly owned rail networks might have democratic boards composed of locally and regionally elected consumer representatives.

One thorny issue is how to balance encouraging local autonomy in terms of ownership with committing to equity and distributional justice. Even where organizing local decision-making is economically efficient, centralized coordination and regulation would be needed to safeguard every citizen's basic economic, social, and cultural rights. The US history of local racial segregation and discrimination reminds us of the need for clearly defined national (and even international) basic economic and social rights. Guaranteeing such social rights would require higher-level state regulation, particularly in such direct-service sectors as health, housing, and energy. Also, local public ownership would need to be set within frameworks of universal constitutional rights to affordable basic necessities across national state jurisdictions.

Even if we accept the basic principles of decentered decision-making, we still need some democratically elected way of dealing with broader macroeconomic decisions made at the national, supranational (such as the EU), and even global level. Consider here as an example a tax on financial speculation. Table 15.2 shows how these different forms of public ownership might be applied across the range of economic sectors. The list is far from exhaustive, but shows how a very different kind of economy might be built around collective forms of ownership and institutions that benefit the community or "general interest" rather than elite groups.

Profiteering and speculation in the financial sector have created massive social inequities over the past three decades without adding to the general common wealth. In place of the private and deregulated model that precipitated the financial crisis in 2007–2008 and subsequent recession, we could develop a very different publicly owned sector. A mix of ownership forms would be consonant with differing needs for and uses of money and credit. State ownership, at a range of scales, could help us reach broader economic stabilization objectives. Today's central banks know how to do this, but going forward we would have to re-democratize them, moving away from "independent" control serving elite interests and putting social goals (creating jobs and reducing unemployment) ahead of austerity and monetary policy driven by inflation.

Below the national or federal level, regional state reserve banks (like Germany's *Landesbanken*, for instance) could be tasked with securing sustainable and balanced local and regional economic development. In the United States, this might mean more autonomy for its regional Federal Reserve banks. In general, we should push for much greater political interference in central bank decision-making, but this should be deliberative and broadly scrutinized. Technical committees and managerial

Table 15.2 What Kinds of Public Ownership Could Be Used in Different Sectors?

Type of Activity	Spatial Organization	Forms of Ownership	Institutional and Regulatory Arrangements
Finance	Local, national, transnational	• Global FSOs for international development • National FSOs for monetary policies • FSOs and LMOs for funding industrial/economic development • COs for housing, finance • PO/EOs for housing, pensions	• Tight regulation and demarcation of separate spheres • Outlawing of speculation and derivatives trading, tax havens • Restrictions on "usury"
Utility industries (e.g., electricity, water, gas)	Local, national, macro-regional	• Combination of LMOs and FSOs	• Possibilities for hybrid forms of ownership at local scale (for example, Denmark)
Public transportation	Local, national, macro-regional	• Combination of LMOs and FSOs	• Public subsidy for public transport • High taxes on private motoring
Public service (e.g., health, education)	Local and national	• Combination of LMOs and FSOs	• Strong national regulatory structure to ensure equal standards between regions • High taxation of private forms and redistribution of income to state run areas
Housing	Regional, local	LMOs and CCs	• National level housing federation to promote public and cooperative ownership • Tax subsidies for public housing projects • Legislation for tighter regulation of mortgage financing and private renting

(Continued)

Type of Activity	Spatial Organization	Forms of Ownership	Institutional and Regulatory Arrangements
Consumer products (e.g., clothing, food, electronic equipment)	• Global production networks • Local/ regionalized food networks	• Consumer and producer cooperatives • Small and family-owned firms	• Ethical trade rules • Living wage standards • Rights of collective association • Tax and other subsidies to stimulate local and carbon-neutral production systems

Source: Derived and updated from Cumbers, *Reclaiming Public Ownership*, 2012, 168, Table 7.2.

appointees could still be drawn from the economics profession (though not just mainstream neoclassical economics), but legislators should set strategic priorities.

National and regional development banks, also state owned, could be tasked with investing in key sectors and initiatives and with promoting training, research, and development—for example, in renewable energy or medical research. Such banks should not be beholden to or even comparable to private commercial banks, but should instead be driven by a broader public interest requirement and tasked with meeting specified social and environmental goals. Reinvented, they might, for instance, support local community development banks and credit unions, or democratized banks.

Utilities also exemplify strategic activities requiring management by and for the whole community. Natural monopolies—such as public transport, electricity, and water supplies—require higher-level coordination to deliver economies of scale. But some can be combined with more local and decentralized forms. Already, many European countries organize water supplies effectively at the municipal or regional scales. Power generation needs national and even supranational coordination of grid networks to, for instance, tackle climate change and eradicate fuel poverty. Once again, confederal structures, with national entities constituted by democratically elected representatives of local and regional public companies, could do the job if more localized forms of ownership were created at the same time.

Such public transportation and public services as health and education should be broadly organized in the public sector, their forms ranging from local community cooperatives to more national forms (such as educational authorities and basic healthcare) where distributive justice, efficiency, and cross-subsidization of poorer groups warrant higher scales of organization. Private ownership and market-based delivery should be kept to a minimum, or, in care and nurturing sectors, outlawed since social rights must take precedence over monetary valuation and commodification. The US health-care system provides the test case example of how not to proceed: its market-based values infringe on human dignity and the right to decent care, and it is also very inefficient, with price fixing and significant public investment hiding market failure, ultimately leading to poor outcomes.

For housing, a more diverse mix of ownership forms would be preferable. Private housing should be allowed but legislation and regulation (e.g., community land trusts, land-value taxes) could challenge its hegemonic and privileged status and free the sector from speculative and financialized interests. A more regulated system, allowing private ownership but reducing speculation, would keep assets affordable for communities and promote the rights of all individuals and families to decent housing. This way, real consumer choice would replace the *faux* choice of speculator-driven subprime markets.

To make this approach work, more finance and investment would have to be channeled toward collective ownership. While cooperative ownership forms could be encouraged, more democratic forms of state ownership as an alternative to mortgage thralldom should be an aspiration of progressive housing governance. Social housing needs to be a lifestyle choice rather than the stigma of a residualized underclass. Hybrid forms of public ownership, part local state and part cooperative ownership, could play an important part.

More diverse forms of collective ownership could also be given greater encouragement in consumer goods sectors. Examples abound of retail chains in Western Europe and Scandinavia that are already cooperatively or employee owned and which provide high level service and product quality (for instance, the UK's John Lewis chain). These enterprises could, however, be subject to stricter ethical rules around employment conditions, fair trade, and environmental best practice, and we will still need competitive markets to provide signals and stimulate innovation.

Transition Time

Given the power of vested economic and political elite interests, the transition to a democratic, publicly owned economy would take considerable political mobilization and dedicated critical engagement with the state apparatus and institutions. The obstacles to the vision laid out here are immense, but the continuing popularity of public ownership among the wider population in opposition to, and despite, the negative rhetoric of the mainstream corporate media is encouraging.

The solutions proposed here all exist already in some form, and public ownership is once again an issue of debate, due to disaffection with our current economic system, its injustices, and inequalities. Within individual economic sectors, forms of public ownership could be introduced relatively quickly—within an electoral cycle—if they were to build on current forms of public ownership and collective forms of organization and excite political will.

The ability to carry out such changes will, of course, vary with the size of the national economy and its openness to international trade. Another variable is how integrated the economy is into the global international division of labor. It will be harder for a Greece than a Germany or United States, but easier in a more advanced smaller economy such as Sweden, which competes less on cost competitiveness than does, say, Vietnam or Bangladesh.

Clearly, variations in current forms of public ownership and capitalism mean that the short-term prospects for advancing democratic public ownership are more feasible in some countries than others. However, even in relatively hostile and advanced neoliberal political economies (say, the United States and the United Kingdom), many of ownership options outlined here already exist. While the public sector has suffered considerable reversals, commitments to cooperativism and mutualism remain strong, often at the local level in opposition to national government initiatives. Thus, given the right political will across geographical scales, with the right government policies, it would be possible over a relatively short period (perhaps a decade) to extend their reach across the entire economy.

Real-World Examples, Experiments and Models

Two real-world examples typify the spirit of the approach suggested here: Norway's model of oil development and Danish experiences with renewable energy.[6] Differing in form and context, both are public ownership regimes with strong elements of economic democracy and public participation, and both highlight the extent to which very different geographical and institutional configurations can provide more participatory forms of economic governance that challenge elite capture. Importantly, the critical mix of state regulation and legislation needed to foster both democratic public ownership and public participation and the collective learning processes employed are replicable.

Norway's Oil Experience: State Ownership, Active Civil Society, and Deliberative Democracy

The "Norwegian model" is rightly acclaimed around the world for its approach to North Sea oil and gas development, particularly for dispersing the benefits throughout the country's economy and society rather than allowing vested interests to capture resources. After almost 40 years of oil development, Norway remains one of the planet's most egalitarian societies and compares particularly favorably on that score with the United Kingdom. It consistently ranks at the top of the United Nations Human Development Index (number one in the rankings in 2018).[7]

Norway's careful husbandry of its oil interests has been a critical part of this success story. Of particular interest here is the state intervention in and public ownership of the development of oil and gas resources. When the North Sea oil fields were discovered in the 1960s, the approach adopted had much in common with Third World countries in dealing with the power of the international oil cartel: a nationalized entity was set up using a "top-down" model of state ownership, initially led by elites within the central state apparatus. However, as the magnitude of oil resources became apparent, a much more broader debate over the impact of oil wealth on Norwegian society and culture developed. In the ensuing process, oil development was placed within a more deliberative and democratic framework, where more progressive agendas on environmental, social development, and workplace health and safety agendas took hold.

Critical to the creation of this approach was an active civil society and a long tradition of viewing natural resource extraction in terms of broader community and social benefits. In Norway's political and cultural context, important ethical and institutional norms regarding the relationship between natural resources and economic interests run very deep. Influenced by the American progressive journalist Henry George, the Norwegian justice minister, Johan Carlsberg, believed firmly that economic rent from natural resource use should not be captured by any private individual or group of private interests but should be the "common property of the people."[8]

Norwegian oil policy created important mechanisms and institutions to secure the national collective interest and ensure that society as a whole benefited from oil and gas and took part in the public debate during the 1970s about the future of the nation's resources. The state's direct financial interest (SDFI) in oil development was established in 1985 to quell fears that Statoil was becoming too powerful and is now managed by a state-owned company, Petero. A separate state oil fund—the "Government Pension Fund Global"—was established in 1990 and is currently worth around £600 billion.[9] This fund has recently been subjected to much tougher ethical investment rules, including divestment from coal-fired energy, giving it a progressive outward-facing role as one of the largest global investment funds.

Two other important institutions were critical in the creation of a more progressive and democratic Norwegian approach to managing oil resources. A Petroleum Directorate was created separate from Statoil and charged with administering, regulating, and controlling oil and gas resources independent of the oil companies. One consequence was the development of the world's safest offshore oil and gas regime from the early 1980s onward. But the Directorate also developed its own professional and technical expertise in all things oil.

The second defining feature was what became known as the Paragraph 10 clause in the legislation creating Statoil. While Statoil was supposed to be a commercial operation at arm's length from government, the clause required the company to present an annual report to parliament on "significant issues relating to principles and policy."[10] As a result, the company and the impact of oil on Norway were under continuing scrutiny and debate into the 1990s.

Many committees in the Norwegian Parliament—including Social Affairs, Foreign Affairs, and Local Government—began considering all aspects of oil development. In the process, they drew on diverse knowledge and expertise from all sectors of civil society, including professional associations, trade unions, fishing and farming interests, and church groups. In this impressive process of deliberation and collective learning, many parliamentarians also developed extensive knowledge of oil affairs. The outcome was probably the most progressive approach to energy development ever seen. Norway committed itself to a "socialized" model of oil, key elements of which were the priority that oil should create a "qualitatively better society" and, crucially, a "moderate rate of oil extraction," with a 90-million-ton ceiling that was not breached until the early 1990s.[11] Additionally, emphasis was put on developing the resource in the most environmentally friendly manner and using oil-extraction revenues to boost Norway's spending on international development.

Denmark's Wind Power Revolution: Diversified and Decentered Public Ownership

If Norway's example shows how an older form of top-down public ownership—a state enterprise—can be embedded in democratic and participatory frameworks of governance, the Danish experience with renewable energy points us toward a diversified and innovative mix of forms of public or common ownership that might enrich democratic processes in the economy.

In energy policy, Denmark has been held up as a model by the International Energy Agency for its far-sighted approach to tackling climate change. The country went from being completely dependent on foreign oil and gas for its energy needs in the 1970s to using renewables for over 20 percent of primary energy production (DEA 2015).[12] The cornerstone of this success was the emergence of a wind power industry that has been at the forefront of Denmark's strategy to increase self-reliance and reduce CO_2 emissions and that also created 20,000 jobs and claimed 50 percent of the world market for wind-turbine manufacturing.[13]

Denmark's success has been based on public ownership and planned interventions, but it is neither a top-down, state-driven process, nor a grassroots achievement. Instead, it reflects the combination of state action, grassroots social mobilization, and diversified public ownership arrangements at different geographical scales. While it reflects some important historical and geographically specific factors, this success story also offers some important general insights for developing more sustainable and democratically based economic forms.

The oil crises of the 1970s exposed Denmark's heavy dependence on imported oil—roughly 90 percent of total energy demand in 1973.[14] Rising oil prices over the decade prompted Danes to rethink energy policy. While the country lacked the vast oil and gas resources of the United Kingdom and Norway, important discoveries in the Danish North Sea translated into reduced imports during the 1980s. However, Denmark still faced significant problems and some hard choices in achieving long-term security of energy supply.

The political struggle over the direction of energy policy was intense. Much of the country's political and business establishment favored nuclear power as an alternative to oil, but a coalition of green, left, and rural communities countered with an alternative vision of a more localized, decentered model based on renewable energy. An important factor in turning away from nuclear was likely the country's traditional interest in wind power. Another factor was that Denmark's engineering and scientific communities showcased the viability of non-nuclear technologies in a populist way, fostering an alternative discourse around "clean" and "pure" energy.

By 1980, the Danish government had embarked on a decisive strategy in support of renewables with a model of decentered and localized forms of collective ownership at the fore. Three critical pillars defined government policy:

- First, government funding for 30 percent of all investment in new wind turbines from 1980 to 1990 gave wind-power producers an important boost.
- Second, the *Energipakken* was introduced, compelling electricity distribution companies to purchase a certain quota of energy supply every year from renewable producers as part of nationally set targets.
- Third, and most pertinent here, local and collective ownership of turbines was encouraged, largely through laws limiting their ownership to those residing in the municipality where the turbine is built. These are known as "residency criteria," or distance regulation laws.

Together, these policies gave the wind power industry a massive boost. Growth was particularly pronounced in the second half of the 1990s

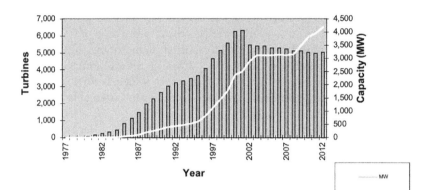

Figure 15.2 Growth in number of turbines and capacity: Denmark 1977–2012.
Source: Danish Energy Agency.[20]

(see Figure 15.2) following adoption of the feed-in-tariff, which other EU countries have since applied.

Although relaxed more recently with the election of more center-right governments, these local ownership laws gave critical political momentum to localized and collective forms of ownership and have had long-lasting effects. They have meant that wind turbine ownership remains dominated by either small-scale forms of private ownership (typically, partnerships among neighbors) or cooperative forms. The first Danish onshore "wind farms," which covered extensive areas and supplied energy to more than a local neighborhood, were all cooperatively owned. At the height of local turbine ownership in the late 1990s, some 150,000 families, around 10 percent of the population, were involved.[15]

Community participation in the ownership and development of the technology has been critical to the growth of renewable energy capacity. Surveys suggest that around 70 percent of the population—far more than any other country—now favors of wind farms, with only around 5 percent against them.[16]

Together, the distance–regulation laws, state support for renewables, and Denmark's localist and collectivist traditions have been important in both dispersing economic power and creating the conditions for greater public participation, deliberation, and economic democracy in the energy sector. The country's electricity-distribution system is also decentralized and cooperative compared to those put in place through nationalization in France and the United Kingdom after 1945. On balance, the model here may be hard to transplant to more centralized energy systems with national grids of older coal, gas, and nuclear power stations. Yet, the dispersed nature of low-carbon energy technologies may still invite more localized forms of organization and ownership to develop.

Today, Denmark's broader electricity system remains heavily decentralized. Around 100 local distribution companies (primarily cooperatively and municipally owned) and 10 regional transmission networks (amalgamations of the 100 local cooperatives) are operating.[17] This means that local cooperative and mutual forms of ownership dominate the electricity distribution system. While a more traditional oil- and coal-fired centralized power-generation system is still around, the state-owned energy company, Dansk Olie og Naturgas A/S, and Vattenfall, a subsidiary of the Swedish state-owned corporation, have helped build localization into power generation.

Boards of municipal, mainly urban companies are appointed by the local government, whereas the mostly rural cooperatives are democratically elected at meetings of consumers. Representatives from the local boards, in turn, elect the board members of regional companies. Overall, the Danish energy network is remarkable for its level of public participation and democratic decision-making and for the way these powers are "decentered" (not bound up in one organization or set of elite institutions). The network's active and knowledgeable civil society around renewable energy and climate change politics represents a progressive force for broader processes of social and environmental change.

Interestingly, some innovative hybrid forms of local public ownership have emerged since 2000, notably the development of partnerships between municipal and publicly owned utility companies, and partnerships between municipal governments and residents' cooperatives. Besides the *Mittlegrunden* wind farm mentioned above, hybrid models are also being encouraged in offshore wind ventures that must offer a 20 percent stake to bespoke local residents' cooperatives.[18]

Conclusion

The model of economic democracy here envisages a mixed economy populated by diverse forms of public ownership. The model stands in opposition to today's increasingly corporatized and financialized system. "Decentering" the economy would encourage the diffusion of economic decision-making and the development of democratic ownership forms ranging from national state to local cooperatives and employee-owned firms. Seven possible forms of public ownership are identified, though these are not exclusive and could be combined in hybrids to further widen democracy through structures that draw multiple stakeholders and interest groups into economic decision-making. No one model of public ownership is applicable in all contexts, but distinctive forms will be appropriate in different economic sectors. This chapter provides a schematic overview of how this model could look in practice across the main sectors of an economy.

Notes

1 For greater elaboration of these issues, see Andrew Cumbers, *Reclaiming Public Ownership* (London: Zed Books, 2012).
2 Cumbers, *Reclaiming Public Ownership*, 145–146.
3 Cumbers, *Reclaiming Public Ownership*.
4 Cumbers, *Reclaiming Public Ownership*, 21.
5 Cumbers, *Reclaiming Public Ownership*, Chapter 8.
6 Descriptions of the models outlined here can be found in greater depth in Cumbers, *Reclaiming Public Ownership*.
7 United Nations Development Programme, "Human Development Reports," United Nations, 2014, http://hdr.undp.org/en/composite/HDI.
8 Helge Ryggvik, *The Norwegian Oil Experience: A Toolbox for Managing Resources* (Oslo: University of Oslo, Centre for Technology, Innovation and Culture, 2010), http://www.sv.uio.no/tik/forskning/publikasjoner/tik-rapportserie/Ryggvik.pdf.
9 "IQ 2016 Quarterly Report," *Norges Bank*, https://www.nbim.no/en/transparency/reports/2016/1q-2016-quarterly-report/.
10 Ryggvik, *The Norwegian Oil Experience*, 100.
11 Ryggvik, *The Norwegian Oil Experience*, 34–35.
12 DEA 2015 *Key Figures from DEA's Preliminary Energy Statistics* Danish Energy Agency, accessed August 2016, http://www.ens.dk/en/info/news-danish-energy-agency/2015-denmark-hits-lowest-energy-consumption-more-40-years.
13 Danish Energy Agency (DEA), *Danish Energy Policy 1970–2010* (Copenhagen: DEA, 2010).
14 Cumbers, *Reclaiming Public Ownership*, 193.
15 Cumbers, *Reclaiming Public Ownership*, 197.
16 Hans Christian Soerensen, Lars Kjeld Hansen, Karin Hammarlund, and Jens Larsen, *Experience with and Strategies for Public Involvement in Offshore Wind Projects* (Brussels: Institute for Infrastructure, Environment and Innovation, 2003).
17 Cumbers, *Reclaiming Public Ownership*, 198.
18 Danish Government, *Promotion of Renewable Energy Act 2008*, 2009, Section 13 (1), p. 5, accessed August 2016, http://www.ens.dk/sites/ens.dk/files/undergrund-forsyning/vedvarende-energi/vindkraft-vindmoeller/havvindmoeller/kystn-aere/promotion_of_renewable_energy_act.1392.2008.pdf.
19 Table derived from *Statistical Bulletin: Ownership of UK Quoted Shares 2014*, Office of National Statistics, London, accessed August 2016, http://www.ons.gov.uk/economy/investmentspensionsandtrusts/bulletins/ownershipofukquotedshares/2015-09-02.
20 Figure drawn from DEA spreadsheet, accessed August 2016, http://www.ens.dk/en/info/facts-figures/energy-statistics-indicators-energy-efficiency/overview-energy-sector/register.

Part 5

Community-Based Pluralist Systems

Relationships are at the core of economic systems. It's hard to keep that in mind when so much modern economic activity involves faceless, soulless entities. Our current economic system was built for speed and efficiency—and without the hard work of building community, cultivating mutually beneficial interactions, and ensuring that the cumulative effects of our economic exchanges don't rend our social fabric and damage our planet.

How does community-building, and the relationship-nurturing that it entails, figure into a reimagined economic system? Can an economy have a heart—not merely the capacity for altruistic actions but the kind of caring that evolves from relationships?

The essays in this section delve into ways system change should evolve from the kind of relationships we want to have and the communities we want to build.

Arguing for a "pluralist commonwealth," Gar Alperovitz, founder of The Democracy Collaborative, asserts that "the central challenge of the emerging era" is building community—not just an economic and political structure but "a new culture of 'we are all in it together.'" Four principles undergird the pluralist commonwealth: democratization of wealth, community as a guiding theme, decentralization, and democratic planning. Democratic control both within enterprises and communities—local, regional, and national—are central to the longer-term design. Embedded in the concept of "community" are localism—in which national powers are devolved to regions and regional powers are devolved to municipal and neighborhood levels—and broad inclusion. Multiple forms of democratic ownership would be encouraged, both allowing for and depending upon a systemic reconstruction that engenders far greater equality, common direction, and community.

James Gustave Speth, the co-chair of The Next System Project at The Democracy Collaborative, envisions a society that has rejected what Tibor Scitovsky called "the joyless economy" and embraced a radically new system to create and sustain joy. Speth explains that joy "comes not from money but from 'other people.' We flourish in a setting of warm, nurturing, and rewarding interpersonal relationships, and within that context we flourish best when we are giving, not getting." As a result, Speth's "new America" is more democratic—designed to encourage and sustain "human solidarity, devoted friendship, and meaningful accomplishment," structured to ensure that economic benefits are shared equitably, and committed to sustaining the "environment ... for current and future generations." Speth proposes interventions that affect all dimensions of life, including cultural values, markets, corporate structures, finance, economic growth, politics, foreign relations, and the military. The result, simply put, is that life is "simpler, people more caring, and less grasping and status-conscious."

Jessica Gordon Nembhard, political economist and professor in the Department of Africana Studies at the City University of New York's John Jay College, describes a cooperative commonwealth, a system of interlocking, grassroots solidarity enterprises that establish and strengthen economic participation from the bottom up. In the cooperative solidarity commonwealth, the economy is centered on need, not profit. Economic and political power are decentralized, and wealth is democratically controlled and distributed. Since "we can't have economic democracy in a racist and sexist society," work on anti-oppression and nonexploitation would be an imperative as communities start cooperatives and control resources. In the United States, this system would be built by local groups of marginalized peoples and their allies. Cooperators would produce much of what they need locally, contributing to ecological and environmental health and sustainability.

Emily Kawano, co-director of the Wellspring Cooperative Corporation in Springfield, Massachusetts, looks at the solidarity economy as a global movement as well as an evolving framework for building a just and equitable economic alternative to capitalism and other authoritarian state-dominated systems. She describes the solidarity economy as an ecosystem of practices—some old, some new, some still emergent—that align with values informed by social movements focusing on anti-racism, feminism, anti-imperialism, labor, poor people, the environment, and democracy. The concept encompasses principles of solidarity, equity, participatory democracy, sustainability, and pluralism. The Solidarity Economy Mapping Project tracks the myriad ways of realizing an economic vision capable of supplanting an ecologically destructive focus on profit with a fabric of mutual economic support.

Ed Whitfield, co-managing director of the Fund for Democratic Communities in Greensboro, South Carolina, suggests a framework for democratizing wealth that calls for enabling human potential currently stifled by exploitative structures and private ownership of productive assets. The goal is total economic democracy and community control over production, so as to place "the wealth created by human labor back into the commons for the benefit of all." It would require creating new relationships among people, new democratic norms and political procedures to establish and defend those norms, and new environmental outcomes that reflect those norms. Cooperative associations and democratically managed community groups would own productive assets, and public financial institutions would control surplus values and investments. Examples include experiments by F4DC in community ownership and community-as-developer, along with a Southern Reparations Loan Fund.

Michael T. Lewis, executive director of the Canadian Centre for Community Renewal, envisions a "cooperative economic democracy"—a new global economic system structure based on "seven principles of resilience": diversity, modularity, social capital, innovation, overlap and redundancy, tight information feedback loops, and ecosystem services (social functions that are essential but have no market value). These principles "mirror the ecological principles, processes, and relationships that render healthy ecosystems resilient." The initiatives that best reflect them have three features, Lewis writes: they engage in local or regional (micro) level action; they interweave providing basic human needs with other system-change endeavors; and they build federations of networks, coalitions, and movements with a shared agenda and greater capacity. Lewis cites as examples the RESO community economic development initiative in Montreal, worker and consumer cooperatives in Emilia-Romagna in Italy, and La Vía Campesina in Latin America. Fully realizing this vision will require revolutionizing goods and services production, and regaining public sovereignty over the money supply to fund the transition to sustainable energy.

Chapter 16

A Pluralist Commonwealth and a Community Sustaining System

Gar Alperovitz

Throughout much of the modern era, the two dominant alternatives to corporate capitalism have been state socialism and social democracy. The former gave priority of place to state-owned economic entities while the latter maintained capitalist institutions and hoped to contain their power through organizing (commonly bolstered by strong labor unions) for robust regulations, health and other social programs, and progressive taxation.

Both models experienced limitations in the latter part of the 20th century, and in some cases succumbed to them. For a time, after the collapse of communism in the East and the retreat of social democracy when confronted by neoliberalism in the West, it was proclaimed that unencumbered corporate capitalism—with all its inequality and environmental costs—was the only game in town, the last system left standing.

Especially since the Great Financial Crisis of 2007–2008, this judgment has begun to change. The rise of right-wing populism, in general, and the presidency of Donald Trump, in particular, have underscored the importance of clarifying critical issues not only of progressive politics, but of systemic design and institutional power relationships that may or may not permit the development of a positive new direction. So, too, the 2016 presidential campaign of Senator Bernie Sanders and the 2018 election of Alexandria Ocasio-Cortez to Congress have stimulated intensified interest in system-altering alternatives that can take us beyond periods of political impasse.

At the same time, a growing array of new proposals (and variants on older proposals) have emerged in response to the challenges facing the current model and the pain being felt in the United States and around the world. Even as politics recasts traditional left-right divisions, some of the oldest questions of political-economy are being debated with renewed seriousness, a clear response to current difficulties. Alternative system-changing directions have emphasized worker-owned or worker self-managed enterprises as a central economic institution, while other community-based designs elevate local small businesses and cooperatives.

Anarchist theories commonly give pride of place to various community forms while playing down larger state and other structures. A far-reaching and many-faceted theoretical debate is under way just below the surface of conventional reporting.

On a parallel track, there has been an explosion of on-the-ground experimentation and new institutional development that includes worker cooperatives (and public support for their development), neighborhood land trusts, new municipal and neighborhood economic structures, public banking efforts, remunicipalization campaigns in the water and energy sectors, public takeovers of large banks, and even the crisis nationalizations of General Motors, Chrysler, and AIG, one of the largest insurance companies and financial institutions in the world.

As this reassessment continues, the following approach begins with three assumptions: first, that any serious trajectory of longer-term development must clarify both its longer-term vision and its explicit values and goals—and especially how both are furthered by alternative institutional designs; second, that any serious trajectory of development must clarify how, specifically, it relates to emerging and fast-developing economic experiments (including not only, for instance, proposed worker cooperative and other institutions, but also larger-scale national and regional structures); and third, any serious trajectory of development must clarify how it can achieve longer-term political and cultural support as an integrated systemwide solution supportive of the values it affirms and the ecological and other limits it faces.

Critical to the latter is the exploration of evolutionary institutional, cultural, and political paths—as opposed to the simple assertion of ultimate (static) designs independent of processes that may achieve those designs. Accordingly, the following discussion is not based on a "fixed" approach to systemic "design" and "architecture," but rather on "evolutionary reconstructive" and related political strategies of (ongoing) development. For this reason, too, it includes numerous illustrations of emerging and evolving forms of institutional change developing throughout the nation.

The Principle of Community

As a guiding theme, the Pluralist Commonwealth emphasizes the principle of community: that we are all in it together. This is important both in terms of the model's institutional design and the political power and culture outcomes the model seeks to promote. Institutionally, it encourages plural forms of democratic ownership (including worker, community, and publicly owned companies alongside small- and medium-scale private firms) both at the neighborhood and the municipal level. Public or joint worker/community/public enterprises operate at the regional and national levels. Such enterprises are also understood to be a basis upon which to build progressive political power, given the institutional vacuum left by the radical decline of labor unions. By distributing ownership more broadly, the model also seeks to disperse systemwide power as an outcome of basic institutional structure.

Similarly, democratic control both within enterprise and within communities—local, regional, and national—is central to the longer-term design. This in turn requires substantial democratic planning. Planning is also required to promote stable communities in which democratic and reciprocal cultural relationships can flourish. In terms of values, the Pluralist Commonwealth seeks to advance equity, racial justice, environmental sustainability, community, liberty, and subsidiarity (that decisions should be made at the most local or decentralized level possible) in the day-to-day operations of the institutions that make up the model.

Especially important are two large-order challenges:

1   Regional decentralization: It is by no means clear that a more participatory political and economic system is possible in a continental system as large as the United States. We often forget that Germany (itself a comparatively large country) is physically smaller than the state of Montana alone[1]; California by itself is the fifth largest economy in the world.[2] There is also growing awareness of the possibilities of longer-term regional-scale decentralization in New England and the Northwest. Texas may also be an outlier, as Hispanic population trends transform current conservative political domination in a regional-scale polity. Seven regional commissions defined other possibilities in the 1960s and 1970s.[3]

2   The nation's history of slavery and publicly enforced racism pose specific challenges different in their degree of intensity and historical depth from those confronted by other advanced nations.

An instructive starting place for a deeper analysis of long-term systemic design is John Stuart Mill's insistence that direct experience with local governance is essential to "the peculiar training of a citizen, the practical part of the political education of a free people."[4] His elaboration was straightforward:

> We do not learn to read or write, to ride or swim, by being merely told how to do it, but by doing it, so it is only by practicing popular government on a limited scale, that the people will ever learn how to exercise it on a larger.[5]

Alexis de Tocqueville similarly stressed that "municipal institutions constitute the strength of free nations. Town meetings are to liberty what primary schools are to science; they bring it within the people's reach, they teach men how to use and enjoy it."[6]

In his call for "strong democracy" the late Benjamin Barber also stressed the role of direct participation in cultivating public-mindedness, and, importantly, of *creating* new future directions—beginning, again, at the local level of everyday community experience. As he observed:

> ...strong democracy relies on participation in an evolving problem-solving community that creates public ends where there were none before by means of its own activity ... In such communities, public ends are neither extrapolated from absolutes nor 'discovered' in pre-existing 'hidden consensus.' *They are literally forged through the act of public participation created through common deliberation and common action* and the effect that deliberation and action have on interests, which change shape and direction when subjected to these participatory processes (emphasis added).[7]

The same judgments about the importance of experience—both within local government and economic institutions—help define critical points of departure for other core values, including ecological sustainability, equality, liberty, and, indeed, the foundational concept of community itself. Put in the negative, if the communities and economic institutions in which Americans work and live out their lives are undemocratically managed, lack a culture of citizen initiative, and accept or condone ecologically destructive practices, great inequality, denials of liberty, and practices and attitudes that undermine a sense of community (that "we are all in it together"), it is difficult to see how the nation as a whole might ever achieve such values.

Put positively, the first critical system question is: how, specifically, might new local institutions nurture and support values of importance to the system as a whole while also helping generate political and institutional support for the necessary systemwide preconditions of a flourishing community existence—including economic stability, planning for equality, the devolution of political power (and democratic accountability of concentrated economic power)—that must ultimately be addressed on a larger scale by larger democratically controlled institutional elements of a comprehensive solution?

A fundamental contention is that if economic practices at the level of the community itself are not, by virtue of institutional design and experience, thoroughgoing in their nurturance of key values, it is unlikely, if not impossible, to expect transformative change at higher levels of the state, region, and nation. In the language of Martin Buber: "A nation is a community to the degree that it is a community of communities."[8]

Critical Challenges and Principles

In addition to the central issue of democracy, four other critical challenges require systemic answers that both begin at the level of community and also help generate value premises and potential structural directions at higher levels of integration. All are highly charged, but also potentially capable of opening radically new possibilities. They include the following:

1   Deep-seated questions of structural racism, changing gender roles, the implications of demographic change, and the economic distress, anger, and alienation of many working-class communities
2   Ecologically sustainable long-term development, climate change, the likely expansion of the US population, and the material production and growth-dependency of the economy over the next decades
3   The impact of ongoing technological change which, on the basis of the 20th century's highly uneven economic history (two world wars, a Great Depression, numerous recessions)—and even leaving aside major new technological advances—is on track to replicate its eight-fold increase in economic output per capita over the coming century[9]
4   The limitations of its more than 200-year-old constitutional design, elements of which have also slowly begun to come into focus for thoughtful reassessment and ultimate revision

The judgments implicit in the arguments of Mill, Tocqueville, Barber, and Buber point to the necessity not only of (1) building democracy on new local footings from the bottom up; but (2) of developing new institutional forms and practices that nurture other critical values, again from the bottom up—which is to say *in everyday life*; and (3) of developing overarching systemwide capacities that both provide economic and institutional support to maintain local community stability and also deal with systemwide economic, ecological, and other planning.

This is not to exclude proposals, for instance, for a "Green New Deal" or "Medicare for All." It is rather to suggest that a system-changing model capable of achieving the larger foundational directions implicit in such proposals (and furthered by them) will ultimately require deeper democratic reconstruction of institutions and political processes at many levels.

The foundational democratic theory of the Pluralist Commonwealth model includes four critical principles that build on evolving forms and structural principles appropriate to the larger challenges: (1) democratization of wealth; (2) community, both locally and in general, as a guiding theme; (3) decentralization in general (including regional-scale devolution of many national institutional capacities); and (4) substantial (though not complete) forms of democratic planning in support of community and longer-term economic, democracy-building, and ecological goals.

Clarity about the foundational concept of community is critical. Unless new cooperative, neighborhood, municipal, and other community-structured forms of democratic ownership are established at the local level, there cannot be a democratic economy in general, nor can foundational experiences for broader development become sufficiently widespread so that a culture of democratic ownership and control can become commonplace throughout the larger system. Changing ownership is a necessary, but not sufficient, condition of establishing the institutional foundations for systemic movement toward genuine equality.

This fundamental judgment has immediate relevance for political-economic institutional design. Importantly, nearly half of the members of any community, on average, are not understood to be "workers" as defined by traditional conceptions of the labor force. Among these are the elderly (24 percent) of whom a majority are former workers; individuals with disabilities (10 percent); individuals providing care for others (8 percent); and students (6 percent).[10] If genuine democracy is a priority (to say nothing of genuine community), the development of local communitywide institutions must be broadly inclusive, designed in ways that bring together the interests not only of workers engaged in production at any particular moment in time, but also of other members of society who have been or will be "workers," as well as the interests of the broader community.

An Ecologically Coherent Culture

By "internalizing externalities" a community-inclusive approach also is critical to the nurturing of economic and institutional power relationships that help rationalize environmental choices. Contrary to situations in which private businesses may pollute—and the community through government must intervene as an opposing regulatory force—when the community itself is directly involved in, for instance, a community owned utility, the question posed is whether it wishes to pay the costs of cleaning up the problems its own activities create. Beginning to move in such a direction is critical to the development of an ecologically coherent culture in everyday life—the necessary local precondition of an ecologically sustainable system in general. To the degree a community or neighborhood owns significant economic enterprises, ecologically sustainable practices become far less contentious. Unlike the conventional regulation of private firms—which inherently creates conflict between public and private interests—in models that include community ownership the regulatory choice is rationalized since the costs of responsible environmental practices are both paid for and simultaneously largely benefit the same entity: the community or municipality that owns the firm.

This principle applies at many different levels of impact: the costs of constraining, eliminating, or substituting for processes that currently generate

CO_2, and other climate-impacting gases commonly create conflict between private corporate owners and regulatory publics. When ownership of the enterprise is anchored in the community of not only the city but the state, region, or nation—*and the impact of its noxious output* again harms the same (larger scale) community—democratic consideration of the dangers, costs, and benefits are rationalized.

Similarly, to the degree the principle of community is normalized, the concept of *the community-through-time, recognizing the needs of future generations*, is also normalized, which is to say paying the costs of eliminating *ongoing climate change and other environmental dangers, again, can both be borne by—and also benefit—the community understood via generational family and other relationships as inherently both present and continuing through time.*

Finally, a flourishing and meaningful community, if developed with care and concern for social relationships and the necessary economic and institutional foundations of such relationships, can reduce the pressures that drive wasteful and unsustainable growth and cultures of envy, competition, and unnecessary consumption.

Models for Systemic Redesign

An initial approximation of a long-term solution to the systemic design challenge based both on the principles stated earlier and on developing real-world institutions would include a specific set of characteristics.

At the level of the local community, economic institutions increasingly and predominantly involve small-scale worker-owned firms, cooperatives, and other forms of democratized ownership. These include credit unions (which currently boast more than 114 million members in the United States)[11]; worker cooperatives—firms owned and democratically operated by their employees—of which hundreds currently operate in America[12]; and a modest proportion of free-standing employee stock ownership plan (ESOP) companies, enterprises that are democratically owned by workers through a particular form of retirement trust.[13]

Important (illustrative) examples of existing public and political support for various democratized economic institutions are now widespread: In New York, the City Council has supported a Worker Cooperative Business Development Initiative with some $5 million in funding for more than a dozen partner organizations.[14] In fiscal year 2017, this translated into the launch of 36 new worker cooperatives and 185 total hires at cooperative firms.[15] In Madison, Wisconsin, the City Council has earmarked $5 million over five years to support cooperative development.[16] Oakland and Berkeley, California have taken steps toward establishing preferential treatment in municipal bidding procedures, technical assistance, and financial support for worker cooperatives.[17] In 2017, the Austin City Council passed a similar ordinance directing the city manager to produce recommendations in support of worker cooperatives, in general, and to ensure that cooperatives can access small business programs, bid on city contracts, and, in particular, act as conversion opportunities for retiring business owners.[18]

In Rochester, New York, Mayor Lovely Warren and the Office of Innovation have launched an incubator for employee-owned businesses—Own Rochester. The city has also announced its own Office of Community Wealth Building (modeled after one in Richmond, Virginia) to combine work on financial literacy and credit access and serve as the city's liaison to Own Rochester.[19] In Jackson, Mississippi, the city government and Mayor Chokwe Antar Lumumba hope to develop "a cooperative bank, a training center, and a cooperative business incubator" as part of a larger effort to address the city's infrastructure needs.[20]

In (small- and medium-scale) cities like Rochester and Jackson, developing municipally supported complexes also aim to strengthen democratic enterprises by helping secure contracts from large "anchor" institutions, especially those dependent in significant part, directly or indirectly, on public funds (such as nonprofit hospitals and universities).

In the United Kingdom, the City Council of Preston, a deindustrialized city of some 140,000 people in the north of England, has partnered with other local public institutions to help direct spending toward cooperatives and other local businesses. Spending by anchor institutions has gone from £38 million to £111 million, while spending in the broader Lancashire county area has increased from £292 million to £486 million.[21] The City Council has also helped establish a credit union and a studio space for local artists.[22] Efforts are underway to establish a network of worker cooperatives by bringing together current and potential cooperative enterprise owners through the Cooperative Guild Network and by promoting employee buyouts as a succession option for retiring owners.[23] In addition, government pension funds have invested £100 million locally.[24] In 2018, Preston was named the most improved city out of 42 studied by the London think-tank Demos and PricewaterhouseCoopers along a range of economic, social, and environmental measures.[25]

In larger cities, similar structural efforts based on principles of inclusive community and involving joint community/worker-owned complexes are being developed at the neighborhood level. Again, these are supported both by municipal government and anchor institutions such as hospitals and universities.

In Cleveland, Ohio, the Evergreen Cooperatives consist of a neighborhood network of worker-owned businesses (including an industrial-scale laundry, an urban greenhouse, and a contractor specializing in energy efficiency) that provide some 500 jobs for local residents.[26] When profitable, the cooperatives also contribute funds to a neighborhood-wide nonprofit organization that operates a revolving loan fund to start additional cooperatives. The network is also stabilized in part by purchasing from local anchor institutions, like the Cleveland Clinic and University Hospitals, that help provide demand for the cooperatives' goods and services.

The overall structure in both small city efforts and neighborhood efforts in larger cities embodies two key principles. First, it institutionalizes a community-inclusive system beyond simple worker ownership since the cooperatives are in part jointly owned by and contribute to a community nonprofit organization. Second, the economic relationships between larger-institution purchasing and local cooperative complexes define a form of partial economic planning to help stabilize communities.

Projected larger-scale institutional elements of a new model beginning at (and building from the democratic experience of) the local level include the following:

Publicly Owned Enterprises and Utilities at the Municipal and Regional Level. A particularly useful illustration is the ongoing community mobilization in Boulder, Colorado to establish a locally owned public utility, freeing itself from the private provider Xcel Energy. The city aims to produce 100 percent clean energy by 2030 and to reduce carbon emissions by 80 percent by 2050.[27] The effort has inspired other communities to follow suit (like Decorah, Iowa, where residents put a municipalization measure on the May 2018 ballot).[28] All told, there have been some 692 documented cases of remunicipalization occurring worldwide since 2000.[29] These include many in the United States, especially in the water sector.[30]

Municipal Internet Systems. More than 500 communities have established full or partial public telecommunications networks, e.g., cable or fiber optic lines operated through public utilities or by local governments.[31] More than 130 communities in 27 states even provide ultra-fast, 1-gigabit services.[32]

City and State-Owned Banks. Since the financial crisis of 2008, cities and states have increasingly taken up the issue of public banking as a way to make the most of their limited budgetary resources. Feasibility studies have been conducted or announced in Santa Fe, New Mexico and Oakland, California.[33] At this writing, new approaches are under active development in Seattle, Philadelphia, Los Angeles, Washington, San Francisco, and many other cities.[34] New Jersey Governor Phil Murphy has made a state-owned public bank a major goal of his new administration.[35] Several candidates in the 2018 California gubernatorial Democratic primary, including incumbent Governor Gavin Newsom, endorsed the idea.[36]

Community Land Trusts (CLTs) have also proliferated. These are nonprofit organizations that provide permanently affordable housing by allowing community members to purchase housing on land owned by the CLT, provided that if the home is resold it must be sold to future owners at an affordable price. A leading example is the Champlain Housing Trust—formed in 2006 through a merger of two large Vermont community land trusts.[37] It is now the largest such effort in the nation, with over 2,000 members housed in rental apartments, co-ops, and shared-appreciation single-family homes and condominiums.[38]

Community Ownership and Management of Methane Collection and Energy Generation Enterprises. For example, the Point Loma Treatment Plant near San Diego captures methane—a potent greenhouse gas—from wastewater and turns it into electricity, saving the city around $3 million annually since 2000.[39] The same approach applies to landfills, roughly 300 of which are publicly owned and capture methane for energy production in the United States.[40]

Community Development Corporations (CDCs). There are some 4,000 of these community-owned enterprises around the country, many of which help revitalize neighborhoods and help provide affordable housing.[41] The New Community Corporation in New Jersey illustrates an earlier model that moves beyond this. It has $500 million in assets, and manages 2,000 units of housing in addition to a shopping center, supermarket, nursing school, and day care centers.[42] The New Community Network also provides workforce training, educational services like GED Prep and English-as-a-Second-Language programs, and mental and behavioral health services.[43]

Community Development Financial Institutions (CDFIs). There are now more than 1,000 credit unions, community banks, loan funds, and other financial intermediaries that are certified as CDFIs.[44] This suggests a direction other financial institutions can take to provide underserved communities access to banking services to buy first homes or to start a business. Illustrative is the Latino Community Credit Union, which was started after attacks on immigrants in Durham, North Carolina.[45] The credit union manages financial services and loans for more than 75,000 members, 65 percent of whom were previously unbanked, 80 percent of whom are low income, and 2,700 of whom have bought their first home through the bank.[46]

Nonprofit Social Enterprises. These are additional examples of broader community-building economic institutional approaches. For instance, Coastal Community Action in Washington has a 6-megawatt, 29-acre wind farm that sells wind power back to its local public utility and is projected to raise $8 million over 20 years for programs related to housing, food security, homelessness, energy assistance, and elderly assistance.[47] The St. Vincent de Paul Society of Lane County in Oregon operates 15 retail thrift stores and other recycling-based businesses—resulting in more than 1,300 units of affordable housing since 1988 and providing funding for homelessness aid, job training, and emergency services for thousands of people annually.[48]

Public Enterprise and Beyond

Such concrete examples illustrate the practicality, diversity, and developing trajectory of increasingly democratic local economic elements of a larger model. In addition, a comprehensive approach would necessarily include such widely understood elements as follows:

- Small-scale private entrepreneurial firms and high-tech innovators
- Nonprofit institutions in general (a sector that now includes roughly 10 percent of the private sector workforce).[49] Among these, particularly important are hospitals, universities, and other quasi-public institutions increasingly structured as nonprofit or public municipal or state enterprises. Hospitals and universities alone account for roughly 7 percent of national economic activity.[50]
- Local elements of regional or national public enterprises structured as joint ventures with local worker, neighborhood, or community-wide participation.
- At higher levels of scale, building on precedents like the Tennessee Valley Authority, regional forms of public enterprise in critical areas would likely be structured as joint ventures—again, with local worker, neighborhood, and/or community-wide participation. As population continues to increase over the next decades, ultimately in a large nation like the United States most national forms would devolve where appropriate to regional-scale joint ventures. Obvious areas of likely decentralization exploration include Appalachia, New England, the Upper Northwest, the state of California, and the state of Texas (particularly as Mexican American voting power increases over time).

Important strategic areas of concern for larger-scale public forms of enterprise include health care (minimally single-payer, i.e. the equivalent of a public insurance company); national- and international-scale banking; and military production. Beyond these, researcher Charlie Cray has offered a partial listing that provides an appropriate starting point for clarifying which firms might usefully be structured over time as (regional or national) forms of public or joint public/community/worker ownership of larger enterprises:

> "Industries which principally rely upon public resources (including taxpayer-funded contracts) or the commons for their very existence (essential services like water; the broadcast media; extractive industries) …
>
> "Industries that serve a compelling national interest (e.g., weapons manufacturers and other contractors whose primary income is derived from federal defense, intelligence and/or homeland security contracts) …

"Other industries (e.g., energy and transportation) with a key role in national security and perceived collective emergencies ...

"Industries that provide an inherently public function structured in a way that protects the broader economy. Examples include the Big Four auditing firms, which have been pressing for a liability cap based on the argument that they are 'too big to fail.' Another option, proposed by Reagan-era Securities and Exchange Commission commissioner Bevis Longstreth, would be to put the SEC in charge of auditing public companies—the way that bank examiners audit banks—a proposal that was included in the original draft legislation creating the SEC.

"Industries where the pressures of 'short-termism' cannot be alleviated by conventional reforms such as changes in executive compensation policies, corporate governance, or an emphasis on strategic planning.

"Recidivist corporations and criminogenic industries that repeatedly break the law, where structural remedies are needed to isolate and/or eliminate the source of such behavior. As Justice Department criminologists have suggested, 'the size and the complex interrelationships of large corporations make it extremely onerous for government agencies to exercise any effective social control'...."[51]

In connection with larger public companies, joint national (ultimately devolved to regional)/community/worker ownership points toward responsive approaches to a number of critical challenges.

- First, publicly accountable enterprises provide a viable answer to destabilizing corporate dislocation of local communities—a practice that undermines local democratic and community practice and culture, *the foundational requirement of any serious democratic reconstruction over time.* The extension of massive subsidies, tax breaks, and other incentives to large corporations, "smokestack chasing" also wastes budgetary resources needed to respond to community priorities and local democratic choice.[52]
- Second, publicly owned enterprises do not face the same Wall Street-driven imperatives to externalize or minimize costs (such as pollution) as private corporations face.
- Third, and critically, such firms do not face Wall Street imperatives to grow or die—a foundational requirement of the era we are entering.
- Fourth, the financial practices and accounts of publicly owned enterprise can be made transparent, open to public scrutiny.
- Finally, and perhaps most importantly, unlike large private corporations, whose lobbying and political contributions distort democracy, the direct political role of large (public) enterprise can be radically reduced.

Beyond this, the transformation of very large (global) corporations into public (national or regional) enterprise can help reduce pressures to intervene diplomatically and militarily in the politics and economics of developing nations.

Public Ownership and Public Planning

Efficient and effective forms of public enterprise are now common around the world. Simply by way of illustration: high-speed rail systems are run by the government in France, Spain, Belgium, German, Italy, the Netherlands, China, and South Korea.[53] Public ownership of airlines is also common: France holds 17.6 percent of Air France-KLM; Sweden, Denmark, and Norway hold a 42 percent stake in Scandinavian Airlines; Israel, 43.48 percent of El Al; and Singapore, 55.6 percent of Singapore Airlines (ranked as one of the world's best).[54] Collectively, the French, German, and Spanish governments own more than 26 percent of Airbus, "the largest aeronautics and space company in Europe."[55]

Much better and faster internet service than that of the US is provided in many countries where public corporations exist side by side with private companies.[56] Public telecommunications companies are conventional in most parts of the world, including in Austria, Japan, Sweden, France, Germany, Switzerland, and Norway.[57]

Banking provides a further illustration both of existing practice worldwide, and the developmental trend toward a new model in the United States from local to national. Public banks are found in France, Germany, Japan, Switzerland, the United Kingdom, and other countries.[58] Germany has more than a thousand cooperative banks and around 400 Sparkassen, or local, publicly owned savings banks.[59]

In the United States, the large publicly owned Bank of North Dakota directly helped the state thrive during the financial crisis and recession, continuing to contribute revenues to the state budget, backstopping local banks with liquidity. As previously noted, public ownership of banks is now on the agenda for serious discussion and implementation in numerous cities and states.[60]

Neighborhood, municipal, state, regional, and national forms of ownership—from cooperative to national public structures—define a pluralist economy involving democratized entities at many levels—i.e., a "pluralist commonwealth." That the model would be overwhelmingly characterized by small- and medium-scale firms is also clear. There are currently an estimated 5.9 million firms in the United States.[61] Of these a mere 0.3 percent currently employ 500 or more employees, and only 0.035 percent of all firms employ more than 5,000 individuals and 0.017 percent employ more than 10,000.[62]

Even if all the significant scale firms were to become either national or regional-level public or joint public-worker-community-owned in structure, the economy would still be overwhelmingly characterized by small-scale firms.

Establishing the necessary institutional preconditions and beginning points for the development of a pluralist model of ownership, democracy, and equality from the bottom up—from community to state to region and beyond—also requires addressing the matter of democratic planning. The question, however, is not whether to plan, but who will control planning, in whose interests, and with what measures of transparency and accountability.

In fact, overt and covert economic planning is now common throughout the current political-economic system. In connection with banking (and Federal Reserve operations), energy, agriculture, health care, transportation, and many other sectors, the terms of reference for development are largely set by de facto and little discussed underlying tax policies, regulatory policies, subsidies, monetary policy, trade policy, and many other public processes (including, critically, research and development leading to major technological breakthroughs from effective drugs to the internet), and these in turn are commonly exploited or de facto significantly controlled by corporate interest groups operating in each sector. Growth is a central goal of much of the current planning effort.

The principle of planning, and many of the current procedures, however, offer a preliminary matrix of practices and institutions upon which a trajectory of development toward different, more sustainable goals can begin to be built.

National forms of de facto planning regularly also occur through government estimating procedures at both the executive and congressional level; through specific national budget allocations (and congressional budget "reconciliation" procedures); through Federal Reserve Board policy decisions; and in major federal research financing in diverse areas. In all these areas, planning decisions central to economic functioning are regularly made, though hardly in a participatory democratic fashion. Similarly, economic activity and production that takes place within large corporations are regularly and routinely planned rather than organized by any kind of market mechanism internal to these giant firms.

Initial steps in the direction of decentralized, democratic planning can be found in the explorations of participatory budgeting—a process by which constituents propose, discuss, and vote on budget allocations, a practice now commonplace in some 1,500 cities around the world and in the United States in New York; Chicago; St. Louis; Boston; San Francisco; and Vallejo, California.[63] Building on these various procedures and experiences, new forms of national planning would likely build up priorities from the community, state, and regional levels to be integrated at the national level into coherent options for democratic choice.

Market processes would inevitably also occur within the bounds of public choices and the directions set for public and quasi-public institutions. As population continues to expand, ultimate devolution to constitutionally defined regional-scale units capable of more democratic forms of decision-making would likely rationalize processes developed and tested in a transitional period of experimentation.

Positive Liberty

Though less commonly discussed, of particular importance are structural and institutional support for substantive (positive) liberty. In contrast to theories of liberty that emphasize the "negative" or "formal" dimensions of liberty (such as the absence of coercion or domination; and specific protections of various "rights"), positive conceptions define liberty more broadly.[64] They include formal legal and Constitutional freedoms, but also "effective" dimensions of liberty—the social and material conditions necessary for independence and true self-determination.[65] Beyond such basics as housing, education, and healthcare, among the most important are material, social, temporal, or psychological aspects, including economic security, free time, and recognition within a community of equals.

A preliminary step is a job guarantee which (like university tenure or the personal economic foundation once offered by a small farm) provides the security commonly required from which to express independence. Another approach supportive of substantive liberty—a basic income— is now widely discussed (and being tested in Finland, the Netherlands, Kenya, Spain, Canada, and Oakland, California).[66] The Alaska Permanent Fund also offers suggestive possibilities; it invests revenue from extractive industries in the state and pays out annual dividends to all eligible state residents as a matter of right.

As technology advances over the coming decades, shortened work weeks and increasing free time offer further opportunities to expand the substance of liberty—*free time to do as one pleases.* (The latter must be understood not only as assuring 'time as liberty' but also free time in support of—and allowing for—much deeper participation in the reconstruction of genuine democracy and a culture of community from the bottom up.)

Although it is a deeply flawed measure, a sense of the possibilities is given by again recalling that GDP per capita increased roughly eightfold during the 20th century.[67] If it increases at roughly the same rate (and leaving aside additional possibilities suggested by new information technologies), the current (at this writing) economy's output of $227,000 for every family of four would be increased in the early part of the next century to the equivalent of roughly $1.8 million.[68] Alternatively, the work week could be radically reduced to the realm of 20 or even 10 hours per week, depending on allocation choices, and still provide very generous income levels for all—*and an ever-expanding potential realm for substantive liberty in a system not constrained to ever-expanding growth.*

These and other possibilities both allow for, but also depend upon, systemic reconstruction that generates institutions that can sustain and nurture far greater degrees of equality, common direction, and community. This returns us to the central importance of rebuilding from the bottom up in ways that not only achieve stability but help reconstruct democracy and a culture of community. They also pose the question of whether new political trajectories (and supporting institutions) might allow for, be informed by, and nurture strong democracy, equality, liberty, ecological sustainability, and other critical values and supportive trajectories of change from the ground up. These must inevitably involve both positive institutional reconstruction and strategies of political power accumulation capable of challenging existing institutions. The two are intimately related both in theory and in developmental practice.

In particular, a serious longer-term strategy must build converging political-economic institutional forms and support in Black, Hispanic, and working-class White (urban and rural) communities. Also needed is a steadily developing sense of the longer-term possibilities of strategic reorientation based on foundational forms and alliances that can help create the basis of new political, cultural, and economic power aimed at such larger common goals as dealing with climate change and reducing the overall growth dynamic.

The unusual demand placed on *long-term strategy* is not simply (as many hold) to develop institutions that are participatory and democratize ownership in the existing economy, but to (1) develop institutions in and of the current economy that also (2) help alter power relationships that can change the current economy in the direction of greater equity and ecological sustainability; (3) refine strategies, based on such relationships, that can help stabilize the foundations of urban as well as rural communities (including especially the targeting of jobs and work to both); (4) allow for cross-community political alliances based on common needs and common class concerns; (5) prefigure, building from the bottom up, a reconstructed culture of community capable of nurturing a new politics, and of dealing with traumatic racial and other realities (including reparative processes); (6) develop a culture, too, of community capable of nurturing a more powerful ecological, gender-equality-based, and cooperative ethic and politics; (7) pave the way for longer-term regional political-economic devolution of the continental system[69]; and (8) construct a culture capable of nurturing and managing the realities of a transition to a largely post-work era of technological abundance.

Addressing the truly pressing challenge of climate change will involve many of these elements, including planning for the future, addressing unequal institutional power relationships, and stabilizing communities. Given the short window of opportunity to transition beyond fossil fuels before humanity spends its remaining carbon budget, the US government could use one of two methods to acquire and retire the top 25 US extractive corporations, remove them as political obstacles to important climate change policies, and transition their operations into producing green 21st-century infrastructure:

1   It could simply buy these enterprises and retire their operations (and their political opposition to regulatory and other strategies aimed at dealing with global warming). The likely costs of a public takeover, though large, are well within the range of what the United States has accepted in other situations of national concern. Purchasing, dismantling, and reorienting the major corporate players (say the top 25 oil, gas, and coal producers) toward the production of necessary green infrastructure would likely be cheaper than the average annual costs of the wars in Iraq and Afghanistan.[70]
2   Modern Monetary Theory also opens up policy possibilities to realize such developments with even less cost to the taxpayer. Public control of corporations sufficient to ensure that they do not resist, lobby against, and campaign against responsible approaches to climate challenges could almost certainly be secured without a full takeover, but rather by gaining a majority equity stake and control of the boards. Moreover, such a takeover could be financed by the same "quantitative easing" practices that have been used to boost the US economy—but this time mobilized to ensure a just transition to a sustainable future.[71]

Power, Culture, and Beyond

The central challenge of community—in building radically new political-economic structures *and a new political power base* from the bottom up, while working steadily to develop a new culture of "we are all in it together"—is the central challenge of the emerging era. Addressing it is a requirement of a revitalized economy and of a culture oriented to ecologically sustainable and radically reduced growth necessities. Establishing such a culture will not be easy. Political theorist Wendy Brown has described the many ways in which neoliberal ideology has eroded or undermined many foundations of our collective, democratic existence as previously political elements of our social life have been "recast in an economic idiom."[72] "These elements," she stresses, "include vocabularies, principles of justice, political cultures, habits of citizenship, practices of rule, and above all, democratic imaginaries."[73]

And economist Samuel Bowles has demonstrated "how people inter-act in markets and other economic institutions... durably shapes social norms and preferences, and these are then generalized to noneconomic domains of life."[74] Ethical considerations like altruism or reciprocity are often "crowded out by policies and incentives that appeal to material self-interest."[75]

Against such ongoing tendencies, establishing new venues in which a culture of community is nurtured from the bottom up becomes a paramount concern.

It is a concern that must be confronted even as the many specific dangers and explicit political, economic, and other institutional and power battles at all levels must be fought—*to and through the period of increasingly obvious political danger.* In the words of the late cultural historian Raymond Williams:

> It is, in practice, for [anyone], a long conversion of the habitual elements of denial; a slow and deep personal acceptance of extending community. The institutions of cynicism, of denial and of division will perhaps only be thrown down when they are recognized for what they are: the deposits of practical failures to live. Failure the jaunty hardness of the 'outsider' will lose its present glamour, as the common experience moves in a different direction.[76]

Ultimately, building new political and institutional power, and a new culture not based on endless growth from the ground up—community by community, region by region—must also confront two of the nation's great moral failings. The first of these involves the cross-cutting challenges that slavery, and subsequent public policy and institutional racism, have brought to the particular history and ongoing reality of the United States. Any serious path toward a new democratic community must deal not only with current discrimination, but with some form of reparations—both material and symbolic.[77]

Reparations are required to address not only the economic exploitation and terror of slavery and Jim Crow, but also the theft of Native American lands, livelihoods, and lives as well as the ongoing reality of systemic racism. A nation founded on white supremacy must face its past squarely if it has any hope of moving beyond to create a meaningful community capable, too, of managing the larger systemic challenges reviewed in this paper.

So, too, must questions of America's role around the world—and of formal and informal, overt, and covert interference in other nations—be addressed in any serious approach to a longer-term transformation. US actions have toppled governments and regularly installed brutal regimes in the 19th and throughout the 20th and early 21st centuries—and in modern times from Cuba in 1898 to Iran in 1953 and beyond in many countries around the world, in general, and in Latin America, in particular.

Wars fought without explicit constitutionally required congressional declaration in support of such efforts in modern times include the Korean War ("Police action"), the undeclared Vietnam war based on the dubiously supported Gulf of Tonkin Resolution, and the undeclared wars in Iraq and Afghanistan.[78]

The reconstruction of the nation's underlying political economy—away from corporate domination, toward democracy and community rebuilt from the bottom up—is itself an important condition of a fundamental change in the nation's global stance.

A transformative systemic model is commonly viewed as being either utopian or revolutionary. The evolutionary reconstructive building of a next system, however, involves the development of ideas, institutional practices, and political power from the ground up to inform *an ongoing reconstructive transformation of real-world experience*—both to change here-and-now relationships and to build political-institutional power and cultural resources for further transformation.

In the decades preceding the New Deal—including the "Red Scare" of 1917–1920 and three of the most conservative presidencies of the 20th century (Warren Harding, Calvin Coolidge, and Herbert Hoover)—experimentation at the state and local levels, in the so-called "laboratories of democracy," laid down institutional precedents and experience for many of the larger systemwide programs that ultimately became the basis of the New Deal. Illustrations abound: Countercyclical public works projects were explored in states like Pennsylvania in 1917.[79] Workers compensation had been passed in 38 states by 1919.[80] Early efforts to establish unemployment insurance date back to Massachusetts (1916) and Wisconsin during the 1920s.[81] Old-age pensions were established in three states by 1923 and six states by 1928.[82]

Similarly, before the federal income tax was established in 1913, Virginia established an income tax in 1909 and Wisconsin passed a state income tax in 1911.[83] Before the 19th Amendment established women's suffrage, 19 states and territories had established full or partial suffrage for women, including Wyoming (1869), Colorado (1893), Utah (1896), Idaho (1896), and Washington (1910).[84]

Over the last several decades—and even in the dark present of the Trump era—there has been and continues to be a flow of positive institutional development building from the bottom up at the local and state level. We have also witnessed explosive financial crises leading to nationalizations following the weakening of regulatory financial controls (a possibility now returning, given the legislative and regulatory undermining of the Dodd-Frank banking laws enacted after the last major crisis).

The system question is not simply one of ultimate design. It *is* that. But it is also, how, specifically, to conceive and then build—to and through the difficulties—a sustainable and democratic next system that is both practical and worth fighting for by virtue of the values it affirms and the institutions in support of such values it builds. The goal is not "a final system," but rather irreversible ongoing systemic transformation of individual and community practice, power, and institutional development at the level of neighborhood, community, region, and nation—upon which even deeper patterns of ecologically sustainable democracy, and community and liberty can be built beyond...

Notes

1 To compare country and US state sizes, see: Daniel Goldstein, "Put the Size of Countries in Perspective by Comparing Them to US States," *Decision Science News*, February 20, 2015, accessed January 23, 2017, http://www.decisionsciencenews.com/2015/02/20/put-size-countries-perspective-comparing-us-states/; *The World Factbook*, "Country Comparison: Area," United States Central Intelligence Agency, accessed November 10, 2016, https://www.cia.gov/library/publications/the-world-factbook/rankorder/2147rank.html; for the size of states listed: "State Area Measurements and Internal Point Coordinates," United States Census Bureau, 2010, accessed November 10, 2016, https://www.census.gov/garea.html.

2 Thomas Fuller, "The Pleasure and Pain of Being California, the World's 5th-Largest Economy," *The New York Times*, May 7, 2018, accessed May 9, 2018, https://www.nytimes.com/2018/05/07/us/california-economy-growth.html.

3 Martha Derthick, *Between State and Nation: Regional Organizations of the United States* (Washington, DC: The Brookings Institute, 1974), 108–133.

4 John Stuart Mill, *On Liberty*, ed. Elizabeth Rapaport (Indianapolis, IN: Hackett Publishing, 1978), 108.

5 John Stuart Mill, "Tocqueville on Democracy in America (Vol. I)," in *Essays on Politics and Culture*, edited by Gertrude Himmelfarb (Garden City, NY: Doubleday, 1962), 200–201.

6 Alexis de Tocqueville, *Democracy in America* (New York: Vintage Books, 1960), Vol. 1, 63, as quoted in Benjamin Barber, Strong Democracy (Berkeley: University of California, 2003 [1984]), 234.

7 Benjamin Barber, *Strong Democracy* (Berkeley: University of California, 2003[1984]), 152.

8 Martin Buber, *Paths in Utopia* (Boston, MA: Beacon Press, 1958), 136.

9 U.S. Council of Economic Advisors, *Economic Report to the President 2000* (Washington, DC: U.S. Government Printing Office, 2000), 23–24, accessed November 9, 2017, http://www. presidency.ucsb.edu/economic_reports/2000.pdf.

10 Matt Bruenig, "Who Was Poor In 2016 and Why Our System Keeps Failing Them," *People's Policy Project*, September 12, 2017, accessed November 17, 2017, https://peoplespolicyproject.org/2017/09/12/who-was-in-poverty-in-2016/.

11 *Monthly Credit Union Estimates: March 2018* (Washington, DC: Credit Union National Association, March 2018), ii, accessed May 4, 2018, https://www.cuna.org/uploadedFiles/Global/About_Credit_Unions/CUMonthEst_MAR18.pdf.

12 Tim Palmer, "US Worker Cooperatives: A State of the Sector," Democracy at Work Institute, accessed November 11, 2017, http://institute.coop/sites/default/files/resources/State_of_the_sector_0.pdf.

13 "A Statistical Profile of Employee Ownership," National Center for Employee Ownership, December 2015, accessed October 4, 2016, http://www.nceo.org/articles/statistical-profile-employee-ownership.

14 Oscar Abello, "NYC's Worker Cooperative Ecosystem Continues to Grow," *Next City*, January 19, 2017, accessed November 11, 2017, https://nextcity.org/daily/entry/nyc-worker-coops-growth.

15 Gregg Bishop and Michael Owh, "Working Together" *Services* (New York: New York City Small Business, 2018), 6.

16 Ajowa Nzinga Ifateyo, "$5 Million for Co-op Development in Madison," Grassroots Economic Organizing (GEO), accessed January 29, 2015, Madison.

17 Michelle Camou, *Cities Developing Worker Co-ops: Efforts in Ten Cities* (Medina: Imagined Economies Project, 2016), 18–19.

18 Oscar Perry Abello, "Austin Council Votes to Boost Worker Cooperatives," *Next City*, April 18, 2017, accessed May 7, 2018, https://nextcity.org/daily/entry/worker-cooperatives-austin-city-support.

19 "Mayor's Office of Community Wealth Building," *City of Rochester*, accessed May 7, 2018, https://www.cityofrochester.gov/wealthbuilding/.

20 Mary Mitchner, "Jackson, Mississippi Bets on a Cooperative Local Economy," *Nonprofit Quarterly*, October 23, 2017, accessed November 13, 2017, https://nonprofitquarterly.org/2017/10/23/jacksonmississippi-bets-cooperative-local-economy/.

21 Aditya Chakrabortty, "In 2011 Preston Hit Rock Bottom. Then It Took Back Control," *The Guardian*, January 31, 2008, accessed March 15, 2018, https://www.theguardian.com/commentisfree/2018/jan/31/preston-hit-rock-bottom-took-back-control.

22 Clifford Singer, "The Preston Model," *The Next System Project*, September 9, 2016, accessed November 14, 2016, https://thenextsystem.org/the-preston-model/; Ed Walker, "GuildMoney Credit Union to be Bankrolled by Preston City Council," *Blog Preston*, January 28, 2014, accessed May 8, 2018, http://www.blogpreston.co.uk/2014/01/guildmoney-credit-union-to-be-bankrolled-bypreston-city-council/.

23 Clifford Singer, "The Preston Model," *The Next System Project*, September 9, 2016, accessed November 14, 2016, https://thenextsystem.org/the-preston-model/.

24 Tom Gann, "Labour's New Economics Conference: Part Five, Local Democratic Economic Strategies," February 28, 2018, accessed March 15, 2018, https://newsocialist.org.uk/labours-new-economics-conference-part-five-local-democratic-economic-strategies/.

25 Richard Partington, "Preston Named as Most Improved City in UK," *The Guardian*, October 31, 2018, accessed November 1, 2018, https://www.theguardian.com/politics/2018/nov/01/prestonamed-as-most-most-improved-city-in-uk.

26 Zoe Sullivan, "New Cleveland Fund Will Acquire Businesses and Sell Them Back to Workers," *Next City*, November 13, 2018, accessed November 13, 2018, https://nextcity.org/daily/entry/newcleveland-fund-will-acquire-businesses-and-sell-them-back-toworkers.

27 "Our Energy Vision," City of Boulder Colorado, accessed November 14, 2017, https://bouldercolorado.gov/energy-future.

28 Donnelle Eller, "Decorah Citizens Group Seeks a Recount on Vote to Create Municipal Utility," *Des Moines Register*, May 7, 2018, accessed May 7, 2018, https://www.desmoinesregister.com/story/news/2018/05/07/alliant-energy-power-decorah-electric-utility-vote-referendum-midamerican-iowa-absentee-ballots/586054002/.

29 Satoko Mishimoto and Olivier Petitjean, *Reclaiming Public Services: How Cities and Citizens Are Turning Back Privatization* (Paris: Transnational Institute, 2017), 8.

30 Mishimoto and Petitjean, *Reclaiming Public Services*, 6.

31 "Community Network Map," Community Broadband Networks, accessed November 14, 2017, https://muninetworks.org/com munitymap.

32 "Community Network Map," Community Broadband Networks, accessed November 14, 2017, https://muninetworks.org/com munitymap.

33 Jimmy Tobias, "What If People Owned the Banks, Instead of Wall Street?," *The Nation*, May 22, 2017, accessed November 14, 2017, https://www.thenation.cothe-banks-instead-of-wall-street/; Ali Tadayon, "Oakland Council to Spend $75,000 for Study into Public Bank," *East Bay Times*, September 28, 2017, accessed November 14, 2017, http://www.eastbaytimes.com/2017/09/28/oakland-to-spend-75k-for-publicbank-study/.

34 Heidi Groover, "Could Seattle Take the Next Step Toward a Municipal Bank?," *The Stranger*, October 16, 2017, accessed November 13, 2017, http://www.thestranger.com/slog/2017/10/16/25472733/ could-seattle-take-the-next-step-toward-a-municipal-bank; Jimmy Tobias, "What If People Owned the Banks, Instead of Wall Street?," *The Nation*, May 22, 2017, accessed November 14, 2017, https://www.thenation.cobanks-instead-of-wall-street/; Oscar Perry Abello, "Taking Steps Toward Public Options for Banking," *Next City*, April 30, 2018, accessed May 7, 2018, https://nextcity.org/daily/entry/taking-stepstoward-public-options-for-banking; Adele Peters, "The Growing Movement To Create City-Run Public Banks," *Fast Company*, January 08, 2018, accessed May 7, 2018, https://www.fastcompany.com/40512552/the-growing-movement-to-create-city-run-publicbanks.

35 John Reitmeyer, "Can Gov.-Elect Murphy Make a go of His Public Bank?" *NJSpotlight*, November 13, 2017, accessed November 13, 2017, https://www.njspotlight.com/2017/11/17-11-12-can-gov-elect-murphy-make-a-go-of-his-public-bank/; Bob Dreyfuss and Barbara Dreyfuss, "Can a Sanders Democrat Win the New Jersey Governor's Race?," *The Nation*, February 22, 2017, accessed November 14, 2017, https://www.thenation.com/article/archive/can-a-sanders-democrat-win-the-new-jersey-governors-race/.

36 David Dayen, "A Public Bank for Pot Entrepreneurs? How about the Rest of Us?," *Los Angeles Times*, February 13, 2018, accessed May 7, 2018, https://www.latimes.com/opinion/op-ed/la-oe-dayen-public-pot-bank-20180213-story.html; Brianna Lee, "Your Guide to the 2018 California Governor's Race," KPCC – Southern California Public Radio, May 7, 2018, accessed May 7, 2018, https://www.scpr.org/news/2018/05/07/82768/2018-election-californias-nextgovernor/.

37 "History," *Champlain Housing Trust*, accessed July 16, 2015, http://www.getahome.org/about/history.

38 "About Us," *Champlain Housing Trust*, accessed January 5, 2018, http://www.getahome.org/about-us.

39 Brad Schweikert, "Is Your Wastewater Going to Waste?" *Sustainable City Network*, November 2, 2010, accessed December 2, 2016, http://www.sustainablecitynetwork.com/topic_channels/water/article_86c69e9c-e6af-11df-9dc9-0017a4a78c22.html.

40 "Landfill Gas Energy Project Data and Landfill Technical Data Detailed File of Currently Operational Projects (2018)," *Environmental Protection Agency*, February 2018, accessed May 8, 2018, https://www.epa.gov/lmop/landfill-gas-energy-prlandfill-technical-data.

41 Alexander Von Hoffman, "Community Development Past and Present," in *Investing in What Works for America's Communities*, edited by Nancy O. Andrews and David J. Erickson (San Francisco, CA: Federal Reserve Bank of San Francisco, 2012), 50.

42 "About," *New Community Corporation*, accessed November 15, 2017, http://www.newcommunity.org/about/; "Frequently Asked Questions," *New Community Corporation*, accessed November 15, 2017, http://www.newcommunity.org/about/frequently-asked-questions-faqs/.

43 "About," *New Community Corporation*, accessed November 15, 2017, http://www.newcommunity.org/about/.

44 "About CDFIs," *CDFI Coalition*, accessed November 15, 2017, http://www.cdfi.org/about-cdfis/.

45 "Latino Credit Union: 2000–2010 Report," *Latino Credit Union*, accessed November 28, 2016, http://latinoccu.org/assets/10-Year-Report-English-Final-cropped.pdf.

46 "Impact," *Latino Community Credit Union*, accessed November 15, 2017, https://latinoccu.org/impact/; "Latino Credit Union: 2000-2010 Report," *Latino Credit Union*, accessed May 8, 2018, http://latinoccu.org/assets/10-Year-Report-English-Final-cropped.pdf.

47 "Coastal Energy Project," *Coastal Community Action Program*, accessed November 15, 2017, project/; "Craft3 and Coastal Community Action Program: Powering the Elimination of Poverty," *Vimeo*, 2014, accessed November 15, 2017, https://vimeo.com/89718788; Kim LaFranchi, *Coastal Energy Project Impact Report* (Grayland, WA: Strategica Development Solutions, 2011), 4.

48 "Mission & History," St. Vincent de Paul Society of Lane County, accessed November 15, 2017, https://www.svdp.us/about-us/mission-history/.

49 "Nonprofits Account for 11.4 Million Jobs, 10.3 Percent of All Private Sector Employment," Bureau of Labor Statistics, U.S. Department of Labor, accessed November 14, 2017, https://www.bls.gov/opub/ ted/2014/ted_20141021.htm.

50 For spending by postsecondary institutions, see: "Fast Facts," National Center for Education Statistics, accessed November 8, 2017, https://nces.ed.gov/fastfacts/display.asp?id=75; For hospital procurement spending see: "Hospitals are Economic Anchors in Their Communities," *American Hospital Association*, January 2017, accessed November 8, 2017, http://www.aha.org/content/17/17econcontribution.pdf.

51 Charlie Cray, "Using Charters to Redesign Corporations in the Public Interest," in *The Bottom Line or Public Health: Tactics Corporations Use to Influence Health and Health Policy, and What We Can Do to Counter Them*, edited by William H. Wiist (Oxford: Oxford University Press, 2010), 305–306. Cray developed this listing in support of an argument for national public chartering. He has since acknowledged that almost certainly public forms of ownership would be required to achieve the goals he sought. Conversation with author and emails.

52 Jia Wang, "Do Economic Development Incentives Crowd Out Public Expenditures in U.S. States?" *B.e. Journal of Economic Analysis and Policy* 16, 1 (2016): 513–538. doi:10.1515/bejeap-2015-0042; Richard Florida, "Handing Out Tax Breaks to Businesses Is Worse Than Useless," *CityLab*, March 7, 2017, accessed February 7, 2018, https://www.citywaste.com/518754/.

53 For France, see: SNCF, "EPIC Status," SNCF, no date, accessed November 6, 2012, http://www.sncf.com/en/meet-sncf/epic-status; For Spain, see: Renfe, "The Company," *Renfe*, no date, accessed November 6, 2012, http://www.renfe.com/EN/empresa/index.html; For Belgium, see: Thalys, "About Thalys," *Thalys*, no date, accessed November 6, 2012, http://www.thalys.com/fr/en/about-thalys/presentation; for Germany, see: Deutsche Bahn, "2000 to 2008: Restructure and Invest," *DB*, January 25, 2012, accessed November 6, 2012, www.deutschebahn.com/en/group/history/chronology/2000_2008.html; For Italy, see: Rail Europe, "Italy: Trenitalia," Rail Europe, no date, accessed November 6, 2012, http://www. raileuropeworld.com/about-us-23/railways/article/italy-trenitalia; For the Netherlands, see: "The Profile of NS," *NV Nederlandse Spoorwegen*, accessed May 8, 2018, https://www.nsannualreport.nl/ annual-report-2017/companyprofile/a1002_The-profile-of-NS, and "Organisation of Corporate Governance at NS," *NV Nederlandse Spoorwegen*, accessed May 8, 2018, https://www.ns.nl/en/about-ns/ corporate-governance/organisation-of-corporate-governance-at-ns. html; For China, see: Keith Bradsher, "High-Speed Rail Poised to Alter China," *The New York Times*, June 22, 2011, accessed November 6, 2012, http://www.nytimes.com/2011/06/23/business/global/23rail.html?pagewanted=all; For South Korea, see: Korail, "Korail Innovation Way," *Korail*, no date, accessed November 6, 2012, http://info.korail.com/2007/eng/ekr/ekr03000/w_ekr03100.jsp.

54 For Air France-KLM, see: "2016 Annual Report" Air France – KLM, 2016, accessed May 8, 2018, http://www.airfranceklm.com/sites/default/files/publications/annual_report_2016_1.pdf; For SAS, see: "SAS Annual Report November 2016–October 2017," SAS Group, accessed May 8, 2018, https://www.sasgroup.net/en/ corporate-governance-report-2016–2017/; For El-Al, see: El Al, "Shareholders as of October 31, 2014," *El Al*, 2012, accessed May 8, 2018, https://www.elal.com/en/About-ELAL/About-ELAL/ Investor-Relations/Pages/Shareholders.aspx; For Singapore Airlines, see: Singapore Airlines, "Stock And Shareholding Information," *Singapore Airlines*, 2018, accessed May 8, 2018, https://www. singaporeair.com/en_UK/us/about-us/information-for-investors/ shareholding-info/; For airline rankings, see: "Top 100 Airlines: 2017," *Skytrax*, accessed May 10, 2018, http://www.worldairlineawards.com/awards/world_airline_rating.html.

55 "Share Price & Information," *Airbus*, accessed May 8, 2018, http:// www.airbus.com/investors/share-price-and-information.html; "About Airbus," *Airbus*, accessed May 8, 2018, http://www.airbus.com/company/about-airbus.html.

56 Ian Bremmer, "The Long Shadow of the Visible Hand," *The Wall Street Journal*, May 22, 2010, http://online.wsj.com/article/SB10001424052748704852004575258541875590852.html; Carlo Cottarelli, *Fiscal Regimes for Extractive Industries: Design and Implementation* (Washington, DC: International Monetary Fund, 2012), 23.

57 Organization for Economic Co-Operation and Development, "Table 2.9. Government Ownership of Public Telecommunication Network Operators," in *OECD Communications Outlook 2011* (Paris, FR: OECD, June 2011), 78–80. http://dwmw.files.wordpress. com/2011/06/oecd-commoutlook-2011.pdf.

58 Meagan Day, "Donald Trump Wants to Gut Protections for Bank Customers. Here's How to Fight Back," *Mother Jones*, March 31, 2017, accessed August 18th, 2017, http://www.motherjones.com/politics/2017/03/public-banking-community-private-banks-wallstreet-oakland-philadelphia-santa-fe/.

59 Christopher Cermak, "How Germany's Three-Tiered Banking System Works," *Handelsblatt Global*, June 09, 2017, accessed August 18th, https://global.handelsblatt.com/finance/how-germanys-threetiered-banking-system-works-779275; "Financial Report 2016 of the Savings Banks Finance Group," *Finanzgruppe Deutscher Sparkassenund Giroverband*, accessed August 18, 2017, https://www.dsgv.de/en/facts/facts-and-figures.html.

60 Deborah M. Figart and Mariam Majd, "The Public Bank Movement: A Response to Local Economic Development and Infrastructure Needs in Three U.S. States," *Challenge* 59 (2016): 462.

61 "2015 SUSB Annual Data Tables by Establishment Industry," United States Census Bureau, September 2017, accessed November 9, 2017, https://www.census.gosusb-annual.html.

62 "2015 SUSB Annual Data Tables by Establishment Industry," United States Census Bureau, September 2017, accessed November 9, 2017, https://www.census.gov/data/tables/2015/econ/susb/2015-susb-annual.html.

63 "PB Map & Process List," *Participatory Budgeting Project*, accessed March 19, 2018, https://www.participatorybudgeting.org/pb-map/.

64 The University of Pavia professor, Ian Carter, explains egalitarian understandings of positive and negative freedom, writing that the

> analysis of constraints helps to explain why socialists and egalitarians have tended to claim that the poor in a capitalist society are as such unfree, or that they are less free than the rich, whereas libertarians have tended to claim that the poor in a capitalist society are no less free than the rich. Egalitarians typically (though not always) assume a broader notion than libertarians of what counts as a constraint on freedom. Although this view does not necessarily imply what [philosopher Isaiah] Berlin would call a positive notion of freedom, egalitarians often call their own definition a positive one, in order to convey the sense that freedom requires not merely the absence of certain social relations of prevention but the presence of abilities, or what Amartya Sen has influentially called 'capabilities.'

See: Ian Carter, "Positive and Negative Liberty," *Stanford Encyclopedia of Philosophy*, August 2, 2016, accessed June 8, 2017, https://plato.stanford.edu/entries/liberty-positive-negative/; See also Axel Honneth, *The Idea of Socialism* (Malden, MA: Polity, 2018), 21–26.

65 Samuel Arnold, "Socialism," *The Internet Encyclopedia of Philosophy*, accessed June 7, 2017 http://www.iep.utm.edu/socialis/#H6, Carol Gould, "Retrieving Positive Freedom and Why It Matters," in *Isaiah Berlin and the Politics of Freedom: 'Two Concepts of Liberty' 50 Years Later*, edited by Bruce Baum and Robert Nichols (New York: Routledge, 2012), 108.

66 Kate McFarland, "Existing and Upcoming BI-Related Experiments," *basicincome.org*, October, 15, 2017, accessed November 16, 2017, basic-income-related-experiments-october-2017/.

67 U.S. Council of Economic Advisors, *Economic Report to the President 2000* (Washington, DC: U.S. Government Printing Office, 2000), 23–24, accessed November 9, 2017, http://www.presidency.ucsb.edu/economic_reports/2000.pdf.

68 Real gross GDP per capita was $56,823 in Q3 2018. See "Real Gross Domestic Product per Capita," *Federal Reserve Bank of St. Louis*, accessed November 13, 2018, https://fred.stlouisfed.org/series/A939RX0Q048SBEA; For the increase in income over the 20th century, see: *U.S. Council of Economic Advisors, Economic Report to the President 2000* (Washington, DC: U.S. Government

Printing Office, 2000), 23–24, accessed November 9, 2017, http://www.presidency.ucsb.edu/economic_reports/2000.pdf.

69 Serious exploration of such directions occurred among leading political scientists during the 1930s. For a brief overview, see Gar Alperovitz, *America Beyond Capitalism: Reclaiming Our Wealth, Our Liberty, & Our Democracy* (Takoma Park, MD: Democracy Collaborative Press, 2011), 65.

70 Gar Alperovitz, Joe Guinan, and Thomas M. Hanna, "The Policy Weapon Climate Activists Need," *The Nation*, April 26, 2017, accessed May 11, 2018, https://www.thenation.copolicy-weapon-climate-activists-need/.

71 For a discussion of quantitative easing and other modern monetary strategies commonly used by central banks around the world, and by the Federal Reserve Board in the United States see: Randall L. Wray, *Modern Money Theory: A Primer on Macroeconomics for Sovereign Monetary Systems* (New York: Palgrave Macmillan, 2015); and Stephanie Kelton, "How We Think About the Deficit Is Mostly Wrong," *The New York Times*, October 5, 2017, accessed November 16, 2018, https://www.nytimes.com/2017/10/05/opinion/deficit-tax-cuts-trump.html. In recent years, financing well over $2 trillion has been developed in support of banking and other needs. For specific ways in which such strategies can be used to finance a buy-out of corporations that add to climate changer dangers, see: Gar Alperovitz, Joe Guinan, and Thomas M. Hanna, "The Policy Weapon Climate Activists Need," *The Nation*, April 26, 2017, https://www.thenation.com/article/archive/the-policy-weapon-climate-activists-need/.

72 Wendy Brown, *Undoing the Demos: Neoliberalism's Stealth Revolution* (Brooklyn, NY: Zone Books, 2015), 42.

73 Brown, *Undoing the Demos*, 17.

74 Samuel Bowles, *The Moral Economy: Why Good Incentives Are No Substitute for Good Citizens* (New Haven, CT: Yale University Press, 2016), 116.

75 Bowles, *The Moral Economy*, 4.

76 Raymond Williams, *Culture & Society, 1780–1950* (Garden City, NY: Anchor Books, 1960), 353.

77 Many of the most significant social policies of the 20th century—including Social Security, the GI Bill, the Fair Labor Standards Act, and Federal Housing Administration policy—advantaged white families while excluding communities of color. For example, Social Security occupational requirements initially excluded 65 percent of African Americans. In terms of housing, UC Santa Barbara Professor George Lipsitz notes that

> The Federal Housing Administration and the Veterans Administration financed more than $120 billion worth of new housing between 1934 and 1962, but less than 2 percent of this real estate was available to nonwhite families—and most of that small amount was located in segregated areas.

The Economic Policy Institute's Richard Rothstein, meanwhile, has demonstrated that such segregation was not simply the cumulate result of countless private decisions, but was in many cases the direct result of government actions: establishing segregated public housing, promoting exclusionary zoning laws, providing FHA guarantees to developers on condition that they did not rent or sell to African Americans, and largely excluding African Americans from federally backed mortgages. At a minimum, the US government must acknowledge and remedy its specific historical injustices. "When government is directly involved, claims for systemic compensation to match systemic harm become most compelling," writes Columbia University historian Ira

Katznelson. "Public policies, after all, have been the most decisive instruments dividing Americans into different racial groups with vastly different circumstances and possibilities." Beyond this, reparations are necessary to address the legacy of slavery, Jim Crow, and the theft of Native American lands and livelihoods, in addition to the ongoing reality of systemic racism. A nation founded on white supremacy must face its past squarely if has any hope of moving beyond it. See: Ira Katznelson, *When Affirmative Action Was White: The Untold History of Racial Inequality in Twentieth-Century America* (New York: W.W. Norton & Company, 2005); George Lipsitz, *The Possessive Investment in Whiteness: How White People Profit from Identity Politics* (Philadelphia, PA: Temple University Press, 2006), 6; Richard Rothstein, *The Color of Law* (New York: W.W. Norton and Company, 2017).

78 For further information on US interventions in support of corporate interests, on the one hand, and anti-democratic forces on the other, see: Stephen Kinzer, *Overthrow: America's Century of Regime Change from Hawaii to Iraq* (New York: Times Books, 2006).

79 Udo Sautter, "Government and Unemployment: The Use of Public Works before the New Deal," *The Journal of American History* 73 (1986): 64.

80 Ann Shola Orloff, "The Political Origins of America's Belated Welfare State," in *The Politics of Social Policy in the United States*, edited by Margaret Weir et al. (Princeton, NJ: Princeton University Press, 1988), 53.

81 Edwin Amenta and Bruce G. Carruthers, "The Formative Years of US Social Spending Policies: Theories of the Welfare State and the American States during the Great Depression." *American Sociological Review* 53 (1988): 663.

82 Edwin Amenta and Bruce G. Carruthers, "The Formative Years of US Social Spending Policies: Theories of the Welfare State and the American States during the Great Depression." *American Sociological Review* 53 (1988): 663–664.

83 Harold Groves, "The Wisconsin State Income Tax," in *The Wisconsin Blue Book* (Madison, WI: Democrat Printing Company, 1933), 51.

84 Mary Schons, "Woman Suffrage," *National Geographic*, January 21, 2011, accessed November 7, 2017, https://www.nationalgeographic.org/news/woman-suffrage/.

Chapter 17

The Joyful Economy
A Next System Possibility

James Gustave Speth[1]

In his 1976 book, *The Joyless Economy*, Tibor Scitovsky saw environmental neglect and other problems as results of a very American pattern of "putting the earning of money ahead of the enjoyment of life."[2] Over four decades later, his observation remains valid. Yet, as explored here, we can transition from a Joyless Economy to a Joyful one.

In the Joyful Economy, the goal of economic life is to sustain, nourish, and restore human and natural communities so that life's material and non-material blessings are available to all. It is a new system of political economy that gives true and honest priority not to profit, production, and power but rather to people, place, and planet. Its watchword is *caring*—caring for each other, for the natural world, and for the future.

Promoting the transition to such a new political economy should be the central task of a new environmentalism.

To guide us, we desperately need a new American Dream—a dream of an America where pursuing happiness doesn't boil down to more getting and spending but to the growth of human solidarity, devoted friendship, and meaningful accomplishment; where the average person is empowered to achieve his or her human potential; where the benefits of economic activity are widely and equitably shared; where democracy and civic participation flourish at all levels; where the environment is sustained for current and future generations; and where the virtues of simple living, community self-reliance, good fellowship, and respect for nature predominate. These traditions may have faded today, but they are not dead. They await us, and indeed they are currently being awakened across America.

"More than a little utopian," some may be thinking. Yes, but a utopian vision is precisely what today's situation requires. Things are so bad that there is no room for pessimism. And as Richard Flanagan asked recently, "What reality was ever created by realists? ... What we cannot dream we can never do."[3]

The Environmentalist's Tale

The public is concerned about many things that can frame the case for this economic and political transformation to a new system of political economy.[4] One is the environment—my brief.

Almost a half-century has flown by since a group of us launched the Natural Resources Defense Council (NRDC). Since then, NRDC and other mainstream US environmental groups have racked up more victories and accomplishments than one can count. I shudder to think what our world would be like had they not.

Yet, despite those accomplishments, the specter of failure is haunting American environmentalism. All of us in the US environmental movement must now face up to a deeply troubling paradox: our environmental organizations have grown stronger and more sophisticated, but the environment has continued to go downhill. The prospect of a ruined planet is now very real. We have won many victories, but we are losing the planet.

Climate change is coming at us very hard. A great tragedy is now essentially unavoidable. Around the world, we are losing biodiversity, forests, fisheries, and agricultural soils at frightening rates. Fresh water shortages multiply. Toxics accumulate in ecosystems, and in us.[5]

But those are global-scale issues, some say; we have done better here at home. In some ways that is true, but the reality is that our domestic environmental challenges are far from met. Half of the freshwater bodies in the US still do not meet the goal of "fishable and swimmable" set for 1983 in the 1972 Clean Water Act.[6] And about half of Americans live with unhealthy levels of air pollutants.[7]

We have protected an area the size of California as designated wilderness, but since 1982 we have lost open space the size of Washington state to development—urban and industrial sprawl—much of it prime agricultural land.[8] Thirty percent of US plants and 18 percent of our animals are now threatened with extinction.[9] And these estimates do not take into account the full impacts of likely climate change. America's record of climate inaction must rank as the greatest dereliction of civic responsibility in the history of the Republic.

Something is terribly wrong. Clearly, more of the same cannot be the answer when we've had decades of more of the same.

Here we are, a half-century after the burst of energy and hope at the first Earth Day, headed toward the very planetary conditions we set out to prevent. Indeed, all we have to do—to destroy the planet's climate, impoverish its biota, and poison its people—is to keep doing exactly what we are doing today, and that's with no economic or population growth. Just continue to release greenhouse gases at current rates, just continue to degrade ecosystems and release toxic chemicals at current rates, and the world in the latter part of this century won't be fit to live in. But human activities are not holding steady at current levels—they are accelerating, dramatically. It took all of human history to grow the $7 trillion world economy of 1950. Now, we grow by that amount in a decade. The potential for much larger and continuing environmental loses is very real.

We American environmentalists must take some responsibility for what has happened. In particular, we did not take stock and adjust to the dangerous new conditions ushered in by the Reagan revolution of 1980, the moment to reassess and reboot, as discussed below.

But our part of the blame is decidedly the lesser part. To chronicle the much larger part, let's begin with lines from Frederick Buell's *From Apocalypse to Way of Life*:

> Something happened to strip the environmental [cause] of what seemed in the 1970s to be its self-evident inevitability.… In reaction to the decade of crisis, a strong and enormously successful anti-environmental disinformation industry sprang up. It was so successful that it helped midwife a new phase in the history of US environmental politics, one in which an abundance of environmental concern was nearly blocked by an equal abundance of anti-environmental contestation.[10]

Nowhere has this disinformation campaign been more important—and successful—than with climate change, all brilliantly documented in Naomi Oreskes and Erik Conway's book, *Merchants of Doubt*.[11]

The disinformation industry that Buell notes was part of a larger machinery of opposition that may have been kickstarted by Lewis Powell's famous 1971 memorandum to the US Chamber of Commerce urging business to fight environmental and other regulations. Powell, then a corporate attorney who would become a Supreme Court justice, urged corporations to get more involved in policy and politics. Since then, well-funded forces of resistance and opposition have done just that. Especially since Reagan became president, virtually every step forward has been hard fought. Along with environmental protection, essentially all progressive causes, even the basic idea of government action in the interests of the people as a whole, have been forcefully attacked.

The story of the conservative assault on environmental protections has now been well told in Judith Layzer's 2012 book, *Open for Business*. As she explained:

> Since the 1970s, conservative activists have disseminated a compelling antiregulatory storyline to counter the environmentalist narrative, mobilized grassroots opposition to environmental regulations, and undertaken sophisticated legal challenges to the basis for and implementation of environmental laws. Over time, these activities have imparted legitimacy to a new antiregulatory rhetoric, one that emphasizes distrust

of the federal bureaucracy, admiration for unfettered private property rights and markets, skepticism about science, and disdain for environmental advocates. By employing arguments rooted in this formula, conservatives have been instrumental in blocking efforts to pass major new environmental legislation or increase the stringency of existing laws.[12]

The growing grip of deep-pocketed opposition explains much of our mounting environmental failure. But this exercise of power and control is merely the political surface of deeper systemic imperatives.

What was the biggest mistake we environmentalists made? As federal environmental laws and programs burst onto the scene in the early 1970s, we eagerly pursued the important goals and avenues those laws opened up. There, the path to success was clear. But in doing so we left by the wayside the more difficult and deeper challenges highlighted by leading environmental thinkers of the 1960s and 1970s—Barry Commoner, Paul Ehrlich, Donella Meadows, and others.[13] They urged us to strike at the root causes of environmental decline by seeking fundamental systemic changes in our prevailing system of political economy. They saw that the problem was the system.

Most of us ignored these calls for systemic change. We missed a particularly important chance to revisit these deeper issues when our momentum stalled after 1980, especially in the Reagan years. Instead, we pursued environmental actions that worked in the 1970s but have since proved no match for the system we're up against. New laws created opportunities to make large environmental gains. But pursuing these changes in the way we did locked us inside the DC Beltway. Once there, inside the system, the need to succeed invited tameness: as Washington became more conservative, mainstream environmentalists had to adjust. In sum, we opted to work within the system of political economy that we found instead of trying to transform the system itself.

Environmentalists truly believed during those decades that the current system can be made to work. But America has now run a half-century experiment testing whether this is true—only to find that it isn't.

Today's environmentalism is fine as far as it goes. The problem has been the absence of huge, complementary investments of time, energy, and money in deeper approaches to change. And here, the leading environmental organizations must be faulted for not doing nearly enough to ensure that these investments in system change were made.

System change is essential because our environmental problems, including climate disruption, are deeply rooted in defining features of our current political economy. These include the following:

- an unquestioning society-wide commitment to economic growth at virtually any cost
- a measure of growth—gross domestic product (GDP)—that includes not only the good but also the bad and the ugly

- powerful corporate interests whose overriding objective is to generate profit and grow, including profit from avoiding the social and environmental costs they create
- markets that systematically fail to recognize these costs unless corrected by government
- government that is subservient to corporate interests and the growth imperative
- rampant consumerism spurred endlessly by sophisticated advertising
- social injustice and economic insecurity so vast that they paralyze action and empower often false claims that needed measures would cost jobs and hurt the economy
- dominant cultural values that are materialistic, individualistic, and anthropocentric
- economic activity now so large-scale that its impacts alter the planet's fundamental biophysical operations

It is clearly time for something different—a new environmentalism that seeks a new economy. And to deliver a new system, we must also build a new politics. New environmental leaders will learn from the ideas of the 1960s and early 1970s, rediscover environmentalism's taproots, and step outside the system to change it before it is too late.

We must once again ask the basic question: What is an environmental issue? Air pollution and water pollution, of course. But what if the right answer is that environmental issues include anything that determines environmental outcomes. Then, surely, creeping plutocracy and corporatocracy—the ascendancy of money power and corporate power over people power—are environmental issues. And more: the chartering and empowering of artificial persons—today's corporations—to do virtually anything in the name of profit and growth; the fetish of GDP growth as the ultimate public good and the main aim of government; runaway consumerism; and vast social insecurity, with half of US families living paycheck to paycheck. Such underlying drivers of environmental outcomes rarely appear on our main national environmental groups' agendas.

The agenda of the new environmentalism should debunk consumerism and commercialism and the lifestyles they offer, turn away from growthmania and a profit-centered economics, redefine what society should be striving to grow, challenge corporate dominance and today's main corporate form and its goals, embrace deep change in the control and the ownership of productive assets, and push against the anthropocentric and contempocentric values that currently dominate American culture.

Environmentalists must also join with social progressives and others in addressing the crisis of low incomes and economic insecurity now unraveling America's social fabric. We should make common cause with those seeking to reform politics and strengthen democracy. We need to fight the vicious circle of income disparities shifting political access and influence to wealthy constituencies and large businesses and further imperiling the democratic process' potential to correct growing income inequality. Environmentalists need to embrace public financing of elections, new anticorruption ethical restrictions on legislatures, the right to vote, tougher regulation of lobbying and the revolving door, nonpartisan Congressional redistricting, and other political reform measures as core agenda items. We must join in campaigns like Move to Amend to forge a new Constitution that recognizes that corporations are not people and money is not speech.

The new environmentalism must work with a progressive coalition to build a mighty force in electoral politics. This will require concerted efforts—grassroots organizing, strengthening groups working at the state and community levels, and both supporting and fielding candidates for public office. It will also require developing new motivational messages and appeals.

Above all, the new environmental politics must be broadly inclusive, reaching out to embrace the concerns of working families and union members, people of color and minorities, frontline communities, family farmers, religious organizations, the women's movement, and other communities of complementary interest and shared fate. Much stronger alliances are needed to overcome walls that separate the environmental community from those working on domestic political reforms, a progressive social agenda, gender equality, racial justice, international peace, consumer issues, world health and population concerns, and world poverty and underdevelopment.

The final goal of the new environmental politics must be to "build the movement." Today, that means networking with other progressives, protesting and taking direct action, demanding accountability from governments and corporations, and taking steps as consumers and communities to realize sustainability and social justice in everyday life.

System Change

In my books, I have made the case for driving systemic changes so deeply that our country emerges with a new system of political economy, one programmed to routinely deliver good results for people, place, and planet. Certainly, the idea of a new political economy is too big to swallow whole. For that reason, system change can best be approached through a series of interacting, mutually reinforcing transitions—transformations that attack and undermine the current system's key motivational structures while replacing these old structures with the new arrangements needed to help human and natural communities flourish.

The transitions sketched below hold the key to moving to a new and joyful political economy. Think of each as a progression from today—from our corporatist, consumerist capitalism—to a much better tomorrow beyond today's capitalism:

- *The Market*: from near laissez-faire to powerful market governance in the public interest; from dishonest prices to honest ones and from unfair wages to fair ones; from commodification to reclaiming the commons, the things that rightfully belong to all.
- *The Corporation*: from shareholder primacy to stakeholder primacy, from one dominant ownership and profit-driven model to new business models embracing economic democracy and goals other than profit, and away from private to democratic control of major investment decisions.
- *Economic Growth*: from growth fetish to post-growth society, from mere GDP growth to growth in social and environmental well-being and growth focused squarely on democratically determined priorities.
- *Money and Finance*: from Wall Street to Main Street, from money created through bank debt to money created by government; from investments seeking high financial returns to those seeking high social and environmental returns.
- *Social Conditions*: from economic insecurity to genuine security; from vast inequalities to fundamental fairness; from racial, religious, and other invidious discrimination to just and tolerant treatment of all groups.
- *Indicators*: from GDP ("grossly distorted picture") to accurate measures of social and environmental health and quality of life.
- *Consumerism*: from consumerism and affluenza to sufficiency and mindful consumption, from more to enough.
- *Communities*: from runaway enterprises and throwaway communities to vital local economies, from social rootlessness to rootedness and human solidarity.
- *Dominant Cultural Values*: from having to being, from getting to giving, from richer to better, from isolated to connected, from apart from nature to part of nature, from near-term to long-term.
- *Politics*: from weak democracy to strong, from creeping corporatocracy and plutocracy to true popular sovereignty and empowerment of marginalized groups.
- *Foreign Policy and the Military*: from American exceptionalism to America as a normal nation, from hard power to soft, from military prowess to real security.

The good news is that we already know a great deal about the policy and other changes needed to propel us in these Directions.[14] Even better, we are already seeing the proliferation of innovative models along many of the lines sketched here, particularly at the local level: sustainable communities, transition towns, solidarity and local living economies, sustainable and regenerative agriculture, new regional and organic food systems, locally owned and managed renewable energy, and community development and investment institutions have been proliferating around the country. We are also seeing the spread of innovative business models that prioritize community and environment over profit and growth—including social and public enterprises, for-benefit business, worker-owned and other co-operatives, and local credit unions—as well as numerous campaigns for fair wages, worker rights, and pro-family policies.[15] Together with new community-oriented and earth-friendly lifestyles, these initiatives provide inspirational models of how things might work in a new political economy devoted to sustaining human and natural communities.

These practical utopians at work and play are bringing the future into the present.

A Change in Values

Describing these transitions, I have stressed the centrality of new values—the evolution to a new consciousness. Although progress can be made before America's dominant culture has been transformed, we simply won't make much headway against our major challenges without this parallel shift in values and culture.

Instead of viewing humanity as something apart from nature, and nature as something to be transcended and dominated, we see ourselves as part of nature, as offspring of its evolutionary process, as close kin to wild things, and as wholly dependent on its vitality and the services it provides.

Rather than seeing nature as humanity's resource to exploit as it sees fit for economic and other purposes, we see the natural world as holding intrinsic value independent of people and having rights, the rights of nature, that create the duty of ecological stewardship.

Instead of discounting the future by obsessing over the short term, we take the long view and recognize our duties to human and natural communities well into the future.

Instead of today's buying into hyperindividualism and the social isolation that results, we reward those who foster community, conviviality, and social solidarity.

Instead of glorifying violence and accepting war unquestioningly, we frown on hatemongering, don't allow it to be a launching pad for careers in broadcasting and politics, and fight against constant warring. We realize women's and LGBTQ rights and racial and ethnic justice in everyday life.

Instead of materialism, consumerism, and the primacy of ever-more possessions, as a culture we give priority to family and personal relationships, learning, experiencing nature, service, spirituality, and living within Earth's limits.

Rather than tolerating gross economic, social, gender, racial, and political inequality, we demand and achieve a high measure of equality in all of these spheres.

We don't need to wait on these changes but can bring them about. "The central conservative truth is that culture, not politics, determines the success of a society," Daniel Patrick Moynihan remarked. "The central liberal truth is that politics can change a culture and save it from itself."[16]

We actually know important things about how values and culture can change. One sure path is, unfortunately, the cataclysmic event—the crisis that profoundly challenges prevailing values and can delegitimize the status quo. The Great Depression is the classic example. It's safe to say that we haven't seen the end of major crises, but they will drive events in the right directions only if we are prepared.

Two other key factors in cultural change are leadership and social narrative. Howard Gardner has written:

> Whether they are heads of a nation or senior officials of the United Nations, leaders ... have enormous potential to change minds ... and in the process they can change the course of history....
>
> I have suggested one way to capture the attention of a disparate population: by creating a compelling story, embodying that story in one's own life, and presenting the story in many different formats so that it can eventually topple the counterstories in one's culture.... The story must be simple, easy to identify with, emotionally resonant, and evocative of positive experiences.[17]

Bill Moyers, a powerful force for good in our country, has written,

> America needs a different story.... The leaders and thinkers and activists who honestly tell that story and speak passionately of the moral and religious values it puts in play will be the first political generation since the New Deal to win power back for the people.[18]

Some evidence suggests that Americans are ready for another story. Large majorities of Americans, when polled, express disenchantment with today's lifestyles and support values similar to those urged here.[19] (Of course, respondents do not always act on the high-minded sentiments expressed to pollsters.)

Another key source of value change is social movements. Social movements are all about consciousness raising, and, if successful, they can help discredit dysfunctional values and old habits of thought and point to new values appropriate to today.

Another way forward to a new consciousness lies with the world's religions. Mary Evelyn Tucker has noted that "no other group of institutions can wield the particular moral authority of the religions."[20] The potential of faith communities is enormous, and they are turning more attention to social justice, peace, climate, and the environment.

Spiritual awakening to new values and new consciousness can also derive from the arts, literature, philosophy, and science. Consider, for example, the long tradition of "reverence for life" stretching back from the Emperor Ashoka more than 2,200 years ago and to Albert Schweitzer, Mahatma Gandhi, Aldo Leopold, Thomas Berry, Terry Tempest Williams, Martin Luther King, Jane Goodall, and others.[21]

Education, of course, can also seed and prepare us for cultural change. Not only formal education but also day-to-day and experiential education, as well as the field of social marketing, can pave the way for change. Social marketing has helped move people away from such bad behaviors as smoking and drunk driving, and its approaches could be applied to other behavior and values changes too.

One proven way forward is to seed the landscape with innovative, instructive models. Besides the proliferation of innovative models of community revitalization and business enterprise already noted here, local currencies, slow money, sanctuary communities, state Genuine Progress Indicators, locavores—all can bring the future visibly into the present. Models like this will grow in importance as communities search for answers on how the future should look, and real-world examples can change minds. Seeing is believing.

In sum, cultural transformation won't be easy, but it's not impossible either.

Joy

The fundamental importance of these changes in values and culture is underscored by the findings of the relatively new field of positive psychology. Studies comparing levels of happiness and life satisfaction among nations at different stages of economic income find that the citizens of wealthier countries do report higher levels of life satisfaction. Yet, the correlation between income and life satisfaction is rather poor, and it is even wobblier when such factors as quality of government are taken into account. And this positive relationship virtually disappears when only countries with GDP per capita over $10,000 per year are considered. In short, once a country achieves a moderate level of income, further income growth does not significantly improve perceived well-being.[22]

Even more challenging to the idea that well-being increases with higher incomes are extensive time-series data showing that throughout almost the entire post–World War II period, as incomes skyrocketed in the US and other advanced economies, reported life satisfaction and happiness levels stagnated or even declined slightly. The consistency of this finding across a broad range of societies is impressive.[23] After reviewing the new evidence, Richard Easterlin and Laura Angelescu conclude pointblank that "there is no significant relationship between the improvement in happiness and the long-term rate of growth of GDP per capita."[24]

But that is not all. Ed Diener and Martin Seligman, two leaders in positive psychology, note,

> Even more disparity [between income and well-being] shows up when ill-being measures are considered. For instance, depression rates have increased 10-fold over the same 50-year period, and rates of anxiety are also rising…. There is [also] a decreasing level of social connectedness in society, as evidenced by declining levels of trust in other people and in governmental institutions.[25]

You may have heard the joke: "Those who say money can't buy happiness just don't know where to shop!" But much data indicate that money can't buy joy or satisfaction in life for the more affluent. As Diener and Seligman put it:

> Economic growth seems to have topped out in its capacity to produce more well-being in developed nations…. Efforts and policies to raise income in wealthy nations are unlikely to increase well-being and might even undermine factors (such as rewarding social relationships or other cherished values) that have higher leverage for producing enhanced well-being.[26]

If extra income contributes so little to well-being and happiness, what exactly does? The answer can be somewhat complicated, but when a founder of the field of positive psychology was asked to state briefly the lessons of positive psychology, his answer was "Other people."[27] We flourish in a setting of warm, nurturing, and rewarding interpersonal relationships. It is with other people—companions of many types—that joy can be found.

The Joyful Economy

Envisioning a better alternative is the first step in realizing it. Can we begin to envision the contours and texture of daily life in the Joyful Economy? We can certainly draw on what numerous communities are striving to do today, along with extensive literature on transition towns, intentional communities, new enterprise forms, and more.[28] Pointers can also be gleaned from positive psychology and our understanding of expressed national and local aspirations. When all this is pulled together, we can see that life in the Joyful Economy will tend strongly toward:

Local Life: Economic and social life will be rooted in the community and the region. More production will be local and regional, with shorter, less-complex supply chains, especially but not only in food and energy supply. Enterprises will be more committed to the long-term well-being of employees and the viability of their communities and will be supported by local complementary currencies and local financial institutions. People will live closer to work and walk and bike more. Energy production will be decentralized, typically with local ownership and management, and overwhelmingly renewable. Socially, community bonds will be strong; neighbors and genuine unpretentious relationships important; civic associations and community service groups plentiful; support for teachers and caregivers high. Personal security, tolerance of difference, and empathy will be impressive. Local governance will stress participatory, direct, and deliberative democracy. Citizens will manage and extend the commons—the valuable assets that belong to everyone—through community land trusts and otherwise.

New Business Models: Locally owned businesses, including worker-, customer-, and community-owned firms, will be prominent. So too will profit/nonprofit and public/private hybrid business models. Cooperatives large and small will flourish. Everywhere, the profit motive will become secondary, often fading entirely, and social and public missions of many stripes will guide enterprises. Investments, frequently promoting import-substitution, will be locally sourced. Business incubators will help entrepreneurs with finance arrangements, technical assistance, and other support. Enterprises of all types will stress environmental and social responsibility.

Plenitude: Consumerism will give way to the search for abundance in things that truly bring happiness and joy—family, friends, the natural world, meaningful work. Recognition will go to those who earn trust and provide needed services to the community. Individuals and communities will enjoy a strong rebirth of re-skilling, crafting, and self-provisioning. Overconsumption will be considered vulgar, replaced by new investment in civic culture, natural amenities, ecological restoration, education, and community development.

More Equality: Because large inequalities are at the root of so many social and environmental problems, measures will be implemented to ensure much greater equality of both opportunity and outcomes. Because life will be simpler, people more caring and less grasping and status-conscious, a fairer sharing of economic resources will come naturally. Livelihoods will be secure, backed by such measures as a guaranteed living income for all.

Real Democracy: Popular sovereignty and government of, by, and for the people will prevail at all levels. Participatory, direct, and deliberative democracy will be commonplace. Following the principle of subsidiarity, government actions will be taken at the smallest, least centralized level that can be effective. Local and regional authorities will be vital in political life, and the saying "the nation-state is too big for the little things and too little for the big things" will be followed in practice. A deepening sense of global citizenship will prevail.

Time Regained: Formal work hours will be cut back, freeing up time for family, friends, hobbies, household productions, continuing education, skills development, caregiving, volunteering, sports, outdoor recreation, and participating in the arts. Life will be less frenetic. Frugality and thrift will be prized and wastefulness shunned. Mindfulness and living simply with less clutter will carry the day. Social bonds will strengthen. The overlapping webs of encounter and participation that were once hallmarks of America, a nation of joiners, will have been rebuilt. Trust in each other will run high.

New Goods and Services: Products will be more durable, versatile, and easy to repair, with components that can be reused or recycled. Applying the principles of industrial ecology, the negative impacts of products throughout their life cycles will be minimized, and production systems will be designed to mimic biological ones, with waste eliminated or becoming a useful input elsewhere. The provision of services will replace the purchase of many goods, and sharing, collaborative consumption, and community ownership will be commonplace. Fewer people will buy, and more will prefer to lend and lease and to make and grow their own.

Resonance with Nature: Energy will be used with maximum efficiency. Zero discharge of traditional pollutants, toxics, and greenhouse gases will be the norm. Green chemistry will replace the use of toxics and hazardous substances. Organic farming will eliminate pesticide and herbicide use. Prices will reflect the true environmental and social costs of the products we consume. Schools will stress environmental education and pursue "no child left inside" programs. Natural areas and zones of high ecological significance will be protected. Environmental restoration and cleanup programs will be the new barn raisers. We will develop a palpable sense that all economic and social activity is nested in the natural world. Biophilic design will bring nature into our buildings and our communities.[29]

Growth Off, Children On, the Pedestal: Growth in GDP and its local and regional variants will not be a priority, and GDP will be seen as a misleading measure of well-being and progress. Instead, indicators of community wealth creation—including measures of social and natural capital—will be closely watched. Special attention will be devoted to children and young people. Their education and receipt of loving care, shelter, good nutrition and health care, and an environment free of toxins and violence, will be our measures of how well we're doing in our communities and as a nation.

Scale and Resilience: Society and economy and the enterprises within them will not be too big to understand, appreciate, or manage successfully. Key motivations will be to maintain a human scale and resilience—the capacity to absorb disturbance and outside shocks without buckling.

"Glocalism": Despite the many ways life will be more local, and in defiance of the resulting temptation to parochialism, Americans will feel a sense of citizenship at larger levels of social and political organization, becoming, importantly, global citizens. We will appreciate the need to bring political accountability and democratic control to the things that can be well handled only at the international level.

Remember here that there are many visions of successful new economies and next systems. The one I have sketched resembles what Paul Raskin has described as "Arcadia." But the Joyful Economy also includes features of what Raskin calls "Agoria," which builds on contemporary social democracy's best features, and "Ecodemia," which takes economic democracy as its premise and stresses worker ownership and socialized control of investment decisions.[30]

Having sketched how life in the next system might look, I'm only too aware that we know far more about where change should be headed than where it will ultimately lead us. But at least we can sketch the questions we must answer to decide whether we are at least moving toward the next system[31]:

Economy

- Does the initiative move an ever-larger share of the economy away from the profit motive?
- Does the initiative assert ever more democratic control over financial investment decisions and the creation of money?
- Does the initiative diversify the ownership of productive assets and enterprises, and promote other forms of economic democracy?
- Does the initiative increase wealth of the public and the community?
- Does the initiative promote a new world of locally owned and employee controlled, earth-friendly, and cooperative enterprises?
- Does the initiative assert more democratic control over the actions, size, governance, and motivations of large corporations?
- Does the initiative promote the growth and health of the commons (not commodifying or capturing its assets for a few only)?
- Does the initiative limit the market to what it does well?

- Does the initiative move away from the growth fetish and GDP worship toward policies that promote discrete, democratically determined priorities, high social and environmental returns, and alternative indicators of human and environmental well-being?

Polity

- Does the initiative increase decentralization and the diffusion of economic and political power? Does it respect the principle of subsidiarity? Does it favor democratic governance at the local and regional levels?
- Does the initiative reverse the evident trends toward corporatocracy and plutocracy, reassert people power over money power, and reclaim government by, for, and of the people—real democracy at all levels from local to global?
- Does the initiative enhance human freedom and protect both liberty and privacy?
- Does the initiative recognize the important role of planning in successful governmental undertakings?
- Does the initiative strengthen the movement for deep change?
- Does the initiative contribute to a more just, peaceful situation internationally and support the global citizens movement?

Society

- Does the initiative increase equality of opportunity and also social and economic equality and reducing poverty?
- Does the initiative promote community, solidarity, care, and inclusion?
- Does the initiative strengthen children and families?
- Does the initiative celebrate human diversity of all forms?
- Does the initiative work against consumerism, materialism, and "affluenza"? Does the initiative help us work and spend less, create and connect more?

Environment

- Does the initiative envision the economy as nested in and dependent on the world of nature, its resources, and its systems of life?
- Does the initiative recognize the rights of species other than humans and otherwise transcend anthropocentrism?
- Does the initiative respond to the threat of global climate change with utmost urgency?
- Does the initiative recognize that environmental success depends on correcting the underlying drivers of environmental decline and

working for deep, systemic change outside the current framework of environmental law and policy?

• Does the initiative respond to global-scale environmental challenges through innovative approaches (like the establishment of a World Environment Organization that is every bit as powerful as the World Trade Organization)?

To cap this discussion of the joyful economy, let me share this remarkable quote from John Maynard Keynes, who mused on possible futures in his 1933 essay "Economic Possibilities for Our Grandchildren." There, he envisioned the day much like ours now, when the economy could provide a decent standard of living for all. Then, he wrote,

> For the first time since his creation man will be faced with his real, his permanent problem—how to use his freedom from pressing economic cares, how to occupy [his] leisure … how to live wisely and agreeably and well….
>
> When the accumulation of wealth is no longer of high social importance, there will be great changes in the code of morals. The love of money as a possession … will be recognized for what it is, a somewhat disgusting morbidity, one of those semi-criminal, semi-pathological propensities which one hands over with a shudder to the specialists….
>
> I see us free, therefore, to return to some of the most sure and certain principles of religion and traditional virtue—that avarice is a vice, that the exaction of usury is a misdemeanour, and the love of money is detestable, that those walk most truly in the paths of virtue and sane wisdom who take least thought for the morrow. We shall once more value ends above means and prefer the good to the useful. We shall honour those who can teach us how to pluck the hour and the day virtuously and well, the delightful people who are capable of taking direct enjoyment in things….
>
> Chiefly, do not let us overestimate the importance of the economic problem, or sacrifice to its supposed necessities other matters of greater and more permanent significance.[32]

How Might It Happen?

In thinking about the need for transformation, I have had to think about a "theory of change"—how transformative change can happen. Deep change can be crisis-driven. Crises wake us from the slumber of routine and shine a spotlight on the current order's failings. Transformative leadership can point beyond the crisis to something better. Systemic changes can be spurred both bottom-up and top-down—from communities, businesses, and citizens deciding on their own to build the future locally and by a fusion of progressive forces developing the political muscle to adopt system-changing policies at the national and international levels.

Here is how it might all come together. As conditions in our country continue to decline, or at best fester, ever-larger numbers of Americans will lose faith in the current system's ability to deliver on its proclaimed values. The system steadily loses support, leading to a crisis of legitimacy. Meanwhile, conventional crises, both in the economy and in the environment, grow more numerous and fearsome. In response, progressives of all stripes coalesce, find their voice and their strength, and pioneer the development of powerful new ideas and policy proposals confirming that the path to a better world does indeed exist. Demonstrations and protests multiply, and a powerful movement for pro-democracy reform and transformative change is born. Locally, people and groups unite to take control of their communities' futures and thus plant the seeds of change through innovative initiatives that provide inspirational models of how things might work in a new political economy devoted to sustaining human and natural communities. Sensing the direction of the moving current, our wiser and more responsible leaders, political and unelected, rise to the occasion, support the growing movement for change, and frame a compelling narrative that makes sense of it all and provides a positive vision of a better America. It is a moment of democratic possibility.

One sure sign that the search for a new political economy has begun is the way that constituencies have formed around new concepts of the economy—including the solidarity economy, the caring economy, the sharing economy, the restorative economy, the regenerative economy, the sustaining economy, the commons economy, the resilient economy, and, of course, the new economy. More and more Americans are discussing the need for a "next system" and a "great transition" and for a "just transition" rooted in racial, gender, and class justice. New conceptualizations and constituencies around "socialism" are forming.

Under whatever names, the needed transformations require institutions to spur and sustain them. The Democracy Collaborative, the Institute for Policy Studies, the Tellus Institute, *Yes!* magazine, the Capital Institute, Friends of the Earth, People's Action, the Labor Network for Sustainability, Jobs with Justice, the National Domestic Workers Alliance, Chelsea Green Publishing, and the Institute for Local Self-Reliance, among others, have taken up the cause. So have organizations strengthening new types of business—the Business Alliance for Local Living Economies and the American Sustainable Business Council, for instance. Joining them are new entities seeking to bring the many "new economy" issues and organizations together, including the New Economy Coalition (at this time, about 200 organizations strong) and the Next System Project that I co-chair. Finally, a number of impressive new economy groups focus on the "next law"—the Sustainable Economies Law Center, the Community Environmental Legal Defense Fund, the Earth Law Center, the New Economy Law Center at the Vermont Law School. This is important work, and it is a privilege to be involved in it.

Whether driven by climate and fossil fuel insults; poverty, low wages, and joblessness; deportation of immigrants and other family issues; mistreatment of women; police shootings; or voter suppression, movements are now challenging key aspects of the system, seeking to drive deep change beyond incremental reform, and offering alternative visions and new paths forward. Some groups are marching in the streets, state capitals, and local congressional offices. Others are supporting people with alternative agendas for public office. New next-system research hubs are forming, and new coalitions are bringing diverse groups together. Strong movements can be found in other countries, and, indeed, many countries are farther along than we Americans are. These are among the grounds for hope, the reasons to believe that real change is possible.

I hope today's young people will not worry unduly about being thought "radical" and will find ways to shorten the long and tortuous path I took. If it seems right to you, embrace it. A wonderful group of leaders and activists who are trying to change the system for the better are building new communities in which we can all participate.

Notes

1 An earlier version of this essay appeared in Melissa Scanlan, ed., *Law for the New Economy: Sustainable, Just, and Democratic* (Northampton, MA: Edward Elgar, 2017).
2 Tibor Scitovsky, *The Joyless Economy* (New York: Oxford University Press, 1992 revision), 210.
3 Richard Flanagan, *The Narrow Road to the Deep North* (New York: Vintage, 2015).
4 As I reported in 2012 in *America the Possible*, among the 20 most well-to-do democracies, the United States ranks last or close to it in 25 major indicators of national well-being. The measures span economic, social, and political performance, just not environmental. See: James Gustave Speth, *America the Possible: Manifesto for a New Economy* (New Haven, CT: Yale University Press, 2012), 1–2.
5 Speth, *America the Possible*, chapter 4.
6 See Environmental Protection Agency, "National Summary of State Information," accessed January 26, 2017, https://ofmpub.epa.gov/waters10/attains_nation_cy.control#total_assessed_waters.
7 See American Lung Association, *The State of the Air 2016*, Key Findings, accessed January 26, 2017, http://www.lung.org/our-initiatives/healthy-air/sota/key-findings/.
8 See United States Department of Agriculture, Natural Resources Conservation Service, "2012 Natural Resources Inventory," *Summary Report*, August 2015, accessed January 26, 2017, http://www.nrcs.usda.gov/Internet/FSE_DOCUMENTS/nrcseprd396218.pdf.

9 See Matt Lee-Ashley and Nicole Gentile, Center for American Progress, "Confronting America's Wildlife Extinction Crisis," October 2015, accessed January 26, 2017, https://cdn.americanprogress.org/wp-content/uploads/2015/10/09142515/WildlifeExtinction-report.pdf.

10 Frederick Buell, *From Apocalypse to Way of Life: Environmental Crisis in the American Century* (New York: Routledge, 2004), 3–4, 10.

11 Naomi Oreskes and Erik M. Conway, *Merchants of Doubt: How a Handful of Scientists Obscured the Truth on Issues from Tobacco Smoke to Global Warming* (New York: Bloomsbury, 2010).

12 Judith Layzer, *Open for Business* (Cambridge, MA: MIT Press, 2012), 4.

13 See James Gustave Speth, *Angels by the River: A Memoir* (White River Junction, VT: Chelsea Green Publishing, 2014), 136–137 and the works cited there. And see James Gustave Speth, *The Bridge at the Edge of the World* (New Haven, CT: Yale University Press, 2008), 116–117.

14 See, e.g. Speth, *America the Possible*. And see the works cited in notes 14 and 27, below.

15 See generally *Yes!* magazine and www.community-wealth.org. And see Gar Alperovitz, *What Then Must We Do? Straight Talk about the Next American Revolution* (White River Junction, VT: Chelsea Green Publishing, 2013) and *America Beyond Capitalism* (Hoboken, NJ: John Wiley, 2005).

16 Quoted in Lawrence E. Harrison, *The Central Liberal Truth* (Oxford: Oxford University Press, 2006), xvi.

17 Howard Gardner, *Changing Minds: The Art and Science of Changing Our Own and Other People's Minds* (Boston, MA: Harvard Business School Press, 2006), 69, 82. See also James MacGregor Burns, *Transforming Leadership: A New Pursuit of Happiness* (New York: Grove Press, 2003).

18 Bill Moyers, "The Narrative Imperative," *TomPaine.com*, January 4, 2007, 2, 5, http://www.tompaine.com/print/the_narrative_imperative.php.

19 Speth, *The Bridge at the Edge of the World*, 163.

20 Mary Evelyn Tucker, *Worldly Wonder: Religions Enter Their Ecological Phase* (Chicago: Open Court, 2003), 9, 43.

21 See Bruce Rich, *To Uphold the World* (Boston, MA: Beacon, 2010); Albert Schweitzer, *Out of My Life and Thought* (New York: Henry Holt, 1933); Aldo Leopold, *A Sand County Almanac* (New York: Oxford, 1949); Thomas Berry (Mary Evelyn Tucker, ed.), *Evening Thoughts* (San Francisco, CA: Sierra Club Books, 2006); E. O. Wilson, *The Creation* (New York: Norton, 2006); and Terry Tempest Williams, *Refuge* (New York: Vintage, 2001). See also Stephen R. Kellert and James Gustave Speth, eds., *The Coming Transformation* (New Haven, CT: Yale School of Forestry and Environmental Studies, 2009).

22 Ed Diener and Martin E. P. Seligman, "Beyond Money: Toward an Economy of Well-Being," *Psychological Science in the Public Interest* 5, 1 (2004): 3–5; Avner Offer, *The Challenge of Affluence* (Oxford: Oxford University Press, 2006), 15–38. See also the diagrams reproduced in Speth, *The Bridge at the Edge of the World*, chapter 6.

23 United States: Jonathon Porritt, *Capitalism as If the World Matters* (London: Earthscan, 2005), 54; United Kingdom: Nick Donovan and David Halpern, *Life Satisfaction: The State of Knowledge and the Implications for Government*, UK Cabinet Office Strategy Unit, December 2002, 17; Japan: Bruno S. Frey and Alois Stutzer, *Happiness and Economics: How the Economy and Institutions Affect Human Well-Being* (Princeton, NJ: Princeton University Press, 2002), 9.

24 Richard A. Easterlin and Laura Angelescu, "Happiness and Growth the World Over: Time Series Evidence on the Happiness-Income Paradox," Institute for the Study of Labor, Bonn, Germany, Discussion Paper No. 4060, March 2009.

25 Diener and Seligman, "Beyond Money," 3.
26 Diener and Seligman, "Beyond Money," 10.
27 Quoted in Martin E. P. Seligman, *Flourish* (New York: Free Press, 2011), 20.
28 See, e.g., Juliet Schor, *Plenitude: The New Economics of True Wealth* (New York: Penguin, 2010); David C. Korten, *The Great Turning* (San Francisco: Berrett-Koehler, 2006); Duane Elgin, *Voluntary Simplicity* (New York: Harper, 2010); David Wann, *The New Normal* (New York: St. Martin's, 2010); Thomas Princen, *Treading Softly* (Cambridge, MA: MIT Press, 2010); Bill McKibben, *Deep Economy* (New York: Times Books, 2007); Jay Walljasper, *All That We Share* (New York: The New Press, 2010); Janelle Orsi and Emily Doskow, *The Sharing Solution* (Berkeley, CA: NOLO, 2009); and Fritjof Capra and Hazel Henderson, *Qualitative Growth* (Institute of Chartered Accountants in England and Wales, jointly published with Tomorrow's Company, 2009), http://www.icaew.com/search?q=capra+and+henderson. And see: The Democracy Collaborative, www.community-wealth.org; Institute for Local Self-Reliance, https://ilsr.org; Next System Project, thenextsystem. org; Beautiful Solutions, https://solutions.thischangeseverything.org; Transition US, www.transitionus.org; US Solidarity Economy Network, https:// ussolidarityeconomy.wordpress.com; BALLE, https://bealocalist.org.
29 See: www.biophilicdesign.net; Stephen R. Kellert et al., *Biophilic Design* (New York: Wiley, 2008); Stephen Kellert, *Building for Life* (Washington, DC: Island Press, 2005); David W. Orr, *The Nature of Design* (Oxford: Oxford University Press, 2004); and William McDonough and Michael Braungart, *Cradle to Cradle* (San Francisco, CA: North Point Press, 2002).
30 Paul D. Raskin, "The Great Transition Today: A Report from the Future," GTI Paper Series. Frontiers of a Great Transiton no. 2 (Tellus Institute, 2006), http://www.greattransition.org/archieves/papers/The_Great_Transition_ Today.pdf.
31 The presentation is adapted from James Gustave Speth, "Getting to the Next System: Guideposts on the Way to a New Political Economy," The Next System Project Report 2, The Democracy Collaborative, October, 2015, 16–18, http://thenextsystem.org/sites/default/files/2017-07/GettingToTheNextSystem.pdf.
32 John Maynard Keynes, "Economic Possibilities for Our Grandchildren," in *Essays in Persuasion*, edited by John Maynard Keynes (New York: W. W. Norton and Company, 1963 [1933]), 365–373.

Chapter 18

Building a Cooperative Solidarity Commonwealth

Jessica Gordon Nembhard

The next system that the United States—and the world—needs is a cooperative commonwealth within interlocking local solidarity economies. Created from the bottom up, building on multiple grassroots cooperative enterprises and democratic community-based economic practices, these networks collaborate and federate from the local to municipal, regional, national, and international levels.

Cooperatives, Cooperative Commonwealths, and Solidarity Systems

Cooperatives are companies owned by the workers or the people who use their services. These member-owners form the company for a particular purpose—to satisfy an economic or social need, provide a quality good or service that the market isn't delivering at an affordable price, or create an economic structure to produce necessities or distribute them more equitably. Cooperatives are jointly owned and democratically controlled enterprises that range from very small entities to large corporations. They are based on the values of self-help, self-responsibility, democracy, equality, equity, and solidarity, as well as accountability and transparency. Cooperative enterprises must operate democratically, according to International Co-operative Alliance principles that include open membership, "one person, one vote" regardless of how much each member invests, continuous education, cooperation among cooperatives, and concern for the community.[1] Depending on the relationship between the member-owners and the entity's purpose, cooperatives can be consumer-owned, producer-owned, or worker-owned (or a hybrid).

A *cooperative solidarity commonwealth* is a system of interlocking cooperative ownership structures in all industries and all economic sectors. In it, cooperatives and other community-based enterprises support one another by building linked supply chains, collaborating on projects, and sharing funding. These interconnections start locally but build into regional, national, and international interlocking structures, as needed.

For example, in a cooperative commonwealth, a credit union helps develop worker cooperatives, provides financial services to cooperative members and low-interest loans to cooperative stores (to, say, buy a building) and housing cooperatives. The cooperative store deposits its money in the credit union and increases its reserves so it can make more community loans. The housing cooperative members run their own management, security, and maintenance companies as worker-owned cooperatives that also service the credit union and the cooperative store, and use the credit union for their financial services. The residents own cooperative sewing factories, catering enterprises, childcare centers, and home-care facilities that sell to and use the other cooperatives' services. The model can also encompass industrial cooperatives in recycling, alternative energy production, laundry services, and manufacturing.

In this interlinked system, everybody is part of several different but connected cooperatives. The interlinked cooperatives help one another out and work together to meet social need. Should, for instance, one cooperative face financial challenges or should the community need additional affordable housing, some of a profitable cooperative's surplus can be directed toward these needs. Bartering, gifting, and fair-trade relationships are all incorporated into these activities and exchanges.

Loosely defined, a "cooperative" can include any kind of economic cooperation in a *solidarity system*. That system, in turn, privileges cooperative ownership and cooperative enterprises that entail a nonhierarchical, nonexploitative, and equitable set of economic relationships and activities geared toward the grassroots—that is of the people (putting them before profit), indigenous, participatory, and based on human needs, humane values, and ecological sustainability.[2] In the solidarity system, surplus, or profit, is shared equitably, through democratic decision-making, and used for the common good. Risks are collectivized, skills are perfected, learning is continuous, and economic practices are both ecologically and commercially sustainable, bringing collective prosperity. Capital is democratized and widely owned or controlled. It is also subordinate to labor, as in David Ellerman's sense (labor rents capital rather than capital renting labor)[3]; and returns go to labor.[4] The solidarity system follows seventh generation thinking, and its members are stewards of the commons, mother earth, and our ecology.[5]

In a solidarity system, marginalized and oppressed people's sense of solidarity (born of similar racial, social, political, cultural, or economic domination and exploitation) motivates them to join together economically to combat oppression and economic exclusion and exploitation. Such solidarity is cohesive and helps establish trust within the group. Empowering its members and giving them voice, the system recognizes the prevalence and evils of racism, sexism, and patriarchy and deliberately counters oppression and exclusion by developing values, policies, and practices to mitigate them.

The notion behind solidarity is that no one group, or one person, can run off with all the "spoils." Instead, wealth and prosperity recirculate in the community. Also, community members, especially those who do the work and need resources to live, decide what happens to those resources. In a system distinguished by shared prosperity, shared decision-making, and collective economic activity, economic democracy spills over into other social and political spaces and enriches civil society, as well as family and individual wellness.

Social Energy

Community resources are not solely financial. Nor are market relationships critical. In fact, we should be able to abolish the price system, as African American scholar WEB Du Bois hoped. In the early 1900s, he declared that African Americans should be at the forefront of creating intelligent cooperation that would dismantle the price system and set up an economy based on and supporting the common good:

> It is now our business to give the world an example of intelligent cooperation so that when the new industrial commonwealth comes we can go into it as an experienced people and not again be left on the outside as mere beggars.... [I]f leading the way as intelligent cooperating consumers, we rid ourselves of the ideas of a price system and become pioneer servants of the common good, we can enter the new city as men and not mules.[6]

In this economic cooperative ecology-of-caring community, the finance capital you bring to an economic venture matters, but so do your other resources and agency, as well as your ability to work, lead, and participate with others (social capital).

Inspired by Du Bois, Curtis Haynes at Buffalo State University uses the concept of social energy.[7] To Haynes, social energy is not just sweat equity—earning equity as you contribute in-kind work—but also the enthusiasm, caring, and persistence put in to support the business and keep it going. Social energy is about the quality of social interactions among cooperators and the energy and in-kind support they provide for the enterprise and their fellow cooperators. Much of the productivity in, and success of, cooperatives and solidarity economy relationships results from that kind of energy and from the quality of social relationships, the trust, and the leadership that such energy builds—not just from the money put in or the hours worked and the personal connections made. It's about exerting agency, putting in time to work together to solve problems and make decisions, and figuring out how and when to take the lead. Understanding that this social energy is just as important as financial contributions is another way to think about a new system and another way to think about how we democratize capital.

The Goals, The Ways, and The Means

A cooperative solidarity commonwealth has three goals. First is creating sustainable economic prosperity for all. Second is eliminating poverty, the opportunity to become a billionaire, economic inequality, racism, sexism, and discrimination. Third is increasing local democratic control over economic activity, capital, and collective wealth. A cooperative solidarity economy aims to embrace economic democracy, humane social and economic values, just and nonexploitative relationships, democratic participation, diversity, equity, ecological sustainability, the dignity of work, the visibility of invisible productivity (particularly child rearing, elder care, and home-making), democratic control over capital, and collective asset ownership, wealth accumulation, and distribution of assets and wealth.

To achieve a cooperative solidarity economy, we need more cooperative ownership and democratic governance of economic enterprises. We also need to make information, education, and training on how to run an enterprise democratically and how to start a cooperative widely available. Then we need to develop interlocking supply chains and federations among cooperative and community-owned enterprises to strengthen and stabilize them. Other key elements are wage solidarity and living wages, profit sharing, affordable housing, free higher education, and criminalizing subprime and predatory lending. Wage solidarity—optimally, a ratio of six to one or less—means equitable wages and salaries in a workplace, eliminating the wide gap between the highest and lowest paid employees. All wages and salaries must be living wages with full benefits and include profit sharing, if not ownership. Without these features, a solidarity economy cannot exist.

In addition, subprime or predatory lending practices (for interest rates greater than 3 percent above prime, for example) and debt peonage (such as share cropping) should be outlawed. These practices keep people in poverty by keeping them in debt or denying them access to capital—two main reasons for low wealth and poverty. Also needed: access to non-predatory capital to help people finance their economic endeavors and contribute their equity to cooperative businesses or cooperative housing. Besides prohibiting predatory lending, society should privilege community development credit unions, cooperative banks, nonexploitative community development financial institutions, and regional public banks. Historically, these financial institutions have community boards, provide affordable financial services, recirculate capital in communities, and practice democratic governance.

As for affordable housing, we should return to policy specified in the 1940s that housing should not cost more than 20 percent of income, since those who pay more than 30 percent are considered "burdened."[8] If law kept housing from becoming commodified or banned the real estate speculation that makes it unaffordable, it would be easier to eliminate poverty and increase economic stability so people could devote more of their income to feeding their families, buying into cooperative businesses, or investing in cooperative business education and development. If the 30-percent rule applied to all housing, we would not need limited equity housing cooperatives, though they could remain one model for home ownership.

Given education's importance, a bachelor's degree should be free—paid for by taxes on pharmaceutical drugs, alcohol, tobacco, and marijuana—with a stipend that covers the cost of living for full-time students. That way, more people would obtain a BA and most students would graduate with little or no debt so they could afford to buy their share in a cooperative business and invest in their communities. In parallel, we need to require cooperative and solidarity economics literacy from kindergarten on, combining age-appropriate content and practical experience with cooperative economics and solidarity principals.

We also need to move from a consumer society to a producer society—producing goods and services to satisfy real needs and not solely for profit. This will mean producing and buying things locally as much as possible and saying goodbye to advertising, especially aggressive advertising. Marketing should return to its roots in information sharing, so that people can learn about and judge which products are best for them and their family or company and coordinate the trade, exchange, and transportation of goods and services. With a focus on education, knowledge, and the common good, we can escape the superficiality and truth-stretching that have become advertising's hallmarks. And without advertising that invites us (and, worse, our children) to think we want and need things that we don't really require or can't afford, the values of a solidarity economy and the skills to engage in democratic economic participation would be easier to impart.

Universal cooperative laws and enabling legislation, along with many of the policy and legal changes mentioned here would greatly help expand cooperative ownership and implement a cooperative solidarity economy. Public bank development, public bank and credit union loans for cooperative development, wealth taxes and foreign transaction taxes to reduce wealth inequality and help fund the new public banks, and nonpredatory interest rate policies are all essential. Models such as Spain's Mondragon cooperative system that used the credit union to drive cooperative development in business development strategies and financing can catalyze the growth of cooperatives[9]—especially with the kind of research and development for cooperative business that the Mondragon credit union, *Caja Laboral Popular*, sponsored.[10]

Any strategy to implement cooperative ownership should start with local grassroots solidarity economic practices that connect with each other and with cooperative businesses, suppliers, procurers, and regional associations. Meanwhile, sectoral associations and regional, national, and international federations need to be developed and strengthened. Along with policies that support solidarity-based business, financial, investment, and educational development, these initiatives will help formalize and enlarge interlocking cooperative enterprises.

Converting current businesses into worker cooperatives is another strategy that does not require starting from scratch. Organizations such as the Democracy at Work Institute and the Ohio Employee Ownership Center have developed scalable models and policies to support this practice.[11] Employees in businesses converting into cooperatives already know how to run the business. They mainly need more exposure to the co-op ownership model, training in democratic business management, and more technical and financial support. This conversion can happen organically, as owners sell to their employees, or through education initiatives that encourage workers to buy businesses from retiring owners.

In the United States, this model will start with low-income people of color and their allies, progressives, and labor. The many countries already engaged in these practices provide useful strategies and models but transforming the United States into a cooperative solidarity economy is imperative since it's the belly of the beast of neocolonialism, neoliberalism, economic inequality, discrimination, and oppression.

The pockets of solidarity economy practices and initiatives that the United States does have need to be continued, strengthened, and expanded. Examples include the Democracy at Work Institute, the Union-Coop Initiative with the United Steel Workers, the One Worker One Vote initiative, the US Solidarity Economy Network, the Federation of Southern Cooperatives, and Cooperative Economics Alliance of New York City.[12] Their like should build alliances and develop trade connections with the global solidarity economy and cooperative movements.

Much of this proposal is immediately practical. We understand how to develop cooperatives; they already exist. Small but strong, the US solidarity economy can be incorporated into the current system. Needed now are more visibility, more capital for cooperative development, more policy support for cooperative business ownership, and more exposure to these models and more education about them. In short, while we have the way, we do not yet necessarily have the will, or even the awareness.

A Multidimensional Transformation

Realistically, it will take 20 to 30 years to slowly develop more cooperatives through conversions and bottom-up development supported by the necessary cooperative-enabling laws. The cooperative ethos has taken hold but not yet spread.

Markets may resist change, but in the solidarity economy they will slowly become less influential, and pricing will be based on need, affordability, and the common good. Everyone will be paid a living wage with full benefits based on wage solidarity. And as owners, all collective enterprise members would decide what to do with the surplus. Indeed, enterprise-level decision-making—not markets or market psychology—will be the major mechanism for balancing economic activity.

As for the mix of enterprises, those cooperatively owned with 1,000 employees or fewer will populate the economy. Most will be small, with 100–250 employees, or even fewer. To start, capitalist corporations will be part of the mix, but these will decrease in size and number and eventually become unwanted and unnecessary (and perhaps illegal), as the cooperatives and solidarity economy develop more and grow stronger. Large corporations will die out since it will become illegal for small groups of people to own huge corporations (especially those with budgets exceeding those of a medium-size municipality or state). The ratio of employees to board directors will increase, as many corporations convert to worker cooperatives, decentralize, and work more closely with their local communities. Federations and regional and national associations representing cooperative solidarity enterprises will replace corporations.

Planning will become democratic and become workplace-based. Regional and national meetings of representatives by sectors and geography will be venues for coordinating individual enterprise planning at municipal, regional, and national levels. In this grassroots-up approach, decisions and policies will spring mainly from local participation, interests, and needs. The overall aim is coordinated decentralized planning.

Meeting need, not fanning growth, will be a priority. Cooperative enterprises will grow in response to need—and opportunity. Instead of increasing the size of any one enterprise, planned growth will mean increasing the number of worker-owned and community-owned enterprises, thus maintaining wage solidarity and democratic governance among smaller units. Big will not necessarily be good. The Gini coefficient will be a more important measurement than GNP.[13] We will measure whether everyone and every family is prosperous, has a safe place to live, can feed itself, enjoys good health, has leisure time and some disposable income, and is not discriminated against.

Money will be created and allocated by credit unions, cooperative banks, and public banks funded by tax revenues and dedicated to nonextractive lending. They will charge overhead or fixed fees on loans rather than outright interest, or engage in profit sharing with the borrower, which will increase returns and thus create new money—a solidarity model rather than an extraction model of earning interest on loans that can hardly be repaid or foreclosing to create new money.[14] Community boards will govern these financial institutions and study ways to effectively practice non-extractive lending.

We will need to act locally but think globally in this new economic system. We will need global inter-cooperation and international accords, particularly between secondary cooperatives and national federations, but also in the realms of business and industrial regulations, and laws and policies. Fair-trade values and policies will govern this environment, and capital flight will shrink or stop. Multinational corporations will be replaced by national and international federations of cooperatives and solidarity enterprises.

In the new solidarity system, work will remain important but not be all-consuming. The workweek will contract to 20 hours—a full-time standard that entails both full benefits and living wages supported by profit-sharing. More people will work and all will have a decent income. Employment will include public works, community organizing, and so-called invisible labor (such as childcare and in-home elder care) so there will be enough work for all.

Organized labor will operate in tandem with cooperative ownership (as it did in the 1880s with the Knights of Labor). The current Union Cooperative model will be expanded, and unions will support worker-owners, helping them focus on their needs and issues as workers, and balancing those with their needs as owners.[15]

More philosophically, work will leave time for caregiving, volunteering, and the continuous learning needed to participate fully in a democratic solidarity system. These values and activities provide for the common good in ways that also produce economic worth. So, banking on social energy, the system will create a society that gives back to the community while continuously learning to do things better and providing for all its members.

Economic Democracy and Values

We can't have economic democracy in a racist, hierarchical, and sexist society that privileges certain races and sexual orientations. Indeed, working on oppression, discrimination, racism, sexism, ableism, and hierarchy within the economic democracy framework is an ingrained imperative. Similarly, the cooperative solidarity commonwealth will require a healthy natural environment on grounds that the economy is nested in, and dependent on, the natural world and its systems of life. Built into the new solidarity system is an understanding that sustainability must include Mother Earth and all meanings of community.

As these imperatives suggest, values must change—those of the ruling elites but also those of grassroots community members who do not yet know, understand, or practice the values of the solidarity economy. With the new model, no one will aspire to be an elite since there will be no ruling elites. We will learn and show by doing—by practicing/engaging in democracy and economic justice. We will need more public education to expose more people to these values and to economic democracy in practice and to teach people a new way of thinking and acting.

Democracy will start in the economic sphere in this model. Since we can't achieve political democracy without economic democracy, this system will focus on establishing and institutionalizing grassroots economic participation, democratic governance, and nonhierarchical and nonexploitative relationships at the enterprise level. Solidarity, equity, and non-exploitation will then bubble up to other levels and other systems.

Government will follow the lead of communities and democratic workplaces. Eventually, government will be controlled by grassroots worker-owners. Worker-owners will assert their leadership by engaging in legislative activity at the municipal, state, regional, and national levels after learning democracy through practice in cooperatives and the solidarity economy.

There is not true democracy without economic democracy, and the fight for economic rights goes hand in hand with the fight for political and civil rights. My book, *Collective Courage*, shows that the African American cooperative economic movement was integral to the long civil rights movement. Many African Americans realized that fighting for political rights was not enough, that they also needed to practice solidarity and cooperative economics for survival, economic stability, and full liberation. Without economic democracy and economic independence, moreover, those who struggled for civil and political rights were easily targeted, undermined, and retaliated against. Similarly, many African American civil rights leaders were first trained in the cooperative movement or practiced or advocated for cooperative economics: their civil rights work, organizing, and leadership in building social movements were often forged in the cooperative movement or developed, at least partly, from practicing cooperative solidarity economics. Then and now, we make the road to cooperative solidarity by doing it.

Real-World Examples, Experiments, and Models

Many elements of the cooperative solidarity commonwealth have real-world exemplars. The Mondragon Cooperative Corporation in Northern Spain, the Emilia Romagna region of Northern Italy, and the state of Kerala in India all include small local worker cooperatives, interlocking systems, and networks of cooperatives supporting each other with strong financial systems and strong enabling policies.

(Continued)

Also, the five-year plan of the Young Negroes' Co-operative League in 1930 (during the height of the Great Depression in the United States) exemplifies the beginnings of a cooperative solidarity commonwealth—though it was never realized. A YNCL pamphlet outlined this five-year plan:

- Five thousand charter members, paying a $1 initiation fee, by 3/15/31
- A council in each community where there are five or more members that establishes a weekly forum to discuss economic problems of the Negro and study consumers' cooperation
- A cooperative enterprise where each council exists, by 3/15/32
- A cooperative wholesale establishment in each state by 3/15/33
- A cooperative bank in each community where there is a council by 3/15/34
- Factories to produce such necessities as clothing, food, and shelter by 3/15/35[16]

More generally, World Social Forum models of the solidarity economy resemble a solidarity commonwealth because they focus on grassroots, informal, nonexploitative economic relationships, and activities. Still other notions of a cooperative commonwealth involving interlocking and networked cooperatives connect less directly with solidarity economy values and do not necessarily address racial and other exploitation.[17] In the late 1960s and early 1970s, the Black Panther Party in the United States practiced economic cooperation and established several cooperatives as part of their "survival programs pending revolution."[18] Later, The Southern Grassroots Economies Project began to assemble a coalition to develop a comprehensive vision to build cooperatives, especially worker cooperatives, in the US South, based on racial equity and solidarity economy values.[19] Most recently, the Movement for Black Lives' Platform included cooperatives in their economic justice platform to not only combat police brutality but also to better the lives of African Americans.[20]

Notes

1 See International Co-operative Alliance, "Co-operative Identity, Values and Principles," ica.coop/en/whats-co-op/co-operative-identity-values-principles.
2 See The US Solidarity Economy Network, https://ussen.org/.
3 David P. Ellerman. *The Democratic Worker-Owned Firm* (Boston, MA: Unwin Hyman Inc., 1990), 206–207. The "new assets and liabilities created in

production" in a worker cooperative accrue to the residual claimants (workers) (207). "The relationship between the worker and the firm is membership, an economic version of 'citizenship', not employment"—the employment relationship is abolished (206).

4 The Mondragon Cooperative Corporation uses slightly revised cooperative principles that include: sovereignty of labor, instrumental subordinate nature of capital, participatory management, payment solidarity, and social transformation. "Labour is the main factor for transforming nature, society and human beings themselves." "Capital is considered to be an instrument subordinate to labour, which is necessary for business development." "The willingness to ensure fair social transformation with other peoples by being involved in an expansion process that helps towards their economic and social reconstruction and with the construction of a freer, fairer and more caring Basque society." See The Mondragon Corporation, "Our Principles": http://www.mondragon-corporation.com/eng/cooperativeerative-experience/our-principles/.

5 Seventh generation thinking suggests that people live, work, and make decisions for the benefit of people seven generations into the future. It is thought of as a way of life that centers on stewardship of the planet and a focus on ecological and environmental concerns. For more on the concept and its origins with the Iroquois tribe, see: Seventh Generation Thinking, "An Iroquois Perspective," in *American Indian Environments: Ecological Issues in Native American History*, edited by Christopher Vecsey and Robert Venables (New York: Syracuse University Press, 1994).

6 William E.B. Du Bois, "Where do we go from Here? (A Lecture on Negroes' Economic Plight)." An address delivered at the Rosenwald Economic Conference, Washington, DC. May 1933. First published in *The Baltimore Afro-American*, May 20, 1933. Reprinted in Andrew G. Paschal, ed., *A W.E.B. Du Bois Reader* (New York: Collier Books, 1971), 162–163.

7 See Curtis Haynes, Jr., "Du Bois and Economic Cooperation," Mimeo, unpublished working paper (Buffalo, NY: Buffalo State College, 1999); and Curtis Haynes, Jr., "An Essay in the Art of Economic Cooperation: Cooperative Enterprise and Economic Development in Black America," unpublished PhD dissertation (Amherst: University of Massachusetts, 1993).

8 Paying more than 30 percent was defined in the 1937 Housing Act as "housing burdened." However, the "maximum rent standard" of the 1940s required that no one pay more than 20 percent of their income in housing. See Mary Schwartz and Ellen Wilson, "Who Can Afford To Live in a Home?: A Look at Data from the 2006 American Community Survey," *US Census Bureau*, http://www.census.gov/housing/census/publications/who-can-afford.pdf.

9 For example, Race Mathews explains this role of the early Mondragon credit union (Caja Laboral Popular) in, "Mondragon: Past Performance and Future Potential." Paper in honor of the late Professor William Foote Whyte, to be presented at the Kent State University Capital Ownership Group Conference Washington, DC, October 2002. https://libertarianism.livejournal.com/1175415.html.

10 Karen Thomas, "Lessons of Mondragon's Employee-Owned Network," *Owners at Work* 12, 1 (Summer 2000): 5–9.

11 See Democracy at Work Institute, "Workers to Owners," http://institute.coop/workers-owners.

12 See The Democracy at Work Institute, www.institute.coop; Union-Coop Initiative, www.cincinnatiunioncoop.org; 1worker1vote, www.1worker1vote.org/about; US Solidarity Economy Network (https://ussen.org/); The Federation of Southern Cooperatives, www.federation.coop; and Cooperative Economics Alliance of New York City, www.gocoopnyc.com/home.

13 Gini Coefficient: "Measure of the deviation of the distribution of income among individuals or households within a country from a perfectly equal distribution. A value of 0 represents absolute equality, a value of 100 absolute inequality." World Bank, *World Development Indicators 2013* (Washington, DC: World Bank). http://data.worldbank.org.

14 For more on nonextractive finance, see The Working World, http://www.theworkingworld.org/us/; and Southern Reparations Loan Fund, https://southernreparations.org/. For more on the Islamic banking model of interest free loans see, Ahmad Ziauddin, *Islamic Banking: State of the Art* (Jeddah: Islamic Research and Training Institute, Islamic Development Bank, 1994). Available, http://www.isdb.org/irj/go/km/docs/documents/IDBDevelopments/Internet/English/IRTI/CM/downloads/IES_Articles/Vol%202-1..Ziauddin..ISLAMIC%20BANKING.pdf.

15 See 1worker1vote, www.1worker1vote.org.

16 See Jessica Gordon Nembhard, *Collective Courage: A History of Cooperative Economic Thought and Practice* (University Park: The Pennsylvania State University Press, 2014), 113–114.

17 See Grassroots Economic Organizing, "The Cooperative Commonwealth," by Frank Lindenfeld: http://www.geo.coop/story/cooperative-commonwealth.

18 See David Hilliard, ed. *The Black Panther Party: Service to the People Programs* (Albuquerque: University of New Mexico Press, 2008). And, John Curl, *History of Worker Cooperation in America* (Toledo, Ohio: Homeward Press, 1980), 45–49: www.red-coral.net/WorkCoops.html.

19 See Southern Reparations Loan Fund website, https://southernreparations.org/, which developed out of the Southern Grassroots Economies Project.

20 See Movement for Black Lives Policy Platform, https://policy.m4bl.org/platform/.

Chapter 19

Solidarity Economy

Building an Economy for People and Planet

Emily Kawano

We stand at the brink of disaster. The fragilities of the 2008 global economic meltdown remain, prompting warnings of another financial collapse, and inequality in wealth and income is at historic highs while burdens continue to fall disproportionately on communities of color and low-income communities. Our ecosystem is in crisis. A growing number of scientists believe that humans are fueling our headlong rush toward the Sixth Extinction; the Fifth Extinction wiped out the dinosaurs.[1]

This is a grim picture of a long-simmering systemic crisis created by our own hands. And yet, crisis is opportunity. Both the Great Depression and the stagflation of the late 1970s spurred profound shifts in the dominant capitalist economic model. The Great Recession too has prompted thinking about new models that can draw us back from the brink. The solidarity economy offers pathways toward an economy that serves people and planet, not blind growth and private profits.

The solidarity economy is a global movement to build a just and sustainable economy. Not a blueprint or a theory, it is an ecosystem of practices—some old, some new, some still emergent—that align with solidarity economy values. The solidarity economy seeks to make visible and connect these disparate practices in an alternative economic system.

Defining the solidarity economy can be challenging, though a broad common understanding is emerging. This paper draws heavily on two perspectives. One is from the Intercontinental Network for the Promotion of the Social Solidarity Economy (RIPESS), which connects national and regional solidarity economy networks on six continents and collaboratively produced a Global Vision for a Social Solidarity Economy (2015). The second is that of the US Solidarity Economy Network (SEN), which since 2007 has been building a coalition of progressive organizations, businesses, and projects.

Solidarity Economy: Vision and Principles

The Solidarity Economy seeks to transform our capitalist system and other authoritarian state-dominated systems into one that puts people and the planet first. The solidarity economy is both an evolving framework and a global movement comprised of practitioners, activists, scholars, and proponents.

The solidarity economy's framework is a relatively recent construct, though built of parts both old and new. The term arose and spread in the late 1980s in Latin America and Europe through such academics as Luis Razeto in Chile and Jean Louis Laville in France.[2] The articulation of the solidarity economy was, in many ways, theory pursuing practice rather than practice conforming to a model. Scholars drew on research and experiences to theorize and systematize the wide-ranging practices that form the foundation of, in the words of the Zapatista, "a world in which many worlds fit."

Examples of the solidarity economy pervade the economy (see Figure 19.1). We see the solidarity economy and all economies as embedded in natural and social ecosystems. Governance, through policies and institutions, shapes the economic system on a macro-level (national or international) and the micro-level (enterprise or community), and the state too must be transformed. As Argentinian economist Jose Luis Corragio put it, "When today we propose a State as a protagonist of a revolution and promoter of another economy and another territorialization, it must be on the assumption that the State itself has changed its political context, that it 'governs by obeying,' following the Zapatista slogan."[3]

Principles

How the solidarity economy's principles are articulated varies by place, but all versions prioritize human and planetary welfare. The US Solidarity Economy Network embraces five principles:

- Solidarity, cooperation, mutualism
- Equity in all dimensions (race, ethnicity, nationality, class, and gender, etc.)
- Participatory democracy
- Sustainability
- Pluralism

It is important to take these principles together. Embraced individually, they are insufficient to undergird a just and sustainable system, and alignment in one dimension does not necessarily signal alignment in others. We can have equity without sustainability, democracy without equity, or sustainability without solidarity. Like any healthy ecosystem, the solidarity economy flourishes with a full spectrum of interconnected principles.

Pluralism

The solidarity economy respects variations in interpretation and practice based on local history, culture, and socio-economic conditions. Similarly, we find national and local variations in how the solidarity economy itself and the strategies for building it are defined. That said, a strong common foundation, as articulated in RIPESS's Global Vision document, draws on the experience and analysis of grassroots networks of practitioners, activists, scholars, and proponents everywhere.[4]

Figure 19.1 An image from an evolving slide presentation created by the Center for Popular Economics (2016).

Solidarity

The solidarity economy is grounded in collective practices that express the principle of solidarity—shorthand for such social interactions as cooperation, mutualism, sharing, reciprocity, altruism, love, caring, and gifting. The solidarity economy nurtures these anti-capitalist values and in all economic sectors assumes forms that are old and new, formal and informal, monetized and non-monetized, mainstream, and alternative. It recognizes such family labor and community nurturing (from cooking and child-rearing to helping neighbors and volunteering) as integral parts of the "real" economy and the bedrock of reproduction and participation in paid work. Unpaid household production accounts for an estimated $11 trillion worth of global economic activity, ranging from 18 percent of the gross domestic product in the US to 42 percent in Australia and 43 percent in Portugal.[5] Solidarity economy policies and institutions support these important non-monetized transactions.

Equity

Many of the real-world practices that comprise the solidarity economy were undertaken by communities struggling against neoliberalism and corporate globalization.[6] For example, in Latin America the debt crisis led to land takeovers by Brazil's Landless Workers' Movement (MST), factory takeovers in Argentina, the *autonomista* movements in Chiapas, Mexico, and the Popular Economic Organizations in Chile.[7]

Opposing imperialism, colonization, discrimination, and patriarchy, the solidarity economy has values informed by social movements focusing on anti-racism, feminism, anti-imperialism, labor, poor people, the environment, and democracy. But while social movements emphasize resisting, the solidarity economy emphasizes building. Both are necessary and interdependent, and they must be better integrated.

In the US, efforts to support and strengthen the solidarity economy must focus on marginalized and oppressed communities. Often invisible, solidarity economy practices do exist in low-income communities, whether community self-provisioning, gardening, child and elder care, mutual aid, lending, or healing. Jessica Gordon Nembhard documents a history of thriving cooperatives in African American communities that died out after coming under racist attack.[8] Other initiatives are highlighted later.

Participatory Democracy

The solidarity economy embraces participatory democracy as a way for people to get involved in their own collective development by localizing decision-making and action as much as possible. This approach, also called *subsidiarization*, invites participation and collaborative problem-solving in communities and workplaces.

In the workplace, the solidarity economy upholds self-management and collective ownership. The RIPESS Global Vision documents some of many workplace expressions of the solidarity economy as "cooperatives (worker, producer, consumer, credit unions, housing, etc.), collective social enterprises, and participatory governance of the commons (for example, community management of water, fisheries, or forests)."

Capitalist enterprises, with their separate owning and working classes, have no place in the solidarity economy. Even if a company seeks a triple bottom line (social, ecological, and financial), the owner ultimately controls the enterprise and profits, and worker participation in decision-making granted by management or negotiated by a union can be taken away or lost. That said, though the solidarity economy's long-term vision is of economic democracy, during the transition alliances with responsible businesses must be built while moving them toward solidarity economy principles.

Sustainability

RIPESS has embraced the concept of *buen vivir* or *sumak qawsay* (living well), which draws heavily on Andean indigenous perspectives of living in harmony with nature and with each other. The Ecuadoran National Plan for Good Living defines it as: "Covering needs, achieving a dignified quality of life and death; loving and being loved; the healthy flourishing of all individuals in peace and harmony with nature; and achieving an indefinite reproduction perpetuation of human cultures."[9]

The solidarity economy upholds the principle of sustainability, and RIPESS has embraced the more radical notion that ecosystems have the legal right to exist, flourish, and regenerate.[10] The rights of Mother Earth (nature) have been enshrined in national constitutions and recognized by communities. Worldwide, we see a spectrum of alignment. For now, we should see the partially aligned as potential strategic allies while heeding the danger of cooptation.

A New Narrative

While conventional economics portrays itself as a science, the economy is a social construction, built on a story or narrative. The central character of capitalism's narrative, homo *economicus* or economic man, is the basis from which economic theory, models, and policies are spun. Our real-world economy builds on assumptions about homo *economicus*—namely, that he is rational, calculating, self-interested, and competitive and has little concern for the community, the common good, or the environment.

Capitalism's one-sided assumptions about human nature and behavior reflect the belief that individuals acting self-interestedly in the market will generate optimal and stable economic outcomes. Of course, even mainstream economists know that homo *economicus* is an unbalanced and unrealistic depiction of human beings, but it simplifies mathematical modeling, justifies laissez faire neoliberalism, and allows economics and behavior in the magic marketplace to be treated "free of" emotion, culture, and social norms.

Conversely, in this economic story, collective action is predestined to fail due to rational self-interest. Garrett Hardin's influential *Tragedy of the Commons* argued that open access to pastureland and other communal resources leads to disastrous overgrazing[11] since even after the maximum number of animals that the land can support is reached, each individual still has incentive to enlarge his herd.

If what is rational for the individual is irrational for the group, small wonder our economic system discourages collective ownership, control, and management. Yet, in 2009, Elinor Ostrom won the Nobel Prize in Economics for documenting the many examples of forests, irrigation systems, fishing grounds, and pastureland that have been managed as commons by their stakeholders more efficiently, sustainably, and equitably than by the state or private owners.[12]

Hardin was wrong, and homo *economicus* is increasingly endangered as the central character in our story of the economy. The new emergent protagonist, homo *solidaricus*, is more complex—both self-interested and solidaristic—and more diverse.

A Metaphor for Change

An apt metaphor for thinking about the social and economic transformation that the solidarity economy seeks is the metamorphosis of a caterpillar into a butterfly.

When the caterpillar spins its chrysalis, its body begins to dissolve into a nutrient-rich soup containing imaginal cells that the caterpillar is born with. These cells have a different vision of what the caterpillar could be—so different that the residual immune system tries to attack them. Still, the surviving imaginal cells find and recognize each other as part of the same metamorphosis and connect to form clusters, work together, take on different functions, and build a whole new creature. As the imaginal cells specialize into a wing or an eye or a leg, they integrate into a whole new organism that emerges from the chrysalis as a butterfly.

In the same way, we can think of the many real-world "solidaristic" economic practices as imaginal cells, operating in isolation in an indifferent or hostile environment. The solidarity economy movement works to help these imaginal cells recognize one another as part of the same project of metamorphosis and to pull together to build a coherent economic system with all the "organs" needed to survive in finance, production, distribution, investment, consumption, and the state.

Drivers of Change: The Need to Proliferate and Integrate

Why are solidarity economy practices proliferating? Social and economic forces, the ecological crisis, and the state all play roles.

Social and Economic Factors

Many people enter the solidarity economy not out of need but because of an ideological or spiritual commitment. They join food and worker cooperatives, community-supported agriculture programs, credit unions, or volunteer projects to expresses their values. For others, practical motivation is reinforced by ideological motivation.

Solidarity economy practices have also often been motivated by hard times or the challenge of survival. These practices have surged over the past four decades in reaction to the long-term crises of neoliberalism, globalization, and technological change, and many scholars have debated the "end of work" as machines replace people, especially men of prime working age.[13] In response, many people and communities have grown weary of making demands on a deaf or underfunded government and have started building their own collective solutions inside and outside the formal and paid economy, creating jobs, food, housing, healthcare, services, loans, and money.

While neoliberalism, globalization, and automation have created a long-term crisis, the economic crisis of 2008 has shaken confidence in neoliberalism to its core. And the window of opportunity provided by the crisis is not closed. Another financial collapse may await, and growing inequality, un-and under-employment, stagnant wages, and precarious labor continue to fuel interest and engagement in such practices as cooperatives, social currencies, community supported agriculture, and participatory budgeting.

The Ecological Crisis

The other long-term crisis driving the solidarity economy's growth is ecological. The growing consensus is that human activity is ushering in a new geological epoch, the Anthropocene (human epoch), in which humans are driving global warming, rising sea levels, intensified hurricanes and tornadoes, ocean acidification, and biodiversity losses.[14] The capitalist system is inherently ecologically unsustainable because it requires every business to maximize profits and grow or be outcompeted and die. Continual growth, in turn, requires ever-increasing and ever more unsustainable levels of consumption. (To RIPESS, the value of "growth" depends on how it is defined and what its goals are.[15])

Solidarity economy responses to drastic ecological changes range from emphasizing local production and consumption to integrating ecological principles into production and agriculture, turning waste into inputs, restoring healthy ecosystems, reducing the carbon footprint, creating tool and toy libraries, providing mutual aid disaster relief, and investing in community-owned energy generation.

In the solidarity economy, protecting nature's rights also means fighting such environmentally destructive practices as fracking. In the US in 2014, the Community Environmental Legal Defense Fund filed the first motion by an ecosystem to intervene in a lawsuit. The Little Mahoning Watershed in Grant Township, Pennsylvania defended its own legal rights to exist and flourish, and wastewater injection wells for fracking were banned as a violation of those rights.[16]

Besides serving as practical tools for combatting ecosystem destruction, the rights of Mother Nature also reflect *buen vivir* in harmony with each other and nature. Worldview shifts like this help drive the solidarity economy's growth.

Government

The solidarity economy's big tent includes those who embrace this framework from an *autonomista* or anarchist perspective and eschew working with the state and those working to transform the state, its institutions, and its policies. There is no "right" way forward but, rather, many paths.

Some local, national, and international governments are fostering the solidarity economy or its components. Support can be direct (through the public sector) or supportive (through legal, tax, investment, and procurement policies). Some US cities support the development of worker-owned cooperatives emphasizing job and wealth creation for low-income and marginalized communities. France, Spain, Portugal, Mexico, Colombia, Ecuador, and Canada's Quebec province have all passed laws or are developing framework legislation that recognizes and supports the solidarity economy.[17] Brazil, France, and Luxemburg have ministries of solidarity economy. Bolivia and Ecuador have enshrined solidarity economy in their constitutions.

Often, government support for the solidarity economy stems from pressure from social movements. Without public pressure, governments only rarely pioneer policies supporting equity, economic democracy, sustainability, and collective action. Also, some government initiatives that support the social economy don't necessarily support the solidarity economy—an important distinction. While the social economy[18] adheres to principles of democratic control by membership, solidarity, primacy of social and member interests over capital, and sustainability,[19] it does not necessarily seek systemic transformation. The solidarity economy does.[20] Beyond that, the far broader solidarity economy encompasses, for example, the transformed state and such non-monetized transactions as care and volunteer labor.

Integrating Solidarity Economy Practices

With a sense of what drives the proliferation of solidarity economy practices, we can now better understand how to integrate them into an interconnected system. Just as the butterfly develops from a chrysalis, this process is one of coming together, specializing, and emerging as a new and different organism. Integration relies on raising public awareness, developing solidarity economy value chains, and capacity building.

Public awareness is a first step in recognizing each other as part of the same project of transformation. While every individual practice need not reflect this view and agenda, building common cause among a substantial portion of practices is vital. This work, already afoot, involves outreach, communication, and education.

Creating solidarity economy value chains means building our own economy by having solidarity economy enterprises source from other solidarity economy producers.[21] For example, the Brazilian cooperative Justa Trama [Fair Chain] produces bags and t-shirts by sourcing cloth from Cooperativa Fio Nobre, which buys raw organic cotton from Coopertextil, and using buttons made of seeds and shells from Coop Acai. Two sewing cooperatives, Univens in Porto Alegre and Coopstilus in Sao Paulo, complete the products. Over all, collaboration has increased sales, landed members long-term contracts, and allowed those with the most need to realize profits.[22] Making this social economy supply chain of producers and suppliers a value chain would require integration with solidarity economy—say, finance from a community bank, distribution through a fair-trade network, settling accounts using social currency, and selling through a community cooperative store.

Where solidarity economy suppliers are few, the need is to make it easy for producers and suppliers to find each other using a Solidarity Economy map.[23] Where these suppliers don't exist, a more diverse ecosystem of solidarity economy producers must be created, particularly in manufacturing.

New York City and Madison, Wisconsin allocated over $3 million and $5 million dollars, respectively, for worker cooperative development aimed at low-income communities and communities of color.[24] In many other US cities, municipal, labor, or grassroots initiatives support the development of worker cooperatives.

Resist and Build

Advocates of the solidarity economy are building, strengthening, and connecting actual practices to show that they are viable, advocate for a supportive environment, create a critical mass for systemic transformation, and build the road by walking. But it is equally necessary to resist our current system's exploitation, injustice, oppression, and destructiveness. To resist and build, to oppose and propose, are two sides of the same coin.

In the US, social movements long favored resistance over building, though that is changing. In the solidarity economy, advocates support improving wages and working conditions but also promote workplaces owned and managed by workers. Of course, solidarity economy redistributional policies—say, land trusts and other limited-equity cooperative housing models—would keep such inequality from ever developing.

The solidarity economy is about people collectively finding ways to provide for themselves and their communities. It is not primarily about the government doing it for them. Instead of a welfare state, government is a partner.

Real-World Examples

The huge foundation of current practices and the many unifying principles underlying the solidarity economy leave much room for diversity and debate. Although the typology presented here may seem straightforward, defining the solidarity economy's boundaries is complicated. Many of these practices straddle multiple sectors. A community-supported agriculture is both production and a collective form of distribution and exchange, and some community gardens straddle production and distribution through gifting surplus. The Solidarity Economy Mapping Project includes only those practices that substantially align with solidarity economy principles and that don't structurally violate solidarity economy principles.

Take the inclusion of worker cooperatives, for example. The seven cooperative principles that most cooperatives follow echo all five solidarity economy principles, and nothing in the worker cooperative form itself violates any of the principles.[25] In contrast, some practices aligned with one or a few principles only (Table 19.1).

Social enterprises, for instance, have a social mission likely to align with principles of equity, sustainability, and solidarity. But capitalist social

Table 19.1 Solidarity Economy Practices by Type

Production	Distribution and Exchange	Consumption	Finance	Governance
Worker cooperatives Producer cooperatives Volunteer collectives Community gardens Collectives of self-employed Unpaid care work	Fair trade networks Community supported agriculture and fisheries Complementary/ Social/Local currencies Time banks Barter or free-cycle networks	Consumer cooperatives Buying clubs Cooperative housing, co-housing, intentional communities Community land trusts Cooperative sharing platforms	Credit unions Community development credit unions Public banking Peer lending Mutual association (e.g. insurance) Crowdfunding	Participatory budgeting Commons/ community management of resources Public sector (schools, infrastructure, retirement funds, etc.)

enterprises with owners or stockholders making all important decisions don't honor the democratic principle of the solidarity economy so are excluded from the typology, even though they may be valuable allies. Some social enterprises that are collectively and democratically owned and managed—say, a business that is run by a nonprofit—do fit in the solidarity economy.

Unpaid care work, as feminists have long argued, should be recognized as economically valuable and deserving of support because society couldn't reproduce without it. Far too often, of course, care labor is performed under oppressive and exploitative conditions perpetuated by patriarchal culture. Including such work in our taxonomy affirms its economic and social value without affirming the patriarchy.

Although the solidarity economy's boundaries are complicated and overlapping, examples from each sector show what aligning principle with practice generally means.

Cooperatives

Worker cooperatives are businesses owned and democratically run by their workers on the basis of one worker one vote. As owners, the workers decide how to use profits—how much to reinvest, save, or "share out" among themselves. Compared to conventional capitalist businesses, worker cooperatives are more resilient and more equitable. Studies of worker cooperatives in Quebec and Canada pegged the five-year survival rate at around

60 percent, compared to 40 percent for conventional businesses.[26] Most worker cooperatives also typically have a low ratio of highest to lowest paid—around 4:1—compared to a US average of 295:1.[27] Worker cooperatives typically pay as well or better and offer greater job security (preferring pay cuts to lay-offs in hard times).

Since the Great Recession of 2008, worker-cooperative start-ups have proliferated, and cities are beginning to invest in worker cooperatives to further inclusive economic development in low-income communities and communities of color.[28] Labor unions are supporting worker cooperative development to help create good jobs and worker-controlled businesses. In 2009, the United Steelworkers began collaborating with Mondragon, the world's most famous cooperative network, to develop union cooperatives in the US, such as WorX Printing in Worcester, Massachusetts. The Cincinnati Union Co-op Initiative (CUCI) is developing a worker-owned farm, food hub, and grocery store.

Self-Provisioning, Urban Homesteading, Community Production, and DIY

The solidarity economy views nonmonetized and nonmarket exchanges as important components of the "real" economy. Throughout the world, women shoulder far more unpaid child-rearing, elder care, cooking, housekeeping, and community volunteer work than men, often on top of paid work. Numerous countries now at least track unpaid care labor, providing leverage for promoting gender equity.

The culture of self-provisioning is burgeoning, spurred by a desire to live more sustainably and by economic unease.[29] Renewed interest in self-sufficiency is driving thousands of people to build their own homes, generate their own power, grow their own food, capture rainwater, raise chickens and bees, organize skill shares or swaps and barn-raisings, and exchange goods and services using social currencies or time banking.

Frithjof Bergmann's concept of New Work, which looks beyond jobs toward community-scale provisioning, has resonated in such job-depleted cities as Detroit.[30] Unlike earlier back-to-the-land and communal living movements, this new vision of community production fully uses the very technologies that are destroying jobs, such as digital fabrication and 3-D printers, to localize production of things as complex as a car,[31] as large as a house,[32] or as personalized as orthodontic retainers.[33]

Distribution Exchange

Social currencies and time banks operate alongside official forms of money and enable the exchange of goods and services through socially created money or time credits. Local money helps boost the community economy by increasing the supply of money and keeping it circulating close to home.

Social currencies have a long global history. The Swiss WIR Cooperative, around since 1934, issues its own money, which is used in $1 billion worth of transactions annually.[34] In western Massachusetts, Berkshares are accepted by over 400 businesses, healthcare services, and farms. Berkshares can be purchased from local banks at a 5-percent discount, which gives people an incentive to buy them and businesses a disincentive to cash them out.

Time banks are a form of electronic exchange in which people earn time credits for each hour worked. A person could earn an hour credit by reading to an elderly person and then spend that credit on a massage or legal service. Dane County Timebank's Youth Court in Madison, Wisconsin and the DC Time Dollar Youth Court Program allow young people volunteering as peer jurors to earn timebank hours exchangeable for tutoring, music, art lessons, and other services. Both social currencies and time banking are burgeoning, partly in response to economic recession and austerity programs.

Community supported agriculture (CSA)supports local small farmers and sustainable agriculture by creating dependable demand for their produce and up-front capital for annual crops. A paid subscription entitles members to a portion of whatever is produced each week. In good years, everyone shares in the bounty and in bad years, the pain. CSA members also enjoy knowing the farm and farmer. By Local Harvest estimates, the US may have over 6,000 CSAs.[35] Some serve low-income people by subsidizing shares through donations from wealthier members. Others, such as Uprising Farm in Bellingham, Washington, keep their share prices low and accept Supplemental Nutrition Assistance Program benefits.

Consumption

Community Land Trusts (CLTs) are nonprofit organizations that create permanently affordable homes by taking housing out of the speculative market. In one variation, the CLT owns the land and leases it to the homeowner for a nominal sum. The homeowner buys the home, not the land, an arrangement that makes home-owning more affordable. In Vermont, Champlain Housing Trust homes cost typically half what comparable open-market properties cost. Owners can sell their houses at a fair rate of return, but the house's price is capped to maintain permanent affordability. CLTs also leases rental units for those who can't afford or don't desire home ownership.

The CLT model also affords protection during economic and housing crises. A 2008 study showed that foreclosure rates among members of eighty US housing trusts were six times lower than the national average, thanks to CLT services and interventions.[36] The success of CLTs has spurred impressive growth, from 160 in 2005[37] to 225 in a 2018 survey.[38] Given housing-market gyrations, this is a model whose time has come.

The Sharing Economy and Platform Cooperativism

The sharing economy would seem to be entirely in keeping with the solidarity economy. And some parts—such as skill-shares, gifting, tool libraries, and other traditional volunteer and care work—do build relationships and community, reduce consumption, and amplify knowledge and skills. More controversial are such capitalist online platforms as Uber, Lyft, and Task Rabbit that enrich the owners on the backs of "freelance" workers who have no job security, health insurance, retirement benefits, vacation time, or workplace protection. Contingent workers like those in this "gig economy" now make up approximately 40 percent of the US workforce.[39]

Platform cooperativism defines a sharing economy approach that leverages many of the same technologies as Uber and Task Rabbit, but with a collective ownership structure and the goal of benefiting multiple stakeholders.[40] One example is Loconomics, a worker-owned version of Task Rabbit, where people can find and offer professional services online.[41]

Finance

Public banking is rapidly gaining support, especially since the financial meltdown of 2008. Public banks are owned by the people through local, state, or national government. They exist to serve the public good, not maximize profits for shareholders.

The Bank of North Dakota is the only state bank currently in operation in the US. Holding all the state's assets and revenues, the bank targets loans toward such state priorities as agriculture, infrastructure, economic development, and education. Unlike the many states where credit-rating downgrades after the financial crisis made it harder to borrow money, North Dakota sailed through the Great Recession with record-high budget surpluses, relying on its state bank for funds that local banks then lent. Revenues (over $300 million in the past decade) all go to its single shareholder—the people of North Dakota. Since 2009, more than 20 states and such cities as Santa Fe, New Mexico, have filed legislation to start or explore the feasibility of a public bank.

Credit unions are financial institutions that are nonprofit cooperatives, owned and controlled by their members/depositors. Most credit unions make personal loans, but some lend to small businesses and start-ups. Community Development Credit Unions provide predominantly low-income communities an alternative to predatory lenders by offering fairly priced loans, non-exploitative pay-day loans, and sound financial counseling and financial literacy education.[42] The number of credit unions decreased from 7,486 in 2010 to 6,143 in 2015,[43] mostly because small credit unions merged with larger ones, but the membership growth rate has increased year after year. Total credit union membership in 2015 topped 105 million, roughly one-third of the US population.[44]

Governance

Participatory budgeting democratizes government budgeting by giving local residents an official say in where public money should go. *Porto Alegre* in Brazil has been a leader in participatory municipal budgeting since 1989, and the model has spread to cities in the US, the UK, Canada, India, Ireland, Uganda, and South Africa. Between 2015 and 2019, according to the Participatory Budgeting Project, residents in various US and Canadian cities decided how to spend $276 million on 432 local projects, ranging from adding bike lanes and supporting community gardens to purchasing a new ultrasound system at a hospital and adding heating stations at train platforms. Channeling increased resources to meet the needs of low-income and marginalized communities, participatory budgeting also encourages people to dive into local issues, build community connections, learn how budgeting works, and practice direct democracy.

The Commons movement seeks to protect and promote resources that we hold in common. Commons proponent Jay Walljasper defines the commons as

> a wealth of valuable assets that belong to everyone. These range from clean air to wildlife preserves and from the judicial system to the Internet. Some are bestowed to us by nature; others are the product of cooperative human creativity.[45]

Socially created commons include such resources as Wikipedia and free software and parks, squares, and other public spaces where people play, relax, and socialize. Not a free for all, a commons requires governance to ensure equitable and responsible use.

Conclusion

Our current economic system is killing us and the planet. To survive, we need a fundamental transformation from an economy premised on *homo economicus*—calculating, selfish, competitive, and acquisitive—to a system premised on solidarity, cooperation, mutualism, altruism, generosity, and love. As we human beings practice and live more fully in tune with these values, we can more fully realize our nature's better angels. There is a strong and diverse foundation upon which to build that stretches across the globe. If we can now recognize each other as parts of the same transformative project, then we can achieve a metamorphosis of our economy and society. Shifting toward the solidarity economy may enable us to pull back from the brink.

Notes

1 On the Sixth Extinction, see: Elizabeth Kolbert, *The Sixth Extinction: An Unnatural History* (New York: Picador, 2014).
2 Jean Louis Laville, "The Solidarity Economy: An International Movement," *RCCS Annual Review* 2 (October 2002), https://journals.openedition.org/rccsar/202; Luis Razeto, "Factor C: la Solidaridad Convertida en Fuerza Productiva y en el Factor Econòmico [Factor C: The Force of Solidarity in the Economy]," 1998 and Luis Razeto, Interview with Luis Razeto. Interview by Esteban Romero. http://cborowiak.haverford. edu/solidarityeconomy/wp-content/uploads/sites/3/2013/07/Interview-with-Luis-Razeto_May-2010.pdf.
3 Jose Luis Coraggio, "Territory and Alternative Economies," *Universitas Forum* 1, 3 (2009): 6.
4 RIPESS, "Global Vision for a Social Solidarity Economy: Convergences and Differences in Concepts, Definitions and Frameworks," February 2015.
5 Nancy Folbre, "Valuing Non-market Work," *UNDP Human Development Report* – Think Piece, 2015.
6 Neoliberalism is a particular model of capitalism that advocates minimizing the role of the state in promoting the common good in favor of giving free rein to big business. Policies include privatization, de-regulation, cutbacks in social welfare programs, and "free" trade, though in reality there is a great deal of flexibility regarding these positions depending on what is beneficial to big business.
7 Esteban Romero, "The Meanings of Solidarity Economies. Interview with Luiz Razeto," May 2010.
8 Jessica Gordon Nembhard, *Collective Courage: A History of African American Cooperative Thought and Practice* (State College: Penn State University Press, 2014).
9 *National Plan for Good Living 2009–2013: Building a Plurinational and Intercultural State,* Summarized Version, The Republic of Ecuador. National Development Plan, Quito, Ecuador, 2010, 6.
10 Shannon Biggs, *Rights of Nature: Planting the Seeds of Change* (San Francisco, CA: Global Exchange, 2012).
11 Garrett Hardin, "The Tragedy of the Commons," *Journal of Natural Resources Policy Research* 1, 3 (2009): 243–253.
12 Elinor Ostrom, "Collective Action and the Evolution of Social Norms," *Journal of Economic Perspectives* 14,3 (2000): 137–158; Elinor Ostrom, *Governing the Commons: The Evolution of Institutions for Collective Action* (Cambridge: Cambridge University Press, 1990).
13 Jeremy Rifkin, *End of Work, The Decline of the Global Labor Force and the Dawn of the Post-Market Era* (Putnam, NY: G. P. Putnam's Sons, 1995).
14 Eckart Ehlers and Thomas Krafft, *Earth System Science in the Anthropocene: Emerging Issues and Problems* (Berlin: Springer, 2006).
15 RIPESS, "Global Vision". op. cit., p. 16.

16 Rights of Nature, Community Environmental Legal Defense Fund, http://celdf.org/how-we-work/education/rights-of-nature.

17 On the French legislation, see: "The 2014 Law on Social and Solidarity Economy: France." *European Commission*, 2014, https://webgate.ec.europa.eu/socialinnovationeurope/en/directory/ france/news/2014-law-social-and-solidarity-economy-%C3%A9conomie-sociale-et-solidaire-%E2%80%93-ess-en.

18 There is considerable confusion about and conflation of social economy and solidarity economy. RIPESS uses the term social solidarity economy which is admittedly confusing, but the RIPESS Charter makes it clear that its meaning is the solidarity economy and the intent is systemic transformation. The use of both social and solidarity is a matter of history and a marriage of convenience.

19 "The Social Economy," Brussels: CEPCMAF, 2002, http://www.amice-eu.org/userfiles/file/2007_08_20_EN_SE_charter.pdf.26.

20 Emily Kawano, "Social Solidarity Economy: Toward Convergence across Continental Divides." *UNRISD*, February 26, 2013.

21 Euclides Mance, "Solidarity-Based Productive Chains," *Curitiba*, November, 2002.

22 Ana Esteves, "Grassroots Mobilization, Co-production of Public Policy and the Promotion of Participatory Democracy by the Brazilian Solidarity Economy Movement," Ph.D. Dissertation, Department of Sociology, Brown University, 2011.

23 "Solidarity Economy Map and Directory," Solidarity Economy Mapping Project.

24 Anne Field, "More Cities Get Serious About Community Wealth-Building," *Forbes*, November 10, 2015, https://www.forbes.com/sites/annefield/2015/11/10/more-cities-get-serious-about-community-wealth-building/#3754fc4151c2; Jennifer Jones Austin, "Worker Cooperatives for New York City: A Vision for Addressing Income Inequality," Federation of Protestant Welfare Agencies, January 2014.

25 "Seven Cooperative Principles," National Cooperative Business Association.

26 Lise Bond et al., "Survival Rate of Cooperatives in Quebec," Quebec Ministry of Industry and Commerce, 1999; Carol Murray, "Co-op Survival Rates in British Columbia," British Columbia Cooperative Association, 2011, http://auspace.athabascau.ca/handle/2149/3133.

27 Alyssa Davis and Lawrence Mishel, CEO Pay Continues to Rise as Typical Workers Are Paid Less, Economic Policy Institute, Issue Brief 380 (June 12, 2014).

28 Nina Misuraca Ignaczak, "It Takes an Eco-system: The Rise of Worker Cooperatives in the US," *Shareable*, July 16, 2014,

29 Juliet Schor, *True Wealth: How and Why Millions of Americans Are Creating a Time-Rich, Ecologically Light, Small-Scale, High-Satisfaction Economy* (New York: Penguin Group, 2011).

30 New Work New Culture website, http://newworknewculture.org/.

31 Esha Chhabra, "The 3D Printed Car That Could Transform the Auto Industry: On Sale in 2016," *Forbes*, December 30, 2015.

32 Mark Molloy, "This Incredibly Cheap House Was 3D Printed in Just 24 Hours," *The Telegraph*, March 3, 2017.

33 Nathan McAlone, "This College Student 3D Printed His Own Platic Braces For $60, And They Actually Fixed His Teeth," *Business Insider*, May 19, 2016, http://www.businessinsider.com/college-student-3d-prints-plastic-braces-for-60-2016-5.

34 W. Wuthrich, "Cooperative Principle and Complementary Currency," trans. Philip Beard, 2004, http://monetary-freedom.net/reinventingmoney/Beard-WIR.pdf.

35 Steven McFadden, "Unraveling the CSA Number Conundrum," *The Call of the Land Blog*, January 9, 2012, https://thecalloftheland.wordpress.com/2012/01/09/unraveling-the-csa-number-conundrum/.

36 "Community Land Trusts Lower Risk of Losing Homes to Foreclosure," *National Community Land Trust Network*, March 17, 2009, http://www.shareable.net/blog/it-takes-an-ecosystem-the-rise-of-worker-cooperatives-in-the-us.

37 Rosalind Greenstein and Yesim Sungu-Eryilmaz, "Community Land Trusts: Leasing Land for Affordable Housing," *Land Lines*, April 2005, 1 www.lincolninst.edu/publications/articles/community-land-trusts.

38 Emily Brown and Ted Ranney, "Community Land Trusts and Commercial Properties," A Social Justice Committee Report for the Urban Land Institute Technical Assistance Program for Atlanta Land Trust Collaborative, 8. Emily Thaden, "The State of Shared Equity Homeownership," *Shelterforce*, May 7, 2018, https://shelterforce.org/2018/05/07/shared-equity/.

39 "Contingent Workforce: Size, Characteristics, Earnings and Benefits," U. S. Government Accountability Office, GAO-15-168R, April 20, 2015, http://www.gao.gov/assets/670/669899.pdf.

40 Trebor Scholz, "Platform Cooperativism: Challenging the Corporate Sharing Economy," *NYC: Rosa Luxemburg Stiftung*, January 2016, http://www.rosalux-nyc.org/wp-content/files_mf/scholz_platformcooperativism21.pdf.

41 Loconomics, http://loconomics.com.

42 Jessica Gordon Nembhard, *Taking the Predator Out of Lending: The Role Played by Community Development Credit Unions in Securing and Protecting Assets*, Working Paper, Howard University, Center on Race and Wealth, August 2010.

43 U. S. Credit Union Profile, Mid Year 2016, *CUNA Economics & Statistics*, 7.

44 U. S. Credit Union Profile, Mid Year 2016, *CUNA Economics & Statistics*, 5.

45 Jay Walljasper, "What, Really, Is the Commons?" *Terrain.org* 27 (Spring/Summer 2011), http://www.terrain.org/articles/27/walljasper.htm.

Chapter 20

Democratizing Wealth in the US South and Beyond

Ed Whitfield

"Democratizing wealth" means struggling to put the wealth initially created by human labor back into a democratically controlled commons for the benefit of all. Basic resources need to be made available to everyone so all have the opportunity to be productive and do for themselves. Wealth should be used in the interest of the people, by the people, and for the people. While this is on its surface an economic outcome, it is also much more.

Democratizing wealth is intimately connected to changing social realities. It will require creating new relationships among people, along with new democratic norms, political procedures to establish and to defend those norms, and new environmental outcomes that reflect those norms. Democratizing wealth calls for enabling the full human potential, which is currently stifled by exploitative structures and the systems of private ownership of productive assets. The existing ownership relationships are made to seem natural, inevitable, and immutable, but, in fact, they are human creations that reflect the desires and interests of particular people at a particular time, which means they can be changed. We need to create a system that recognizes that the private control of nature and the accumulation of the wealth created by labor means that a few people have virtual control of the means of life of everyone else. We need a system where nature and wealth are owned and utilized for the common good.

We at the Fund for Democratic Communities (F4DC) do not have a roadmap to the future. We recognize that we live in a dynamic world, where future changes do not announce themselves in an orderly way. Besides the challenges of having to change the world when it is already in flux, our core belief in authentic democracy keeps us from presenting full outlines of what communities should do. The ultimate directives for the future, and clarity on the path forward, must and will instead emerge from communities engaged in meeting their own needs and elevating the quality of community life. Government and enabling policies have roles to play, but the struggle for policies needs to flow from the people engaged in the concrete practice of creating new possibilities and fighting for their success. With the proper information, and by examining a range of possibilities, communities can choose and implement the policies and programs for the change that they need. F4DC's role is to help process information, help share alternatives, and find some of the needed resources. We stand firmly with the people of the most marginalized communities to build a world that is democratic, sustainable, just, and fair for all.

Democracy and SASH

In the long term, what is needed is a new commons that includes both the natural world and finance. Both the earth—which was here before all of us—as well as the creations of social activity made from the earth, should be available democratically to us all.

We have a long way to go. Today, nature and the surplus value created by labor are privately appropriated and held as the personal or corporate property of individual owners. Just as many early societies had no concept of private land ownership, an economically just society would ban the theft of nature and its consequent ownership, as well as the theft of the products of the labor of others.

The new commons can come about through the development of financial structures and business entities that will reflect new relationships of democratic ownership and control. By "democratic" we mean "of, by, and for the people." The people decide how the basic decisions are to be made (of the people), then they decide that they themselves are the ones to make those decisions (by the people), and that the decisions are to be made in the interests of the people as a whole (for the people). This is a simple concept, but it is not a simple process.

Democracy is not brought into existence simply by establishing voting processes, though it will often involve voting. If the process is manipulated so that the interests of the powerful elite are satisfied to the detriment of the common people, then the process is not really democratic. If the process is compromised by lack of access to information and the weight of misinformation and prejudices, then the process is not truly democratic. Often, people think of democracy from the standpoint of simply registering their opinions. But if opinions cannot be challenged and do not have to be reconciled with the opinions of others, opining is not enough. Indeed, the most important aspect of democracy is people thinking together, sharing information, raising questions, and resolving their differences and thereby developing shared understandings and a common direction.

We at F4DC think of democracy as requiring the adoption of a certain Spirit, along with the Arts, Sciences and Habits of standing with the whole and being in the community, for the community. We call that "SASH." If any one of those components is missing, the democratic project is likely to falter. Democratizing wealth requires a thoughtful and intentional approach to the question of how to balance the community's interests with those of the individual or the corporation. This balancing act ranks among our greatest challenges.

Inspiring by Example

To democratize wealth, we must together build concrete examples of useful, sustainable economic enterprises as existence proofs, to show that new ways of approaching democratic ownership are possible. Examples can unleash the imagination and energy of those of us who don't even dream of other realities beyond today's exploitative hierarchical relationships.

At F4DC, we are working with others to develop new institutions that will inform people's understanding and behavior. We are building such community-owned or worker-owned cooperative businesses. Our efforts have included the Renaissance Community Cooperative grocery store (RCC) and such non-extractive democratic financial institutions as the Southern Reparations Loan Fund (SRLF), a part of Seed Commons: A Community Wealth Cooperative.

The RCC, which opened in 2016 and, sadly, closed in 2019, was a full-service community-owned grocery store serving a working class African American neighborhood in Greensboro, NC. The first such project in the country, this project was initially criticized by experts in the field of cooperative food store development because the community was identified as being too black, too poor, and too uneducated for a successful food cooperative. Their demographic model dismissed neighborhoods like the one we were working in as having "weak demographics." This community was a food desert—its previous grocery store closed in 1998. Community members organized immediately to try to retain that store, or get another corporate chain grocery store to replace it and had to mobilize again a few years later to join with others from across Greensboro to advocate for the closure of a solid-waste landfill that was lowering property values and the quality of life.

The community won the fight against the landfill and a second fight when a new, more conservative city council considered reopening it. But still no grocery store—until F4DC shared the idea of opening a cooperative grocery store themselves. Since the community came together around the possibility, approximately 2.5 million dollars in funding was secured from multiple sources: one hundred dollar membership/ownership fees, owner loans from co-op members, Community Development Financial Institution (CDFI) funding from Shared Capital Cooperative, non-extractive patient lending from Regenerative Finance facilitated through The Working World and the Southern Reparations Loan Fund, a challenge grant from the City of Greensboro, two large church donations, and some small foundation grants. The store, which closed in early 2019 due to revenue shortages, was still worth the seven-year effort: it helped reshape thinking within the food cooperative world about the need to address black working-class food deserts. Other efforts across the country were inspired by the RCC's fight for respect within the coop world, and now many residents of that Greensboro neighborhood stand ready to put even more effort into the next community effort.

The SRLF is developing into a democratic financial institution rooted in three basic principles:

- Radical inclusivity, which means making loans available for cooperative economic development to communities that would otherwise not be considered.
- Non-extractive finance, which means making loans that will not make the borrower financially worse off than before, even if the enterprise for which they borrow money does not succeed. Not accepting prior assets as loan collateral is one way to do this.
- Maximizing community benefit, which means not focusing on maximum profit, but, instead, on maximizing the value to the whole community.

The SRLF functions in the US South, using investments from individuals and institutions that understand the need to place capital at the disposal of underserved communities to repair some of the historical and ongoing damage done by the exploitative economic system. Incorporated in North Carolina, SRLF began with a single loan officer trying to cover an area of nearly one million square miles of the 14 former southern slave states and Oklahoma. Today, SRLF is a regional network of local loan funds with independent branches in place or developing from the Delta region of Mississippi to the border areas of Kentucky and West Virginia. A functioning board of representatives from the local funds works with a support network including the national Seed Commons and regional assistance within SRLF to support lending in West Virginia, Mississippi, North Carolina, Florida and have plans in place to support grassroots cooperative efforts in marginalized communities in Louisiana, Tennessee, Georgia, and Kentucky. Rather than simply making yes or no decisions on loans, we look to say "yes" or "not yet." If there is a specific reason for "not yet," we try to provide or secure the needed technical assistance. Presently, F4DC is funding the SRLF staff while we work to affiliate with other like-minded local loan funds to develop a financial cooperative.

The RCC project and the SRLF create existence proofs of new possibilities. The RCC story, in spite of its premature ending, has still inspired people to try to build food cooperatives in traditionally overlooked neighborhoods; the SRLF, to build financial institutions along sustainable democratic lines.

Projects like these help build the political power needed to spread and protect new approaches to livelihoods and democratic wealth. New policy frameworks will emerge from concrete struggles to create new structures, and as people come to realize what is possible and build new democratic models, they will then work to create new policies that support them. Policy is important and the political struggle to change it must be led by people who have engaged in practical efforts to change the basic nature of community wealth accumulation, but policy change doesn't have to come before practice.

The relationship between values, culture, and consciousness and the systems that produce them and are affected by them is reflexive. It is said that we can *think our way into new ways of acting*, but we can also *act our way into new ways of thinking*. Both parts of this proposition are true. Both are important. Keeping groceries flowing into a food desert at least for a few years was possible because struggles around other local issues in Greensboro had succeeded and because a new consciousness and enthusiasm emerged from work on the cooperative store. The community has learned about the possibility and importance of doing something for itself.

Cooperative Enterprises

The basic form of business structure that we advocate is the cooperative. It has built into its principles the ideas of democratic ownership and governance. In cooperative structures, where enterprises are collectively and democratically owned and democratically governed for the benefit of the group rather than an entrepreneurial owner, the surplus is at the disposal of the many, not just the fortunate few. In an economy of cooperatives, income won't necessarily need to be equalized if the opportunities to increase one's income are fairly available to the many and everyone has enough to meet their needs.

While the role of individual genius and entrepreneurship is appreciated and should be rewarded, it should not entail the ongoing extraction of value from other people's labor. The idea that some of us live by work and others live by owning isn't legitimate. All who can contribute to society should. Conjoining private property ownership to so-called "public ownership" produces a hybrid in which the differential in power between the two parts puts one at a significant disadvantage. Public enterprises that are publicly owned and publicly governed are in many ways an ideal.

The most productive economic landscape will include both small and moderate-sized enterprises, partly because scaling direct democracy is difficult. Networks of small and moderate-sized enterprises create fewer opportunities for undemocratic, command-based development than gigantic enterprises, which claim economies of scale but don't allow for democratic management.

The upper limit of moderate-sized enterprises is a couple of thousand employees. Much larger than that and democracy goes out the window! Enterprises of that size are big enough to build automobiles and airplanes, or, better, wind turbines and electric rail cars. Networks of mid-sized enterprises could fix crumbling infrastructure. The argument that certain big projects need still larger enterprises ignores the fact that efficiency often requires bigger enterprises to break down into more manageable sections. It is important to think about scale if we care about the concentration of power and wealth.

Very large corporations need to come under the democratic control of public bodies. If they are too big to fail, then they are too big to exist and should be broken up. Both the Tennessee Valley Authority or General Motors (before it collapsed) are cases in point. To the extent that super-sized enterprises are needed at all, their management should be regulated, governed, and controlled by government, itself controlled by the people.

Local Focus

Although cooperative structures can be networked to reach larger scales, starting local is not just a pragmatic decision related to the cooperative movement's current level of development. Democratizing wealth means trying to meet local economic needs in the local economy rather than producing goods for export. In turn, meeting needs locally is the necessary foundation for other forms of economic development.

Just what are these needs? Besides the fundamentals of food, clothing, and shelter, communities will have their own standards. (In the United States, a house with no flush toilets wouldn't seem right, for instance.) Beyond shared standards for what's acceptable, local needs will also include water and sewage, transportation infrastructure, an education system, a healthcare system, and energy.

Typically, government covers water/sewage, transportation infrastructure, and pre-college education while much of higher education (apart from community colleges and state universities), healthcare, and energy are handled by private businesses. In a sophisticated, complex, and mature community thinking about building an economy that meets people's needs, members must think about how all these components interact. As small independent business units, cooperatives can only partially address the need for democratizing wealth and the economy. That said, preferred treatment—both incentives and preferential purchasing—by local government can expand cooperatives' reach and success.

Currently, local government bids out infrastructure construction to local contractors and developers. In the economy F4DC envisions, local government contractors are cooperatively based and local government privileges cooperative businesses over private for-profit businesses in procurement. For instance, most government-run water-treatment and sewage-treatment facilities are funded from tax revenues for infrastructure and usage fees for services. Since these services need to be carefully regulated for the community's safety, most oversight should be handled by staff hired by local elected government bodies tending to the public good instead of profit. Most of this work should not be privatized. Instead, whatever local government employees can't do directly, such as a capital improvement or major infrastructure development, should be contracted out to worker-owned enterprises.

Similarly, building and repairing local infrastructure should be handled by cooperative business interests wherever possible and financed by public or cooperative banking. As it now stands, this costly and typically lucrative work is almost always financed by private banks and done by private developers and local contractors running for-profit enterprises. In this transfer of money from the public sphere into the private sphere, taxes or borrowed money repaid through taxes provide profit to individual and corporate entrepreneurs and bankers. If infrastructure were directly financed through taxation, or by borrowing from publicly owned, democratically controlled banks or credit unions, interest payments on the public debt would go to the public through democratically controlled institutions.

The intention of Mayor Chokwe Lumumba in Jackson, Mississippi was to do just this. In his town of under 175,000 people, the Environmental Protection Agency in 2013 was requiring three to four billion dollars' worth of infrastructure work on the water and sewage system.[1] Before his untimely death, Lumumba worked toward privileging the development of worker cooperative businesses to handle the bulk of these contracts. It remains to be seen when the local community there can get back on track with this visionary plan now that his son, Chokwe Antar Lumumba, has been elected and is working to pursue similar policies, but, either way, this potential exists for communities nationwide.

Along with infrastructure, higher education and healthcare are two of the larger scale and more stable portions of many communities' economies. In many cities and towns, the college and the hospital are the area's largest employers. Thinking about a more just economic system, we should consider this local development opportunity in two ways—as the economic activity of an enterprise itself, including all the operations that can be democratized, and as the procurement of supplies and services on a scale affecting other businesses' prospects.

Democratizing the enterprise means supporting the organizing efforts of the institutions' employees, giving them greater control over the conditions of their labor, whether in a profit-making or a sustainably run not-for-profit mode. At some point, it might make sense to develop alternative institutions parallel to the existing institutions, but organized cooperatively from the beginning. Another possibility is organizing cooperative universities and hospitals.

As for their huge purchasing power, many colleges and hospitals buy enough goods and services to warrant the creation of medium-scale businesses to enter that market. Cleveland's Evergreen Cooperative and its relationship to the Cleveland Clinic, Case Western Reserve University, and University Hospitals exemplify how this can work. Making universities and hospitals anchor institutions for building cooperative businesses is also being examined in Western Massachusetts. Since businesses built to provide goods or services for anchor institutions might be totally dependent on the anchor institutions for their survival, cultivating other customers will be important.

Community Finance and Investment

A just economic system would put the ownership of productive assets in the hands of community groups or democratic cooperative associations to meet community needs. Banking, the process of extending credit to finance production, should also be democratic. At smaller scales, a democratic economy would also include credit unions, where individuals' surplus could be used for productive lending or as a personal cushion for a rainy day. At the larger scale, bigger public banks and other community development institutions based on non-extractive principles are needed. At both scales, lending decisions should depend on whether the loan can be paid back from related revenues and on the business activity's importance to the community. Funds should be made available to cooperative entities and either royalty payments equaling a percentage of net profit should be made, or fixed interest charged after the activity becomes profitable, with the principal being repaid on a realistic schedule. The royalty or interest would cover lending's administrative costs and supplement the fund.

Investment is a somewhat more complex proposition due to questions of ownership and power. Investment currently implies part ownership, and, presumably, part control of governance. Many investors want to control what they own. Others are interested only in the monetary return on their investment, but that poses a problem if they also want control, especially for enterprises that need to turn a profit and remain sustainable while meeting human needs. In a new system in which individuals are not allowed to appropriate the surplus created by others and in which surplus is held in common, that surplus would no longer be invested for profit as now conceived. Any investing would need to be in the form of "preferred shares" which have no decision-making power. In this new system, the power of owners with deeper connections to the enterprise would not be diluted.

The owners of economic surplus should be those who produce it and the communities they are a part of. The moral justification for the community to receive and control the accumulated surplus is that the production of surplus from human labor requires a nurturing and supportive community. The community should be the basic unit of analysis, where the quality of lived experience is measured and maximized.

Good Work

Workers may be able to work less as automation continues but they will have to organize themselves differently.

The amount of time people spend in socially maintained productive activity, compared to leisure, recreation, family, and personal time, has varied widely throughout history and among cultures. Eight hours of work, eight of sleep, and eight of time with family and community at leisure every day with two days off for family activity and rest sounds good. But few use their time this way exactly, and it's certainly not the only way we could order work. Rather than having a guaranteed annual income, basically an expanded welfare system, why not shorten the typical workweek and allow more people to participate community life?

A shorter workweek also seems more appealing than allowing some people to be productive workers in society and get paid for it, while others are simply consumers enabled by a free check. With a guaranteed income, we socialize consumption while allowing production to remain private and making it hard to balance social power.

Other work-related issues need attention too. Today's organized labor movement is weak largely because many workers don't see it as representing their interests so much as creating another exploitative elite. Highly paid union spokespeople for organized labor only rarely speak to the dreams and aspirations of working people. These officials are part of an exploitative system they are almost powerless to change; their job is to create labor peace. When the US economy was stable or growing and large corporations reaped huge profits, many corporations made lucrative deals with their unions. But the new economic realities are different: both domestic trade deals that reward the corporate exportation of jobs and changing world economic realities make it difficult for corporations to pay concessions to organized labor. With declining membership and less give during negotiations, organized labor is weaker than it has been at any time since the Great Depression.[2] The idea that dues check-off and the ability to negotiate a closed shop are the main demands of labor simply does not speak to the lived experiences of working people. Removing the old system's roots in different economic realities to make way for a better bargain will be hard, as will organizing workers who have never been unionized.

Wealth, Poverty, and the Commons

Poverty today is rampant because many communities lack the wealth to allow everyone to be productive and meet community needs. If we again think of the commons as embracing both the natural bounty of the earth and the wealth created by labor, we can see how having this resource available fairly and democratically to all would be key to eliminating poverty. Here, the aim isn't to divide wealth into small parcels and distribute them to all, but rather to democratize access to the aggregate. Dividing and apportioning large assets to individuals as shares raises the specter that all such assets might be re-accumulated by individuals who make advantageous deals with other stakeholders.

An example is the massive Black land loss that has resulted when properties sold to satisfy the conditions of joint ownership prove hard to sell in subdivided pieces. This problem can also be seen around the world. Some economists, such as Hernando de Soto Polar, have suggested dividing communally held lands for individual ownership so that they can be mortgaged for loans.[3] But this division could well precipitate the foreclosure of many such loans and lead to the transfer of ownership to the banks who took the land as collateral. Large parcels of land and large amounts of productive capital might best be utilized in the aggregate with democratic control rather than being parceled out for individual ownership.

Reclaiming or recreating commons is a major challenge since many people have been convinced of the "tragedy of the commons." This theory posits that the successful community use of the commons is impossible despite the historical record of the commons prior to the enclosure movement. The late economist Elinor Ostrom has proved the theory wrong by showing how effective and long lasting effective commons management has historically been.[4] Success, she found, requires clearly deciding the roles and responsibilities of stakeholders through an agreed-upon democratic process and establishing monitoring processes that regulate the fair use of the commons for all.

Environmental Justice, Not Green Shopping

Some environmental activists insist that the US environmental crisis is rooted equally in mass consumption and corporate production. But US consumers can't buy their way out of our global environmental fix. The fundamental decisions about what is made, how much of it is made, and through what processes it is made are not decisions made by the public, but rather in corporate boardrooms where maximizing the bottom line is the only goal. The idea that consumers can just stop buying things that cause pollution or deplete resources misses the point. Consumers are manipulated through high-priced marketing that creates demand unnaturally. Only public control of production will put the public in full control of consumption.

Other environmentalists juggle the question of whether the environment matters more than economic justice. Suggesting economic justice requires further development that necessarily entails more environmental damage, they further claim that saving the earth is more important than eliminating inequity. Two problems undermine such arguments. First, they imply that economic justice will require more development activity that will be polluting or otherwise destroy Earth's resources. Second, they assume that economic justice is nice in theory but not worth going to great trouble to attain, suggesting that human life lost to hunger is less important than life lost to pollution and climate change. The truth is that justice may be found in more democratic development to meet human needs, rather than increased production to increase profit. Intelligent paths to democratic development that do not necessarily produce polluting environmental outcomes are open.

The other problem with pitting the environment against the economy is that it assumes that Earth itself is being damaged by economic development. What we are destroying is the Earth's capacity to support human life. When people lack access to the means of producing or purchasing food, the economic injustice leading to starvation is just as dangerous to human potential as water and air pollution. It is among those whose economic privilege makes their starvation unthinkable that the simple choice can be made of the environment over the economy.

Many environmentalists have moved beyond the false dichotomy of economic development versus ecological health. Forming partnerships with economic development groups helps. F4DC works with such environmental groups as The Chorus Foundation, The Climate Justice Alliance (CJA), and Grassroots Global Justice Alliance on a "just transition" to a world that's both environmentally and economically healthy. Until the current system of ownership, power, and privilege is overturned in favor of a wealth democracy, the challenge is to connect with others in the political struggle to get current governments to take environmental concerns seriously.

At every step in building a democratic economy, the environmental consequences of economic activity deserve close attention. The decisions made should be informed by the best available understanding of the consequences. Ours should be a standards-based environmental consciousness. We need to decide what is permissible based on its consequences and our best understanding of our roles and responsibilities in the world. Earth itself will survive even our complete annihilation as a species. It is the planet's capacity for human habitation that is at risk.

Reparations for Communities

There is a need to right historic inequities. Reparations are owed to communities that have been systemically stripped of the wealth they produce. We do not have to wait for the current government to accept responsibility for past wrongs and implement reparations. Individuals with access to wealth and philanthropic concentrations of wealth can voluntarily make their wealth available as reparations to these drained communities. The Southern Reparations Loan Fund, the Southern network of Seed Commons: A Community Wealth Cooperative, works to build relationships with such individuals and put their wealth back within marginalized communities.

Other efforts at repairing historical discrimination have taken different approaches. The *Pigford vs. Glickman* class action discrimination suit charged the US Department of Agriculture with discriminating against Black farmers. In the original suit, individual Black farmers won claims that were generally $50,000 or less if they could prove that they were treated differently from a white farmer in a similar situation during a very specific period.[5] While this approach was not called "reparations," it models one way to make repairs for the damage of slavery and discrimination.

Yet, the class action approach has two serious flaws. For one, its basis is in individual injury when the injury was to a community. For another, it asks for proof of a specific connection to that injury when the connection is through hundreds, even thousands, of damaged relationships and outcomes compounded for decades or even centuries. As Ben Burkett of the Mississippi Association of Cooperatives has said of the Pigford payments, it would have been better to pool the funds in a trust so they could be borrowed against and used for business development.[6] As it was, much of the money was spent as consumption that did not enhance the community's ability to become producers.

The most meaningful reparations would come as a correction to the lack of development in communities where labor and the surplus it creates were stolen. Development funds for creating new enterprises and the expansion and modernization of current enterprises in disadvantaged communities would require democratic access to wealth.

Liberty and Justice for All

The drive toward perfect equality is not necessarily desirable since people's energy levels and appetites differ. And equity and fairness don't require equality. But they do require fair opportunity. The problem with today's undemocratic economic system is that it denies the overwhelming majority the opportunity to use their skills, energy, and interest to be productive members of the community. The system syphons off the excess of people's production above the bare minimum required to carry on and allows a small minority to accumulate it. The injustice is that a small minority sees everyone else as simply instrumental to its drive for ever-increasing accumulation and ever-increasing power.

Forming cooperatives, instituting community ownership and finance, and integrating concern for the future into our decisions are all key steps to realizing economic democracy. But constitutional change is needed too. The current US constitution compromised the interests of the northern industrial exploiters with those of the southern slavocracy. Portions of the constitution do reflect attempts to expand its beneficiaries beyond the initial narrow elite—privileged white men with property and political voice. The Bill of Rights too and later the Thirteenth, Fourteenth (though compromised by recent attempts to justify corporate personhood), and Fifteenth Amendments are certainly progressive. But a society rooted in freedom, equity, and human development is needed now. In particular, the US constitution's fixation on preserving property rights needs to be understood as a defense of both the theft of native land and the ownership of enslaved Africans as chattel slaves.

A starting point in this critical democratic exercise of considering a new founding document should be preserving liberty—provided that individual liberty does not mean elevating the individual above the community and privilege individual property over the social process of its production and the social needs it serves. What should be promoted and protected is the kind of liberty needed for each person to express his or her full humanity, which can be expressed only in relationship with other people. The individual finds real freedom within community. Our legal structures need to reflect the broadly held values and concomitant ethical rules that would have us treat others with the same respect that we ask for ourselves. Without interfering with others, we should all be free to pursue our dreams and aspirations. This is the purpose of democratizing wealth.

Of course, it takes political power to bring about constitutional change and the other features of wealth democracy. This power is vested in local, state, regional, and national government entities, and it needs to be directed to serve the needs and interests of all the many communities within their jurisdiction. Government power should enhance freedom and facilitate the possibility for everyone to be productive and have expanded agency. For their part, citizens need to question the relationships among the personal, corporate, public, governmental, and community forms of power.

Locally, more efforts for direct democracy are needed. There is no other way to open up discussions leading to choices beyond those twisted and restricted by the elite to serve their interests. One democratizing option is participatory budgeting, in which citizens and communities directly determine how a portion of tax revenues is spent. Nationally, voting for "the lesser of the two evils," without engaging in the elevated political discourse needed to move national elections beyond evil, isn't enough. More principled dialogue is needed, perhaps grounded nationwide in local activity to identify local priorities, gain political experience, and encourage local leaders to move up and form new national structures.

Here a word about race is in order. The divisions and disparate treatment between people of different skin color, ethnic heritage, religious belief, and national origin divide the United States and weaken grassroots communities struggling for human dignity and opportunities to meet their needs. Slaves freed after the Civil War understood that enslavement meant that the product of their labor was taken without consent and that freedom was the ability to keep and use the product of one's own labor. This understanding highlights the fact that we are still not truly free. But it also gives us a way of knowing what is missing. Those formerly enslaved community leaders who met with military and federal government leaders asked for land and equipment, not money. The promise was made of 40 acres. While this promise was broken, what matters here is that this "ask" was for production units, not consumption units. Being made whole was thought of as having the land and equipment needed to produce something.

There is nothing inherently discriminatory about difference. "Race" differences, such as skin color, do not naturally produce racism any more than differences in eye color or hair color do. It is the existence of racism. The disparate treatment and double standard of access in a society based on heritage is what produces "race," the idea that there are essential differences between people based on color or national origin. Enunciated in Barbara and Karen Fields' book *Racecraft*, this distinction helps us see what needs to be done to end racist thought and action.[7] What the Fields show is that the acceptance of essentialized notions of racial difference pervades US society—just as notions about witchcraft once bedeviled the Puritans—and that thinking that race differences are produced by a person's race and not by racism damages our ability to correct the racist practices long accepted as natural. When democratic access to community wealth is made the universal norm, the need to perpetuate the divisiveness fostered by racism wanes. With careful amends made for past racism, people's natural capacity to recognize and respect each other can be unleashed.

In Crisis, Opportunity

As the economic crisis intensifies, more market failures come to light, and more people start questioning government's role in protecting the rich, we would like to build the movement necessary to get government involved in institutions that model a more rational approach to development. Political progress isn't smooth and linear, and both cataclysmic events and social and economic crises change the nature of public discourse. The national dialogue after the economic crisis of 2008 was at a higher level than it had been during and after the Cold War, and the discourse on the role of the 1 percent versus the 99 percent in the United States has recently opened a more realistic way of looking at what had been euphemistically called "opportunity" and "freedom" in describing capitalism. The Occupy movement also triggered discussions about the concentration of wealth and power and the struggle to expand direct democracy.

Changing the nature of public discourse, community groups, organizations, government bodies, and individuals have been searching for new approaches and solutions. One positive force is renewed interest in self-sufficiency, social justice, and the movements that promote them. From the development of the Black church to the rise of mutual aid societies, and, later, the Garvey movement, we see a consistent thrust toward oppressed communities seeking and finding ways to do for themselves.[8]

F4DC's theory of social justice movements holds that they have three fundamental components: Resistance (R), Advocacy (A), and Doing for ourselves (D), or RAD. Resistance and advocacy are institutionalized in many social justice organizations. The power that hurts us and can crush us can and must be resisted. *Resistance* work is necessary for our survival. The power that can be diverted to help us meet our needs and satisfy our desires can, and should, be directed. This direction of power is advocacy. *Advocacy* allows us to make the best use of the concentrations of power outside of ourselves. Another key to understanding power is that we ourselves can wield it, that not all power has to be in the hands of others. It is the realization that we too can have human agency and provide for the things that we need, as well as do many of the things that we want. This drive is to have the power needed to *Do for ourselves*.

Many social justice movements in the United States, particularly since the Civil Rights Movement, are deeply committed to Resistance and Advocacy but not to the possibilities of what we can Do for ourselves. That ability is limited by the concentration of wealth, but the democratization of wealth addresses that limitation by making wealth democratically available.

In periods of general stability, little thought is given to what we can accomplish without directly involving the powerful, but amid crises many more minds are open to the need and the possibility for change. And new economic crises are definitely coming. Social historians and economists predict a major, systemwide and potentially catastrophic socioeconomic crisis soon, lending urgency to the need to create examples of new models while offering a better path to those focused simply on resistance. We can't predict the full-blown crisis' exact arrival, but we can prepare for it.

Conclusion

Our aim is to help create a world where each person can reach their full human potential as a productive creative individual, a carrier of the culture and an expressive agent of individual and community development. We want everyone to be able to fully contribute by using the tools and resources that should be available to us all to meet our needs and elevate the quality of life within our community. Democratizing wealth will entail sharing control of the tools that multiply our individual efforts. The current system, neither sustainable nor humane, must be replaced by economic democracy through our continuing collective efforts.

Notes

1 United States, *Drinking Water Infrastructure Needs Survey and Assessment: Fifth Report to Congress* (2013), http://purl.fdlp.gov/GPO/gpo46211.
2 For information about membership decline over time, see: Pew Research Center, "American Unions Membership Declines as Public Support Fluctuates," February 20, 2014, http://www.pewresearch.org/fact-tank/2014/02/20/for-american-unions-membership-trails-far-behind-public-support/.
3 For more on Hernando de Soto Polar's approach to land, see de Soto, Hernando, *The Mystery of Capital: Why Capitalism Triumphs in the West and Fails Everywhere Else* (New York: Basic Books, 2000).
4 Elinor Ostrom, *Governing the Commons: The Evolution of Institutions for Collective Action* (New York: Cambridge University Press, 1990).
5 Tadlock Cowan and Jody Feder, "The Pigford Cases: USDA Settlement of Discrimination Suits by Black Farmers." *Congressional Research Service Report for Congress*, May 29, 2013, http://nationalaglawcenter.org/wp-content/uploads/assets/crs/RS20430.pdf.
6 Andrianna Natsoulas and Beverly Bell, "Fighting Racism from the USDA, Black Farmers Gain Power through Co-ops," *Truthout*, October 13, 2015, http://www.truth-out.org/opinion/item/33208-fighting-racism-from-the-usda-black-farmers-gain-power-through-co-ops.
7 Karen E. Fields and Barbara Jeanne Fields, *Racecraft: The Soul of Inequality in American Life* (New York: Verso Books, 2012).
8 For more on self-sufficiency and African American cooperatives, see Jessica Gordon Nembhard, *Collective Courage: A History of African American Cooperative Economic Thought and Practice* (University Park: The Pennsylvania State University Press, 2014).

Chapter 21

Navigating System Transition in a Volatile Century

Michael T. Lewis

A blessed unrest is roiling across the planet; millions of creative, innovative, indignant, dedicated, hopeful individuals are cogitating, communicating, animating, educating, innovating, agitating, and advocating for change. Banding together in diverse groups, organizations, and movements, they are trying to figure out how to navigate the unprecedented economic, social, ecological, and cultural challenges of the 21st century. *Unprecedented* is the key word. Never in human history have we been so challenged.

Key Trends Defining Our Time

Four crosscutting and interrelated trends frame and justify the claim that our time is like no other:

1 *Climate Change*: The climate crisis is the *preeminent* threat to the survival of all life. The latest data available (1999–2017) through the U.N. Office for Disaster Risk Reduction estimates approximately 90 million people were affected by climate-related disasters and $2.45 trillion in economic losses realized.[1] From only three regions—Sub-Saharan Africa, South Asia, and Latin America—the World Bank warns, over 140 million climate migrants will be on the move.[2] We either grasp the nettle and take on the difficult political, economic, and social changes necessary or, down the line, face exponentially greater consequences. The laws of chemistry and physics simply aren't negotiable.

2 *Degraded and Threatened Ecosystems*: We currently extract resources 60 percent more rapidly than nature can replenish them, meaning that we would need 1.7 earths to sustain our current annual consumption rates.[3] Over the last 40 years WWF reports a 60 percent decline in the size of populations of mammals, birds, fish, reptiles, and amphibians.[4] Degraded eco-systems are losing their capacity to support life.

3 *The Third Industrial Revolution: The Zero Marginal Cost Society*: In the 18th and 19th centuries, coal, steam power, and the telegraph radically shrunk distance and increased connectivity. The discovery of oil, the

telephone, and the automobile ushered in a second industrial revolution, further shrinking time and space while enhancing connectivity. Gargantuan investments in power generation and distribution networks gave rise to large vertically integrated corporations. Centralized capital and power, combined with the concentrated power within one barrel of oil, created previously unimaginable economies of scale. Mass production drove down the marginal cost of each unit of goods produced. Profits skyrocketed. Costs plummeted. Cheap goods multiplied and consumption exploded, fed by technical innovations and rising wages.

The third industrial revolution is radically shrinking space and time again as the internet juggernaut joins up with the accelerating transition to renewable energy. An Oxford University study of over 700 occupations found that 47 percent (over 60 million jobs in the US) are susceptible to automation within 20 years.[5] Job insecurity, already a scourge, will increase.

This perilous revolution also holds promise. Renewables will fuel the transition to a low-carbon energy. A more balanced relationship among human beings and the biosphere appears possible. And decentralized, distributed, autonomous energy flows could enable diverse, democratic, dematerialized, equitable, and sustainable ways of living together on the planet. But realizing this positive shift is far from certain.

4   *Money, Debt, and Finance: Major Obstacles to Navigating the Transition*: Massive investment in renewables and other sectors fueling the transition is central to addressing our climate and ecological crises and livelihoods' accelerating precariousness. But financing those investments poses a real conundrum. The communications revolution, coupled with financial deregulation, has given rise to a worldwide casino of speculative finance ten times the value of global gross domestic product (GDP) and almost completely dissociated from the real economy or the transition challenges we face.

Adding fuel to the fire, *governments have given over their sovereignty to create debt-free money*. Private banks now issue 95 to 97 percent of the money supply, registering the debt on loans as assets on their balance sheets while we borrowers, private and public, pay the bank huge sums in compound interest. German researchers estimate that 35 percent of the costs of goods and services are the embedded costs of compound interest working its way across the economy's supply chains.[6] Moreover, they estimated, $600 million *per day* in interest payments flows from the bottom 80 percent of the population (wealth-wise) to the top 10 percent.

Put all this together with stagnant wages, cost of living increases, tax revenue decreases, soaring debt, elites hiding out in tax havens, and intensifying austerity measures and the circle becomes vicious. Economic demand declines, business risk increases, and access to credit shrinks. Even so, the systemic, debt-driven compulsion to grow regardless of natural systems' limits remains, propelling us toward mutually assured destruction.

Navigating Our Way to the New System

Can the forces of "blessed unrest" secure fairness on a livable planet? Are the diverse innovations now developing and spreading merely tentative steps in the right direction, or are they vital strides? What keeps us from scaling up their impact? What system changes could expand their contribution to a just transition to a low-carbon future? We must ask and we must find out.

The contours of the new system *are* being revealed. But gains are hard fought. They take time, energy, talent, and resources—requirements vividly revealed in the examples of "cooperative economic democracy" shared here.

Cooperative Economic Democracy and the Solidarity Economy

Cooperative economic democracy (CED) is a framework of concepts, values, practices, and models that elevates:

- Resilience over growth.
- Cooperation over competition.
- Sufficiency over efficiency.
- Well-being over the right to possess.
- Fairness and equity over the freedom of markets, trade, and capital.
- Decentralized and democratic ownership over concentrated private ownership.
- The commons over the inalienable rights of private property.
- Our dependence on nature over our right to dominate it.

These are not theoretical propositions. They are choices about what matters most as we co-construct a collective capacity to address the challenges before us.

Many features of cooperative economic democracy mirror the ecological principles, processes, and relationships that render healthy ecosystems resilient. The next system must be guided by the same kind of ecological resilience based on diversity, modularity, innovation, overlap and redundancy, tight feedback loops, and accounting for ecosystem services (see Box).

Since the "next system" must also be guided by a resilient socio-political system, the emerging Solidarity Economy movement's efforts to target unmet human needs deserves notice here.

The Solidarity Economy traces partly back to a categorization of human activity into the private, the public, and civil society (see Figure 21.1). Each system has its own values, priorities, and core animating logic (simplified here but, in reality, blurred and interactive). In the First System are private ownership and the profit motive. In the second are public service and the planned provision of goods and services, usually through government authority. In the third are the social purposes of self-help, mutual aid, and reciprocity.

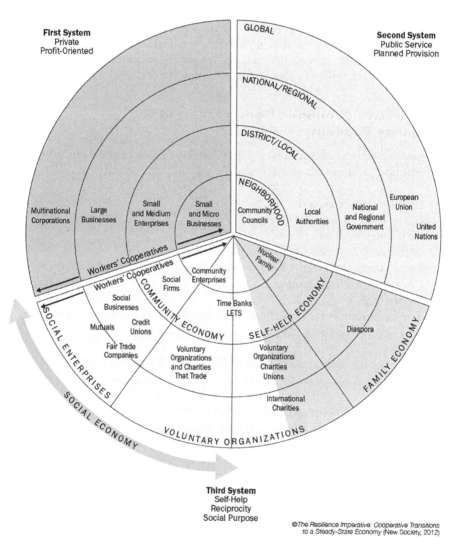

Figure 21.1 Three systems of the economy.

The Seven Principles of Resilience

- *Diversity:* A resilient world would promote and sustain diversity in all forms (biological, landscape, social, and economic). Diversity is a major source of future options and thus of a system's capacity to respond to change and disturbance in different ways.
- *Modularity:* A resilient world's components would each operate and be modified independently of the rest. Avoiding the risk of system-wide shocks that comes with total connectivity, modularity enables a resilient system to mitigate or absorb disaster's repercussions.
- *Social Capital*: A resilient world would promote trust, well-developed social networks, and leadership. The resilience of social-ecological systems stems from the human capacity to meet challenges together, making trust, strong networks, and leadership critically important.
- *Innovation:* A resilient world would emphasize learning, experimentation, locally developed rules, and embracing change. Instead of resisting change counter-productively, a resilient system helps people willing to change, thus fostering innovation.
- *Overlap:* A resilient world would have institutions whose governing structures incorporate "redundancy." By increasing the diversity of responses possible amid disturbance and crisis, redundancy increases systemic flexibility and makes adaptation more flexible.
- *Tight Feedback Loops:* A resilient world would possess tight (but not too tight) information feedback loops. Information on the impact of a process or event flows back to the system so it can self-correct and, also, we can detect thresholds before crossing them.
- *Ecosystem Services:* A resilient world would consider and assess all the ecosystem services that the market economy currently disregards. Whatever the market economy does not price, it does not value.

Note here how much third-system creativity originates in failures or inaction in the other two spheres—especially in the so-called "social economy," which combines social purpose with market-based trading.

In contrast to neoliberal ideologues, social economists argue that reciprocity should be the shaping principle in the management of markets, trade, and capital, that community and social benefit should be integral to any "value proposition," and that the diversity of the commons should outrank the homogeneity hard-wired into mass markets. For some, the social economy is a "construction site" for strategies, tools, and institutions that can challenge the hegemony of the first and second systems.

All that said, the solidarity economy has a more strategic role amid today's challenges. It presumes that some people, organizations, businesses, and governments are beginning to perceive the world differently and that each system has some creative actors who share (imperfectly) the values of social justice, inclusiveness, ecological sustainability, and deeper, democratic forms of participation.

The Solidarity Economy cuts across all three systems (see Figure 21.2). While the circle of intersection is relatively small at present, its implications wax huge.

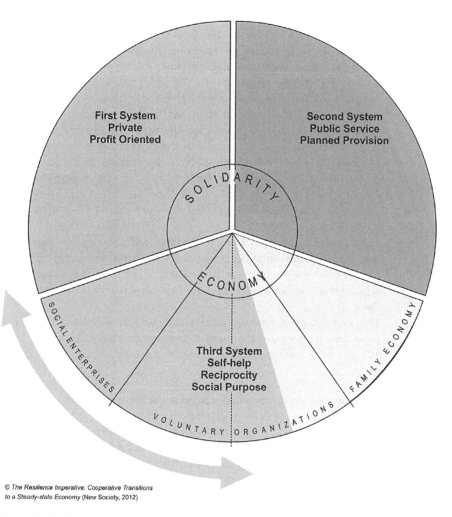

© *The Resilience Imperative: Cooperative Transitions to a Steady-state Economy* (New Society, 2012)

Figure 21.2 The solidarity economy.

Consider, for example, the Seikatsu Consumer Co-operative in Japan. Since 1965, it has been reshaping relationships between consumers and private food producers dedicated to ecological farming methods and fair prices. The cooperative has also transformed the supply chain: processing, packaging, recycling, and distribution are performed by both private firms and 600 worker-owned firms (with 17,000 worker-owners). This "values-added" supply chain has, as of 2012, produced 1600 products to cutting-edge ecological standards,[7] and the cooperative is branching out to social care and renewable energy.

As we learn to respect and live within Earth's limits, the Solidarity Economy compels us to craft transformative strategies, alliances, and partnerships based on social purpose, mutual aid, and reciprocity. The social economy's role in making this happen is important but not exclusive. Working only with just-like-us partners within our own "system silo" won't be enough to take us from profit-driven economic growth to a steady-state economy. Instead, we must advance the common good collaboratively.

Pathways to a New System: Action at Multiple Scales

The principles of cooperative economic democracy and the strategic orientation of the solidarity economy are manifest worldwide in initiatives that differ dramatically in scale, sector, and structure. The best of them share three salient features.

First, they entail local or regional (micro) level action but also seek to influence macro-level policies and systems that advance their priorities. Challenging and working against today's rules of the game, they seek ways to diffuse and scale up the impacts achieved in a particular neighborhood, sector, or enterprise.

Second, the provision of basic human needs must be interwoven with other endeavors that further the transition. Expanding alternative ways to provide food, energy, shelter, and social care is essential to bettering people's everyday lives but requires reclaiming finance, reclaiming the commons, and localizing and democratizing ownership.

Third, these initiatives build federations of networks, coalitions, and movements with a shared agenda and greater capacity. Facing inevitable resistance from status-quo interests and power, the transition will be a long hard-fought effort requiring joint action.

RESO: Transformative Place Shaping

RESO *(Regroupement économique et social du Sud-Ouest)* is a community economic development corporation in Montreal started in 1982 with organizing efforts to revitalize Point St. Charles, a depleted neighborhood.

By 1984, organizers had established a community economic development organization named PEP *(Programme économique of Pointe-Saint-Charles)* and secured a modest sum of seed money to pursue small business development through training and a loan program. New businesses and jobs were created, though far fewer than those meanwhile lost, so from 1986 on PEP changed its focus to business retention and supports to stem the flow of capital, business, and jobs from the community.[8]

PEP also provided strategic leadership in building a broader coalition of community and labor organizations, aiming to produce a more comprehensive strategy for helping poor neighborhoods and addressing unemployment. This difficult, dynamic, and very public process forged a strategy owned and supported by a cross-section of interests in the city. In 1989, PEP became a community economic development corporation for the five poorest neighborhoods in southwestern Montreal.

Revitalizing a territory impoverished by the mainstream economy requires thinking about the key economic and social functions critical to a healthy community (see Figure 21.3). RESO's three priorities were planning, research, and advocacy related to neighborhood interests; building local ownership and developing the capacities and skills of people to work

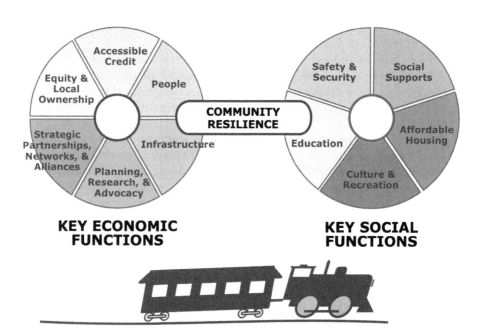

Figure 21.3 To rev up the engine of community revitalization, put social and economic development on the same track.

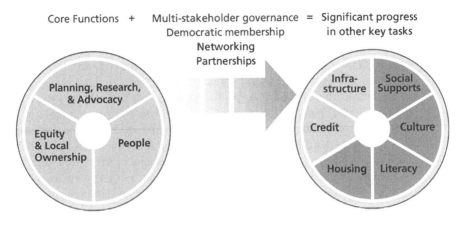

Figure 21.4 RESO's development system.

in local businesses; and positioning itself to significantly influence several other key economic and social domains (Figure 21.4).

Initially, RESO strove to revitalize an impoverished community, inspired largely by US community development corporations. RESO's focus then expanded to include shaping rapid economic growth to favor the neighborhood's social, economic, and environmental interests.

Much of RESO's success traces to its structure for enabling citizens and sector stakeholders to become full players in their own development process. RESO's membership elects four representatives from community organizations, two from labor, two from small business, one from large business, one from finance, and two citizen members at large. In 2012, RESO had about 1,500 RESO members—a good share of the roughly 80,000 people who live in the five neighborhoods.[9]

Another factor in RESO's success was the role of provincial, local, and federal governments. RESO won over government and other partners by mobilizing community resistance as needed, advocating for the neighborhoods' key priorities, *and* getting results. After a protracted and sometimes rocky start, RESO secured a resource flow to support its staff, invest in community priorities, and build up its strategic networking and partnership development. The state—local, Provincial and Federal—became an important partner. Credit was increased. Infrastructure investment generated local benefits. Literacy, housing, and social supports and cultural enterprises flowered, and the devastating leakage of capital and businesses from the community ended.

RESO richly illustrated how cooperative economic democracy can be advanced locally through organizing, democratic ownership, and multisectoral partnerships. Over the years as the breadth and depth of RESO's multi-functional capacity increased, these partnerships started to extend their reach even farther. For example, in Griffintown, a sub-zone in one of the five neighborhoods, RESO organized and advocated for a plan to deploy investment, expand the urban commons, and increase opportunities for community and collective ownership.

Unfortunately, as RESO began to make inroads in Griffintown, an increasingly neoliberal government came to power in Quebec. Early in its mandate, it cut budgets by 40 percent and realigned mandates to change the approach to territorial development. Supports for multi-stakeholder Community Economic Development corporations in urban and rural areas were emasculated. Municipal led and delivered services were mandated to provide direct services with 40 percent less money. Not surprisingly, the pattern of development in Griffintown, with no countervailing power, devolved into the common redevelopment practices: chic restaurants, destruction of historical buildings, speculative condo developments, and, inevitably, displacement.

Even so, RESO's model proved itself over a 30-year period. Citizens and stakeholders democratically shaped the places where they live and work and their collective capacity was further extended by federating with others, politically and operationally.

In a context where climate, ecological, and socio-economic challenges are mounting, pro-active measures to reduce emissions and advance adaptation are vital. Without multi-stakeholder capacity located in specific territories, the question becomes whether a just transition and broadly based adaptation planning and implementation can be realized.

Social Solidarity Cooperatives in Italy: Transforming the Social Care Sector[10]

In Emilia-Romagna, a northern Italian province of four million, the cooperative movement has over decades extended a multi-stakeholder service model into social care. In Bologna (population 376,000), six in ten residents belong to one or more cooperatives. In Imola (population 100,000), 115 local cooperatives account for 60 percent of local economic output. Democratically owned enterprises are part of virtually every economic sector.

Beginning in the 1970s, unemployment rose in Italy, and public services, including social care, were slashed. The crisis prompted families and care workers to envision "social solidarity cooperatives"—social care organizations supported and governed by service recipients, their families, the paid staff, and the volunteers. By 1990, there were 1,800 cooperatives.

In 1991, a three-year campaign to change cooperative law and to further diffuse the model bore fruit. New legislation defined "social cooperatives" as pursuing the community's general interest and advancing social inclusion by managing social, health, and educational services. Two types were recognized:

- *Type A* delivers social, health, and educational services, mainly for local authorities. Workers and volunteers make up to half the primary members. Public sector bodies can preferentially contract Type A services.
- *Type B* focuses on getting disadvantaged people into the labor market. At least 30 percent of the cooperative's workforce must be disadvantaged. Members include workers, volunteers (up to 50 percent), and family members.

Four principles guide the social cooperative approach. Clients and family members participate in the design, content, and delivery of services. Each organization may have no more than 100 members, lest strong social ties fail to develop. Managers are accountable to members. And services are delivered within a defined geographical area. These innovations were amplified by tax incentives embedded in legislation in 1991.

Also aiding this growth is a social care consortium that makes support services available to cooperative members. Besides providing market and back-office services, technical assistance and training, and pooled resources that boost contracting capacity, the consortium has speeded up expansion of the model cost-efficiently by developing financing tools that link cooperative and ethical banks with local authorities.

Today, some 15,000 social cooperatives employ hundreds of thousands of Italians and annually generate hundreds of millions of Euros.[11]

What does this experience tell us about system change dynamics?

- Crises breed innovation. In Emilia-Romagna's case, rising unemployment and state cuts to public services mothered invention.
- Sectoral consortia can create a shared infrastructure of administrative, training, and technical services to reduce risk and costs and accelerate the diffusion of innovation.
- The rapid diffusion and scaling of a proven model requires mobilizing citizens, stakeholders, and networks to demand more effective policy and legislation.

Together, these factors can drive system change (see Figure 21.5).

Figure 21.5 Emilia-Romagna's consortia by sector.

Weaving Cooperative Economic Democracy into the Energy Transition

The importance of rapidly expanding renewable energy is self-evident, and its development and use is picking up speed and attracting investment. In this good news, however, lurks the real danger that capital seeking to centralize and control energy provision will co-opt the transition. Arguably justifiable in the fossil fuel era, such domination is unjustifiable now, as amply demonstrated in Denmark and Germany, where policy has fostered diverse distributed–ownership models.[12]

Decentralized, democratic forms of local and regional ownership represent a strategic choice of unquestionable importance. First, in the long-term process of increasing local and regional self-reliance and resilience, ownership means capturing cash flow and surplus to reinvest in the energy transition and other challenges, including adaptation to climate change. Second, democratic ownership reduces inequality by shifting the distribution of economic benefits to a broader population. Third, distributing ownership opportunities broadens the base for mobilizing human talent, energy, and capital to accelerate the transition. Fourth, households and businesses won't embrace energy conservation unless citizens are systematically engaged where they live and work.

The four examples that follow show how important these assertions are.

Going Fossil-Fuel-Free in Sweden: The Efficacy of Democratic Ownership by a District Municipality[13]

Kristianstad in southeastern Sweden is a district municipality covering 1,300 square kilometers of prime agricultural land and consisting of 25 communities of from 150 to 33,000 residents each. In 1999, its elected representatives decided to become the western world's first fossil-fuel-free municipality. Within nine years, Kristianstad had halved its use of fossil fuels and was producing renewable energy for export.

How? First, Kristianstad's political leadership articulated and held on to the vision. Second, staff planning and coordination, citizen engagement, and partnership development gave the vision backbone. Third, municipally owned energy and waste-management companies put all the pieces together, designing and executing smart and profitable projects to realize the vision in partnership with the private and public sectors.

Crucial to Kristianstad's strategy has been the capture of diverse waste streams to produce biogas—enough to run the entire municipal transportation fleet. Also, the 41,000 residents of two large towns also use wood chips from waste and thinnings in combined heat-and-power systems for district heating. Wood- and straw-based fuels feed mini-district heating systems and individual buildings in smaller communities. Together, these methods ensured 130,000 tons less carbon annually by 2014.[14] In addition, by 2008 wind power in Kristianstad was generating enough electricity to power 6,500 average American homes. Output sufficient for 50,000 homes is already ramping up for on-shore wind, and the same target has been set for future off-shore wind farms.

As Lennart Erfors, Kristianstad's climate strategist notes, fossil-fuel freedom is saving householders and the municipal government money. Municipally owned businesses are making money, reducing carbon, and delivering public benefits while systematically reinvesting in the energy transition.

Retrofitting Germany's Built Environment: National Framework Linked to Tailored Public Bank Financing[15]

In 2009, a United Nations Environment Programme report showed that some 30 percent of global annual carbon and 40 percent of all greenhouse gas (GHG) emissions came from buildings.[16] While not all such emissions can be stanched, carbon output can be cut substantially while generating jobs in energy conservation.

Germany is a leading example of national energy-conservation policy and incentives—part of that country's commitment to reducing GHG emissions by 80–95 percent (relative to 1990 levels) by 2050. The federal government has established energy-efficiency standards, incentives for retrofitting buildings, and regulations for new building construction, and the German state development bank *Kreditanstalt für Wiederaufbau* (KfW) ties financial goals to energy metrics. Homes that meet stringent standards for reducing energy consumption qualify for partial mortgage financing at ultra-low rates. And repayment bonuses upon completing work go as high as 17.5 percent of the total cost.

Between 2001 and 2012, 2.1 million energy-efficiency home loans totaling €45 billion were issued, reducing CO_2 emissions by 156 billion tons. From 2009 to 2012, between 280,000 and 960,000 housing units were retrofitted annually under this program, creating several hundred thousand jobs each year. The latest measures between 2006 and 2018 reflect the ongoing progress.[17]

- 5.4 million housing units: 9.45 million-ton CO_2 reduction (75 percent existing stock and 25 percent new units)
- 3,300 state, local government, schools: 480,000-ton CO_2 reduction
- Since 2015, 4,700 commercial buildings: 408,400-ton reduction

In 2018 alone, €2 billion was invested to advance efficiency in the built environment.

Kirklees, UK: Penetrating Energy Conservation to the Local Householder[18]

Frustrated with the British government's piecemeal energy-efficiency programs, the government of Kirklees in West Yorkshire joined a European pilot program in 2000. SAVE (Specific Actions for Vigorous Energy Efficiency) sought to build local capacity to reduce carbon emissions across the European Union. The local government's obligation was to establish an arms-length social enterprise to develop and carry out integrated community-based energy conservation. In return, SAVE would pay half the costs.

Kirklees Energy Services (KES) swiftly developed into a one-stop shop, providing energy- conservation services promoted door to door. Credit unions offered preferential loans to participating householders, and local authorities and power utilities funded generous rebate programs, making the uptake by householders nearly painless. Installation contractors were vetted and prequalified and paid referral fees to KES.

In 2008, KES put everything it had learned into a package it could extend to low-income areas. In 2009, additional investment came from the Warm Zones Program, a national strategy to reduce fuel poverty and carbon emissions. By July 2010, some 71,000 homes across the borough received an energy audit. By 2012, fully 132,000 had undertaken retrofits, creating over 160 jobs. Households saved £9–10 million per year in energy costs. Annual carbon emissions fell by 55,000 tons. Every pound that local authorities and the Warm Zones Program invested in KES's work leveraged another five pounds in energy-efficiency investments.

Since KES evolved into a community interest company and now works across England with local authorities, commercial, government and housing association partners. Services have expanded to include renewable energy installations and a range of technical- and policy-related services. In 2018 lifetime fuel bill savings were US$ 63.3 million and lifetime reduction of carbon emitted was 85.1 million tonnes.[19]

British Columbia: GHG Reductions by SMEs[20]

Climate Smart, a social enterprise based in Vancouver, British Columbia, helps small- and medium-sized businesses (SMEs) reduce their carbon emissions. At the core of its approach is a well-designed training, software, support, and coaching program.

Since its modest beginning as a pilot project of Eco-Trust Canada in 2007, Climate Smart has trained over 800 firms throughout the economy. Its programming has permanently averted the release of over 97,000 tons of GHG emissions annually (equivalent to removing over 22,000 passenger vehicles from the road). Each ton eliminated generates on average $397 in savings to participating firms, a collective savings of $38.5 million.

Even gains as impressive as these barely scratch the surface. Since SMEs generate 27 percent of metro Vancouver's GHG emissions, Climate Smart is now concentrating on three approaches to accelerate local innovation:

- Strategic collaborations with partners that serve or sell to large groups of SMEs—local governments, credit unions, ports, and airports. Climate Smart tailors its value-adding turnkey program to the business community its partners serve.
- Mining its performance data so more businesses can grasp the costs savings of competitors that are reducing GHG emissions.
- Working with the provincial government on fiscal tools to complement the provincial carbon tax and incentivize SME investments in training, technology, retrofitting, and improved processes.

The municipality of Kristianstad, Germany's public bank KfW, Kirklees Energy Services in the UK, and Climate Smart in Canada all speak to the strategic importance of decentralizing the capacity to plug the manifold nooks and crannies through which GHGs escape into our atmosphere. All illustrate the importance of working across the public, private, and civil society sectors and indicate the efficacy of cooperative economic democracy.

A Values-added Approach to Transforming the Food System[21]

The year was 1965: a small group of women started discussing the quality, safety, and the security of their food supply. Worried about farmland being lost, farmers struggling to earn a living, the ever-increasing use of pesticides, and the trend toward more and more imports to Japan, these women decided to approach a local farmer with a simple question. *Would you provide us with fresh food that is chemical-free in return for a fair and just price?* He said yes, but had one condition. The women had to buy all his product and handle distribution.

Thus was born a partnership or, in Japanese, "teikei" which, Seikatsu's leaders say, carries with it a profound colloquial meaning: "Food with a farmer's face on it."

The new project started collectively purchasing food to achieve social, economic, and ecological values. The so-called Hans, each five to fifteen strong, met regularly to plan food purchases and distribution. As their numbers grew, representatives of each Han started to meet to plan and aggregate their purchasing and to better coordinate with farmers involved. Eventually, the first Seikatsu Consumer Cooperative, was formed to coordinate and extend the work. Now 32 consumer cooperatives—with close to 400,000 members— have, in turn, federated nationally into the Seikatsu Union Club (SUC).

SUC now generates annually over $1 billion in sales. And 600 collective enterprises involving 17,000 worker owners are involved in processing and distribution. Even more impressive, the club has over $450 million in equity, much of it derived from individual members, who each pay $11 a month into an equity account until they have contributed $3,500—true solidarity-based finance. These accounts assure financial stability, prompt cooperative members to view themselves as co-producers and co-investors in a fair and sustainable food system, and help participants as *citizens* preserve and defend their democratic rights and autonomy.

A Japanese super-box store may stock as many 300,000 products. The average in a Japanese food cooperative is 9,000. In Seikatsu, it's 1,600 items— mainly basic nutritious staples. This less-is-more approach reduces waste food, waste plastic, and wasted shipping energy. Similarly, the processors Seikatsu works with must use one of eight specified types of returnable bottles, reducing recycling costs and carbon by 2,000 tons annually. If such a rule were applied across Japan, the carbon reduction would total 600,000 tons.

As co-investors and co-producers in the food system's transformation, the Seikatsu cooperative demonstrates a "values added" strategy with great potential in the other sectors it is entering: elder care, green energy, and now childcare.

Seikatsu means "Living People," an apt name for those working long and hard to build a resilient food system that is decentralized yet connected and federated, that sets ecological standards that consumers and producers respect, that is founded on the fundamental value of fair price and fair trade, and that creates and reinforces our interconnectedness as human beings and our ultimate dependence on the ecological services nature provides.

The Politics of System Change: Federating to Construct the Next System

Building the kinds of alternatives described here is essential to ushering in the next system, but the way forward is guaranteed to be contentious.

Cooperative economic democracy has encountered resistance from special interests while extending its reach and scope. Fortunately, inspiring examples of organizing for political effectiveness exist.

The Chantier: Quebec's Federated Construction Site for the Social Solidarity Economy

How can people whose ultimate goal is moving toward an economy based on care, sustainability, democracy, and inclusiveness find the right organization to join?

- *Consider the kinds of businesses that might be included at the table.* Consider a community-owned radio station, or a nonprofit business that is recycling waste and employing a workforce that is 80 percent people with disabilities. Consider cooperative and nonprofit childcare centers. Consider a group of artisans operating a social enterprise to advance their art. Consider a cooperative organized to provide affordable high-quality home care to ailing elders. Consider a multi-sector federation of cooperatives.
- *Consider the type of community-based infrastructure that could help build more solidarity businesses.* Consider community development corporations committed to revitalizing economically marginalized neighborhoods and rural areas. Consider a network of community-controlled organizations providing loans and technical assistance to small businesses and social enterprises otherwise hard-pressed to gain access to credit.
- *Consider the kinds of organizations that could add the clout and resources needed to help convince governments that business as usual can and must give way to a fairer, more democratic economy.* Consider a federation of labor unions with a deep history of defending workers' rights. Consider social movements—women's, anti-poverty, aboriginal, environmental, and others—joining together to press for change. Consider a province-wide federation of housing cooperatives aiming to expand affordable housing. Consider the key networks evolving around local food, sustainable production, and low-carbon consumption of energy.
- *Consider what financing institutions and mechanisms would be needed to unleash social entrepreneurial energy and create innovative products/services so as to expand the number of people producing, consuming, and acting within a framework of solidarity and transition.* Consider a federation of credit unions owned by a membership that includes 80 percent of a province's citizenry. Consider labor-sponsored funds for investing in small- and medium-sized businesses. Consider community and social enterprise loan funds operating in local communities.
- *Finally, consider what role academics and university researchers might play in a movement for significant economic change.* What might the diverse array of such researchers and experts contribute if they focused their research on questions important to leaders and practitioners from all these other groups?

Just imagine what all of these groups sitting at a common table with a common purpose might accomplish. If you do, you have begun to envision what the *Chantier de l'économie sociale* has become.

A network of networks, the Chantier (or "construction site of the social economy") emerged out of a budget crisis in Quebec in the mid-1990s. When the provincial premier announced plans to convene an economic summit of government and business leaders, civil society demanded to be at the table. Its ranks included women's organizations protesting policies that deepen poverty and exclusion, and community development corporations (CDCs) working to revitalize poor urban neighborhoods. Both groups contended that, along with opposition, new kinds of coalitions—like RESO, described above—were needed to propose and advance democratic, decentralized, proactive approaches to economic and social development.

These groups won a seat at the 1996 summit table for the first time, and by the summit's end, they had forged agreements with government, the private sector, and the labor movement. Once politically recognized, they created a task group to create Chantier.

Figure 21.6 depicts the first ten years of its evolution: the scope of its vision, its major functions, and the diversity of the networks that governed its work. The Chantier member networks represent hundreds of organizations, which in turn represent hundreds of thousands of members committed to promoting Solidarity Economy.

Partnerships with local development organizations in urban and rural areas, the province's major cooperative technical assistance organizations, and networks of sector-specific social enterprises are key to support for the planning, development, and coaching of new social enterprises and cooperatives.

Chantier's formal partnerships with university researchers are strategic: documenting what is and is not working, codifying best practices, building the rationale for and details of innovative financing tools, mapping the field and project results, and undertaking policy research and development. This work has helped establish the social solidarity economy's credibility.

The Chantier has formed two financing vehicles. *Réseau d'investissement social du Québec* (RISQ) is a $10-million investment fund that flowed directly from the 1996 summit commitments made by the private sector, labor-sponsored investment funds, and the Quebec government. Financing only collective enterprises, RISQ has leveraged other sources of financing, including loan funds from local development organizations and credit unions.

Ten years on, the Chantier created a second financial instrument, the FIDUCIE ("trust" in English). Capitalized to the tune of $48.8 million, this social venture fund is a combined investment of the federal government, two trade union-owned investment groups, and the Quebec Government.[22] The fund bridges the gap between financial markets and social economy enterprises by pooling risk and reduces financing costs for both

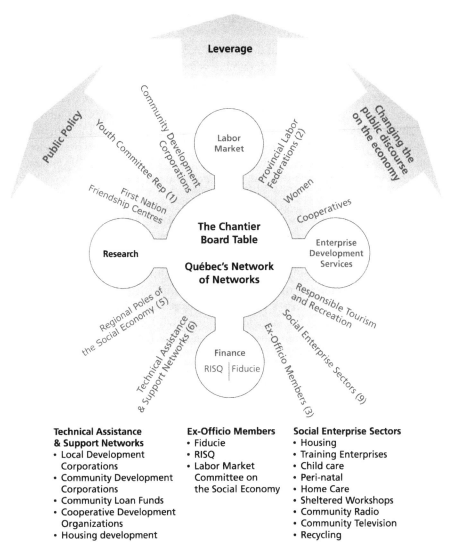

Leverage

Labor Market

Provincial Labor Federations (2)

Public Policy

Youth Committee Rep (1)

Community Development Corporations

First Nation Friendship Centres

Changing the public discourse on the economy

Women

Cooperatives

The Chantier Board Table

Research

Québec's Network of Networks

Enterprise Development Services

Responsible Tourism and Recreation

Regional Poles of the Social Economy (5)

Technical Assistance & Support Networks (6)

Social Enterprise Sectors (9)

Ex-Officio Members (3)

Finance

RISQ | Fiducie

Technical Assistance & Support Networks
- Local Development Corporations
- Community Development Corporations
- Community Loan Funds
- Cooperative Development Organizations
- Housing development

Ex-Officio Members
- Fiducie
- RISQ
- Labor Market Committee on the Social Economy

Social Enterprise Sectors
- Housing
- Training Enterprises
- Child care
- Peri-natal
- Home Care
- Sheltered Workshops
- Community Radio
- Community Television
- Recycling

Figure 21.6 Quebec's Chantier de l'economie sociale.

investors and enterprises. Qualifying social enterprises receive "patient capital product" loans with a 15-year capital repayment moratorium that can be used for working capital and to buy, build, or renovate real estate.

RISQ and the other technical assistance organizations work to improve management capacity and worker skills. Along with FIDUCIE's stakeholders, these organizations are helping develop a cadre of competent social entrepreneurs, and several university-based diploma and degree programs in Quebec now offer leadership training that will expand the social solidarity economy.

Born of a virtuous circle of opposition and proposition, the Chantier has woven together a dynamic federated development system in less than two decades. It has adeptly leveraged resources and advanced an agenda that yields concrete results. As needed, it still uses opposition effectively too. When a new government tried to increase the cost to parents of Quebec's high-quality nonprofit, cooperatively run childcare system, the Chantier helped mobilize 25,000 people who within one week forced government to back down.[23] This approach lets Chantier protect its gains while enlarging the social economy's economic and political space in Quebec.

La Via Campesina: Building a Global Movement for Food Sovereignty[24]

La Via Campesina (LVC) grew out of the radical erosion of rural peasants' life in Latin America in the second half of the 20th century. Policies of the World Bank and the International Monetary Fund (IMF), coupled with the fossil-fuel-intensive "green revolution" damaged small farmer agriculture across Latin America. Government's moves to transform food into an export commodity to earn foreign currency abraded social and economic relations between rural people and the state while the IMF forced heavily indebted governments to cut services as a condition of borrowing from northern capital markets. Markets opened up, commodity-based agriculture spread, and cheap subsidized food from the North was dumped in the South. All the while, prices paid to farmers serving local and regional markets slid.

Local and regional organizing coalesced in 1992 with the formation of a Latin America-wide network of peasants and farmers joining hands to resist destruction and build a new model. As those with small- to medium-sized farms began to understand the forces at work, organizing across borders accelerated. In 1993, 70 leaders of peasant and farmer organizations meeting in Belgium formally committed to work together to defend their rights and resist neoliberal assaults on local food producers.

From the outset, LVC acted strategically, as its ground rules attest:

- NGOs, foundations, and aid agencies cannot be members.
- No financial support is accepted that is conditional on the donor's participation in members' decision-making.
- Only the LVC can represent member interests in any forum.

LVC is militant and makes clear demands. Conflict—aggressive debate and protest—is understood as an important tool for building a critical mass for positive change.

LVC's adversarial strategy is balanced by positive propositions hammered out through extensive discussion and debate. Although this process takes time, the LVC has shaped and organized the largest global social movement in human history, involving some 500 million families who belong to 148 organizations in 69 countries.[25]

Food sovereignty is the LVC'S central concern. Local and national markets are the priority, and LCV asserts that countries have the right to define their own food, farming, and agricultural policies, regardless of World Trade Organization (WTO) rules. It argues that food plays a central role in addressing poverty; preserving rural life, economies, and environments; and managing natural resources sustainably. It contends that prices must be fair to both producers and consumers and proposes maximum limits on farm size, the abolition of seed patenting, and equitable local control over seeds, land, water, and forests.

LVC's building phase was characterized by the militant assertion of its viewpoint in many settings—most notably, international meetings of the WTO, the IMF, and the World Bank. Attempts by the World Bank and WTO to co-opt the movement through jet-setting dialogues were rejected, though LVC considers the Food and Agriculture Organization (FAO) of the United Nations as a safe space for developing sound agricultural policies.

LVC's current internal priorities are to strengthen local and regional leadership to help members themselves mobilize. One initiative is extending the reach of LVC training schools, women's training centers, and political education. Another is establishing regional secretariats to strengthen the organizations of weaker members. An LVC university now trains the sons and daughters of peasant farmers to accelerate and sustain the transition away from fossil-fuel-intensive agriculture, imparting practical skills while stressing the difference between food sovereignty and the dominant agricultural model.

In all, LVC has employed a three-pronged approach. It *resists* a globalized food system in which food is merely another commodity. It *builds* decentralized and democratic food systems based on fair price, fair trade, and sustainability. It *advocates* from the local to the global. It dramatically exemplifies what it takes to build a sophisticated new politics that has system change as a core priority.

Federating to Expand our Leverage

Federating our organizations to better advance cooperative economic democracy and to advance macro-system changes is vital to any transition (Figure 21.7). Globalization, the neoliberal mantra, must give way to *glocalization*. Via Campensina illustrates one way of organizing coalitions that federate across scales, sectors, and movements into a multi-nodal but unifying political force for system changes at all levels. As the renowned community organizer, Saul Alinsky, often emphasized: if you're not organized you won't contend.

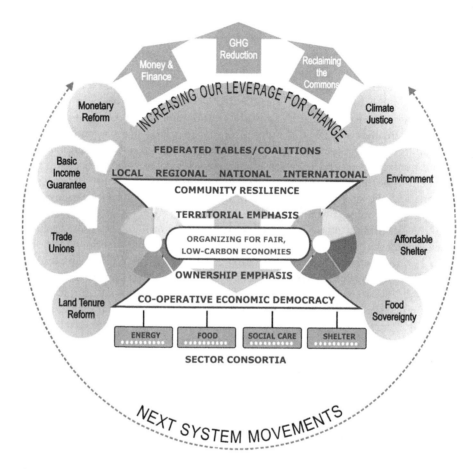

Figure 21.7 Co-operative economic democracy organizing for transition.

Goals and Strategies Aimed at Macro-Level Change

To explore strategic options for addressing the four major issues before us—climate change, the ecological crises, the peril and promise of the third industrial revolution, and debt-based money and finance—let's consider four propositions.

- If unchecked, climate change will severely disrupt human life at every level, distorting and displacing our capacity to advance a transformative agenda by diverting us into sheer coping with triage.

- At every level, efforts to broaden and deepen cooperative economic democracy must be designed to reduce greenhouse gas emissions, increase ecological restoration, secure basic minimum incomes, and transform people's relationship with money, finance, and debt.
- We must find ways to federate our resistance and advocacy to advance macro-level system change in all four domains.
- Members of diverse networks and alliances must reflect on these propositions and develop a common agenda for acting on them.

What follows is a selection of interventions related to each the four trends this paper addresses.

Climate Change: Minimize investments that contribute to GHGs and maximize investments that reduce them to limit global warming to 1.5–2 degrees Celsius.

1   Annually increase the price of carbon to systematically reduce fossil fuel dependence.

- Tax carbon emissions from all fossil fuels in proportion to carbon content.
- Start carbon taxes low so individuals and institutions can adjust. Then raise taxes substantially and briskly on a pre-set trajectory so investors, consumers, and governments have stable expectations.
- Use some carbon tax revenue to offset unfair burdens to lower-income households.[26]

2   Terminate fossil fuel subsidies country by country and worldwide.

- Deploy recaptured subsidies to key investments aimed at reducing GHG emissions, especially phasing out coal, devoting $100 billion to the energy transition and climate adaptation in economically disadvantaged countries, and providing low-cost financing to facilitate decentralized and democratic ownership of renewable energy.
- Take account of this investment's consequent savings—estimated at $5.3 trillion in 2015—on the environment and human health.

3   Tax the top 10 percent of Carbon Emitters (which contribute 45 percent of global emissions).

- Tax high-end consumers of air travel to fund the energy transition in poor countries.

4   Accelerate the Transition to Renewable Energy.

- Step up investment in renewable energy and smart transmission grids within a policy framework that increases the diversity and distribution of ownership.

5   Retrofit the Built Environment.
  • Invest systematically in retrofitting all residential and commer-
    cial buildings to maximize efficiency in energy use and carbon
    reduction.
Degraded and Threatened Ecosystems: Maximize ecosystem protec-
tion and restoration, partly to mitigate climate change.

1   Invest in Ecological Protection and Restoration.

  • Invest first in sequestering carbon, conserving water, and increas-
    ing soil fertility, aimed at the same time to reduce artificial inputs.
  • Invest over time in permaculture and agroforestry initiatives that
    restore degraded environments through water conservation, soil
    restoration, and revegetation (e.g. food forests).
  • Create the financing, educational, and technical supports needed
    to transition away from current ill-advised agricultural practices
    and land use.

The Third Industrial Revolution: Move toward the Zero Marginal
Cost Society.

1   As end goals, use the tightly connected neural network now revolu-
    tionizing manufacturing to drive marginal energy costs to near zero
    and realize the potential for the decentralized, low-cost, resource-
    efficient, autonomous, and democratic production and distribution of
    goods and services.[27]
2   Institute basic minimum income guarantees (BIG) at the local/regional
    and national levels to reduce the negative impacts of job loss and dislo-
    cation. For examples, look to projects under way in Holland, India, and
    Brazil and to BIG advocacy networks in Canada (BIEN) and Switzerland.

Money, Debt, and Finance: Regain sovereignty over the money supply
and fund the energy transition.

1   Increase government issue of debt-free money even though doing so
    will slow growth and invite deflation.
2   Channel investment to public, private, civil society, and scientific
    spheres specified in a transition mandate.

Conclusions

In advancing cooperative economic democracy as a framework of concepts and values, I have given short shrift to some important issues. Ownership (especially of land), diverse financing and regulatory options that
would end the current casino mentality, and gross waste, especially by the
military establishment, all deserve attention.

What I have tried to do is sketch the urgent and complex challenges society faces, adaptable examples of viable transitional projects, and the role alternative financing strategies play in navigating our way to the systemic changes needed to ensure our collective survival with solidarity and dignity intact.

Notes

1 "Economic Losses, Poverty and Disasters: 1998–2017", United Nations Office for Disaster Risk Reduction, October 10, 2018, https://www.unisdr.org/archive/61121.

2 "Groundswell: Preparing for Internal Climate Migration", World Bank, March 19, 2018, https://www.worldbank.org/en/news/feature/2018/03/19/meet-the-human-faces-of-climate-migration.

3 Global Footprint Network, 2018, https://www.footprintnetwork.org/our-work/ecological-footprint/.

4 "Living Planet Report: 2018" World Wildlife Fund, https://www.worldwildlife.org/pages/living-planet-report-2018.

5 Carl Benedikt Frey and Michael A. Osborne, *The Future of Employment: How Susceptible are Jobs to Computerisation* (Oxford: Oxford University Programme on the Impacts of Future Technology, 2013), http://www.oxfordmartin.ox.ac.uk/downloads/academic/The_Future_of_Employment.pdf.

6 Margrit Kennedy, *Interest and Inflation Free Money* (Seva International, 1995), 30–31, accessed March 29, 2016, http://userpage.fu-berlin.de/~roehrigw/kennedy/english/Interest-and-inflation-free-money.pdf.

7 Research conducted by the author for: Michael T. Lewis and Pat Conaty, *The Resilience Imperative: Cooperative Transitions to a Steady State Economy* (Gabriola, BC: New Society Publishers, 2012), 136; Steve Dubb, "Seikatsu Club Consumers' Co-operative Union," Interview of Seikatsu Club Co-op Delegation from Japan, The Democracy Collaborative, August 2012, http://community-wealth.org/content/seikatsu-club-consumers-co-operative-union.

8 Stewart Perry and Michael T. Lewis, *Reinventing the Local Economy: What 10 Canadian Initiatives Can Teach Us about Building Creative, Inclusive & Sustainable Communities* (Centre for Community Enterprise, 1994), 138–157.

9 Michael T. Lewis and Pat Conaty, *The Resilience Imperative*, 174. Canada: New Society Publishers.

10 This section is abridged from Lewis and Conaty, *The Resilience Imperative*, 251–257.

11 "36,000 new Jobs were Created in Italian Cooperatives in 2012," CECOP, December 6, 2012, accessed March 24, 2016, http://www.cecop.coop/36-000-new-jobs-were-created-in. Between 2007 and 2011 the number of employees increased 17.4 percent. The number of 15,000 jobs was estimated by pro-rating the percentage increase over four years to correspond with the 2008 number cited—13,000 jobs.

12 Policies for several countries are identified at http://www.res-legal.eu/search-by-country/denmark/.

13 Unless otherwise noted all material in this section is drawn from: Michael T. Lewis, "The Path to Fossil-Fuel-Freedom," Centre for Community Renewal, June 18, 2012, accessed March 24, 2016, http://www.communityrenewal.ca/path-to-fossil-fuel-freedom#sthash.qjFWjXBA.dpuf.

14 "Converting Waste into Energy in Kristianstad, Sweden," Rocky Mountain Institute, June 12, 2014, https://rmi.org/blog_2014_06_12_converting_waste_into_energy_in_kristianstad_sweden/.

15 Unless otherwise noted, this section derives from: Justin Ritchie, "How Germany's State Development Bank Finances Energy Transition," 2013, prepared for BC-Alberta Social Economy Research Alliance, http://auspace.athabascau.ca/bitstream/2149/3537/1/FTRC_EfficiencyHouseGermany.pdf.

16 "Buildings and Climate Change: Summary for Decision-Makers," United Nations Environment Programme (UNEP), 2009, accessed March 24, 2016, http://www.unep.org/sbci/pdfs/SBCI-BCCSummary.pdf.

17 Energiewende Direct, Federal Ministry for Economic Affairs and Energy, February 21, 2019, https://www.bmwi-energiewende.de/EWD/Redaktion/EN/Newsletter/2019/02/Meldung/direkt-answers-infographic.html.

18 Unless otherwise noted, all material in this section is drawn from: Mike T. Lewis, "Kirklees, UK: An Area-based Approach to Energy Efficiency, Housing Affordability, and Jobs," Centre for Community Renewal, June 18, 2012, accessed March 24, 2016, http://communityrenewal.ca/sites/all/files/resource/i42011MAY20_KES.pdf.

19 YES Energy Solutions, Annual Report, April 2017–March 2018, pg 4 https://www.yesenergysolutions.co.uk/userfiles/files/CIC-Report-2017-18---FINAL-compressed-file.pdf.

20 Unless otherwise noted, all material in this section is drawn from: Elizabeth Sheehan and Michelle Bonner, "En Route to Paris: From the Ground Up – How Small Businesses are Cutting Carbon and Growing the Economy," Climate Smart, accessed March 24, 2016, https://climatesmartbusiness.com/2015/10/22/en-route-to-paris-from-the-ground-up-how-small-businesses-are-cutting-carbon-and-growing-the-economy/.

21 Research conducted by the author for: Lewis and Conaty, *The Resilience Imperative*. Numbers and quotations from the author's discussions with Seikatsu leadership and fact checked by Yvon Porier and Ian McPherson, two are experts.

22 Alex Nicholls, Rob Paton, and Jed Emerson, *Social Finance* (Oxford: Oxford University Press, 2015), 480.

23 The Canadian Press, "Roads Blocked and Day Care Disrupted as Quebec Unions Protest against Charest," *Child Care Canada*, December 11, 2003, accessed August 22, 2019, https://www.childcarecanada.org/documents/child-care-news/04/01/roads-blocked-and-day-care-disrupted-quebec-unions-protest-against-c.

24 Unless otherwise noted all material in this section is drawn from Maria Elena Martinez-Torres and Peter M. Rosset, "La Via Campesina: The Evolution of a Transnational Movement," *Global Policy Forum*, February 8, 2010, accessed March 24, 2016, https://www.globalpolicy.org/social-and-economic-policy/world-hunger/land-ownership-and-hunger/48733-la-via-campesina-the-evolution-of-a-transnational-movement.html; See also, Peter M. Rosset, *Food is Different: Why We Must Get the WTO Out of Agriculture* (Halifax, Nova Scotia: Fernwood, 2006).

25 Statistics on the size and makeup of La Via Campesina come from A.A. Desmarais, "The Via Campesina: Peasants Resisting Globalization," PhD diss., University of Calgary, Dept. of Geography, 2003.

26 See "CTC's Paris Summit Letter: A Call to Paris Climate Negotiators: Tax Carbon," Carbon Tax Center, November 29, 2015, accessed March 29, 2016, http://www.carbontax.org/?s=Paris+letter.

27 See Richard Heinberg, "Renewable Energy after COP21: Nine Issues for Climate Leaders to Think about on the Journey Home," Post Carbon Institute, https://www.postcarbon.org/renewable-energy-after-cop21.

Part 6

Commoning, Cooperation, and Participatory Planning

Few think of the US economy as "planned." True, certain political decisions are made about what types of economic activities are incentivized (through tax or regulatory policies), but enterprises mostly make strategic plans on their own to pursue profit. Yet, their plans—especially those of huge transnational corporations—can have a cross-cutting impact on the larger economy. To the extent that the well-being of the general populace and the environment is taken into consideration, it happens after the fact to address the consequences of economic activity, and, even then, nearly always within the political parameters drawn by those with the most wealth and power. The grand plan seems to be to allow wealth accumulation without due regard for the impact on people and the planet.

Advocates of this kind of US-style capitalism would argue that the absence of "economic planning" allows for innovation and flexible responses to public wants and needs. They point to the planned Communist economies of the 20th century as a cautionary tale of how top-down, multiyear plans left these countries flat-footed amid unexpected change, unable to pivot to meet new needs or opportunities, and unable to harness the creativity of the people the plans ostensibly existed to benefit.

Neither the capitalist economy free-for-all—perhaps more accurately, the "free-for-some"—nor the authoritarian "planned economy" allows for a third possibility: an economy shaped not by the whims of the state or by moneyed interests, but by the shared concerns and aspirations of the people. Instead of feeling as if they have to fight the prevailing economic powers to protect themselves and meet their needs, people become the economic power. The writers in this group of essays imagine the ramifications of that transformation.

A core question is, "Who should own what?" David Bollier, director of the Reinventing the Commons Program at the Schumacher Center for a New Economics, explores the scope and role of the commons—"at once a paradigm, a discourse, an ethic, and a set of social practices"—as a starting point for envisioning an alternative to neoliberal capitalism. The commons are shared resources, "common wealth" owned and stewarded collectively by all, and Bollier argues for an expansive definition of what is in the commons and thus excluded from market commodification. No "tragedy of the commons" would arise to justify privatization, Bollier argues. Rather, a commons-based new system would be flexible, controlled by communities and responsive to their needs, and would "integrate production, governance and bottom-up participation into new sorts of institutions." Economics, governance, politics, and culture would be blended, and based on decommodification, mutualization, and the organization and control of resources outside of the market.

Building on the concept of the commons, John Restakis, an independent researcher and consultant on international co-op and community economic development, emphasizes the "social control of capital" as "the linchpin of system change" in his call for a pluralist, cooperative commonwealth based on the principle of economic democracy. His model embodies a civil socialism in which states act as "partner states" but democratically structured civil institutions make up the economy's organizational basis. Such institutions would include public banks chartered to support cooperatives and collectives as the dominant enterprise model. Restakis also calls for restructuring and democratizing social care, the social economy, and social markets that facilitate the creation of social relationships through which people receive services. In this commonwealth, new information and communications technology would enhance an emerging "generative democracy" that mirrors the ethos that has given the world such digital commons resources as open source software and Wikipedia.

Michael Albert's vision of participatory economics, or "parecon," aims to "provide an institutional setting that facilitates future people deciding for themselves what their own conditions of life and work should be." In parecon, Albert—a prolific author on the topic—advocates for four new core economic institutions and arrangements: self-managing councils and federations, equitable remuneration, "balanced job complexes" that would help ensure "classless" workplaces where all jobs are equally empowering, and "a self-regulating allocation alternative to both markets and central planning that is compatible with its other three defining features." Albert's model depends on decentralized, participatory planning for the mutually beneficial allocation of goods and services. "The participatory vision does not assume a population of omniscient and morally saintly people," he writes. "Instead, simple structures enable, facilitate, and make such results the rational, personal, and community-serving aim of everyone."

Robin Hahnel, an economics professor who has worked closely with Michael Albert, fleshes out the participatory economics model. Participatory economic planning would take place in various stakeholder councils. Long-run development and investment planning would be carried out mostly by federations of industry and consumer councils, Hahnel suggests, while an annual planning procedure would determine which worker councils will produce which goods and services for consumption by which consumer councils. To come to a consensus on a feasible plan, these councils would rely on accurate estimates of the full social costs of producing goods and services, and the opportunity costs of using different capital goods, categories of labor, and natural resources and services. To make this planning process possible, Hahnel writes, "we must convince the majority that ordinary people are perfectly capable of managing our own economic affairs without either capitalist employers or commissars to tell us what to do."

Chapter 22

Commoning as a Transformative Social Paradigm

David Bollier

Facing up to our time's many profound crises, we see a conundrum with no easy resolution: how can we imagine and build a radically different system while living within an incumbent system that aggressively resists transformation? Our challenge is not just articulating attractive alternatives, but also identifying credible strategies for actualizing them.

The commons—at once a paradigm, a discourse, an ethic, and a set of social practices—holds great promise in cracking this conundrum. More than a political philosophy or policy agenda, the commons is an active living process. It is less a noun than a verb because it is primarily about the social practices of *commoning*—the acts of mutual support, conflict, negotiation, communication, and experimentation needed to create systems to manage shared resources. This process integrates production (self-provisioning), governance, culture, and personal interests.

In this brisk overview of the commons and commoning, I explain the theory of change that animates many commoners—especially those trying to tame capitalist markets, steward natural systems, and mutualize the benefits of shared resources. I offer a commons-based critique of the neoliberal economy and polity, a vision of how the commons can bring about a more ecologically sustainable and humane society, and a tour of the major economic and political changes that commoners seek and the principal means for pursuing them. I then speculate about some implications of a commons-centric society for the market/state alliance ("the system"), asking how a world of commons provisioning and governance would change the polity and address the interconnected pathologies of relentless economic growth, concentrated corporate power, consumerism, unsustainable debt, and cascading ecological destruction.

Goals of the Commons Movement

For starters, let me state clearly the commons movement's goal. Commoners aim to reclaim their "common wealth," both material and political. They want to roll back the pervasive privatization and marketization of their shared resources—from land and water to knowledge and urban spaces—and reassert greater participatory control over those resources and community life. They want to make certain resources *inalienable*—protected from sale on the market and conserved for future generations. This project—reversing market enclosures and reinventing the commons—seeks to achieve what state regulation has generally failed to achieve: effective control of abusive, unsustainable market behavior.

Although the terms of engagement vary, countless activist communities around the world are resisting the neoliberal economy and creating commons-based alternatives. The mounting momentum of this activity may escape notice because conflicts occur at many levels from the local to the transnational, in diverse resource domains, and sometimes they are self-described in terms other than the commons language. Yet, all dissent from the grand narrative of free-market ideology and its near-theological belief in "self-made" individualism, expansive private property rights, constant economic growth, government deregulation, capital-driven technological innovation, and consumerism. Commoners see this belief system as the engine of the extractive market economy that is destroying ecosystems, undermining democracy, disempowering communities, and dispossessing individuals, especially the poor and vulnerable.

Since conventional political venues tend to be structurally rigged against systemic change, commoners focus more on creating their own alternative systems outside of the market and state. Without abandoning either progressive change or conventional politics and regulation as vehicles for self-defense, they recognize their inherent limits. Electoral politics and policy-driven solutions tend to be expensive, expert-driven, legalistic, bureaucratically inflexible, and politically corruptible at best, and truly corrupt right now.

Carving out protected spaces for their own initiatives, commoners engage with policy only as politically necessary or feasible. Instead of looking to state authorities as guarantors or administrators of their interests, commoners typically seek direct sovereignty and control over their cities, neighborhoods, food, water, land, information, infrastructure, credit and money, social services, and much else. By demonstrating the superiority of commons-based systems (say, free or open-source software development, local food provisioning, cooperatives, and alternative currencies), commoning creates quasi-independent, socially satisfying alternatives to capital-driven markets.

The more profound influence of the commons may be cultural. Commoning regenerates people's social connections with each other and with nature. It helps build new aspirations and identities. By giving people significant new opportunities for personal agency far beyond those of the consumer, citizen, and voter, the commons embodies wholesome cultural values that meld responsibility and entitlement. Transcending market culture, commoning cultivates new cultural spaces and inner subjective experiences that are far more socially empowering than consumerism, conventional politics, or ideology. Ultimately, commoning is not so much a fixed philosophical vision or policy agenda as it is engaged collaboration in building successful commons. As conceptual artist Jenny Holzer says: "Action creates more trouble than words."

What the Term "Commons" Means

To understand the subversive, strategic power of the commons, one must first understand the tangled modern usage of the word "commons." For nearly half a century, much of the educated public considered the commons a failed management regime associated with government coercion. This idea traces back to a famous essay written by biologist Garrett Hardin in 1968, "The Tragedy of the Commons," in the journal *Science*. In Hardin's parable, sharing pasture on which no single herder has a "rational" incentive to limit his cattle's grazing[1] led inevitably to selfish behavior: each farmer grabbed as much of the common resource as possible, resulting in its overuse and ruin and illustrating the case for allocating private property rights to natural resources. But what Hardin was describing was *not* a commons, but an open-access regime or free-for-all in which everything is free for the taking. In a commons, a distinct community governs the resource and its usage. Commoners negotiate their own rules of access and use, assign responsibilities and entitlements, monitor use, penalize free riders, and take other steps to maintain the commons. Commons scholar Lewis Hyde has puckishly called Hardin's "tragedy" thesis "The Tragedy of Unmanaged, Laissez-Faire, Commons-Pool Resources with Easy Access for Non-Communicating, Self-Interested Individuals."[2]

Political scientist Elinor Ostrom at Indiana University helped rescue the commons from the memory hole to which mainstream economics had consigned it. From the 1970s until her death in 2012, she documented the many ways in which hundreds of communities, mostly in rural settings in poorer nations, manage natural resources sustainably. Ostrom answered the all-important question of "how a group of principals who are in an interdependent situation can organize and govern themselves to obtain continuing joint benefits when all face temptations to free-ride, shirk or otherwise act opportunistically."[3] In her landmark 1990 book, *Governing the Commons*, she identified eight key design principles for successful commons and explored ways to diversify and nest governance (what she called "polyarchy") to empower bottom-up initiative and decision-making.[4] For her work, she became the first woman to win the Nobel Prize in Economics. Coming on the heels of the 2008 financial crisis, the honor may have been bestowed to showcase that ongoing social *relationships* play as significant a role in economics as impersonal market *transactions*. In any case, Ostrom's research laid the groundwork for this reconceptualization of both economic analysis and the role of the commons in it—without taking the next step, political engagement.

Unfortunately, to this day, most mainstream politicians and economists channel Hardin, not Osrom, and see the commons as an inert, unowned resource. Too few acknowledge the reality of a commons as a dynamic, evolving social activity: commoning. In practice, a commons consists not just of a resource, but of a *community* that manages a *resource* by devising its own *rules, traditions, and values*. All three are needed. In short, the commons must be understood as a living social system of creative agents.

This type of discourse is unsettling to conventional academics because it moves the entire discussion out of the familiar economistic framework based on *Homo economicus* and rational actors. It opens the door to what they regard as the vagaries of anthropology, psychology, sociology, geography, and other "soft," humanistic sciences. This makes it more difficult to build the tidy quantitative, mechanical models that economists and policymakers prize so highly. When there are so many idiosyncratic local, historical, cultural, and intersubjective factors at play, propounding a universal typology of commons seems impossible.

Today's commons discourse seeks to rescue the messy realities of human existence and social organization from the *faux* regularities and worldview of standard economics, bureaucratic systems, and modernity itself. The complicated reality is that a commons arises whenever a given community decides it wants to manage a resource collectively, with an accent on fair access, use, and long-term sustainability. This can happen in countless unpredictable ways. Indeed, commons have arisen in such improbable contexts as community theater, open-source microscopy, open-source mapping to aid humanitarian rescue, and hospitality for migrants. Each of these "world-making" communities is animated by its own values, traditions, history and intersubjectivity.

Once we acknowledge that the ontological premises of a commons matter—that commoners inhabit a different social reality than that presented by economists, for example—we enter a new cosmology of social phenomena. The accent is on dynamic, living *relationships* (including with the Earth), and not on episodic transactions among decontextualized objects, each with fixed, invariable traits. The commons can be understood only as an evolving, holistic living system, and that requires new heuristic methods for understanding commons (and the world). The idea of socially enacted patterns, as described by Christopher Alexander's idea of pattern languages, is an excellent methodology for this task.[5]

In the world of the commons, enacting an ontological shift, or "OntoShift," is precisely the point. Commoning is about building human spaces in which the local, the distinctive, and the historical *matter.* Unique experiences, vernacular traditions, cultural values, and geographies must be recognized and privileged. The commons, then, is a language and socio-political-economic project for honoring the *particularity* of lived experience—and more, for honoring *the generative and intrinsic human value of such particularity*. An Indigenous commons will, of course, differ from an urban commons, and both will differ from, say, the Wikihouse design community. Together, such various commons form what Arturo Escobar calls a "pluriverse."[6] As evolutionary scientists are finding, the baseline reality of the human species is a shared DNA that manifests itself in many highly varied local adaptations, so why can't our economic and political institutions reflect this fact?

The commons paradigm asks us to cross an important ontological threshold—but mainstream political and economic players in Western industrial societies adamantly refuse to do so. Consider the West's disdain for the idea of "nature's rights," "biocultural protocols," and self-determination for local communities (and even for nations that choose to protect their ecosystems in defiance of trade treaties). The commons names a set of social values that lie beyond market price and propertization. They honor informal, tacit, experiential, intergenerational, ecological, and even cosmic realities that cannot be comprehended by rational actor theory in economics, say, or the neo-Darwinian survival-of-the-fittest narratives informing neoliberal economics.

In this sense, the commons challenges the worldview of the liberal bureaucratic state and conventional science, both of which treat ecosystems and humans as more or less fungible and commodifiable resources. Our labor is treated as a "human resource" to be bought and managed; bee pollination is seen as one of "nature's services" that can be priced; and even life forms can now be patented and owned. By insisting upon the inalienability of living systems and their intrinsic (non-tradeable, shared) value, the commons makes radical demands for system change that are not just political and economic, but cultural and ontological.

Why the Commons Discourse Matters

This review of the modern history of commons discourse sheds light on the "theory of change" that the commons movement is seeking to enact. The language of the commons is, first, an instrument for reorienting people's perceptions and understanding. It helps name and illuminate the realities of market enclosure and the value of commoning. Without this language, these two social realities remain culturally invisible or at least marginalized—and therefore politically inconsequential.

Commons discourse provides a way to articulate moral and political claims that conventional policy discourse ignores or suppresses. Using the concepts and logic of the commons also helps bring into being a new cohort of self-aware commoners who can recognize their mutual affinities and shared agenda. The discourse helps people assert their sovereign values and priorities in systemic terms. More than an intellectual nicety, the coherent philosophical narrative of the commons helps commoners recognize when capital is playing one interest off against another: nature versus labor, labor versus consumers, consumers versus the community. Through the language and experiences of commoning, people can start shedding the constrictive social roles of "employee" and "consumer" and live more integrated lives as whole human beings. In contrast to the divide-and-conquer tactics that capital deploys to neutralize demands for change, the holistic commons vision helps diverse victims of market abuse recognize their shared victimization, develop a new narrative, cultivate new links of solidarity, and build a constellation of working alternatives driven by a different logic.

Economics and the Commons

As already implied here, the commons movement seeks to change our very conception of "the economy." Rather than consider "the market" as an autonomous "natural" realm of society somehow apart from the Earth's natural systems and our social needs, commoners seek to integrate the social, ecological, and economic. In *The Great Transformation*, Karl Polanyi explains how market culture in the 17th through 19th centuries gradually supplanted kinship, custom, religion, morality, and community to become society's primary ordering principle.[7] That transformation must be reversed; unfettered capital and markets must be re-embedded in society and made answerable to it. Through commoning, we must subordinate capital investment, finance, production, corporate power, and international trade to societal needs.

Along with allied movements, the commons movement seeks to develop institutions and norms for a post-capitalist, post-growth order. This means confronting the monoculture of market-based options with a richer, more vibrant sense of human possibilities than the producer/consumer dyad affords. A book that Silke Helfrich and I edited, *Patterns of Commoning*, profiles several dozen fascinating successful commons that draw on various human capacities and social forms. These include community forests, local currencies, Fab Labs, municipal water committees, farmland trusts for supporting local family farming, Indigenous "biocultural heritage" areas for stewarding biodiversity, permaculture farming, "omni-commons" structures that provide administrative/legal support to commons-based enterprises, and many others.[8]

There is hope, as well, in the multi-stakeholder co-operative model, which successfully provides social services to people in Quebec, Italy, and Japan. Cooperative forms also need to supplant proprietary digital platforms now dominated by Facebook, Uber, Lyft, Airbnb, Task Rabbit, Mechanical Turk, and other "sharing economy" ventures that are privatizing and monetizing the fruits of social cooperation. A major new effort to invent co-operative models for online platforms—"Platform Cooperativism"—has spread around the world since its launch in 2015.[9]

Commoners everywhere are pioneering important institutional innovations that seek to replace exploitative proprietary market platforms and corporate structures. Some examples:

- *Buying clubs and reconfigured production/supply chains for mutual benefit,* such as the clothing production system developed by the Solidarity Economy in Italy and the Fresno [California] Commons that is re-inventing the regional food supply chain through a commons-based trust
- *State-chartered stakeholder trusts,* such as the Alaska Permanent Fund and the new models proposed by Peter Barnes, that mutualize the revenues generated by state-owned resources
- *Open source programming communities* that freely share code and sometimes are supported by affiliated foundations led by respected community elders
- *Global peer production design and local manufacturing communities* that are creating modular, low-budget cars, farm equipment, furniture, and other physical products

A significant unresolved problem for many of these commons-based institutions is access to credit and revenues. Conventional banks and financial institutions, even social and ethical banks, find it difficult to lend to commons that are not profit-seeking commercial enterprises. An open source design and manufacturing ecosystem, for example, has no intellectual property to offer as collateral to a bank, and so it can't obtain capital to develop or produce more "products"—fuel-efficient, open-source vehicles, or cheap locally sourced farm equipment. Fortunately, many near-forgotten historical models of cooperative finance are being rediscovered and blended with new technologies to support commons. These include novel DIY credit systems, alternative currencies, and crowdfunding platforms like Goteo in Spain. Interest-free credit of the sort developed by JAK Bank in Sweden is being adapted to service local transition economies while others are exploring new types of crowd-equity schemes for commons.[10]

The basic point is that a post-capitalist vision for finance and money is fitfully emerging. Self-organized commons are poised to create their own value-accounting and exchange systems, including currencies and credit, which could enable them to bypass many of the pathologies of conventional debt-driven lending and market-based production.

As conventional bank and finance systems start imploding under the weight of capitalism's contradictions, and as new digital technologies and commons-based communities demonstrate new cooperative options, mu-tualized finance holds great promise.[11] Similarly, commoners could reap huge gains if government control of the ability to create money were recaptured from the private banking sector (which creates most of the US money supply through its loans). Recovering this power would enable the redirection of money to serve public democratically determined needs rather than the narrow profit-making goals of commercial lenders.[12]

The large diversified realm of common-based production based on *indirect* reciprocity, in contrast to markets, also holds promise. Participation in timebanks, open source networks, co-learning communities, and artistic commons (to name only a few) are generally not based on one-to-one exchange, but on personal commitments to the community as a whole—a "pool and share" approach. Often patronized as the "voluntary sector" or "do-gooding," these convivial communities (in the sense described by Ivan Illich) are in fact socially productive workhorses.[13] They perform many services in caring, humane, and low-cost ways.

The "new economy" that commoners seek to build is not so much an economy as a blended hybrid of the social, the economic, and peer governance. The resulting system, as seen in scores of examples, is more transparent and controllable by communities, more flexible, and locally responsive. It is regarded as trustworthy and socially concerned and is less prone to creating the negative externalities routinely generated by markets.

Many progressives tend to assume that state law and public policy—top-down systems—are the most effective, rapid way to achieve system change. These tools, while often necessary, have a diminishing effectiveness and trustworthiness in today's networked world. It is exceedingly difficult to achieve transformational change through conventional political institutions now paralyzed by bureaucratic norms, partisan gridlock, and high jurisprudential barriers.

The big challenge for commoners, therefore, is to build and federate their models into larger collaborative social ecosystems. Since national governments allied with large corporations may be reluctant to support this approach, cities will quite likely become the key movers. This is already apparent in Barcelona, Amsterdam, Seoul, and Bologna, among other cities, where commons initiatives are flourishing.[14] These experiments speak to the limitations of centralized command-and-control systems in a networked age.[15] In his book *The Utopia of Rules*, anthropologist/activist David Graeber argues persuasively that the singular failure of the left has been its inability to imagine functional, human-scale alternatives to bureaucracy and foster citizen initiative, participation, and innovation—"strong democracy"—that has everyday meaning and impact.

The new system will have to embrace peer cooperation on distributed networks to do work that bureaucracy so often bungles. This is not a matter of "reinventing government," but of integrating production, governance, and bottom-up participation into new sorts of commons institutions. Economic and technological trends are clearly headed in this direction, as documented by Yochai Benkler in *The Wealth of Networks*; Jeremy Rifkin in his *Zero Marginal Cost Society*; and Michel Bauwens in the P2P Foundation wiki and blog.[16] Network-based or -assisted commons can provide a vital infrastructure for building a new social economy of participatory control and mutualized benefit. Coordinating bureaucratic systems with network-based commons remains a difficult challenge, but many "Government 2.0" experiments are already exploring the possibilities.

The beauty of many commons-based innovations is their quasi-autonomy; they do not necessarily require government, law, or policy to move forward. They can bypass conventional political venues. Law, policy, and procurement could certainly facilitate the growth of a Commons Sector, and some government policies that privilege market incumbents and criminalize commoning certainly need to be eliminated. But commons-based systems of provisioning and services have already shown their great capacities to meet needs in innovative ways.

Ramifications for Society, Environment, and Polity

The economic/provisioning vision sketched here obviously has far-reaching implications for inequality, ecosystems, gender and race relations, and the polity. So, then, how would a commons-centric society deal with these issues?

Wealth and Income Inequality. When people's basic needs can be met through a system that is not driven by debt and profit-seeking, the grotesque inequalities of wealth and income that neoliberal capitalism produces can be reduced. The point of commoning, after all, is to *de-commodify* or *mutualize* the provisioning of needs so that the needs of all are met. The late alternative monetary expert Margrit Kennedy once estimated that up to half the cost of essential goods and services sold in the market represents debt. If a family can reduce its dependence on conventional markets and credit, then its cost of living can decline dramatically, along with its vulnerability to predatory corporate behavior.

The de-commodification and mutualization of daily life can occur through many commons-based systems. Community land trusts take land out of the market to reduce housing costs. Cooperative finance alternatives reduce exposure to high-interest rates and debt. Cooperatively produced goods and services reduce costs and enhance quality, as do shared infrastructure for energy, transportation, Internet access, social media platforms, and open and commons-based systems for software code, data, information, scientific research, and creative works.

Social Justice and Racial and Gender Equality. Focused on governance, provisioning, and social cooperation, the commons paradigm does not speak directly to racial, ethnic, or gender concerns. However, the commons paradigm is keenly focused on inclusiveness and social solidarity, and so can go beyond the formal legal rights that liberal democracies provide but don't necessarily honor. Markets ignore human need and zero in on consumer demand, making anyone without the money to express consumer demand marginal or invisible. But commons are dedicated to meeting people's basic material needs first, and to doing so in socially committed and inclusive ways. Just as many African American communities used cooperatives to build dignity and respect while meeting material needs,[17] so the commons has a core commitment to social need, fairness, and respect.

As for women, children, and families, commons historian Peter Linebaugh has noted that

> birth, nurturance, neighborhood, and love are the beginnings of social life. The commons of the past has not been an exclusively male place. In fact, it is one very often where the needs of women and children come first. And not 'needs' only but decision-making and responsibility have belonged to women from the neighborhoods of industrial slums to the matriarchy of the Iroquois confederation to the African village.[18]

In a commons, "care work" is primary. By contrast, capitalist markets and economics routinely ignore the world of household life and social conviviality essential to a stable, sane, rewarding life. Market economies regard these essentials as free self-replenishing resources—"pre-economic" or "non-economic" resources without standing that can be ignored or exploited at will. In this sense, the victimization of women in care work resembles the victimization suffered by commoners, colonized persons, and nature. All generate important non-market value that capitalists depend on without truly valuing. As a 1980 United Nations report stated with savage clarity:

> Women represent 50 percent of the world adult population and one third of the official labor force, they perform nearly two thirds of all working hours, receive only one tenth of the world income and own less than 1 percent of world property.

German writer Ina Praetorius recently projected "care work" onto a much larger philosophical canvas in her essay, "The Care-Centered Economy: Rediscovering What Has Been Taken for Granted."[19] Praetorius suggests using the importance of "care" to imagine new structural priorities for the entire economy, helping to reorient economic institutions and behaviors.

The commons is an obvious vehicle for advancing these ideas because it honors nonmarket care as an essential category of value-creation.

Ecosystem Stewardship. Whatever the shortcomings of any individual natural resource commons, its participants realize that they must work with them, not against them. Unlike markets, commoners treat "the environment" as a dynamic living system that enframes their lives, not as a commodity. They generally have far less incentive than corporations to over-exploit natural systems and much greater incentive to respect and sustain nature for collective benefit.

Small-scale natural resource commons that revolve around forests, fisheries, pastures, groundwater, and wild game are enormously important in rural regions of marginalized countries.[20] These commons also tend to be far more ecologically benign than the energy-intensive industrial agriculture of the "developed" world. Yet, even though an estimated two billion people worldwide rely on commons to meet everyday needs, they are ignored by leading economics textbooks because no market activity or capital accumulation is taking place—only production for household use.[21]

In these small commons, the bedrock of a more ecologically mindful economy, people are not motivated by money but by "affective labor"—a term geographer Neera Singh uses to describe commons-based forest management.[22] Here, people's sense of self and subjectivity is intertwined with their biophysical environment. They take pride and pleasure in becoming stewards of local resources. This is why affective labor in a commons matters—it changes how we perceive ourselves, our relationships to others, and our connection to the environment.

The Polity and Governance. What type of polity could possibly host and "govern" a wide universe of commons? The very question implies a radical shift in the state's character and role. As its limited capacity to meet needs becomes more acutely evident, engendering public distrust, the state will need to delegate powers to allow more bottom-up, commons-based initiatives to flourish.

One promising solution is "commons/public partnerships" (CPP) that are instigated by and for ordinary people, not business interests, in cooperation with state institutions. A CPP is an agreement of long-term cooperation around specific functions, such as providing an urban Wi-Fi service (Guifi.net in Catalonia), city bureaucracies working closely with citizen groups (the Co-City Protocols developed in a number of Italian cities), and managing a renewable energy coop as a citizen/state collaboration.

Such collaborations can also occur at large, transnational scales, as demonstrated by the Drugs for Neglected Diseases Initiative (DNDi), a partnership among commoners, states, and research institutes to develop affordable new drugs. Commoning as a new sort of "micro-behavior" can lead to new types of "macro-institutions" that enact new types of large-scale governance. Two other examples: Wikipedia, with more than

80,000 volunteer editors around the world, and La Via Campesina, the international network of peasant farmers.

These innovations in governance and provisioning parallel some profound discoveries over the past generation in the evolutionary sciences and complexity science. Both fields validate the reality of bottom-up social organization and governance and confirm that some of the most stable, resilient forms of governance are distributed, peer-based, and collaborative. This topic is explored at greater length in my book with Silke Helfrich, *Free, Fair and Alive: The Insurgent Power of the Commons.*[23] Here, the basic point is that human communities can evolve higher, more complex forms of organization without the direct control of a central sovereign or bureaucracy: such emergence is a bottom-up theory of governance.[24] Within a sufficiently defined and hospitable set of parameters and conditions, stable forms of self-organization based on local circumstances can arise. Self-actualized order, internal governance, and creative evolution happen all the time in biophysical and chemical contexts, as complexity science has documented. Elinor Ostrom's findings about countless self-organized commons can be considered another instance of this phenomenon. Effective governance need not be imposed through a comprehensive grid of uniform general rules embodied in formal state law and administered through legislators, regulators, and courts. With the right "fitness conditions"—a stable context, shared needs, a sufficient diversity of symbiotic agents—governance can emerge naturally, on its own, through the active participation and consent of the governed at the relevant scale.

Of course, there are differences between a network-based governance regime and a polity. But the very idea of a polity may need to evolve if we are to get beyond the current dysfunctionalities of nation-state governance. Tech platforms of commoners could complement or partially substitute for state authority, much as corporations have been chartered by the state, ostensibly to serve the public good. New governance forms will have to emerge as commons become more prevalent and mature, requiring new types of state support and coordination. Inevitably, this new polity will not be comprehensible to the old order.

Conclusion

Because the commons movement is a pulsating, living network of commoners around the world, it is difficult to set forth a definitive blueprint or predict the future. The future paradigm can arise only through evolutionary co-creation. Still, we can already see the expansive, self-replicating power of the commons idea as embraced by highly diverse groups: Francophone commoners in eight countries who hosted a commons festival with more than 300 events, urban activists who are reconceptualizing the "city as a commons," Croatians fighting enclosure of their public spaces and coastal lands, Greeks developing a "Mediterranean imaginary" of the commons to fight neoliberal economic policies, Indigenous peoples defending their ethnobotanical and biocultural traditions, digital activists mobilizing to devise new forms of platform cooperativism, and so on. The commons language and framework helps develop unexpected new synergies and forms of solidarity.

As a meta-discourse that has core principles but porous boundaries, the commons can speak at once to the worlds of politics, governance, economics, and culture. Importantly, unlike the state or the market, it can also speak to the alienation associated with modernity and to people's instinctive needs for human connection and meaning. The commons paradigm offers a deep philosophical critique of neoliberal economics, with hundreds of convergent examples. But in this action-oriented approach to system change, everything depends on the energy and imagination of commoners, and would-be commoners, to develop this globally networked living system.

The anonymous Invisible Committee in France has observed that

> an insurrection is not like a plague or forest fire—a linear process which spreads from place to place after an initial spark. It takes the shape of music, whose focal points, though dispersed in time and space, succeed in imposing the rhythms of their own vibrations.

That describes the unfolding odyssey of the commons movement, whose rhythms are producing a lot of resonance.

Notes

1 Garrett Hardin, "The Tragedy of the Commons," *Science* 162, 3859 (December 1968): 1243.
2 Lewis Hyde, *Common as Air: Revolution, Art and Ownership* (New York: Farrar, Straus and Giroux, 2010), 44.
3 Elinor Ostrom, *Governing the Commons: The Evolution of Institutions for Collective Action* (New York: Cambridge University Press, 1990), 42.
4 Elinor Ostrom, *Understanding Institutional Diversity* (Princeton, NJ: Princeton University Press, 2005); Joanna Burger, Elinor Ostrom et al., *Protecting the Commons: A Framework for Resource Management in the Americas* (Washington, DC: Island Press, 2001).
5 Christopher Alexander, Sara Ishikawa, Murray Silverstein, Max Jacobson, Ingrid Fiksfahl-King, and Shlomo Angel, *A Pattern Language: Towns, Buildings, Construction* (New York: Oxford University Press, 1977). See also David Bollier and Silke Helfrich, *Patterns of Commoning* (Amherst, MA: Commons Strategies Group, 2015).
6 Arturo Escobar, "Commons in the Pluriverse," in Bollier and Helfrich, *Patterns of Commoning*, 348–360.
7 Karl Polyani, *The Great Transformation: The Political and Economic Origins of Our Time* (Boston, MA: Beacon Press, (1944) 2014).

8 Bollier and Helfrich, *Patterns of Commoning.*

9 Trebor Scholz, *Platform Cooperativism: Challenging the Corporate Sharing Economy* (New York: Rosa Luxemburg Siftung, 2015). http://www.rosalux-nyc. org/wp-content/files_mf/scholz_platformcoop_5.9.2016.pdf. See also Platform Cooperativism conference website, http://platformcoop.net.

10 David Bollier and Pat Conaty, *Capital for the Commons: Strategies for Transforming Neoliberal Finance Through Commons-based Alternatives* (Berlin: The Commons Strategies Group, 2015).

11 Bollier and Conaty, *Capital for the Commons.*

12 Mary Mellor, *Debt or Democracy* (London: Pluto Press, 2015); Mary Mellor, *The Future of Money: From Financial Crisis to Public Resource* (London: Pluto Press, 2010); Frances Hutchinson, Mary Mellor, and Wendy Olsen, *The Politics of Money: Towards Sustainability and Economic Democracy* (London: Pluto Press, 2003).

13 Ivan Illich, *Tools for Conviviality* (New York: Harper & Row, 1973).

14 Shareable, *Sharing Cities: Activating the Urban Commons* (Oakland, CA: Tides Center/Shareable), 2018. https://www.shareable.net/sharing-cities.

15 David Graeber, *The Utopia of Rules* (Brooklyn, NY: Melville House, 2015).

16 Yochai Benkler, *The Wealth of Networks: How Social Production Transforms Markets and Freedom* (New Haven, CT: Yale University Press, 2005), http://public. eblib.com/choice/publicfullrecord.aspx?p=3419996; Jeremy Rifkin, *The Zero Marginal Cost Society: The Internet of Things, the Collaborative Commons, and the Eclipse of Capitalism* (New York: Palgrave Macmillan, 2014); See P2P Foundation, "Michael Bauwens," http://p2pfoundation.net/Michel_Bauwens/ Full_Bio.

17 Jessica Gordon Nembhard, *Collective Courage: A History of African American Cooperative Economic Thought and Practice* (State College: Pennsylvania State University, 2014).

18 Peter Linebaugh, "Stop, Thief!" Onthecommons.org, April 14, 2014, http:// www.onthecommons.org/magazine/stop-thief.

19 Ina Praetorius, "The Care-Centered Economy: Rediscovering What Has Been Taken for Granted," *Heinrich-Böll-Stiftung* 7 (April 2015), https://www. boell.de/en/2015/04/07/care-centered-economy.

20 See, e.g. the holdings of the Digital Library of the Commons at http://dlc. dlib.indiana.edu/dlc.

21 Paul A. Samuelson and William D. Nordhaus, *Economics*, 17th edition (New York: McGraw-Hill, 2001); Joseph E. Stiglitz and Carl. E. Walsh, *Economics*, 3rd edition (New York: W.W. Norton, 2002); "Securing the Commons: Securing Property, Securing Livelihoods," International Land Alliance website, http://www.landcoalition.org/global-initiatives/securing-commons.

22 Neera Singh, "The Affective Labor of Growing Forests and the Becoming of Environmental Subjects: Rethinking Environmentality in Odisha, India," *Geoforum* 47 (2013): 189–198.

23 David Bollier and Silke Helfrich, *Free, Fair and Alive: The Insurgent Power of the Commons* (Gabriola Island, BC: New Society Publishers, 2019).

24 Weston Burns and David Bollier, *Green Governance: Ecological Survival, Human Rights and the Law of the Commons* (Cambridge: Cambridge University Press, 2013).

Chapter 23

Cooperative Commonwealth and the Partner State

John Restakis

Among capitalism's many critics, it is standard procedure to state that neoliberalism has failed and that without a new paradigm for how economies work, human societies will collapse under the weight of an unsustainable and environmentally catastrophic capitalist system.

The International Monetary Fund (IMF), neoliberalism's most powerful apostle over the past 40 years, has now admitted that perhaps its signature ideology has been oversold and that free market ideology's costs may have outweighed the touted benefits. Whether this signals a fundamental shift in thinking or a tactical maneuver to preserve the status quo is a matter of political perspective. My bet is on the latter.

In fact, neoliberalism has not failed. True to its principles, it is succeeding marvelously in its ultimate purpose—maximizing wealth to the owners of capital. The problem is that these principles are not just unsustainable—they are pathological,[1] and their dominance in our culture has literally deprived people of the capacity to imagine any alternative. Indeed, the absence of alternatives from public debate is one clear symptom of the crisis we are in.

We have entered an age where it is entirely likely that change—in whatever form—will come not from political effort by social movements, but rather from the collapse of the current system. The consequences of global warming, growing inequality, disappearing civil liberties, and the consolidation of the surveillance state all point to the need for political mobilization on a scale not seen since the uprisings of the mid-1800s.

Needed now are a vision and a plan to challenge and transform our current system's underpinnings. That means the recovery of economic and political sovereignty by nations, the radical curtailment and redistribution of wealth, the social control of capital, the democratization of technology, the protection of social, cultural, and environmental values, and the use of state and civil institutions to promote economic democracy. Above all, it means the evolution of new forms of governance that deliver decision-making power to citizens.

A tall order. But if the grievances polarizing societies across the globe are not channeled into constructive pathways to reform, toward positive visions of society that people can believe in, and ways of life that have meaning beyond self-aggrandizement and money worship, what comes next will be a nightmare, fueled by rage and resentment. In the toxic politics of the US, and in the rise of populist neofascist movements across Europe, we are already witnessing the harbingers of dark times ahead.

Thankfully, the elements of a new imaginary are all around us. The outlines of a humane political economy in which personal fulfilment and community well-being are conjoined are also visible in innumerable cooperative and social enterprises that are showing daily that social values can be the basis for an economics in which the common good prevails. Ethics can be a basis for a new economic order.

This essay describes elements of political economy that are indispensable for system change. This includes the forms by which such an economy might function, the roles of citizens and the state, the role of technology, and examples of how these ideas may be realized in the provision of social care, the creation of money and social investment, the creation of social markets, and the containment of corporate power. With our political order in crisis, with regressive policies growing daily, thinking about what comes next can ensure that urgent actions taken now reflect a long-term vision that makes what we do today meaningful and coherent.

Cooperative Commonwealth

The form of political economy advocated here is a pluralist, *cooperative commonwealth* based on the principle of economic democracy in service to the common good. Its purpose is to reinforce and reward human solidarity, to care for the planet, to nurture community, and to support the fullest realization of our aspirations as social beings.

Cooperative commonwealth is not a new idea. It has been expounded for over 150 years by both theorists and practitioners. From the ideas of Robert Owen and William Thompson in the cooperative movement's early years to the guild socialists of the interwar years, to current theorists of peer-to-peer production networks and the commons, an economy based on collectively owned, democratically organized, and self-governing cooperative enterprises and institutions has been a central pillar of the socialist alternative to capitalism.

But there are many brands of socialism. What I propose is a form of civil socialism wherein democratically structured civil institutions are the organizational basis of the economy, as opposed to forms of state socialism, which are organized around centrally planned systems controlled by the state.

Civil socialism blends elements of these two modalities—state and non-state economic organization—through civil mobilization and empowerment. The form of cooperative commonwealth advocated here is pluralist. It leaves room for small and medium firms that are privately owned and for publicly owned enterprises. Cooperative entities are actively encouraged and supported, but other types of enterprise are also free to operate. The only strictures on privately owned small- and medium-sized businesses are that they treat employees fairly and don't attempt to control markets or adopt practices that harm society or the environment.

In other words, the term "cooperative commonwealth" is not a hegemonic system. A plurality of enterprises is fundamental not only to the health of an economy but also to the health of cooperatives and commons. Moreover, imposing a purely cooperative model of economy would require the use of force, thus corrupting the model. Enforced cooperation is an absurdity and doomed to failure as has been shown repeatedly everywhere governments have tried it.[2]

The Commons

The commons refers to any resource whose use is freely accessible to a community of users and which, in turn, they manage in common. A commons is not owned in the conventional sense. Rather, its value lies in the fact of its free and open access. It is the antithesis to enclosure of a resource for private benefit. Instead, a commons is based on the social ethics of interdependence and cooperation and the value of a commons is generated through the practice of sharing. Most importantly, a commons is the product of those social relationships that enable this use.

Traditionally, commons have referred to such natural goods as water, fisheries, forests, and pastures that help sustain collective living. But the concept has been broadened to include such non-material common resources as knowledge, culture, free software, and the Internet since concepts like open access and collective management can be applied to them too.

The principle of protecting the commons is central to the aims of cooperative commonwealth. For Indigenous peoples dispossessed of their lands, commons rights are the only means of securing survival. More generally, the principle applies to the inheritance of society as a whole—the protection and stewardship of public resources.

The commons are an irreplaceable resource for regenerating a society's store of social capital, for validating and manifesting the idea of social solidarity, and for anchoring both the values and the operations of civil society. That means that protecting and expanding the commons instead of commodifying them must be a basic aim both of civil society and of government.

Foremost among these sovereign powers are:

1   The power to control the production of money.
2   The power to control the operations of capital and to prevent the evasion of social responsibility, including the evasion of tax.
3   The power to preferentially support local enterprises and the forms by which local economies might develop.
4   The power to withhold permission for firms to operate if they contravene the public interest or fail to secure a social mandate.
5   The power to regulate markets and to promote or protect different types of market (public, commercial, social, etc.).
6   The power to render as commons the infrastructure and resources deemed essential to the public good, including natural resources, energy, knowledge, culture, and such basic human services as education and health care.

The recovery of these powers by governments is a precondition not only for the democratization of economies, but also for the democratization of the state. But it is only a beginning. The transition to cooperative commonwealth requires the powers of state and citizenry to be radically realigned and the collective wealth of a society—including its productive capital—mobilized into a collective resource for the common good.

Above all, civil society as a whole must establish the means, apart from the state apparatus and the confines of electoral systems, to organize and express collective interests and to hold governments accountable. The state must serve civil society, not the reverse.

The Role of the State

The state's power to help or hinder transition to new forms of political economy is self-evident. Less clear is whether the state is *by nature* antithetical to the forms of direct democracy advocated here. The key questions related to systems change are whether institutional power legitimated by popular consent can be achieved in forms other than a state and whether some form of radically altered state could act as a transition mechanism to more comprehensive forms of democratic organization.

Two responses are needed. The first involves challenging and radically reforming the established role and operations of the state by democratizing its operations, thus creating what might be called the Partner State. The second involves an autonomous process of self-organizing and direct democracy by citizens and communities locally, regionally, and supra-regionally to implement *stateless* democracy in actual practice, whether or not the state is formally transformed.

The Partner State

The idea of the Partner State proceeds directly from the principle that civil society is the source of political legitimacy in a democracy. In this view, the state serves civil society by advancing and protecting the common good. Above all, the Partner State is an enabling state, existing mainly to maximize civil society's capacity to create social value and to act as the primary agent in the formation of public policy. The Partner State enlarges the scope of personal autonomy and liberty and guarantees personal economic security while reinforcing the social bonds that build healthy communities and a vibrant civil society. Central to this process is the democratization of the state itself.

Traditionally, the state has been viewed as the final arbiter in regulating and operating three broad economic sectors in society—the private sector (which seeks profit), the public sector (which promotes equality by collecting and redistributing taxes), and the social economy (whose purpose is the promotion of social solidarity and the creation of community). It accomplishes this by generating social relationships whose purpose is the creation of social value (Figure 23.1).

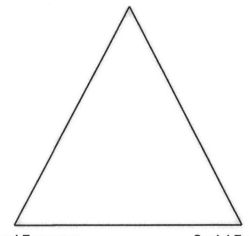

Capitalist Market Economy
(Neoliberal State)
Values: Efficiency, profit maximization
Economic Principles: Exchange of equivalents (price mechanism)

Centralized Economy
(Socialist)
Values: Equality
Economic Principles:
Redistribution/well-being

Social Economy
(Partner State/
Cooperative Commonwealth)
Values: Social solidarity
Economic Principles:
Reciprocity/mutuality/well-being

Figure 23.1 Models for economic activity.

In theory and practice, the Partner State is the first state formation in which civil society and social economic values predominant in the management of economic and social policy. Indeed, its cooperative nature and the radical realignment of its relationship to civil society in general and the social economy in particular define the Partner State.

The Social Economy

The social economy is far more than the use of self-help strategies at the economy's margins to help the poor and disadvantaged, as some believe. And the social economy is not merely a collection of economic self-defense measures against the failures and depredations of the free market economy. Rather, the social economy represents a wholly different conception of economics in which market forces and economic practice serve social or collective interests, rather than those of capital or the individual. It shows that markets can (and do) operate for both commercial and *non*-commercial social ends.

The social economy embodies the social principles of reciprocity, mutuality, and common benefit. Cooperatives, commons, charitable organizations, and diverse community and social service organizations represent these values to one degree or another. Overall, the defining characteristic of social economy organizations, including hybrids, is that they produce primarily for social benefit.

The social economy continuously generates new mechanisms for producing social value, especially social services. *Extrapolating and diffusing this idea of production for social value, and replicating the organizations and institutions that embody it, are the means of democratizing economies and the state's operations and institutions.*

Public policies that explicitly recognize and advance the social economy's principles are thus indispensable in any transition to a new political economy. Moreover, as unchecked automation leads to massive unemployment and the welfare state erodes, these policies must be interpreted and advanced within the context of whole system change and form part of a comprehensive public policy ecosystem that is large enough, and effective enough, to respond to the challenges.

The Partner State also reorients government's role toward the private economy and public-sector operations. The private and public sectors retain essential economic and social roles, and the profit motive and private business have their place. But in the Partner State, the roles and powers of the market and the public sector are counterbalanced by the primacy of the common good as the basis for public policy. Serving the common interests of the whole society, the Partner State synthesizes and facilitates, implementing the rules and providing the resources that the private economy, enterprises, civil society institutions, and the social economy need to flourish.

Yet, the primary reason for advocating a radical transformation of the state is not to generate a new form of centralized power. It is to create new forms of decentralized, non-state, *civil* power. A Partner State supports this process, especially in the design and delivery of human services and the provision of social care.

Beyond the Welfare State

The application of social economy principles and the emergence of democratic, distributed, and user-controlled systems of social care allows societies to move social welfare beyond both the welfare state and the privatization of care. This shift depends on the rise of civil networks, on new forms of social innovation, and on civil society's centrality in promoting the common welfare.

Policies that promote cooperation and the growth of civil networks for social benefit have proven successful in strengthening social economy organizations' capacity to produce social services and increase related employment. In Quebec, where government funds 85 percent of the costs of daycare programs delivered by solidarity cooperatives and other social economy organizations, this sector is the province's fourth largest employer. Italy's social cooperatives compose only 2 percent of nonprofits, but provide 23 percent of jobs in that sector.[3] In Bologna, 87 percent of social services are provided by social cooperatives under contract to the municipality.[4]

Within the broader market economy, cooperatives and other social economy organizations have prospered when access to basic capital resources—owned and controlled by the social economy—has been bolstered by progressive tax policy, enabling legislation, education and professional development, and, most of all, the support of civic associations that can identify and address the collective needs of their community or sector. Multi-stakeholder structures that represent a broad range of actors working in concert have been key to this success.[5]

Generative Democracy

Just as there are varying kinds of socialism, there are many forms of democracy. The term "generative democracy," denotes a form of democracy in which citizens are directly engaged in the *production* and *control* of the goods and services they require for their personal and collective well-being. In contrast, citizens in conventional forms of democracy are merely entitled to *receive* certain benefits by virtue of their representative power in government—a critical difference. Applied to all forms of public goods and services, generative democracy is a radically new form of governance and the Partner State is key to its emergence.

How can this be achieved?

This process can begin most effectively with the democratization of the institutions and services currently provided by the state, especially social care and human services. A focus on social care as a pathway to systemic change is strategically important for these reasons:

1   Everyone (except, possibly, the very wealthy) is affected by social care systems and has a stake in their operation.
2   Everyone who chooses can play a proactive and transformative role in the proposed democratic alternative.
3   Examples of democratized social care systems are already in use and offer concrete lessons for the evolution of new models.
4   Democratized social care systems transform the state's basic institutions and operating rationale and their introduction entails fundamental and far-reaching reforms in the political economy as a whole.
5   The democratization of social care systems and their reconstruction as forms of protected commons precludes their privatization and commodification for profit.

The same process of democratization can be applied to energy, public finance, education, housing, information and communications technology (ICT), environmental protection, food and agriculture, and national security, including policing.

Social Care in the Partner State

Three main legal and policy instruments are needed to make the social economy a full partner as envisaged in the Partner State. First is the emergence of a true social market that enlarges the power and scope of the social economy and its organizations.[6] Second is the creation of civil and community-based institutions that mediate between government and individuals in the creation of social goods and services. Third is the progressive democratization of public goods and services through the transfer of institutional control from state bureaucracies to democratically governed civil bodies.

Legislation governing the creation of cooperative and other social economy organizations sorely needs reform. Even in the most advanced states, public policy rarely aims to distribute power more effectively between the state and the citizenry. Since user-controlled systems for providing human services address the highly specific needs of individuals very effectively,[7] social economy organizations' role in social care delivery should in particular be recognized in statutory provisions, including:

•   The recognition and promotion of user-controlled social cooperatives and multi-stakeholder structures as unique models for providing social care.

- The recognition and promotion of mutual interests for serving the common good by local public authorities and social care cooperatives, with particular emphasis on social inclusion and service to the most vulnerable.
- The implementation of tax and financing policies that support the operation of social cooperatives and other social institutions for the promotion of human services and the development of public policy.
- The creation of local and regional civil councils that manage the collaboration and co-construction of human services through the joint participation of civil and governmental bodies.
- The adoption of participatory budgeting—including free and open access to government data—for human services at local, regional, and national levels.
- The restriction of public funding exclusively to non-profit and democratic, user-controlled organizations providing essential human and social services.

A prime example of this approach to the decentralization and democratization of human services is in Italy.[8] There, social cooperatives have a special mandate to provide social care services to the whole community, not just their members. Social cooperatives work closely with local government authorities to identify service needs, design services, and negotiate the terms of service delivery, including budgets, performance monitoring, and quality control.

Realizing this vision entails reclaiming fundamental sovereign governmental powers that have been undermined by deregulation, privatization, and global trade agreements that seek to entrench the power and privileges of corporations and the elites that control them.

Both processes must be organized and led by progressive forces in civil society simultaneously.

In modern times, the regulatory role of the state has swung from the promotion of either the private sector through its support of the capitalist economy, or the redistributive function of government through state control of economic planning. Both are flawed. The first submits the public and social economies and the public interest to the requirements of capital; the second submits the private and social economies to the needs of centralized planning and the controlling bureaucracies of the state. Both models come at unsustainably high economic and social costs.

The co-design and delivery of social care is supported through a system of subsidiarity: local authorities identify service needs and commission service provision through accredited cooperative or other non-profit service groups. In turn, a complex infrastructure of consortia and cooperative networks enable user-controlled cooperatives to organize and scale up from local to municipal and regional levels of operation.

At each level, government decision-making and planning are counterbalanced by a commensurate level of organization representing the interests of service users and workers in service design and delivery. In effect, the social economy has generated a parallel system of representative civic organization that collaborates with the state and holds it accountable with respect to the provision of social care to citizens.

The co-construction of public goods and services through an institutional framework fosters the public/social partnerships at the heart of The Partner State. The underlying need, then, is for a policy framework that radically recasts the state's role from one of dominating control over the production of public goods and services, to one of *promoting and enabling the civil production of goods and services as a form of protected commons.*

Social Markets

It is not possible to advance a convincing theory of the social economy without a corresponding theory of a social market that corresponds to it and provides its economic foundation. Without a social market supporting and reflecting the values and operations of the entities that comprise it, the social economy remains a vaporous and half-realized idea.

What then *is* a social market?

Just as a commercial market makes possible the types of production and exchange relations that generate surplus value (profit), a social market facilitates the creation of social relationships whose purpose is providing services to people. As opposed to the production of exchangeable goods and services for commercial value, social markets sustain the production of *relational goods* for social value.

Relational goods are non-material goods that are products of the interpersonal relationships created between people. Human services examples include social care, education, counseling, and health care. Relational goods are produced and consumed by those interacting in the relationship; the relationship *itself* is the primary object and benefit. Thus, while relational goods are goods, they are not *commodities*. The sale of a relational good immediately destroys its relational, or social, character. This implies that while they have social value, they have no market price. How then can they be valuated and exchanged in a market?

What are needed are new social and economic policies that recognize and enlarge the social and mutual foundations of the social economy. These policies and the market they create must be based on the principles at the heart of social economy organizations and of the social economy— *reciprocity, mutuality,* and *social benefit.*

The creation of sustainable social markets entails:

1 The ability of social economy organizations to raise capital by issuing social capital shares or using social currencies.
2 The development of social market exchanges that facilitate the valuation and exchange of non-commercial social goods and services.

3   The provision of social financing controlled by civil institutions independently of both the state and the private sector.
4   The operation of civil institutions to support of research, education, training, organization, and the continuous development of social economy organizations.

Of all the challenges impeding the social economy's growth and potential, the difficulty in accessing and controlling capital is surely the most crippling and deserves immediate attention. Of the many ways that public policy can expand social economy organizations' capacities, rethinking and reforming tax policy ranks among the most important and potent.

One approach is to provide tax benefits and exemptions for investments in social economy organizations. Tax-exempt contributions sourced from within civil society would mitigate social economy organizations' dependence on the state and lessen the perpetual rationing of capital when state funding is tight. But for this to happen, the outmoded idea of non-profits as organizations whose goals are incompatible with the generation and utilization of capital (profit) has to be left behind.

All enterprises, whether commercial or social, must generate a profit (or surplus in the case of co-operatives) to survive. The question is: to what purpose is this profit or surplus put? Is it private or social? The case of cooperatives clearly shows how profit can be a social good as well as a private one.

Cooperatives are a form of social economy organization whose surplus is collectively owned and utilized by its members for their mutual benefit. When non-profits reinvest their surplus in community services, this too is profit transmuted into a common good. And just as private capital is bent on privatizing social wealth, the social economy focuses on ways to *socialize* capital.

A social economy understanding of the market and profit makes it possible to rethink non-profit legislation. Why not allow non-profits to issue shares to raise capital, accumulate capital in the form of undistributed reserves for the pursuit of social ends, and invest in fellow social economy organizations and institutions that share the same purpose? The development of social purpose capital now possible in cooperatives should be extended to the whole of the social economy, with the proviso that this asset's use be transparent and democratically accountable to contributors and service users.

Without such accountability, capital accumulated by an organization for social purposes could be diverted to pursue private interests—as is sometimes the case with non-profits that have no structure for accountability to stakeholders. What is central in protecting the pursuit of social ends is not the conventional prohibition on accumulating and distributing profit, but rather the social constraint imposed by democratic accountability on the use of that profit.

One example of a social market, operating through the use of a social currency, is Fureai Kippu. This reciprocity-based time-banking system was developed in 1995 in Japan to provide care for the elderly. Fureai Kippu literally means "Ticket for a Caring Relationship" and refers to the ticket or credit earned by volunteering time to help seniors with physical, home, and emotional care.[9]

According to 2012 unpublished estimates, 148 or the 391 operating branches of Fureai Kippu are run by independent small grassroots groups and another 84 are run by local government or quasi-government bodies. The remaining 159 branches are run by two non-profit organizations with wider networks whose branches accept credit transfers. The largest Fureai Kippu organization, the Nippon Active Life Club (NALC), has over 30,000 members in 133 branches nationwide.

Fureai Kippu's strict time-banking model tracks earned credits and then reimburses volunteer time accordingly. In some branches, earned credits are redeemed in services for the volunteer or relatives. In others, volunteers receive a combination of earned time credits and cash. In both models, dependent users of services may pay a small user fee if ill health or incapacity keeps them from earning time credits, and such fees fund any cash payments to volunteers.

Like time-banking initiatives elsewhere, Fureai Kippu generates positive impacts on top of the obvious social benefit of providing good care to the elderly.[10] Benefits include building personal relationships and expanding social connections, improving participants' mental and physical health; promoting mutuality and responsibility in the care of vulnerable people; and, helping to create a more equal relationship between caregivers and recipients. Requiring Japanese citizenship, the systems is no panacea, but it does offer a civil model of care that is more cost-effective, flexible, and humane than expensive "top- down" models typically associated with state care provision.

The social markets generated by reciprocity-based exchange systems like Fureai Kippu show how producing social value can spawn an entirely new form of market. There is no reason why vouchers or other mechanisms for valuing and exchanging service to others or to the broader community could not be extended throughout a society's entire social fabric. Aided by civil institutions that organize and coordinate reciprocal exchanges, social markets can valorize socially beneficial services.

Along with the production of social value, the evolution of social markets requires making a universal citizen's income a basic right so all individuals could devote some of their time to the production of social goods and services.[11] This right would also ensure that immaterial cultural wealth, such as fine art, music, craftsmanship, and knowledge creation, can be sustained and offer viable livelihoods outside the capitalist market.

Returning to tax rates more like those of the 1950s–1960s (upwards of 47 percent for corporations), taxing capital gains and wealth as well as income, and eliminating tax loopholes and offshore tax havens could easily finance a universal basic income. Redistributing wealth in this way would eliminate the economic insecurity and precarity that currently haunts growing numbers of citizens in capitalist economies.

Money and Investment

If economic democracy is the basis for an alternative to capitalism, the linchpin to system change is social control over capital, especially the creation of money and the management of investment.

When the Bank of England disclosed in 2014 that money in modern economies is created by commercial banks creating new debt, most people were duly surprised that these banks weren't still simply lending out the money they receive from depositors.[12] Since money is created by banks in the form of new loans, disguised as deposits, which are then circulated as currency, the mere *creation* of money has become an endless source of wealth delivered to the owners of private banks through the interest charged on loans. As Thomas Picketty has shown, this system is the primary source of wealth inequality in our societies.[13]

It need not be so. Money can be conceived as a public good. The creation of a publicly owned bank responsible for generating debt-free money as a public resource has been tested and was for decades (1935–1974) the operating model for the Bank of Canada, which used interest-free money to finance such major infrastructure projects as the St. Lawrence Seaway, the Trans-Canada Highway, public housing, financial aid for veterans, and the development of the federal health care system. Other examples of publicly owned banks include the Reconstruction Finance Corporation (1932–1957) and the Bank of North Dakota in the US, the Central Bank of New Zealand, and Kreditanstalt für Wiederaufbau (KfW) in Germany.

If governments today are trapped in debt and unable to invest in public services and public infrastructure, it is partly because they borrow their money from private banks at interest. For 108 years (1867–1974), the Government of Canada's accumulated debt was nearly a flat line, amounting to just over $21 billion.[14] But around 1974, the federal debt began to grow exponentially and by 2017 the debt had ballooned to 671.25 billion. Not coincidentally, 1974 was the year that the Government of Canada was persuaded by the Bank for International Settlements (BIS) to start borrowing from private creditors, on the false pretext that borrowing from public banks at very low interest rates would cause inflation.[15] The change to private sector financing made public debt soar, and now the interest on the national debt of 84 percent of GDP is the single largest item in the federal budget.[16]

Once again putting public banks in charge of money creation and of financing public spending is fundamental to exerting social control over capital and the financial sector. Nothing would prevent private banks from lending for private ventures. But with a public bank setting low interest rates, private banks would occupy a specific—and contained—niche in the private capital market that could function without compromising the flow of credit necessary for businesses to operate. Strict controls on speculative banking and separating high-risk investment banking from savings banks, as the Glass-Steagall Act in the United States once provided, would further contain risk.

Besides supplying private banks with currency at interest, a public bank would be a key source of investment capital for the social economy and, on grounds that social economy enterprises primarily provide social benefit, would offer social enterprises lower rates of interest than those available to profit-making banks and capitalist enterprises. This provision alone would promote the growth of the social economy. Other forms of cooperative and social financing, including credit unions and other community capital organizations, could also be supported with preferential taxation and public policies to encourage the growth of financial institutions owned and controlled by their users and by local communities.

Promoting social control of capital could also entail the creation of localized social currencies. While a nationally accepted currency establishes a national economy's monetary foundation, other forms of social currency are extremely effective at promoting local economic development, especially amid economic crises and shortages of conventional credit. Social currencies—whether Greenbacks in the US, Wörgl town currency in Austria, WIR cooperative currency in Denmark, or the Patacónes currency in Argentina—have been used to increase the circulation of local goods and services without incurring new debt.

While recognizing that social control over capital requires, at minimum, the establishment of public financial institutions, the governance structure of these institutions is what makes them transparent and accountable. One way to establish democratic control is to organize a publicly owned Central Bank as a multi-stakeholder public utility based on a federated structure representing different stakeholders and different levels of service, from the local to district and regional levels. This model is currently used by the credit union system, which federates local credit unions into regional and national administrative bodies that are democratically accountable to their member cooperatives.

In a multi-stakeholder structure, a public central bank could have a board selected by the financial organizations that it serves, including locally constituted cooperative banks (credit unions), registered community capital organizations, private banks, and government representatives. As a public benefit utility, a publicly owned and democratically structured central bank would be far more responsive to the public interest through its direct accountability to the civil, state, and private interests it is required to serve.

Corporations

The question of social controls over the size and influence of corporate power has a long history. Beginning in the late 1800s, the rise of monopolies in such key sectors of the American economy as railroads and transport, oil, coal, banking, telecommunications, and agriculture prompted government to prevent the control of markets by corporations and to protect the principle of free competition. Federal anti-trust laws, what the Supreme Court called a "charter of freedom," were passed to break up monopolies and preserve Americans' freedom to start businesses and participate in economic life.[17] As stated by Republican Senator John Sherman, author of the landmark Sherman Anti-Trust Act of 1890, "If we will not endure a king as a political power we should not endure a king over the production, transportation, and sale of any of the necessaries of life."[18] More recently, US anti-trust legislation has been used to keep Microsoft from dominating the software industry and digital communications. Clearly, there are strong precedents for limiting the power of huge corporations to dominate markets.

The remaining question is whether measures like those adopted in the late 19th century to curtail the rise of cartels are feasible today. With the passage of decisions such as Citizen's United by the US Supreme Court, and millionaires and billionaires dominating all branches of government, it is doubtful whether even existing statutes can be enforced to limit corporate power in the economy.

Regardless, we must still consider alternatives. Certainly, applying anti-monopoly legislation to limit the size and influence of capital is crucial to a pluralist economy like that envisaged here. Also needed is a mechanism for democratizing and distributing the accumulated wealth and organizational resources of large corporations and for diversifying the private sector. Here are a dozen ways to accomplish this:

1 Enterprises over a certain size (say, 500 employees), or controlling more than a maximum allowable percentage of a market, must divest and subdivide into separate enterprises.
2 The ownership of subdivided enterprises must first be offered to employees, giving them a right of first refusal.
3 No enterprise may be sold to a third party without first being offered for purchase to its employees.
4 No enterprise may apply for bankruptcy without first being offered to its employees for takeover and turnaround.

5 In cases in which employees are insufficiently interested in ownership, legislation requires worker representation on the company's boards of directors, as in Germany now.
6 The provision for worker representation on company boards applies to *all* enterprises over a certain size (perhaps ten employees), whether privately or publicly owned.
7 By law, all employees working in enterprises of ten employees or more must be represented by unions.
8 In private enterprises, profit-sharing with employees—over and above wages—must be mandatory.
9 A living wage for all employees, whether of private companies, public corporations, or cooperatives, is mandatory.
10 All enterprises, regardless of their structure, must set aside a portion of their profits in a common trust to be used to finance possible subdivision of the enterprise and transition to worker ownership.
11 On pain of fines or closure, all enterprises must operate in accordance with provisions that clearly account for the impact of their operations on both the natural and the social environment. Negative externalities must be identified through compulsory social and environmental audits and their costs incorporated and covered by the operations of the enterprise.
12 In addition to formal incorporation, all enterprises must base their operations on a formal social charter that is revocable if these other 11 provisions are contravened.

These measures would minimize the domination of any one enterprise model over markets and the economy and would also establish a regime in which workers gradually become owners and shareholders in the enterprises that employ them. Wealth would be distributed more fairly among those who contribute to its creation, and the rights of individual entrepreneurs and private businesses to participate in the economy would be ensured within a framework of sustainable social and environmental values.

Information and Communications Technology

Re-visioning production for social benefit is greatly influenced by the unprecedented organizational changes ushered in by the Information and Communications Technology (ICT) revolution. The emergence of *generative democracy* in particular embodies the features and possibilities of a new, distributed paradigm of production that new technologies make possible.

Social economy organization's structures, principles, and aims enable these organizations to make cooperative economic democracy work by activating social relations that both reflect and reinforce their principles and aims. This is where the distributive cyber logic of digital technology meets the distributed social logic of democratic practice.

In the early 20th century, the state's governance and production systems were modeled on the knowledge economies of industrial capitalism and the private corporation—mass production and the eclipse of artisanship, the Fordist assembly line, and the managerial principles of Taylorism, which de-skilled and dehumanized manual labor while concentrating design and operational control in a technical and managerial elite. Workers and consumers became mute objects in an impersonal productive system. This classic, centralized, top-down governance model was demanded by the industrial technology of the time and promoted by such influential figures as Andrew Ure.[19]

The ICT revolution has demolished—and reversed—the centralizing logic of this old model. Emergent technology relies on the conscious production and application of globalized knowledge in a continuous process of innovation through decentralized and distributed production networks.[20] ICTs have returned the focus to the individual and their personal connections. What persists, however—particularly in the public sector—are the old authoritarian power structures that struggle to manage and direct the design and provision of services in an economy that thrives on open rather than proprietary knowledge and on the cooperative social and economic networks spawning new forms of cooperative production. The digital commons and the free open source software movement (FOSS) are archetypes of this open and distributed social architecture, and demands for citizen participation in government decisions and access to state information reflect the dynamics of a new era.

Other aspects of state/civil relations affected by ICTs include:

- The relations of information in the Partner State's operations, in terms of both open information flows between partners and civil partners' access to the state's know-how.
- The way the state gains its information about civil society/economy to inform the planning and delivery of its services.
- The information economy *within* the state and the degree to which the creation and access to information are open and coordinated among government sections and agencies.
- The access to global know-how on public services by government and its agencies and civil society.
- The development of new forms of distributed production and the potential for their decentralization to the social economy.

In turn, these crucial elements of the state's social economy of knowledge need to be seen in the context of radical changes in contemporary capitalist production, distribution, and corporate organization in the age of ICT. These include:

- The shift from mass production to mass customization and the proliferation of product variety.

- The orientation of just-in-time production systems around consumer demands, and the shift from the supply push of Fordism to the demand pull of post-Fordism;
- The increase in "produsage" and consumer involvement in design, production, and service delivery.
- The flattening of organizational hierarchies and the distribution of complex planning and operations from the center to the periphery.
- The redesign of information flows within organizations and between organizations and their suppliers and markets, along with innovations in stakeholder involvement.
- The use of ICT in data mining to further customize marketing, crowd sourcing of innovative ideas, and the design and performance of products.

These changes are now well established in the private market and in the social economy in the field of social care.[21] However, their adoption has lagged in the public sphere. Any discussion of increased democracy and participation in state operations must take account of the changes that have been powered by the diffusion of ICT, coupled with the democratic governance structures of social economy organizations such as social cooperatives. This is not to say that what is good for the private economy is equally good for the public. The point here is how technology can harness the volition and interests of the individual, or the community, in the production of goods and services that respond to what people actually need and want. Here, technology design and democracy are closely linked. The issue of democratic control and accountability is very different in the construction and operation of nuclear power plants than it is with distributed energy systems based on, say, small-scale wind turbines or mini hydro. To use ICT merely to replicate centralized and hierarchical systems is to misunderstand these technologies' revolutionary potential to transform citizens and communities from commentators or informants on service design and construction into proactive and autonomous generators of services.

The privatization of public services has transferred much of the operational know-how and data to the private sector, leaching the state of professional capacity and knowledge and reducing the scope for citizen and workforce participation in public life. An alternative path starts with redesigning public service systems so that they are more open to citizen engagement and the incorporation of social knowledge.

Actions premised on citizens' capacity to influence government's behavior and priorities takes the transition to a new political economy beyond the formulation of new governance systems and their implementation through public policy. It involves broad-based political mobilization and protracted struggle at a scale not seen for generations—if ever.

Political struggle and the transition to new forms of political economy must occur at two levels simultaneously. One is the level of nations and national governments, where social affiliations and people most identify. The second is the global level of international networks and power circuits that ultimately determine the trajectory of political and economic development.

The evolution of transnational networks that embody a new paradigm of social and economic development—consider the pioneering Fairtrade movement here—is already far advanced. Yet, the transformative potential of online communities that utilize cooperative and commons systems to produce and share knowledge and other immaterial goods is a new modality altogether, one that could increase political mobilization, raise awareness, and flatten the hierarchical power structures that characterize capitalist production systems.[22]

Stateless Democracy

Is a political system in which generative democracy, cooperative commonwealth, and the revolutionary potential of new technologies combine to sustain a political economy dedicated to the common good even possible?

One answer might lie in the Rojava Revolution. When the Arab Spring ignited the insurgencies across the Arab world in 2011, the Kurdish people of the Rojava region in northern Syria initiated a revolution of their own. The social, economic, and political changes implemented in the three cantons known collectively as the Autonomous Regions of Rojava are unlike anything previously seen in the Middle East or the Arab lands, and they hold valuable lessons for those considering what a radical economic and political democracy might look like.

Jettisoning the obsession with national statehood that has bedeviled the Middle East, the Rojava Revolution rejects the state as inherently anti-democratic and an instrument of oligarchic control, capitalist exploitation, and gender oppression.[23] As described by Abdullah Ocalan, Rojava's Democratic Confederalism is:

> ...based on grass-roots participation. Its decision-making processes lie with the communities. Higher levels only serve the coordination and implementation of the will of the communities that send their delegates to the general assemblies.... the basic power of decision rests with the local grass-roots institutions.[24]

The system's foundation rests on the *communes*, voluntary citizen councils operating in neighborhoods, districts, municipalities, and cantons. In this nested system, representatives in the upper administrative tiers are elected from the citizen councils operating at more localized levels. Committees in each commune manage local community projects while larger projects, including infrastructure, are handled cooperatively by the canton and the communes. While the Rojava uses a parliamentary system to manage the cantons' legislative, political, and juridical affairs, the day-to-day practice of democracy is directly in citizens' hands, and each canton has its own autonomous Legislative Assembly. In a reversal of traditional federal principles, all decisions of the elected parliaments must be endorsed by the local councils before being implemented.

A complementary feature of Rojava's civil structure is a political coalition, the Movement for a Democratic Society or TEV-DEM, that congregates all the major civil-society organizations, whether political, religious, youth-oriented, academic, or ethnic. The citizen councils and TEV-DEM jointly comprise an autonomous civil society check on administrative operations. Thus, direct democracy occurs primarily within the context of non-state *civil* space, which in turn informs and validates the decisions to be carried out by the Democratic Self Administration. In short, this stateless democracy operates within the whole society, not just electoral institutions.

The Kurds of Rojava are also constructing a cooperative economy to organize and provide essential goods and services, especially focusing on food and agriculture. Hundreds of cooperatives are being established with support from TEV-DEM and the citizen councils. A small business and family-run private sector exists, but the overall aim is to maintain economic pluralism and to distribute as widely as possible the ownership, control, and benefits of economic activity to prevent the domination of the economy and markets by capital and the many outside interests competing for control of the region.

In Rojava, we can see how a form of Partner State with a clear aim of democratizing governance through the mobilization and empowerment of civil society could be achieved. While central authority remains for administrative purposes, it will "shift from controlling to coordinating and unifying the parts that make up the whole." With the gradual build-up of civil institutions and the transfer of decision-making authority to decentralized and self-managing civil bodies, the democratization of the state is closely linked to the democratization of the economy.

Admittedly, this model of direct democracy is hard for many to imagine in the context of large populations and pervasive centralized institutions. But the enhanced power of communication, knowledge sharing, and collaboration using digital platforms makes democratic decision-making at regional, national, and even international scales possible. ICT's promise applies to the operation of cooperative enterprises, the extension of cooperative economies and commons, and participatory decision-making in governance systems.

Yet, important as these tools are, they are not the ultimate form of the democracy we seek. In the end, the aim is to strengthen and preserve true, face-to-face communities; create enriching and empowering occupations and workplaces; and restore the intimate bonds of caring and service to others that give life depth. Cooperative commonwealth is an empty slogan without the physical communities where the principles of human solidarity and care for the planet come to life.

Conclusion

There has always been an element in society that forecasts the demise of human civilization—perhaps such worrying is hardwired into human consciousness. But today an overwhelming weight of scientific evidence shows that the world is amid an existential crisis from which there may be no return. Global warming is a fact of life, a new era of species extinction has begun, and the only debate now appears to be over how much damage human societies and the environment can endure. And there can be little remaining doubt that the driving force of environmental catastrophe is global capitalism.

The need for a new system is no longer only a moral imperative with respect to social justice. Human societies have always had to defend against the predatory instincts of those who would monopolize and control the means of life. Today, the imperative is existential. Unless civil societies create the means to democratize economies and exert social control over capital, neither politics nor economics will solve our collective human dilemma. The real issue is whether, and how, this systemic shift might come about.

Some argue that this shift is already under way in the emerging digital democracies that prefigure a new form of economy and a more open and equitable society. This view is optimistic and borders dangerously on techno-determinism. But it does reflect a deep and abiding sense that centralized, authoritarian systems of control—whether economic or political—must be challenged and overcome by genuine forms of democracy.

The power and privilege of elites must somehow be ended. Ruling classes are most dangerous, however, in times of crisis and impending collapse. The viciousness with which their interests will be protected is proportional to the threat posed by real prospects for change. Thus, just when radical reforms to the world's economic systems are desperately needed, what we witness is ever greater concentrations of wealth for the privileged accompanied by austerity and growing precarity for everyone else. The expropriation of public wealth by capital has become the new world order.

Ironically, something like a global New Deal would serve the long-term interests of the wealthy far better. But global elites appear caught up in a feeding frenzy coupled with a siege mentality: those in a position to will take as much as they can for as long as they can even if it means taking the world down with them.

Quite possibly, the only route to system change is the implosion of the global capitalist system, prompted by economic and environmental crises. The question then becomes what will take its place. Will it be the solidary forms of humane societies—of cooperation, reciprocity, mutual aid? Or will it be the tribalisms that thrive on competition, aggression, and the oppression of the weak? The outcome depends on the endurance of the alternatives we are creating now and whether we can mobilize politically to bring them to fruition.

Those of us working for system change must seek two outcomes—both of which entail exactly the same vision and work.

One aim is to create system change within the institutional framework of the current system. This means shifting political structures, public policies, power relations, and the narrative of our collective worldview. Through political organizing on a massive scale and a vision of economic democracy founded on the primacy of the common good, something like a Partner State could emerge.

The other aim is the creation of those models of humane economies that embody a new vision and carry it forward, regardless of the wider political environment. It is the realization of the change we seek in every space and opportunity that presents itself. It is a continuous and never-ending process and, as always, driven by the natural human impulse for social justice.

We must aim for the first outcome and prepare for the second.

Notes

1 George Monbiot, "Neoliberalism – The Ideology at the Root of all Our Problems," *The Guardian*, April 15, 2016, https://www.theguardian.com/books/2016/apr/15/neoliberalism-ideology-problem-george-monbiot.
2 The evidence of this is clear in the damage done to the operations and the reputations of cooperatives in such places as the former satellite states of the Soviet Union, or in postcolonial governments of Africa or Latin America, where cooperatives were used as proxies of the State.
3 Tito Menzani and Vera Zamagni, "Cooperative Networks in the Italian Economy," *Enterprise & Society* 11, 1 (March 2010): 98–127.
4 Restakis, *Humanizing the Economy: Co-operatives in the Age of Capital* (Gabriola, BC: New Society Publishers, 2010), Chapter 5.
5 Restakis, *Humanizing the Economy: Co-operatives in the Age of Capital.*
6 For a fuller discussion on social markets, see: John Restakis and Margie Mendell, "Public Policy for a Social Economy," *FlOK Society*, 2014, http://floksociety.org/docs/Ingles/3/3.2.pdf.
7 Restakis, *Humanizing the Economy: Co-operatives in the Age of Capital*, Chapter 6.
8 Restakis, *Humanizing the Economy: Co-operatives in the Age of Capital*, Chapter 6.
9 Sawayaka Welfare Foundation (SWF), 1993.
10 Gill Seyfang, "Time Banks: Rewarding Community Self-help in the Inner City?," *Community Development Journal* 39, 1 (2004): 62–71; Ed Collom,

"The Motivations, Engagement, Satisfaction, Outcomes, and Demographics of Time Bank Participants: Survey Findings from a U.S. System," *International Journal of Community Currency Research* 11 (2007): 36–83, http://dx.doi.org/10.15133/j.ijccr.2007.004; Lucie Ozanne, "Learning To Exchange Time: Benefits and Obstacles To Time Banking," *International Journal of Community Currency Research* 14, A (2010): 1–16, http://dx.doi.org/10.15133/j.ijccr.2010.002.

11 Note here the need to consider Universal Basic Income as a policy that *follows* the establishment of a Partner State, rather than a policy enacted in the current set up whereby the control of governments by capital interests could allow the use of UBI to eliminate existing social safety nets and create an even more precarious and dependent citizenry.

12 Michael McLeay, Amar Radia, and Ryland Thomas, "Money Creation in the Modern Economy," American Monetary Institute, Quarterly Bulletin, 2014, http://www.monetary.org/wp-content/uploads/2016/03/money-creation-in-the-modern-economy.pdf.

13 Thomas Piketty, *Capital in the 21st Century*, trans., Arthur Goldhammer (Cambridge, MA: The Belknap Press of Harvard University Press, 2014).

14 Qualicum Institute, http://qualicuminstitute.ca/federal-debt/.

15 Ellen Brown, "Oh Canada! Imposing Austerity on the World's Most Resource-rich Country," April 1, 2012, https://ellenbrown.com/2012/04/01/oh-canada-imposing-austerity-on-the-worlds-most-resource-rich-country/.

16 Where Your Tax Dollar Goes, Department of Finance Canada, http://www.fin.gc.ca/taxdollar06/text/html/taxdollar06_-eng.asp.

17 Appalachian Coals, Inc. v. United States, 288 U.S. 344, 359–60 (1933): "As a charter of freedom, the act has a generality and adaptability comparable to that found to be desirable in constitutional provisions."

18 Bills and Debates in Congress Relating to Trusts, Fiftieth Congress to Fifty Eighth Congress.

19 Restakis, *Humanizing the Economy: Co-operatives in the Age of Capital.*

20 Yochai Benkler, *The Wealth of Networks: How Social Production Transforms Markets and Freedom* (New Haven, CT: Yale University Press, 2007).

21 Restakis, *Humanizing the Economy: Co-operatives in the Age of Capital.*

22 Bauwens, "Why the P2P and Commons Movement Must Act Trans-Locally and Trans-Nationally," P2PF Wiki, http://wiki.p2pfoundation.net/Why_the_P2P_and_Commons_Movement_Must_Act_Trans-Locally_and_Trans-Nationally.

23 Abdullah Ocalan, *Democratic Confederalism*, International Initiative (London: Transmedia Publishing, 2011), http://www.freeocalan.org/wp-content/uploads/2012/09/Ocalan-Democratic-Confederalism.pdf.

24 Ocalan, *Democratic Confederalism.*

Chapter 24

An Introduction to Participatory Economics

Michael Albert

People now fighting economic injustice have no right to decide how future people should live. But we do have a responsibility to provide an institutional setting that helps future people decide for themselves what their own conditions of life and work should be. To this end, participatory economics—or parecon, or participatory socialism, whichever name you prefer—describes the core institutions required to generate solidarity, equity, self-management, and an ecologically sound and classless economy.

Parecon proposes self-management by workers' and consumers' councils, federated by industry and region, as society's primary venues of economic decision-making. "Self-management" means people and groups have decision-making influence in proportion to how much the decision in question affects them.

If an issue overwhelmingly affects just one person, that person should make the decision—albeit often in context of broader guidelines already decided by a wider range of affected participants. In the case of issues affecting overwhelmingly a work team, that work team should decide—again, typically abiding by broader guidelines addressing, say, the duration of the workday and the overall plan for production.

Sometimes the best way to get self-management is to seek consensus. Other times, a simple "one person, one vote" majority rule or other method may be better. A key self-management principle is that participants must not only have appropriate say, but must also understand the circumstances and information needed to develop relevant opinions, engage in relevant discussions, and set workable agendas.

Parecon-ish equity means you get more income for working harder, longer, or under worse conditions, as long as you are producing things people want.

Imagine two people who do the same job, for the same duration, at the same intensity, under the same conditions, and so, by the above norm, have the same income. Now, suppose one person wants more income to consume more. Parecon recognizes that people's tastes for consumption goods and services will vary. But, says parecon, what makes the accumulation of more income fair is if the person wanting more arranges to work longer or harder or under worse conditions.

Conversely, suppose a person doesn't care as much about consumption of goods and services, but wants more free time. Parecon says that fair compensation practices should allow that person to arrange to work fewer hours and take a smaller share of the social product. Overall, the benefits and costs any economic actor faces should be the same as those faced by everyone else because we are all entitled to comparable conditions of life. The impact on "conditions of life" of work plus consumption taken together as a whole should be the same for everyone.

Consider a would-be surgeon who has to undertake a college education, medical school, and an internship prior to becoming a practicing surgeon earning a surgeon's pay. The surgeon's pay needs to be very high, claims the professional economist, journalist, or teacher, or we'll have a shortage of surgeons, and the same is true for being a lawyer, accountant, professor, high-level designer, scientist, and so on. Lacking high pay to attract new members, experts tell us, these (expert) professions will die for want of people doing them.

Suppose that instead of simply accepting the expert's familiar claim, we test it. Think of telling a student leaving high school and hoping to be a surgeon that a big change in society has made it the case that surgeon's salaries, instead of being $600,000 a year, are henceforth going to be $80,000 a year. Will the student then reject the idea of going to college, attending medical school, and being an intern before becoming a surgeon because he or she could immediately begin a life-long career working in a coal mine, for the same $80,000 a year, or even for more? Try asking some students as I have done many, many times. None will say they will switch—not one. And this is even without noting that in a participatory economy education is free and higher education is remunerated as work. Incentives are needed precisely when one is being asked to do something more onerous, or more time consuming, or more intense. But you don't need an incentive to work shorter hours, at lower intensity, or under less onerous conditions.

Because some time, even in a worthy economy, has to go to work that isn't as intrinsically rewarding as playing, studying, resting, or being with family, and some time even has to go to downright onerous work that is intrinsically unpleasant and unfulfilling, even when we understand and are motivated by the benefits the work bestows on society, incentives matter. Parecon provides them.

The additional information issue, often overlooked, is this: Some socialists might reply to the above, "No, we don't need to correlate income and work. We just need people to understand the importance of each role and what the responsible, moral choice to make is, and they will act on that understanding." The person adds,

> I get that parecon has incentives which will yield a wonderful allotment of people's energies and a distribution of the social output that is

just, fair, and rewarding for all. But even so, I believe we can get that same allotment without bribing folks with payment for labor. That is demeaning, so why should we have payments?

A first answer is that thinking of income rights as bribery is a bit strange, unless we are talking about income as it is in vile economies. But more tellingly, if we disconnect work from income by having people work however much and at whatever they want while also having them consume however much and whatever they want, without requiring a connection between the two decisions, we won't get as good an allotment as with the participatory approach. People will typically choose to work too little for the social good to be optimally met and will likewise choose to take too much from the system, which will fail to deliver because the available output will fall well short of available demands for income.

This shortfall of work and the excess of demand will not occur because people are greedy, lazy, or irresponsible, but because in this setting people will have no way to know what is responsible and moral, and they will not and should not wish to mistakenly police themselves into working too much or having too little income.

Moreover, good people in a good economy should in fact prefer to work fewer hours, less intensely, and under less onerous conditions for a given income. And the same people should want to receive more income, for a given number of work hours, intensity, and onerousness.

Indicating that they want less work and more income is in fact critically important to the economy innovating to make that happen, to the extent that (i) it is possible and desirable to do so and (ii) consistent with acceptable social and ecological implications.

No one can know—in the abstract—what is a fair amount to offer to produce, or what is a fair amount to ask to consume, because what is fair depends hugely on the available tools, resources, knowledge, needs, desires, and so on. Fairness is not prescribed on a tablet but instead has to emerge from a discussion of what people want as their income, working conditions, and working hours. By disconnecting production and consumption decisions, we would lose the means of knowing what is responsible, leaving people to curb their own appetites and desires rather than express them. It probably shouldn't need saying, but for completeness: people being able to receive income from merely doing anything they want is also hugely problematic. I would like to play professional tennis at Wimbledon, but as it would have no social value it should not be remunerated.

Without indications not just of people wanting x (where x is some good such as a product, some leisure, a type of work, clean air, and so on) but of how much they want x relative to their other preferences, there is no way for producers to know how much x it is appropriate to produce, or where to invest.

Something close to self-managing councils and equitable remuneration is very often adopted in real circumstances by at least some real workplaces. Worker cooperatives have no owners and typically don't reward property, power, or output, but instead tend to equalize wages and utilize a workplace council for decisions. So do occupied factories, as in hundreds of instances in Argentina not so long ago. In such cases the owner either leaves, or is ejected, or didn't exist from the outset. Salaries are equalized but then typically vary for duration. Councils function democratically and often use the flexible means described above, with teams deciding their own circumstances and using different tallying for different situations.

However, a problem often arises. In time, initial excitement starts to dissipate. Workers start to skip council meetings. A few people wind up determining options. Income differentials enlarge. Alienation ensues. And, finally, participants blame themselves. "This is who we are," they think. "It must be in our genes to have growing disparities of income, power, and circumstance. We tried for a better world. It didn't work. There really is no alternative."

To counter this depressing outcome, participatory economics balances all jobs so they each have roughly the same overall empowerment effect. What does this look like? How does it prevent the dissolution noted above?

In corporate divisions of labor, about 80 percent of the workforce perform jobs whose component tasks are overwhelmingly disempowering. These jobs tend to fragment workers from each other, separate workers from information about decisions, involve workers in rote and repetitive activity, and in all these ways cause a steady decline in workers' skills, confidence, knowledge of workplace relations, and familiarity with making choices. The other 20 percent of the workforce performs jobs whose tasks typically enhance ties to others, increase social skills, provide access to decision contexts, enlarge confidence and knowledge of workplace relations, and, in general, empower people to participate in and impact decisions.

Parecon's claim is that this corporate division of labor creates a class division between those who monopolize empowering work, the "coordinator class," and those who are left with overwhelmingly disempowering work, the working class. The coordinators' position in the economy conveys advantages, up to and including ruling class status in "coordinatorism" (often called 20th-century socialism).

When adopted in occupied factories or in cooperatives all over the world, the corporate division of labor leads to 20 percent of the workforce not only setting agendas and choosing actions, but eventually reimposing inequitable incomes that ultimately lead to ruling class status for themselves. This is all the old crap coming back. It is the cause of the dissolution of gains in so many situations. For this reason, in addition to self-managing councils and equitable remuneration, participatory economics says we need a new division of labor called "balanced job complexes" if we are to have real self-management and real classlessness.

The fourth defining feature participatory socialism offers has to do with arriving at an optimal level of workplace and consumer inputs and outputs and their distribution throughout the economy. History offers three main choices for such allocation decisions: markets, central planning, and voluntary self-regulation.

Markets intrinsically impose antisocial motivations and inequitable remunerative norms as well as vast power differentials and ecological suicide. They violate self-management, and elevate a coordinator class above workers.

Central planning intrinsically creates that same class division, and even more obviously violates self-management. It also tends to violate ecological preservation and accrues excess wealth for the planners (and the whole coordinator class) while promoting obedience and domination that in turn spread to other areas of life.

Voluntary self-regulation is a wonderful sentiment, but as a method for resource allocation, it typically assumes away important underlying complexities. For people to self-regulate in accord with worthy values and real possibilities requires a means for people to determine what qualifies as worthy choices regarding both work and consumption, a context that makes people's well-being depend on and enhance the well-being of others, and a process that apportions self-managing say to each. In fact, parecon's participatory planning is built on the idea of viable, collective self-regulation. That is precisely what it delivers, but without assuming away complexities.

The inclusion of corporate divisions of labor subverts the prior attainment of council-based self-management and equitable remuneration by the intrinsic class implications the monopolization of empowering work imposes on all actors. That is why we need balanced job complexes.

Similarly, choosing either markets or central planning subverts the prior attainment of council-based self-management, equitable remuneration, and balanced job complexes as a result of the psychology, operational behaviors, and ensuing class implications these allocation methods impose on all actors. That is why participatory socialism proposes a cooperative, negotiated, self-regulating allocation alternative to both markets and central planning that is compatible with its other three defining features.

Good allocation requires wise and informed collective self-regulation to arrive at optimal levels of economic inputs and outputs that meet needs and develop potential while fostering solidarity, enhancing equity, and enacting self-management. It must do so in light of an accurate awareness of the true social and ecological costs and benefits of all of our choices.

This is a big list of virtues, but it is what participatory socialism claims to achieve with participatory planning. Workers' and consumers' councils present proposals, and implement collective self-management by interactively and cooperatively refining them by negotiating levels of inputs and outputs that are consistent with and depend on the norms of equitable remuneration and labor apportionment to balanced job complexes. That is, they collectively self-regulate.

There is no top or bottom. There is no center. There is no competitive rat race. Solidarity is produced by the requisites of the process, as is self-management. And yet the participatory vision does not assume a population of omniscient and morally saintly people. Instead, simple structures enable, facilitate, and make such results the rational, personal, and community-serving aim of everyone. That is participatory economics.

Yet, to exist in a society participatory economics needs that society to have compatible culture and community, kinship and education, polity, and adjudication. These matters are no less important than economics, and vision for these aspects of life must be compatible with one another as with economics vision, just as economics must also be compatible with new relations of these other facets of life.

And finally, having a vision for economy as here summarized, or for polity, culture, or kinship, or even all combined, is one thing. Attaining it is another. A participatory socialist vision must, to prove its worth, inform strategy for change. That's a topic for further exploration.

Chapter 25

Participatory Economics and the Next System

Robin Hahnel

Neoliberal capitalism is not working well for most of us. Growing inequality of wealth and income is putting the fabled American middle class in danger of becoming a distant memory as American children for the first time face economic prospects worse than those their parents enjoyed. We suffer from more frequent financial "shocks" and linger in recession far longer than in the past. Education and healthcare systems are being decimated. And environmental destruction continues to escalate as we stand on the verge of triggering irreversible, even cataclysmic, climate change.

Yet, amid escalating economic dysfunction, new economic initiatives are sprouting up everywhere. Diverse "new" or "future" economy initiatives all reject the economics of competition and greed and aspire instead to develop an economics of equitable cooperation that is environmentally sustainable. What they also have in common is that these initiatives must survive in a hostile economic environment. Helping these exciting and hopeful future economy initiatives grow and stay true to their principles will require us to think more clearly about what kind of "next system" these initiatives point toward.

Each council and federation must revise and resubmit its own proposal until it meets with approval from the other councils. How does the approval process work?

Present economies are not just environmentally unsustainable, they are crashing vital ecosystems at breakneck speed. Absent a massive Green New Deal in the next several decades that replaces fossil fuels with renewable energy sources and dramatically increases energy efficiency in agriculture, industry, transportation, and the built environment, humans risk the lemmings' proverbial fate.

The question we should ask about any economic system now is whether its basic institutions and decision-making procedures afford creative ideas and proposals about how to relate to the natural environment a fair and friendly hearing. The profit motive ignores many environmental effects unmeasured in commerce and drives producers to expand or die. Markets encourage economic activities that pollute and discourage activities that preserve and restore valuable ecosystems; they promote throughput-intensive private consumption at the expense of less throughput-intensive social consumption; and they promote consumerism at the expense of leisure—all to the detriment of the environment.

If capitalism is fast-tracking environmental destruction and it can't accept or act on ideas for better relating to the natural environment, can the basic institutions of a participatory economy create a setting and incentives that promote judicious relations with the natural world? When organic farming, recycling, locally grown produce, smart growth, public transportation, energy conservation, solar and wind power, more leisure, and more public and fewer private goods are proposed in a participatory economy, will they be discriminated against, as they often are in capitalism, or afforded a fair hearing?

How? If the long-run plan calls for more overall investment, the amount of consumption available to the present generation in this year's annual plan falls accordingly. If the long-run plan calls for reducing the automobile fleet and expanding rail service in the future, the amount of investment and productive resources this year's annual plan can allocate to worker councils making automobiles shrinks while that allocated to worker councils making trains grows. If the long-run plan calls for reducing national carbon emissions by 25 percent over five years, the national consumer federation must reduce the amount of allowable carbon emissions in each of the next five annual plans accordingly. Major changes in the energy, transportation, and housing sectors, as well as conversions from polluting to "green" technologies and products, are all determined by the long-run planning process, where federations can express preferences for investments in environmental protection and restoration as easily as they can ask for investments that facilitate future increases in private consumption.

Annual participatory planning is designed to estimate the detrimental and beneficial effects of economic choices on the environment accurately and incorporate them into the overall costs and benefits that must be weighed. Long-run participatory planning makes issues of intergenerational equity and efficiency as clear as possible. Moreover, longer- and shorter-run planning processes can be integrated: information revealed during subsequent annual planning processes can replace mistaken information used initially in longer-term plans, which can be revised as more accurate information becomes available. But even so, there is no guarantee that future generations and the environment might not be slighted. Some, like Dr. Seuss's Lorax, will have to speak up in the long-run participatory planning process when they see peers neglecting future generations and the environment.

The model of a participatory economy is a concrete and comprehensive proposal for how any national economy might be organized to best promote economic democracy, economic justice, solidarity, and environmental sustainability while using scarce productive resources and labor efficiently. Since it is unlikely this proposal would be taken up in every country at the same time, those who do would have to coexist in a global economy where many countries are still capitalist. But how?

The same logic applies to international financial investment. Global efficiency gains can be realized when investment raises productivity more in the borrowing country than it would in the lending country. As long as the interest rate distributes more than half of the benefit to the less developed country, international financial investment is consistent with reducing global inequality. Naturally, a participatory economy would play a leading role in an international coalition to make the 50-percent rule a cornerstone of a "new international economic order." But even before the global economic system is reformed to be fairer, nothing stops a participatory economy from taking part in international trade and investment to its own benefit without violating its fundamental commitment to economic justice as long as it abides by the 50-percent rule.

To be sure, taking more of our increases in labor productivity as leisure rather than consumption, and substituting less throughput-intensive consumption goods for more throughput-intensive goods is crucial to avoiding further environmental degradation. And a participatory economy promotes both these changes. But even without these changes, labor productivity and the economic well-being it bring could continue to rise as fast as throughput efficiency rises without putting increased strain on the natural environment.

A participatory economy requires replacing private corporations and markets with social ownership and participatory planning. And, a popular majority must support these changes for a fully democratic economy to work. That means in most countries a transition strategy spanning decades will be necessary. Yet, this may not be true everywhere.

Likewise, at any time the Cuban government could turn the Committees for Defense of the Revolution (CDRs) into neighborhood consumption councils, and replace its antiquated authoritarian planning system with participatory planning—and thereby at long last unleash the creative self-managing capabilities of Cuban workers and consumers. Progressive political parties that won elections in other Latin American countries such as Bolivia, Ecuador, Brazil, Chile, and Uruguay during the "pink tide" could also have taken steps toward implementing various parts of a participatory economy, as could the government of Andres Manuel Lopez Obrador in Mexico today.

Only when a majority is sufficiently disgusted by corporate rule, and confident that workers and consumers can manage and coordinate their own economic affairs, will it be possible to leave capitalism in the dustbin of history and launch an economic system supportive of sustainable, equitable cooperation. In most of the world, this will happen only when economic reform movements—the labor movement, the anti-corporate movement, the environmental movement, the consumer movement, the poor people's movement, and the global justice movement—have all grown more powerful by earning the support of far more people than they have today. And it will be possible only when the public has seen many more successful experiments in equitable cooperation—worker-owned cooperatives, consumer-owned cooperatives, community-supported agriculture initiatives, egalitarian and sustainable intentional-living communities, community land trusts, community development corporations, cities practicing participatory budgeting, B-corps, socially responsible investment funds, or enterprising municipalities that capture the new wealth created by city planning for the citizenry instead of ceding it to landlords and developers.

We needn't fear for lack of potentially game-changing crises in the future. Financialized capitalism, capitalism running on fossil fuels, plutocratic capitalism—in short, modern day neoliberal capitalism—can be counted on to run roughshod over majority interests and produce economic and environmental crises in the process. But these crises will help move us forward only if they lead to larger reform movements and more experiments in equitable cooperation. Crises undermine confidence in ruling elites and dominant institutions, but if new progressive political leadership isn't ready to fill the vacuum with new institutions, the result will simply be increased popular cynicism.

The vision or model of a participatory economy outlined here demonstrates that a coherent, feasible, and desirable next economic system is perfectly possible and rebuts the "disenabling" myth that "There Is No Alternative" (TINA) to capitalism and command planning.[1] The model is not a transition strategy or program to take us from today's economics of competition and greed to an economics of equitable cooperation. But it does point to the kinds of institutions and practices that might and so has implications for strategy.

Goals

The institutions and decision-making procedures of a participatory economy are designed to promote economic democracy, economic justice, environmental sustainability, and human solidarity—all while achieving economic efficiency. Unfortunately, most economic visionaries who support these goals remain vague about concrete particulars. That's a serious mistake since which economic institutions and procedures are appropriate typically depends on how one defines them. Here, *economic democracy* means decision-making input in proportion to the degree one is affected, *economic justice* means compensation commensurate with one's efforts or sacrifices, *sustainability* means protecting the natural environment *and* ensuring that future generations enjoy overall economic conditions at least as favorable as today's, human *solidarity* means consideration for the well-being of others, and economic *efficiency* means using scarce productive resources and human capabilities wherever they yield the greatest social well-being.[2]

Major Institutions

The defining institutions of a capitalist economy are private ownership of the means of production, limited liability corporations, and markets. In contrast, the major institutions in a participatory economy are *social ownership* of the productive "commons," *democratic worker councils and federations, neighborhood consumer councils and federations,* and a *participatory planning procedure* that these councils and federations use to coordinate, or plan, their interrelated activities.

Social Ownership

In a participatory economy, everything needed to produce our way of life belongs equally to everyone. While individuals own personal property, everything we need to produce goods and services is owned in common. Common ownership of our natural environment extends to "vital sinks" as well as natural resources (the *natural commons*), an increasingly complex array of useful manufactured artifacts (the *produced commons*), productive knowledge or know-how (the *information commons*), and all the useful talents and skills needed to deploy all this natural and produced wherewithal to productive ends. All of this "commons for modern times" is treated as a joint inheritance—what Joel Mokyr calls a "gift from Athena"— bequeathed to us all by countless past generations.[3]

Democratic Councils and Jobs

Worker Councils

In a participatory economy, every worker in a workplace has one vote in the worker council, the enterprise's ultimate decision-making body. Just as stockholder meetings, where a share of stock equals a vote, are ultimately "sovereign" in a capitalist corporation, the worker council, where each worker-member has one vote irrespective of seniority, is sovereign in a participatory economy. That said, worker councils can grant authority over some decisions to groups of disproportionately affected workers, and workers can still tap others' expertise as needed to make decisions.

Balanced Jobs

Every economy organizes work into jobs that define what tasks a single individual will perform. In hierarchical economies, the majority of jobs contain mostly undesirable and disempowering tasks, while a few jobs have mostly desirable and empowering tasks. But does it have to be this way? If some workers sweep floors all week, year in and year out, while others attend planning meetings nonstop, is it realistic to believe that the two groups will equally affect workplace decisions simply because all have one vote in the worker council? To prevent enterprise democracy from atrophying, job-balancing committees within worker councils—not outside bureaucracies—should include more and less desirable tasks, and more and less empowering tasks in all jobs. The idea isn't to rotate everyone through every task, or eliminate specialization, or give each worker more tasks, but to include some appropriate empowering tasks in everyone's job description and distribute unpleasant tasks more fairly. Obviously, job balancing committees would need to take technological, skill, and psychological considerations into account.

Compensation According to Effort or Sacrifice

As long as work requires workers to make sacrifices, those who sacrifice more should receive extra "consumption rights" commensurate with the sacrifices they make. To implement this conception of economic justice, worker councils would give members an "effort rating." Worker councils would have leeway in how they go about this, but there is one restriction. So workers aren't tempted to award workmates, undeservedly high ratings in exchange for like treatment, the average effort rating awarded by councils to their members must be capped.[4]

Consumer Councils and Federations

In a participatory economy, every household in a neighborhood has three important roles and responsibilities. First, it submits a consumption request, together with effort ratings of household members who work and consumption allowances of members who are too young or old to work or are disabled. Second, it participates in discussions about, and votes on, which neighborhood public goods to request. Third, it votes for recallable representatives to higher level federations of consumer councils at the ward, city, state, regional, and national levels, where delegates discuss which higher level public goods to request during the planning procedure. Individual requests for additional consumption due to special need and requests to borrow and consume more than an effort rating or allowance warrants are also handled through procedures established by each neighborhood council. Organizing consumers into councils and federations that participate on an equal footing with worker councils in participatory planning empowers people as both consumers and workers, eliminating the notorious bias in market economies against expressing one's preferences for collective consumption.

Participatory Planning

An annual "participatory planning" procedure determines which worker councils will use which parts of the productive commons to produce the goods and services that consumer councils and federations will consume.[5] More particularly, an "iteration facilitation board" (IFB) first announces the final values from the previous year's plan for the opportunity cost of using each kind of capital (natural, produced, and human), the social cost of producing every good and service, the damage caused by every pollutant, and the social benefits of each consumption good and service. Based on these values, each worker and consumer council, and each federation of consumer councils, submits a "self-activity proposal" for what that council or federation wants to do this year. Then the IFB tabulates the overall excess demand or supply for each capital stock, produced good, and pollutant, and raises its estimate of the opportunity or social cost for anything in excess demand, and lowers its estimate for anything in excess supply. Based on these revised estimates of opportunity and social costs, councils and federations revise and resubmit new self-activity proposals until a feasible plan is reached—until, that is, there is no longer excess demand for any natural resource, any kind of physical capital, any category of labor, any intermediate or final good or service, or permission to emit any pollutant.

Consumption council proposals are easily evaluated by multiplying the quantity of every good or service requested times the current estimate of the social cost of producing a unit of the good or service, and then summing to estimate the overall cost to society of meeting the consumption requests. This result is compared to the average effort rating plus allowances of consumption council members requesting the goods and services. A neighborhood council whose members have above average work effort ratings and/or consumption allowances approved is entitled to a consumption bundle that costs society more than the average. By the same token, a neighborhood council with lower than average effort ratings and/or allowances qualifies only for a consumption bundle costing less than the average. This way, whether a consumption proposal is "socially responsible" is easy for the council making the proposal and all other councils to know.

Worker council production proposals are evaluated by comparing the estimated social benefits of their outputs to the estimated social cost of their inputs. In any planning round, a production proposal's social benefits are calculated simply by multiplying quantities of proposed outputs by current estimates of their social benefits and then summing. The social costs of a production proposal are calculated by multiplying inputs requested by current estimates of their opportunity or social costs, including current estimates of the damages from pollutants emitted, and then summing. If the social benefits exceed the social costs—that is, if the *social benefit to cost ratio* (SB/SC) of a production proposal exceeds one—everyone else is presumably made better off by approving the worker council's proposal. If the ratio is less than one, the opposite is true unless the numbers fail to capture something. Just as the estimates of opportunity and social costs make it easy to determine whether consumer council requests are fair or unfair, the social benefit-to-cost ratio makes it easy to see whether production proposals are socially responsible.

Elsewhere, my colleagues and I have demonstrated that each round of this social iterative procedure will begin with more accurate estimates of opportunity and social costs and benefits than the previous round, and that worker and consumer councils and federations will be induced to whittle their self-activity proposals down until an efficient feasible plan is reached.[6] Most importantly, because estimates of opportunity and social costs and benefits are immediately available to all, no central planner is needed to give final approval or disapproval. Councils can vote "yea" or "nay" on other councils' proposals without time-consuming evaluations or contentious meetings, except in occasional cases requiring special review.

In essence, the planning procedure boils down to this: worker councils making proposals are asking permission to use particular parts of productive resources that belong to everyone. In effect, their proposals say:

> If the rest of you, with whom we are engaged in a cooperative division of labor, agree to allow us to use productive resources owned by all as inputs, then we promise to deliver the following goods and services as outputs for others to use.

When consumer councils make proposals, they are asking permission to consume goods and services whose production entails social costs. In effect, their proposals say: "We believe the effort ratings co-workers gave us indicate that we deserve to consume goods and services whose production entails an equivalent level of social costs."

The planning procedure clearly reveals when a worker council production proposal is inefficient or when a consumption council proposal is unfair, and it allows other worker and consumer councils to nix such proposals. But initial self-activity proposals, and all proposal revisions, are entirely up to each worker and to the consumer council. This aspect of participatory planning, which distinguishes it from all other planning models, is crucial if workers and consumers are to enjoy meaningful self-management.

In sum, a participatory economy is a planned rather than a market system. Long-run development decisions, investment decisions, and allocation of user rights over the productive commons are all made via participatory planning procedures and *not* left to be determined by the laws of supply and demand. Nor is there a market for labor. People can apply to become members and work in any worker council they choose. And worker councils are free to hire new members from applicants as they please. But *nobody's pay can be determined in advance at the time of hiring.* Pay is determined only after work has been done and co-workers rate one another's efforts. So there is free labor mobility, but pay rates are not determined by the law of supply and demand.

Finally, the planning procedure eliminates the well-known bias in market economies against public goods in favor of private goods. In every round of proposals, requests for public goods are made by different levels of consumer federations at the same time and on the same basis that requests for private consumption are made. Unlike in market economies, in participatory planning it is just as easy to express desires for public as private consumption.

Economic institutions and systems designed to help people figure out how to cooperate with one another in mutually beneficial and equitable ways differ profoundly from those that compel people who want to cooperate to compete against one another instead. Many have swallowed the myth that authoritarian planning is the only alternative to markets. Our participatory planning procedure demonstrates that this gospel is nothing more than a myth. Participatory planning is a feasible and practical alternative to both market competition and command planning.

Protecting the Natural Environment

Protecting the Environment in Annual Plans

As long as producers and consumers are not forced to bear the costs of pollution resulting from their decisions, we will over-pollute. But participatory planning internalizes the negative external effects of pollution, making polluters pay. One social cost estimated when each round of planning begins is the damage caused by releasing a unit of every pollutant, and worker councils who propose to release the pollutant are charged for the damage while residents are compensated for any damages suffered. If members of a worker council propose to emit x units of a particular pollutant, they are charged the current estimate of the damage per unit released times x—just as they are charged y times the social cost of producing a ton of steel if they propose to use y tons of steel, and just as they are charged z times the opportunity cost of an hour of welding labor if they propose to use z hours of welding labor. All these costs are weighed against the social benefits of whatever outputs they propose to make.

At the same time, the "community of affected parties" (CAP) living in the region affected looks at the current estimate of damages caused by a unit of the pollutant and decides how many units can be emitted. The answer may be none, but if the CAP allows X units of a pollutant to be emitted in the region, then the CAP is "credited" with X times the estimate of damages from one unit of the pollutant, and CAP members get to consume more than they would otherwise. Tolerating some adverse effects from pollution is treated as a burden people choose to bear, worthy of compensation, just as the burdens people take on in work deserve compensation.[7]

Protecting the Environment in Long-Run Plans

Treating pollution and environmental preservation in an "incentive compatible" way in annual participatory planning is a major accomplishment and significant improvement over the way market economies behave. But while this may settle environmental accounts efficiently and equitably for all taking part in the annual participatory planning process, what protects the interests of future generations? How can we avoid intergenerational inequities and inefficiencies while preserving economic democracy when much of the toll from environmental deterioration will fall on the unborn, who have no voice today?

The interests of future generations, which include the future state of the natural environment, must always be protected by the present generation. In a participatory economy, intergenerational efficiency and equity related to the environment must be achieved in the same way intergenerational efficiency and equity are achieved in all other regards--through self-restraint exercised in democratic deliberations during the investment and development planning processes.[8]

There is no way to guarantee that members of the present generation will take the interests of future generations sufficiently to heart or choose wisely for them. For example, a development plan to replace cars with trains for our descendants might prove to be a mistake should cars powered by electricity produced by renewables rather than fossil fuels turn out to reduce carbon emissions just as much while affording more convenience. Nor can we make sure that the present generation will not, like Louis XV, simply decide, Après moi, le deluge (After me, the deluge). Still, we can hope that people who practice economic justice among themselves in the participatory economy will practice it on behalf of their children, grandchildren, and great grandchildren as well. We can hope that people used to permitting pollution only when the benefits outweigh the costs will apply the same principle in their long-run planning when considering future costs and benefits And we can hope that when choices are presented in ways that clearly show when favoring themselves would be unfair to their descendants that people will be too ashamed to put themselves first.

Additional Features that Protect the Environment

Apart from planning procedures, other features of a participatory economy make it more likely that people will treat the natural environment judiciously.

First is the egalitarian distribution of wealth and income: nobody will be too poor and desperate to value environmental preservation over material consumption. There will be no destitute colonists cutting down and burning valuable rain forests because they have no other way to stay alive. There will be no poverty-stricken communities that acquiesce to host unsafe toxic waste dumps because they are desperate for jobs and income. An egalitarian distribution of income and wealth also means nobody will be rich enough to buy private environmental amenities while leaving the public environment to deteriorate.

Second is a system that minimizes the use of material incentives and emphasizes rewards for social serviceability, greatly diminishing environmentally destructive conspicuous consumption. Ample evidence corroborates that what Juliet Schor calls "competitive consumption" drives many to consume far beyond the point where additional consumption generates enough well-being to offset the cost of lost leisure.[9] There is good reason to believe this phenomenon will die out in a participatory economy.

Third is an allocative system that provides productive resources to workers as long as the social benefits of their work exceed the social costs—including the environmental costs. This eliminates the competitive rat race for producers to accumulate and grow despite adverse environmental consequences. In short, there is no unhealthy and environmentally destructive "growth imperative" in a participatory economy.

International Trade and Investment

The guiding principle for how any participatory economy should interact with other economies is the 50-percent rule. International trade can be advantageous if there are true differences in opportunity costs among countries. Where such differences exist, the terms of trade distribute the efficiency gain from international specialization between trading partners. Any participatory economy should trade if there are truly efficiency gains to be had. However, given its commitment to economic justice, a participatory economy should secure terms of trade that distribute more than half of the efficiency gain to the less developed country. If the trading partner is more developed than the participatory economy, it should simply fight for the most favorable terms of trade it can secure. But if the participatory economy is richer than a trading partner, it should accept terms that distribute more of the benefit from trade to its trading partner. The 50-percent rule allows for mutual benefit while reducing global inequality.

Economic Decentralization: How Much?

When the social opportunity costs of producing goods differ by country or region within a country, specialization and trade can be mutually beneficial. Today's division of labor, however, often decreases efficiency both internationally and within countries. Since commercial prices systematically fail to register external effects, countries and regions too often specialize in producing goods in which they have comparative *dis*advantages. Typically, the commercial costs of transportation don't include the full social cost of moving goods, also leading to overspecialization. Responding to this dysfunctional overspecialization, many visionary economists call for decentralizing more economic activity and increasing local self-sufficiency.

Unlike many who preach the virtues of localism, supporters of participatory economics are resolutely *agnostic* about how self-sufficient versus how integrated different geographical areas should be. Often, more internal diversification and self-sufficiency would move us in the right direction. But just *how much* more self-sufficient should economies become? When push comes to shove, local visionaries invariably concede that local regions would be only *semi*-autonomous. That answer leaves two crucial questions unanswered: How large is *semi*? And how would the *semi* part be coordinated?

Participatory planning procedures are the best way to answer both questions. How self-sufficient and how integrated economies will turn out to be under procedures proposed here is difficult to say in advance or in general. That said, the procedures proposed for engaging in long-run development planning, investment planning, and annual planning are appropriate ways to find the right mixture of self-sufficiency and integration, and the participatory planning process outlined here is far superior to the market as a way for *semi*-autonomous regions to arrange whatever degree of dependency proves mutually advantageous.[10]

Enterprises: How Big?

Supporters of participatory economics are also agnostic about how large production units should be. While some visionaries cringe at the idea of any large-scale production units, sometimes economies of scale can be significant. In those cases, worker councils with thousands of members may be appropriate.

It is important to distinguish here between true economies of scale in production and commercial, financial, and monopoly advantages that large producers enjoy in capitalist economies. Many large corporations today are big only because that gives them advantages over smaller firms in advertising, financing, and pricing—not because of production efficiencies. Since large worker councils in a participatory economy will not enjoy any such advantages, and since devising participatory decision-making procedures for large groups is harder than for small groups, doubtless we'll find fewer large production units and more small- and medium-sized production units in a participatory economy than there are today. In principle, though, our model finds nothing wrong with large organizations *per se,* and the participatory planning procedure is well suited to discovering if and when larger production units make sense.

Work Week: How Long?

Many visionaries emphasize how much shorter the work week will be when productivity is increased and what Herman Daly calls "uneconomic growth" is eliminated, explaining that everyone will have more time for civic engagement, family, and personal development. A participatory economy will stimulate increases in productivity while eliminating pressures to overconsume.

We need not speculate about how either countries or individuals will choose between consumption and leisure in a participatory economy. Clearly, the national choice will likely depend on a country's level of economic development. But in both more and less advanced economies the length of the standard work week should be decided democratically by people living in any participatory economy, and individuals should be free to work more or fewer hours than whatever standard is set.

Growth: Good or Bad?

Exactly what in the new economy is worth "growing"? As long as we are talking about growth of economic *well-being,* why not continue to grow indefinitely?

A participatory economy will not only distribute well-being far more equally but should also increase the growth rate of well-being per capita. What can*not* continue to grow without limit is what ecological economists call environmental *throughput*—natural resources used as inputs in production processes along with wastes and other material outputs of production stored in natural repositories or "sinks." But material inputs taken from nature and material outputs deposited back in nature are not the same as economic well-being. Assuming a constant population and no change in hours worked, throughput will not increase if throughput efficiency increases as fast as labor productivity.[11]

Time Frame and Theory of Social Change

Take Venezuela. At the turn of the century conditions were ripe for implementing major features of a participatory economy. A government pledged to build "twenty-first century socialism" enjoyed majority support from the electorate. What Venezuelans' called their "social economy" already contained many of the building blocks necessary to build a participatory economy. What Venezuela lacked was a campaign to replace market relations with participatory planning among the cooperatives, assemblies, communal councils, community clinics, *misiones*, and people's food stores that comprised the social economy sector. Once the social economy had been consolidated and integrated by participatory planning among its parts, and once it had proved its superiority, a popular government in Venezuela could have extended the social economy to replace the dysfunctional private and state sectors.

Elsewhere, had the Syriza-led Greek government not submitted to a draconian neoliberal austerity plan, but instead had the courage to launch its own economic recovery plan, that program could have created worker and neighborhood councils and initiated participatory planning. The same would be true for a Podemos-led government coming to power in Spain, or a Left Bloc government in Portugal. However, in the US and most countries, popular support for replacing not only neoliberal capitalism, but capitalism itself, will take many decades to build.

Without successful experiments in equitable cooperation like these, people will never move beyond reform, which never fully solves problems and can always be rolled back. On the other hand, without much larger reform movements, experiments in equitable cooperation will remain isolated and never reach enough people. Broadly speaking, the answer is more powerful reform movements and campaigns, combined with more and larger experiments in equitable cooperation. Neither alone will succeed, but fortunately each helps mitigate predictable pitfalls in the other.[12]

The goal is clear enough: We must convince the majority that ordinary people are perfectly capable of managing our own economic affairs without either capitalist employers or commissars to tell us what to do. We must convince that majority that groups of self-managing workers and consumers have what it takes to coordinate their own division of labor through participatory, democratic planning, rather than abdicating this task to the market system or central planners. But how this goal will be achieved, and how people will defend the progress they make from powerful and entrenched elite interests when they move to thwart the will of the majority, will vary greatly from place to place.

Notes

1 For more information about participatory economics online readers should go to www.participatoryeconomics.info. The most up-to-date book explaining the model is Robin Hahnel, *Of the People, by the People* (Portland, OR: Soapbox Press, 2012).

2 For justifications of these definitions and their use, see Robin Hahnel, *Economic Justice and Democracy: From Competition to Cooperation* (London: Routledge, 2005), chapters 1 and 2; Robin Hahnel, "Economic Justice," *Review of Radical Political Economics* 37, 2 (2005): 131–154; and Robin Hahnel, *Green Economics: Confronting the Ecological Crisis* (Armonk, NY: M.E. Sharpe, 2011), chapter 3.

3 For a fuller exposition and justification of this conception of social ownership, see Robin Hahnel, "Participatory Economics and the Commons," *Capitalism Nature Socialism* 26, 1 (2015): 31–43.

4 Caps could be equal for all worker councils, or, alternatively, the average effort rating for each council could be 100 times the ratio of the social benefits of the outputs it delivered last year to the social costs of the inputs it used. Capping average effort ratings for councils eliminates any incentive for workers on an effort rating committee to inflate the ratings they award.

5 The annual planning procedure takes place in the context of an investment plan that has already determined what investment goods will be produced in the coming year. It also takes place after the stocks of natural capital, produced capital, and human capital available for use in the coming year are known.

6 The participatory planning procedure will yield an efficient outcome even when there are externalities and public goods while the general equilibrium of a competitive market economy will not. For technical discussions, see Michael Albert and Robin Hahnel, *The Political Economy of Participatory Economics* (Princeton, NJ: Princeton University Press, 1991), chapter 5; Michael Albert and Robin Hahnel, "Socialism As It Was Always Meant to Be," *Review of Radical Political Economics* 24, 3&4 (1992): 46–66; Michael Albert and Robin Hahnel, "Participatory Planning," *Science & Society* 56, 1 (1992): 39–59. Helped by a grant from the Institute for Solidarity Economics in Oxford, England, researchers from the System Science Department at Portland State University are analyzing a computer simulation of the planning procedure to study its convergence properties, including how robust the iterative planning procedure is even when traditional "convexity" assumptions break down.

7 See Robin Hahnel, "Wanted: A Pollution Damage Revealing Mechanism," *Review of Radical Political Economics* 49, 2 (2017): 233–246 for more on this procedure and the ways it will: reduce pollution to "efficient" levels, satisfy the "polluter pays principle," compensate pollution victims, and induce "communities of affected parties" to reveal the true extent to which they are damaged by pollution–none of which market systems accomplish.

8 For a discussion of how to best organize investment and long-run development planning, see Hahnel, *Of the People, by the People*, chapter 16.

9 Juliet Schor, *The Overspent American* (New York: Basic Books, 1998).

10 For a sympathetic critique of eco-localist visions, see Robin Hahnel, "Eco-localism: A Constructive Critique," *Capitalism, Nature, Socialism* 18, 2 (2007): 62–78.

11 See Robin Hahnel, "Environmental Sustainability in a Sraffian Framework," *Review of Radical Political Economics* 49, 3 (2017): 477–488, which demonstrates this result in a Sraffian framework and explains how it can help distinguish sense from nonsense in the steady-state and de-growth literatures.

12 For more on theories of social change and transition strategy, see Robin Hahnel, part 4 in *Economic Justice and Democracy: From Competition to Cooperation* (New York: Routledge, 2005), and Robin Hahnel and Erik Olin Wright, part 2 in *Alternatives to Capitalism: Proposals for a Democratic Economy* (London: Verso Books, 2016).

Part 7

The Emerging New Economy

In communities around the world, new economic systems are not futuristic ideas mused upon in essays and debated in lecture halls and conference rooms. They are being built right now, by people who have taken it upon themselves to lead the rebuilding of economic structures that meet community needs and reflect community values. The authors of the essays in this section number among them.

The efforts they described here are small in the context of the systems that they are seeking to upend and replace. Their stories include setbacks, mistakes, and adjustments. But the experiences they describe attest to the reality of system change—a road that is often jagged, mostly uphill, and traveled by people convinced that the destination is real and worth the journey.

These essays also underscore the fact that much of the work of system change is animated by the drive to root out systemic racism and sexism. Racial inequity is a core characteristic of global capitalism, manifest in the high unemployment and poverty rates in much of Africa and of people of African descent in America. The patriarchy woven into capitalism's DNA means that even five decades after the 1960s rallying cries of "women's liberation," women on average in 2019 still earned just 79 cents for each dollar men earned.

Arising from a feminist critique of political economy that rejects its features of dominance and subordination, J.K. Gibson-Graham and members of the Community Economies Collective (CEC) write about their work around the world to make real their vision of "community economies." By this, they mean "the ongoing process of negotiating our interdependence." That negotiation, in their view, revolves around six "coordinates": survival, surplus, transactions, consumption, commons and investment. One set of strategies deployed in their work and executed through research and collaborative mapping projects activates a politics of language to describe economic diversity and make current ethical economic practices visible. A second set "broaden[s] the horizon of economic politics so that ethical economic practices might multiply." More than a dozen projects illustrate how these collective actions work in practice, including the creation of community-supported fisheries in Maine and the diverse economic practices of cooperation implemented in post-Soviet Russia.

Kali Akuno and Sacajawea Hall write as leaders of Cooperation Jackson, which they describe as "a scrappy little project" in Jackson, Mississippi that "is striving to make a big impact in the prefigurative development of the next socioeconomic system." They are developing what they call "eco-socialism," defined as "a classless socioeconomic system in which humans live in balance with nature." The economy would feature collective ownership of the means of production, democratic planning, and production tuned to meet social needs within ecological limits. Four cooperative institutions form the core of Cooperation Jackson: a federation, an incubator, an "economic democracy" school, and a financial institution. Their solidarity economics strategies and practices range from the establishment of a community land trust and a "community production cooperative" that offers training in digital fabrication to help for low-income residents improving their living standards through better managing and more sharing of resources.

Meanwhile, in Boston three leaders of the Boston Ujima Project—Aaron Tanaka, Nia K. Evans and Libbie Cohn—make reparations the focus of their vision and work on radical systems change. Reparations, they write, is not simply economic compensation for the labor stolen, lives taken, and opportunities lost to slavery and institutionalized racism. It is also about building the "new and reciprocal relationships of repair and accountability necessary to address the continued effects of slavery and to prevent similar harms from being perpetuated." The Boston Ujima Project is "robustly grounded in a reparations frame": members of Boston's working-class communities of color work together to identify economic development priorities and to allocate finance capital through a participatory process designed to favor the historically marginalized and impoverished. A long-term goal of the Ujima Project is to reform the Boston city charter and "transition city government from a shepherd of racialized capitalism toward an organ of deep democracy and self-determination of historically exploited communities."

Zitto Kabwe, a member of the Tanzanian Parliament from the opposition party Alliance for Change and Transparency (ACT-Wazalendo), offers lessons from his country's experience after then-President Julius Nyerere in 1967 issued his landmark "Arusha Declaration," which put forward an African socialist vision as a path to liberation from economic as well as political colonialism. For 25 years, Tanzania followed its precepts, with government control of the economy on behalf of the people. But, as Kabwe explains, starting in the late 1970s external events and internal missteps combined to send the economy into crisis. By 1986, the country accepted bailout terms set by the International Monetary Fund and the World Bank, which among other things demanded the privatization of the Tanzanian economy. With privatization came the "foreignization" of outside private capital, and then deindustrialization when that capital chose to leave. In 2015, Kabwe's party issued the Tabora Declaration, a call for a return to the socialist principles of the Arusha Declaration in a 21st-century context. While the Tabora Declaration suggests a role for private capital and entrepreneurship that Nyerere's original proclamation did not, the core rejection of capitalist domination holds. "Socialism is the absence of exploitation of the people by those who own their economy," Kabwe concludes. "What is bad in that?"

Chapter 26

Cultivating Community Economies
Tools for Building a Livable World

J.K. Gibson-Graham, Jenny Cameron, Kelly Dombroski, Stephen Healy, Ethan Miller, and the Community Economies Collective

---

The Community Economies Collective (CEC) seeks to bring about more sustainable and equitable forms of development by acting on new ways of thinking about economies and politics. The Collective challenges two problematic aspects of how "the economy" is understood: seeing it as inevitably capitalist and separating the economy from ecology. The ultimate aim is to help mobilize social transformation to a "post-capitalist politics," but we believe in starting where we are and building other worlds with what is at hand by identifying, gathering, and amplifying ethical economic practices that already exist and betoken "the world we want to live in."

Key Commitments

• The CEC embraces anti-essentialist thinking. Instead of reducing the world to a few key determinants, we understand the world as shaped by multiple and interacting processes, only some of which we can apprehend. We are open to the unexpected and the unknown, to the small and seemingly insignificant.
• The CEC affirms that lives unfold in a "pluriverse," not a "universe." There are a range of solutions and strategies for change and multiple pathways toward more sustainable and equitable worlds.
• Like others seeking ethical relationships instead of an end state, the CEC is involved in ongoing learning and in "becoming ethical subjects" through negotiation with human and "earth others" (species, ecologies, landscapes and seascapes).

These commitments have evolved from critical engagements with a range of political and intellectual traditions, especially J.K. Gibson-Graham's feminist critique of political economy. Just as feminist theory liberated the category "woman" from its subordination to "man," we work to liberate non-capitalist economic activities from subordination to "capitalism."

Anti-essentialist Marxian political economy has been another formative influence on the CEC's work. Marx's analysis of "class as a process" (of producing, appropriating, and distributing surplus) helps us unpack the diversity of economies within any historical or geographic context, deconstructing capitalism and opening up radical possibilities for heterogeneous economies. We employ both anti-essentialist Marxism and post-structuralist feminism as strategies to "queer" the economy and society, resisting the alignment of aspects of identity (whether of class, gender, sexuality, or race) into seemingly intractable "structures" that prevent alternative ways of seeing and being.[1]

Our engagement with these traditions has convinced us that radical transformation is possible and that the way stories or narratives of transformation are constructed matter since they can help bring about the worlds they describe instead of closing off possibilities. We cultivate representations of the world that *inspire, mobilize,* and *support* change efforts even while recognizing today's formidable challenges.

Community Economies

The term "community economy" often refers to localized business activity. In sharp contrast, to us it means the active, ongoing, and open-ended negotiation of interdependence with all life forms, human and nonhuman. We see community as a never-ending process of being together, struggling over the boundaries and substance of togetherness, and coproducing this togetherness in complex power relations. We emphasize *process,* not *product.* We ask whether the dynamics of being together are *obscured* and made difficult to challenge and change or made *explicit* and opened for collective democratic negotiation and transformation.

In conventional usage, "economy" often refers to a system of formal commodity production and monetary exchange. Our use of the term is much broader. The "eco" in economy comes from the Greek root *oikos,* meaning "home" or "habitat," while "nomy" derives from *nomos,* meaning management. We view economy as referring to all of the practices that allow us to survive and care for each other and the earth. Economy, understood this way, refers to the ongoing management—and therefore negotiation—of human and nonhuman ecological relations of sustenance. What we call "economic practices" don't sum to a single system or boil down to one particular logic or rationality (individual utility maximization, for example). Rather, they are diverse, complex, and contextually situated, animated by multiple motivations and relational dynamics.

Building on these understandings, "community economy" names the ongoing process of negotiating our interdependence. It is the explicit democratic co-creation of the diverse ways in which we collectively *make* our livings, *receive* our livings from others, and provide *for* others. To help make these complex negotiations clearer, we identify a cluster of ethical concerns or "coordinates" for community economies:

- Survival: What do we really need to survive well? How do we balance our survival needs and well-being with those of others and the planet?
- Surplus: What's left after our survival needs have been met? How do we distribute this surplus to enrich social and environmental health?
- Transactions: What is the range of ways we secure things that we cannot produce ourselves? How do we conduct ethical encounters with human and non-human others in these transactions?
- Consumption: What do we really need to consume? How do we consume sustainably and justly?
- Commons: What do we share with human and non-human others? How do we maintain, replenish, and grow this natural and cultural commons?
- Investment: What do we do with stored wealth? How do we invest it so that future generations may live well?

The following (alphabetized) examples provide just a snapshot of existing initiatives that are negotiating these ethical concerns.

Alter Trade Japan

Alter Trade Japan (ATJ) is a global network that uses *transactions* as a vehicle to help people *survive well* and protect their natural and cultural *commons*. ATJ was formed in the late 1980s as a long-term trade initiative that would take over from the short-term emergency relief work of the Japan Committee for Negros Campaign, which was supporting starving sugarcane farmers on Negros Island who had lost their livelihood when the international sugar market collapsed. ATJ has since expanded to source a range of fairly produced foodstuffs for Japanese consumer cooperatives. Products include natural sea salt from the once-threatened saltpans of France, olive oil from Palestine, "eco-shrimps" from Indonesia, and Balangon bananas from the Philippines.

The Chantier de l'économie sociale, Québec

The Chantier is a nonprofit entity that serves existing and new enterprises in Quebec's social economy, particularly through *investment* strategies. It has developed two financial tools for social economy enterprises that channel *surplus* into shared social outcomes. The *Réseau d'investissement social du Québec* (Social Investment Network of Quebec) helps finance social economy enterprises during start-up, consolidation, expansion, or restructuring. The *Chantier de l'économie sociale* provides loans for social economy enterprises (especially those with under 200 employees). Representing "quasi-patient capital," these loans don't have to be repaid for 15 years. By Chantier estimates, more than 7,000 collective enterprises (cooperatives and nonprofit businesses) in Québec now provide over 150,000 jobs and contribute over 8 percent of the province's GDP. Critical to Chantier's operations is the board, which comprises representatives from associations of social economy enterprises, the main labor federations, the cooperative movement, the women's movement, social and environmental movements, and Québec-wide associations of First Nations and Inuit peoples.

Hepburn Wind

Hepburn Community Wind Park Co-operative (Hepburn Wind) exemplifies community-driven *investment* used to help shift toward more sustainable *consumption* practices and to distribute *surplus* for social benefit. Based in rural Victoria, Australia, Hepburn Wind owns two turbines with a combined capacity of 4.1 megawatts—enough electricity to power 2,300 homes in a country with one of the world's highest levels of per capita consumption of coal. The cooperative's 2,000 members contributed AUD\$9.8 million to the wind farm. Over half of these members are local residents for whom minimum shares cost \$100 (compared to \$1,000 for non-local members). The Victorian state government also provided grants totaling \$1.7 million and a community-run bank provided a \$3.1 million loan. The initiative's surplus is returned to members as dividends. Community projects also receive a share of the surplus with \$15,000 per turbine being used annually for local environmental, recreational, cultural, and educational projects.

Kerala

For over 50 years, the southern Indian state of Kerala has been negotiating how to *invest* to enable people to *survive well*. Rather than applying a business-focused investment strategy (with elusive trickle-down benefits), Kerala has invested directly in people's well-being. Thanks largely to its investment, some 94 percent of births are now attended by health professionals and the infant death rate is lower than that for African Americans in Washington DC. The total fertility rate is two births per woman, and the population growth rate is below replacement level. As a result, Kerala's female-to-male sex ratio is 109 to 100, compared to 91 to 100 in India as a whole. Education is another priority, including investment in schooling for boys and girls and adult literacy projects. As a result, Kerala has a 90-percent literacy rate. Kerala now has a skilled workforce but lacks the jobs to match so many educated Keralites seek employment overseas. And although physical health has improved across the board, mental health problems are reflected in the high suicide rate. This example reflects how building a community economy is an ongoing process of negotiating dilemmas along the way.

Montreal Protocol on Substances that Deplete the Ozone Layer

With concerted international action on climate change progressing slowly, what can we learn from other efforts to *common* such open access resources as the atmosphere? From the early 1970s warnings had been raised about the effects of ozone-depleting chemicals. The urgency of the problem became evident in 1985 with images being captured of the hole in the ozone layer over Antarctica. Only two years later, in 1987, the Montreal Protocol on Substances that Deplete the Ozone Layer was agreed to, and in 1989 it came into force. Rapid action resulted, not only by nation states and their negotiators, but also by a "community of concern" (scientists, unionists, multinational corporations, media reporters, ordinary citizens, and others). By 2005, the Montreal Protocol had resulted in a 95-percent reduction in the production and consumption of ODCs by all 191 countries that ratified the Protocol. This case offers some hope that global *commoning* can yield rules and protocols to protect our life-sustaining atmosphere.

Strategies for Cultivating Community Economies

The Community Economies Collective has developed strategies to help cultivate community economies. The first strategy activates a politics of language to describe economic diversity and make current ethical economic practices visible. The second suite of strategies activates a politics of the subject and a politics of collective action. Both strategies broaden the horizon of economic politics so that ethical economic practices might multiply.

Strategy I: Situating Today's Economic Politics within a Diverse Economy

Our first strategy uses a language of the *diverse economy* to expand the scope for economic action and legitimate economic politics across a broad front. Textual and visual forms of language play a crucial role in generating new ways of seeing and acting. Currently, the language of economy is dominated by an essentialist vision of capitalism: wage labor, commodity production for markets, and profit-seeking capitalist enterprise are seen as the *real economy*. Our anti-essentialist and non-deterministic language of economy unsettles this singularly capitalist representation of the economy.

A vast and varied array of economic practices support life in the world. The Diverse Economy Iceberg is one way of representing how economic practices are far more diverse than mainstream economics suggests, involving a wide range of people, processes, sites, and relationships (Figures 26.1 and 26.2).

Figure 26.1 The Diverse Economy Iceberg. Image by Ken Byrne, 1999.

Figure 26.2 One way to organize the economic activities below the tip of the iceberg. Image by James Langdon, 2013.

The language of the diverse economy allows us to identify spaces for negotiation and to demonstrate why saying that we live in a capitalist world or system is to negate other possible worlds already all around us. Within a diverse "more than capitalist" economy, we can discern multiple pathways to these other possible worlds.

One way we promote a language of economic diversity is through the use of five identifiers related to work, business, markets, property, and finance. Each includes a range of economic practices, including familiar or mainstream "Western" practices, those with some mainstream characteristics but also a twist (e.g., in-kind labor payments or green capitalist firms), and those well outside of what is usually considered "economic" (e.g., volunteer work or gifting).

These identifiers serve two purposes. First, they highlight current economic diversity and feature practices that are intrinsically ethical (e.g., cooperatives, fair and direct trade) along with those that are neutral but potentially ethical (e.g., household flows, sweat equity), or immoral (e.g., slavery, feudalism). Second, highlighting this diversity helps identify economic practices that might undergird a community economy. Neither comprehensive nor definitive, these identifiers are instead "works-in-progress," prompts to help us see the possibilities that are all around, and triggers for conversation and discussion.

The Politics of Work: Surviving Well Together

People use various labor practices to survive. In a *community economy*, we consider not just how these practices might enable an individual or household to survive, but also how they affect other people and the environment. For example, reliance on paid work in that minority of the world that is sometimes called the "developed world" has led to an emphasis on material well-being to the detriment of social, community, spiritual, and physical well-being. And everywhere the flow-on effects of reliance on paid work have encouraged unsustainable consumption that harms other people and environments (Figure 26.3).

The diverse labor identifier helps pinpoint practices that households, communities, and civic institutions might adopt to improve well-being for people and planet. For example, wouldn't reducing time spent in paid labor and substituting other types of labor (such as self-provisioning and volunteering) provide social, community, spiritual, physical, and environmental well-being along with material well-being? This is certainly the wager of those now taking steps to improve life by redefining work—by, say, cutting back on paid work, taking lower paid but less stressful jobs, or moving to less expensive regions. Their fellow travelers are groups involved in the simplicity living movement, employers supporting the 30/40 workweek, and NGOs lobbying for a 21-hour workweek.

DIVERSE LABOR IDENTIFIER

PAID LABOR

ALTERNATIVE PAID LABOR

Self-employed
Cooperative
Indentured
Reciprocal Labor
In-kind
Work for welfare

UNPAID LABOR

Housework
Family care
Neighborhood Work
Volunteering
Self-provisioning
Slave labor

Figure 26.3 Diverse labor identifier.

Other types of important actions in this domain include:

- Campaigns for fair work and wages (such as living wage and anti-sweatshop campaigns)
- Basic Income Grants that directly contribute to household survival and potentially free up time and resources for civic engagement, care of social and environmental commons, and creative activities
- Government supports that help everyone survive (such as universal healthcare, free education, affordable housing, public transport, caregivers' payments, paid family leave)
- Initiatives for sharing essentials (such as co-housing, carpooling, or food-sharing)

Such actions certainly connect with established political movements. Yet, most such movements tend to focus on one type of labor activism: unions seek fairer wages and better conditions for paid labor, anti-slavery movements seek the abolition of forced labor, and small business organizations seek conditions favorable for self-employment. In a community economy, what gets negotiated is the interconnection of different struggles. For example, what impact do increased wages in one sector or nation have on working conditions in others? Or on planetary well-being?

The Politics of Business: Distributing Surplus to Increase Well-being

Various business or enterprise types can generate new wealth (or surplus). In the most familiar, the capitalist enterprise, workers produce surplus value that the capitalist owner privately appropriates and distributes. Alternative capitalist enterprises distribute surplus also to other ends (such as for environmental care, for groups that are disadvantaged). In a *community economy*, surplus is produced under safe and fair working conditions, decision-making about surplus is democratic and involves those who produced it, and the surplus furthers social and ecological well-being (Figure 26.4).

Worker-owned cooperatives are a standout example of enterprises in which the workers who produce the surplus also decide how to distribute it. With their strong social and environmental ethos, most worker-owned cooperatives direct the surplus to further the well-being of others. In a community economy, such cooperatives are mainstays and so are the organizations that promote and support their development, such as the US Federation of Worker Cooperatives, The Working World, the Australian Business Council of Cooperatives and Mutuals, and Solidarity Economy initiatives. Also important are networks of cooperatives, such as Mondragon Corporation, Evergreen Cooperatives, and the Network of Bay Area Cooperatives.

DIVERSE ENTERPRISE IDENTIFIER

CAPITALIST

ALTERNATIVE CAPITALIST

Green capitalist firm
Socially responsible firm
State-run enterprise

NONCAPITALIST

Cooperative
Social enterprise
Self-employed business
Slave enterprise
Feudal estate

Figure 26.4 Diverse enterprise identifier.

Enterprise politics can also play other roles in a community economy:

- Employee Stock Ownership Programs (ESOPs) can help enterprises become more participatory by democratizing ownership.
- Social enterprises can directly address social and environmental well-being.
- More ethical forms of capitalist enterprise (such as B Corps) can direct surplus toward social and environmental well-being.

Institutional shifts (such as a new legal form in the UK, the Community Interest Company) can help promote and support the development of more ethical enterprises. Changes to the taxation system can also be an important incentive, as it has been in Italy and Spain, where tax legislation favors the development of cooperatives.

The Politics of Markets: Encountering Others through Diverse Transactions

Capitalism and markets are frequently conflated by champions and critics alike. Anti-market forces bemoan "commodification" of the living world while market champions decry the market-distorting effects of social and environmental regulation and activist interference. Conflating markets with capitalism marginalizes the many other ways that people and communities exchange goods and services. In a *community economy*, what gets negotiated is how all parties (including nonhuman others) are affected by the exchange of goods and services, inside the market and out (Figure 26.5).

Identifying different forms of transactions lets us see all the ways individuals and communities exchange things to survive. We can then explore the ethical negotiations involved: how might exchange relationships support individuals and communities in both giving and receiving? How might ecological and social concerns be valued and accounted for in markets and other exchanges?

Mainstream markets are woven into the cultural fabric of many societies. Particularly in cultures like that of the US, the supermarket and discount stores play to our senses and appeal to our thriftiness. Yet, as Annie Leonard points out in *Story of Stuff,* contemporary consumer culture has shallow roots—a couple of generations. Could it be that consumers are developing new habits—using new markets to connect with places and one another, using peer-to-peer exchange networks to recycle goods and services? Could it be that we are developing spaces for ethical connection and negotiation? Consider these examples:

- The expansion of ethical local markets—whether farmers' markets, other "buy local" initiatives, or ethical buying guides—that take into account the well-being of others

DIVERSE TRANSACTIONS
IDENTIFIER

MARKET

ALTERNATIVE MARKET

Fair trade and direct trade
Reciprocal exchange
Alternative currency
Local trading system
Community-supported agriculture
Barter
Underground economy
Informal market

NONMARKET

Household flows
Gift giving
Gleaning
State allocations
Hunting, fishing, gathering
Theft, poaching

Figure 26.5 Diverse transactions identifier.

- The expansion of ethical international markets (e.g., fair- and direct-trade networks) that respect the well-being of others
- The expansion of ethical reciprocity in such varied forms as community-supported agriculture or fisheries or performing arts, complementary currencies, and principled discarding through Freecycle and other networks

The Politics of Property: Commoning Diverse Resources

The dominant discourse has been promoting private property as the most efficient and just way to use and conserve things of value. One such trope has been Garrett Hardin's infamous "tragedy of the commons," a phrase based on a fictitious grazing commons ruined as individuals pursued their own self-interest. Hardin came to regret not saying the "unmanaged commons." The real tragedy was the lack of practices of care and management of the commons, not commoning itself. It has been up to such researchers as Nobel Prize winning economist Elinor Ostrom to document how communities have developed complex norms and practices to manage common resources, sometimes for centuries (Figure 26.6).

DIVERSE PROPERTY IDENTIFIER

PRIVATE

ALTERNATIVE PRIVATE

State-owned
Tenanted
Ninety-nine-year lease
Customary
Community-managed
Community trust

OPEN ACCESS

Atmosphere
Water
Open ocean
Ecosystems services

Figure 26.6 Diverse property identifier.

In a *community economy* people talk to one another, develop protocols or rules governing the access and use of resources, and collectively exercise responsibility to care for land, water, forests, fisheries, intellectual property, educational and health systems, languages, and much else. Looking at the rules around the use and care of commons changes our understanding from a noun (commons are simply there) to a verb (commoning is something we do).[2]

Identifying different forms of property allows us to see how people are developing social relations of commoning divorced from tenure. These include:

*   Initiatives to common private property (such as voluntary conservation agreements to protect private land from development in perpetuity or efforts to remunicipalize privatized water systems)
*   Initiatives to common open access resources, such as the atmosphere (in the case of the Montreal Protocol) or fisheries (in the case of the Nauru Agreement Concerning Cooperation in the Management of Fisheries of Common Interest)
*   Efforts to resist enclosure by defending common resources (ranging from making the Human Genome Project a scientific commons to legal struggles to maintain Antarctica and outer space as *terra communis*)

The Politics of Finance: Investing in Futures

The past decade has revealed the global financial system's unstable and speculative nature. Many have paid the price for loosening financial rules and agreements made after the Second World War. Only "the one percent" seem to have benefited, with the disparity in wealth distribution burgeoning over the past decade. Given this backdrop, in finance it is hardest to envision *community economies*. Yet, communities *are* investing surplus to address current challenges and build a common future. Examples range from such online innovations as crowdsourcing to the revival of more traditional forms of financial support, such as informal rotating savings groups. Investment strategies make it possible to move away from short-term speculation toward more prudent and future-oriented investment (Figure 26.7).

Identifying diverse forms of finance makes us aware of the multiple monetary and non-monetary resources available to secure and sustain better social and ecological well-being now. Only then can we really see how communities are accessing diverse forms of finance and ways that

**DIVERSE FINANCE
IDENTIFIER**

**MAINSTREAM MARKET
FINANCE**

**ALTERNATIVE MARKET
FINANCE**

State banks
Government-sponsored lenders
Credit unions
Microfinance
Friendly societies
Community-based financial
institutions

NONMARKET FINANCE

Sweat equity
Community-supported business
Rotating credit funds
Family lending
Donations
Interest-free loans

Figure 26.7 Diverse finance identifier.

policy and legislation could be changed to make it easier for enterprises, organizations, and communities to invest in a common future. This is why entities innovating with financial tools are so important (including the Chantier de l'économie sociale, Québec, Charity Bank in the UK, and Australia's community banking movement).

Other ways that communities are innovating with investment opportunities include:

- Peer-to-peer financing (including traditional Rotating Credit and Savings Organizations or ROSCAs, the pooling of migrant remittances as capital for alternative development pathways, and online financial support)
- Do-it-yourself financing (ranging from community-issued scrips and community investment notes to the use of reciprocal labor as capital)
- Ethical investment and divestment (including the current push for such institutions as universities to divest from fossil fuels)
- Redirecting government revenue toward life-sustaining rather than life-destroying activities (including using tax revenues for social infrastructure and environmental initiatives)

Strategy 2: Broadening the Horizon of Economic Politics

Our anti-essentialist approach encourages us to broaden the horizon and scope of economic politics. Transformation, we contend, can occur over various timespans and geographic scales and can stem from actions both organized and disorganized. Consider here how social movements around feminism and sexual identity have remade society. In just two-and-a-half generations, these movements have transformed the meaning of gender and sexual identity and thereby transformed how lives are being lived. Such social movements illustrate how thinking and acting differently in discreet locations can have global consequences. They also highlight the value of politically connecting the dots between seemingly small and isolated actions and scaling them out through adaptation, translation, and reinterpretation.

This understanding of change also affords a distinctive take on more familiar forms of economic politics. When the economy is framed in terms of capitalism, and when capitalism is presented as spreading across the globe, it seems that the only alternative is an equivalent globally organized anti-capitalist struggle. This diminishes the potential of the local in economic politics. Conversely, framing the economy as comprising diverse practices opens up multiple sites as places of economic struggle and makes us see that what seems global is actually occurring in multiple locales and that what seems local can be globally networked and connected.

Strategies for broadening economic politics build on the first strategy—activating a politics of language—to help shed light on diverse and ethical economic practices. Here the aim is to help people recognize themselves as economic agents with the capacity to enact economic change through collective political action. Below, we provide examples of how members of the Community Economy Collective have deployed this approach.[3]

Place-based Action Research

The Collective has developed methods of participatory research for generating alternative economic development pathways in places and regions where mainstream economic growth has faltered. Academic and community researchers work with other local residents, particularly those most marginalized by capitalist development, on new social enterprises, community-supported production and marketing, and commons management.

Community Partnering in a Deindustrializing Region

In an action research project in Australia's Latrobe Valley, led by Jenny Cameron and Katherine Gibson, the language of diverse economy was combined with asset-based community development to reframe retrenched mining and energy workers, unemployed youth, and needy welfare recipients as people with multiple gifts of the head, hands, and heart. Also, this supposedly problem-beset region was reframed as having an array of physical, associational, and people assets that might form the basis of a new economic development pathway. Supported by workshops and field trips, local residents (including community researchers) built a small cluster of community-based initiatives. The *Shifting Focus* method was then used with groups of residents from marginalized neighborhoods on the urban fringe of Brisbane, Australia. This project was funded by the Australian Research Council and Latrobe City Council.

Community Partnering in the Philippines

Building on the first Community Partnering project, action research involving Katherine Gibson, Amanda Cahill and Ann Hill was undertaken in two poor, labor-exporting, rural communities in the central Philippines. Local residents, supported by community researchers, university researchers, and NGO representatives, worked together to establish community-based social enterprises. The project's website (communitypartnering.info) offers training tools for people and organizations interested in developing local economies by putting people first, building on local assets and strengths, forming new partnerships, experimenting with social enterprises, and extending support networks. Unlad Kabayan

Migrant Services Foundation Inc., was a partner in this project, which the Australian Research Council and AusAID funded.

Hybrid Collective Research Method

Drawing from the experiences of Community Partnering (and the Networking Community Food Economies project, discussed below), Jenny Cameron, Katherine Gibson and Ann Hill refined the action research approach to recognize how human and non-human others can work together as acting subjects. Three critical interactions undergird this method: gathering, which brings together those who share concerns about an issue; reassembling, in which material gathered is rebundled to amplify particular insights; and translating, through which reassembled ideas are taken up by other like-minded collectives.

Collaborative mapping

CEC members have worked with community researchers using Geographic Information System (GIS) mapping techniques to make the number and spatial extent of ethically informed economic activities visible. This strategy has been used to highlight solidarity economies and urban and marine commons.

Mapping the US Solidarity Economy

This project identified the spatial distribution, impact, and significance of solidarity economy practices in the US. The team of Craig Borowiak, Stephen Healy, Marianna Pavlovskaya, and Maliha Safri collated national data and produced an interactive map of solidarity entities, including producer, worker, and consumer cooperatives, credit unions, cooperative housing, and other entities that emphasize shared solidarity economy values. The researchers produced detailed maps of Philadelphia, New York, and Worcester, Massachusetts and explored the distribution of solidarity activity in relation to demographic features. The team also used economic modelling to quantify the impact of solidarity economy activity and conducted interviews to understand the cultural and political significance of solidarity economy entities to cities and states. The project was supported by the National Science Foundation.

Commons Sensor App

Commons-sensor is a mobile-friendly website developed by Open Local and the Parramatta Collaboratory (in association with Louise Crabtree, Katherine Gibson and Stephen Healy) to allow citizen researchers to enter photographic, quantitative, and descriptive data about their physical, cultural and knowledge commons and to record how commons are accessed, used, and cared for. Using "open street maps" as a base map, the sensor is adaptable to many locations worldwide.[4]

Reclaiming Marine Commons through Participatory Mapping

This project used participatory mapping techniques to engage fishing communities in the Northeast US around their use and stewardship of marine resources. The "Atlas Project," funded by National Oceanic and Atmospheric Administration through the Northeast Consortium and led by Kevin St Martin, asked fishing community members to map and assign cultural, historical, environmental, and economic meanings to those marine areas on which their communities depended. Community-based mapping exercises visually linked coastal economies and consumption practices to at-sea fishing grounds, habitats, and ecosystems, fostering a rethinking of fishers and fish as interdependent members of a local marine commons and community economy. This work led to new standards for mapping "communities at sea" for use in fisheries management and Marine Spatial Planning.

Assemblage Research

Assemblage research acknowledges the role of non-humans and materiality in world-making. It also recognizes that the local and global are outcomes of particular networks and associations, not inherent qualities or capacities. Some projects attempt to include other-than-human as potential allies in creating community economies, tracing and creating connections between what is traditionally seen as discrete, isolated, or local with processes and practices elsewhere.

Reassembling Marine Livelihoods in the Northeast US

In the Northeast US, CEC researchers Rob Snyder and Kevin St Martin have engaged fishing communities, marine scientists, and fisheries policy-makers around concern for community sustainability. Present and future community and commons livelihoods have been prioritized in numerous new initiatives. The nation's first community supported fisheries (CSF) initiative in Port Clyde, Maine links consumers, fishers, and the marine commons through a direct marketing scheme similar to community supported agriculture. There are now over 30 CSFs in the US. In another initiative, coastal communities reframed local production, services, and utilities as commons resources open to inventive solutions (e.g., community owned wind energy or shared broadband access).

Urban Agroecology Assemblages in the Philippines

CEC researcher Ann Hill is examining urban agroecology initiatives in Manila and urban Mindanao, where people are working with typhoons, rivers, plants, vegetables, "waste" materials, and digital media to grow ethical economic food futures. This research highlights how people, materials, and more-than-human forces can work together to create more liveable worlds.

Resilience Assemblages in Monsoon Asia

When economic crisis or disaster hits Monsoon Asia, such economic practices as sharing, reciprocity, and resource pooling come to the fore in the recovery and relief effort. Research by Katherine Gibson, Ann Hill, and Lisa Law sheds light on cases where these economic practices have been innovatively harnessed to diversify livelihoods and build economic and ecological resilience, highlighting ways that human and nonhuman materialities and subjectivities have combined to strengthen resilience.

Developing New Metrics

Indicators and metrics measure and count "what matters." But too many reduce social life's complexity to bare numbers of use in neoliberal governance. To develop more progressive indicators and metrics, researchers use an approach of generating discussion of lived practices and incorporating users' experiences in new indicators.

Metrics for Taking Back the Economy

In *Take Back the Economy*, J.K. Gibson-Graham, Jenny Cameron, and Stephen Healy provide inventories, metrics, and accounting frameworks that reframe the economy and prompt self-reflection and learning influenced by human and earth others. In every dimension of the economy—work, business, markets, property, and finance—new and current measuring and accounting technologies are presented to highlight the ethical dimensions of economic decision-making (Figure 26.8).

Place-based Indicators for Gender Equity and Economic Change

In partnership with NGOs and community groups in Solomon Islands and Fiji, Michelle Carnegie, Katherine Gibson, and Katharine McKinnon generated a Pacific-based understanding of gender equity. The project sought to widen understanding of the economy and better represent diverse Pacific ways of life and livelihood. The diverse economy's gendered

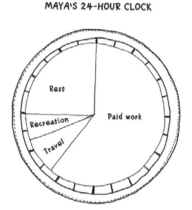

MAYA'S 24-HOUR CLOCK

WELL-BEING SCORECARD

MAYA'S WELL-BEING	1	2	3
Material			X
Occupational		X	
Social	X		
Community	X		
Physical		X	

Figure 26.8 An example of a well-being scorecard.

division of labor was represented as a floating coconut, and researchers developed culturally grounded community-level indicators to track the gender-equity impacts of economic change and development programs.

Learning to Be Affected

Building on the work of Bruno Latour and others with a post-humanist vision of agency, researchers are creating connections and encounters that offer new ways of learning from the world's entirety of human and non-human conditions. This process of co-constitution produces new body-worlds perhaps capable of living in the world differently, more lightly, less exploitatively.

Manifesto for Living in the Anthropocene

We acknowledge the tragedy of anthropogenic climate change. It is important to tap into the emotional richness of grief about extinction and loss without getting stuck in the "blame game." Allowing for the expression of grief and mourning, the CEC adopts a reparative rather than a purely critical stance toward knowing. The essays in this Manifesto, co-edited by Katherine Gibson, Deborah Bird Rose, and Ruth Fincher, focus on new types of ecological economic thinking and ethical practices of living.

Guarding Life through Alternative Hygiene Practices

Research by Kelly Dombroski shows how mothers and other caregivers in China, Australia, and New Zealand learn to sense babies' signs and signals

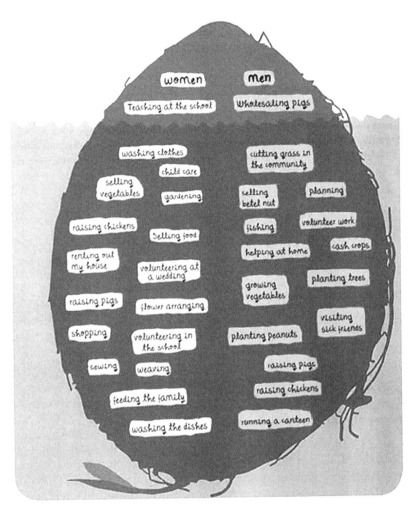

Figure 26.9 The "floating coconut" of gender roles in the Solomon Islands and Fiji.

for impending "elimination," making diapers almost unnecessary. Some mothers see this as a way of "guarding life" (the Chinese ideogram for hygiene) for babies; others see it as guarding life for people and the planet.

Networking Community Food Economies

This research project—led by Jenny Cameron and based on field trips by community gardeners to each other's plots to learn more about a nascent network of community gardens in Newcastle, Australia—revealed ways that community gardeners were responding to climate change and enacting both climate politics and post-capitalist food politics.

Reading for Difference

In the modern development imaginary, diverse economic practices have been positioned as "traditional," "rural," and largely superseded. By reading against the grain of modernization, Community Economy scholars make diverse economic practices visible, accessible, and widely available—an asset that community members, policy-makers, and development practitioners can mobilize.

Reading for Cooperation in Post-Soviet Russia

This research by Marianna Pavlovskaya investigated diverse non-capitalist economic practices and property relations that have developed in pro-capitalist Russia in the last two decades, examining the complexity of economic and social relationships within Russian and migrant households, Indigenous communities, and industrial and agricultural enterprises. By reading for difference, Pavlovskaya identified cooperative economic practices that support non-exploitative livelihoods. She analyzed the class, gender, and racial/ethnic dimensions of these grounded ways of establishing economic and social justice and solidarity.

Reading for Difference in Forest Ecologies and Economies

Elizabeth Barron and Marla Emery have worked with local communities in the Northeast US and Scotland to document how local ecological knowledge is used in the gathering of wild plants and fungi. This work centers on acknowledging and validating different forms of environmental knowledge to demonstrate how diverse forest practices involve ethical decision-making around care of the environment, thereby contributing to human-non-human community building.

Reading for Postdevelopment Practices

Research by Katharine McKinnon engages critically with development practice and offers insights into new ways to practice development that sidestep some of the harmful effects of mainstream approaches. Highlighting examples of place-based and politically engaged modes of development practice offers pathways toward new forms of professional engagement.

Reading for Different Manufacturing Cultures

Katherine Gibson, Stephen Healy, Jenny Cameron, and Joanne McNeill are conducting case studies of Australian manufacturers "doing business" in innovative ways (e.g., environmental responsibility, employee participation, wealth sharing or social inclusion). The firms include multinational capitalist enterprises, family and private businesses, producer cooperatives and social enterprises. Representatives from the firms have collaborated with the researchers to generate a vision for manufacturing in the 21st century that links firm viability with environmental sustainability and economic justice.

Reframing

Drawing on insights from psychoanalytic practice, researchers use reframing techniques to give new meaning and value to people's lives and potentially spark willingness to explore collective actions.

Reframing Our Economies, Reframing Ourselves

The Rethinking Economy project (led by Julie Graham with a team including Stephen Healy) sought to reframe the economy to illuminate the hidden alternative and non-capitalist activities in the Pioneer Valley Region of Western Massachusetts. Funded by the National Science Foundation, academic and community researchers struggled with the familiar vision of capitalist dominance and the sense of powerlessness that it engenders. Research training helped the team feel more comfortable with both the uncertainties and possibilities of non-capitalist spaces, relationships, and processes.

Reframing Care

Kelly Dombroski, Stephen Healy, and Katharine McKinnon are reframing economies of care in maternity and early childhood. Through reframing and the development of shared language, this project seeks a way out of the entrenched ideological conflict between the medical and natural birth paradigms that interferes with efforts to provide good care. It uses digital ethnographies and deliberative forums to explore and transform the social, economic, and material relationships that make good care possible.

Reframing Disaster

The 2010 and 2011 earthquakes in Christchurch, New Zealand devastated the city's central business district. Once the rubble was cleared and the fences around unsafe buildings dismantled, the emptied lots became gravel parking spaces awaiting the prolonged rebuild. But the earthquakes also unleashed great innovation and community action, and the central business district was also the site of quirky cooperative creative arts and solidarity-economy transitional projects that united shell-shocked people. This project, involving Gradon Diprose, Kelly Dombroski, and Stephen Healy, attempts to tell this happier alternative story, alongside similar stories of creative arts "commoning" in New Zealand.

Notes

1 Other intellectual and political debts include Socialism, Anarchism, Radical Democracy, Queer Theory, Ecological Humanities, Science and Technology Studies, Political Ecology, and Indigenous Studies.
2 We acknowledge the important work of *Next System Project* co-contributor David Bollier on commoning.
3 The materials discussed are available through communityeconomy.org.
4 See commons-sensor.openlocal.org.au.

Chapter 27

Building Economic Democracy to Construct Eco-socialism from Below

Kali Akuno and Sacajawea Hall

In a small corner of Jackson, Mississippi, a scrappy little project is striving to make a big impact in the prefigurative development of the next socio-economic system that will help guide humanity's continuing evolution and transcend the oppressive and exploitative capitalist social order now threatening with extinction humanity and all complex life on our precious planet. This project aims to synthesize the practices and institutions of the social and solidarity economy in combination with permacultural design, digital fabrication, and energy democracy, thus establishing economic democracy on a municipal level to inspire and help build eco-socialism from below on a national and international level. The name given to this scrappy little project is the Jackson-Kush Plan, and the organization leading its advancement is Cooperation Jackson.

What, you might ask, is *eco-socialism*? And why is Cooperation Jackson aiming to build it? Loosely defined, eco-socialism describes a classless socioeconomic system in which humans live in balance with nature. Exchange value would be subordinated to use value by organizing production primarily to meet social needs and the requirements of environmental protection and ecological regeneration. To build an ecologically rational society along these lines requires the collective ownership of the means of production, democratic planning to enable society to define the goals of production and investment, and a new technological production structure that meshes with societies' plans and stays within the earth's ecological carrying capacity. In turn, building such a democratic culture necessitates the transformation of social relations, particularly those of production and reproduction, through deliberate and intentional struggles to eliminate white supremacy, settler colonialism, colonialism, imperialism, patriarchy, heterosexism, speciesism, and all systems of domination, oppression, hierarchy, extraction, and exploitation.[1]

However, before we get to eco-socialism and the overarching challenge ahead, we must first establish concrete examples of economic democracy. So, what is economic democracy? In short, it is the democratization of our economy's basic production structures. This transformation starts with the democratization of our workplaces, the institutions of finance and investment, and the distribution of goods and services within the market. More specifically, economic democracy calls first and foremost for transforming our workspaces into worker cooperatives: we must break capital's stronghold on the institutions of finance and investment by establishing capital controls and creating such institutions as public community banks. At the same time, we must struggle to bring investment institutions under democratic control, particularly on the local level through such practices as participatory budgeting in the public arena. Economic democratization also entails expanding the practices and institutions of the solidarity economy and the commons—whether through community land trusts, time banking, community currencies, solidarity markets, or other means.[2]

With these basic definitions and parameters in mind, the question becomes how to move from our immediate, short-term economic democracy pursuits toward our comprehensive long-term pursuit of economic democracy. Our strategy is to make Jackson a comprehensive Transition City through the agency of our Jackson Just Transition Plan.

Structure and Projects

To fully grasp our program and strategy, it is critical to understand Cooperation Jackson's structure and reason for being. In brief, Cooperation Jackson is the sum total of four interconnected and interdependent institutions:

- *A Federation of Emerging Local Cooperatives and Mutual Aid Networks:* The Federation comprises numerous interconnected and interdependent worker, consumer, and community cooperatives cooperating as one overall, coherent, but democratic, body. Various mutual aid institutions and practices reinforce the Federation's solidarity and provide multiple ways to exchange value, labor, and time to improve the quality of life of all of Federation and community members.
- *A Cooperative Incubator:* The Incubator is Cooperation Jackson's start-up training and development center. The Incubator aids new cooperators with basic training, feasibility studies, business plan development, financing, training in democratic management, and more.
- *A Cooperative School and Training Center:* Its Economic Democracy School ensures that Cooperation Jackson serves the social transformation by continually broadening the social consciousness of all its cooperators and enhancing their skills, abilities, and overall capacities to act as conscious actors in improving their social context and environment.
- *A Cooperative Financial Institution:* The financial institutions we are building will be used to start and strengthen all Cooperation Jackson operations and serve as a means of self-capitalization and democratic investment to expand the initiative.

All of Cooperation Jackson's programs and strategy are presently executed through five intentionally interlocked and interdependent focal points, including various campaign initiatives, projects, and programs. These include:

1   The development of self-managed green-worker cooperatives and an extensive network of mutual aid and social solidarity programs, organizations, and institutions, such as community land trusts. This programmatic approach is translated into transformative policy aimed at making Jackson a *Solidarity City*.
2   The development of an Eco-Village, community energy production, and sustainable methodologies and technologies of production and ecologically regenerative processes and institutions. This programmatic approach is translated into transformative policy aimed at making Jackson a *Sustainable City*.
3   The development of a network of 3D print factories that anchor community production cooperatives and institutions. This programmatic approach is translated into transformative policy aimed at making Jackson a *Fab* (or Digital Fabrication Laboratory) *City*.
4   The development of an all-embracing, class-oriented Union Cooperative to build genuine worker power from the ground up in Jackson. This programmatic approach is translated into transformative policy aimed at making Jackson a *Workers City*.
5   The development of a Human Rights Institute to craft a human rights charter and commission for Jackson. This programmatic approach is translated into transformative policy aimed at making Jackson a *Human Rights City*.

The transformative policy components attached to each of the focal points are critical since none of the system(s) change processes described here can be sustained in a non-revolutionary context unless the state supports and reinforces them. Such support means providing legal justification, incentives, and resource allocation, and monitoring and enforcement from the civilian institutions that monitor government's conduct and performance.

All these transformative policy components are fundamentally articulations of "non-reformist reforms." Such reforms were first concretely formulated by the French socialist Andre Gorz, who posed the formulation to bridge our short-term engagements for social justice in everyday life and our longer-term vision for an anti-capitalist world.[3] Gorz's formulation centers on struggling for demands and reforms that improve conditions in people's immediate lives while subverting the logic of the capitalist system, upending its social relations, and diluting its strength. Non-reformist reforms seek to create new logic, new relations, and new imperatives that create a new equilibrium and balance of forces to weaken capitalism and enable the development of an anti-capitalist alternative. This aim is exactly what Cooperation Jackson's transformative policy components seek to accomplish.

Complementary Institutions and Practices

No one practice or form associated with the solidarity economy alone can transform the capitalist economy and build economic democracy as a transitional alternative. In our view, we must develop and employ several complementary and reinforcing practices and forms of solidarity economics at once to subvert dynamics of the capitalist system, logic and imperative.[4] Accordingly, Cooperation Jackson is currently building or aiming to build these complementary solidarity institutions and practices:

Community Land Trust (CLT): A CLT is a democratic nonprofit corporation that stewards and develops land and other community assets on behalf of a community. Cooperation Jackson's primary objective in developing this institution is to acquire and decommodify as much land as possible in Jackson to take it off the capitalist market.

Community Saving, Lending, and Investing: This practice includes community-controlled financial institutions ranging from lending circles to credit unions. We are creating new grassroots funds in our community and supporting several existing ones; the need is to create our own finance capacity, given that few "traditional" financial institutions will lend to poor Black people with little, no, or bad credit. We have borrowed ideas heavily from Italy's Mondragon,[5] prioritizing the work of creating a self-reinforcing financial institution to gain maximum control over capital and its deployment for Jackson's collective benefit.

Price-based Mutual Credit: Mutual credit is a form of barter in which a network of creditors and debtors lend to and borrow from each other through various forms of direct exchange and account for the goods and services exchanged. Our model draws heavily on the experiences of the Mutual Aid Network (MAN) in Madison, Wisconsin[6] in creating a credit system denominated in either the national currency (US dollar) or our local alternative currency (as described below). This mutual credit system will be transferable and practical for the community's working-class people doing business with standard capitalist-oriented firms that willingly participate in the system.

Time Banking: Time banking is a method people can use to exchange services using time as currency instead of money. This practice of valuing everyone's time equally, no matter the task, allows everyone to help produce value in the community and assures that typically undervalued or unappreciated skills and services get their due. Our main aim in building this practice is to elevate women's often unpaid work and to allow those presently excluded from the monetary economy to join the emerging solidarity economy on an equal footing so they can access the goods and services needed to improve their overall quality of life.

Poshterity Budgeting: "Poshterity" is personal and community budgeting that explores ways to design and utilize various value-exchange options to replace monetary need. This practice helps people to improve their standard of living and quality of life by identifying where, when, and how to use their limited resources to maximum effect. Broadly utilized, this practice helps end poverty's stranglehold on the vast majority of Jackson's residents.

Alternative Currency: An alternative currency is any form of currency used as a substitute for the national currency, in our case the US dollar. In the United States, private individuals, corporations, or nonprofit community institutions create such currencies as a counterbalance to the standard currency's use. Alternative currencies enhance the market mobility and access of those who—lacking jobs and other sources of income—have limited access to standard currency. Pursuing this practice buttresses our cooperatives and financial institutions and helps our city amid budgetary crises support the struggle to retain the Black majority and Black political power against the pressing threats of gentrification, displacement, and privatization.

Tool Lending and Resource Libraries: Tool libraries allow community members to check out or borrow tools, equipment, and "how-to" instructional materials, either free of charge (with community norms and conditions) or for a rental fee (also with norms and conditions). Pursuing this practice eliminates aspects of overconsumption in our community and gives more people access to the things they need to engage in critical work projects and improve their quality of life.

Participatory Budgeting: According to two of the leading researchers and advocates in the field, Mike Menser and Juscha Robinson,

> Participatory budgeting consists of a process of democratic deliberation and decision-making in which ordinary city residents decide how to allocate part of a public budget through a series of local assemblies and meetings.... community members determine spending priorities and elect budget delegates to represent their neighborhoods, budget delegates transform community priorities into concrete project proposals, public employees facilitate and provide technical assistance, community members vote on which projects to fund, and the public authority implements the projects.

When citizens direct municipal budgets and set investment priorities, documented benefits include "more equitable public spending, higher quality of life, increased satisfaction of basic needs, greater government transparency and accountability, increased levels of public participation (especially by marginalized residents), and democratic and citizenship learning."[7] In Jackson, we are developing this practice to humanize governance and to institutionalize equity processes throughout government.

Community Energy Production: Community Energy is the cooperatively owned and democratically managed production and distribution of energy from such renewable sources as sunlight, wind, geothermal, and biophotovoltaics[8] (which produce energy directly from plants). Renewable energy can be used for direct consumption and production or sold to the public energy utility grid. In Jackson, we are developing this practice to reduce our community's carbon footprint, to contribute concretely to the development of sustainable energy systems, and to create energy self-reliance and self-determination in our community.

All of these solidarity institutions and practices are in very rudimentary stages of development. As of mid-2019, our main priorities are building three interrelated and interconnected initiatives to incorporate all of these practices and advance economic democracy in Jackson. First is expanding our *Community Production Cooperative*, our light manufacturing digital fabrication factory and education center. Second is creating a model of off-grid sustainable housing—the *Ewing Street Eco-Village Pilot Project*. And third is laboring, through *People's Grocery and Food Security Complex*, to end food apartheid in our community and boost food security in West Jackson.

The Eco-socialist Future

Hard work and ambitions aside, this work to construct economic democracy in Jackson is at best a small step toward an eco-socialist future. Reaching that will take the agency and collective power of the multinational working class on a global level—building worker- and community-owned and self-managed cooperatives, organizing worker-led labor unions that own and control their workplaces, and forming people's assemblies in communities or municipalities to deepen democracy.

Part of this larger program must be a plan to reduce the production and consumption of various consumer goods. The program should also eliminate the planned obsolescence built into the life cycle of all modern consumer products, from cars to cell phones, a practice that enriches corporations and drives resource extraction.

This larger program must also expand the production of public goods and services held in common, ending the false scarcities that capitalism produces. Designing cities around mass transit could reduce the need for individual cars. Collective urban farms and edible lawns could ensure greater local food sovereignty while drastically reducing emissions for food transport and storage.

We must also implement "regenerative production" standards, replacing extractivist logic with regenerative logic. For every resource we extract and use, we must either replace it or create conditions for it to regrow or regenerate itself. This could mean, for example, planting three trees for every tree cut, rehabilitating damaged habitats, and reintroducing species harmed by extractive industries.

Given the capitalist system's expansive drive, restoring Earth's natural habitats will be no small feat. In practice, restoration will involve regenerating our soils, massive reforestation, and ocean-cleaning projects.

The transition to waste-free methods of production, distribution, consumption, and recycling must be front and central in any program of constructing eco-socialism. This shift will be easier if accompanied by local material sourcing, local production, and localized supply and value chains. We must ramp up recycling, reuse, and composting while reducing downstream waste in landfills and incinerators, both of which release greenhouse gases.

We need comprehensive zero-waste and recycling processes for all nonperishable products, and producers must bear primary responsibility for compliance. One option is requiring corporations to invest in the production of fully recyclable or reusable products and to fully internalize the costs of including disposable components—say, plastic or cardboard wrappings—rather than passing them on to consumers and the public.

Some new production methods will require new technology. We need massive public funding for open-source research into the development of carbon-neutral production techniques for the industrial and consumer goods needed to ensure a high quality of life for billions of people. Several young technologies are headed in the right direction. For instance, digital fabrication—in which computers direct production—allows for decentralized manufacturing and uses far less material than traditional processes.

This larger shift—in Jackson and the rest of the world—will necessitate learning and incorporating a mixture of Indigenous and sustainable methods of production drawn from pre-capitalist cultures. Far from a call to return to pre-capitalist production, this is a call to press forward with the full range of scientific knowledge that humanity has accumulated—for example, drawing on the more durable and sustainable methods of concrete production used in ancient Rome or on ecologically sound food cultivation methods from the Incas and Aztecs.

To stop runaway climate change and save the species and habitats that can still be saved, we must now fully open our imaginations and dig deep into the reservoirs of our accumulated knowledge to enact comprehensive systems change over the next 10 to 15 years.

Given the tremendous obstacles our ancestors have overcome over the past 200,000 years—from extreme ice ages to super-volcanic eruptions to the genocidal spread of global capitalism—we know we have the capacity to cope and flourish. But will we develop the necessary will and organization? Cooperation Jackson believes we can and must, and we are working as hard as we can to play our part in our small little corner of this precious earth.

Notes

1 Aspects of this definition are drawn from *Ecosocialism: A Radical Alternative to Capitalist Catastrophe* by Michael Lowy and *Red-Green Revolution: The Politics and Technology of Ecosocialism* by Victor Wallis.
2 Aspects of this definition were drawn from *After Occupy: Economic Democracy for the 21st Century* by Tom Malleson.
3 For more information see, *Strategy for Labor: A Radical Proposal*, by Andre Gorz, and *Activism and Social Change: Lessons for Community Organizing* by Eric Shragge.
4 For more information see *Envisioning Real Utopias* by Erik Ollin Wright, and *Alternatives to Capitalism: Proposals for Democratic Economy* by Robin Hanhnel and Erik Olin Wright.
5 For more information see, Mondragon at http://www.mondragon-corporation.com/eng/ and *New Paths to Socialism: Essays on the Mondragon Cooperatives and Workplace Democracy, Green Manufacturing, Structural Reform and the Politics of Transition* by Carl Davidson.
6 For more information about the Mutual Aid Network, see http://www.mutualaidnetwork.org/gears/.
7 This definition came from "Participatory Budgeting: from Puerto Alegre, Brazil to the US," by Mike Menser and Juscha Robinson, https://www.scribd.com/document/16362300/Participatory-Budgeting-and-the-Solidarity-Economy.
8 For more information on biophotovoltaics, see https://biophotovoltaics.wordpress.com.

Chapter 28

How We Build the Movement for Reparative Economic Democracy

Aaron Tanaka, Nia K. Evans, and Libbie Cohn

Tall tales of a happy Thanksgiving dinner notwithstanding, the origin of the United States' contemporary economic system rests on the relations forged between early European settlers and the Indigenous communities they decimated, the African people they enslaved and tortured, and the land and resources they stole. Despite generations of resistance, these relationships generated for European settlers the wealth and leisure upon which American democracy was established. US politics continues to be defined by these legacies of dehumanization and extraction, which also underlie aspects of the global economy in which the United States plays an outsized role. This is why our vision for radical systems change focuses on the movement for reparations, which demands justice for and a reckoning with these most fundamental aspects of the US economy.

The struggle for reparative justice for slavery dates back at least as far as 1897, when ex-slave Callie House organized formerly enslaved people across the South and established one of the nation's first campaigns for reparations. Building on House's work, civil rights leader Audley "Queen Mother" Moore dedicated her life to the cause, forging the modern reparations movement with an influence that reverberated throughout the civil rights and Black power eras. Moore's focus on local organizing, both domestically and internationally, radically expanded the political project of reparations to encompass diverse plans for and conceptions of the demand for reparative justice throughout the African diaspora.

Toward the end of her life, Moore worked with the National Coalition of Blacks for Reparations in America (N'COBRA). Among other activities, they together championed a bill by Representative John Conyers (H.R. 40), introduced in 1989 and in every Congress since, which if passed would establish a formal commission to study and develop proposals for reparations. Thanks most recently to the work of the Movement for Black Lives and the advocacy of journalist Ta-Nehisi Coates, among many others, the demand for reparations is receiving renewed national attention.

What exactly is at stake? And what is the debt owed? From the narrow perspective of commodity production, the present value of labor extracted from enslaved Black people is estimated at $5.9 to $14.2 trillion. The value of land stolen from Indigenous Americans is inestimable: nearly all original wealth creation was capitalized by "subsidies" secured through land theft and the enslavement and genocide of Indigenous Americans.

Debates about reparations are often framed around the unworkability of determining *financial compensation in proportion to injury* for slavery or genocide. Framing the debate in this way limits our conception of reparative justice for harms committed over several hundred years of state-sanctioned violence. Payment and material transfer of resources to the harmed communities are a necessary and essential part of reparations, but *only a starting point for a broader engagement with the question of reparative justice*. Rather than focusing the debate on the technical viability of calculating payment, the reparations movement demands political and cultural space for conversation, led by the communities that experienced the harm, about how the United States can build the new and reciprocal relationships of repair and accountability necessary to address the continued effects of slavery and to prevent similar harms from being perpetuated. Within this effort, it is also necessary to address the question of what our next economic system must look like.

A broader framework for reparations could take various forms. The Movement for Black Lives cites the United Nations' Guidelines on the Right to a Remedy and Reparation in its own recently published Reparations Toolkit, particularly these five categories:

1   Restitution (i.e., restoring those harmed to the original state as far as possible)
2   Compensation (to the extent economically assessable)
3   Rehabilitation (medical, psychological, and legal services)
4   Satisfaction (including cessation of all continuing violations, public apology, commemoration)
5   Guarantees of Non-Repetition

Concrete proposals for meeting these five categories of reparation could include the policy demands outlined in the 2016 Movement for Black Lives Policy Platform. The demands include:

- full and free access for all Black people to lifetime education
- a guaranteed minimum livable income for all Black people
- corporate and government reparations focused on healing ongoing physical and mental trauma, and ensuring access to and control of food sources, housing, and land
- mandated public school curricula that examine the impacts of colonialism and slavery, and honor Black collective struggles and triumphs
- the immediate passage of H.R. 40, among other policy proposals

More generally, reparative justice is a process in which impacted communities take the lead in determining what justice looks like for them, while the people, institutions, and governments that have perpetuated and benefited from their harm help to realize those visions.

What would our national economy rebuilt along these reparative lines look like? If we implemented the proposals laid out in the Movement for Black Lives Policy Platform, how would our nation and our relationships be transformed? From where we stand today, how do the practices of economic democracy and solidarity economy move us toward implementing this reparative framework?

By asking these questions, we aim to anchor possibility in the world of the possible while grounding our visions for the future in our history, values, and work. The starting point for this work is centering Black, Indigenous, and other communities of color so as to develop and sustain economic practices founded on collective wealth building, cooperative relationships, and structures of accountability.

Often, that means building on rich legacies of innovation and organizing within Black liberation struggles. From early mutual aid societies led by freed people to Black-owned worker and farm cooperatives aimed at keeping money in Black communities to the wide array of cooperative economics practiced during the Civil Rights movement, Black Americans, like many other oppressed communities of limited means, have pooled their resources to feed, clothe, and provide for collective needs while acquiring assets for long-term community self-sufficiency. Facing eviction and other forms of economic retaliation for political organizing, movement leaders from WEB Du Bois, Marcus Garvey, and A. Philip Randolph to Ella Jo Baker and Fannie Lou Hamer at times advocated and practiced cooperative economics and democratic ownership as part of their broader visions for liberation.

It is as important now as ever to support the development of economic and democratic practices through which communities reorient their relationship to capital, control their own assets, and break dependence from the dominant, extractive economy. One prime example is the Boston Ujima Project, under the wing of the Center for Economic Democracy. Modeling deliberative democracy, this project is developing new forms of investment that prioritize the self-determination of working-class communities of color receiving investment in decisions about where investment is most needed. Although reparative justice in this venture is rooted primarily in the history of Black liberation struggles in the United States, this work accords with the aims of Indigenous movements for land rights and restitution, as well as intersectional femme and feminist leadership.

Translating Values to Practice: The Boston Ujima Project

What will it take to transition our current economy from a globalized system of extraction benefitting 1 percent of humans to an economy by and for all people?

Like all disruptive and lasting social change, such a transition will require radical imagination among progressive movements to build visions, resources, and power for alternatives to our current economic regime, the courage and leadership of the frontline communities most harmed by the economy, and sweeping shifts in public opinion.

The Boston Ujima Project focuses on place-based community organizing strategies to build a broad-based movement for economic rights. We do not position our work as reparations in action but rather as robustly grounded in a reparations frame. The project addresses the social and economic injustices and crises our communities face today while seeding and growing capacity to implement systemic change. The Ujima model prefigures post-capitalist visions inspired by many of the theorists, economists and practitioners featured in this volume and by the rich histories of Black, Indigenous, and women's liberation struggles in the United States and across the globe. Marrying theory with practice, the process aims to improve people's quality of life, create relationships of mutual accountability, and build power in working-class communities of color and among their allies. As a collective experiment, it risks failure to deepen our collective knowledge and strengthen our movements.

Capital Allocation, Governed Democratically

In December 2018, after three years of research, popular education, and base-building, the Boston Ujima Project's 400-plus members launched a first-of-its-kind democratic investment fund and cooperative economics ecosystem. In Ujima's ecosystem, members of Boston's Black and working-class communities of color work together to identify economic development priorities and to allocate finance capital through a participatory process that models local reparative alternatives to capitalist economics.

As North Carolina-based social justice activist Ed Whitfield often remarks, the unfulfilled promise of 40 acres and a mule established the demand for reparations not as a redistribution of consumption goods (such as Happy Meals or Bentleys), but as a transfer of the control of capital assets to enable long-term economic independence for formerly enslaved people. Consistent with this reparative framework, Ujima participates in efforts to democratize "access to capital," such as capitalizing co-ops and community land trusts, while also applying democracy to the prior step in the economic supply chain—allocating and governing capital itself.

Ujima's investment fund is managed democratically through neighborhood assemblies attended by hundreds of Ujima members. The annual cycle begins with a neighborhood planning process. Residents identify both local enterprises they would like to support and businesses operating with harmful or extractive practices. Applying their intimate knowledge of their neighborhood's geography and land-use patterns, and of the needs and wishes of their family, friends, and neighbors, residents brainstorm the types of retail businesses, community infrastructure, and real estate projects they want to help seed and succeed in their neighborhoods.

Ujima membership is comprised of voting members and non-voting solidarity members. All members are welcome to participate in the assembly process, but only voting members can participate in governing and allocating the funds. While voting status is limited only by residence in Boston, Ujima's racially and economically privileged members are encouraged to opt into the nonvoting solidarity membership to center Ujima's governance with our core constituency of working-class residents of color. Most do.

Ujima's membership structure also decouples investment size from investor influence. All members are encouraged to invest what they can afford, and the investments of nonmembers and non-voting solidarity members go toward amplifying the impact of voting members' collective allocation decisions.

In its first 18 months, Ujima hosted five neighborhood assemblies and engaged over 550 members and local residents in planning and voting on Ujima's "next economy" strategies. Members to date have collectively established labor, environmental, and ownership standards for Ujima-supported enterprises and ratified a list of community companies and local needs to drive investment. Within the Ujima cooperative economics ecosystem, members have also launched a time bank and a local currency to better circulate skills and spending within Ujima's business and community partners.

The project's reparations framework informs the structure of Ujima's capital fund, which aims to raise $5 million over two years. Pooling capital from Ujima's members and allies, as well as from wealthier accredited investors, philanthropic groups, large institutions, and government, Ujima offers higher returns to its nonaccredited investors, while positioning wealthier investors to absorb lower returns with higher risks. In effect, the Ujima Fund upends the capitalist risk-return relationship by redefining risk to include the financial and class position of Ujima's community investors.

The capital fund structure, together with Ujima's democratic assembly process and tiered membership, offers one local economic model for centering and uplifting the needs and interests of working-class communities of color. Participating in Ujima's investment fund and cooperative economics ecosystem means engaging with economic democracy to advance and embody reparative justice. These structures, together with the arts and cultural organizing that completes the Ujima ecosystem, create space for debate and for conversation about rebuilding relationships of accountability and reparative justice.

Arts and Cultural Organizing: Joining Past and Future

Economy is more than governance and resource allocation. Ujima engages with the deeply and long-held beliefs of friends, family members, community members, colleagues, and a wider public. It aims to be inviting, not didactic or dismissive, since such beliefs are deeply felt and not just stated. To be compelling and get accepted, Ujima's invitation must move people, producing a cultural shift by expanding the shared sense of what is considered normal and possible. Accordingly, Ujima centers and uplifts arts and cultural organizing—alongside more traditional organizing—to encourage people to use song, dance, images, and creative word play to make sense of our economic and political relationships.

Early in 2017, three artists—Cierra Michele Peters, Jax Gil, and Sarah Rejouis—expressed interest in forming an independent, autonomous artist and cultural network in parallel development with Ujima. The first collaboration was a dance party with live painting but no agenda, a slightly different approach from organizing community members around a particular cause, problem, or fear. In this way, daily life infused organizing, and people found another entry point into Ujima's proposed world.

Later in 2017, after a membership drive, Ujima created an Arts & Cultural Organizing Member Team. To date, the team has hosted a conversation on artist space, identified by Ujima members as a community need, planned a second party, and begun creating zines to orient people to Ujima Arts & Culture and Ujima writ large.

Another cultural foray has been the BlackTrust Chuck Turner Arts & Lecture Series on the intersections of race and finance. Honoring community organizer and former Boston city councilor Chuck Turner and highlighting trust in and among Black people, the series excavates histories of Black liberation struggles that include cooperative economics, thereby linking the past and the future, revaluing old ways of being and of staking our claim. Here, the key idea is that what people have done before they can do again.

The first lecture was a marriage of minds. Political scientist and urban planner Phil Thompson took the stage with actress, writer, and comedian Obehi Janice, who opened the talk by reading a scene from an original composition, *Ole White Sugah Daddy*. Also in the series, director Charlotte Brathwaite showed her original film, *Only When It's Dark Enough*

Can You See The Stars, and political economist Jessica Gordon Nembhard spoke about the subject of her book, *Collective Courage*, tracing the history of Black cooperative businesses in the United States. Combining lectures with other art forms results in a nice night out, providing a different type of conversation than a traditional community meeting--and another entry into Ujima's proposed world.

With Emerson College, Ujima is developing a role-playing game that allows participants to practice the perspective-taking, deliberation, and collaboration necessary for meaningful shared governance. Now in its fourth iteration, the game is being adapted from a board game to a digital format.

Through arts and cultural organizing, Ujima attends to every aspect of economic democracy as it is experienced, tasted, heard, seen, and felt.

Vision for the Future: Reforming the City Charter

As Ujima creates a cultural framework and economic infrastructure to build community capacity for self-governance at the neighborhood scale, the Center for Economic Democracy (CED) supports the natural extension of these experiments in direct democracy to municipal governance. If Ujima is a democratic intervention in the private capital markets, such practices as municipal participatory budgeting offer analogous processes in the governance of public tax dollars. While recognizing the theoretical debates on striking the right balance between planned and market economies, CED drives concrete initiatives to model reparations and direct democracy in both.

In building a community appetite for economic democracy through the governance of a collective fund, Ujima's democratic spillover effect is already evident in the growing citywide movement for public control of city investments. Three months after launching the Ujima Fund, a hundred community members packed Boston City Hall demanding and winning initial commitments to divest city treasury dollars from private prisons and fossil fuels. Ujima participants also called for the formation of a municipal public bank to direct public investments to such democratically controlled financial institutions as Ujima.

While efforts like participatory budgeting and public banking embody economic democracy in the public sector, municipal charter reform is a unifying strategy to advance a broader range of democratic reforms. The aim is to transition city government from a shepherd of racialized capitalism toward an organ of deep democracy and self-determination of historically exploited communities.

CED's current research and exploration in rewriting Boston's city charter touches everything from the community control of policing, resident approval of city contractors, and the democratic governance of public land allocation to housing and development. As Ujima and other partners like the national housing rights alliance Right to the City cocreate ongoing neighborhood assemblies as sites for community governance, municipal charter reform would not only imbue these grassroots bodies with formal power, but also use these resources as essential infrastructure for 21st-century democracy.

At the core of a municipal charter reform strategy is an effort to assert a more fundamental right to community and economic self-governance. We contrast this right with protective rights like freedom of speech, and positive rights to human needs like education or clean water. Rather than rallying for fair or responsible provisions of the economic pie, a charter reform strategy asserts a right to democratically govern local land, labor, and capital for communities to meet their own collectively determined needs and dreams.

To assert these rights at the municipal level, we are forced to expand our terrain of struggle. The right to govern American cities faces preemption by state law and constitutions, which are in turn restrained by federal policy and the US constitution itself. In this way, we view our attempts at prefiguring economic democracy in Boston's private and public sectors (Ujima and charter reform, respectively) as necessary steps in compelling a sustained and forceful cultural movement to reroot our juridical foundations through the federal constitutional adoption of a new regime of global democratic rights.

There is no guarantee that a society that is democratically self-governed would not be as cruel, unequal, or self-destructive as the world our corporate overlords have constructed for us today. In fact, one can easily point to the global trend of white nationalism and patriarchy to convincingly warn us of the dangers of direct democracy.

Reparations, as a result, are more than a moral obligation but are a strategic necessity for a transition to a new economy. As a framework that seeks to purge the original poisons that run through America's body politic as a settler colonial slave state and to repair and heal, reparations systemically combat a culture of domination with the antidote of self-determination, which in turn sows our ancestral seeds for a new economy. Ujima's working-class members of color will not always make the most impactful or successful investment decisions. And as membership numbers and the financial stakes rise, conflicts, factions and fissures could emerge. But we believe that it is within our right, our gifted capacity, and even our duty as humans to govern for ourselves. In reclaiming our lives from politicians and CEOs, we learn the limits and possibilities of our collective efforts and evolve our abilities to inhabit the futures we deserve to create.

Chapter 29

The Arusha Declaration
The Case for Democratic Socialism 50 Years On

Zitto Kabwe

This chapter is adapted from a speech delivered in Swahili in Arusha, a city in northeastern Tanzania, on March 25, 2017. As leader of the opposition party ACT (Alliance for Change and Transparency)-Wazalendo, Zitto Kabwe highlights the parallels between ACT's economic objectives and the socialist vision outlined in the original "Arusha Declaration," which was delivered by Tanzania's founding president Julius Nyerere in 1967.

On February 5, 1967, Tanzania's founders gathered in Arusha and heard President Julius Nyerere deliver what came to be known as the Arusha Declaration.[1] Fifty years later, that statement still inspires debate in this country, in Africa and across the world.

Professor Issa Shivji, a distinguished scholar in this country, calls the Declaration a revolutionary statement, explaining, "Without a doubt, the Declaration was among the revolutionary documents to come out of and to shape the African continent." The words from the Declaration—"We have been oppressed enough, we have been exploited enough and we have been disregarded enough"—are words that were sung by every downtrodden Tanzanian, and up to today; they still resound in our hearts.

The Arusha Declaration was the first sign of an African wanting to take control of his life and to show the world that African Socialism can drive social and economic development. There is no other African country that was able to motivate its citizens to take control of their country more than Tanzania through the Arusha Declaration. The Declaration was rooted in the fundamental principles of equality, humanity, and African unity, and it was held together by its core commitment to a system of collective production. Thus, the government of the day decided to take over ownership of the commanding heights of the economy, to take control of production, distribution, and redistribution. This approach endured for 25 years after the Arusha Declaration was issued. After that, though, Tanzania turned and went down a neoliberal path, which it has followed for the past 25 years.

Arusha versus Tabora Declarations: Socialism Then and Now

On June 13, 2015, ACT-Wazalendo issued the Tabora Declaration,[2] which aims to renew, expand on, and adapt the Arusha Declaration for Tanzania's 21st-century context. In a meeting of the party's National Executive Committee, we agreed to review the 25 years during which Tanzania honored the Arusha Declaration and the 25 years since its core principles were abandoned. We said, "It is our responsibility to ensure that, in 2017, we commemorate the 50 years of the Arusha Declaration."

The aim of our party is not to endorse the Arusha Declaration wholesale; far from it. We will critique it where we see it was misguided. But we will also revisit what was valuable in the Declaration, and what has been lost. We should treat it as a living document, one whose spirit can be revived and redeployed to address the challenges of our time.

Socialism and Its Realization

Many people interpret socialism according to their own unique perspective, and indeed, each country can adapt socialism in whichever way it sees is best suited to the local context.

The core socialist commitment enshrined in the Arusha Declaration is to *oppose exploitation*. The Declaration affirms,

> A socialist country is a country of workers. There is no capitalism or tribalism. There are no two classes of people: the lower class who live from their work and an upper class who live from the work of others.

The Tabora Declaration, in reviving the Arusha Declaration, shares the commitment to eradicate exploitation. It states, "In a country with Democratic Socialism, there is no exploitation, meaning each person works according to her capacities and is remunerated according to her needs." In the Arusha Declaration, it was said, "Each worker will get a fair remuneration for the work she has done, and the incomes of various workers will not differ much." In the Tabora Declaration, we say that the government, through its tax regime, must correct for the income inequality between the haves and the have nots.

In both cases, therefore, opposition to exploitation comes with an ambition to fight inequality, albeit through different means. The socialism of the Arusha Declaration aims for there to be no big difference in income while the Tabora Declaration explains that it is the Government's responsibility to correct for these differences through its tax policies. We will return to this discussion of "inequality" a little later.

Another core principle of socialism, according to the Arusha Declaration, is that the commanding heights of the economy should be owned and controlled by farmers and workers "operating through their government and cooperative unions." This commitment led the government to pursue a major nationalization drive after the Declaration was announced. It nationalized banks, mines, insurance companies and various other domestic and foreign businesses. It also invested in industry, especially to add value to our agricultural goods, for instance, through cotton ginning and textile manufacturing. A total of 12 textile factories were built, creating thousands of jobs. The government also launched leather tanning factories as well as cashew, sugar, and coffee processing factories. In short, our nation's founders wanted to move our economy beyond the production of raw materials alone. All of this we accomplished together as a Nation, using either our domestic revenue or loans and development assistance from abroad. Our country was taking off.

But then we took a downward turn. By the late 1970s, the war against Idi Amin's Uganda, the second oil price shock and the negative consequences of some of our own mistakes—like abolishing autonomous cooperatives—sent the economy into crisis. After initially resisting, in 1986, our country accepted the bailout conditions stipulated by the International Monetary Fund (IMF) and the World Bank. Among those conditions was the privatization of our productive enterprise, both what we had nationalized and what we later built ourselves. Starting in 1996, we began to sell all the factories we had built through our collective effort. These were privatized and given away to a few individuals, many of them foreign. We started to see banks, which we had all owned as a nation, being sold off at throwaway prices. What we witnessed was not privatization alone, but also the "foreignization" of our economy and its deindustrialization. Today there is not even a single cashew processing factory in operation as the new owners of the privatized industry failed to keep it running. The same situation applies to the old cotton milling and textile factories.

In its Tabora Declaration, ACT-Wazalendo reflects on this history. We take stock of our current economic realities and reconsider how to achieve an inclusive economy today. Consequently, the Declaration outlines a vision of an economy *overseen by the State, not owned by the State*. It stipulates that "many people [should] own parts of the economy through their cooperative unions and associations." This focus on cooperatives and associations reflects a desire to build a socialism that is truly democratic and, therefore, truly socialist. This is a socialism where the State does not own and control the economy in the name of the people but where the people are organized to own and control the economy for themselves, with the State merely facilitating this organization.

In this vein, we can distinguish between the concept of a public versus a state-owned enterprise. For example, we often refer to the Tanzania

Electric Supply Company (Tanesco) as a public enterprise, which strictly speaking, is incorrect. Tanesco is a state-owned enterprise because the government owns 100 percent of that company. That government could be a capitalist government or a dictatorship. But if Tanesco were owned by the Tanesco workers or a workers' cooperative or even a social security fund using worker contributions, we could say that Tanesco is a public enterprise because it is owned by the people themselves. The apartheid government of South Africa had a 100 percent stake in the national electricity utility, yet you cannot say that the proponents of apartheid were socialists.

This reflection on ownership and control is key to any reconsideration of socialism to mark this 50th anniversary of the Arusha Declaration. In 1981, Tanzania's ruling party, under Nyerere's continued leadership, affirmed that "self-criticism and criticism of each other is a revolutionary weapon." The truth is that, despite the many achievements to come out of the Arusha Declaration, we shut our eyes to the reality that, in the end, we were building State Capitalism and not Democratic Socialism. The Tabora Declaration aims to ensure a socialism rooted in democratic control, with the State helping to coordinate and support this new system.

Is Socialism Possible in Today's World?

The answer to the above question is yes, but each country needs to adapt its own form of socialism to suit the prevailing context. As it is, we see a great variety of socialist and capitalist economic systems and equally varied forms of democratic and authoritarian control. In China, for instance, state-owned companies compete with private companies in a market, and we have seen the largest state-owned companies turn into major multinationals. In Scandinavian countries, privately owned companies compete in a market economy, but the government ensures that all important social services are available to the entire population. These services include education, health, and social security. The top income tax rate goes up to 50 percent, and voters accept this policy because they receive free services without means-testing.

As noted above, the particular version of socialism endorsed in the Arusha Declaration emphasized equality of income as a central pillar of socialism. The view of our country's founders was that workers should be the dominant class and that, in a socialist country, capitalists should not exist. Fifty years later, the situation has changed dramatically as the income members of Tanzania's private sector elite receive far exceeds what the average person earns.

Today, though, we are not able to shrink or eliminate the private sector in the way Nyerere's government—at times—appeared to desire. Instead, the Tabora Declaration observes,

The economy must have people who innovate and create new productive enterprise, and they must be paid for their entrepreneurship without being exploited for their work. Just as the workforce is paid a salary, entrepreneurship earns a profit. However, it is the responsibility of the State to curb *the excessive accumulation of wealth* through the tax system.

The Declaration then emphasizes, "In the kind of socialist country we want to build, the Government—through its tax policies and other interventions—redresses the income inequality between the haves and the have-nots."

The big difference, then, between the Arusha Declaration and the Tabora Declaration is the latter's recognition of the economic contribution made by those with capital. However, both declarations share a similar perspective on the danger large income and wealth inequalities pose to society. Beyond its emphasis on redistribution, moreover, the Tabora Declaration does question the dominance of private ownership, if not its very existence. As noted above, it advocates the parallel expansion of co-operative and more democratic forms of ownership.

The issues of inequality and redistribution are central to discussions of political economy, not just in Tanzania or Africa but worldwide. Champions of a free market believe that the market dynamic, the efforts of private individuals and economic growth are the only appropriate determinants of income distribution. Capitalists lobby for a small government, one that does not intervene in the economy because the market is supposed to reward everyone in line with their effort. By contrast, supporters of (an orthodox) socialism believe that the only way to remove people from poverty is to engage in political and social struggle so that government takes over the means of production by nationalizing the commanding heights of the economy and by instituting a system in which workers are paid enough to live a decent life. The capitalist way is hegemonic across the world today. Tanzania tried this more orthodox socialist route for 25 years, and because of international pressures and the influence of domestic capitalists, abandoned that path. The construction of a market economy has since led to spiraling inequality within Tanzanian society.

Even within capitalist core countries, a big discussion has emerged about their economic system. The emergence of someone like Sen. Bernie Sanders in the United States, someone who openly identifies as a socialist, is evidence that the debate over the best economic system is no longer an ideologically one-sided debate. Only those with ideologically bankrupt views can think that socialism is dead and buried. Rapidly growing inequality both within and between countries is fueling tensions and the search for a new economic system, one inspired by socialist traditions.

We are trying and will continue trying to adapt this discussion to the Tanzanian context. This means examining whether the policies currently being implemented help reduce inequality. Indeed, a key reason why poverty persists despite Tanzania's robust economic growth lies with the economic strategies we are pursuing in this country. They do not help the average Tanzanian. Available statistics show that from 2002 to 2012 the economy grew by an average of 7 percent, but the poverty rate was reduced by only 2.1 percentage points, from 35.6 percent to 33.4 percent. It is clear Tanzania's rapid growth benefited few people, and those who did benefit were primarily the wealthy. It is equally apparent that this notion that countries need economic growth above all else is flawed.

Neglect of the Peasant Majority

An article I wrote in 2012, "The Bottom 30 Million," addressed the question of why Tanzanians are poor despite our country's great wealth. That article concluded that Tanzanians are poor because our leaders decided it should be so, pursuing policies that benefit the privileged few, many of whom live in cities, while abandoning the rural majority living in relative poverty.

One reason that economic growth does not translate into job creation is that the sectors of the economy that are growing fastest have no strong link with the average citizen. These sectors include mining, construction, communications, and finance. The sector that involves the most people, the agriculture sector, is not growing fast enough to reduce poverty. In 2015, the agriculture sector grew by only 2.3 percent. According to economic experts, to significantly reduce the level of poverty in Tanzania, the agriculture sector needs to grow by over 8 percent for three consecutive years and then to keep growing by an average of 6 percent for another 10 years.

So why now is the agriculture sector not growing fast enough to reduce poverty in Tanzania? The answer is that our leaders don't want it to. Tanzanians' poverty is the result of a choice by our leaders to pursue policies that raise the incomes of the haves while immiserating the have-nots, the rural majority. Granted, poverty is caused by many things. Geographical factors, for instance, play a role. But poverty also comes from being impoverished. It results from the political decisions of the national government in question, as well as international pressure, which undermine people's efforts to access basic services like education, health, and water and, even more important, to ensure food security.

The majority of Tanzanians are impoverished by policies that contravene the core principles of the Constitution of the United Republic of Tanzania. Article 9 calls for the pursuit of socialism and Self-Reliance. The aim of the Constitution is,

To facilitate the building of the United Republic as a nation of equal and free individuals enjoying freedom, justice, fraternity and concord, through the pursuit of the policy of socialism and Self Reliance which emphasizes the application of socialist principles while taking into account the conditions prevailing in the United Republic. Therefore, the state authority and all its agencies are obliged to direct their policies and programmes towards ensuring... (i) that the use of national wealth places emphasis on the development of the people and in particular is geared towards the eradication of poverty, ignorance and disease; (j) that economic activities are not conducted in a manner that may be result in the concentration of wealth or the major means of production in the hands of the hands of a few individuals.[3]

Since we discarded the Arusha Declaration, these constitutional aims have been disregarded, the result being that now a few individuals have accumulated a vast amount of wealth while many are left with no property at all.

The ruling party, Chama Cha Mapinduzi (CCM), has impoverished the rural population. In 1991, 28.1 percent of residents in the city of Dar es Salaam were poor. In 2007, 16 years later, 16 percent of Dar residents lived in poverty. Turning to the rural population, in 1991, 40 percent of Tanzania's rural population was poor. Sixteen years later, 37 percent were still mired in poverty.

The poor who live in Dar es Salaam or other towns can escape poverty by taking advantage of the various opportunities available in urban areas. Transport infrastructure, new industries and job opportunities are concentrated more in towns than in rural areas. Education and health services are better in towns, and even teachers and health workers have piled into the cities, fleeing the villages where there is now a dangerous shortage of these workers. The urban poor are not destitute. The rural poor, despite working hard, do not have the opportunity to lift themselves out of poverty.

The country's economic system is such that the price for agricultural produce is set in the towns while rural populations must accept the prices set for manufactured goods from those same towns. Agricultural cooperatives, which were once strong and supported by enabling state policies, are now largely neglected and only a shadow of their past selves. Rural roads are in a terrible state of disrepair or do not exist at all. Social services like education, water and health are poor. Electricity is completely lacking in 96 percent of villages.

But the politicians who divide up the resources of this country say there is not enough money for rural electrification to promote small-scale industry and value-addition for agricultural goods, to support cooperative expansion, to supply clean and safe water to improve health and reduce the time rural women spend searching for water, or to build rural roads so that farmers can get their produce to market. When it comes to building schools, dispensaries, and health centers, rural people are told to build them themselves, to volunteer.

Tanzanian Workers Bled Dry

In Tanzania, there are 2.1 million employed in the formal sector, which is only 9 percent of the Tanzanian workforce. Of these workers, 1.4 million or 67 percent are employed in the private sector and 700,000 or 33 percent in the public sector. Their income comes from their salary and various allowances. Ninety-one percent of Tanzanians work in the informal sector and finding a record of their income is a challenge. Even so, we know that many are self-employed as farmers, small business owners, fisherfolk, pastoralists, small-scale miners, and service providers of various kinds. It is important to emphasize that many Tanzanians are in neither formal nor informal employment. According to "The State of the Economy in 2015," a report published by the Ministry of Finance, only 60 percent of Dar es Salaam residents are in formal or informal employment, and 40 percent have no work at all.

Focusing on the formal sector, we can see from official government tax receipts that, despite the relative scarcity and precarity of formal employment, workers contribute more than owners of capital to State coffers. In the financial year 2016–2017, all public and private sector workers together contributed a total of 3 trillion shillings compared to owners of capital contributing only 900 billion shillings through taxes on interest, profits, and capital gains. Even if you look at the past two years, you will see that in 2015–2016 companies contributed 773 billion shillings while workers contributed 2.2 trillion shillings, and in 2014–2015 companies contributed 600 billion shillings and workers 1.9 trillion shillings in tax to the government. So, if we focus on revenue from income tax, then the rich contribute only a quarter of the total while workers contribute two thirds. This exacerbates the vast inequality in society.

Companies Pay Less Tax Than Workers

Why it is that workers contribute more than capital owners is a question we will return to. The primary reason, though, is that capitalists have many opportunities to evade tax while workers do not have that option.

Workers' tax contribution is taken straight out of their salary along with other deductions, like for social security and health insurance. These tax deductions start at 9 percent for the lowest income earners and go up to 30 percent for the highest earners. Workers' tax contributions are, thus, a source of revenue that the government is certain to collect. It is formal sector workers who carry the entire tax burden for workers in this country. But why is it that the amount of tax collected from companies is small compared to the tax collected from workers?

For companies, corporate tax is 30 percent of each company's profits. But the revenue collected through this tax is very low, as observed, 600 billion shillings only for the financial year 2016–2017 or 4 percent of total revenue collected by the Tanzania Revenue Authority.

This situation is not unique to Tanzania. As Thomas Piketty explains, "Although corporation tax rates are between 40–50 percent of profits in western countries, corporate tax revenue does not exceed 2.5–3 percent of GDP."[4] An important reason for this limited contribution is the prevalence of tax loopholes, which as Piketty writes, pervade the whole global tax system. These loopholes are the main way companies avoid tax, especially multinational corporations.

African countries have been greatly affected by the international tax system and the resultant flow of wealth taken from Africa overseas. In the Tabora Declaration, ACT discussed this misfortune, which African governments have failed to address. There have been some valuable interventions, though, notably by former President of South Africa, Thabo Mbeki. Mbeki writes,

> In the book Africa's Odious Debts: How Foreign Loans and Capital Flight Bled a Continent, the writers Leonce Ndikumana and James Boyce show that over the last 40 years, a total of $11.4b was stolen from Tanzania using various means. This is equal to an average of $285m stolen per year from 1970 to 2010. The largest portion of this money is looted by large foreign companies that do business and invest in this country.

The Africa Progress Panel, along with Mbeki's High-Level Panel on Illicit Financial Flows, established by the UN Economic Commission for Africa, have explained that Africa loses more than $50 billion per year due to the transfer of money overseas, licit and illicit, especially by multinational companies.

An estimated 30 percent of the continent's financial wealth is parked in tax havens according to the book The Hidden Wealth of Nations, written by Gabriel Zucman, a lecturer at the London School of Economics. In that book, Zucman draws on statistics from UBS, which confirm that roughly $150 billion taken from Africa has been stashed in Swiss banks. The cumulative GDP of all countries in the East Africa Community is $147.3 billion, so the African money in Switzerland is more than the GDP of Tanzania, Kenya, Uganda, Rwanda, and Burundi combined. That money is equal to five times the cost of building the Inga Dam in Congo, which could generate enough electricity for the entire African continent.

What tax loopholes enable these financial flows out of African economies? There is something called Base Erosion and Profit Shifting, which refer to the way multinational companies, when they invest here in this country, routinely register their profits in other countries with a lower tax rate and so don't pay any tax at all in Tanzania or else pay a negligible amount. For example, when calculating their tax, companies subtract the cost of interest on loans, insurance, and administrative costs and what is left is the profit on which they are taxed. These companies purchase these services—financial and administrative—from sister companies and double the costs, thereby transferring money as if to pay for these expenses and, in the process, greatly reducing their tax burden. It is due to these methods that, for instance, mining companies operating in Tanzania were not paying income tax.

Legal tax loopholes aside, there are also plenty of instances of outright corruption and tax evasion. Parliament's Public Accounts Committee ordered an investigation into the tax avoidance carried out by multinational corporations, and discovered that almost every sector was affected by this scourge. One case involved cashew exports. In 2011, Tanzania sold cashews to India. The Tanzania Revenue Authority's records show that we exported 80,000 tons of cashews at a price of $1,000 per ton, earning a total of $80 million. The committee's investigation showed that, according to India's tax records, they purchased $120 million worth of cashews from Tanzania because they bought 120,000 tons. This means that 40,000 tons were not recorded by our customs, so those selling cashews avoided paying an export levy worth over $12 million. Also, these cashew-exporting companies avoided income tax on more than $40 million worth of earnings.

In sum, companies have many ways of underpaying tax, thereby enabling their owners to accumulate wealth and further exacerbating wealth inequalities, national and global. If firm steps are not taken, this inequality will continue to rise and will endanger this country's security and wellbeing.

ACT-Wazalendo emphasized this issue of reforming the tax system in Tanzania's 2015 general election campaigns, promising to

> introduce a new international tax system to prevent multinational corporations from eroding their tax base by fully participating in all international campaigns to reform the international tax system, including through tax treaties with other countries to prevent tax avoidance and to build the capacity to prevent tax avoidance.

Do We Need a Return to Socialism?

Our country has been done a huge amount of harm due to our leaders' narrow thinking and the endorsement of an economic system that exploits our people and resources. To advocate socialism is apparently a sin or a regression to the 1970s, yet our economic system is still run by imperialist countries. Imperialism is the system imposed by powerful countries on weaker nations.

African countries still need socialism to fight back against international exploitation. Without developing the right thinking, how will we fight imperialism? We have the good example, outlined above, of financial extraction from the continent. If you understand imperialism, you will understand why we lose billions of dollars overseas, and you cannot understand imperialism without understanding its counter, the theory of African socialism and socialism in general.

So, will socialism take us backwards? Socialism is not poverty. Socialism is the absence of exploitation of the people by those who own their economy. What is bad in that?

Let me conclude by quoting the words of Mwalimu Julius Nyerere. "Now a few Africans," he once said, amidst the liberalizing reforms of the 1990s,

> You govern Tanzanians by force and without hope, then you think they will stand by peacefully hoping for the best. But if that hope runs out, there will be social unrest, and I will be surprised by these Tanzanians if they do not riot.

Notes

1 The Arusha Declaration on Socialism and Self-reliance, 1967, Dar es Salaam: Publicity Section, TANU.
2 The Tabora Declaration on the Politics of Democratic Socialism, 2015, Dar es Salaam: ACT-Wazalendo.
3 "Constitution of the United Republic of Tanzania: April 26, 1977" (as Amended to June 30, 1995).
4 Thomas Piketty and Arthur Goldhammer, *Capital in the Twenty-first Century* (Cambridge, MA: Harvard University Press, 2014).

Questions for Authors of Works on New Models and Systems

These questions were developed to guide authors contributing to *The New Systems Reader*.

1 *Core Goals*. Briefly, what are the principal, core goals your model or system seeks to realize? [Partly, this is a question about the scope of the conceptualization you have developed, so be sure to note whether it speaks to economic, social, political, and environmental outcomes or only some of these.]

2 *Major Changes*. What are the principal changes you envision in the current system—the major differences between what you envision and what we have today?

3 *Principal Means*. What are the principal means (policies, institutions, behaviors, whatever) through which each of your core goals is pursued?

4 *Geographic Scope*. What is the geographic area covered by the model? If the nation-state, specify which ones or what category you address.

5 *Temporal Scope*. Recognizing the large uncertainties, if there is a transition to the revised system about which you write, what would you suggest as a timeframe for the new system to take shape? Where on the spectrum from imminently practicable to purely speculative would you place your proposals?

6 *Theory of Change*. What factors or forces might drive deep change toward the system you envision? What is the explicit or implicit theory of change in your work? What is the importance of crises? Of social movements? Of available examples of change? What's the biggest problem or impediment for adoption of your model?

7 *Some Specifics: Economy*. Insofar as your work addresses the nature of the economy, how (if at all) do the following fit into the future you envision?

  a How are productive assets and businesses owned? Does ownership differ at different scales (community, nation, etc.)? Do forms of ownership vary by economic sector (banking, manufacturing, health care, etc.)?

b   How are public and private investment decisions made?

c   What is the role of private profit and the profit motive? Who owns and controls economic surplus?

d   What is the role of the market for goods and services? For employment? Other?

e   What is the role of planning in your model? How is it structured? How, if at all, made democratic?

f   How are the international economy and economic integration handled?

g   How do you address economic localization, globalization, decentralization, 'glocalization,' and similar issues? Where is the primary locus of economic life?

h   How do economic competition and cooperation play out?

i   Do commodification, commercialization, and the commons surface in your analysis?

j   How is private property handled in your analysis?

k   What mix of business enterprise sizes do you envision?

l   How do you envision the future of the large corporation and what specific measures do you envision for corporate governance and control, internal and external?

m   What role do you see for innovative corporate forms, coops, public enterprise, social enterprise, and public–private hybrids?

n   What is the evolution of the workweek (hours worked, say, per year)?

o   What is the envisioned future of organized labor?

p   What are the roles of economic growth and GDP as a measure of growth in your system? What is the priority of growth at the national and company levels?

q   How is money created and allocated?

8 Some Specifics: Society

a   How do you envision the future course of income and wealth inequality? What factors affect these results? How do you envision the future course of economic poverty? What factors affect these results?

b   Are special measures envisioned to protect and enhance children and families? To advance the underprivileged? To promote care-giving and mutual responsibility?

c   How do racial, ethnic, and religious justice figure in your work?

d   What role do gender and gender issues play in your work?

e   What, specifically, is the role of community in your model? What measures and factors affect community health, wealth ('social capital'), and solidarity, and how central are local life, neighborhoods, towns, and cities?

f   Do you envision a change of values, culture, and consciousness as important to the evolution of a new system? If so, how do these changes occur?

g   What are the roles of the consumer, consumerism, and advertising in the system you envision? Self-provisioning? Sharing, renting, and bartering?

h   How do "leisure" activities—including volunteering, care-giving, continuing learning—figure in your work?

9 *Some Specifics: Environment*

a   If your system addresses environmental concerns, how do you conceptualize "the environment"? Do you envision the economy as nested in and dependent on the world of nature and its systems of life?

b   Do you address a rights-based environmentalism (e.g. right to clean water) and the idea that nature has legal rights? Do we have duties to other species and living systems? Are any of your goals non-anthropocentric?

c   Do you envision addressing environmental issues outside the current framework of environmental approaches and policies (e.g. by challenging consumerism, GDP growth, etc.)?

d   How do you handle environment-economy interactions, trade-offs, and interdependencies?

e   How do you address transnational and global-scale environmental challenges?

f   Does your work explore the links between large-scale environmental challenges (like climate change) and other economic and political issues?

10 *Some Specifics: Polity*

a   To what degree would your proposed model require Constitutional change? What specifically might be required or recommended?

b   Does your model have anything to say about liberty and how it may or may not relate to the design of your model? And how, specifically, is liberty nurtured and protected?

c   How does your model address questions of political and institutional power?

d   How does your model deal with problems of scale? How much decentralization does it include for large systems? How would decentralization be structured?

e   Does your work address issues of foreign policy, international relations, regional integration, military policy and spending, war, and peace, i.e. the international context of the new system? If so, how?

f At different political levels, what polity and what political conditions are implicit or explicit in getting to success?

g There is an ongoing critique of representative government and exploration of direct, "strong," and deliberative democracy. Does any of this figure in your framework? If so, how?

h Milton Friedman, among others, believed that only a crisis produced real change. Another old expression is that "good government is just the same old government in a helluva fright." Do you examine crisis-driven political change and crisis preparedness?

i How central is government in the future you envision, both in getting there and staying there?

j In the system you write about, what are the appropriate levels of government expenditure or government as a share of the economy and how are these levels achieved?

k Do you envision social movements as important in driving political change and action? If so, can you elaborate on how this happens?

11 Real-World Examples, Experiments and Models

a Are there specific real-world examples or experiments you can point to that embody your model or system or exemplify important elements of your approach?

b Are there other models that you see yourself aligned with or close to yours?

Index

Made in the USA
Middletown, DE
22 April 2021